PART I
THE CLASSICAL PERIOD

I - THE HELLENIC STYLE

ATHENS, 5TH CENTURY B.C.

"We are all Greeks." So said Shelley in the preface to his play *Hellas*. "Our laws, our literature, our religion, our arts, have their roots in Greece." Merely the mention of such key words as *mythology*, *philosophy*, *democracy* points immediately to their Greek source. So also do the familiar forms of architecture, sculpture, painting, poetry, drama, and music have their taproots in the age-old soil of Hellas, the land where the Hellenic style was nurtured and brought to fruition.

In Athens, for a brief span of time were concentrated the creative activities of many men of genius—leaders who made Athens the first democracy in a world of tyrants, philosophers who were seeking to understand the world in which they lived, and artists who conceived daring expressions in stone, word, and tone. In 480 B.C., the Athenians had turned the tide against the powerful Persians, but only after their city had been reduced to rubble. Without hereditary rulers, government rested on the shoulders of the citizen class, and the rule of the *demos*, the people, became the order of the day. Here the statesman Pericles and the future philosopher Socrates heard the wisdom of Anaxagoras, who taught that the universe was governed by a supreme mind that brought form

out of the chaos of nature; and that man, as the measure of all things, by thinking for himself could likewise bring order into human affairs. After the destruction of their city, the Athenians, boldly facing the future, instead of reconstructing their old temples and statuary, launched a new building program that surpassed anything the world had ever seen and that was to serve as a classical model for all generations to come.

Like many other ancient cities, Athens had developed around an *acra*, or hill, that had first served as a military vantage point. As in other cities, a long-ago victory on this fortified hilltop, known as the *acropolis* (Fig. 1), had been attributed to divine intervention, and in the popular mind the acra had become a sacred place, to be crowned with a suitable monument—just as the brow of a warrior responsible for a heroic deed had been adorned with the kingly diadem. Civic buildings, palaces, and temples had been erected, and the people in the city below looked up with pride toward the acropolis that recorded their history, represented their aspirations, and had become the center of their religious and civic ceremonies. From

(above) *Priestess Burning Incense*, side panel of "Ludovisi Throne." *c.* 470 B.C. Marble, 34″ high. National Museum, Rome.

General History B.C.

c.1600–c.1100		Mycenaean Period
	c.1184	Fall of Troy to Achaeans
	c.1100	Dorians and Ionians invaded Greek peninsula, conquered Achaeans. End of Mycenaean Period, beginning of Hellenic civilization
c.950–	c.800	Proto-Geometric Period; Homeric epics (?)
c.800–	c.650	Geometric Period; Homer; Eastern contacts
	776	First Olympic games
	c.700	Hesiod wrote *Theogony* (basis of Greek mythology)
c.650–	c.500	Archaic Period
	534	Playwriting competitions began at Athens
	c.494	Persians under Darius invaded Greece
	c.490	Athenians defeated Persians at Marathon
	480	Persians under Xerxes defeated Spartans at Thermopylae
		Athens sacked and burned
		Athenians defeated Persian fleet at Salamis
	477	Delian League founded under Athenian leadership
c.461–	429	Pericles (490–429) ruled Athens
	454	Delian League treasury moved to Athens
437–	404	Peloponnesian Wars between Athens and Sparta
	413	Athenians defeated at Syracuse, Sicily
	404	Athens fell to Sparta. End of Athenian empire
	387	Plato founded Academy
359–	336	Philip of Macedonia gained control of Greek peninsula
	336	Alexander the Great succeeded Philip as king of Greece
	335	Aristotle founded Lyceum
335–	323	Alexander the Great conquered Near East, Asia Minor, Persia, and India
	146	Corinth destroyed by Romans
	86	Athens sacked by Romans under Sulla

A.D.

	c.100	Plutarch (c.46–c.125) wrote *Parallel Lives*
c.140–	150	Pausanius visited Athens. Later wrote description of Greece
	529	Athenian schools of philosophy closed by Emperor Justinian

Architecture and Sculpture B.C.

	c.650	Ionic temple of Artemis built at Ephesus
	c.600	Kouros from Sounion carved
	c.550	Korai of Samos carved
	c.530	Archaic Doric temples built at Athens, Delphi, Corinth, Olympia
	c.489	Doric temple (Treasury of Athenians) built at Delphi
	c.470	Charioteer of Delphi cast
c.470–	c.450	Zeus (Poseidon?) cast
c.465–	457	Temple of Zeus built at Olympia
	450	Phidias appointed overseer of works on Athenian acropolis
449–	440	Temple of Hephaestus (Theseum) built
447–	432	Parthenon built by Ictinus and Callicrates
		Parthenon sculptures carved under Phidias
437–	432	Propylaea built by Mnesicles
427–	424	Temple of Athena Nike built by Callicrates
421–	409	Erechtheum built by Mnesicles
	334	Choragic monument of Lysicrates built

A.D.

	c.117	Temple of Olympian Zeus completed

Philosophers B.C.

c.582–	c.507	Pythagoras
500–	428	Anaxagoras
485–	411	Protagoras
469–	399	Socrates
427–	347	Plato
384–	322	Aristotle

Historians B.C.

c.495–	425	Herodotus
c.460–	395	Thucydides
c.434–	c.355	Xenophon

Sculptors B.C.

c.490–	c.432	Phidias
c.460–	c.450	Myron active
c.460–	c.440	Polyclitus active
c.390–	c.330	Praxiteles
c.350–	c.300	Lysippus active

Painters B.C.

c.480–	c.430	Polygnotus (noted for perspective drawing)
	c.440	Apollodorus, the "shadow painter," flourished (modeled figures in light and shade)

Dramatists and Musicians B.C.

525–	456	Aeschylus
496–	406	Sophocles
480–	406	Euripides
c.444–	380	Aristophanes

1. Acropolis, Athens (view from southwest).

the beginning, the Athenian acropolis was never static, and its successive buildings reflected the city's changing fortunes. Once it had been the site of the palace of Erechtheus, a legendary hero and king. Its shift from a military citadel and royal residence to a religious shrine, especially sacred to Athena as the city's protectress, is described by Homer when he notes in the *Odyssey:* "Therewith grey-eyed Athene departed over the unharvested seas, left pleasant Scheria, and came to Marathon and wide-wayed Athens, and entered the house of Erechtheus."

Spreading out from the base of the acropolis was the *agora* (Fig. 2), a meeting and a market place, with its colonnades, public buildings, market stalls, gardens, and shade trees. This ten-acre square was the center of the city's bustling business, social, and political life. Here could be found country folk selling their wares, citizens discussing the news, foreign visitors exchanging stories, and magistrates conducting routine city affairs. "You will find everything sold together in the same place at Athens," wrote the poet Eubolus in a humorous vein, "figs, witnesses to summonses, bunches of grapes, turnips, pears, apples, givers of evidence, roses, . . . honeycombs, chickpeas, lawsuits, . . . myrtle, allotment-machines, irises, lamps, water-clocks, laws, and indictments." And he could well have added "philosophies of life," for the agora was the place where philosophers settled the prob-

2. Agora, Athens. (Left, re-construction of Stoa of Attalus II of Pergamon, *c.* 150 B.C.)

lems of the universe. On a typical day, Socrates could be heard arguing with the sophists, whom he called "retailers of knowledge," for, as his pupil Plato was to point out, the merchandising in the agora was "partly concerned with food for the use of the body, and partly with food of the soul which is bartered and received in exchange for money." The sophists were concerned primarily with the art of persuasive speech, but some professed to teach wisdom as well. As manipulators of public opinion, they often became intellectual opportunists who would use any line of reasoning so long as it turned their trick. In his disputations, Socrates showed that sophistry was more a matter of quibbling on the surface over words than of penetrating profoundly into the deeper world of ideas. By pricking some of the sophists' pomposities with the sting of his wit, Socrates gained his immortal reputation as the "gadfly" of Athens.

On the southern slope of the acropolis was the theater of Dionysus (see Fig. 3), the sanctuary dedicated to the god of wine and frenzy and patron of the drama, and where the ancient poetic festivals were held. Here, more than 2,000 years before Shakespeare, the people of Athens gathered to enjoy the plays that mirrored their world in dramatic form and, annually, through their applause to pick the winner of the coveted poetry prize that had been won no less than 13 times by Aeschylus, the founder of heroic tragedy. Sophocles, his successor and principal poet of the Periclean period, quickened the pace of Greek drama by adding more actors and actions; Euripides, last of the great tragic poets, ran the gamut of emotions, endowing his plays with such passion and pathos that they plumbed the depths of the human spirit. After the great Periclean age was past, the comedies of Aristophanes proved that the Athenians still were able to see the humorous side of life.

Above the theater, on the rocky plateau of the acropolis, was a leveled site, about 1,000 feet long and 445 feet wide, where the temples were constructed. Under Pericles, this was a place of ceaseless activity by builders, sculptors, painters, and other craftsmen. The necessary materials were available in abundance: Paros and other Aegean islands yielded good stone; from nearby Mt. Pentelicus came the fine-grained, cream-colored marble ideal for building and carving; Mt. Hymettus in Athens itself had a blue-white stone, excellent for embellishments; while the dark-gray limestone of Eleusis could be used for contrasting effects. As the buildings rose stately in size and fair in form, the craftsmen, declares Plutarch in his biography of Pericles, were "striving to outvie the material and the design with the beauty of their workmanship, yet the most wonderful thing of all was the rapidity

of their execution. Undertakings, any one of which singly might have required, . . . for their completion, several successions and ages of men, were every one of them accomplished in the height and prime of one man's political service."

Pericles had the wisdom to foresee that the unity of a people could rest on philosophical idealism and artistic leadership as well as on military might and material prosperity. A seafaring people, the Athenians had always looked beyond the horizon for ideas as well as goods to add luster to their way of life. In the Delian confederation, once the Persian threats were ended, they joined with the broader community of Greek-speaking peoples of the mainland, the Aegean islands, and the coast of Asia Minor not only to defend themselves but also to achieve a cultural unity. With the Delian treasury brought to Athens and its ample funds available for her building program, the city was assured leadership in the arts as well as in other practical and idealistic enterprises. Thus Athens became a city whose acknowledged wealth was in its dramatists (Aeschylus, Sophocles, and Euripides), its architects (Ictinus, Callicrates, and Mnesicles), its sculptors (Myron, Polyclitus, and Phidias), and such painters and craftsmen as Polygnotus and Callimachus.

The acropolis was, then, both the material and spiritual treasury of the Athenian people, the place which held both their worldly gold reserves and their religious and artistic monuments. Work continued with unabated enthusiasm until by the end of the 5th century B.C. the acropolis had become a sublime setting, worthy of the goddess of wisdom and beauty, and the pedestal that proudly bore the shining temples dedicated to her.

ARCHITECTURE

The Acropolis and the Propylaea

On festive occasions, the Athenians would leave their modest homes to walk along the Panathenaic Way (Fig. 5), the main avenue of their city, toward the acropolis. As the procession moved diagonally across the agora, to the right all could see the Hephaesteum (Fig. 6) on a low hill. Today the best preserved of all Greek temples, it was dedicated to Hephaestus (Vulcan), god of the forge and patron of metalworkers. He shared his temple with Athena in her role as protectress of arts and crafts that brought fame to the artisans who lived in the adjoining potters' quarter, known as Ceramicus. Ahead, towering above them, was the supreme shrine—the acropolis where they worshiped their gods, commemorated their heroes,

(above) 3. Acropolis, Athens. Reconstruction drawing as of end of 2nd century A.D. (Theater of Dionysus, 4th century B.C., upper right; Odeion of Herodes Atticus, 2nd century A.D., lower left.)

(right) 4. Acropolis, Athens, plan. (A. Propylaea; B. Temple of Athena Nike; C. Parthenon; D. Erechtheum.)

(below) 5. Agora (with Panathenaic Way), Athens. Reconstruction. Royal Ontario Museum, Toronto.

(top) 6. Hephaesteum ("Theseum"), Athens. *c.* 449–430 B.C. Pentelic and Parian marble, 104 × 45′.

(above) 7. MNESICLES. Propylaea (view from east), Acropolis, Athens. 437–432 B.C.

(left) 8. Propylaea. Cross section (after H. D'Espouy).

9. ICTINUS and CALLICRATES. Parthenon, Athens. 447–432 B.C. Pentelic marble, *c.* 228 × 104′; columns 34′ high.

and recreated themselves. Accessible only by a single zigzag path up the western slope, the ascent was never easy. In Aristophanes' *Lysistrata*, a chorus of old men bearing olive branches to kindle the sacred fires chant as they mount the hill: "But look, to finish this toilsome climb only this last steep bit is left to mount. Truly, it's no easy job without beasts of burden and how these logs do bruise my shoulder!"

As the procession neared the summit, the exquisite little temple of Athena Nike (Fig. 15) appeared on a parapet to the right, and ahead was the mighty Propylaea (Fig. 7). Built entirely of Pentelic marble except for some dark contrasting Eleusinian stone in the frieze, this imposing structure was a spacious gateway with wings extending on either side to an overall width of about 156 feet. An enclosure on the left was a picture gallery, and an open room on the right contained statuary. In the center was the portico consisting of six Doric columns with the middle two spaced more widely apart as if to invite entrance. Between the columns facing the city and the corresponding ones on the opposite side facing the acropolis plateau was an open vestibule with columns of the more slender Ionic order (Fig. 8), which permitted greater height and space for exhibitions and the waiting crowds. The axis of the Propylaea paralleled that of the Parthenon, an exception to the usual self-containment of Greek buildings of the Hellenic period but justified by the Propylaea's function as a gateway rather than an independent building in its own right.

Through the portals of the Propylaea the procession entered the sacred area. Amid the revered monuments to the gods and heroes and looming above them was the colossal statue of Athena Promachus, said to have been fashioned by Phidias

from the bronze shields of defeated Persian enemies, the tip of her spear gleaming brightly enough to guide homecoming sailors over the seas toward Athens. On the right was the majestic Parthenon; on the left the graceful Ionic Erechtheum.

The Parthenon

At first glance, the Parthenon (Fig. 9) seems to be a typical Greek temple. Such a shrine was originally conceived as an idealized dwelling to house the image of the deity to whom it was dedicated. Under a low-pitched gabled roof, the interior was a windowless oblong room called the *cella*, in which the cult statue was placed. The *portal*, or door, to the cella was on one of the short ends, which extended outward in a *portico*, or porch, faced with columns to form the façade. Sometimes columns were erected around the building in a series known as a *colonnade*. The construction was simple: a platform of three steps, the top one known as the *stylobate*, from which rose the upright *posts* that supported the *lintels*, or horizontal beams. When these columns and lintels were made of marble, the weight and size of the superstructure could be increased and the *intercolumniation*, or span between the supporting posts, widened. The history of Greek temple architecture was largely the refining of this *post-and-lintel* system of construction, which permitted the architects a steadily increasing freedom.

The capital of the Doric column is in three parts: the necking, the echinus, and the abacus (Fig. 10). The purpose of any capital is to mediate between the vertical shaft of the column and the horizontal entablature above. The *necking* is the first break in the upward lines of the shafts,

10. Comparison of Doric and Ionic Orders.

though the fluting continues up to the outward flare of the round, cushionlike *echinus*. This, in turn, leads to the *abacus*, a block of stone that squares the circle, so to speak, and smoothly effects the transition between the round lower and rectangular upper members. Above the columns and below the roof is the *entablature*. Directly above the abacus is the *architrave*, a series of plain rectangular blocks stretching from the center of one column to that of its neighbor to constitute the lintels of the construction and to support the upper parts of the entablature—frieze, cornice, and pediment. At this point, sculpture is called into play for decorative purposes, beginning with a carved band known as a *frieze*. In the Doric order, the frieze is made up of alternating triglyphs and metopes. The rectangular *triglyphs* are so named because of their three grooves (glyphs), two in the center and a half groove on either side. They are the weight-bearing members, and by rule, one is placed above each column and another in the interval between. The sameness of the triglyphs contrasts with the differently carved relief panels of the *metopes*. This alternation results in an interesting visual rhythm, which illustrates the classical principle of harmonizing the opposites of unity and variety. The frieze is protected by the overhanging *cornice* (and enhanced by its shadow), and the *raking cornice* rises

gablelike from the side angles to the apex in the center. One triangular space enclosed by the cornices is called the *pediment*, which is recessed to create an indented space in which free-standing sculpture can be placed to climax the decorative scheme.

On close inspection, the Parthenon is not so much a typical Greek temple as it is the culmination of the long evolution of the Doric order with variations adapting it to the needs of its time and place. Since the Parthenon was to serve both as a shrine to Athena and as the treasury of the Delian League, the plan called for a double cella. The larger room on the east was to house Phidias' magnificent gold-and-ivory cult statue of Athena and that on the west was to be the treasury. It was this western cella that technically was the *parthenon*, or chamber of the virgin goddess; later the name was given to the whole building. The outer four walls of the cella were embellished by a continuous frieze, a decorative device borrowed from the Ionic order. A *peristyle*, or colonnade, of free-standing columns completely surrounded the temple, the columns being placed far enough outward from the cella walls to permit an *ambulatory*, or passageway. On each side, along its 228 feet of length, were 17 columns, and along the 104-foot width in front and back were 8 columns—hence the Parthenon is called octastyle. (The number of columns used on the portico of a Greek temple was determined by the size of the building rather than by any rigid rule, 6 being the usual number, although some temples had as few as 2, others as many as 10 and 12.) On both the east and west ends of the Parthenon, between the outer colonnade and the entrance portals to the cella, were 6 additional columns that formed the inner porticos.

Except for such details as the timbered roof beneath the marble tiles and the wooden doors with their frames, the entire Parthenon was built of Pentelic marble. When freshly quarried, this fine-grained stone was cream colored, but as it has weathered through the centuries its minute veins of iron have oxidized, so that today the color varies from light beige to darker sepia tones depending on the light. In the original design, bright colors played an important part. The triglyphs were tinted dark blue and parts of the molding were red, as is known from ancient sources. The sculptured parts of the metopes were left cream colored, but the backgrounds were painted. In the frieze along the cella walls, the reins of horses were bronze additions, and the draperies of figures here and on the pediments were painted. Such facial features as eyes, lips, and hair were done in natural tints.

For sheer technical skill, the workmanship of the Parthenon is astonishing. No mortar was used

anywhere; the stones were cut so exactly that when fitted together they form a single smooth surface. The columns, which appear to be monoliths of marble, actually are constructed of sections called *drums*, so fitted and held tight by square plugs in the center that the joinings are scarcely visible. To insure harmonious proportions, the design is based on the mathematical principle of the golden section, a flexible system of dividing lines into extreme and mean ratios. Just how it was applied is now unknown, but far from being a cut-and-dried formula, the golden section obviously allowed much latitude in actual practice.

In the Parthenon the orderly organization of verticals and horizontals, the relationship of length and breadth to height, the ratio of the solid masses of the columns to the open voids between them—all are according to tradition. A unit of measure known as the *module* was used to assure the orderly relation of parts and whole. Such modules were not fixed measures like yards and feet but flexible units, such as the diameter or radius of a column. In keeping with the Greek ideal of the structural integrity of single buildings, the module was varied from structure to structure.

While the Parthenon was built according to geometrical laws, many subtle variations from the norm reveal that it was a living geometry based on experience rather than on a textbook. Close examination reveals that what appears to be straight and correct is in reality a complex series of harmonious convex and concave curves. To accommodate the building to its rocky site, to correct certain optical illusions, as well as to create the appearance of vitality and flexibility in what otherwise would become a cold exercise in geometry, the architects Ictinus and Callicrates found a solution that is psychologically and aesthetically rather than mathematically correct. If completely level, for instance, the long straight line of the stylobate would seem indefinite to the eye, and might even appear to sag slightly under the weight of the masonry. To give it a feeling of having a beginning, a middle, and an end (as well as to correct a possible optical distortion), the architects caused the stylobate to rise slightly upward and flare outward on each of the four sides. From the corners to the center on the short ends the rise is about 2¾ inches and on the long sides, about 4 inches.

If all columns were equal in diameter, those on the corners when seen against the sky would appear slimmer and weaker than those viewed against the cella walls. Hence, to promote the feeling of structural solidity and the effect of a closed composition, the corner columns are thicker and closer together than those in the center. The slight convex curve of each column, technically called *entasis*, begins at the base, swells to a point about one third of the height, then tapers gradually toward the top. Entasis creates an impression of elasticity as if, by analogy, the "muscles" of the columns bulge a bit as they carry their load. The outer surfaces of the columns have twenty grooves, called *flutes*, which form concave vertical channels from the bottom to the top of the shaft. Fluting serves several purposes, the first being to correct an optical illusion. When seen in bright sunlight, a series of ungrooved round columns appears flattened. The fluting also maintains the round appearance, makes a constant play of light and shadow, and creates a number of graceful curves to please the eye. Through the increased number of vertical lines, the visual rhythm is quickened, and the eye is led upward toward the sculpture of the entablature.

No column, moreover, is exactly parallel to its neighbors, and the columns as well as the cella walls slant slightly inward to avoid the appearance of top-heaviness and promote the feeling of stability. It has been estimated that if the lines of columns and walls were continued upward, they would meet at a point about a mile above. Columns and walls thus seem to come together in a communal effect of converging cooperation. That all was part of the original subtle design is known from the writings of the Roman architect Vitruvius, who apparently had access to the lost book on the Parthenon by Ictinus. More than mere dimensions, however, the Parthenon has proportions. With its deviations from mathematical exactness, all rigidity is banished, and the temple becomes an example of active equilibrium and mobile stability rather than a static study in geometry. It is, in short, a work of art, not just an example of skillful engineering.

In its time, the Parthenon stood out as a proud monument to Athena and her people and a realization of Pericles' ideal of "beauty in simplicity." Begun in 447 B.C. as the first edifice in that great statesman's building program, it was dedicated during the Panathenaic festival ten short years later at a time when the star of Athens was still in ascendancy. It, as well as its companion buildings on the acropolis, would be standing today with only the usual deteriorations owing to the passage of time were it not for a disaster in the year 1687. At that time, a Turkish garrison was using the Parthenon as an ammunition dump, and during a siege by the Venetians a random bomb ignited the stored gunpowder, blowing out the central section. From that time on, the Parthenon has been a noble ruin. Today, after numerous partial restorations, its outline is still clear, and in its incomparable proportions and reserved poise it remains one of the imperishable achievements of the mind of man.

11. Mnesicles(?). Erechtheum (view from southeast, with Propylaea on the left), Athens. *c.* 421–409 B.C. Pentelic marble, 37 × 66′.

The Erechtheum

After Phidias' gold-and-ivory statue was so handsomely housed in the Parthenon, the city fathers wished to provide a place for the older wooden statue of Athena that was thought to have fallen miraculously from the sky. They also wished to venerate the other heroes and deities that formerly shared the acropolis with her. Hence a new building of the Ionic order (Fig. 11) was undertaken. It was described in the city records as "the temple in the acropolis for the ancient statue."

The site chosen was that where Erechtheus, legendary founder of the city, had once dwelled. As recounted by Homer: "And they that possessed the goodly citadel of Athens, domain of Erechtheus the high-hearted, whom erst Athene daughter of Zeus fostered when Earth, the grain giver, brought him to birth;—and she gave him a resting place in Athens in her own rich sanctuary; and there the sons of the Athenians worship him with bulls and rams as the years turn in their courses. . . ." It was also the spot where Athena and the sea god Poseidon were supposed to have held their contest for the patronage of the land of Attica and the honors of Athens, and which is depicted in the sculptures on the west pediment of the Parthenon (Fig. 26). As they asserted their claims, Poseidon brought down his trident on a rock whereupon a horse, his

gift to man, sprang out. A spring of salt water also gushed forth to commemorate the event. When Athena's turn came, she brought forth the olive tree, and the gods awarded her the victory. Later, Erechtheus, whom she protected, tamed the horse and cultivated the olive that gave the Athenians oil for their cooking, butter for their bread, ointment for their bodies, and fuel for their lamps.

Since the sacred olive tree, the salt spring, the mark of Poseidon's trident on the rock, and the tomb of Erechtheus were all in the same sacred precinct, the architect Mnesicles had to design the temple around them, a fact that makes the plan of the Erechtheum (see Fig. 4) as complex as that of the Parthenon is simple. The rectangular interior, some 31½ feet wide and 61¼ feet long, had four rooms for the various shrines on two different levels, one 10¾ feet higher than the other. Projecting outward from three of the sides were porticoes, each of different dimensions and design. That on the east has a row of six Ionic columns almost 22 feet high. The north porch (Fig. 12) has a like number but with four in front and two on the sides; while the smaller porch on the south (Fig. 13) is distinguished by its six sculptured maidens, the famous caryatids, who replace the customary columns.

Unlike those of the Doric order, Ionic columns (Fig. 10) are more slender and have their

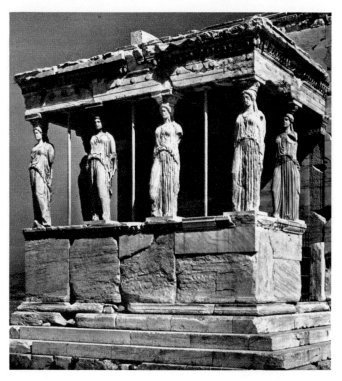

12. MNESICLES(?). Erechtheum (north porch), Athens. 35'2" wide.

13. MNESICLES(?). Erechtheum (south porch), Athens. Caryatids 7'9" high.

greatest diameter at the bottom. Their shafts rest on a molded base instead of directly on the stylobate, and they have 24 instead of 20 flutings. Most striking, however, is the Ionic capital with its scroll-like volutes. The fine columns of the north porch (Fig. 12) rest on molded bases carved with a delicate design. The necking has a band decorated with a leaf pattern; above this comes a smaller band with the egg-and-dart motif, and after the volutes a thin abacus carved with eggs and darts. The columns support an architrave divided horizontally into three bands stepping slightly inward, a continuous frieze rather than the alternating Doric triglyphs and metopes; and above rises a shallow pediment without sculpture. A greatly admired and much-imitated doorway leads into the cella of the Erechtheum. Framed with a series of receding planes, the lintel above combines each of the decorative motifs that appear elsewhere in the building. As seen in the band that runs around the cella (Fig. 14), these include (from lower to upper) the honeysuckle, bead-and-reel, egg-and-dart, bead-and-reel, and leaf-and-tongue.

Facing the Parthenon, the south porch of the Erechtheum, with its caryatids (Fig. 13), is smaller than the others, measuring only some 10 by 15 feet. Above three steps rises a 6-foot parapet on which the six maidens, about one and a half times larger than life, are standing. In order to preserve the

proportions of the building and not appear to overburden the figures, the frieze and pediment were omitted. Grouped as if in a procession, the figures infer a stately forward motion, with three on one side lifting their right legs and those on the other, their left. The folds of their draperies suggest the fluting of columns; and, while the maidens seem solid enough to carry their loads, there is no hint of stiffness in their stances. And just as the cella frieze of the Parthenon reenacts the Panathenaic

14. Erechtheum. Decorative band showing honeysuckle, bead-and-reel, egg-and-dart, bead-and-reel, and leaf-and-tongue motifs. Glyptothek, Munich.

15. CALLICRATES. Temple of Athena Nike, Athens. *c.* 427–423 B.C. Pentelic marble, 17′9″ × 26′10″.

built about 390 B.C., had a circular colonnade of 20 Doric columns outside and 10 Corinthian columns inside. The oldest surviving Corinthian structure in Athens is the Choragic Monument of Lysicrates (Figs. 16, 17), now located at the foot of the acropolis. Too ornate for the generally restrained Hellenic taste, the Corinthian had to wait for Hellenistic and Roman times to reach its full development, as seen in the ruins of the Temple of Olympian Zeus (Fig. 18).

SCULPTURE

The Parthenon Marbles

The Parthenon sculptures have a special significance, because they rank high among the surviving originals of the 5th century B.C. The extant Parthenon statuary falls into three groups: the high-relief metopes of the Doric frieze, the free-standing pediment figures, and the low-relief cella frieze. Phidias' celebrated gold-and-ivory cult statue of Athena has long since disappeared, and inferior later copies convey little of the splendor attributed to it by the ancients. As architectural sculpture, the friezes and pediments should not be judged apart from the building they embellish. By providing diagonal lines and irregular masses as well as figures in motion, they offset the more static vertical and horizontal balances of the structural parts. The original location of these sculptures must also be kept in mind by the modern viewer: they were intended to be seen outdoors in the intense Greek sunlight and from the ground some 35 feet below (not out of context in the artificial light of a museum and at eye level).

Since the entire Parthenon project was completed in little more than a decade, Phidias, its presumed designer, could have had time to do little more than make sketches for his assistants to work from. He may have done some examples in each group, and the best of the sculptures are sometimes attributed to him. The result is a model of simplicity and restraint, and the marbles complement the building as a whole rather than assert themselves independently. The workmanship reveals the unevenness common to all group projects. Some sculptures show the hand of a master; others are routine products of artisans. But the fact that the metopes were finished first, then were surpassed by the cella frieze, and both, in turn, were eclipsed by the later pedimental sculptures shows that the work did not aim at standardization but rather at a continuous approach to the ideal of excellent craftsmanship.

festival, so these maidens well may be related to the ritual of the Erechtheum. A sculptural fragment from an older temple on the acropolis shows a priestess leading a procession in which four maidens balance a long chest on their heads. Since the temple bears the name of their warrior king, the caryatids seem to suggest a ceremony honoring the heroic dead.

On their acropolis, the Athenians brought to the highest point of development two distinct Greek building traditions—the Doric with the Parthenon, and the Ionic with the Erechtheum and the Temple of Athena Nike (Fig. 15). By combining the two architectural orders in the Propylaea and enshrining them separately in the Parthenon and the Erechtheum, the Athenians symbolized that their city was the place where the Dorian people of the western Greek mainland and the Ionians of the coast of Asia Minor across the Aegean Sea had for centuries lived together in peace and harmony and through the generations had become one people. In the following century, another order was added: the Corinthian. Taller and more tree-like than the Ionic, the columns of the Corinthian order are distinguished by their ornate capitals with double rows of acanthus leaves and fernlike fronds rising from each corner and terminating in miniature volutes. The Tholos at Delphi (Fig. 47),

(left) 16. Choragic Monument of Lysicrates, Athens. 334 B.C. Pentelic marble. Podium 13′ high, 9½′ square; shrine 20′ high, 7′ in diameter.

(right) 17. Choragic Monument of Lysicrates (after Stuart and Revett).

18. Temple of Olympian Zeus, Athens. 174 B.C.–A.D. 130. Pentelic marble, columns 56½′ high.

The metopes of the Doric frieze play an important part in the architectural design of the Parthenon by providing a welcome variety of figures to relieve the structural unity, and their diagonal lines contrast well with the alternating verticals of the triglyphs and the long horizontals of the architrave and cornice just below and above. In order to take full advantage of the bright sunlight, these metopes were done in *high relief*, a technique by which the figures are deeply carved so as to project boldly outward from the background plane. The subject is the battle of the

(below) 19. *Centaur Abducting Maiden*, metope from Parthenon frieze. 447–441 B.C. Marble, 3′ 11″ × 4′ 2″. Louvre, Paris.

(bottom) 20. PHIDIAS(?). *Lapith and Centaur*, metope from Parthenon frieze. 447–441 B.C. Marble, 3′ 11″ × 4′ 2″. British Museum, London.

Lapiths and centaurs after a centaur has kidnapped a Lapith bride at a wedding feast (Fig. 19). In one of the most skillfully executed (Fig. 20), the rich spreading folds of the mantle form a fine unifying framework for the human figure, and, in turn, both make a striking contrast with the awkward angularity of the grotesque centaur.

The inner frieze (Figs. 21–25) that ran along the outer walls of the cella was a continuous band about 3¾ feet high, over 500 feet in length, and included some 600 figures. Since this frieze was placed behind the colonnade and directly below roof level, where it had to be viewed close by at a steep upward angle, some sculptural adjustments were called for. The technique, of necessity, was *low relief*, in which the figures are shallowly carved. Because shadows in this indirect light are cast upward, the frieze had to be tilted slightly and cut so that the lower parts of the figures project only 1¼ inches from the background plane, with the relief gradually becoming bolder toward the top where the figures extend outward about 2¼ inches. The handling of space, however, is so deft that as many as half a dozen horsemen are depicted riding abreast without confusing the separate spatial planes. The horses, when seen at eye level, are too small in comparison with their riders. When viewed from below and in indirect light, however, they would not seem out of proportion. The use of color and metal attachments for such details as reins and bridles also helped accent parts and protected the clarity of the design. All the heads, whether the figures are afoot or on horseback, are kept on the same level in order to preserve the unity of the design as well as to provide a parallel with the architectural line. (This principle, known as *isocephaly*, will also be encountered in later Byzantine art [see Figs. 124, 137, and Plate 8].)

The cella frieze, unlike the traditional mythological subjects elsewhere in the Parthenon sculptures, depicts the Athenians themselves participating in the festival of their goddess. The scene is the Greater Panathenaea that took place every four years. Larger than the annual local procession because it included delegations from other Greek cities, the Greater Panathenaea was also the prelude to more elaborate poetical and oratorical contests, dramatic presentations, and games. On the western side (Figs. 21, 22), which is still in place, last-minute preparations for the parade are in progress as the riders ready their mounts. The action, appropriately enough, starts just at the point where the live procession, after passing through the Propylaea, would have paused to regroup. The parade then splits in two, one file proceeding along the north and the other along

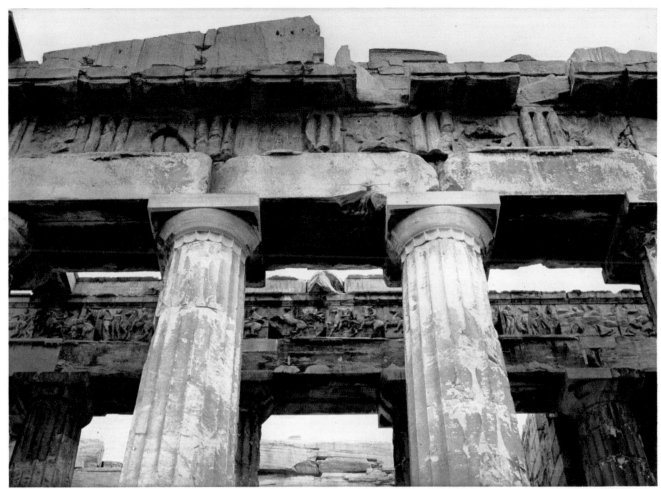

21. Parthenon. Frieze of west cella. *c.* 440 B.C. Marble.

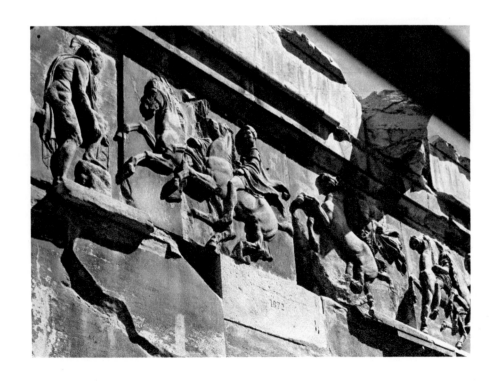

22. *Horsemen*, detail of Parthenon west cella frieze. *c.* 440 B.C. Marble, 3'7" high.

(above) 23. *Procession of Maidens*, detail of Parthenon east cella frieze. *c.* 440 B.C. Marble, 3′ 7″ high. Louvre, Paris.

(left) 24. *Poseidon and Apollo*, detail of Parthenon east cella frieze. *c.* 440 B.C. Marble, 3′ 7″ high. Acropolis Museum, Athens.

the south side. After the bareback riders come the charioteers; and, as the procession approaches the eastern corners, the marshals slack the tempo to a more dignified pace. Here are musicians playing lyres and flutes, youths bearing wine jugs for libations, and maidens walking with stately tread (Fig. 23). The two files then converge on the east side, where magistrates are waiting to begin the ceremonies. Even the immortal gods, as seen in the panel depicting Poseidon and Apollo (Fig. 24), are present to bestow their Olympian approval on the proceedings. The high point of the ritual comes in the center of the east side with the presentation of the *peplos* (Fig. 25), the saffron and purple-tinted mantle woven and embroidered by chosen maidens to drape the ancient wooden image of Athena.

The pedimental sculptures, in contrast to the friezes, are free-standing figures, carved in the round. The themes of both pediments have to do with Athena, that on the west (Fig. 26), facing the city, depicting her triumph over Poseidon (see p. 12) and that on the east pediment (Fig. 27) recounting the story of her miraculous birth, the event that was celebrated each summer at the Panathenaea. While but a few fragments of the western pediment remain, enough survives of its eastern counterpart to convey a good idea of its original state.

From various sources it is known that the eastern scene is Mt. Olympus, and Zeus, father of the gods, was seated in the center. On one side stood Hephaestus, cleaving open the head of Zeus to let

(top) 25. *Presentation of Peplos*, detail of Parthenon east cella frieze. *c.* 440 B.C. Marble, 3′ 7″ high. British Museum, London.

(below) 26. *Contest of Athena and Poseidon for the Land of Attica.* Reconstruction of Parthenon west pediment. Acropolis Museum, Athens.

28. Parthenon. East pediment figures. *c.* 438–432 B.C. Marble. (above) *Sun God's Horses*, lifesize; (below) *Dionysus*, over lifesize; (opposite page) *Demeter and Persephone*, 4′ 10½″ high; *Iris*, 5′ 8″ high. British Museum, London.

27. *Birth of Athena*. Reconstruction of Parthenon east pediment. Acropolis Museum, Athens.

Athena spring forth in full battle array. The sudden appearance of the goddess of wisdom, like a brilliant idea from the mind of its creator, disturbs the Olympian calm. As the news spreads from the center to the sides, each figure is in some way affected by the presence of divine wisdom in their midst. Iris, the messenger of the gods (Fig. 28), rushes toward the left with a rapid motion as revealed by her windswept drapery. Seated on a chest, Demeter and Persephone are turning toward her, and the rich folds of their costumes bespeak their attitudes and interest. The reclining Dionysus, with his panther skin and mantle spread over a rock, is awakening and looking toward the sun god Helios, the horses of whose chariot are just rising from the foaming sea at break of day. On the opposite side are three goddesses (Fig. 29) whose postures bring out their relationship to the composition. The one nearest the center of the pediment, aware of what has happened, is about to rise, while the middle figure is starting to turn toward her. The reclining figure at the right, still in repose, is as unaware of the event as is her counterpart Dionysus on the far left. Like the feminine group on the left, these figures constitute a unified episode in the composition, and their relation to the whole is made clear in the lush lines of their flowing robes. This undulating linear pattern, and the manner in which it transparently reveals the anatomy of the splendid bodies beneath, mark a

29. Parthenon. East pediment figures. *c.* 438–432 B.C. Marble. (above) *Three Goddesses*, over lifesize; (left) *Moon Goddess' Horse*, lifesize. British Museum, London.

high point in the art of sculpture. At the far right, the chariot of the moon goddess Selene was seen descending. Now only the expressive downward-declining horse's head remains to show by his spent energies that it is the end of the day.

Perhaps the most admirable aspect of the whole composition is the ease and grace with which each piece fulfills its assigned space. Fitting suitable figures into a low isosceles triangle and at the same time maintaining an uncrowded yet unified appearance was a problem that long occupied Greek designers. One over-lifesize figure, such as Apollo, usually dominated the center, with seated or crouching figures on either side and reclining ones in the acute side angles. The pediment space of the Parthenon stretched about 90 feet and rose over 11 feet in the center. The rising and setting sun and moon chariots defined the time span as that of a single day, while the setting of Mt. Olympus and the single event supplied the identity of time, place, and action in keeping with the classical

unities (a principle that will be treated more fully in the section on drama). The ascending and descending chariots gave a contrasting upward and downward movement on the extreme ends, while the reclining and seated figures led the eye to the apex where the climax took place. The subsequent action dispersed the middle figures centrifugally once more toward the sides. The varied postures, rich plastic modeling, and flowing lines connect all the figures with such a unified motion that, even though the center ones are now missing, the meaning is quite clear.

Taken as a whole, the Parthenon marbles present a picture of the Greek past and present plus aspirations for the future. The attempt to interpret the dark ancient myths of a people into more enlightened contemporary terms is to be found here in the sculptures as well as in Greek philosophy, poetry, and drama. The metopes on the east portray the primeval battle of the gods and giants for control of the world, and the triumph of the Olympians hailed the coming of cosmic order out of chaos. The metopes on the south show the Lapiths, oldest inhabitants of the Greek peninsula, subduing the half-human centaurs with the aid of the Athenian hero Theseus. This victory signals the ascendancy of human ideals over the bestial side of human nature. In the north group, the Homeric epic of the defeat of the Trojans is told, while in the west metopes the Greeks are seen overcoming the Amazons, those ferocious women warriors who symbolized the Asiatic enemies and, in this case, allude to the Athenian defeat of the Persians at Marathon. In the east pediment, the

birth of the city's patroness Athena is seen; while the west pediment tells the story of the rivalry of Athena as goddess of the intellect and Poseidon, patron of maritime trade, suggesting the conflict of two ways of life—the pursuit of enlightenment and of material wealth. The Panathenaic procession of the cella walls brings history up to date by depicting a contemporary subject. Here the proud Athenians could look upward and see their own images carved on a sacred temple, an echo of the living procession that marched along the sides of the temple on feast days. The climax came after they had gathered at the east portico and the portals of the temple were opened to the rays of the rising sun, revealing the image of the goddess herself. Shining forth in all her gold-and-ivory glory, Athena was the personification of the eternal truth, goodness, and beauty for which her faithful followers were striving. With her help, the forces of Greek civilization had overcome the ignorance of the barbarians. The bonds between the goddess and the citizens of her city were thus periodically renewed, and the Parthenon as a whole glorified not only Athena but the Athenians as well.

The Course of Hellenic Sculpture

The tremendous distance traversed by the art of sculpture from the archaic, or preclassical, phase prior to the 5th century B.C. to the end of the Hellenic style period in the mid-4th century can be seen clearly when examples are compared. The *Kouros* (Fig. 30) represents the archaic sculptural type of youthful athlete, victor in the games, moving toward the temple to dedicate himself. The advancing left foot provides the only suggestion of movement in the otherwise rigid posture. The anatomy of the torso is severely formal and very close to the block of stone out of which it was carved. The wide shoulders and long arms attached to the sides provide a quadrangular framework; the long vertical line from the neck to the navel divides the chest; while the diamond-shaped abdomen is defined by four almost straight lines, a heritage of the formalized geometrical conventions of the archaic period.

The *Doryphorus*, or *Spear Bearer*, by Polyclitus (Fig. 31), in contrast, moves with greater poise and freedom. Originally in bronze, it is now known

30. *Kouros*, from Sounion. *c.* 615–590 B.C. Marble, 11′ high. National Museum, Athens.

31. POLYCLITUS. *Doryphorus (Spear Bearer)*. Roman copy of original of *c.* 450–440 B.C. Marble, 6′ 6″ high. National Museum, Naples.

(left) 32. PRAXITELES. *Hermes and the Infant Dionysus.*
c. 340 B.C. Marble, 7' 1" high. Museum, Olympia.
(Compare Plate 1.)

(bottom) 33. *Charioteer*, from Sanctuary of Apollo,
Delphi. *c.* 470 B.C. Bronze, 6' 11" high. Museum,
Delphi.

only through routine marble copies. The sculptor
was renowned in ancient times for his attempts to
formulate a canon, or rational theory of proportions, for the human figure. The exact way Polyclitus' theory operated is not known, but the
Roman architect Vitruvius mentions that beauty
consists "in the proportions, not of the elements,
but of the parts, that is to say, of finger to finger, and
of all the fingers to the palm and wrist, and of these
to the forearm, and of the forearm to the upper arm,
and of all the parts to each other, as they are set
forth in the Canon of Polyclitus." Just as the
Parthenon had its module derived from a unit of
the building, so Polyclitus took his module from a
part of the body. Whether it was the head, the
forearm, or the hand apparently varied from statue
to statue. Once adopted, however, the whole and
all its parts were expressible in multiples or fractions of the module. As Vitruvius illustrated the
canon, the head would be one eighth of the total
height; the face one tenth, subdivided, in turn,
into three parts: forehead, nose, and mouth and
chin. The forearm would be one quarter the height,
and the width of the chest equal to this length of
forearm. Like the optical refinements of the
Parthenon, however, Polyclitus' canon was not a
mechanical formula but one that allowed for some
flexibility, so that the dimensions could be adjusted
for a figure in movement or for one designed to be
seen from a certain angle.

Praxiteles' *Hermes and the Infant Dionysus*
(Fig. 32; Plate 1), coming at the close of the
Hellenic period, is the epitome of poise and polish.
Unlike the rather studied *Doryphorus*, Hermes rests
his weight easily on one foot, and the relaxed
stance throws the body into the familiar S-curve, a
Praxitelean pose widely copied in later Hellenistic
and Roman statuary. From the stiffness of the
stolid archaic *Kouros* and the strength of the
stocky *Doryphorus*, the sculptor Praxiteles has arrived at complete plastic mastery of his material.
Through the soft modeling and suave surface
treatment, Praxiteles suggests the blood, bone, and
sinews beneath the skin and gives his cold marble
material the vibrancy and warmth of living flesh.

The *Charioteer of Delphi* (Fig. 33) and the *Zeus*
found at Artemision (Fig. 34; Plate 2)—two of the
rare Hellenic bronze originals—and the Roman
marble copy of Myron's lost bronze *Discobolus*, or

Discus Thrower (Fig. 35), reveal a transition in style from quiet monumentality to energetic action within a 20-year timespan in the mid-5th century. The splendid *Charioteer* once was part of a larger group that included several horses, and, although in action, the figure is given something of the monumentality and equilibrium of a fluted column by the vertical folds of its lower garment. The commanding figure of *Zeus*, poised to throw a thunderbolt, reveals in its powerful musculature the massive reserves of strength of a truly godlike physique. In Myron's *Discobolus*, the taut yet resilient muscles of the athlete are poised momentarily between a backward movement and forward thrust. The vigorous motion is admirably contained by the curved arms that enclose the composition and confine the activity to a single plane.

The archaic *Kore* from Samos (Fig. 36), sometimes called "*Hera*" *of Samos*, is one of a file of maidens, originally in a temple courtyard, carrying small animals as votive offerings. Her severely cylindrical figure is quite abstract in that everything extraneous has been eliminated and only the essential formal and linear elements retained. The rhythmically repeated vertical lines of the skirt contrast with the ingenious curves of the upper

(above) 34. *Zeus (Poseidon?)*. *c.* 460–450 B.C. Bronze, 6′ 10″ high. National Museum, Athens. (Compare Plate 2.)

(top) 35. MYRON. *Discobolus (Discus Thrower)*. Roman copy after bronze original of *c.* 460 B.C. Marble, life-size. National Museum, Rome.

(right) 36. *Kore*, from Samos. *c.* 550 B.C. Marble, *c.* 5′ 3″ high. State Museums, Berlin.

(above) 37. PHIDIAS. *Athena Lemnia.* Roman copy after original of *c.* 450 B.C. Marble, *c.* 6′ 6″ high. Body, Albertinum, Dresden; head, Civic Museum, Bologna.

(right) 38. PRAXITELES. *Aphrodite of Cnidos.* Roman copy after original of *c.* 320 B.C. Marble, 6′ 8″ high. Vatican Museum, Rome.

(below) 39. *Birth of Aphrodite,* center panel of "Ludovisi Throne." *c.* 470 B.C. Marble, 4′ 8″ wide. National Museum, Rome.

drapery to create a pleasing linear design. The *Athena Lemnia* (Fig. 37) is a superior marble copy of Phidias' original bronze statue that stood on the Athenian acropolis. Phidias here created a mood that is more lyrical than epical, and in ancient sources the statue was referred to regularly as "the beautiful." The serene profile, softened by the subtle modeling, surely approaches the ideal of chaste classical beauty. Praxiteles' *Aphrodite of Cnidos* was proclaimed by Greco-Roman critics as the finest statue in existence. Now known only through such an inferior copy as Figure 38, the "smile playing gently over her parted lips" and the "soft melting gaze of the eyes with their bright and joyous expression" that the Roman writer Lucian so admired in the original can now only be imagined. Praxiteles, however, departed from the draped goddesses of the previous century by boldly portraying the goddess of love in the nude. By so doing, he created a prototype that influenced all subsequent treatment of the undraped female figure.

Three relief panels show in yet another way the course Greek sculpture took. The *Birth of*

Aphrodite (Fig. 39) depicts the goddess of love rising from the sea. A pleasant linear rhythm is created by the combination of curved, straight, and zigzagged lines of the drapery. Some naturalistic detail is included in the rocks of the shore, but formal considerations dominate the composition with the interaction of the attendants bending inward and the arms and breasts of Venus stretching outward. The noble restraint and pensive attitude of the panel portraying *Athena* (Fig. 40) yields at the end of the century to the informal treatment of the *Goddess Adjusting Her Sandal* (Fig. 41). The dignified calm of the erect Athena has now melted into the graceful, relaxed posture of the figure bending downward. Whatever rigidity there was in the perpendicular lines of the earlier example has given way to the fluid rippling drapery of the later relief where, through the transparent, clinging drapery, the illusion of a moving, breathing body beneath is achieved.

DRAMA

Greek drama was a distillation of life in poetic form, represented (or imitated, to use the ancient term) on the stage. In these vivid presentations, members of the audience through their representatives in the chorus became vicarious participants in events happening to a group of people at another time and in another place. Like all great works of art, Greek drama can be approached on many different levels. At one, it can be a thrilling story of violent actions and bloody revenge. At another, it is a struggle between human ambition and divine retribution, or a conflict of free will and predestined fate. At still another level, it becomes a moving experience that ennobles through lofty language and inspired poetry. Plots were always taken from mythology, heroic legends, or stories of royal houses. Since these age-old themes were forms of popular history known in advance, the dramatist could concern himself with more purely poetic functions than plot development. He could provide dramatic commentaries on old tales, reinterpreting them in the light of recent events. He could thus inspire by conjuring up the heroic past, as did Aeschylus in *The Persians*; express individual sentiments in the light of universal experience, as did Sophocles in *Antigone*; invite reexamination of ancient superstitions, as did Euripides in *The Bacchants*; or remind that present difficulties had parallels in time past and, by showing that it has ever been thus, place current problems in broader historical perspective.

The origins of the Greek dramatic form were rooted in the religious rites associated with the worship of Dionysus (the Bacchus of Roman

40. *Athena*, relief from Acropolis, Athens. *c.* 445 B.C. Marble, 18″ high. Acropolis Museum, Athens.

41. *Goddess Adjusting Her Sandal*, relief from balustrade of Temple of Athena Nike, Athens. 410–407 B.C. Marble, 42 × 20″. Acropolis Museum, Athens.

mythology), the god of wine and revelry, whose cult festivals coincided with spring planting and fall harvesting seasons (see Fig. 43). From primitive magical practices, the rituals gradually grew in refinement until they became a vehicle for powerful creative expression. When theaters came to be built, they were located in a precinct sacred to Dionysus. His altar occupied the center of the circular *orchestra* where the chorus sang and danced, and the audience which gathered paid their tribute to him by their presence.

In the beginning, Greek drama had only a chorus, whose function, according to the philosopher Nietzsche, was to conjure up the divine vision in which it "beholds its lord and master Dionysus . . . [and] sees how he, the god, suffers and glorifies himself." The vision beheld by the chorus eventually came to be acted out, and the alternation between group *choruses* and individually declaimed *episodes* became the basis of the dramatic form. Put another way, the choral songs were at first a group narration of great deeds. Later, the words attributed to the hero were sung and mimed by the leader of the chorus. Then a second and a third actor were added, and the dialogue of the enacted episodes achieved parity with the alternating choruses. Hellenistic and Roman drama were to upset this classic balance by emphasizing the action and roles of individual performers, but in Hellenic times the collective voice of the chorus and that of the principal actors were equal in importance. As the group chanted its *strophes* and *antistrophes* (turns and counterturns), it effected transitions from scenes, reminded of the past and foretold the future, reflected public opinion, voiced the dramatist's own commentary, and, above all, by acting as its proxy, made the audience feel a part of the play.

The Theater of Dionysus at Athens (see Fig. 3), like the better preserved one at Epidaurus (Fig. 42), had an *auditorium* hollowed out of a hillside to accommodate about 18,000 spectators. The semicircular tiers of seats half surrounded the orchestra and faced the *skene*, a scene building or raised platform, on which the actors played their roles. The skene had a permanent architectural façade with three doors for the actors, while the chorus entered and exited at the corners below. The stylized face of the skene, suggesting a temple or palace, was suitable for most dramatic situations, since the action almost always took place in the open. The chorus, for example, usually represented worshipers at a shrine, townspeople or petitioners before a palace, a mob, or a group of prisoners, while the actors moving in and out of the portals above took the parts of priests, heroes, or members of royal families. When the situation demanded another setting, the chorus or an actor would paint the scene with a few words so that other sets were unnecessary.

A typical Greek play opens with a *prologue*, spoken by one of the actors. The prologue sets the scene, outlines the plot, and provides a taking-off point for the action that is to follow. The substance of the drama then unfolds in a sequence of alternating choruses and episodes (usually five episodes enclosed by six choruses) and concludes with the *exodus* of the chorus and an *epilogue*. Actors wore masks of general types that could be recognized instantly by the audience. The size and outdoor location of the theaters made facial expressions ineffective, and the swift pace of Greek drama requires the player of a king or peasant to establish immediately a type and character. The masks were equipped with megaphones that helped project the voices, though the acoustics of the bowl-shaped

42. Theater, Epidaurus. *c.* 350 B.C. 373′ in diameter, orchestra 66′ across.

theaters are generally excellent. Masks also proved useful when an actor took more than one part, bringing him immediate acceptance in either role.

Restraint and simplicity were the rule in Greek staging. As with the later Elizabethan theater, scenery was conspicuous by its absence. The only visual illusion seems to have been the *mechane*, a crane that lowered to the stage those actors portraying gods. This *deus ex machina*, or god from the machine, in later times became a convenient way of solving dramatic problems that were too complex to be worked out by normal means. Direct action, moreover, never occurred on stage. Any violent deed took place elsewhere and was reported by a messenger or another character. The plays proceeded by narration, commentary, speculation, dialogue, and discussion. All these devices—plot known in advance, permanent stage setting, use of masks, offstage action—served two principal purposes: to accent the poetry of the play and to give the freest possible scope to the spectator's imagination. But while Greek drama is a complex of choral song, group dances, mimed action, and dialogue coordinated into a dramatic whole, poetry always is the central dramatic agent. It should also be noted that the Athenians experienced their plays and poetry only in oral presentations. While manuscript copies of literary and philosophical works were available to scholars, books in the modern sense did not exist. Much of the beauty and power of the plays was derived from the heightened experience of poetic declamation as well as from the Greek tongue itself. Not an accentual language, Greek admits of a wide variety of metrical patterns capable of expressing every nuance of action and mood. In reading a Greek drama in translation, therefore, one must let one's imagination supply the melody, color, and flowing rhythms of the original language as well as the missing factors associated with a live theatrical production.

The scope of Greek drama was tremendous, extending from majestic tragedy of heroic proportions, through the pathos of *melodrama* (in its proper meaning of drama with melody) and subtle satires (or satyr plays), all the way to the riotous comedies of Aristophanes. Conflict is always the basis for dramatic action, and the playwrights set up tensions between such forces as murder and revenge, crime and retribution, cowardice and courage, protest and resignation, human pride and humility. When, for instance, a hero is confronted with his destiny, the obstacles he encounters are at once insurmountable and necessary to surmount. In the conflict that follows, the play runs a gamut of emotions and explores the heights to which human life can soar and the depths to which it can

43. SCHOOL OF SCOPAS(?). *Dionysian Procession*. 4th century B.C. Marble. National Museum, Athens.

sink. In Sophocles' *Oedipus Rex*, the hero starts at the peak of his kingly powers and ends in the abyss of human degradation. Each character in a true drama, moreover, is drawn three dimensionally so as to reveal a typically human mixture of attractive and repulsive, good and bad, traits. The *protagonist*, or central character, can fulfill the necessary conditions of tragedy only when he portrays some noble figure—one "highly renowned or prosperous," as Aristotle puts it—who is eventually brought to grief through some flaw in his own psychological make-up and by some inevitable stroke of fate. The reasons for this must be made apparent to the audience gradually through the process of "causal necessity." A common man's woes might bring about a pathetic situation but not a tragic one in the classical sense. When a virtuous hero is rewarded or the evil designs of a villain receive their just deserts, obviously there is no tragic situation. When a blameless man is brought from a fortunate to an unfortunate condition or when an evil person rises from misery to good fortune, there is likewise no tragedy because the moral sense is outraged.

Under Aeschylus, its founder, Greek tragedy sought to comprehend the mystery of the divine will, often so inscrutable to man—as in his *Agamemnon*. By establishing a working relationship between man and his gods, Aeschylus tried to reconcile the conflict between the human and the divine and find a basis for personal as well as social justice. The implications of the early Aeschylean tragedy were thus strongly ethical, showing clearly that the drama was still identified in his mind with theological thought. The forms of Sophocles' plays were distinguished by their impeccable craftsmanship, while their lofty content was based on the course of human destiny as seen in the light of the moral law of the universe.

Euripides, said the philosopher Aristotle, sought to show men as they are, while Sophocles had depicted men as they ought to be. In some ways, the works of Euripides may not be so typical of the Hellenic style as those of Aeschylus or Sophocles, but his influence on the subsequent development of the drama, both in Hellenistic and later times, was incalculably greater. *The Bacchants*, the last of his ninety-odd plays, was written at a time when the darkness of disillusionment was descending on Athenian intellectuals toward the end of the disastrous Peloponnesian war, and in it he gives voice to some of the doubts and uncertainties of his time. Like most masterpieces, it is in some respects atypical, while in others it seems to stem from the deepest traditional roots of the theater's origin. Despite some inner inconsistencies and a certain elusiveness of meaning, *The Bacchants* has all the formal perfection and grandeur of utterance of the loftiest tragedies. The strange wild beauty of the choruses, the magic of its poetry, and the complex interplay between the human and divine wills endow it with all the necessary ingredients of the theater at its best.

After the great days of Aeschylus, Sophocles, and Euripides were over, Aristotle, with knowledge of their complete works instead of the relatively few extant examples known today, wrote a perceptive analysis of tragedy and more broadly of art in general in his treatise *Poetics*. According to him, true drama, as indeed all other works of art, must have form in the sense of a beginning, a middle, and an end. Unity of time, place, and action is also desirable. Sophocles' *Oedipus Rex*, for example, takes place in a single day (albeit a busy one); all the scenes are set in front of the palace at Thebes; and the action is direct and continuous without subplots. Other Greek plays encompass a longer span of time and have several settings. But, as Aristotle pointed out, these unities were useful but by no means hard and fast rules. In the episodes, convention held that three actors on stage at one time was the maximum. If the play required six parts, the roles were usually apportioned among three actors. As the action proceeds, the conflict between *protagonist* and *antagonist* emerges, and the play should rise to its climax in the middle episode. Through the proper tragic necessity, the hero's downfall comes because he carried the seeds of his own destruction within his breast. After this turning point, the well-planned anticlimax resolves the action once more into a state of equilibrium. Tragedy, according to Aristotle, had to be composed of six necessary elements which he ranked as follows: Plot, "the arrangement of the incidents"; Character, "that which reveals moral purpose"; Thought, "where something is proved to be or not

to be"; Diction, "the metrical arrangements of the words"; Song, "melody holds the chief place among the embellishments"; and Spectacle. Finally, Aristotle summed up his definition of tragedy as "an imitation of an action that is serious, complete, and of a certain magnitude; in language embellished with each kind of ornament, the several kinds being found in separate sections of the play; in the form of action, not of narrative; with incidents arousing pity and fear, wherewith to accomplish its *katharsis* [purgation] of the emotions."

MUSIC

The word *music* today carries with it the connotation of a fully mature and independent art. It must be borne in mind, however, that symphonies, chamber music, and solo instrumental compositions, where the focus is almost entirely on abstract sound, are relatively modern forms. The word *music* is still used to cover the union of sound with many other elements, as in the case of popular songs, dance music, military marches, and church music. It also describes the combination with lyric and narrative poetry, as in songs and ballads; with bodily movements, as in the dance and ballet; and with drama, as in opera.

In ancient Greece, *music* in its broadest sense meant any of the arts and sciences that came under the patronage of the muses, those imaginary maidens who were the daughters of the heavenly Zeus and the more earthly Mnemosyne. Since Zeus was the creator and Mnemosyne, as her name implies, the symbol of memory, the muses and their arts were considered to be the results of the union of the creative urge and memory, half divine, half human. This was simply a fanciful way of saying that music was recorded inspiration. As Greek civilization progressed, the muses, under the patronage of Apollo, god of prophecy and enlightenment, gradually increased to nine, and the arts and sciences over which they presided came to include all the intellectual and inspirational disciplines that sprang from the fertile minds of this highly creative people —lyric poetry, tragic and comic drama, choral dancing, and song. Astronomy and history were also included. The visual arts and crafts, on the other hand, were protected by Athena and Hephaestus—intelligence tempered by fire. Plato and others placed music in opposition to gymnastic or physical pursuits, and its meaning in this sense was as broad as our use of the words *liberal arts* or *culture*.

The Greeks also used *music* more narrowly in the sense of the tonal art. But music was always

intimately bound up with poetry, drama, and the dance and was usually found in their company. At one place in the *Republic*, Socrates asks: "And when you speak of music, do you include literature or not?" And the answer is in the affirmative. Thus, while it is known that the Greeks did have independent instrumental music apart from its combination with words, evidence points to the fact that the vast body of their music was connected with literary forms. This does not imply, of course, that music lacked a distinct identity or that it was swallowed up by poetry, but rather that it had an important and honored part in poetry. Plato, for example, inquires: "And I think that you must have observed again and again what a poor appearance the tales of the poets make when stripped of the colours which music puts upon them, and recited in simple prose. ... They are like faces which were never really beautiful, but only blooming; and now the bloom of youth has passed away from them?"

Greek music must therefore be considered primarily in its union with literature, as illustrated in the vase painting *Instruction in Music and Grammar in an Attic School* by Douris (Fig. 44). The clearest statement of this again is found in the *Republic*, where it is pointed out that "melody is composed of three things, the words, the harmony [by which is meant the sequence of melodic intervals], and the rhythm." In discussing the relative importance of each, Plato states that "harmony and rhythm must follow the words." The two arts thus are united in the single one of *prosody*—that is, the melodic and rhythmic setting of a poetic text. The Greek melodies and rhythms are known to have been associated with specific moods, or *modes*— scales constructed by adjusting the pitch of tones within the octave as with the more modern major and minor modes. The great variety of Greek modes allowed poets and dramatists to elicit a gamut of emotional responses from their audiences. And while ethical and emotional orientations have changed over the centuries, the basic modal and metrical system of the Greeks has, in effect, continued through all subsequent periods of Western music and poetry.

Music, in both its broad and narrow senses, was closely woven into the fabric of the emotional, intellectual, and social life of the ancient Greeks, and the art was considered by them to have a fundamental connection with the well-being of individuals personally as well as with their social and physical environment. There is no more eloquent tribute to the power of art in public affairs than that made by Socrates who said "when modes of music change, the fundamental laws of the State always change with them." Education for young people in Greece consisted of a balanced curriculum of music for the soul and gymnastic for the body. The broad principle of building a sound body is still one of the ideals of education. Even the welfare of the soul after death had musical overtones, since immortality to many Greeks meant being somehow in tune with the cosmic forces, and being at last able to hear the "music of the spheres." All these notions had to do with the idea of the physical nature being some way in harmony with the metaphysical, and the soul being an attunement of the body. According to the Greek myth of Orpheus, who is depicted in a fine red-figured vase of the early 5th century B.C. (Plate 3), music even had the miraculous power to overcome death. This thought found an enduring place in Western literature, and no writer has

44. DOURIS. *Instruction in Music and Grammar in an Attic School.* Red-figured painting on the exterior of a kylix. *c.* 470 B.C. State Museums, Berlin.

expressed it more sensitively than Shakespeare in *The Merchant of Venice* (Act V, Scene 1):

> . . . look, how the floor of heaven
> Is thick inlaid with patines of bright gold:
> There's not the smallest orb which thou behold'st
> But in his motion like an angel sings,
> Still quiring to the young-eyed cherubins;
> Such harmony is in immortal souls;
> But, whilst this muddy vesture of decay
> Doth grossly close it in, we cannot hear it.

The most important Greek contribution to music is without doubt a theoretical one—that of coordinating the mathematical ratios of melodic intervals with their scale system. The discovery, attributed to Pythagoras, showed that such intervals as the octave, fifth, and fourth had a mathematical relationship. This can easily be heard when a tuned string is stopped off exactly in the middle. The musical interval between the tone of the unstopped string and the one which is divided into two equal parts will then be the octave, and the mathematical ratio will be 1:2. Then if a segment of the string divided in two parts is compared with one of a string divided into three parts, the resulting interval will be the fifth, and the ratio 2:3. If one compares the tone of the triply divided string with one divided into four parts, the interval will be the fourth and, the ratio 3:4. Hence, mathematically 1:2 equals the octave; 2:3, the fifth; 3:4, the fourth; 8:9, the whole tone; and so on. Music to Pythagoras and his followers thus was synonymous with order and proportion and rested on a demonstrably rational basis. This tremendous discovery seemed to be a key that might unlock the secrets of the universe, which, they reasoned, might likewise be reduced to numbers and be constructed according to the principles of a musical scale. This idea found its way into all aspects of Greek intellectual life, and even Plato built up a conception of the cosmic harmony of the world on these musical principles in his *Timaeus*. It is possible that the architects also incorporated these laws into the proportions and designs of their buildings. The Roman architect Vitruvius, for instance, was thoroughly familiar with Greek musical theory.

Knowledge of Greek music must be gleaned from a variety of sources, such as occasional literary references, poetry and drama, visual representations of musical instruments and music-making in sculpture and painting, theoretical treatises, and some very fragmentary surviving examples of the music itself. When all the separate sources are combined, a faint notion of what Greek music actually was like can be gleaned. From them, it is apparent that music's highest development undoubtedly was found in its union with the drama.

The Athenian dramatist was by tradition responsible for the music, the training of the chorus, and the staging of his play as well as for the writing of the book. In addition to all this, he often played one of the roles. The great dramatists, therefore, were composers as well as poets, actors, playwrights, and producers.

In reconstructing the Greek drama, one must imagine a Greek audience to whom the drama was a lively aural and visual experience of choral singing and dancing, of vocal and instrumental music, as well as of dialogue and dramatic sequence. Today, with all the choruses and dances missing, such a play as *The Suppliants* of Aeschylus is like the libretto of an opera without the musical score. It is so clearly a lyric drama that the music itself must have been the principal means by which the poet conveyed his meaning. Euripides' *The Bacchants*, on the other hand, has far greater intrinsic dramatic substance, but even here the emotional intensity of the individual scenes often rises to such a pitch that music had to take over where the words left off—just as when a person is so overcome with feeling that words fail and he resorts to inarticulate sounds and gestures.

The weight of the musical expression fell primarily on the chorus, which was the original basis of the dramatic form and from which all the other elements of the drama evolved. We have at last realized, said Nietzsche in his analysis of Greek drama, "that the scene, together with the action, was fundamentally and originally conceived only as a *vision*, that the only reality is just the chorus, which of itself generates the vision and speaks thereof with the entire symbolism of dancing, tone, and word." The chorus performed both in stationary positions and in motion, accompanied by mimetic gestures as it circulated about the orchestra where the choral songs, dances, and group recitatives took place around the altar of Dionysus. The forms of the choruses were metrically and musically very elaborate and were written with such variety and invention that repetitions either within a single play or in other plays by the same poet were very rare.

Interestingly enough, the sole surviving relic of Greek music from the 5th century B.C. is a fragment of a choral *stasimon*, or stationary chorus, from Euripides' *Orestes*. All ancient Greek manuscripts come down through the ages from the hands of medieval scribes who omitted the musical notation of the earlier copies because it was no longer comprehensible to them. In this instance, the musical notation was included, but all that is left is a single sheet of papyrus now perforated with age. From ancient accounts, however, it is known that the music of Euripides differed considerably from

that of his predecessor Aeschylus and his contemporary Sophocles. Euripides was educated in the "new" music by Timotheus, while Sophocles received his instruction from the more conservative rival Lampros. The new music was considered more ornate and was criticized because it was so complex that the words were unintelligible. The text was thus on its way to becoming of as little consequence as that of an opera chorus of today, while traditionally it had dominated the music. Evidence to support this development is found in the literary content of Euripidean choruses, which sometimes have little or no direct connection with the action.

Fragmentary though this scrap of evidence is, these few notes from Euripides' *Orestes* are enough to tell their own story. Since the intervals called for are in half and quarter tones, it means that Euripidean choruses were musically complex enough to demand highly skilled singers. The mode is mixolydian, which is described by Aristotle in his *Politics* as being "mournful and restrained." The words that accompany the fragment perfectly express this sentiment, and, when properly performed, it still conveys this mood. Other than this single relic of choral recitative, the music of the 5th century must remain mute to our ears, and we can only echo the words of Keats in his "Ode on a Grecian Urn": "Heard melodies are sweet, but those unheard are sweeter."

IDEAS

Each of the arts—architecture, sculpture, painting, poetry, drama, and music—is, of course, a distinct medium of expression. Each has its materials, whether of stone, bronze, pigments, words, or tones. Each has its skilled craftsmen who have disciplined themselves through years of study so they can mold their materials into meaningful forms. But every artist, be he architect, sculptor, painter, poet, dramatist, or musician, is also a child of his time, who in youthful years is influenced by the social, political, philosophical, and religious ideas of his period and who, in turn, during his maturity contributes creative leadership in his special field. No art exists apart from its fellows, and it is no accident that the Greeks thought of the arts as a family of sister muses. Architecture, to complete itself, must rely on sculpture and painting for embellishments; sculpture and painting, for their parts, must search for congenial architectural surroundings. Drama embraces poetry, song, and the dance in the setting of a theater. This was all quite clear in ancient times, as Plutarch quotes Simonides as

saying, "Painting is silent poetry; poetry is painting that speaks." When the philosophers Plato and Aristotle discoursed on the arts, they looked for common elements applicable to all. And they were just as keen in their search for unity amid the multiplicities of art as they were for unity among all the other aspects of human experience.

Certain recurring themes appear in each of the arts of the Hellenic period as artists sought to bring their ideals to expression. Out of these themes emerges a trio of ideas—humanism, idealism, and rationalism—that recur continually in Athenian thought and action. These three ideas, then, provide the framework that surrounds the arts and encloses them in such a way that they come together into a significant unity.

Humanism

"Man," said Protagoras, "is the measure of all things." And, as Sophocles observed, "Many are the wonders of the world, and none so wonderful as man." This, in essence, is humanism. With himself as yardstick, Hellenic man conceived his gods as perfect beings, immortal and free from physical infirmities but, like himself, subject to very human passions and ambitions. The gods likewise were personifications of human ideals: Zeus stood for masculine creative power, Hera for maternal womanliness, Athena for wisdom, Apollo for youthful brilliance, Aphrodite for feminine desirability, and so on down the list. And because of his resemblance to the gods, Hellenic man gained greatly in self-esteem. When gods were more human, as the saying goes, men were more divine.

The principal concern of the Greeks was with human beings—their social relationships, their place in the natural environment, and their stake in the universal scheme of things. In such a small city-state as Athens, civic duties devolved on each individual. Every responsible person had to concern himself with politics, which Aristotle considered to be the highest social ethics. Participation in public affairs was based on the need to subordinate personal aspirations to the good of the whole state. A man endowed with great qualities of mind and body was honor-bound to exercise his gifts in the service of his fellowmen. Aeschylus, Socrates, and Sophocles were men of action who served Athens on the battlefield as well as in public forums and theaters. One responsibility of a citizen was to foster the arts, and under Athenian democracy the state itself, meaning the people as a whole, became the principal patron of the arts.

Politically and socially, the Athenian's life was balanced between an aristocratic conservatism and

a liberal individualism, which were maintained in equilibrium by the democratic institutions of his society. His art reflects a gravitational pull between this aristocratic tradition, which resisted change and emphasized austerity, restraint, and stylization in the arts, and the new dynamic liberalism, which opposed conservatism with greater emphasis on emotion, a desire for greater ornateness, and naturalism. The genius of Phidias was that he was able to achieve a golden mean between these opposites, and the incomparable Parthenon and its sculptures were the result.

Humanism also expressed itself in kinship with nature. By personifying all things, animate and inanimate, the Greeks tried to come to terms with unpredictable natural phenomena and to explain the inexplicable. With their forests populated with elusive nymphs and satyrs, their seas with energetic tritons, and their skies with capricious zephyrs, they found an imaginative way of explaining some of the forces beyond their control. These personifications, as well as the conception of the gods as idealized human beings, created a happy condition for the arts. By increasing his understanding of nature in all its aspects, Hellenic man also enhanced his own humanity. Even when the scientific philosophers sought to reduce the universe to basic matter—earth, air, fire, water —man's body and soul were still identified with the basic stuff of the natural world. To create an imaginary world that is also a poetic image of the real world will always be one of the pursuits of the artist. And the Greeks thought of art as a *mimésis* —that is, an imitation or representation of nature. Since this also included human nature, it implied a re-creation of life in the various mediums of art.

Particularly congenial to this humanistic mode of thought was the art of sculpture. With the human body as the point of departure, such divinities as Athena and Apollo appeared as idealized images of perfect feminine and masculine beauty. Equally imaginative were such deviations from the human norm as the goat-footed Pan, the half-human half-horse centaurs, and the myriads of fanciful creatures and monsters that symbolized the forces of nature. The Greeks were more thoroughly at home in the physical world than the later Christian peoples who believed in a separation of flesh and spirit. The Greeks greatly admired the beauty and agility of the human body at the peak of its development. In addition to studies in literature and music, Greek youth was trained from childhood for competition in the Athenian and Olympic games. Since it was through the perfection of their bodies that men most resembled the gods, the culture of the body was a spiritual as well as a physical activity. The nude body in action at

gymnasiums was a fact of daily experience, and sculptors had ample opportunity to observe its proportions and musculature. The result is embodied in such well-known examples as the statues of athletes attributed to Polyclitus, such as the *Doryphorus* (Fig. 31), the *Discobolus* by Myron (Fig. 35), and the *Scraper* by Lysippus (Fig. 45). As an instrument of expression, the male nude reached a high point in the 5th century B.C., but the female form had to wait for similar treatment until the succeeding century.

45. LYSIPPUS. *Apoxomenos (Scraper)*. Roman copy after original of *c.* 330 B.C. Marble, 6′ 9″ high. Vatican Museum, Rome.

Any humanistic point of view assumes that life here and now is good and meant to be enjoyed. This attitude is the opposite of medieval asceticism, which denied the joys of this life as snares of the devil, believing that true good could be attained only in the unseen world beyond the grave. While the Greeks had no single belief about life after death, the usual one is found in the underworld scene of Homer's *Odyssey* when the shade of the hero's mother explains that "when first the breath departs from the white bones, flutters the spirit away, and like to a dream it goes drifting." And the ghost of Achilles tells Odysseus that he would rather be the slave of the poorest living man than reign as king over the underworld. Greek *steles*, or gravestones, usually depicted the deceased in some characteristic worldly attitude—a warrior in battle, a hunter with his favorite horse or dog, or a lady choosing her jewelry (Fig. 46).

The spiritual kingdom of the Greeks was definitely of this world. They produced no major religious prophets, had no divinely imposed creeds, no sacred scriptures as final authority on religious matters, no organized priesthood. Such mottoes inscribed on the sacred stones of Delphi as "Know thyself" and "Nothing in excess" were suggestions that bore no resemblance to the thunderous "Thou Shalt Nots" of the earlier Ten Commandments. Knowledge of their gods came from Homer's epics and Hesiod's book of myths. The character and action of these gods, however, were subject to a wide variety of interpretations, as is clear from the commentaries of the 5th-century drama. This nonconformity bespoke a broad tolerance that allowed free speculation on the nature of the universe. Indeed, the Greeks had to work hard to penetrate the divine mind and interpret its meaning in human affairs. Ultimately, their ethical principles were embodied in four virtues—courage, meaning physical and moral bravery; temperance, in the sense of nothing too much or, as Pericles put it, "our love of what is beautiful does not lead us to extravagance"; justice, which meant rendering to each man his due; and wisdom, the pursuit of truth.

Just as the Greek religious outlook sought to capture the godlike image in human form, so also did the arts try to bring the experience of space and time within human grasp. Indefinite space and infinite time meant little to the Greeks. The modern concept of a nation as a territorial or spatial unit, for instance, did not exist for them. Expansion of their city-state was not concerned with lines on a map but with a cultural unity of independent peoples sharing common ideals. The continuous flow of time also seemed unreal, and their unconcern with a precise historical past is evidenced in

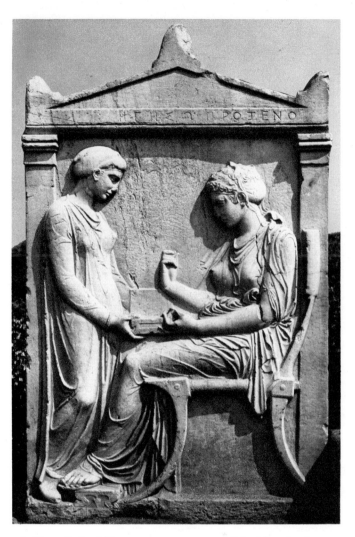

46. *Grave Stele of Hegeso. c.* 410–400 B.C. Marble, 4′ 11″ high. National Museum, Athens.

the imperfection of their calendar and in the fact that their historians Herodotus and Thucydides were really chroniclers of almost-contemporary events. Their geometry was designed to measure static rather than moving bodies, and their visual arts emphasized the abiding qualities of poise and calm. Greek architecture humanized the experience of space by organizing it so that it was neither too complex nor too grand to be fully comprehended. The Parthenon's success rests on its power to humanize the experience of space. Through its geometry, such visual facts as repeated patterns, spatial progressions, and intervalic distances are brought within easy optical and intellectual grasp. The simplicity and clarity of Greek construction were always evident to the eye, and by defining the indefinite and imposing a sense of order on the chaos of space, the architects of Greece made their spaces clearly intelligible.

Just as architecture humanized the perception of space, so the arts of the dance, music, poetry, and drama humanized the experience of time. These arts fell within the broad meaning of *music*, and their humanistic connection was emphasized in the education of youth, because, as Plato says, "rhythm and harmony find their way into the inward places of the soul, on which they mightily fasten, imparting grace, and making the soul of him who is rightly educated graceful." The triple unities of time, place, and action observed by the dramatists brought the temporal flow within definite limits and are in striking contrast to the shifting scenes and continuous narrative styles of later periods. The essential humanism of Greek drama is found in its creation of distinctive human types; in its making of the chorus a collective human commentary on individual actions of gods and heroes; in its treatment of human actions in such a way that they rise above individual imitations to the level of universal principles; and, above all, the creation of tragedy, in which the great individual is shown rising to the highest estate then plunging to the lowest depths, thereby spanning the ultimate limits of human experience. In sum, all the arts of Greece became the generating force by which Athenian man consciously or unconsciously felt himself identified with his fellow citizens and with the entire rhythm of life about him. Through the arts, human experience is raised to its highest level; refined by their fires, the individual is able to see his world more clearly in the light of universal values.

Idealism

When an artist faces the practical problems of representation, he has two main courses open to him: he can choose to represent objects either as they appear to the physical eye or as they appear to the mind's eye. In one case, he emphasizes nature, in the other, imagination; the world of appearances as opposed to the world of essences; reality as contrasted with ideality. The avowed realist is more concerned with *concretion*—that is, with rendering the actual, tangible object that he sees with all its particular and peculiar characteristics. The idealist, on the other hand, accents *abstraction*, which is to say he eliminates all extraneous accessories and concentrates on the inner core, the essential qualities of things. A realist, in other words, tends to represent things as they are; an idealist, as they might or should be. Idealism as a creative viewpoint gives precedence to the idea or mental image, tries to transcend physical limitations, aspires toward a fulfillment that goes beyond actual observation, and seeks a concept closer to perfection.

Both courses were followed in the Hellenic style. One of Myron's most celebrated works was a bronze cow said to be so natural that it caused amorous reactions in bulls, and calves tried to suckle her. Such a work would certainly have been in line, in the literal sense at least, with the Greek definition of art as the imitation of nature. In contrast, the painter Parrhasius agreed with Socrates that, since it was impossible to find perfection in a single human model, it was necessary to "combine the most beautiful details of several, and thus contrive to make the whole figure look beautiful."

The case for idealism is argued in Plato's dialogues. He assumes a world of eternal verities and transcendental truths but recognizes that perfect truth, beauty, and goodness can exist only in the mental world of forms and ideas. Phenomena observed in the visible world are but reflections of these invisible forms. By way of illustration, parallelism is a concept, and two exactly parallel lines will, in theory, never meet. It is impossible, however, to find anything approaching true parallelism in nature, and, no matter how carefully a draftsman draws them, two lines will always be unparallel to a slight degree and, hence, will meet somewhere this side of infinity. But this does not destroy the concept of parallelism, which still exists in the mental image or idea of it. Plato's *Republic*, to cite another example, is an intellectual exercise in projecting an ideal state. No one knew better than the author that such a society did not exist in fact and probably never would. But this did not lessen the value of the activity, and the important thing was to set up goals that would approach his utopian ideal more closely than did any existing situation. "Would a painter be any the worse," he asks, "because, after having delineated with consummate art an ideal of a perfectly beautiful man, he was unable to show that any such man could ever have existed? ... And is our theory a worse theory because we are unable to prove the possibility of a city being ordered in the manner described?" His idealistic theory, however, leads Plato into a rather strange position regarding the activities of artists. When, for instance, they fashion a building, a statue, or a painting, they are imitating, or representing, specific things that, in turn, are imitations of the ideal forms, and hence their products are thrice removed from the truth. The clear implication is, of course, that art should try to get away from the accidental and accent the essential, to shun the transitory and seek the permanent.

Aristotle, for his part, distinguished between various approaches in art. In his *Poetics*, he

Plate 1. PRAXITELES. *Hermes and the Infant Dionysus. c.* 340 B.C.
Marble, 7′1″ high. Museum, Olympia. (See p. 24.)

Plate 2. *Zeus (Poseidon?)*. *c.* 460–450 B.C.
Bronze, 6'10" high. National Museum, Athens. (See p. 24.)

observes that "it follows that we must represent men either as better than in real life, or as worse, or as they are. It is the same in painting. Polygnotus depicted men as nobler than they are, Pauson as less noble, Dionysius drew them true to life. . . . So again in language, whether prose or verse unaccompanied by music. Homer, for example, makes men better than they are; Cleophon as they are; Hegemon the Thasian, the inventor of parodies, . . . worse than they are." Aristotle also applied the same standard to drama, pointing out that "Comedy aims at representing men as worse, Tragedy as better than in actual life." In the visual arts, the distinction, then, is between making an idealized image, a realistic image, or a caricature. And it is clearly implied that the true artist should be concerned only with the ideal.

At its high point in the latter half of the 5th century B.C., the Hellenic style was dominated by the idealistic theory. The Greek temple was designed as an idealized dwelling place for a perfect being, and by its logical interrelationship of lines, planes, and masses, it achieves something of permanence and stability in the face of the ephemeral and haphazard state of nature. In portraying an athlete, a statesman, or a god, the Hellenic sculptor concentrated on typical or general qualities rather than on the unique or particular. This was in line with the Greek idea of personality, which it was felt was better expressed in the dominating traits and characteristics than in individual oddities or peculiarities. In sculpture, as well as in all the other arts, the object was to rise above transitory sensations to capture the permanent, the essential, the complete. Thus the sculptor avoided representing the human being in infancy or old age, since these extremes of immaturity and postmaturity implied incompleteness or imperfection and hence were incompatible with the projection of ideal types. The range of representations extends from athletes in their late teens through images of Hermes, Apollo, and Athena, who are conceived in their early maturity, to Zeus, father of the gods, who appears as the fully developed patriarch in all the power of mature manhood. It must also be remembered that few of the Hellenic sculptor's subjects were intended to represent human beings as such. The majority were fashioned to represent gods, who, if they were to be cast in human form, must have bodies of transcendent beauty.

In some way, even the intangible tones of music participated also in the ideal world by reason of the mathematical relationships on which they are based. A melody, then, might have something more permanent than its fleeting nature would indicate. One of the main functions of the drama was to create ideal types, and, while the typical was always opposed to the particular, somehow the one arose from the other. The interpretation of this interplay was assigned to the chorus, and the drama as a whole shared with the other arts the power of revealing how the permanent could be derived from the impermanent; how the formula could be extracted from the process of forming; how an abiding quality could be distilled from the state of universal flux; how the type could be found in the many specific cases; and how the archetype could arise from the types.

In the extreme sense, the real and ideal worlds represent blind chaos and perfect order. Since the one was intolerable and the other unattainable, it was necessary to find a middle ground somewhere along the line. Glimpses of truth, beauty, and goodness could be caught occasionally, and these intimations should help man to steer a course from the actual to the ideal. By exercising the faculties of reason, judgment, and moral sense, man can subdue the chaotic conditions of his existence and bring closer into view the seemingly far-off perfection.

The Socratic theory of education, expressed in the balance between gymnastic for the body and music for the soul, was designed as a curriculum leading toward this end. The Greek temple, the nobly proportioned sculptural figures, the hero of epic and tragedy, and the orderly relationships of the melodic intervals in music are one and all the embodiments of this ideal. Politician, priest, philosopher, poet, artist, and teacher all shared a common responsibility in trying to bring it closer to realization. As Socrates said: "Let our artists rather be those who are gifted to discern the true nature of the beautiful and graceful; then will our youth dwell in a land of health, amid fair sights and sounds, and receive the good in everything; and beauty, the effluence of fair works, shall flow into the eye and ear, like a health-giving breeze from a purer region, and insensibly draw the soul from earliest years into likeness and sympathy with the beauty of reason."

Rationalism

Rational and irrational forces exist within every society as well as every person. The question remains whether the state or individual tries to solve problems by reason or emotion. "Things are numbers," Pythagoras is supposed to have said, and by this statement to have affirmed that something solid and permanent underlies the shifting appearances of things. A few generations later, Anaxagoras went a step farther by stating

that "mind has power over all things that have life." His disciple Socrates continued the argument and kindled in his followers a burning love of truth, not because truth was useful for worldly success but because truth is an ideal to be pursued for its own sake. The good life in the heyday of Greek civilization embraced not only the ethical principles of courage, temperance, and justice but also wisdom, a virtue achieved by the free exercise of man's rational faculties.

In the Hebraic and Christian traditions, mortal error lay in transgressions of the moral law, but to the Greeks, original sin was a lack of knowledge. The tragedy of Oedipus in Sophocles' drama *Oedipus the King* is his ignorance that does not permit him to know when he is murdering his father, marrying his mother, and begetting children who are also his own brothers. His downfall therefore comes through his ignorance, and his fate is the price he has to pay. In *The Bacchants*, the general theme is the conflict between the known and the unknown. Agave is led to murder her own son because she voluntarily surrenders her reason to an irrational cult. Her son Pentheus' downfall comes because his reason was not strong enough to comprehend the emotional and irrational forces that motivated the lives of the members of his family and his subjects. In order to bring these factors under control, they had first to be understood, and therefore Pentheus lacked the wisdom and tolerance necessary in a successful ruler. The entire Greek philosophical tradition concurred in the assumption that, without the knowledge and the free exercise of the faculty of reason, there is no ultimate happiness for mankind.

By thinking for themselves in the spirit of free intellectual inquiry, the Greeks in considerable measure succeeded in formulating reasonable rules for the conduct of life and its creative forces. This faith in reason also imparted to the arts an inner logic of their own, since when a craftsman's hands are guided by an alert mind, his work can penetrate the surface play of sense impressions and plunge to deeper levels of experience. For all later periods, this balance between the opposites of reason and emotion, form and content, reality and appearance becomes the basis for any classical style. For such subsequent classical movements as the Renaissance and 19th-century neoclassicism, the guiding principle is symmetry, proportion, and unity based on the interrelationship of parts with one another and with the whole.

The qualities of balance, clarity, and simplicity that the Greeks set up as standards of excellence in all the arts depended upon the selective faculty of a well-ordered mind. As Plato put it, "beauty of style and harmony and grace and good rhythm depend on simplicity,—I mean the true simplicity of a rightly and nobly ordered mind and character." Plato's attitude toward the arts that did not meet these specifications was highly critical. And since inspiration as well as rule is a necessary condition of creativity, Plato was afraid that some works of art tended to be more the product of divine madness than of reason. Aristotle, without compromising his rational position, was able to distinguish between historical and poetic truth, fact and fancy. But poetic license was severely criticized by Plato. He was disturbed, for instance, by such architectural refinements as the entasis of columns and the tilting of walls for purposes of creating the appearance of perfection by carefully calculated distortions. Since only the world of mathematics seemed fixed and logical, the world of appearances was deceptive, as proved by such illusions as a straight stick appearing bent when thrust into water. The artist, to Plato, was one who sometimes seemed to minister to the deficiencies rather than the strengths of human nature. "Thus," he writes, "every sort of confusion is revealed within us; and this is that weakness of the human mind on which the art of conjuring and of deceiving by light and shadow and other ingenious devices imposes, having an effect like magic." The philosopher also pointed out that "in works either of sculpture or painting, which are of any magnitude, there is a certain degree of deception; for if artists were to give the true proportions of their fair works, the upper part, which is farther off, would appear to be out of proportion in comparison with the lower, which is nearer; and so they give up the truth in their images and make only proportions which appear to be beautiful, disregarding the real ones." Furthermore, that which is true of the deviations of visual lines applies also to the variations in the rhythms of recited poetry and performed music. If mathematical regularity prevails, the result is dull and mechanical. In music, pitch must also waver slightly in order to approximate the human voice and sound natural and interesting. This Plato also considered irrational, and he felt that the only hope was for "the arts of measuring and numbering and weighing [to] come to the rescue of human understanding." It follows that the excellence or inferiority of the several arts then depends upon the manner in which they make use of mathematical principles.

In spite of the suspicions of the philosophers, the Hellenic artists were no less concerned than Plato with the pursuit of an ideal order, which they felt could be grasped by the mind through the medium of the senses. Greek architecture, in retrospect, turns out to be a high point in the rational solution to building problems. The post-

and-lintel system of construction, as far as it goes, is eminently reasonable and completely comprehensible. All structural members fulfill their logical purpose, and nothing is hidden or mysterious. The orderly principle of repetition on which Greek temple designs are based is as logical in its way as one of Euclid's geometry propositions or Plato's dialogues. It accomplishes for the eye what Plato was trying to achieve for the mind. The tight unity of the Greek temple met the Greek requirement that a work of art be complete in itself. Its carefully controlled but flexible relationships of verticals and horizontals, solids and voids, structural principles and decorative embellishments give it an inexorable internal consistency. And the harmonic proportions of the Parthenon reflect the Greek image of a harmoniously proportioned universe quite as much as a logical system.

Sculpture likewise avoided the pitfalls of rigid mathematics and succeeded in working out principles adapted to its specific needs. When Polyclitus said "the beautiful comes about, little by little, through many numbers," he was stating a rational theory of art in which the parts and whole of a work could be expressed in mathematical proportions. But he also allowed for flexible application of the rule, depending on the pose or line of vision. By such a reconciliation of the opposites of order and freedom, he reveals the sculptor's kinship with his philosophical and political colleagues who were trying to do the same for other aspects of Athenian life.

Rational and irrational elements were present in both the form and content of Greek drama, just as they were in the architecture of the time. In the Parthenon, the structurally regular triglyphs were interspersed with panels showing centaurs and other mythological creatures. The theme of these sculptures was the struggle between the Greeks as champions of enlightenment and the forces of darkness and barbarism. In the drama, the rational Apollonian dialogue existed alongside the inspired Dionysian chorus. However, even in the latter, the composition of intricate metrical schemes and the orderly and complex arrangements of the parts partake of rationalism and convey the dramatic content in highly ordered form. In the dialogue, the action of the episodes must by rule lead inevitably and inexorably toward the predestined end, just as the lines and groupings of the figures must do in a composition like that on the east pediment of the Parthenon. In the union of mythological and rational elements, tragedy could mediate between intuition and rule, the irrational and rational, the Dionysian and Apollonian principles. Above all, it achieves a coherence that meets Aristotle's critical standard of "a single action, one that is a com-plete whole in itself with a beginning, middle, and end, so as to enable the work to produce its proper pleasure with all the organic unity of a living creature."

Just as the harmony of the Parthenon depended on the module taken from the Doric columns, so Polyclitus derived his proportions for the human body from the mathematical relationship of its parts. In similar fashion, melodic lines in music were based on the subdivisions of the perfect intervals derived from the mathematical ratios of the fourth, fifth, and octave. So also the choral sections of the Greek drama were constructed of intricate metrical units that added up to the larger parts on which the unity of the drama depended. In none of these cases, however, was a cold crystallization the desired effect. In the architecture of the Hellenic style, in the statues of Polyclitus, in the dramas of Aeschylus, Sophocles, and Euripides, and in the dialogues of Plato, the rational approach was used principally as a dynamic process to suggest ways to solve a variety of human and aesthetic problems.

It was also the Greeks who first realized that music, like the drama and other arts, was a mean between the divine madness of an inspired musician, such as Orpheus, and the solid mathematical basis on which the art rested acoustically. The element of inspiration had to be tempered by an orderly theoretical system that could demonstrate mathematically the arrangement of its melodic intervals and metrical proportions. Finally, it should always be remembered that the chief deity of the city was Athena, goddess of knowledge and wisdom. Even such a cult religion as that of Dionysus, through the Orphic and Pythagorean reforms, tended constantly in the direction of increased rationalism and abstract thought. While Athena, Dionysus, and Apollo were all born out of a myth, their destinies found a common culmination in the supreme rationalism of Socrates and Plato, who eventually concluded that philosophy was the highest music.

CONCLUSION

As the Athenians looked into the mirror of their arts, they well could have reflected on the long road they had traveled from the dark past of prehistory, with all its primitive practices and mythological superstitions. In the light of their radiant present, they confidently shared the direction of their world with their gods who, to be sure, were immortal but not all-powerful. Since even deities had limitations, man's help was urgently needed. The constant search for justice and wis-

dom was bringing the divine and human worlds closer together into a single universal harmony, and in the process, the gods were humanized and men reached out toward divinity.

The Socratic notion of truth, for example, was not brought down from a mountain or imposed from above by either man or god. It was evolved with practice and effort by the application of rational principles in a dialectical, or give-and-take, process. Since the arts of the Athenians were addressed to reasonable beings, they were more persuasive if they possessed the qualities of balance, order, and proportion than if they attempted to impress by the ponderous mass of a pyramid or the colossal height of a projected tower of Babel. Athenian idealism found expression in a trinity made up of the eternal verities of truth, beauty, and goodness, each in its way a facet of the ideal oneness attainable by the mind of man. The approach to these ideals was not through mystical rites but through the process of dialectics, aesthetics, and ethics. Through these avenues, it was possible to discern on the distant horizon an intellectual, beautiful, and moral living space, broad enough to insure the expansion of Athenian institutions and arts into a sphere of excellence seldom equalled and never excelled by men before or since.

Such, then, was the remarkable configuration of historical, social, and artistic events that led to this unique flowering of culture. Circumstances, however, conspired to bring about a decline of political power, although Athens was destined to remain the teacher of Greece, Rome, and all later peoples of Western civilization. And the words of Euripides still sound a ringing note down the corridors of time:

Happy of old were the sons of Erechtheus,
Sprung from the blessed gods, and dwelling
In Athens' holy and untroubled land.
Their food is glorious wisdom, they work
With springing step in the crystal air.
Here, so they say, golden Harmony first
Saw the light, the child of the Muses nine.

47. THEODORUS OF THOCAEA. Tholos, Delphi. *c.* 390 B.C. Marble, diameter *c.* 49′.

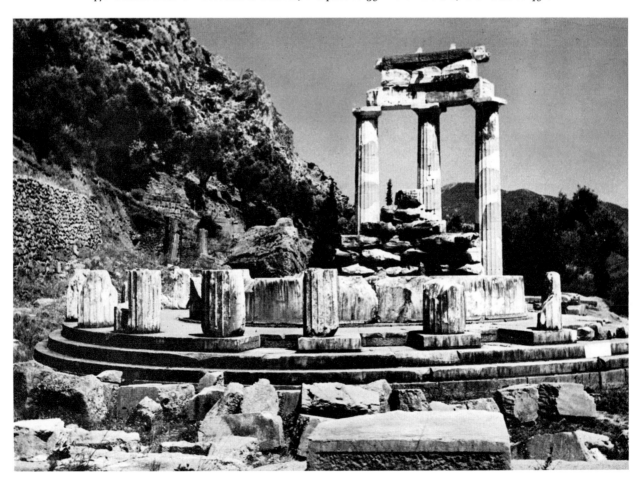

2 - THE HELLENISTIC STYLE

PERGAMON, 2ND CENTURY B.C.

Like the earlier city of Athens, Pergamon (or Pergamum) in Asia Minor developed around its acra, the fortified hilltop that became the residence of its rulers and a sanctuary. The Pergamene acropolis was a geographical site with even greater natural advantages than that of Athens, and it played a significant role in the growth of the city. Strategically located on a plain near the Aegean Sea, Pergamon developed a prosperous export trade. The fertile plain, formed by the confluence of three rivers, was easily defensible from the hill; and the city itself, surrounded as it was by the wide sea, high mountains, and precipitous ravines, was impregnable except from its southern approach. Here, in a situation of unusual beauty, grew the city that was to play such an important role in the Hellenistic period.

After Athens fell to Sparta in 404 B.C., Greece veered away from the small democratic city-state as the basic political unit toward more autocratic forms of government. Philip of Macedon first succeeded in bringing the mainland of Greece into a single kingdom; then his son Alexander the Great embarked on a course of conquest leading to a short-lived empire. With great centers separated as widely as Syracuse on the island of Sicily,

Alexandria on the banks of the Nile, and the cities of Asia Minor on the east coast of the Aegean, Greek thought and attitudes became more varied and international in scope. The Hellenistic period proper covers the two centuries between the death of Alexander in 323 B.C. and the Roman conquest of Greece in 146 B.C., but in effect it continued through a transitional Greco-Roman era down to 27 B.C., the beginning of the Augustan Age in Rome. Throughout these two centuries, cultural leadership remained in the hands of the Greeks, but as they came in contact with such a variety of native influences, their culture became progressively more cosmopolitan. Hence the distinction is drawn between the earlier and purer Hellenic and the later more diffused Hellenistic styles.

In Asia Minor, significant art centers developed at Halicarnassus, Ephesus, Rhodes, and especially at Pergamon. The unique position of the latter was owing largely to the energy and political sagacity of the Attalid kings, whose early recognition of the rising power of Rome led to an advantageous alliance with that city of the future. Perga-

(above) BOETHOS. *Boy with Goose*. Roman copy after Greek original of 2nd century B.C. Marble, 3′ 7″ high. Glyptothek, Munich.

41

General Events B.C.

359–	336	Philip of Macedon gained control of Greece
	336	Philip assassinated; succeeded by son, Alexander the Great
334–	323	Alexander's conquests in Near East, Asia Minor, Persia, and India
	331	City of Alexandria, Egypt, founded
	323	Alexander the Great died
323–	275	Alexander's generals divided empire: Ptolemies in Egypt, Seleucids in Syria and Palestine, Attalids in Pergamon
241–	197	Attalus I ruled as king of Pergamon Defeated Gauls in Galatia Allied kingdom with Rome Erected monument commemorating victory over Gauls Patron of First School of Pergamene sculpture
197–	159	Eumenes II, king of Pergamon Defeated Gauls Power of kingdom at zenith Founded Pergamene library Commissioned Altar of Zeus Patron of Second School of Pergamene sculpture
159–	138	Attalus II, king of Pergamon Patron of painting
	146	Roman conquest of Greece
138–	133	Attalus III, king of Pergamon Willed kingdom to Rome
	129	Pergamon became a Roman province

Architecture and Sculpture

359–	351	Mausoleum at Halicarnassus built; frieze by Scopas and School
323–	146	Hellenistic Period proper; 146–27 transitional Greco-Roman period; great centers of culture at Alexandria, Pergamon, Antioch and Rhodes
c.306		*Winged Victory of Samothrace*
c.250		*Venus de Milo (Aphrodite of Melos)*
c.228		First School of Pergamon Attalus I's monument celebrating victory over Gauls
183–	174	Second School of Pergamon Eumenes II's Great Altar of Zeus
c.100		*Laocoön Group* done at Rhodes by Agesander, Athenodorus, and Polydorus.

Philosophers and Scientists

c.341–	c.270	Epicurus, founder of Epicureanism
c.336–	c.264	Zeno of Citium, founder of Stoicism
	c.321	Aristoxenus of Tarentum, musical theorist, flourished
	c.300	Euclid flourished
c.287–	213	Archimedes

Painters and Sculptors

c.359–	c.351	Scopas active
	c.330	Apelles, court painter to Alexander, flourished
	c.200	Boethos active

mon was thus both an important center of civilization in its own right and one of the principal bridges over which the Greek tradition passed into the Roman Empire.

A planned Greek city rather than an improvised jumble of buildings and houses apparently goes back no further than the middle of the 5th century B.C. The fame of "wide-wayed Athens" rested on its Panathenaic Way (Fig. 5), a street about twelve feet broad. Just wide enough for five or six men to walk abreast, it facilitated the processions to the acropolis, theaters, and market place. Otherwise the streets of Athens were narrow alleys barely broad enough for a man with a donkey cart. Without pavement of any kind, they must have been as dry and dusty in summer as they were damp and muddy in winter and spring. The Athenian residential section was only a mass of mud-brick houses in which rich and poor lived side by side in relative squalor. Only in the agora and on the acropolis was there a sense of spaciousness. But even here buildings were planned with full attention to their individual logic and little or none to their relationship as a group. Each building thus existed independently rather than communally.

Such Greek cities in the vicinity of Pergamon as Miletos and Priene (Fig. 48) are known to have been laid out in gridiron fashion with streets crisscrossing at right angles and with city blocks of regular size. A writer of the time describes a Roman city (Fig. 49) or military camp as being "four-sided and equal-sided, while details of its street planning and its general arrangement are

(above) 48. Priene, city plan (after von Gerkan).

(right) 49. Timgad, Algeria. Airview of Roman city, 2nd century A.D.

precisely parallel to those of a city." From this it is evident that he was comparing the camp with a normal Greek city of his time. St. John also adopted this gridiron plan for his visionary new Jerusalem, which he described in Revelations as being surrounded by a great wall with twelve gates, three on each side. "And the city," he wrote, "lieth four-square, and the length is as large as the breadth" (Rev. 21: 12).

Greek city plans, while a vast improvement on their haphazard predecessors, were based on the application of an inflexible geometrical pattern that paid little or no attention to the irregularities of the natural site. When a hill was within the city limits, as at Priene (Fig. 48), the streets sometimes became so steep that they could be negotiated only by precipitous stairways. While the residential sections of the ancient city of Pergamon have only now begun to be excavated, it is known that they followed such a regular system. Under Eumenes II, the city reached its largest extent, and the thick wall he built around it enclosed over 200 acres of ground—more than four times the territory included by his predecessor. A system of ducts that brought in an ample water supply from nearby mountain springs was sufficient for a population of 120,000 and was the greatest of its kind prior to the Roman aqueducts.

The main entrance to Pergamon was from the south through an impressive arched gateway topped by a pediment with a triglyph frieze. Traffic was diverted through several vaulted portals that led into a square, where a fountain refreshed travelers. From here, the road led past the humbler dwelling places toward the large lower market place, which bustled with the activities of peddlers and hucksters of all sorts. This market was a large open square surrounded on three sides by a two-story colonnade behind which were rows of rooms that served for shops. Moving onward, the road went past buildings that housed the workshops and mills in which pottery, tiles, and textiles were produced. Homes of the wealthier citizens were located on promontories off the main streets overlooking the rest of the city. At the foot of the acropolis another square opened up, which could boast of a large city fountain and a fine view.

On a dramatic site almost 1,000 feet above the surrounding countryside rose the Pergamene acropolis (Fig. 50), a commanding citadel that ranked among the most imposing in the Greek world. Up the slopes of the hill, on rising terraces supported by massive retaining walls and fortifications, were the buildings and artifacts that gave the city its reputation as a second Athens. By ingenious use of natural contours, the Pergamenes had developed settings for a number of buildings, which not only were outstanding as individual edifices but which, by means of connecting roadways, ramps, and open courtyards, were grouped into a harmonious whole. Here on a succession of rising levels were gymnasiums, athletic fields, temples, assembly places, public squares, wooded groves, and an amphitheater. Above them all, flanked by watch towers, barracks, arsenals, storage houses, and spacious gardens, stood the royal residence.

50. Acropolis, Pergamon. Reconstruction by H. Schlief. (below) Detail of Altar of Zeus.

ARCHITECTURE

On the three lowest of the artificially created terraces of the Pergamene acropolis were a series of open grounds, enclosed by colonnades and buildings, which comprised a triple gymnasium—one for each general age group. The spacious outdoor areas included a playground for boys, an athletic field, and a race course. Provision was also made for dressing rooms, baths, and indoor sports. And, as the education center of the city, the gymnasium also included classrooms and lecture halls. It is significant that such gymnasiums provided mental as well as physical exercise. Their pleasant locations in groves and gardens, in fact, were responsible for the names of such famous schools of phi-

losophy as Plato's Academy and Aristotle's Lyceum, just as the *stoa*, or shady colonnade facing a public building (see Fig. 2), became the name of the Stoic school of thought. At the Pergamon gymnasium, statues have been found of such mythological figures as Asclepius, son of Apollo and physician of the gods, and Hygeia, daughter of Asclepius and guardian of the health of growing youths, as well as sculptured representations of athletes at their games. A small adjacent temple was dedicated to one of the patron deities of sports, possibly Hermes, the fleet-footed messenger of the gods, or Heracles, mythological paragon of strength; and nearby were statues of Nike, goddess of victory, altars for votive offerings, and busts of prominent athletes who won the Olympic and other Greek games.

Above the gymnasium was the upper agora (Fig. 50, lower left), an open square that served both as an assembly place and as a market for such quality merchandise as the renowned Pergamene pottery and textiles. Above the agora was the broad marble-paved terrace on which stood the Altar of Zeus with its famous frieze depicting in marble slabs the battle of the gods as personifications of light and order against the giants as representatives of darkness and chaos. Dating from about 180 B.C., this artistic triumph of the Eumenian period was proclaimed by many contemporary authorities as one of the seven wonders of the ancient world. Since both its structure and sculp-

tures are of major importance, this edifice will be discussed in the following section.

On the next higher level, above the Altar of Zeus, was the precinct dedicated to Athena Polias, or Athena protectress of cities and guardian of laws and city life. Her shrine (Fig. 50, center) was a graceful Doric temple, smaller than the Parthenon, with six-columned porticoes on either end and ten columns on each side. This level was framed by an L-shaped, two-storied colonnade that formed an open courtyard in which stood the bronze monument that celebrated the victory of Attalus I, father of Eumenes, over the Gauls (Figs. 51–54). This colonnade served also as the façade of the great library of Pergamon, which appropriately was placed here in the precinct of Athena, goddess of reason, contemplation, and wisdom. The most precious part of the library was housed in four rooms on the second-story level stretching about 145 feet in length and 47 in width. On their stone shelves, some of which are still extant, rested the ancient scrolls, estimated to have numbered about 200,000 at the time of the Attalids. The Pergamon library ranked with that of Alexandria as one of the two greatest libraries of antiquity. Later, after the major portion of the Alexandrine collection of half a million volumes had been burned in an uprising against Caesar, Mark Anthony made a gift to Cleopatra of the entire library of Pergamon.

One of the principal industries of the city, incidentally, was that of the preparation of the skins of sheep and calves for writing purposes. The product was called by the Romans *pergamena*, from which our English words *pergamenous* and *parchment* are derived. Thus the names of both the city and one of its main products were synonymous with writing materials and books. Parchment still continues to be identified with scholarship and learning in the traditional sheepskins of college diplomas. In ancient times, great commercial as well as scholarly rivalry raged over the comparative merits of Alexandrian papyrus (or paper) and the Pergamene parchment. Owing to its greater permanence, posterity has reason to be grateful for the more enduring quality of parchment.

Below the Athena precinct was the theater (Fig. 50, center left), which was constructed under Eumenes II about 170 B.C. The auditorium, with its 78 semicircular tiers of stone seats that could accommodate 10,000 spectators, was carved out of the hillside. Below was the traditional circular section of the orchestra, where the chorus performed around a small altar dedicated to Dionysus, and the rectangular scene building for the actors.

Just as the Attalid kings dominated the life of their city and constituted the apex of the social pyramid of their kingdom, so the royal residence crowned the highest point in their capital city. Later, after the realm came under the domination of Rome, part of the palace was demolished to make way for the large Corinthian temple honoring Emperor Trajan that is shown in the top foreground of Figure 50. From their hilltop summit the kings of Pergamon could survey much of their rich domain. From the mountains to the north came the silver and copper that furnished the metal for their coins—so necessary in promoting trade and paying soldiers. From the same region came also supplies of pitch, tar, and timber —greatly in demand for the building of ships—as well as marble for their buildings and sculptures. A panorama thus unfolded around them, starting with the heights of Mt. Ida and the surrounding range (down whose slopes flowed the streams that watered the fertile valleys and broad plains), all the way to the bright waters of the shining Aegean Sea, beyond which lay the shores of the Greek motherland.

Like Croesus, the Attalids of Pergamon were famed for their fabulous wealth, and "rich as an Attalid" was a phrase used by Horace and other Roman writers. But by later standards, the Attalids lived comparatively modestly, and the residence generally referred to as the "royal palace" was actually a loose constellation of small buildings, set amid wooded groves and gardens, that shifted from time to time with the changing fortunes and dignities of the kings. Included in the group were living rooms opening out into columned courtyards, chambers devoted to the dynastic cult, a barracks for the royal guard, a treasury, and various storerooms for goods, grain, and arms. What the decorative scheme must have been like in the time of Eumenes II is suggested by the mosaic floors (Figs. 64, 65). The love of display, however, was less in evidence in royal residences than in the great public buildings the Attalids erected and in the ostentatious gifts they made to such cities as Athens and Rome. More important to the Attalid kings than the size and luxury of their dwelling was the close link with the temples of the gods that its location afforded. Both symbolically and practically, their residence was located here in order to dominate the city that spread out below them. From there all eyes would be attracted to the magnificent group of edifices, thus causing the populace to look upward psychologically as well as actually toward the place of the kings and gods who ruled over their lives.

The planning of Pergamon thus cleverly promoted the idea of the monarchy towering above it. There, topographically as well as politically, stood the king, aloof from his people and associated by them with the gods. Even while living, he was

accorded such divine prerogatives as a cult statue, with perfumed grain burning on an altar before it, and an annual celebration in his honor. This semidivine status, connected with the king's right to rule, served the practical social purposes of commanding obedience to his laws, facilitating the collection of taxes (often under the guise of offerings to the deities), and uniting the peoples and factions who lived under him. Assisting in this deification were the intellectuals and artists the king attracted to his court, whose works were regarded with awe by the multitude. Native and foreigner alike were overwhelmed by the vast impressiveness of the architecture and sculpture.

The pomp and display that marked Hellenistic life was a distinct departure from the simplicity and nobility of the more austere 5th century B.C. Grandeur became the grandiose, and many monuments were erected not to revere the gods but to honor kings who, even in their own lifetimes, assumed semidivine status. The accent was no longer on the abstract idealism and universality of the earlier period but on the glorification of individuals. With the changing times, however, definite advancements in the art of building were taking place. Domestic architecture was emphasized, and Pergamene architects went beyond the simple post-and-lintel method of the Hellenic period by employing the arch and vault in city gates and in underground water and sewer systems. Architecturally as well as culturally, Pergamon forged the link between the Greek and Roman periods. Such was the picture of the brilliant city with thousands of statues, sculptured reliefs, painted murals, and books; and peopled with philosophers, scholars, writers, artisans, and pursuers of luxury and pleasure.

SCULPTURE

While sculptural works of all kinds are known to have existed in profusion throughout the city of Pergamon, the examples that claim the attention of posterity were located on two of the terraces of the acropolis. In the Athena precinct just below the royal residence, bounded by the temple on one side and the L-shaped colonnades of the library on two others, was a spacious courtyard in which Attalus I erected the sculptural monuments commemorating his victories. The groups he commissioned were in place during the last quarter of the 3rd century B.C. On the terrace below, in the first quarter of the 2nd century B.C., his son and successor Eumenes II built the Altar of Zeus (Fig. 55) with its famous frieze. Historically, the two periods have been distinguished as the First and Second schools

of Pergamon, but since they were separated by less than half a century, some sculptors possibly worked on both projects, and if not, they must have had a hand in training their successors. All the bronze originals of the First School have disappeared and can be studied only in the marble copies made by later Hellenistic or Roman artists. Most of the sculptures from the Second School survive, because of the fortunate results of the late 19th-century German excavations, and may be seen today in the Pergamon Museum in East Berlin.

The principal works of the First School were two large monuments in bronze, each of which was composed of many figures. One commemorated the victories of Attalus over the neighboring Seleucid kingdom, but only a few details of this group survive. The other honored his earlier and greater victory over the nomadic tribes of Gauls, which swept down from Europe across the Hellespont into the region north of Pergamon. From this province, called Galatia after them, the Gauls were a constant threat to the Greek cities lying to the south. While his predecessor had bought them off by paying tribute, Attalus I refused this expedient. He met their subsequent invasion with an army, and the outcome of the battle, fought about thirty miles to the east of Pergamon, was decisive enough to repel the Gauls for a generation. Its consequences were felt far and wide, and all the cities and kingdoms of the Greek world breathed a little easier.

The fierce Gauls had inspired such general terror that their defeat was associated in the popular mind with something of a supernatural character. The name of Attalus was everywhere acclaimed as *Soter* (Savior), and after incorporating the lands he had gained, he assumed the title of king. Thereafter, as King Attalus the Savior, he continued to capitalize on his fortunes by embarking on a program of beautifying his city with the services of the best available Greek artists. Sharing the same patroness, Pergamon began to acquire the status of a second Athens, and its ruler that of a political and cultural champion of Hellenism over the barbarians. Not content with adding to the renown of his city, Attalus made donations of treasure and works of art to other Greek centers, especially Athens. There he paid tribute to the ancient capital by erecting on its acropolis a monument celebrating four great victories—that of the gods over the giants, the early Greeks over the Amazons, the 5th-century Athenians over the Persians, and, of course, his own over the Gauls —thus linking his kingdom more closely with the long unbroken chain of Greek culture. The copies and fragments of struggling giants, dead Amazons, wounded Persians, and dying Gauls that have been

(top) 51. *Dying Gaul*. Roman copy after bronze original of *c.* 225 B.C. Marble, 3′ high, 6′ 3″ long. Capitoline Museum, Rome.

(above) 52. *Dying Gaul* (back view).

found all over the Mediterranean region testify to the fame of this Athenian group. It is a curious commentary on the taste and temper of Roman times that replicas only of the unfortunate victims were made, while the proud victors, probably riding in triumph on horseback, were overlooked.

At Pergamon, however, Attalus' monument was devoted solely to the occasion on which he was the victor. It was a large collective group that rested on a circular platform some 10 feet in diameter. In the center rose a cylindrical base, about 7 feet high, on which were placed the victorious Pergamenes and their leader, while their vanquished

opponents were found below on three descending steps. Parts of the monument can be seen in numerous museums, the *Dying Gaul* and the *Gaul and His Wife* being the most famous of the parts.

The *Dying Gaul* (Figs. 51, 52) is a fine example of Hellenistic pathos. The mortally wounded warrior has agonizingly dragged himself out of the thick of the battle to struggle alone against death. His eyes are fixed on the ground where his sword, the trumpet he has sounded for aid, and other pieces of his equipment are lying. He supports himself weakly with one arm, proud and defiant to the end, while his life's blood flows slowly out of the

(left) 53. *Gaul and His Wife.* Roman copy after bronze original of *c.* 225 B.C. Marble, 6′ 11″ high. National Museum, Rome. (right) 54. *Gaul and His Wife* (view from the right).

gaping wound in his side. The anguished expression in the face is portrayed with an intensity not hitherto encountered in Greek art. The strong but rude musculature of his powerful body, so different from that of the supple Greek athletes, marks him as a barbarian. Further contrast is found in his hair, which is greased so heavily that it is almost as thick as a horse's mane, in the moustache (never worn by the Greeks or Romans), and in the collar of twisted gold worn around his neck. All these carefully recorded details show the interest of the period in individuals as such, in the features that distinguished one people from another, and above all, in the artist's desire to awaken the sympathies of the observer. Thus by the process of empathy, the sculptor invites the involvement of the observer in the situation. The contemporary audience would have felt both attraction and repulsion toward such a subject and hence would have experienced a strong emotional reaction. The litter of the battle-

field beside the Gaul, as well as other realistic details, is not used so much for its own sake as to convey a sense of immediacy in the experience of the beholder. At the same time, the viewer was invited to look beyond the physical wounds and behold the spiritual anguish of the proud but defeated warrior, who is so reluctant to accept his fate.

The expressive impact of the *Gaul and His Wife* (Figs. 53, 54) is no less powerful. The custom of the Gauls was to take their women and children with them on their campaigns. Realizing his defeat, and too proud to be taken a slave, this Gaul has just killed his wife and looks apprehensively over his shoulder at the approaching enemy as he plunges his sword into his own neck. The mood of despair is heightened by the sweeping lines of the woman's drapery, which droops downward in deep folds and casts dark shadows. In both these surviving representations, strong feeling is aroused in the

(above) 55. Altar of Zeus (restored). Begun *c.* 180 B.C. Marble, 120′ wide, 112′ long. Podium including frieze 18′ high. Pergamon Museum, Berlin.

(right) 56. Altar of Zeus, plan.

observer by the noble figures who stare death so courageously in the face.

To the Second School of Pergamon are assigned all the works that fall within the reign of Eumenes II, the patron under whom Pergamon achieved the highest point of its power and glory. Like his father before him, Eumenes II had his victories over the Gauls, and he continued the tradition of erecting votive works with the Altar of Zeus (Fig. 55). It was at once the greatest single monument of the city and one of the few top-ranking architectural and sculptural works of the Hellenistic period. It, too, was intended to glorify the position of the king and to impress the entire Greek world with Eumenes' contribution to the cause of Hellenism in the struggle against the barbarians. Because of the assiduous efforts of the German excavators, it is possible to appraise the Altar of Zeus almost as an original. Beginning in 1878, piece by piece each fragment was painstakingly unearthed, and after a half-century of study, the entire monument was reconstructed in the Pergamon Museum in Berlin. Famed throughout the ancient world, the Altar was described in the early years of the Christian era by St. John as "Satan's seat" (Rev. 2: 13). The reference seems to have been prompted by the resemblance of the

structure to an immense throne and by the pagan gods and demons depicted in the frieze. While the principal interest is focused on the sculpture, the building also commands architectural interest.

The actual altar on which animal sacrifices and other offerings were burned was a large stone podium standing in the inner courtyard. As seen in the ground plan (Fig. 56), the altar was surrounded by a U-shaped enclosure known as a *temenos*. The building rested on a *podium*, or platform, with five steps, above which was the great frieze more than 7 feet in height and 450 feet in length, running continuously around the entire podium, bending inward on either side of the stairway, and diminish-

ing in size as the steps rose (Fig. 57). Below, the frieze was framed by a molding and, above, by a *dentil range*. These bricklike blocks served also to support an Ionic colonnade that surrounded the structure and paralleled the frieze. Above the colonnade was a friezeless entablature with a second dentil range supporting the roof, and crowning the whole was a series of free-standing statues of gods and mythological animals placed at various points along the outer edges of the roof.

The concept of space that underlies the Altar of Zeus differs from that of the 5th century. In the earlier period, the altar was placed outside the temple, and rituals took place against the exterior colonnades. In the Hellenistic period, the concept of space included an interest in depth. Thus, in the case of the Altar of Zeus, the spectator looked into the interior of a courtyard that enclosed the altar, and not toward a background plane. The wider space between the columns also invited the eye toward the interior, whereas the closer inter-columniation of the 5th century promoted the continuity of the plane. Since the Hellenistic concept embraces the same structural members as the previous Greek style, the Altar of Zeus is more a variation on 5th-century forms than a radical departure from them. The columns, entablatures, and interior walls, consistent with the Greek tradition, clearly define the spatial limits, and there is as yet no hint of the unbounded or infinite.

The general effect produced by the Altar of Zeus as a whole is that of a traditional Greek temple—the Parthenon, for example—turned upside-down. The simple dignity of the older Doric temple depended upon its structural integrity. The columns served the logical purpose of supporting the upper members, and the sculptured sections were high above where they embellished but did not dominate the design. At Pergamon, the traditional order was inverted. Since the frieze was considered more important, it was put below, to be seen more easily at almost eye level. For the sake of tradition, the colonnade was included, but it was placed above the frieze where it had no structural purpose. Structurality as a guiding principle had yielded to decoration for its own sake, and the art of architecture, in effect, had given way to the art of sculpture. In the case of the Parthenon, the decorative frieze was included to give some variety to what might otherwise have been a monotonous unity. The Altar of Zeus, on the other hand, with the overwhelming variety of the frieze, has the regularity of a colonnade to preserve the unity. The quiet Greek architectural drama, in other words, has now become an architectonic melodrama.

The subject of the frieze is the familiar battle of the gods and giants. In a depicting of this scene, it was customary to include just the twelve Olympians and an equal number of opponents,

57. Altar of Zeus, detail of west bastion.

but here the unprecedented length of available space demanded a much larger array of participants. Almost certainly scholars of the library were called upon to compile a catalogue of divinities, together with their attendants and attributes, in order to have enough figures to go around. This mythological proliferation, however, apparently taxed the knowledge of the average Greek, because visual footnotes were provided by carved names beside the unfamiliar figures. Further intellectual influence is found in the allegorical treatment of the ancient battle theme. Literal belief in the gods as such was largely a thing of the past, and the local scholars interpreted them as personifications of the forces of nature, the gods representing orderly and benign phenomena and the giants representing such calamities as earthquakes, hurricanes, and floods.

On the inner part of the podium, facing the stairs, the action starts with the divinities of the earth who are summoned forth to take part in the struggle that is to decide the overlordship of the world. Zeus and his fellow gods are locked in mortal conflict with his father Chronus, who is supported by the wicked titans and giants. Moving parallel with the stairs, the action proceeds along the south. Here, in the brightest sunlight, the giants are depicted as forces of darkness in combat with the spirits of light. Helios, the sun god, is shown as a charioteer driving four horses. Fighting with him are Hemera, winged goddess of day, her brother Aether, spirit of air, the moon goddess, and others.

From this side the transition is made to the realm of the sky, and around the corner on the east, as the climax of the composition, the Olympians are found. First among them is Hecate, accompanied by her dog, which is biting one of the giants. Next is Artemis, the heavenly huntress, who fells her foe with an arrow. Then comes Zeus himself, to whom the altar was dedicated, and nearby is Heracles, father of Telephus, the legendary founder of Pergamon. In keeping with his Olympian position, Zeus is the only god who takes on three titans simultaneously. In a series of four slabs (Fig. 58), his powerful figure, wrapped in a swirling mantle, is rearing back to smite the giants with his spear and thunderbolts. While most of Zeus' arm is missing, his hand is seen in the upper left corner of the panel. The titan in the lower left has already been overcome by a thunderbolt, which is depicted as a pointed spear with a handle of acanthus leaves. The second giant is on the other side, his body tense with terror before the blow falls. In the slab to the right, Porphyrion, king of the titans, is shown from the back. From his animal ears to his serpent legs, he is a fearsome, terrible sight as he shields himself with a lion skin from both Zeus' eagle above and the forthcoming thunderbolts.

58. *Zeus Hurling Thunderbolts*, detail of Altar of Zeus frieze. *c.* 180 B.C. Marble, 7′ 6″ high.

(top) 59. *Athena Slaying Giant*, detail of Altar of Zeus frieze. *c.* 180 B.C. Marble, 7′ 6″ high.

(above) 60. *Goddess Throwing Jar of Snakes*, detail of Altar of Zeus frieze. *c.* 180 B.C. Marble, 7′ 6″ high.

Next comes the fine group depicting the part played by Athena, protectress of the city (Fig. 59). Her figure is shown in the second slab, with a shield on her left arm while she grasps a winged giant by the hair with her right and forces him to earth where her sacred serpent can inflict the mortal wound. A moment of pathos is provided by the giant's mother, the earth goddess Gaea, who is seen as a torso rising from the ground. Though she is on the side of the gods, the earth mother implores Athena with her eyes to spare the life of her rebellious son. Gaea's attributes are seen in the horn of plenty she carries in her left hand, a cornucopia filled with the rich fruits of the earth—apples, pomegranates, and grapes with vine leaves and a pine cone. Over her hovers the goddess Nike, symbolizing the victory of Athena.

From this climax in the sky, the action on the shadowy north side gradually descends into the realm of the water spirits, who drive the fleeing giants around the other corner of the stairway into the sea where they drown. Here are the representations of the rivers of Greece. Among the latter is a goddess who is generally identified as Nyx, a water sprite, or Styx (Fig. 60), the spirit of the river that separates the realm of the living and the dead. In her hand is a jar of snakes that she is about to hurl against her adversary. It is possible that here reference is made to an incident in a naval battle in which the fleet of Eumenes II was opposed by that of the famous Hannibal. The Carthaginians resorted to a unique method of warfare by collecting

ARTS AND IDEAS

THE ANCIENT MEDITERRANEAN WORLD

Danube R.

BLACK SEA

Byzantium (Constantinople) • BITHYNIA

MACEDONIA

THRACIAN SEA

SAMO—THRACE

PHRYGIA

Mt. Olympus ▲

LEMNOS

• Troy

AEGEAN SEA

• Pergamon

THESSALY

PHRYGIA

Thermopylae ▲

Chios

LYDIA

• Smyrna

Mt. Parnassus ▲ Thebes

CHIOS

IONIA

Delphi ▲

Eleusis • Marathon

Corinth

Mycenae • • Piraeus

ANDROS

Ephesus •

• Tralles

• Priene

• Miletus

CARIA

Olympia • Argos • • Tiryns

AEGINA

DELOS

Halicarnassus

ARCADIA

Sparta •

SALAMIS

NAXOS

Epidaurus •

MELOS

PAROS

Cnidus •

• Rhodes

PELOPONNESOS

Cythera •

RHODES

CYPRUS

Candia •

Mt. Ida ▲

Knossos •

CRETE

Cyrene •

Alexandria •

EGYPT

Memphis •

Nile R.

CONTENTS

All creative activity begins in the mind's eye and ear of the artist. A work of art that does not communicate meaning is stillborn. Art, then, is a two-way process involving both creator and re-creator. The intensity of the observer's activity, to be sure, may be less than that of the artist, but the experience nevertheless consists of the dynamic activity of responding when the viewer, reader, and listener conjure up corresponding sets of perceptions, images, and impressions on their own. To play his part in the creative act, the re-creator must learn the visual, verbal, and auditory vocabularies that make communication possible and that make the finer nuances of sight and sound distinguishable. Imagination and knowledge must be summoned up to supply the frame of reference and the aura that once surrounded the work of art in its original context. Hence it is necessary to know, for instance, the period and style, the social and religious circumstances, the type of patronage and social position of the artist. These pages, then, are written to guide the viewer, reader, and listener as he seeks understanding.

The expanded chronologies, as before, are like theater programs, giving the times, events, and places of action, as well as casts of characters before the curtain rises on the dramas of the various style periods. Chapter introductions set the scene for the creative activity to be described. Finally, the sections on ideas try to come to grips with the complexities of motivation, interpretation, and meaning.

The adventurous creative life is lived in that no-man's-land between instinct and thought, between feelings and concepts, between emotions and ideas, between shadow and light, between reverie and reason. As the poet Carl Sandburg asked: When does this "borderland of dream and logic, fantasy and reason, where the roots and tentacles of mind and personality float and drift" suddenly crystallize in the shape of "a scheme, a form, a design, an invention, a machine, an image, a song, a symphony, a drama, a poem?" After a lifetime of creative activity, Sandburg added, he was still "trying to learn to read, to see and hear, and to write." On this note the author wishes the reader well on this adventurous journey among masterpieces.

ACKNOWLEDGMENTS

The author wishes to express heartfelt gratitude to the many teachers, colleagues, students, and friends who have contributed so much over the years to the realization of this complex project. He especially wishes to thank his colleagues Professors Abraham Veinus and Sidney Thomas for invaluable insights; Aubrey Garlington, Ann Powell, Frank Macomber, Don Randel, Eugene Wolf, and Mark Zucker for innumerable suggestions; Professor Kenneth J. Conant for opening the rich stores of his knowledge of medieval times and for the plan and elevation of the Cluny Abbey; Professors Robert Branner of Columbia University, Homer F. Edwards of Wayne State University, Colin Eisler of the Institute of Fine Arts, New York University, Evelyn Helmick of the University of Miami, John Knowlton of Connecticut College for Women, and Cornelius Vermeule of the Museum of Fine Arts in Boston for their learned and astute comments on various parts of the manuscript; Chancellor William P. Tolley and Deans Frank P. Piskor, Erik H. Faigle, and Frederic J. Kramer of Syracuse University for their active interest and facilitation of the needed leaves of absence for research; David Thomas for researching the caption legends and reading galley proofs; Jean Wolf for her meticulous work on the index and her watchful proofreading eye; and Coy Ludwig and Calvin Hennig for preparing parts of the typescript. Finally, to the hardworking staff at Holt, Rinehart and Winston I offer my thanks for steering a steady course through the treacherous waters of editing, illustrating, and producing the third edition of *Arts and Ideas*.

spirit of the whole people is reflected. While kings, dynasties, and dictators rise and fall, and political revolutions and battles seem abruptly to settle the affairs of men, the arts, as the expression of the living unity and spirit of man, do not die—though they may have their periods of rise and decline—but go on to reveal the continuity of life. Ultimately what matters in art, as Lionel Venturi pointed out in the case of painting, "is not the canvas, the hue of oil or tempera, the anatomical structure, and all the other measurable items, but its contributions to our life, its suggestions to our sensations, feeling and imagination." Romain Rolland has rightly observed: "Art, like life, is inexhaustible; and nothing makes us feel the truth of this better than music's ever-welling spring, which has flowed through the centuries until it has become an ocean."

Through the study of the arts in relation to the life and time out of which they spring, a richer, broader, deeper humanistic understanding can be achieved. The past, as reflected in the arts, exists as a continuous process, and any arbitrary separation from the present and future disappears in the presence of a living work. True critical appraisal of art, or indeed of any other human activity, can never be a catalogue of minutiae, a record of isolated moments. Understanding can come only when one event is related to another, and when their sum total is absorbed into the growing stream of universal life from which each particular moment derives its significance. In their natural relationship, the arts become the study of people reflected in the ever changing images of man as he journeys across historical time, as he expresses his attitudes toward himself, his fellowmen, and the universe, as he searches restlessly for reality, and as he ceaselessly strives to achieve the ideals that create meanings for life.

The third edition of *Arts and Ideas* is in both content and format the result of much searching, researching, and soul-searching. The quest for finer illustrations, updated scholarship, new light on old works of art, more penetrating analyses has led far and wide. Chapter 20, almost entirely new, has been rethought, rewritten, and expanded to reflect the growing complexity and accelerating dynamics of the art of the 20th century. Approximately 700 illustrations, some 250 more than in the previous edition, now make it possible to reproduce virtually every work of painting, sculpture, and architecture that is either cited or discussed in the text. The 64 color plates and the gravure process used for reproducing the black-and-white illustrations are new to this edition of *Arts and Ideas*. Color and gravure are advantages in printing technology that create a more accurate and subtle reproduction of the distinctive characteristics of the mosaic, fresco, tempera, and oil media, as well as a more convincing suggestion of the qualities of texture and depth in sculpture and architecture.

The reader should keep in mind, however, that even under the most ideal conditions, photographs, like phonograph recordings, are only approximations —shadows and echoes of reality. The miniature pages of medieval manuscripts become the same size as immense murals; lifesize statues in the round are shrunk and flattened to the two dimensions of the printed page; and the proportions and spatial expanses of architecture are only dimly felt through photography. Furthermore, objects placed in museums—statues of gods and goddesses formerly enshrined in temples, altarpieces that once graced Renaissance churches—are now seen in impersonal circumstances and are classified coldly as "works of art." Originally they were never conceived as art objects at all, but as sacred images that inspired reactions of reverence and awe in all who beheld them. Until recently no artist ever consciously painted a picture with the idea that it would hang in a museum. So it calls for imaginative powers to conjure all the possible meanings a work may have had, and to divine the vital forces inherent in a great work of art that make it significant to the contemporary observer.

Only the educated eye and the disciplined imagination can overcome the deficiencies of reproductions and compensate for the dissociation and detachment of works of art from the life and times in which they were produced.

agencies and private contributors have joined forces to erect in New York the Lincoln Center "acropolis" that embraces a complex of opera houses, concert halls, theaters, libraries, museums, and educational centers.

Whenever a center has attained a degree of civilization, has developed a prosperous economy, has given birth to a number of promising individuals, has fostered an adequate educational system, has in its midst groups of artists and master craftsmen, a significant cultural expression may occur. When this happens, it is usually because some personality of powerful convictions has reacted so strongly to the challenge of his time that he is catapulted into a dominating position. Various explanations have been advanced, such as the "great-man theory," which holds that outstanding persons stamp their image upon an age, and that genius is the primary causal influence on history. Social realists, however, contend that environmental forces shape the characters and actions of the individuals involved. The truth probably lies somewhere between these extremes of nature and nurture, and the interplay between powerful personalities and the stimulus of their times brings about the explosion commonly described as genius.

Techniques of production are the private problems of particular craftsmen. Composition, however, is common to them all. An architect puts building materials together, a poet words, a musician tones. But contrary to the views of some purists, they do not do so in a vacuum of self-expression but in order to communicate thoughts, fantasies, social comments, satirical observations, self-revelations, images of order, and the like. Their works—temples, statues, murals, odes, sonatas, symphonies—are addressed not to themselves but to their fellowmen.

The artist's choice of medium, his way of handling materials, the language with which he expresses his thoughts, his personal idioms and idiosyncrasies, his mode of vision, his manner of representing his world, all add up to a vocabulary of symbols and images that define his individual style. In a broader sense, however, a style must include similar expressions in many media, whether in visual, verbal, or tonal forms. Artists, working within a given time and place, share a sociocultural heritage; therefore, it follows that each has a common point of departure. In the arts, as in politics, there are conservatives who try to preserve traditional values, liberals who are concerned with current trends, and progressives who point to coming developments. The individual artist may accept or reject, endorse or protest, conform or reform, construct or destroy, dream of the past or prophesy the future, but his taking-off point must be his own time. The accents with which he and his contemporaries speak, the vocabularies they use, the symbols they choose, the passion with which they champion ideas, all add up to the larger synthesis of a style.

A positive approach, then, can be established on the coincidence of *time, place,* and *idea.* Artists, while working in separate fields, are an integral part of a society, living within a certain geographical and temporal center, and collaborating to a greater or lesser extent. The closer the coincidence, the closer the relationship will be. Composite works of art—forums, monasteries, cathedrals, operas—are always collaborative in nature and must to a considerable degree have mutual influences. Liturgical needs, for instance, must be taken into account in the design of a cathedral, and the sculpture and pictorial embellishments must fit into the plan and iconography of the structure. Hence, in one *time* and in one *place,* the arts of architecture, sculpture, painting, music, and liturgy share a common constellation of *ideas* in relation to the contemporary social order and its spiritual aspirations.

True history, then, is no mere record of dates, treaties, battles, kings, and generals. Aristotle long ago recognized this vital fact when he placed poetic truth higher than historical truth. The political life of a nation is but one phase of its whole life. If one desires to understand the spirit and inner life of a people, one must look at its art, literature, philosophy, dances, and music, where the

PREFACE

Arts and Ideas is a study of the principal styles of Western art as mirrored in selected masterpieces of architecture, sculpture, painting, literature, and music. The book's purpose is not to provide a comprehensive history of the arts but to point out and explore the main stream in Western styles as they crystallized in major centers of civilization at moments of high cultural achievement. Thus, specific works of art are placed in the foreground, but they are also examined in their relationships to one another and against the background of ideas that animated the life of their times.

Because an artist must, perforce, represent his world, his society, and his place in the universe as he himself sees it, his work becomes a representation of his times from a particular point of view. His temple, statue, picture, or poem is an indication of how a sensitive member of that society thinks, feels, dreams, imagines, communicates. In this light a building is not merely a pile of sticks and stones, no matter how interesting a shape it may assume, but an environment for the ordered activity of his fellowmen. Sculpture and painting represent the visage of an age, as well as man's fears and hopes in the form of symbols and images. In poetry and music the inner rhythms, the joys and sorrows, of the human heart are heard. The artist begins the creative process with the vanishing point of the void—empty space and undefined time—then *composes* in the literal sense of selecting materials, placing them together, building them up. The procedure is from the singular toward the plural, from unrelatedness to relatedness, and eventually toward the order and unity of a style.

The search for unity within historical periods, or at least for a coherent grouping of diversities, is crucial for both style definition and art criticism. Cultural expressions, in the manner of the classical unities of Greek drama, usually occur within definite limits of time, place, and action. The search for the underlying ideas that motivate human activities can often reduce to basic simplicity what appears on the surface as a confusing multiplicity of directions. And because the arts are usually experienced simultaneously not separately, it is often wiser to seek understanding from many directions rather than from one. If a common configuration of ideas can be found, then aspects that previously proved baffling may suddenly fall into place and acquire meaning.

Such ideas may be initiated by artists themselves either individually or as a group or by single or collective patrons endowed with sufficient discernment, means, and energy to pursue projects to completion. Such a patron might be a ruler with the vision of Pericles, who presided over the cultural climax of ancient Athens; an enterprising medieval abbot or bishop who envisaged a great monastery or cathedral complex; a family of merchant princes, such as the Medici, who brought Renaissance Florence to its creative peak; or a religious order like the Jesuits, who spread the Counter Reformation baroque style in the wake of their missionary endeavors. The 20th century has witnessed the Commonwealth of India commissioning Le Corbusier to construct Chandigarh, an entirely new capital city of the East Punjab, complete with every public and private facility. In New York, the heirs of a modern industrialist have contributed an architectural complex in Rockefeller Center that compares in grandeur with the imperial forums of ancient Rome. And many public

Library of Congress Catalogue Card Number 68-12011

2664654

1 2 3 4 5 6 7 8 9 0

THIRD EDITION

ARTS AND IDEAS

WILLIAM FLEMING Syracuse University

HOLT, RINEHART AND WINSTON, INC.

New York • Chicago • San Francisco • Toronto • London

Plate 3. *Orpheus among the Thracians. c.* 440 B.C.
Attic red-figured vase. State Museums, Berlin. (See p. 31.)

Plate 4. *Hercules Finding His Infant Son Telephus*. A.D. *c.* 70.
Fresco from Herculaneum, probably a copy after a Pergamene original of 2nd century B.C.
National Museum, Naples. (See p. 56.)

poisonous snakes, packing them in terracotta jars, and hurling them onto the decks of the Pergamene ships. Finding their vessel filled with writhing serpents, the sailors jumped overboard and swam for shore. This historical episode, while not very flattering to local pride, nevertheless was in keeping with the theme of the frieze. Whatever the explanation, this fine figure with her flowing drapery and vigorous attitude is one of the best realized of the entire frieze.

Around the face of the west side and up the stairs are other creatures of the sea. The tumultuous action thus opens and closes on the terrestrial plane, starting on the other side of the stairway with the divinities of the land and ending here with those of the sea. They are separated by the expanse of the wide steps as well as by their placement at the beginning and the end of the dramatic conflict.

The frieze as a whole is a technical feat of the first magnitude and was executed by a school of sculptors, many of whose names are inscribed below as signatures for their work. In addition to the figures, such details as swords and belt buckles, saddles and sandals, and the cloth for costumes are carved and polished to simulate the textures of metal, leather, and textiles, respectively. The bold high-relief carving, deep undercutting that allows the figures to stand out almost in the round, and rich modeling effects that make full use of light and shadow reveal complete mastery of material. To sustain such a swirl of struggling forms and violent movement over such a vast space is a minor miracle. The traditional Doric frieze could depend for unity on the momentary action in the metopes regularly interrupted by the static triglyphs. Here the unity relies on the continuity of the motion itself. The slashing diagonal lines and sharp contrasts of movement are grouped into separate episodes by the device of coiling snakes. Winding in and out they are at once the visual punctuation marks that separate the scenes and the connecting links of the composition, leading the eye from one group to another and promoting a sense of constant writhing motion.

Facing the inner court where the altar stood was a later and less pretentious frieze that told the story of Telephus, the mythological founder of Pergamon, whom the Attalids claimed as an ancestor. Just enough fragments remain to tell of its manner and treatment. The narration is handled like an epic poem, and its design shows unmistakable signs of literary influence. While the great frieze maintained the unities of time, place, and action, the Telephus frieze is subdivided into a sequence of biographical episodes set in a variety of locations depicted by reliefs in the background. The tree and rocks of *Hercules Discovering His Son Telephus Being Suckled by a Lioness* (Fig. 61), for example, locate the scene in a wild and mountainous region. Since the flow of time and shift of locale are closer to actual experience than were the stylized classical unities, the frieze takes yet another step in the direction of realism. It is also the earliest known example of such treatment and points toward such later Roman narrative friezes as that on Trajan's Column (Figs. 106–108).

Comparing the great frieze with the *Dying Gaul* and *Gaul and His Wife*, one can note a style trend from the First and Second schools. Both allude to the perennial wars between the Pergamenes and Gauls. But, in contrast to the almost morbid preoccupation with pain in the earlier monument, the gods on the Altar of Zeus slay the giants with something approaching gaiety and abandon. Instead of sympathy for the victims, the viewer's reaction is wonder at the marvelously ingenious ways the gods invent to dispatch their enemies. Both accent pathos, but in the earlier examples the compassion of the observer is elicited simply and directly. While the great frieze deals with the battle of the gods and giants, it is a thinly disguised allegory of the war between the Pergamenes and Gauls. The Pergamenes in the guise of the gods have become superhuman figures, while the giants, whose features bear close resemblance to the Gallic types of the earlier period, are now

61. *Hercules Discovering His Son Telephus Being Suckled by a Lioness*, detail of "Telephus Frieze," Altar of Zeus. *c.* 150 B.C. Marble, *c.* 3′ high. Pergamon Museum, Berlin.

monsters. Instead of the frank realism of the previous generation, the tale is told in the language of melodrama accompanied by visual grandiloquence. It is put on the stage, so to speak, and done with theatrical gestures and histrionic postures. The emotional range is enormous, beginning with the stark horror of monsters with enormous wings, animal heads, snaky locks, long tails, and serpentine legs, which recall the grotesque prehistoric creatures who inhabited the primordial world. After being terrorized by the sight of such bestial forms, the contemporary audience must have melted into sympathy for the earth mother pleading mercy for her monstrous offspring, and then gone from tears to laughter at the inept antics of some of the clumsy giants. And after hissing the villains, the viewers must have applauded the gods galloping to the rescue. Yet it is good theater since it includes dramatic oppositions, such as the graceful feminine forms (Fig. 60 for example) amid the carnage of the battlefield. The simple realism of the First School,

62. *"Farnese" Hercules*. Roman copy after Lysippus' original of 325–300 B.C. Marble, 9′ 9¾″ high. National Museum, Naples.

however, has become exaggerated. In the case of bodily types, the functional physique of the *Dying Gaul* has become the Herculean power of the professional strong man who is more at home in the arena than on the battlefield. The continuation of this trend is seen in the later example of the muscle-bound figure of the *"Farnese" Hercules* (Fig. 62).

In the case of the whole structure of the Altar of Zeus, it was pointed out that the perception of depth entered into the architectural composition, with the eye being drawn into an enclosed interior. Likewise with the sculpture, the eye does not move only from side to side, as in a plane, but is constantly led back and forth into spatial depth. Because it was painted blue, the marble background is no longer a solid boundary but dissolved into atmosphere. To escape the plane, some of the figures of the great frieze project outward in such high relief as to be almost in the round; others even step outward from the frieze and support themselves by kneeling on the edge of the steps (Fig. 57). The heavy shadows cast by the high-relief carving further intensify this effect. Thus the two-dimensional plane of the Hellenic style was expanded here to suggest some recession in depth.

A general comparison of Hellenistic with the Athenian art of the 5th century B.C. leaves one with the impression of discord rather than harmony; a magnitude that overwhelms rather than dimensions constrained within limited bounds; a wild emotionalism in the place of a rational presentation; virtuosity triumphing over dignified refinement; melodrama superseding drama; variety in ascendance over unity. The Athenian culture, in short, placed its trust in man; the Hellenistic, in superman. No longer the master of his fate, Hellenistic man was engulfed in the storms and stresses of grim circumstances beyond his control.

PAINTINGS, MOSAICS, AND THE MINOR ARTS

Owing to the enduring qualities of stone, more ancient sculpture has survived than art works in any other form. Buildings were torn down for their materials and replaced by others. Statues in bronze, precious metals, and ivory were intrinsically too valuable to survive as such. Libraries of antiquity either were burned or had their volumes disintegrate in the course of time, so that their books survive only in imperfect copies made by medieval scribes or as fragmentary quotations in other volumes. The musical notation contained in ancient manuscripts was not understood by these copyists and eventually was omitted. Mosaics and pottery have fared better, but they, too, were either broken up or carried off by conquerors and collectors. Of all the major visual arts in antiquity, however, painting has suffered most from the ravages of time, and the number of surviving examples is sufficient to give only a hint of what this art must have been at its best. Because of this situation, the impression is easily gained that sculpture was the most important of all the arts. Literary sources, however, attest to the effectiveness and the high esteem in which painting was held by the ancients. The fame of individual painters and the critical praise for their works make it clear that painting was considered on a par with architecture and sculpture.

Two renowned painters were known to have been active in Athens during the 5th century B.C. One was Polygnotus who worked out the principles of perspective drawing, so that his pictures created the illusion of three dimensions and the recession of planes in depth. Apollodorus, "the shadow painter," was the other, who was famed for his use of light and shade and the finer gradations of color. Pausanias, a writer in Roman times, described some murals of Polygnotus, which were in the Propylaea at Athens and elsewhere, and gave longer and more detailed accounts of them than he did of the sculptures on the acropolis. He also mentions many paintings at Pergamon and describes an especially famous one of the *Three Graces* (Fig. 63). The influence of these painters, however, survives to a limited extent in the copies that were made of their masterpieces, and in the vase painting that was done by ceramic craftsmen in imitation of their methods. The latter is, however, only a by-product of the main art and must be considered the work of artisans rather than that of independent artists.

The excavated fragments at Pergamon reveal that the interior walls of temples and public buildings frequently were painted with pictorial panels and had streaks of color that realistically imitated the texture of marble. Other scattered fragments of paintings show that the Pergamenes loved bright colors, such as yellows, pinks, and greens that contrasted with deep reds, blues, and browns. The palace paintings used motives of actual animals, such as lions and charging bulls, and of imaginary ones, such as tritons and griffins. Interiors of rooms were often decorated with painted friezes similar to sculptural ones; and walls, especially of small rooms, were painted with panels, columns, and pilasters, which cast realistic shadows in order to create the illusion of spaciousness. The writers of antiquity mention that the subjects of paintings were often drawn from mythology or from literary sources, such as the *Odyssey* and the like. It is also known that Hellenistic painting frequently dealt

63. *Three Graces*. Early 1st century A.D. Probably a copy after a Pergamene original of 2nd century B.C. Fresco. National Museum, Naples.

in *genre scenes*—that is, casual, informal subjects from daily life.

While both Attalus I and Eumenes II were closely identified with the great sculptural developments, their successor Attalus II was primarily interested in painting. He acquired a large collection by purchase and by sending his artists to various centers to copy famous works that he could not buy. An inscription reveals that Eumenes II sent artisans to Delphi to assist in the repair of its theater; and that Attalus II in 140–139 B.C. dispatched three painters there to restore a famous painting, possibly one which he had previously caused to be copied.

Although the original paintings no longer exist, and only fragments of mosaics and vase painting survive, well-preserved copies of Pergamene work have been found in the Greek cities of southern Italy, notably Herculaneum. This city supposedly was founded by Hercules, whose son Telephus founded Pergamon, and a "family" relationship existed between the two centers. Herculaneum, in fact, became a later middle-class edition of the earlier richer and aristocratic Pergamon. Both Herculaneum and nearby Pompeii were suddenly buried in a rain of cinders and a hail of volcanic stone that accompanied the eruption of

64. HEPHAISTON. Mosaic with (below) detail from Palace of Attalus II. *c.* 150 B.C. Whole, 28' square. Pergamon Museum, Berlin.

Mt. Vesuvius in A.D. 79. When rediscovered in the 18th century, many paintings and mosaics were found to have been preserved almost intact. The taste of both cities was Hellenistic in orientation, and the well-to-do patrons, preferring tried-and-true traditional subjects, usually commissioned copies of famous paintings rather than original works.

The *Three Graces* (Fig. 63) and *Hercules Finding His Infant Son Telephus* (Plate 4) are adaptations of Pergamene originals. In the Plate, the winged figure in the upper right is pointing out to Hercules his son Telephus, who is seen in the lower left among wild animals and suckling a doe. The place is Arcadia, personified by the stately seated figure. Beside her are the fruits of the land, and at her back a playful faun is holding a shepherd's crook and blowing the panpipes. The coloring for the most part is sepia and reddish brown, relieved by lighter blue, green, and whitish tints. The figures appear against the background plane of the sky that projects them forward in the manner of relief sculpture. The drapery and modeling of the flower-crowned Arcadia recall the carving of a marble relief, while the powerful musculature of Hercules' body is cast in the manner of a bronze statue in the round.

Since ancient sculpture usually was painted in vivid colors, and reliefs sometimes had landscapes painted in the backgrounds, the arts of painting and sculpture obviously were closely identified in the Hellenistic mind, and they should per-

haps be thought of more as complementary arts than as independent media. Paintings were more adaptable to interiors, while weather-resistant stone made marble reliefs better for out-of-doors. From the extant evidence, it is clear that the visual intention and expressive effect of both arts were closely associated, and that neither could claim supremacy over the other.

Mosaics, the art of which goes back to remote antiquity, were highly favored at Pergamon for the flooring of interiors and for wall paneling. As with later Roman work, geometrical patterns were preferred for floors, while representations of mythological subjects, landscapes, and genre scenes were

65. Mosaic from Palace of Attalus II, detail. *c.* 150 B.C. Pergamon Museum, Berlin.

used for murals. Two almost perfectly preserved mosaics have been found in the ruins of the palace of Attalus II. Such compositions are formed of small cubes or pieces of stone, marble, or ceramic known as *tesserae* that are set in cement. One mosaic by the artist Hephaiston (Fig. 64) that covered the entire floor of a room has a blank center surrounded first by a colorful geometrical design of black, gray, red, yellow, and white marble tesserae. Beyond this is a wavelike pattern of black and white. Then enclosing the whole is a border about a yard wide with a foliated design of such rich variety that in its 44-foot expanse there is no repetition. Against a dark background are intertwined colored flowers, exotic lilies, vine leaves, and various fruits, all with delicate shadings. In some places grasshoppers are feeding on acanthus leaves; in others small winged Cupidlike *putti*, or boys symbolizing love, are playing among the vines. An interesting touch is the signature of the artist "Hephaiston made it"—words that appear as if on a piece of parchment, three corners of which are fastened down by red sealing wax, while the fourth curls up and casts a shadow on the floor. The other mosaic from the same palace (Fig. 65) has a pattern of beribboned festoons of fruit and green branches embellished by birds and butterflies.

Copies of many Pergamene designs have been found at Herculaneum, Pompeii (Fig. 66, for example), Naples, and Rome. The floor mosaic depicting the Persian warrior Darius fleeing from the forces of Alexander the Great after his defeat in the battle of Issus is a Pompeian mosaic version of the

66. *Defeated Persians under Darius*, detail from *Battle of Issus*. Mosaic copy after a Hellenistic painting. Width of detail *c.* 10½'. National Museum, Naples.

1st century B.C. after an earlier Hellenistic painting of renown. According to Pliny the Elder, the most famous mosaicist of antiquity was Sosus, who was active at Pergamon. Among his most widely copied designs was one of doves drinking from a silver dish, and a favorite for dining-room floors (Fig. 67) showed vegetables, fruit, fish, a chicken leg, and a mouse gnawing on a nut.

Pergamon, as has been said, was noted for its textiles, particularly the woolens used for carpets and curtains. A rich brocaded cloth with interwoven gold threads was known all over the ancient world as *vestes attalicae*, a name that indicated its manufacture in the royal mills. Special chemical and mineral dyes made Pergamene cloth unique. Metalwork, such as silver bowls, bronze medallions, and coins, reveal the Pergamene craftsmen as being adept in the arts of embossing and chasing, as do also their cameos—gems engraved with miniature portraits.

Pergamon was also known as a ceramic center. The clay of the region was well adapted to the making of everything from bricks and tiles to pottery of all sorts. A type of pottery, known as Pergameneware, originated here and was distinguished by its bright varnished surfaces in colors of rich reds with variations in coral, orange, and brownish shades. The large quantities of surviving terracotta figurines, varying from a few inches to a full foot in height, indicate their popularity in individual homes. The figurine medium, being particularly adaptable to informal treatment, was used largely for genre scenes, such as children playing, mothers nursing their young, intoxicated satyrs, and grotesque old people going to market with their wares (see Fig. 76). Such a work as Boethos' *Boy with Goose* (see p. 41) shows a humorous treatment, as the boy is pretending he is Hercules, and, in proportion to his size, the goose becomes a giant. In common with the practice of the time, artisans and craftsmen circulated among various centers, and those trained in Pergamon were in wide demand and enjoyed a particularly high reputation.

MUSIC

Pergamon was identified with the musical tradition of that nearby northern Asia Minor region known as Phrygia, which had its own characteristic idioms, modes, rhythms, scales, and instruments. As early as the 5th century B.C., the Greeks in Athens were divided in their musical views as to the relative merits and propriety of the native Dorian tradition and the increasing influence coming from foreign centers. In particular, the wild and exciting music of Phrygia was gaining in popular favor. The melodies in the Phrygian mode apparently induced strong emotional reactions, and the introduction of a musical instrument called the Phrygian pipe had a similar effect in inflaming the senses. This pipe was a double-reed instrument with a peculiarly penetrating sound, somewhat like the modern oboe. Properly, the single version of the pipe is known as the *aulos* and the double version (shown in Fig. 68) as the *auloi*. In English translations of ancient Greek words, both are often incorrectly translated as flute. The Dorian music, on the other hand, was associated with such stringed instruments as the lyre and the cithara, the latter being mistranslated as the harp.

Both the lyre and the cithara in the Dorian music and the aulos in the Phrygian were used principally to accompany the songs, melodies, and choruses of the two modes and only to a much lesser extent were played as solo instruments by skilled performers. Lyre playing was especially associated in the Dorian tradition with the Apollo cult, and the Greeks attributed to this body of music the quality of *ethos*, or ethical character; the aulos, as the instrument of Dionysus, was associated with *pathos*, or strong feeling, and had a sensuous quality conducive to enthusiasm. To the Athenians, this meant a division in their aspirations and ideals—one instrument and mode of singing were associated with clarity, restraint, and moderation; the other with emotional excitement and aroused passions.

The resultant division of opinion was expressed in the many sculptural representations of the musical contest between the Olympian Apollo and the Phrygian satyr Marsyas. According to an ancient myth, Athena was the inventor of the aulos. One day as she was playing, however, she caught sight of her reflection in a pool of water.

So displeased was she with the facial grimaces the aulos caused her to make that she threw it away in disgust. Marsyas, happening along, found it and was so enchanted by its sounds that he challenged Apollo, the immortal patron of the muses, to a contest. The god chose to play on the dignified lyre, won the contest handily, and proved once again that mortals are no match for the gods. As a punishment he had his challenger flayed alive.

A 5th-century B.C. representation of the myth attributed to Myron shows Athena, calm and disposed, disdainfully throwing away the instrument which distorted her fine features, while Marsyas raises his hands in surprise. A 4th-century relief from Mantineia of the school of Praxiteles (Fig. 68) represents the contest in progress. On one side, calmly awaiting his turn, is the seated Apollo with his lyre; on the other, Marsyas is ecstatically blowing on the aulos. Between them is the judge, or music critic, standing patiently but with knife in hand. The Pergamene versions left out the contest and showed the victorious Apollo on one side, the unfortunate Marsyas (Fig. 70) in the center strung up by the wrists to a tree and, on the other side, the crouching figure of a Scythian slave (Fig. 69), whetting a knife with keen anticipation. The choice of the punishment as the part of the myth to be represented—and the evident enjoyment with which this Hellenistic artist tackled his gruesome subject—obviously was designed to tear the emotions to shreds.

The punishment of Marsyas must have reflected the views of those who disapproved of

68. *Contest of Apollo and Marsyas.* Relief from Mantineia, Greece. *c.* 350 B.C. Marble, 3′ 2¼″ high. National Museum, Athens.

(below) 69. *Knife Sharpener*. Roman copy after Pergamene original. Marble, lifesize. Uffizi, Florence.

(right) 70. *Marsyas*. Roman copy after Pergamene original. Marble, lifesize. National Museum, Rome.

Phrygian music and wished to preserve the ancient traditions. One measure of their hold on the people is found in the attitude of the philosophers who were concerned with maintaining balance and order in the state. Plato, for one, would not admit aulos players into his ideal state, because he considered the instrument "worse than all the stringed instruments put together." He was most emphatic about his preference for "Apollo and his instruments to Marsyas and his instruments." But even the complex stringed instruments were eliminated in favor of the simple lyre and cithara for use in the city, and the pipe to keep the shepherds happy in the country. But while he rejected the aulos, Plato made a curiously human concession in retaining the Phrygian melodies. The two musical modes allowed in the ideal state were the Dorian, which he called the "strain of necessity," and the Phrygian, which was the "strain of freedom." The first was "warlike, to sound the note or accent that a brave man utters

in the hour of danger and stern resolve"; clearly a type of military music is implied. However, maintaining such heroic resolve at all times was apparently too much to expect even of the citizen of his utopia, and Plato therefore allowed the Phrygian music "to be used by him in times of peace and freedom of action, when there is no pressure of necessity."

Aristotle, while for the most part agreeing in his musical views with Socrates and Plato, took exception to this, and said: "The Socrates of the *Republic* is wrong in retaining only the Phrygian mode along with the Dorian, the more so because he rejects the [aulos]; for the Phrygian is to the modes what the [aulos] is to musical instruments —both of them are exciting and emotional.

Poetry proves this, for Bacchic frenzy and all similar emotions are more suitably expressed by the [aulos] and are better set to the Phrygian than to any other mode." It must be pointed out that Aristotle did not reject the Phrygian mode altogether, but only in the case of the education of youth. For this he strongly recommended only the Dorian music, since it was the "gravest and manliest." The Phrygian might produce too much enthusiasm, while the Dorian was more likely to result in a "moderate and settled temper."

In spite of the philosophers and their dire warnings, the stimulating Phrygian music made rapid headway, and in Hellenistic times it was the dominant musical style. The calm, simple, and dignified Dorian tradition of the past, which Plutarch called the age of "beautiful music," was gone, and the wilder, more frenzied strains of Phrygia had taken its place. Their effects can readily be seen in the sculptural representation of a *Satyr Playing the Scabellum* (Fig. 71). The satyr cult flourished in Phrygia, and this statue as well as other satyr types have been traced to a Pergamene origin. Holding the clashing metal *scabellum*, or cymbals, in his hands and stamping on a castenet-like percussion instrument attached to one foot, the satyr is performing an orgiastic dance with wild abandon. The physical tension seen in the lines of the torso reflects the frenzied Dionysian rhythm that seems to electrify his whole body. This image of youthful passion makes it easy to understand why the austere thinkers felt that the music which produced such a reaction lacked ethos.

While historical facts about the actual musical life of Pergamon are few, it is known that here, as in other Hellenistic centers, the practice of music was accorded a high place in the arts. Both boys and girls received musical instruction in their educational institutions, and sang hymns as they marched in processions or participated in religious observances. The curriculum included the teaching of musical notation and the chanting of poetry to the accompaniment of the cithara. The chief educator of the city, the gymnasiarch, was also expected, among his other duties, to arrange for the appearances of visiting poets and musicians.

The Hellenistic era was one of increasing professionalism in activities that had previously been performed by free citizens as part of their public duties and honors. Participation in athletic contests and performances of certain dances, which earlier had been done only by those of noble birth, were taken over by specialists who often commanded high fees for their services. Professional associations, known as the Dionysiac *technites*, had a membership made up of stage managers, actors, mimes, dancers, and musicians who par-

ticipated in theatrical productions. These groups functioned as guilds, or unions, and the master craftsmen accepted talented apprentices who understudied them. The Attalids and other Hellenistic monarchs promoted and protected these technites with an eye toward improving and maintaining the quality of their theatrical and musical performances.

Tralles, one of the cities of the Pergamene kingdom, provides some general information and one of the best musical examples of antiquity. Less than 100 miles from Pergamon as the crow flies, Tralles was a subject-city of the Attalids, who there maintained a residence which usually was occupied by the high priest of the city as their representative. This Phrygian town was saved from the threat of defeat and enslavement at the hands of the Gauls by the victory of Eumenes II in 168 B.C. Like many other cities of the region,

71. *Satyr Playing the Scabellum*. Roman copy after Hellenistic original. Marble, lifesize. Uffizi, Florence.

Tralles was so grateful for its deliverance that it instituted annual gymnastic and musical festivals in honor of the Pergamene kings. One of these was the Panathenaea, which honored Athena as the protectress of Pergamon; another was the Eumenaia, which feted the monarch himself. From inscriptions it appears that the Eumenaia was principally a musical contest.

At Tralles, in the latter part of the 19th century, a tombstone was unearthed that bore an inscription of some four lines of poetry accompanied by clear musical notation. It was an epitaph inscribed on a slab of stone by a man named Seikolos for the grave of his wife Euterpe. On transcription it turned out to be the words and music of a short but presumably intact tune in the Phrygian mode from the 2nd century B.C. After hearing about the wild and orgiastic character of Phrygian music, the reader will find this short song a model of sobriety. The mood, in fact, is more melancholy than intoxicating, and since it was carved on a tombstone, the elegiac character is quite appropriate.

This delightful little song, well over 2,000 years old, was of a popular type known as a *skolion*, or drinking song, which was sung after dinner by the guests as the cup was passed around for toasts and libations to the gods. The word *skolion* is derived from the Greek meaning zigzag and referred to the manner in which the lyre and cup were passed back and forth, crisscrossing the table as each of the reclining guests sang in his turn. The simplicity of this example marks it as the type of song expected to be in the social repertory of every acceptable guest rather than as one of the more elaborate ballads intended to be sung by professional entertainers. In spirit and mood it is not unlike the familiar "Auld Lang Syne," and the occasions on which it was sung would parallel those when we sing the venerable Scottish air. The substance of the words is the universal one of eat, drink, and be merry for tomorrow we die, which expresses a convivial philosophy of the Epicurean type. Technically, it is in the Phrygian mode with the upper and lower extremes falling on *e'* and *e*, thus spanning an octave. The tone most often stressed

is *a*, which thus becomes the mean between the higher and lower reaches of the melody and consequently functions as its tonal center.

IDEAS

Many striking differences have been noted between the Hellenistic and earlier Hellenic styles. As the names indicate, both are Greek; but the Hellenic was a more concentrated development of the small city-states of the Greek mainland, whereas the Hellenistic is a combination of native Greek and such regional influences as those of the Near East, North Africa, Sicily, and Italy. The diffusion of Hellenistic art over several centuries and the entire Mediterranean world makes any quest for stylistic unity difficult. It is remarkable, in fact, that there is any unity at all. The style contrast between Hellenic and Hellenistic, moreover, is never one of polar extremes but rather a tilting of the cultural scale in one direction or another. The universal and social humanism of Athens becomes the particular and personal *individualism* of Pergamon and other centers. The noble Hellenic idealism breaks down into a *realism* that looks at the world more in terms of immediate experience than under the aspect of eternity; the uncompromising rationalism of Socrates, Plato, and Aristotle yields to an *empiricism* of scientists, scholars, and artists interested more in the development of methods and techniques and the application of knowledge to practical affairs than in the adventurous spirit of free inquiry. The tendencies that underly the various art enterprises at Pergamon in particular and the Hellenistic period in general, then, are to be found in a pattern of interrelated ideas, of which individualism, realism, and empiricism are components.

Individualism

As one phase of humanism, the individualistic bias of Hellenistic life, thought, and art contrasted strongly with the broader social accent of the

Skolion of SEIKOLOS (2nd or 1st century B.C.)   (after Kunkel)

(left) 72. Mausoleum at Halicarnassus. 339–351 B.C. *c.* 86 × 106'. Reconstruction drawing.

(below) 73. *Mausolus*, from Mausoleum of Halicarnassus. 339–351 B.C. Marble, 9' 10" high. British Museum, London.

Hellenic period. In politics, the rough-and-tumble public discussions of free citizens and decisions arrived at by voice vote were superseded by the rule of an inner circle of oligarchs headed by a king who enjoyed semidivine status. The cult of personal hero worship that started with Alexander the Great and continued with the kings that succeeded him in the various parts of his far-flung empire was reflected in the popular biographies of great men; in the building of lavish temples and monuments glorifying not the ancient gods but monarchs and military heroes, such as the famous Mausoleum (Fig. 72) for King Mausolus of Halicarnassus (Fig. 73); in the sculptor's accent on individual characteristics, diverse personality traits, and racial differences. In the earlier Hellenic centers, poets, playwrights, and musicians were mainly skilled amateurs; even in sports the accent was on active participation. In the Hellenistic period, however, a rising spirit of professionalism is noted in the fame of individual writers, actors, virtuosos, and athletes, with the result that people became passive spectators rather than active participants.

The search for truth in Athens was a gregarious activity of argumentation participated in by all comers in public squares or in the shady groves of an academy or lyceum where Plato and Aristotle discoursed with colleagues and students. Truth, it was felt, could not be arrived at individually but only through give and take, question and answer, examination and cross-examination, dialogue or dialectical process. In Hellenistic times, these strenuous mental gymnastics gave way to the more personal contemplation and self-reflection of the Stoic and Epicurean philosophies. The thought of Epicurus found ready acceptance in the rich and flourishing cities of Asia Minor. Epicurus had taught that the highest good was "freedom from trouble in the mind and from pain in the body" and that the pursuit of pleasure was the goal of life. The austere idealism of Socrates thus gave way to a comfortable hedonism. But since some pleasures exceed others, the mind and critical faculties are needed to distinguish among those that give more lasting satisfaction. Epicurus also held that happiness for the individual lay in the direction of the simple life, self-containment, and withdrawal from public affairs. This, in effect, denied the social responsibilities of citizenship and encouraged escapism and extreme individualism.

Since the state controlled so much of the public weal, Hellenistic man found greater enjoyment in his personal and home life. Poverty had been deemed an honorable estate in ancient Athens, where rich and poor lived as neighbors in modest homes. Hellenistic wealth, however, allowed a more luxurious standard of living for a larger percentage of the population. Hellenistic architects,

74. Hellenistic house, reconstruction drawing and plan.

then, took special interest in domestic dwellings (Fig. 74); painters and mosaicists were called upon to embellish the houses of the well-to-do; sculptors created figurines with informal, sometimes humorous, subjects, such as Boethos' *Boy with Goose* (p. 41), because they were more adaptable to the home than monumental formal works; together with potters and other craftsmen, all worked to contribute to the life of luxury and ease of a frankly pleasure-loving people.

The Hellenistic artist was more interested in exceptions than rules, in the abnormal than the normal, in types than archetypes, in diversity than unity. In portraiture, he noted more the physical peculiarities that set an individual apart, not those that united him with others. Even the gods were personalized rather than generalized, and the choice of subjects from daily life showed the artist's increased preoccupation with informal, casual, everyday events. He was also more concerned with environmental influences on man than with man's being able to rise above his limitations. The Hellenistic artist, by recognizing the complexity of life, gave his attention to subtle shades of feeling and to representing the infinite variety of the world of appearances.

Hellenistic thought entered on a new emotional orientation. Instead of looking for the universal aspects of experience that could be shared by all, Hellenistic philosophers held that each man has his own feelings, ideas, and opinions entirely different from those of others. In this every-man-for-himself attitude, each must decide what is good and evil, true and false. Instead of seeking a golden mean between such opposites as harmony and discord as did their Hellenic predecessors, Hellenistic philosophers became psychologists analyzing the self and laying bare the causes of inner conflict. The joy, serenity, and contentment of the Hellenic gods and athletes were social emotions that could be shared by all. The sorrow, anguish, and suffering of Hellenistic wounded warriors and defeated giants were private, subjective feelings that separated a man from his fellows and invited inward reflection. It was an old variation on the theme—laugh and the world laughs with you, weep and you weep alone. Artists turned from the ideal of self-mastery to that of self-expression, from the concealment of inner impulses to outbursts of feeling—in short from ethos to pathos. It was said of Pericles that he was never seen laughing and that even the news of his son's death did not alter his dignified calm. A strong contrast to this Olympian attitude is provided by the late Hellenistic *Laocoön Group* (Fig. 75), where the balance of reason and emotion is replaced by a reveling in feeling for its

75. AGESANDER, ATHENODORUS, and POLYDORUS OF RHODES. *Laocoön Group*. Late 2nd century B.C. Marble, 8′ high. Vatican Museum, Rome.

own sake. What is lacking in self-restraint and regard for the limitations of the sculptural medium, however, is amply made up for by the vigor of treatment and virtuosity of execution.

The preoccupation of Pergamene artists with such painful and agonizing subjects as the defeated Gauls, the punishment of Marsyas, and the battle of gods and giants reveals the deliberate intention to involve the spectator in a kind of emotional orgy. Misfortune becomes something that can be enjoyed by the fortunate who participate in the situation with a kind of morbid satisfaction. La Rochefoucauld said: "We all have the strength to endure the misfortunes of others"; and Aldous Huxley observed that when the belly is full men can afford to grieve, and "sorrow after supper is almost a luxury." In the spirit of Stoic philosophy, life and suffering were to be endured with a sort of grim satisfaction akin to a form of morbid enjoyment. The artists of the great frieze of the Altar of Zeus, for instance, show incredible inventiveness in the ways and means they found for the gods to inflict pain and death. The composition approaches an almost encyclopedic inclusiveness in the various modes of combat by the gods and the capacity for suffering by the giants. Nothing like it appears again in art until the Romanesque *Last Judgments* and Dante's *Inferno*.

Realism

The increasing complexity and quicker pulse of Hellenistic life weakened the belief in the underlying unity of knowledge and abiding values that produced the poise of Hellenic figures and the impassive calm of their facial expressions. The world of concrete experience was more real to Hellenistic man than one of remote abstract ideals. In his more realistic view of things, he looked to variety rather than unity and took into account individual experiences and differences. Hellenistic artists sought to present nature as they saw it, to render minute details and ever finer shades of meaning. The decline of idealism was not necessarily the result of decadence, so much as it was a matter of placing man's activities in a new frame of reference, reexamining his goals and redefining basic human values. Confronted with the variety and multiplicity of this world, the Hellenistic artist made no attempt to reduce its many manifestations to the artificial simplicity of types and archetypes. The Hellenic artist portrays man standing aloof and rising above his environmental limitations, but in Hellenistic art man finds himself in the midst of the natural and social forces that beset him on all sides, and he is inevitably conditioned by them. The writhing forms on the great frieze reveal some of the conflicts and contradictions of Hellenistic man. His gods became projections of his own psychological problems. The earlier Hellenic gods appeared to have the world well under control, and the poised Zeus (Fig. 34) of the 5th century B.C. shows no sign of stress or strain as he hurls his thunderbolt. The deities of the Altar of Zeus, on the other hand, are fighting furiously, and things seem to verge on getting out of hand.

In the Athenian architecture of the 5th century B.C., each building, however well in harmony with its site, was an independent unit, and the architects were little concerned with any precise relationship to nearby buildings. Indeed, to have admitted that one structure was dependent upon another in a group would have diminished its status as a self-contained whole and thus rendered it incomplete by Hellenic standards. On the Athenian acropolis, each temple had its own axis and its independent formal existence—in keeping with the conception that each separate work of art must be a logical whole made up only of the sum of its own parts. Only such concessions to nature as were necessary for structural integrity were made. To man alone belonged the power of creating symmetrical form and balanced proportion, and the perfection of each building had to stand as a monument to the mind of man and, as such, to rise above its material environment rather than be bound by it. Hellenistic architecture moved away from the isolated building in the ideal sense of its being a self-contained unit toward a realistic recognition that nothing is complete in itself but must always exist as part of an interrelated pattern. City planning is therefore in this sense a form of realism, and Hellenistic buildings were considered as part of the community as a whole. In the case of the Pergamene acropolis, the relationship of each building was carefully calculated not only in regard to its natural surroundings but to its place in the group.

In sculpture, the members of each group were likewise subject to their environment, and man is portrayed as an integral part of his surroundings. In such reliefs as the Telephus frieze, the painting-in of a natural background places man constantly in reference to specific locations. By using higher relief, Hellenistic sculpture becomes more dependent on changing light and shade for its expressive effect, allows for movement in more than one plane, and suggests greater depth in space. In earlier sculpture, a figure always bore the stamp of a type and personality was subordinate to the individual's place in society. A warrior, for example, had a well-developed physique, but his as to render every nuance of the flesh. The *Old Market Woman* (Fig. 76), for example, reveals the body of a person worn down by toil. The bent back, sagging breasts, gnarled limbs are the results of the physical conditions under which she has had to live. In the handling of materials, the older Hellenic sculptors never forgot that stone was stone. But their realistic zeal often led later Hellenistic craftsmen to force stone to simulate the softness and warmth of living flesh. The story of the legendary sculptor Pygmalion who chiseled his marble maiden so realistically that she came to life could have happened only in the Hellenistic period, and the sensuous figure of the *Aphrodite of Cyrene* (Fig. 77) surely bears this out. The easy grace and charm with which Praxiteles had rendered his gods and goddesses (Figs. 32, 38) find a culmination in such elegant and polished figures as this Aphrodite and the famous *Apollo Belvedere* (Fig. 78).

(above) 76. *Old Market Woman*. 2nd century B.C. Marble, 4′ 1½″ high. Metropolitan Museum of Art, New York (Rogers Fund, 1909).

(right) 77. *Aphrodite of Cyrene*. Roman copy of *c.* 100 B.C. after Praxitelean original, found at Cyrene, North Africa. Marble, 5′ high. National Museum, Rome.

face and body bore no resemblance to a specific person. He could be identified by a spear or shield and was more a member of a class than a person in his own right. The Hellenistic desire to render human beings as unique personalities and not as types necessitated a masterly technique capable of reproducing such particular characteristics as the twist of a mouth, wrinkles of the skin, physical blemishes, and individualized facial expressions. Faces, furthermore, had to appear animated and lifelike, so that the subject of a realistic portrait could be distinguished from all others. Fidelity to nature also meant the accurate rendering of anatomical detail. Like a scientist, the sculptor observed the musculature of the human body with precision so

78. *Apollo Belvedere*. Roman copy after Greek original of the late 4th century, B.C. Marble, 7′ 4″ high. Vatican Museum, Rome.

In all Hellenistic sculpture, the human subject is related to the forces that shape his character and mold his flesh. All the minute physical and psychological conditions that vary the bodies and minds of men, women, and children are taken into account. Yet the end result was managed so that the dignity and status of the art was maintained by rising above the letter of realism in order to portray the spirit of the subject or theme represented. Hellenistic emphasis on realism appealed greatly to the forthright Roman conquerors of Greece, and its appeal to these men of action was largely responsible for the ultimate survival of these Pergamene sculptures.

Empiricism

The rationalism of Hellenic thought as developed by Socrates, Plato, and Aristotle had emphasized the spirit of free intellectual inquiry in

a quest for universal truth. Epicureanism and Stoicism, by contrast, were practical philosophies for living. The abstract logic of the earlier period yielded to an empiricism that was concerned more with science than wisdom, in bringing together the results of isolated experimentation, and in the application of knowledge to the solution of practical problems. More broadly, Hellenistic empiricism stressed fact gathering, the cataloguing of source materials in libraries, scholarly research, collecting art works, and developing critical criteria for judging the arts.

Epicurus, by eliminating the notion of divine intervention in human affairs, and by his physical explanations of natural phenomena, laid the philosophical basis for a scientific materialism. Hellenistic mathematics extended as far as conic sections and trigonometry, and such astronomers and physicists as Archimedes and Hero of Alexandria knew the world was round as well as its approximate circumference and diameter. Hellenistic scientists had a solar calendar of 365¼ days, invented a type of steam engine, and worked out the principles of steam power and force pumps. Indeed, the modern mechanical and industrial revolutions might well have taken place in Hellenistic times had not slave labor been so cheap and abundant. The progressiveness of the period is also seen in its commercial developments that led to new sources of wealth.

This scientific attitude found brilliant expression in the musical field by the development of the theoretical basis of that art. While philosophers and mathematicians of the earlier period had made many discoveries and had had brilliant insights into the nature of music, it remained for the Hellenistic mind to systematize them and construct a comprehensive and coherent science of music. Under Aristoxenos of Tarentum, a disciple of Aristotle, and under Euclid, the theory of music reached a formulation so complete and comprehensive that it became the foundation for Western music. While it is impossible to go into the intricacies of the Greek musical system here, one should keep in mind that it was in this theoretical field more than any other that a lasting musical contribution was made.

After establishing his great library, Eumenes II gathered about him many of the outstanding Greek scholars of his day. They were dedicated to the task of preserving the literary masterpieces of bygone days, making critical editions of the works of ancient poets and dramatists, selecting material for anthologies, cataloguing collections, copying manuscripts, writing grammatical treatises, and compiling dictionaries. In their scholarly endeavors, they upheld the works of the ancients above the writers of their own time, and as a consequence their literary production began to be addressed more to other scholars than to the people at large. Such a restricted audience of cultivated readers could not be supplied by Pergamon alone but had to be sought for all over the scattered Greek world. By mutual consent, the pure and majestic Attic Greek of Pericles, Euripides, and Plato became their "common dialect" and the artificial medium of communication between the cultured classes. With this emphasis on a tongue that was no longer spoken, the living language in which writers could address their fellow citizens began to be regarded as a local dialect.

This was the period of classifiers and organizers in all departments, and the spirit of research was in the air. As a result, creativity in the arts began to be stifled by a growing spirit of antiquarianism. The literary life of Pergamon, for instance, was devoted more to scholarly pursuits than to creative writing, and erudition eventually became a substitute for inspiration. The influence of the library and its scholars was felt in the visual arts as well. The magnitude of the design of the great frieze of the Altar of Zeus demanded the collaboration of scholars, and the completeness of the undertaking shows evidence of the spirit of research. The sculptures are, in fact, a catalogue of mythology, which even includes the obscure names of the individual giants. The labeling of the figures of the frieze in the manner of visual footnotes and annotations contrasts markedly with

that of the Parthenon. At that time, any Greek would have recognized the principals in the cast, and the supporting members were left to the imagination, since they served mainly in the aesthetic capacity of filling in the extra space. As in the case of literature, the Hellenistic visual arts no longer stemmed from the experience of a local community by deriving their spirit and substance from the spoken word and the common religious experience. They were addressed, on the contrary, to an educated class who were sophisticated enough to understand them. The theory of art for art's sake therefore took over.

Like their literary colleagues, the sculptor and the painter were confronted for the first time with a museum filled with noted works from the glorious past that commanded increasing admiration from their contemporaries. In their zeal for collection, the Attalid kings had even carried on extensive excavations which brought to light many works that the 5th century B.C. had thought better to bury. Fortunately, this spirit of looking to a past golden age was not carried to the point of entirely excluding contemporary creative activity. Many artists of the time, however, had to devote their energies to making copies of famous works of the past, such as those by Myron, Phidias, and others, which were placed in the halls of the great library.

The interest of the patrons extended also to the historical and critical aspects of the visual arts, just as it had done in the case of literature and music. This had the positive result of formulating aesthetic standards and setting up critical criteria

79. *Imperial Procession*, detail of Ara Pacis Augustae, Rome. *c.* 13 B.C. Marble, 5′ 3″ high.

80. Ara Pacis Augustae (Augustus' Altar of Peace), Rome.
c. 13–9 B.C. Marble, *c.* 35' square.

so necessary in the evaluation process. In the earlier period artists did not enjoy the high social position they had in Pergamon and other Hellenistic cities at this time. Hence the theorizing about taste and the development of aesthetic judgment proved that now, in contrast with the earlier period, artistic products were at last worthy of the attention of the highest intellectual and social circles. The collector became a judge and connoisseur, and hence engendered a state of mind in which standards of value and aesthetic expression were regarded as important intellectual pursuits.

THE ROAD TO ROME

A reputation for learning had direct bearing on the political purposes of the Pergamene government. The more renowned their capital became for its intellectual and cultural enterprises, the higher its prestige in the Greek world would be. The career of Eumenes II's brother, who eventually succeeded him as Attalus II, is a case in point. As a skillful general, he was invaluable to the Pergamene regime, yet at the conclusion of a successful war he took five years off to study philosophy at the academy in Athens. Furthermore, the proudest boast of the Attalids after their military victories was that they were the saviors of Hellenism from the barbarians. This claim, of course, had to be fortified by the development of their capital as a center of arts and letters. To

advertise the cultural achievements of his realm, Eumenes II chose his librarian, the famed grammarian Crates of Mallos, as his ambassador to Rome. By his championship of humanistic learning, and by stimulating Roman desire for more knowledge about Greek philosophy, literature, and art, Crates made a lasting impression on the future world capital.

With literary talents being diverted into the editing of manuscripts, scholars delving into the history of the past, art collectors digging for buried treasure, and musicians writing theoretical treatises, Pergamon was well on its way toward becoming an archive and a museum. In time, this antiquarianism was bound to lead artistic developments into a stylistic eclecticism and to reduce aesthetic procedures to academic formulas and rules—all of which is symptomatic of a hardening of the artistic arteries and the eventual decline of the creative powers. When, therefore, in 133 B.C. Attalus III willed his kingdom to Rome, he was actually presenting that city with a living museum. The vast art holdings of the Attalids soon were on their way to Italy, where the interest and admiration they commanded, when they were shown in public exhibitions, were destined to have a powerful effect on the taste of the Roman people. Accompanying them were many of the Hellenistic craftsmen who were to embellish the new world capital with carvings, such as those of the Altar of Peace (Figs. 79, 80), an architectural descendant of the Great Altar of Zeus and one of the earliest monuments of the Augustan Age.

3 - THE ROMAN STYLE

ROME, 2ND CENTURY A.D.

The Antonine Age was "the period in the history of the world during which the condition of the human race was most happy and prosperous. . . ." So wrote Gibbon in *The Decline and Fall of the Roman Empire*. Under Trajan, Hadrian, and Marcus Aurelius, continues the great historian, "the Empire of Rome comprehended the fairest part of the earth and the most civilized portion of mankind." This benign state of affairs Gibbon attributed to the Romans' genius for law and order, their cultivation of tolerance and justice, and their capacity for wise government.

The Arch of Trajan at Benevento (Figs. 81, 82) recalls some of this vanished grandeur by proclaiming the virtues and accomplishments of the first great emperor of Gibbon's chosen period. Commissioned by the Roman Senate to celebrate the completion of the Via Traiana, a 200-mile highway over the mountains that linked Rome with the large port of Brindisi, the arch honored an outstanding achievement in engineering as well as the chief engineer of the empire. Such a gateway, marking as it did the start of the long road toward the East, challenged the Romans' imaginations to envisage lands that lay beyond the seas and reminded them that their city was not a self-contained unit. Roman awareness that their individual destinies, as well as those of their city and state, were closely bound up with the surrounding territories found logical expression in just such a monument. Among ancient city-states Rome was unique in its solution of the problem of how to maintain its municipal integrity and at the same time manage a far-flung empire. In evolving the institutions by which this political unity could be made compatible with such wide human diversity, the Romans achieved their greatest social distinction.

Monumental arches usually marked the conclusion of a successful military campaign, by which distant barbarian tribes were subdued or some new civilized people brought into the Roman orbit. In the case of the Arch of Titus in Rome, the returning conqueror, together with his army, a train of captives, and the trophies of war, passed through the arch with the plaudits of the multitudes ringing in his ears. In keeping with this martial theme, the sculptural panels on one side of the passageway of the arch show Titus after his conquest of Palestine, driving his chariot in the grand procession, preceded by the goddess Roma and followed by senators and representatives of the Roman people. On the other side are servants

(above) *Trajan*. A.D. *c*. 100. Marble portrait head, lifesize. Museum, Ostia.

71

General Events B.C.

	753	Legendary date of Rome's founding
c.616–	c.509	Etruscan period. Tarquin kings reigned
	c.500	Roman Republic founded; Tarquins dethroned
	c.450	Romans colonized Italy
	390	Rome sacked by Gauls
280–	275	Greek power in southern Italy weakened
264–	241	First Punic War; Rome annexed Sicily, Corsica, Sardinia
218–	201	Second Punic War; Hannibal invaded Italy; Carthage ceded Spain to Rome
150–	146	Third Punic War; Carthage destroyed; African province created
	133	Pergamon bequeathed to Rome
100–	44	Julius Caesar. Conquered Gaul (58–51); crossed Rubicon, occupied Rome, became dictator (49); Forum of Julius Caesar begun (c.48); campaigned in Egypt, Asia Minor, Africa, Spain (48–45); Julian calendar introduced (45); assassinated (44)
c.50–	c.10	Vitruvius active; wrote treatise *De Architectura*
	43	Second Triumvirate formed—Antony, Octavian (Augustus), Lepidus
	31	Naval battle at Actium; Antony and Cleopatra defeated
27–A.D.14		Augustus (Octavian) reigned. As Octavian founded principate, took name of Augustus, beginning of Empire; built Forum and Mausoleum of Augustus, Ara Pacis, Baths of Agrippa, Theater of Marcellus, Basilica Julia
	4	Birth of Jesus; crucified c.A.D.29

A.D.

54–	68	Nero reigned. Built Baths of Nero, Domus Aureus
	70	Titus captured Jerusalem; temple destroyed
	79	Vesuvius erupted; Pompeii, Herculaneum destroyed
79–	81	Titus reigned. Colosseum finished; Temple of Vespasian, Arch of Titus built
96–	180	"Antonine Age," or "Era of Five Good Emperors" (Nerva, Trajan, Hadrian, Antoninus Pius, Marcus Aurelius). Roman Empire reached pinnacle of power and prosperity

98–117		Trajan reigned. Dacian campaigns (101–106); harbor at Ostia built (103); Via Traiana between Benevento and Brindisi, and Baths of Trajan built (110); Forum of Trajan and Column erected, Arch of Trajan at Benevento begun (113); conquered Armenia, Parthia, Empire's boundaries extended to Persian Gulf and Caspian Sea (113–117)
c.100–	c.120	Apollodorus of Damascus, architect, active
104–	105	Stone bridge over Danube built by Apollodorus
117–	138	Hadrian reigned. Temple of Olympian Zeus at Athens completed (117); Roman Pantheon built (120–124); Villa of Hadrian at Tivoli built (c.120–127); Hadrian's tomb begun (135)
138–	161	Antoninus Pius reigned. "House of Diana" at Ostia built
161–	180	Marcus Aurelius reigned. Stoic philosopher, author of *Meditations* (c.174); died near Vienna
	217	Baths of Caracalla built

B.C. 80–A.D. 14 "Golden Age of Roman Literature"

106–	43	Cicero, statesman, orator, essayist
c.96–	55	Lucretius, poet, philosopher, *On Nature of Things*
87–	57	Catullus, lyric poet
70–	19	Vergil, *Aeneid, Eclogues*
65–	8	Horace, *Odes*
59–A.D.17		Livy, *History of Rome*
43–A.D.17		Ovid, *Art of Love, Metamorphoses*

A.D. 14–117 "Silver Age of Roman Literature"

3 B.C.–A.D.65		Seneca, philosopher, dramatist
c.20–	66	Petronius, *Satiricon*
23–	79	Pliny the Elder, naturalist, encyclopedist
c.50–	c.90	Epictetus, Stoic philosopher
35–	95	Quintilian, *Institutes of Oratory*
40–	c.102	Martial, epigrammatist
c.46–	120	Plutarch, *Parallel Lives*
55–	c.117	Tacitus, historian, *Annals, Germania*
c.60–	c.135	Juvenal, *Satires*
62–	113	Pliny the Younger, writer, administrator; delivered *Panegyric* to Trajan before Roman Senate (100)
75–	c.150	Suetonius, *Lives of Twelve Caesars*
	c.160	Apulius flourished, philosopher, *Golden Ass*
c.160–	c.230	Tertullian, Christian apologist

(left) 81. Arch of Trajan, Benevento. A.D. 114.

(below) 82. *Trajan Sacrificing*, detail of Arch of Trajan, Benevento. A.D. 114.

bearing the seven-branched golden candelabra and the sacred trumpets the emperor had plundered from the temple at Jerusalem (Fig. 83).

Trajan's Arch was modeled architecturally after that of Titus, including such details as the attached *Composite* columns, a Roman combination of the Ionic and Corinthian orders. It differs in spirit from the Arch of Titus, however, in that the sculptures celebrate the arts of peace rather than those of war. The reliefs that so liberally cover its surface were arranged in characteristic Roman fashion so as to inform and instruct as well as to delight the eye. On the side facing the town of Benevento and more-distant Rome (Fig. 81), the panels deal with Trajan's domestic policy. He is seen making land grants in the newly conquered Danube region to veterans of his wars; standing in the midst of prosperous merchants grateful for the new harbor he built for them at Ostia, the port of Rome; and receiving the acclamation of the Senate and the people in the Roman Forum. Across the lintel moves a triumphal procession, and on either side of the keystone hover victories with crown and banners. Above, Jupiter and Juno and Minerva (known in Roman mythology as the Capitoline Triad) are seen extending their welcome to the emperor. As a gesture of approval, Jupiter is turning over his thunderbolt to Trajan, a recognition of the latter's great power as well as a sign that the adulation of the emperor was replacing the worship of the old Olympian deities. This group is placed next to the inscription, which adds to Trajan's usual string of titles that of *Optimo*, the best, which is said to have pleased him especially since he shared it only with Jupiter.

On the side toward the seaport are the scenes pertaining to Trajan's foreign policy. Germany is seen taking the oath of allegiance; various Oriental rulers are sending tributes through their envoys; and the emperor is establishing state-sponsored benefits for the relief of poor children. Above, a figure symbolizing Mesopotamia is paying him homage, and the divinities of the Danube territory are welcoming him. The inside passage of the archway is similarly decorated. One side shows a group of happy, well-fed children and their parents, all grateful for the benefits bestowed upon them. The other shows Trajan participating in a sacrificial observance before setting out on the new highway for eastern conquests (Fig. 82). Although each panel depicts a separate episode, unity is achieved in the repetition of the imperial personage. Variety is obtained by shifting the human and geographical environment. Changes of place are indicated partly by the activities and partly by the backgrounds, which signify a setting in Rome by some familiar buildings, a country place by trees, and a remote locality by exotic river gods. The subject matter is obviously propaganda for imperial rule—even to the extent of sometimes showing Trajan as a figure of superhuman size—but the restrained manner of presentation keeps this aspect from becoming too blatant. The actual sculpture is technically well handled, though there is a tendency to accent linear detail at the expense of unity and repose.

While monumental arches were nonutilitarian in purpose, their form exemplifies the building principle that underlies the Roman achievements in architecture. With the arch the Romans constructed their vaults and domes that carried architecture forward well into modern times. The fact that Trajan's Arch was built in a provincial town south of Rome on the road to and from the great centers of the East—Athens, Pergamon, Alexandria, Ephesus, and Antioch—is a reminder of the route by which the heritage of the classical Mediterranean world became a part of Western cultural tradition. By military conquest, by annexation, by inheritance, and by voluntary action —one by one the proud old city-states and kingdoms became a part of greater Rome. Likewise all

83. *Spoils of Jerusalem*, detail of Arch of Titus, Rome. A.D. 81. Marble, 7′ 10″ high.

the ideas, institutions, and art forms of this vast region were sifted through the ingenious Roman mind, and, together with notable contributions of her own, Rome gradually achieved a culmination of culture, expressed in her literature, architecture, and sculpture, that could compare favorably with the political eminence of her great empire.

ARCHITECTURE

Forum of Trajan

Shortly after his accession as emperor in A.D. 98, Trajan began a grandiose project in Rome: the construction of a new forum (Fig. 84). Just as the empire had grown in his time to its greatest extent, so the population of Rome had risen to over a million, creating a need for larger and more imposing public buildings. The old Forum Romanum of the Republic had long been inadequate, and several extensions had been undertaken in the early years of the Empire. But Trajan's project was so ambitious that it equaled all previous forums combined, bringing the total area covered by such structures to over 25 acres. Needless to say, its magnificence was in every way comparable to its size. Trajan entrusted the project to Apollodorus, a Greek architect-engineer from Damascus, famous for the construction of a stone bridge over the widest part of the Danube before Trajan's second Dacian campaign. But Apollodorus' Greek origin did not necessarily indicate a Hellenistic bias on the emperor's part; all other known architects in Rome at this time (including those who collaborated on the project) were Romans, and Apollodorus was thoroughly conversant with Roman building tradition.

(top) 84. Forum of Trajan, Rome. Reconstruction by Bender. c 920 × 620'. Museo della Civiltà Romana, Rome.

(above) 85. Forum of Trajan, plan. A.D. c. 113–117.

A forum is actually a typically Roman conception, combining a system of open courtyards and buildings grouped in a specific relationship. A glance at the plan of the Athenian acropolis (Fig. 4) shows that the Parthenon and Erechtheum had little more in common than the site on which they stood. But no part of a forum existed in isolation, and in the case of Trajan's Forum everything was conceived from the beginning on a large scale and with an eye to symmetry. From the ground plan (Fig. 85), one can see that the whole was bisected by a central axis running from the

86. *Equestrian Statue of Marcus Aurelius.* A.D. 161–181. Gilt bronze, 9' 10" high. Piazza del Campidoglio, Rome.

In the case of the Forum of Trajan, Apollodorus had problems to solve before he could start to build. Clearing such a large space in a densely populated city meant demolishing many blocks of houses. The site, moreover, was the valley between the Quirinal and Capitoline hills. If the usual interpretation of the inscription on Trajan's Column is accepted, that monument was erected "to show posterity how high rose the mountain leveled by the Emperor." In practical terms, this would mean that more than 100 feet was cut off the Quirinal hill and carted away to make room for the courtyard and basilica. The remaining part was then terraced as a site for the market buildings, which extended up the hillside.

Entrance to the Forum was made through a majestic triple archway into the large paved quadrangle, enclosed on three sides by a wall and colonnade and on the fourth by the Basilica Ulpia, whose entrances stood opposite those of the archway. Standing in the exact center of the open square was an impressive bronze statue of Trajan on horseback. Though no longer extant, it is known to have resembled the surviving bronze equestrian portrait of Marcus Aurelius (Fig. 86), who sits astride his splendid mount with an equilibrium worthy of the patient Stoic philosopher and the throughtful mien of the author of the widely read *Meditations*. Flanking the square on the east and west sides were semicircular recesses known as *exedrae* outlined by tall Doric columns. Similar in shape were the series of market stalls rising upward into the two hills. The best preserved are those on the Quirinal side, which were six stories in height and constructed of brick (Fig. 87). On the forum floor were more than 150 booths—for vegetables, fruits, and flowers; above were large vaulted halls where wine and oil were stored; spices and imported delicacies were sold on the third and fourth floors; the fifth was used to distribute food and money out of the imperial treasure; and on top were tanks supplied by fresh water from an aqueduct where live fish could be bought.

Adjacent to the open square was the Basilica Ulpia, of which only the rows of broken columns (Fig. 88) remain. The term *basilica* was applied rather generally to large public buildings and is approximately equivalent to the modern use of the word *hall* to refer to a place for meetings. Since court sessions were also held in a basilica, the term *hall of justice* is likewise related to one of its functions. As an architectural form, the Roman basilica is one link in the long chain of Mediterranean structures that began with domestic dwellings, Egyptian hypostyle halls, and Greek temples and continued with Christian basilicas.

center of the arched gateway, through the middle of the square, through the entrance to the basilica (whose axis is at right angles to the whole forum), to the base of the column, and finally up the steps of the temple to the altar at the back.

The forum idea apparently evolved from an open city square that combined the facilities of a market and a meeting place. By degrees, the buildings around it were put to administrative uses, and space was allotted for political centers, law courts, triumphal arches, commemorative monuments, and temples. Various historians have pointed to prototypes in the older agoras of Greek cities, in the city plans of smaller Roman settlements, and in Roman military camps. As these facilities developed, however, they became a typical Roman institution. And because the Senate, the center of political debate, met in the Roman Forum, a forum has since been identified with parliamentary bodies and a meeting of minds.

(left) 87. Forum of Trajan, Rome. Northeast exedra and market hall. A.D. *c.* 113–117.

(below) 88. Column of Trajan and ruins of Basilica Ulpia, Rome. Column of Trajan, A.D. 106–113. Marble, 97′ high.

89. Basilica Ulpia, Rome. A.D. 113. Reconstruction drawing of interior.

90. Court at base of Trajan's Column, Rome. Reconstruction drawing.

The large rectangular interior of the Basilica Ulpia (Fig. 89), named for Trajan's family, was marked by a double colonnade in the Corinthian order that ran completely around the building, supporting a balcony and a second tier of columns that, in turn, supported the beams of the timbered roof. This large central hall served as a general meeting place as well as a business center. The semicircular interior recesses called apses, possibly roofed over with hemispherical vaults and set apart from the central hall by screens or curtains, housed the courts of law. The decorative scheme of the building included the lavish use of polychrome marbles. The steps at the entrances were of *giallo antico* stone, and the flanking columns were of matching yellow marble. The exterior and interior walls were liberally faced with varicolored marble panels, and the floor was done in rich mosaic patterns. In the double colonnade the shafts of the columns on the ground floor were of red granite, while their Corinthian capitals were carved from white stone. Pausanias' description of the "roof of bronze" probably meant that the decorative scheme had been completed with some form of metal embellishments.

Beyond the basilica were two libraries, one for Greek and the other for Latin scrolls, separated by a courtyard that enclosed the base of Trajan's Column (Fig. 90), the sculpture of which will be discussed shortly.

After Trajan's death his adopted son and successor, Hadrian, built at the end of the main (left) 91. "Maison Carrée," Nîmes, France. 16 B.C. Marble, 59 × 117' at base, podium 11' high, columns 30½' high.

(below) 92. *Augustus of Prima Porta. c.* 20 B.C. Marble, 6' 8" high. Vatican Museum, Rome.

axis of the Forum the Corinthian temple that climaxed the grand design. Architecturally, it was a large-scale version of the Maison Carrée (Fig. 91) at Nîmes in southern France. Like other Roman temples, this one honoring Trajan and the Maison Carrée rested on podiums and had porticoes in the front, which were much more prominently featured than those in Greek temples. The well-preserved example at Nîmes likewise shows only the columns of the portico standing free, while the rest are attached to the cella, indicating that columns were needed less for structural strength than for embellishment.

The practice of deifying rulers and erecting temples to them was widespread in Hellenistic times, and began in Rome as early as the reign of Augustus. The type of statue that stood in such a temple can be seen in the portrait of Augustus (Fig. 92), which was found near Prima Porta. He stands in the imposing attitude of an imperator addressing his troops. Carved on the cuirass, or metal breastplate of his armor, are scenes in low relief recounting the outstanding achievements of his reign and pictures of the gods and goddesses who conferred their favors upon him. At his side is a cupid astride a dolphin, one of the symbols of Venus (see Fig. 77), which alludes to the divine origin of the Julian family. Vergil, the principal poet of his period, traced Augustus' ancestry all the way back to Aeneas, the legendary founder of Rome, whose father was the mortal Anchises but whose mother was none other than the immortal Venus. In a similar vein is the head of Trajan

93. *Porcia and Cato*(?), portraits of a Roman couple. *c.* 1st century B.C. Marble, 27″ high. Vatican Museum, Rome.

(p. 71), a fragment possibly from a full-length statue. Resolute and far seeing, this is a portrait of a born leader of men.

Much of Roman religion was a family affair, honoring the living *pater familias* as well as the nearer and more remote ancestors. A room in every household was set aside for this purpose, and the custom was responsible for a whole genre of sculpture, such as the portrait busts entitled *Porcia and Cato* (Fig. 93). In contrast to the generalized and somewhat idealized image of Augustus as the statesman and imperator, this unpretentious portrait of ordinary citizens is remarkably realistic. Both kinds of sculpture, however, served essentially the same purpose—one as the image of the father of a family in a simple household, the other for the veneration of a great man in a temple. The paternalistic emperors were felt to deserve the universal reverence of the whole Roman family, since they were considered *pater patriae*, or fathers of their country. Erecting a temple to a distinguished Roman emperor was done in much the same spirit as building the Washington Monument or the Lincoln Memorial in Washington, D. C. Certain days were set aside for the offering of food and drink in simple family ceremonies; on the day for honoring the emperor, the rites at his temple were more formal, occasionally including animal sacrifice, a procession, festivities, and amusements. Religion to the

Romans was the tradition and continuity of the family and, in the larger sense, the history and destiny of Rome itself.

With the exception of the temple, the Forum of Trajan was completed during his lifetime and was dedicated by him for the use of the people of Rome in A.D. 113. The whole, then, is made up of parts—the triumphal entrance archway, the courtyard and its equestrian statue, the mercantile buildings, the Basilica Ulpia, two libraries, a monumental column, and the temple—all adding up to an architectural composition on a grand scale, designed to accommodate a hierarchy of activities. Beginning with a shopping center and place to transact business, the Forum continued with a general meeting place and the halls of justice, moved on to places for quiet contemplation, study in the libraries and the reading of history in visual form on the column, and, finally, came to rest in the precinct for the veneration of the emperor and the worship of the Roman gods.

Imperial Baths

While the forums took care of the more serious pursuits of his people, Trajan never forgot that circuses often were as important as bread in promoting the happiness of his subjects. One of every emperor's duties, in fact, was to provide for public amusement out of his private purse. Only the very wealthy could afford entertainment in their own homes, so the people as a whole had to look for their recreation outside. To this end many baths, theaters, amphitheaters, arenas, and stadiums had been built all over the city. The variety they encompassed has never been surpassed, and to this day the highest praise that can be given an elaborate public festival is to call it a "Roman holiday."

Imperial baths provided the people with far more than hot, cold, and tepid swimming pools. They offered such other facilities as dressing rooms, gymnasiums, restaurants, bars, and shady walks. Guests also could attend plays, witness athletic contests, listen to public lectures, read in one of the libraries, or stroll about the galleries where statuary and paintings were exhibited. The baths were, in short, the people's palaces where the sociable citizenry could enjoy together the things that only the rich could afford separately. Favored also as places to show the booty and souvenirs carried off during foreign conquests, the baths are the sites where much ancient statuary has been found, notably the *Laocoön Group* (Fig. 75). These baths also had important hygienic advantages; and with the habit of daily bathing firmly (below) 94. Cross (or groin) vault.

(bottom) 95. Baths of Caracalla, Rome, plan. A.D. 211–217. 750 × 380'.

(right) 96. Baths of Caracalla. Reconstruction drawing by Spiers.

Bay

established, the people of Rome probably were cleaner than those of any other city.

Trajan added to the already existing public baths a large establishment also built by Apollodorus. Although the ruins of his *thermae* (baths) are not so well preserved as the later baths of Caracalla and Diocletian, enough is known to establish a clear picture of what they were like. Only a degree smaller than the later examples, their facilities were on a comparable scale. The large central hall was the earliest known use of concrete cross vaulting, the principle of which can be studied in Figure 94 and in the similar central hall of the Baths of Caracalla (Figs. 95, 96), which measured 183 feet in length with an open space between the walls of 79 feet. From the illustration, it can be seen that the barrel vault that runs lengthwise is three times intersected at right angles by shorter vaults extending across the width of the hall. Besides spanning larger interior spaces without the obstruction of supporting piers and columns, this type of construction had the additional advantage of ample lighting through the clearstory windows, which were provided with thin strips of translucent yellow marble in lieu of glass. Modern architects, when erecting such huge edifices as the Union Station in Washington, D. C., and Grand Central Terminal in New York City, found no better models among large secular structures than these Roman baths.

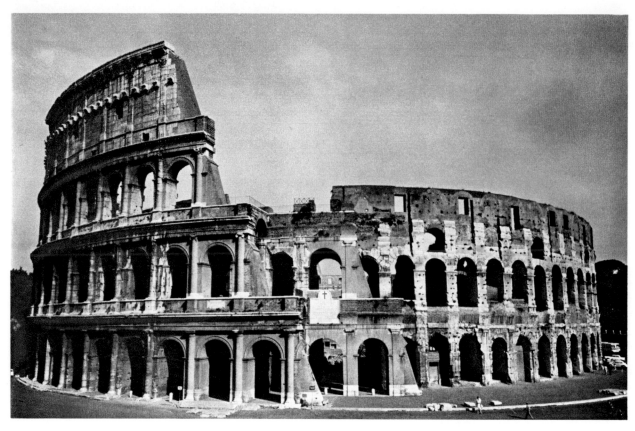

97. Colosseum, Rome. A.D. 72–80. Long axis 620', short axis 513', height 160'.

Colosseum, Aqueducts, and Apartment Houses

Other places, such as the Colosseum (Fig. 97), which dates from the late 1st century, were the scene of more garish forms of mass amusement, including gory gladiatorial contests between men and wild beasts. The oval form of the Colosseum covers about six acres and could seat about 50,000 spectators at one time. Around its circumference run some 80 archways, which served so efficiently as entrances and exits that the entire bowl could be emptied in a matter of minutes. The Roman talent for organization is not only evident here in such practical respects but extends to the structure and decorative design. Three architectural orders are combined in the successive stories of the same building. The attached columns on the lower range are the "home-grown" variation of the Doric, known as the Tuscan; those on the second tier are Ionic; on the third, Corinthian; while on the fourth, which rises to a height of 157 feet, are found shallow, flat Corinthian piers known as pilasters between which run a row of sockets for the poles over which a canvas awning was stretched to protect the spectators from sun and rain. The building material was a concrete

made from broken pieces of brick, small rocks, volcanic dust, lime, and water. It could be poured into molds of any desired shape and when dry was as hard as natural stone. The exterior was originally covered with marble facing, and the entire structure would be in good condition today had it not been used later as a quarry for building materials right up to the 18th century. In spite of this, the Colosseum is still one of the most imposing ruins to survive from Roman times, and its popularity as a prototype can be seen in the numerous football stadiums on college campuses.

In order to assure an ample water supply for his thermae, Trajan found it necessary to improve the old system of aqueducts and to add a new one, 35 miles long, that is still in use today. A more beautiful example of a Roman aqueduct is the Pont du Gard at Nîmes (Fig. 98), which survived from the 1st century A.D. A system of underground and open concrete channels was constructed to bring water from its mountain source to the town 25 miles away. Functioning on the principle of gravity, the ducts were sloped in the desired direction, and in this instance the water was carried almost 300 yards across the valley at a height of more than 160 feet. The graceful lower range of arches support a bridge that is still in use, while the upper series of large and small arches support the water channel.

The most ambitious of Trajan's civil-engineering projects, however, was the construction of a port at Ostia about 15 miles from Rome. It was a complicated system of breakwaters and canals connected with Rome by the Tiber River, and it provided facilities for export and import trade as well as an anchorage for the Roman fleet. Ostia rapidly grew into one of the most important commercial centers of the 2nd century, and recent excavations have uncovered some of its warehouses, theaters, baths, and many other public and private buildings. Of major interest are the ruins of apartment houses that reveal the type of multiple-family dwelling place in use at that time both in Ostia and Rome. In contrast to the more leisurely and rambling Mediterranean country villas found at Pompeii, the so-called "House of Diana" (Fig. 99) shows a close-knit, economically spaced, well-planned building of five stories, which has a strikingly modern look. Because the house was located on a street corner, the ground floor had rows of shops along two sides. The second floor

(above) 98. Pont du Gard, Nîmes, France. Early 1st century A.D. *c.* 902′ long, 161′ high.

(left) 99. "House of Diana," Roman apartment house at Ostia. A.D. *c.* 150.

(below) 100. "House of Diana," Roman apartment house at Ostia. Reconstruction drawing by Gismondi.

provided small apartments for the shopkeepers and their families, and each apartment was connected by separate steps to a shop below. In the reconstruction drawing (Fig. 100) two entrances can be seen on the right. One led into the center courtyard, which provided light for the inner rooms and a fountain. The other led to a staircase, which gave access to the upper floors. The most desirable apartments would have been those with the balconies on the third floor. In the time of Constantine, Rome was known to have had almost 50,000 apartment houses, some of which rose as high as eight stories, and only about 1,700 private town houses.

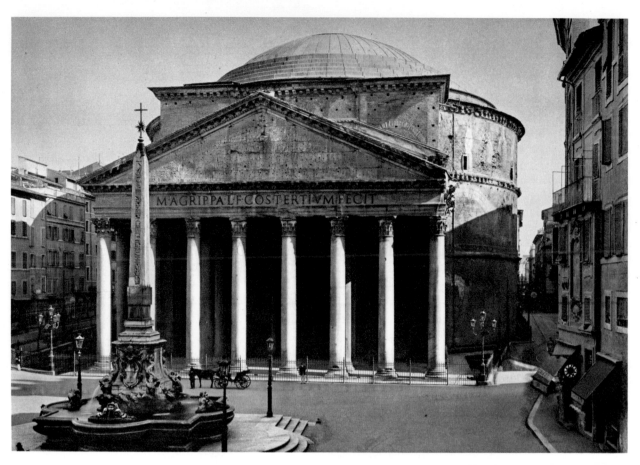

101. Pantheon, Rome. A.D. *c.* 120. Portico 101' wide, 59' high.

The Pantheon

The Roman sense of social organization also was extended to religion with the Pantheon (Fig. 101). While the name implies a temple to all the gods, in effect the Pantheon became a shrine for the chief deities, since the Roman pantheism included such a great number of them. The family or clan was the root of Rome's secular and religious life. The *pater familias*, as the lord of the household and head of the family, was entitled to domestic veneration. This patriarchal structure was extended to the state under the emperor, who was, in turn, the *pater patriae*, or father of his country, and entitled to public honors just as the *pater familias* was in his private domain of the household. Overall on the universal scale presided Jupiter with his Olympian family under whose total embrace the world was ruled with Rome as its leader. To house their divine deliberations and to allow Romans to propitiate them on proper occasions, the Pantheon was projected in Hadrian's reign. As the inscription over the architrave reads, the original structure was erected by Agrippa, Augustus Caesar's administrative aide. All but the portico had been destroyed by fire, however, and it was Hadrian who reconstructed the Pantheon as the domed cylindrical shrine one sees today. Unlike his predecessor Trajan, Hadrian was a man of thought rather than action. He took special delight in disputations with philosophers, and he is known to have prided himself on his architectural acumen. Apparently he had a direct hand in designing this distinguished edifice. The boldness of its conception, as well as its masterly execution, mark it as one of the glories of world architecture.

The builders first constructed a cylindrical base, the walls of which are 20 feet in thickness. Eight large recesses were left in it, one to allow for the entrance vestibule and the others to provide niches for the largest altars. To furnish support for the massive dome, a group of relieving arches and abutments were embedded in the wall to discharge its great weight. The concrete for the dome was poured in adjoining sections, and as it dried, it became one solid mass of stone, thus justifying description as an artificial monolith. Entrance is made through the octastyle Corinthian portico of Agrippa's earlier building, which measures a little over 100 feet in width. So huge a structure could easily have been just an overwhelming mass

Plate 5. GIOVANNI PAOLO PANNINI. *Interior of the Pantheon, Rome. c.* 1750.
Oil on canvas, 50 ½ × 39″. National Gallery of Art, Washington, D.C. (Kress Collection). (See p. 85.)

Plate 6. *View of a Garden. c.* 20 B.C. Wall painting from Villa of Livia at Prima Porta. National Museum, Rome. (See p. 93.)

of brick and concrete. Its solid exterior proportions actually do very little to relieve this general impression, but the fact that it was conceived primarily as an *interior* enclosing a definite space, and not as the solid mass which surrounds it, saves the day (Fig. 103, Plate 5).

The Pantheon's geometry is based on the union of a cylinder and a hemisphere over a circular ground plan (Fig. 102), with the interior diameter and the height of the dome both being a little more than 140 feet. The clarity of form achieved by the visible equality of horizontal and vertical dimensions, as well as by the simplicity of design, is evident to the casual eye. The satisfying sense of spatial proportion and the harmonious impression of the interior are based on a union of applied scientific skill and aesthetic feeling. In the Pantheon as well as in the central hall of the Baths of Caracalla (Fig. 96), the Romans advanced architecture to the point where it achieved significant interiors. Unlike other classical temples, the Pantheon invited entrance. The inner surface of the dome is characterized by *coffers*, indented panels which serve the dual purpose of diminishing the weight of the dome and furnishing the basis for its decoration. In the center of each coffer was a gilded bronze star, a motif that related the dome symbolically to the sky. Much of the once-resplendent interior, with its walls sheathed in varicolored marbles of glowing ochre with red, green, and black contrasts, is still visible. Gone, however, are the gilded-bronze tiles that once spread across the coffered inner dome like an expansive starry firmament mirroring the heavens. The sole source of light is the single 29-foot round opening in the middle of the dome. This *oculus*, or eye, as it was called, can be interpreted as an allusion to the all-seeing eye of heaven. Soaring almost 150 feet above the colorful mosaic flooring, it creates a great shaft of illumination that bathes the interior in light of high intensity.

As seen today, the Pantheon exterior is stripped of its former rich and colorful marble covering. The bronze plates of the portico ceiling, the gilded bronze tiles that covered the entire exterior of both the drum and the dome, and the monumental statues of the gods within have all disappeared in the course of time. Despite mutila-

102. Pantheon, plan.

103. Interior, Pantheon. Diameter 142′, height 140′, walls 20′ thick. Engraving by Piranesi. Metropolitan Museum of Art, New York. (Compare Plate 5.)

Voussoir

Force   Force

104. True arch, and barrel (or tunnel) vault.

tions, however, the Pantheon is the best-preserved single building that survives from the ancient world and the oldest structure of large proportions with its original roof intact. It holds its own as one of the world's most impressive domed buildings in spite of such outstanding competition as Hagia Sophia in Constantinople (Figs. 134, 136), the Cathedral of Florence (Fig. 263), St. Peter's in Rome (Fig. 324), and St. Paul's in London (Fig. 453). Its descendants are legion—the Villa Rotonda (Fig. 339), Thomas Jefferson's home at Monticello, the rotunda he designed for the University of Virginia (Fig. 501), the Pantheon in Paris, certain features of the Capitol rotunda in Washington, D. C., and the Low Memorial Library at Columbia University in New York, to name but a few.

The Roman Architectural Contribution

The Roman contribution to architecture was fourfold: (1) building for use, (2) development of the arch and vault as a building principle, (3) emphasis on verticality, and (4) design of significant interiors. In the first case, Roman architecture was marked by a shift in emphasis from religious buildings to the civil-engineering projects that had such an important bearing on the solution of the practical problems of the day. This did not mean that the Romans neglected their shrines and temples or that they lacked religious feeling. As in the 19th and 20th centuries, however, the main architectural expression was to be found in secular rather than religious structures. In this category come the basilicas, aqueducts, roads, bridges, even the sewer systems, which so admirably served the utilitarian purposes of the Romans.

Second—and perhaps most important of all—was the Roman exploitation of the possibilities inherent in the arch as a building principle to implement the above objectives. The construction of a true arch by means of the wedge-shaped blocks known as *voussoirs* can be seen more easily in Figure 104 than explained in words. When such arches are placed side by side in a series, the resulting arcade can be used for such structures as aqueducts and bridges, as seen in the Pont du Gard (Fig. 98). When placed in a series, from front to back, the result is a barrel vault (also called a tunnel vault), which can be seen in the Arch of Trajan at Benevento (Fig. 81) and which was useful for roofing interiors. When two such half-cylindrical vaults intersect each other at right angles, as seen in Figure 94, the result is referred to as a cross vault (or groined vault). This is the principle that is used so advantageously in the central halls of the Baths of Trajan and Caracalla. When a series of arches span a given space by intersecting each other around a central axis, the result is a dome, as exemplified in the Pantheon (Fig. 103). In greatly oversimplified form, these constitute the technical principles that underlie the Roman architectural achievement.

Third, by their technical advances they were able to increase the height of their buildings in proportion to the growing size of their large structures. The six-story mercantile buildings of Trajan's Forum were an impressive demonstration of the practical advantages of such verticality, which allowed the combination of many small shops into a single structure in a crowded city location. The multifamily apartment houses in Ostia and Rome were also cases in point. The trend was to be seen in the additional height that imparted such pleasing spatial proportions to the halls in the Baths of Trajan and Caracalla as well as the Pantheon—all made possible by cross vaulting and the dome.

Last, the enclosing of large units of interior space was made necessary by the expansion of the city's population. The direction of architectural thought in meeting this need can easily be seen by contrasting a Greek agora with the Forum of Trajan, a Hellenistic theater with the Colosseum, or the Parthenon with the Pantheon. Special attention to space composition and the problems of lighting are in evidence in the planning of such interiors as those of the Basilica Ulpia, the Pantheon, and the halls of the great baths. In all instances, the increasing Roman awareness of the value, tangibility, and reality of the spatial medium is discernible.

SCULPTURE

Spiral Frieze of Trajan's Column

To commemorate Trajan's victories in the two campaigns against the Dacian people of the lower Danube region, a monumental column (Fig. 105) was erected in his Forum by the Senate and people of Rome. It was placed in the small opening off the Basilica Ulpia between the two libraries (see Figs. 85, 88). Its base was originally surrounded by a colonnade (Fig. 90) that supported an upper gallery from which better views of the sculptures could be obtained. The diameter of the column varies from 12 feet at the base of its shaft to 10 feet at the top. As a whole it rose to a full height of 128 feet, including the 18-foot base, the 97-foot shaft, and a 13-foot colossal statue of Trajan that originally stood at the top. The latter has long since disappeared and has been replaced by one of St. Peter. Inside the column is a circular staircase that winds upward to the top and is lighted by small windowlike slits cut into the frieze. According to tradition, Trajan chose the monument as his burial place, and his ashes were placed in a chamber at the base of the column.

The column itself is of the Doric order and is constructed in several sections of white marble. Its surface is entirely covered by a spiral band, carved in low relief, which winds from bottom to top in 23 revolutions. Reading from left to right, the story of the two Dacian campaigns unfolds in a continuous strip about 50 inches wide and 218 yards long in which more than 2,500 human figures make their appearance, in addition to horses, boats, vehicles, and equipment of all kinds.

The hero of the story is, of course, the soldierly Trajan, who is shown fulfilling his imperial mission as the defender of Rome against the encroachments of the barbarians. The Empire was always willing to include any people who accepted the values of Mediterranean civilization, but it could tolerate no challenge. When an important kingdom was founded in Dacia, Trajan regarded it as a threat and set out forthwith to bring it under Roman control. While it took two campaigns to do the job, the lasting result of this Romanizing process is reflected in the name of one of the nations of the region—Romania. Trajan's brilliance as a commander was well known, and on this column and other similar monuments his reputation certainly did not suffer for lack of advertisement. In the frieze, he invariably is present and consistently is portrayed as a resolute figure in complete command of the situation at all times. Sharing top billing with their general is the Roman army; and their opposite numbers are Trajan's antagonist, the Dacian king Decebalus, and his barbarian hordes.

The beginning of the campaign is placed on the banks of the Danube in a Roman encampment guarded by sentries and supplied by boats

105. Trajan's Column, Rome. Cross section. A.D. 106–113. Marble, column 97' high, spiral frieze 656' long.

(left) 106. *Trajan's Campaign against the Dacians*, detail of Trajan's Column. A.D. 106–113. Marble, height of frieze band *c.* 50".

(below) 107. *Trajan Addressing Troops*, detail of Trajan's Column. A.D. 106–113. Marble, height of frieze band *c.* 50".

(Fig. 106). As the Romans set forth across a pontoon bridge, a river god personifying the Danube rises from a grotto and lends his support by holding up the bridge. From this point onward the action moves with singular directness toward the inevitable climax: the triumph of Roman arms. The ensuing scenes show Trajan holding a council of war; clad in a toga pouring a libation to the gods; and standing on a tribunal as he addresses his troops (Fig. 107). The army is shown pitching a camp on enemy soil; burning a Dacian village; and in the midst of battle. At the psychological moment Jupiter appears in the sky, throwing bolts of lightning at the enemy to disperse them in all directions. The aftermath is then shown with the soldiers crowding around the emperor and holding up the decapitated heads of the enemy; surgeons are seen caring for the wound-

ed; and Winged Victory makes her appearance.

At the making of peace Trajan is shown seated in judgment on the left, while the still-defiant Decebalus stands on the far right in front of the wall of the Roman camp. Between them are the representatives of the vanquished people prostrating themselves before their conqueror and imploring his mercy. Here the protagonist and antagonist of the drama confront each other directly in a single scene in the middle of the frieze (Fig. 108), which serves as an interim summary of the action up to this point. On this occasion Trajan made a lenient peace, which gave the king of the Dacians his chance to regather his forces, thus making a second campaign inevitable. At the conclusion of the story near the top of the column, Decebalus is shown falling on his sword; his head is brought to Trajan as a trophy; the barbarians take refuge across a river; and, finally, a personification of Night is seen hovering over a desolate landscape.

The scenes are designed to promote the continuous flow of action as smoothly as possible. For reasons of clarity the scenes have to be differentiated, and the artist does this through some ninety separate appearances of Trajan, which always signal a new activity. Other devices employed are an occasional tree, to set off one scene from another, and new backgrounds that are indicated in some places by a mountain, in others by a group of buildings, and so on. The comparison of this type of spiral relief has aptly been made with the form of the unfolding papyrus and parchment scrolls that the educated Romans were accustomed to read. Trajan is known to have written an account of his Dacian campaigns, much as Julius Caesar had done in the case of his Gallic wars, but the document is lost. Since commentaries on this bit of history are so fragmentary, the column has become one of the principal sources of information about it. The impression the viewer receives is so vivid that he feels almost as if he had experienced the campaign with Trajan.

The reliefs have a definite affinity to literature in their manner of telling a story by the process of visual narration. The methods that the Romans used in such cases have been distinguished as "the simultaneous" and "the continuous." The first is the same as that used by the Greeks in the east pediment and frieze of the Parthenon, for example, where all the action takes place at a given moment that is frozen into sculptural form. The simultaneous or isolating method thus observes the classical unities of time, place, and action. The continuous, or cyclic, method was developed by the Romans for just such a series of scenes as Trajan's wars. The unity of action is obtained by the telling of a life story, or it can be broadened to include a couple of military campaigns, as in this instance. The unities of time and place are sacrificed as far as the whole composition is concerned but are preserved in the separate scenes. While the origin of this continuous style is still a matter of scholarly dispute, none has challenged the effective use the Romans made of it. Its spirit is close to their keen interest in historical and current events, and its value for the purposes of state propaganda is obvious.

Despite the direct narrative content, the style is not realistic. For his effects, the artist depended upon a set of symbols as carefully worked out as the words used by writers of epics. The use of a series of undulating lines, for example, indicates the sea; a jagged outline on the horizon stands for a mountain; a giant rising up out of the water represents a river; a wall can mean either a city or a camp; and a female figure whose draperies are folded in the shape of a crescent moon informs the observer that it is night. In such symbolism, liberties with perspective inevitably occur, and it is quite usual

108. *Trajan Accepting Surrender of Decebalus*, detail of Trajan's Column. A.D. 106–113. Marble, height of frieze band *c.* 50".

to find a man taller than a wall and an important figure, such as that of the emperor, much greater in size than those around him. This technique does not preclude such clearly recognizable things as the banners of certain Roman legions as well as the details of their shields and armor. But there is a sharp stylistic differentiation between the approach in this case and the obvious realism of the relief on the Arch of Titus (Fig. 83). The Trajan frieze points unmistakably in the direction of the pictorial symbolism employed later by early Christian and medieval artists, who doubtless were influenced by it.

Much of the work will seem crude if placed beside the sculptures of Hellenistic artists who were still active in Rome (see Fig. 112 as an example). But this relief is clearly and intentionally an example of Roman popular art, and as such it was addressed to that large segment of the populace that was not accustomed to getting its information and enjoyment from books. Its location between two libraries also indicates a recognition that history could come from pictorial sources as well as from Greek and Latin scrolls. The elegant and placid forms of Greek gods were not apt to arouse the emotions of those Romans who sought amusement in the gladiatorial contests held in the Colosseum. While the educated minority could admire dignity and restraint in their sculpture, the vast majority had to be aroused by just such an energetic direct-action story as this, involving people like themselves. Thus viewed, Trajan's frieze is fresh, original, and astonishingly alive.

The artist who designed the frieze was clearly a master of his medium, who was able to depict with ease in extremely low relief whole armies, pitched battles, and the surrounding landscapes and sky. The care in execution is consistently carried out, and, even though the reliefs at the top were almost completely out of view, the workmanship remains the same. Standing in its prominent location from Trajan's time to the present, this column and the similar one of Marcus Aurelius have had incalculable influence on later art. The continuous mode of visual narration was taken over directly into the catacomb paintings of the early Christians; was continued in illuminated manuscripts, religious sculptures, and the stained glass of the medieval period; and can still be found going strong in the comic strips of daily newspapers. Even the motion picture owes a certain debt to the technique worked out here in the 2nd century A.D. In this book, examples of the direct influence of this narrative mode include the mosaics relating the story of Christ in the church of Sant' Apollinare Nuovo in Ravenna (Figs. 121, 122); the Bayeux Tapestry, which tells the story of the Norman conquest of England (Figs. 194–198, Plate 11); Giotto's (?) frescoes on the life of St. Francis of Assisi (Figs. 243–245); Michelangelo's Sistine Chapel ceiling murals (Figs. 314–321, Plate 23); and the studious duplication of Trajan's Column made under Napoleon for the Place Vendôme in Paris (Fig. 497).

LITERATURE AND MUSIC

While the time of Trajan could boast of no writers of the caliber of Cicero, Lucretius, Vergil, or Horace, it could at least point with pride to some of its eminent men of letters. Quintilian, author of the famous text known as the *Institutes of Oratory*, had influenced directly or indirectly a group of writers including Pliny the Younger, a persuasive orator and graceful letter writer; Tacitus, the historian; Juvenal, the satirist; and Suetonius, who was responsible for the gossipy but informative *Lives of the Twelve Caesars*. Plutarch, though a Greek, must also be listed among the major writers of the period, especially for his perceptive series of biographies of Greek and Roman statesmen, the *Parallel Lives*.

A very vivid picture of the life of a Roman of the patrician class is found in the correspondence of Pliny the Younger. As a senator and holder of important offices under Trajan, he enjoyed a wide acquaintance with many men of affairs. As a man of means he was able to enjoy all the refinements of a style of living that was highly luxurious even by modern standards. His civic duties required him to pass much of his time in Rome, but, like so many others of his class, he preferred to live in more rural surroundings. His country estates were scattered from one end of the Italian peninsula to the other, and he took special pride in the beautiful villas he built on them. Two that he especially liked were located on Lake Como. One he called Tragedy, because it commanded a grand view from its lofty situation; the other he named Comedy, because it was more intimately built on the lakeshore and more conducive to sport. "You may fish yourself," he wrote to a friend, "and throw your line out of your room, and almost from your bed, as from a boat."

Pliny's descriptions of his villa near Florence and another near Ostia are so detailed that architects have been able to reconstruct them with considerable exactness. The pleasures available at his Tuscan estate included hunting, supervising the farming, strolling about in gardens, exercising and playing games in the gymnasium, banqueting, and swimming, for which there were no less than three pools, including a warm one in the sun and a cool one in the shade. Pliny was not one to neglect the pleasures of the mind, which in his case included reading in his extensive library, conversing and corresponding with stimulating friends, and collecting objects of art that took his fancy. His enthusiasm for the latter pursuit is expressed in one of his letters. "I have lately purchased with a legacy that was left me, a statue of Corinthian bronze," he informed a friend. "It represents an old man in a standing posture. The bones, the muscles, the veins, and wrinkles are so strongly expressed, that you would imagine the figure to be animated."

Because of the Ciceronian eloquence he had developed as a pupil of Quintilian, Pliny was chosen by the Senate to make the welcoming speech on the occasion of Trajan's first arrival in Rome after his accession as emperor. The *Panegyric* he delivered was a veritable triumphal arch of flowery oratory. His later correspondence with Trajan, when he served as governor of the distant province of Bithynia, is as businesslike and direct as the speech to the Senate was ornate and devious. Pliny wrote to his superior with a proper note of deference, and Trajan's replies were always terse and to the point. In a typical exchange Pliny asked whether it would be advisable to rebuild the baths in one of the towns under his jurisdiction. The complete text of Trajan's reply was as follows: "If the erecting a public bath will not be too great a charge upon the Prusenses, we may comply with their request; provided, however, that no new tax be levied for this purpose, nor any of those taken off which are appropriated to necessary purposes."

The practice of poetry and music enjoyed higher favor among the educated Roman amateurs than did dabbling in the visual arts. Suggesting a plan for a building or some of the details of its decorative design was all right for a patrician, but from there on it was the architect's and carpenter's business. With sculpture and painting, a wealthy man could make an imposing impression as a collector, but the actual chiseling and daubing were something for artisans and slaves. When it came to the writing of verse or singing to the accompaniment of the lyre, however, amateurs abounded in the highest ranks of society right up to the emperors themselves. While Trajan's recreations seem to have been as strenuous as some of his military activities, those of his immediate successors included literary and musical pursuits. Hadrian wrote poetry in both Greek and Latin, but it remained for the last of the Antonines, Marcus Aurelius, to make an enduring reputation as a writer and philosopher. Hadrian, Antoninus Pius, and Caracalla were proficient on the cithara and hydraulic organ. Their musical prowess, however, was not destined to put that of their famous predecessor Nero into the shade.

While much is known about Roman literature, no actual examples of Roman music survive. All knowledge about it must be gleaned from occasional literary references, from sculptures, mosaics, and wall paintings that show music-making situations, and from some of the musical instruments themselves. From these sources, it is clear that the Romans heard much music and that no occasion, public or private, was complete without it.

A mosaic showing a small Roman instrumental ensemble performing in an amphitheater during a gladiatorial contest has been found in recent excavations in North Africa (Fig. 109). One musician is shown playing the long, straight brass instrument known as the *tuba*, or trumpet;

109. *Gladiatorial Contest*, showing orchestra with hydraulic organ, trumpet, and horn players. Mosaic from Zliten, North Africa. A.D. *c.* 70.

two others are playing the circular *cornu*, or horn; while still another is seated at the *hydraulus*, or water organ. Equipped with a rudimentary keyboard and stops, this highly ingenious instrument produced sounds by forcing air compressed by two water tanks through a set of bronze pipes. Some of these instruments were ten feet high. They were used mainly in open-air arenas where their tone must have resembled that of the calliopes, once so popular in old-fashioned circus parades. Other Roman instruments can be seen in Figure 110. The woman at the left is playing the *tibia*, a version of the Greek aulos; the central figure is clapping together the metal plates known as cymbals; and a drum player is seen at the right.

In keeping with the Roman idea of grandeur, the size of their musical instruments was greatly increased. Marcellinus described a performance in which hundreds of players took part, some of whom were said to have performed on "lyres as big as chariots." Owing to their usefulness in warfare, an ever-increasing volume of sound was demanded of wind instruments. Battle signals were relayed by means of trumpet calls, and the more the legions, the bigger and brassier became the sound. This is borne out by Quintilian, who asks a typical rhetorical question, then proceeds to answer it with a characteristic flourish: "And what else is the function of the horns and trumpets attached to our legions? The louder the concert of their notes, the greater is the glorious supremacy of our arms over all the nations of the earth." The large audiences accustomed to gather in amphitheaters also played a part in the stepping up of the volume of individual instruments and in the development of sizable vocal and instrumental ensembles. Writing in the 1st century A.D., Seneca notes that the size of the vocal and instrumental ensembles was such that sometimes the singers and players in the arena outnumbered the audience. Soloists would be lost in such vast surroundings, and there are descriptions of large groups of singers accompanied by wind instruments of various kinds and the hydraulic organ.

Quintilian also points out some of the practical applications of music to the art of oratory. He particularly emphasizes the development of the voice because "it is by raising, lowering, or inflexion of the voice that the orator stirs the emotions of his hearers." He then cites the example of one of the great speakers of the past who had a musician standing behind him while making his speeches, "whose duty it was to give him the tones in which his voice was to be pitched. Such was the attention which he paid to this point even in the midst of his most turbulent speeches, when he was terrifying the patrician party."

Literary sources point to a high degree of musical activity in Rome during the 2nd century A.D. From the number of Greek-trained singers, instrumentalists, and mimes who were active, clearly the Greek tradition was still very much alive. In its more austere forms, however, Greek art could have appealed only to the aristocratic minority. Hence, like so many other Greek artistic practices, music was adapted to the needs and uses of a large cosmopolitan center that embraced a great variety of tastes. Pliny casually mentions what entertainment was like in a cultivated household, when he chides a friend for not appearing at a dinner to which Pliny had invited him. After describing the menu he had missed, Pliny tells his friend that he was to have been "entertained either with an interlude, the rehearsal of a poem, or a piece of music," whichever he would have preferred.

Music was also a part of every theatrical performance, and, while the Roman drama omitted the chorus that the Greeks had stressed, its dialogue was interspersed with songs accompanied by the tibia. Such musical portions, however, were not composed by the dramatists, as they had been in the Athenian tradition, but were delegated to specialists in this field. The importance of choruses and bands for military morale was not overlooked, and a functional type of military music existed in addition to the trumpet calls to battle. Popular ensembles played music at games and contests, and strolling street musicians (Fig. 110) were part of the everyday scene.

110. DIOSKOURIDES OF SAMOS. *Street Musicians*, mosaic from Herculaneum. *c.* 100 B.C. National Museum, Naples.

The fact that not a single note of any of this music exists today testifies that Roman music was primarily a performing art. While the practicing musicians may very well have composed their own songs and pieces or made variations on traditional tunes, none seems to have been concerned with committing them to paper—and if one had done so, the later church fathers would very likely have seen to it that these pagan melodies were committed to the flames. So, like the folk music that existed only in oral tradition until the advent of modern notation and recording devices, the art died with the people who practiced it.

IDEAS

As a part of the mainstream of classical culture, Roman civilization shared many of the basic ideas that produced the Hellenic and Hellenistic styles. Significantly, the Romans widened the scope of the arts to include not only works that were aimed at the connoisseur but also those that carried broad mass appeal. The two ideas that differentiate the Roman from earlier aspects of the classical styles and dominate the Roman expression in the arts are the genius for organization and the frank spirit of utilitarianism, evidenced in a conception of the arts as a means to popular enjoyment and the solution of practical problems.

Organization

The Roman ability to organize is shown in the building up of a systematic world order, which embraced a unified religion, a unified body of laws, and a unified civilization. Military conquest was, to be sure, one of the means employed, but the allowance of a maximum of self-government to subject peoples, a wide latitude to local customs, even to tribal and cult religions, is proof of the Roman's psychological realism and toleration. Their desire for external unity did not imply internal uniformity, and their frank recognition of this fact was at the root of their success as administrators. With this ability to organize their religious, legal, social, and governmental institutions, their greatest contribution in the arts clearly would lie in the direction of architecture. This organizational spirit, moreover, is revealed most decisively in their undertaking of large public-works projects, such as the building of roads, ports, aqueducts, and the like. It is also seen in their manner of grouping buildings on a common axis, as in the Forum of Trajan, which

was so directly in contrast to the Hellenic idea of isolated perfection; in the organization of business activities in common centers, and the various forms of recreation in the baths; in the technical application and development of all the possibilities of construction by means of the arch and vault; in the combination of the Ionic and Corinthian capitals to form the Composite order, their only distinctive contribution to the classical orders; in the combination of three orders on the exterior of the same building, as in the Colosseum where the Tuscan-Doric order is used on the first story, Ionic on the second, and Corinthian on the third and fourth; in the development of the multifamily apartment house; in the attention given to the efficient assembling and dispersing of large numbers of people in such buildings as the Colosseum; in the invention of a supermarket, such as the six-storied example in Trajan's Forum; and finally, in the erection of a supertemple for the principal gods, as in the Pantheon.

The same organizational spirit is reflected in the expansion of interior space, as in the Basilica Ulpia, the Pantheon, and the great halls of the baths, in order to accommodate ever-larger numbers of people. The Greek idea had been to define space in planes, and the exteriors of their temples were designed as backdrops for processions and religious ceremonies. Those who worshiped Athena at the Parthenon were concerned primarily with its external colonnade, not the interior. Space in this sense was defined but not organized, but in the Pantheon, interior space was enveloped and made real (Plate 5). To the Greeks, space always remained a formless void, but the Romans recognized the possibilities of molding three-dimensional space, enclosing it and endowing it with significant form. Among the many ways they sought to enhance this spatial feeling are a sensitivity to scale; a tendency to design buildings in related structural units; an exploitation of color by the use of polychrome marbles, which livened interiors and which added to the perception of depth; a use of illusionistic wall paintings to suggest the third dimension (Plate 6); and an increased attention given to lighting problems. All this the Romans accomplished without sacrificing the classical clarity of form. The same feeling, furthermore, is carried over into sculpture where the tangibility of the spatial environment is reflected in the backgrounds of reliefs by means of buildings and landscapes that suggest depth, whereas the 5th-century B.C. Grecian style consciously omitted any such frame of reference. In addition to this, the organization of time into a temporal continuum, as in the cyclical series presented on the Column of Trajan, shows a new concept of sequential order translated into the pictorial medium.

Still another facet of this Roman organizational ability is found in the allowance for a wide range of taste in the arts. There were styles that appealed to the educated few and those that held the attention of the untutored populace of the middle and lower classes. In one case it was directed to the eye and ear of the connoisseur, and in the other it was frankly popular in its appeal. The conservative tastes of the first group harkened back to the tried-and-true values of Greek art; hence they either collected antique statuary and paintings, or they commissioned new works to be executed in the older style. Exquisite Greek craftsmanship held little interest for the majority, who needed something like a large bronze equestrian statue or a monumental triumphal arch to capture their attention. In Trajan's Forum, due allowance was made for this variety of taste, with the Greek and Latin libraries placed on either side of a court and a column in between, where the story of Trajan's campaigns was related in a carefully worked out popular language of symbols designed to awaken the curiosity of the multitude.

The disdain of the conservative group for popular art was well stated by Athenaeus, a Greek scholar and teacher who resided in Rome *c.* A.D. 200. He championed the virtues of the older cultural tradition and frequently made unflattering comparisons between the higher standards of the past and those that prevailed in his day. "In early times," he wrote, "popularity with the masses was a sign of bad art; hence, when a certain aulos-player once received loud applause, Asopodorus of Phlius, who was himself still waiting in the wings, said 'What's this? Something awful must have happened!' The player evidently could not have won approval with the crowds otherwise.... And yet the musicians of our day set as the goal of their art success with their audiences." Just as in the case of architecture, sculpture, and painting, the Romans were heirs to the Greek musical tradition. The ancient theories survived in philosophical speculation, and Greek music teachers were employed by preference in the homes of the wealthy. The only musical compositions to survive from this period, for instance, are three hymns by Mesomedes, a Greek musician attached to Hadrian's court. Those who cultivated this more austere style felt that music was meant to educate and elevate the mind, but the popular taste lay in quite another direction.

The music making that Athenaeus and his conservative group scorned was obviously the very kind that the majority of Romans enjoyed at their public festivals, military parades, games, sporting contests, races, and to some extent the theater. The modern parallel would be the cleavage that exists between audiences interested in chamber music, symphony concerts, and the opera, and those attracted by bands at football games, Broadway musicals, and popular jazz. What the Romans accomplished here was to broaden the base of the appeal of the arts and gear them to a number of different types of audience. They thus succeeded in providing for the entertainment of a large city population, just as their buildings and civil-engineering projects took care of their physical needs.

Utilitarianism

In referring to the administrations of the last two Antonine emperors, Gibbon declared that "their united reigns are possibly the only period of history in which the happiness of a great people was the sole object of government." The basis of this claim is to be found in the way the Romans managed to steer a middle course between the Scylla of Greek theoretical abstractions about the nature of an ideal state and the Charybdis of religious speculation on the joys of the world to come, which was to characterize the subsequent Christian phases of the empire. Speculation on the eternal verities could edify the mind, but the understanding of human behavior was rewarded by more immediate advantages. In the late Antonine Age, Rome had reached an equilibrium based on an acceptance of the Stoic doctrine of "live and let live" and the Epicurean idea of pleasure as an index to the highest good. The transfer of these individualistic doctrines to the forms and policies of a government meant a high degree of tolerance and a recognition that the standard of excellence in either a law or a work of art was the greatest good to the greatest number. The construction of elegantly proportioned temples was therefore not so important as the building of new aqueducts. Maintaining a luxurious private palace was secondary to providing people's palaces, such as the public baths and theaters. A private collection of sculpture was subordinate to public exhibitions in city squares and galleries, where the statues could be seen and enjoyed by many. A play, poem, or piece of music that awakened only the sensibilities of the cultured minority did not rank so high on this scale as those that were applauded by the multitude. In short, the practical arts were favored over the decorative arts; material goods superseded more remote spiritual blessings; and utility was in the

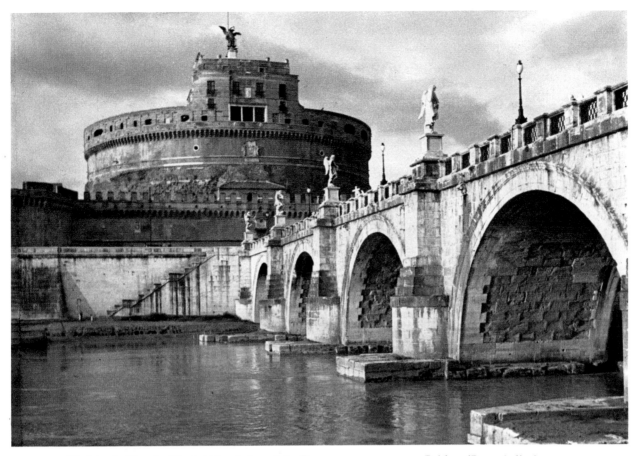

111. Hadrian's Tomb (Castel Sant' Angelo), Rome. A.D. 135-139. Bridge (Pons Aelius), A.D. 134.

ascendance over abstract beauty (though it must be remembered that the two are by no means mutually exclusive).

Since the Romans were little concerned with ideal forms, it was not an accident that their greatest successes were in the arts of government rather than in the fine arts. As Vergil said in the *Aeneid*: "Let others melt and mold the breathing bronze to forms more fair ... or trace with pointed wand the cycled heaven, and hail the constellations as they rise; But thou, Oh Roman, learn with sovereign sway to rule the nations." As was said earlier, the art which was most congenial to Roman aspirations was that of architecture, especially in its utilitarian aspects as found in the field of civil engineering. Building a 200-mile highway over the mountains, moving part of a hill over 100 feet high to make way for a forum, providing a sewer system for a city of over a million inhabitants, bridging the Danube at its widest point, perfecting such a new building material as concrete—all these were taken in stride.

When it came to sculpture, the Romans saw that subject matter served the purposes of the state by extolling the virtues and deeds of the emperors. Such epic poems as the *Aeneid* performed a similar service in the literary medium; and, as Quintilian said, the loud sounds of the brass instruments proclaimed the glory of Roman arms. Other applications of this utilitarianism are found in the brilliant exploitation of such technical devices as the arch and vault. Their success in solving practical problems is proved by the number of roads, aqueducts, and bridges, such as the Pons Aelius (Fig. 111), that are still serving their purpose today. In sculpture the application of the continuous-narrative method to the telling of a story was progressive, in that it promoted the sense of continuity in the temporal dimension and anticipated later Christian and secular pictorial forms. The development of such a practical form of verbal communication into the art of letter writing, beginning with Cicero and continuing with the younger Pliny, was the literary facet of the same idea. Finally, when Quintilian pointed out how the art of melody could be applied to oratory by the use of a pitch pipe to give the speaker a more persuasive tone, the cycle was complete.

Effective as this utilitarianism was, it was purchased at the price of conflict between structure and decoration, extrinsic and intrinsic values, and the purposive and nonpurposive aspects of art.

The Romans built and decorated well, but the two activities somehow failed to achieve a harmonious coexistence. This is well illustrated by the somewhat hollow claim of Augustus, who in an earlier period had boasted that he found Rome a city of brick and left it a city of marble. Actually, Rome was still a city of brick and concrete under an Augustan marble veneer. Neither material needs a disguise, or even an apology, as proved by the rhythmical grace of the functional arches of the Pont du Gard. Hence Augustus had no need to imply that Roman structures were solid marble like the Parthenon. As a whole, then, Roman architecture was at its best when it stuck to its frank utilitarianism, undertook vast engineering projects, and successfully solved the practical problems of construction.

CONCLUSION

Older cultural centers, such as Athens and Pergamon, were so far off the beaten track that their more restrained classical purity did not exert any appreciable influence on the forms of Western art until the archeological discoveries of the 18th and 19th centuries. All intervening phases of classicism were, in effect, revivals of the Roman style. With the establishment of the Roman building methods, Western architecture was firmly set on its course, and it steered in substantially the same direction until the technological discoveries of the 19th and 20th centuries. Consequently, it must be emphasized once more that Rome was the gateway through which all the styles, forms, and ideas of Mediterranean civilization passed in review. After being transformed by the process of selectivity—and with flashes of genuine originality—into a uniquely Roman configuration, they proceeded onward through the arch into medieval culture by way of the new Roman imperial capitals of Byzantium in the East and Ravenna in the West. When Rome declined as the center of world empire, it still remained the capital of Christendom. As the object of pilgrimages, its architectural, sculptural, and literary monuments were bound to exert a massive influence on the rulers, people, and artists who gravitated at one time or another toward the city. Because of this enduring preeminence throughout all subsequent phases of Western culture, no important city exists without a bit of Rome in it. It is therefore with full justification that Rome has been and still continues to be called the Eternal City.

112. Tellus Panel, detail of Ara Pacis Augustae, Rome. "Earth" (in center), "Air" (at left), "Water" (at right). 13–9 B.C. Marble, c. 5′ 3″ high.

PART II
THE MEDIEVAL PERIOD

4 - THE EARLY ROMAN CHRISTIAN AND BYZANTINE STYLES

RAVENNA, LATE 5TH AND EARLY 6TH CENTURIES

Many an old Roman coin bears the inscription *Ravenna Felix*, Happy Ravenna. By a felicitous stroke of fate, this previously unimportant little town on Italy's Adriatic coast became the stage on which the great political, religious, and artistic dramas of a century and a half of world history were enacted. Ravenna was, in turn, the seat of the last Roman emperors of the West, the capital of a barbarian Ostrogothic kingdom, and the western center of the East Roman Empire. A more unprepossessing site could hardly be imagined. To the east lay the Adriatic Sea, to the north and south wide deltas of the River Po, and the only land approach was through marshes and swamps. Yet when the barbarian hordes had Rome under constant harassment, it was this very isolation that led Emperor Honorius to abandon Rome in A.D. 402 and seek in Ravenna a fortress where his hard-pressed legions could be supplied by the East Roman Empire through the nearby port of Classe. But with all its natural advantages, Ravenna could hold out against the barbarians only until the year 476, when Odoacer succeeded in entering the all-but-impregnable city and putting an end to the West Roman Empire. The Ostro-

gothic kingdom of Theodoric, Odoacer's successor, was even more short-lived, and Ravenna fell once more in 540, when Justinian's armies of the East Roman Empire conquered the Italian peninsula and for a brief time reunited the old empire. Meanwhile a third force, the more enduring power of the Roman papacy, was becoming increasingly influential.

Diverse historical traditions as well as wide geographical distances separated Rome in the west, Byzantium in the east, and the nomadic Ostrogoths in the north. Early in the 4th century, after he had made Christianity an official state religion, Emperor Constantine had moved his court to Byzantium, christening the city the "new Rome." Later, this second capital was called Constantinople in his honor, and soon the East and West Roman empires were going their separate courses. With the encroachments of the northern barbarians, a three-way struggle for power began among Justinian, Theodoric, and the pope.

More than the sea stretched between Ravenna and Constantinople, higher mountains than the Alps stood between it and the restive northern barbarians, and greater obstacles than the Apennines

(above) *Christ as Orpheus*. 4th century A.D. Marble, *c.* 40¼″ high. Byzantine Museum, Athens.

99

Rome

284–	305	Diocletian, emperor
306–	337	Constantine, emperor
	313	Edict of Milan legalized Christianity
	c.313	Lateran Basilica begun on site of present San Giovanni in Laterano
c.324–	c.333	Old St. Peter's Basilica begun on Vatican Hill
c.330–	c.350	Tomb of Santa Costanza, daughter of Constantine. Later rededicated as church
c.332–	c.340	Sta. Maria Maggiore Basilica begun
c.340–	397	St. Ambrose; bishop of Milan
340–	420	St. Jerome; translator of Latin Vulgate Bible
354–	430	St. Augustine; bishop of Hippo (North Africa); author of *Confessions* (397), *City of God* (426)
	385	San Paolo fuori le Mura (St. Paul's outside the Walls) Basilica built. Destroyed by fire 1823 and rebuilt
	402	Rome abandoned by Emperor Honorius as capital of West Roman Empire
	410	Visigoths sacked Rome
	455	Vandals sacked Rome
	476	Odoacer sacked Rome; fall of West Roman Empire
590–	604	Gregory the Great, pope; liturgy of Roman Catholic Church codified; Gregorian chant established

Ravenna

395–	423	Honorius, West Roman emperor
	402	Ravenna, under Emperor Honorius, became capital of West Roman Empire
c.402–	450	"Neonian" Baptistry for Roman Christians
c.425–	c.440	Mausoleum of Galla Placidia
c.475–	524	Boethius; Theodoric's minister; translator of Greek treatises; author of *Consolations of Philosophy*
	476	Odoacer conquered Ravenna; Fall of West Roman Empire

476–	540	Ravenna capital of Gothic kingdom
476–	493	Odoacer, king
c.480–	575	Cassiodorus; Theodoric's minister; after 540 founded monastery at Vivarum, Italy
	490	Church of Sant' Apollinare Nuovo begun
493–	526	Theodoric, king
	c.526	Mausoleum of Theodoric built
	c.527	Church of San Vitale begun
c.533–	539	Church of Sant' Apollinare in Classe built
	540	Belisarius entered Ravenna; end of Theodoric's Ostrogothic kingdom
	546	Maximian appointed archbishop of Ravenna; ruled as Byzantine exarch
	547	Church of San Vitale completed
	556	Archbishop Maximian died

Byzantium (Constantinople)

c.324–	c.330	Constantine made Byzantium capital of East Roman Empire
	325	First Council of Nicea
329–	379	St. Basil; bishop of Caesaria; liturgist of Eastern Orthodox Church
c.345–	407	St. John Chrysostom; patriarch of Constantinople; liturgist of Eastern Orthodox Church
518–	527	Justin, East Roman emperor
527–	565	Justinian the Great, East Roman emperor
	c.527	Church of SS. Sergius and Bacchus begun
	c.527	Church of San Vitale begun at Ravenna
532–	537	Church of Hagia Sophia built by architects Anthemius of Tralles and Isidorus of Miletus
	533	Justinian's *Digest of Laws*
534–	540	Belisarius, Justinian's general, conquered Italy
	540	Belisarius entered Ravenna; end of Theodoric's Ostrogothic kingdom

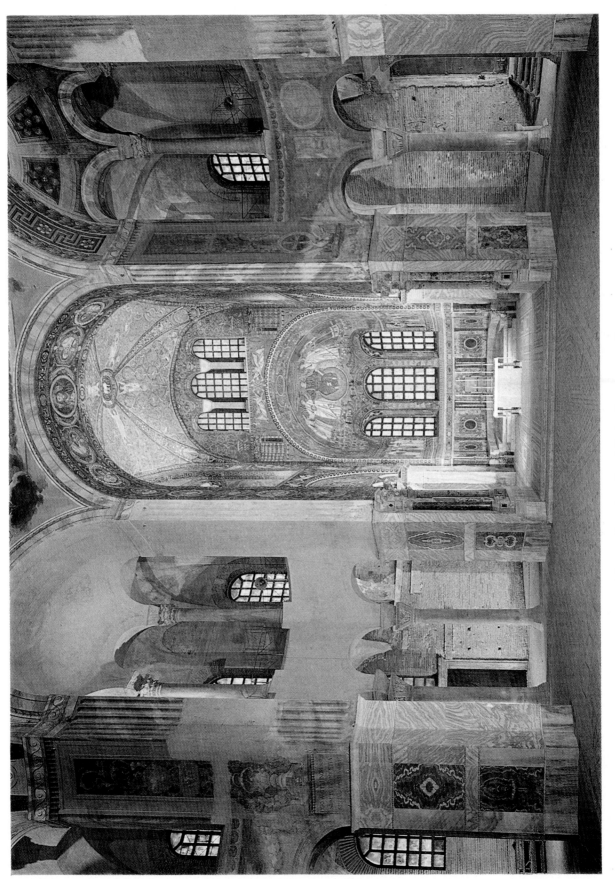

Plate 7. Interior, San Vitale, Ravenna. 526–547.
Outer octagon 115′ in diameter, inner octagon 54′9″. (See p. 112.)

Plate 8. *Empress Theodora and Retinue. c.* 547. Mosaic. San Vitale, Ravenna. (See p. 114.)

separated it from Rome. Metaphysical barriers, in fact, proved more impassable than seas or mountains, because this was the age that was laying the foundations of basic religious beliefs, and in some respects the controversies in Ravenna foreshadowed the later separations of Christianity into Eastern Orthodox and Roman Catholic and Catholic and Protestant denominations. At this time, the main doctrinal battle centered on the nature of the Trinity, and especially on Christ's role as the second person in the Trinity. The Ostrogoths, having been converted by Arius of Alexandria (c. 256–336), believed that, since He was created by God the Father, Jesus was subordinate and not of one substance with God. In spite of this denial of the Trinity, the Arians revered Christ as the noblest of created beings, but human rather than divine. In Byzantium, it was held that Christ as the Incarnated Word was of one single substance with the Father and hence of divine nature only. The Roman papacy found a middle ground between the two extremes and took the position that, since the Word was made flesh, Christ possessed both divine and human natures and was a full member of the Trinity. Today, such theological controversies seem remote, but in the early centuries of Christianity they were of sufficient intensity to shake empires, depose kings, and cause decades of war.

Paralleling the political and religious controversy, a conflict of art styles took place within Ravenna as successive rulers built and embellished the city. In the 6th century, Ostrogothic Arian heretics, Byzantine patriarchs, and members of the Roman hierarchy, together with the schools of artists each patronized, had different cultural heritages, different aesthetic goals, and different ways of looking at the world. During the days when the Roman Empire was united, cultural influences came from all parts of the Mediterranean world, and, with due allowance for regional diversity, Roman art achieved a recognizable unity. But with the disintegration of Roman power, the adoption of Christianity as an official religion, and the separation of the Empire into eastern and western centers, a reorientation in the arts took place. Though there were many overlapping elements, owing to a common heritage, two distinct styles began to emerge. Hence, when reference is to all the art of this period, the designation will be "early Christian"; the term "Early Roman Christian" will be used to distinguish the Western style from the declining old pagan Roman arts, on the one hand, and from the subsequent Romanesque and Gothic styles of the later medieval period on the other; and "Byzantine" will designate the parallel Eastern style.

ARCHITECTURE AND MOSAICS

Ravenna's replacement of Rome as a capital city demanded a building program that would transform a minor town into a major metropolis. No ruler could afford to be outdone by his predecessors. Hence, the West Roman emperors and Empress Galla Placidia, whose tomb is seen in Figure 113, erected significant secular and reli-

113. Mausoleum of Galla Placidia, Ravenna. c. 425. 49 × 41'.

gious structures. Then the barbarian king Theodoric, after he came to power, sought to be more Roman than the Romans. As he wrote to an official in Rome, he wished his age to "match the preceding ones in the beauty of its buildings." And the great Justinian, after the Byzantine conquest, made architectural contributions commensurate with his imperial dignity.

As a capital city with a cosmopolitan population, Ravenna received diplomatic representatives from every part of the Mediterranean world. Each embassy had to build not only a residence for its delegation but also a church so that its specific form of worship would have an appropriate setting. As a result, Ravenna had dozens of churches for the many Christian sects—for the separate Byzantine rites of such eastern cities as Constantinople, Antioch, and Alexandria; for the various Roman, Gallic, and Spanish liturgies of the West—and also a synagogue for the Jews. Had all these buildings survived, Ravenna today would be a complete museum of 5th- and 6th-century Mediterranean architecture. Unfortunately, all but a few fragments of the secular buildings have perished with the passage of time, but the remaining religious structures—churches, baptistries, memorial chapels, and tombs—reveal the rich artistic fruits born of a synthesis of Roman and Byzantine forces. The surviving buildings at Ravenna, together with their rich decorative details, are an excellent index to the art forms of this important transitional period between the classical and medieval worlds. In this proud heritage, the city can still be called Happy Ravenna.

Sant' Apollinare Nuovo and the Oblong Basilica

Theodoric included in his building program a church for his own Arian sect. Originally dedicated by him to "Our Lord Jesus Christ," this church (Fig. 115) today bears the name of Sant' Apollinare Nuovo, honoring Apollinarus, patron saint of Ravenna and, by tradition, the disciple and friend of St. Peter. The floor plan (Fig. 116) is a severely simple one, with a division of space into a vestibule entrance, known as the *narthex*; a central area for the congregation to assemble, known as the *nave*, separated from the side aisles by two rows of columns; and a semicircular *apse*, which framed the altar and provided seats for the clergy. Older pagan temples, with their small dark interiors, were not suitable models for Christian churches that had to house large congregations. Ancient Greek ceremonies had taken place outdoors around an altar with the temple as a backdrop. The principal architectural and decorative elements of the classic temples—colonnades, frieze, pediments—faced outward. The Christian basilica turned the Greek temple outside in, leaving the exterior quite plain, and concentrated attention on the interior colonnades and the painted or mosaic embellishments of the walls and semidomed apse.

The most complete of these early Christian basilicas was Old St. Peter's (Fig. 117), so called because it was razed in the 16th century to make way for the present basilica of Bramante, Michel-

114. Interior, Mausoleum of Galla Placidia, Ravenna. *c.* 425. 39 × 33′.

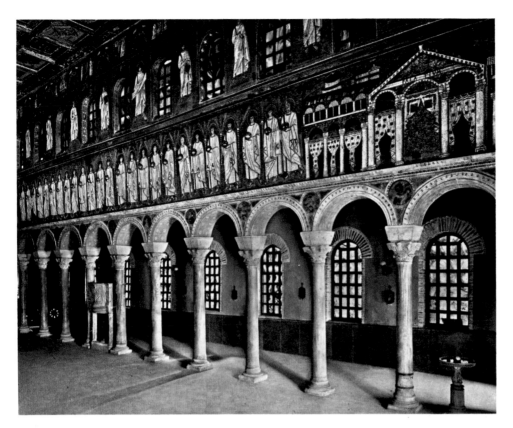

(left) 115. Interior, Sant'
Apollinare Nuovo, Raven-
na. c. 493–526.

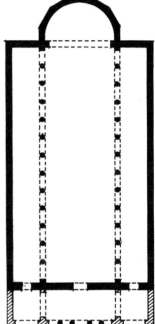

116. Sant' Apollinare
Nuovo, plan.

Kenneth Conant

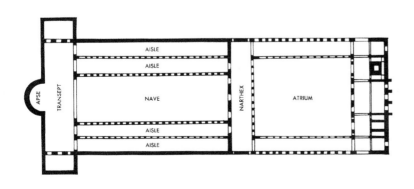

AISLE

AISLE

APSE TRANSEPT NAVE NARTHEX ATRIUM

AISLE

AISLE

(above) 117. Old St. Peter's
Basilica, Rome. c. 333. Grand
axis c. 835′ long, transept 295′
wide. Restoration study by
Kenneth J. Conant.

(left) 118. Old St. Peter's, plan.

angelo, and Maderno (Fig. 324). Planned from the year 326, when it was dedicated by Constantine, built over the presumed tomb of the Apostle, and as the largest church of the period, Old St. Peter's, until its demolition, ranked as the key monument of Western Christendom. To provide for all Christian activities, it brought together elements of Roman domestic, civic, and temple architecture into a new harmonious composition. Approached by a flight of steps, entrance to the *atrium* was made through an arched gateway. This open courtyard, derived from old Roman country villas, was surrounded by roofed arcades supported by columns; it provided space for congregations to gather, facilities for the instruction of converts, and offices for church officials. In its center was a fountain for the ceremonial washing of hands. The side of the atrium toward the church became the narthex that serves as a frontispiece to the church proper. Through the portals of the narthex, entrance was made to the nave and side aisles. This spacious, 80-foot-wide nave resembling the rectangular law-court halls of Roman public basilicas, was flanked on either side by two 30-foot-wide aisles and a procession of columns that led the eye along its 295-foot length to the *triumphal arch* (so called because of its derivation from similar Roman imperial structures). Beyond this was the wide *transept*, the "arms" set at right angles to the nave and an area that functions as a second nave,

and the semicircular apse. The ground plan (Fig. 118), then, was roughly T-shaped or cruciform, resembling a long Latin cross with short arms. From beginning to end, the design of Old St. Peter's swept along a horizontal axis of 835 feet and opened out at its widest point in the 295-foot transept.

Vertically, a basilica (Fig. 119) rises above the nave colonnades through an intermediate area called the *triforium* that extends to the level of the roofing over the side aisles, above which is the clearstory with its rows of windows that light the interior and its masonry that supports the wooden beams of the shed roof. In keeping with the sheltered and inward orientation of these early basilicas, no windows gave view on the outside world; those at the clearstory were too high and too deeply set to allow even a glimpse of the sky. It was inner radiance of the spirit rather than natural light that was sought.

Various parts of the basilica form acquired symbolic meanings in keeping with the teachings of the Christian faith. Such a basilica as St. Paul's outside the Walls (Fig. 120) literally was oriented so that the congregation faces the rising sun—to commemorate the Eastertide resurrection of Christ. The ground plan in the shape of the Latin cross signified the crucifixion. The nave, its name derived from the Latin *navis* (ship), symbolically transported the believers as they passed in the

119. Typical early Roman Christian basilica.

120. San Paolo fuori le Mura (St. Paul's outside the Walls), Rome. *c.* 386 (destroyed by fire *c.* 1823; new building from 1825). 390 × 200'; 100' high.

communion procession through the arch of triumph to the haven, or heaven, of salvation, which is reflected in the semidome of the apse and which was customarily decorated with stars and a celestial vision of Christ in Glory (Fig. 178).

Sant' Apollinare Nuovo, unlike Old St. Peter's which had to accommodate a standing congregation of 40,000 or more, was designed as the private chapel of Theodoric's palace. Only the nave remains intact, all other parts being restorations or later additions. As such, its modest architecture would attract only passing attention, but the magnificent mosaics that decorate its nave wall are of major importance in art history. Although they present a harmonious design, the mosaics actually were made in two different periods and styles.

The mosaics of the earlier period were commissioned by Theodoric and are of Early Roman Christian craftsmanship. "Send us from your city," Theodoric had written through his secretary Cassiodorus to an official in Rome, "some of your most skilled marble-workers, who may join together those pieces which have ·been exquisitely

divided, and connecting together their different veins of color, may admirably represent the natural appearance." After Justinian's conquest, the church was rededicated and all references to Arian beliefs and Theodoric's reign were removed. Half a century later, part of the frieze above the nave arcade was replaced by mosaics in the Byzantine style.

Completely covering both walls of the nave, the mosaic work is divided into three bands (see Fig. 115). Above the nave arcade and below the clearstory windows, a wide and continuous mosaic strip runs the entire length of the nave in the manner of a frieze. It depicts two long files of saints (the Byzantine part) moving in a majestic procession from representations of Ravenna on one side and Classe on the other (the Early Roman Christian part). The second band fills the space on either side of the clearstory windows with a series of standing toga-clad figures. At the top level, panels depicting incidents in the life of Christ alternate with simulated canopylike niches over the figures standing below. Both the middle and upper bands are of Roman workmanship, and the scenes in the upper band constitute the most (above) 121. *Good Shepherd Separating the Sheep from the Goats. c. 520.* Mosaic. Sant' Apollinare Nuovo, Ravenna.

(right) 122. *Last Supper. c. 520.* Mosaic. Sant' Apollinare Nuovo, Ravenna.

complete representation of the life of Christ in early Christian art. On one side, the story of the parables and miracles is told, among them the *Good Shepherd Separating the Sheep from the Goats* (Fig. 121), an allusion to the Last Judgment. In this and other scenes Christ appears youthful, unbearded, with blue eyes and brown hair. On the opposite side, scenes of the passion and resurrection are presented. In the *Last Supper* (Fig. 122) showing Christ and the disciples reclining in the manner of a Roman banquet, He is seen as a more mature and bearded figure. In all instances He has the cruciform halo with a jewel on each arm of the cross to distinguish Him from the

attending saints and angels. His dignified demeanor and purple cloak also tend to show Him in the light of royal majesty. Standing like statues on their pedestals, the figures in the middle band are modeled three dimensionally in light and shade and cast diagonal shadows. They apparently were once identified by inscriptions over their heads, and the removal of their names suggests they may have been prophets and saints revered by the Arian Christians.

The great mosaic frieze above the nave arcade starts on the left and right of the entrance with representations of the port of Classe and Ravenna, respectively. In the crescent-shaped harbor with three Roman galleys riding at anchor, Classe is seen between two lighthouses. Above the city walls some of the ancient buildings are discernible, and from the gate issues the procession of virgin martyrs. On the opposite side is Ravenna with Theodoric's Palace (Fig. 123) in the foreground. Under the word *Palatium* is the central arch where once was an equestrian portrait of Theodoric. Under the other arches, outlines and vestiges of heads and hands indicate that members of his court were also portrayed, and Theodoric was again depicted in the city gate at the right. But when the Ostrogothic kingdom came to its abrupt end, these personages were replaced by simulated Byzantine textile curtains. Above the palace are several of Theodoric's buildings with the Church of Sant' Apollinare Nuovo itself on the left and the domed Arian Baptistry (see Fig. 128) on the right. The rest of the frieze apparently pictured events

of Theodoric's reign that were obliterated after the Byzantine occupation and replaced with the files of saints issuing from the gates of the two cities.

As with the cella frieze of the Parthenon, this procession reflects the ritual that regularly took place in the church. According to the early custom, the congregation gathered in the side aisles, with women on one side and men on the other. At the offertory they went forward through the nave to the altar carrying with them their gifts of bread and wine for the consecration. In a stylized way, the procession frieze reenacts this part of the service on a heavenly level. On the left, 22 virgins (Fig. 124) are led forward by the Three Wise Men to the throne of the Virgin Mary, who holds the Christ Child on her lap. Arrayed in white tunics with richly bejeweled mantles, the virgins carry their crowns of martyrdom in their

123. *Theodoric's Palace. c. 520.* Mosaic. Sant' Apollinare Nuovo, Ravenna.

124. *Procession of Virgin Martyrs. c. 560.* Mosaic. Sant' Apollinare Nuovo, Ravenna.

hands as offerings. In a similar manner, 25 male martyrs on the right are escorted by St. Martin of Tours into the presence of Christ, who is seated on a lyre-backed throne. The eye is led along by the upward folds and curves of their costumes as they tread a flowered path lined with date palms that symbolize both Paradise and their martyrdom. All is ineffably serene and no trace of their earthly suffering is seen. Their heads, though tilted differently to vary the design somewhat, are all on the same level in keeping with the Greco-Byzantine convention of isocephaly. Only St. Agnes is accompanied by her attribute, the lamb; otherwise the faces reveal so little individuality they could not be identified without the inscriptions above.

A completely different artistic feeling is revealed when these Byzantine figures are compared with the earlier Roman work in the bands above. The unshaded lines of the Byzantine design form a frankly two-dimensional pattern, while the garments of the Roman personages fall in natural folds that model the forms they cover in three-dimensional fashion. All the figures in the upper two bands wear simple unadorned Roman togas, while the saints below are clad in luxurious, ornate Byzantine textiles decorated with rare gems. The Roman figures appear against such natural three-dimensional backgrounds as the green Sea of Galilee, hills, or a blue sky. The Byzantine virgins and martyrs, however, are set against a shimmering gold backdrop with uniformly spaced stylized palms. The candor, directness, and simplicity with which the Roman scenes are depicted likewise contrasts strikingly with the impersonal, aloof, and symbolic Byzantine treatment of the nave frieze. Differences of theological as well as stylistic viewpoints are involved, since the Arian-Roman panels accent the Redeemer's wordly life and human suffering, and the Byzantine frieze accents His divinity and remoteness from mundane matters.

The art of *mosaic*, in general, depends for its effectiveness on directing the flow of light from a myriad of tiny reflectors. After the placement of the panels, the design, and the colors have been determined, the mosaicist must take into account both the natural source of light from windows and artificial sources from lamps or candles. Accordingly, he fits each *tessera*, or small cube made of glass, marble, shell, or ceramic, onto an adhesive surface, tilting some this way, others that, so that a shimmering luminous effect is obtained. Fresco painting had been widely used for wall decorations of underground chapels in the catacombs and in Early Roman Christian churches even before Christianity became an accepted religion of the Roman Empire. But when Christianity acquired the prestige and wealth to employ the foremost architects, mosaics were preferred to fresco. Unlike fresco painting or stained glass, mosaics are especially well adapted to dimly lit interiors. Capable of catching even the faintest ray of candlelight, they can convey the impression of radiance emanating from within the church rather than from without. In an age accustomed to look beyond the world of reality, the mosaic medium was ideal for conjuring up other-wordly visions and directing thoughts toward the invisible world of the spirit. Mosaics are even more closely allied with architecture than either sculptures or paintings. While the latter, except in the case of frescoes, are detachable, a mosaic is actually the surface of a wall or a floor. Photographs convey only a faint impression of the true beauty and emotional appeal of mosaics. Their shimmering, kaleidoscopic color changes must be seen in their original settings to be fully appreciated.

San Vitale and Central-type Structures

Little more than a year's time elapsed between the death of Theodoric and the accession of Justinian as emperor in Constantinople. Almost immediately at Ravenna, Justinian undertook in absentia the laying of the foundation stone of San Vitale (Fig. 125). In the statecraft of that day, the building of a church that would surpass anything undertaken by Theodoric served as an assertion of Justinian's authority in Italy and evidence of the weakened power of Theodoric's Ostrogothic successors. At first Justinian's position in the capital of the West Roman Empire was anything but certain, and the project languished. Eventually, the use of force was needed to assert his Italian claims, and his armies entered the city in the year 540. Thereafter, construction of San Vitale proceeded apace, and seven years later the church was ready for its dedication by Archbishop Maximian. Its plain red brick exterior is proof that as little attention was paid to the outside of San Vitale as to that of any other church of the period. But with its rich polychromed marble walls, carved alabaster columns, pierced marble screens and other delicate details, and, above all, its sanctuary mosaics, San Vitale is a veritable jewel box.

Architecturally, San Vitale is a highly developed example of the central-type church, differing radically from Sant' Apollinare Nuovo. Yet, as the ground plan (Fig. 126) shows, it has all the usual features of the basilica, including a narthex entrance, circular nave, surrounding side aisles,

125. San Vitale (exterior of apse), Ravenna. *c.* 526–547. Diameter 112'.

126. San Vitale, plan.

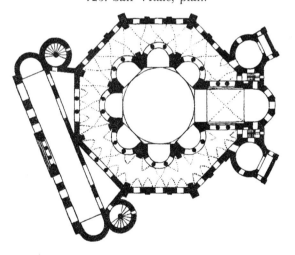

and a triumphal arch leading into a sanctuary with an apse and two side chambers. The striking difference, however, between an oblong basilica and a centralized church is the direction of the axis. In the former, the axis runs horizontally through the center of the building dividing the church lengthwise into equal halves, the eye being led toward the apse; in the central-type building the axis is vertical, leading the eye upward from the central floor space to the dome. Were it not for the addition of the oblong narthex on the west and the apse on the east, San Vitale would be a simple octagon. The two side chambers of the apse are usually associated with Eastern Orthodox churches, and their presence here points to the fact that San Vitale was designed as a theater for the Byzantine liturgy. The northern chamber was designated the *prothesis*, to indicate its use as the place where the communion bread and wine were prepared for the altar. In Eastern Orthodox usage, the sacrificial aspect of the mass assumed a dramatic character, and the sacramental bread was "wounded, killed, and buried" on the table of the prothesis before it appeared on the altar, where it symbolized the resurrection of the body. The southern chamber is called the *diakonikon* and served as the vestry and as a place to store the sacred objects used in the orthodox service.

In order to understand San Vitale and central-type churches, one must look at similar buildings at Ravenna and elsewhere. While the ancestors of the oblong basilica were Roman domestic and public buildings, the centralized church derives from the ancient circular tombs of the *tholos* type, such as the one at Delphi in Greece (Fig. 47). Later examples are seen in Hadrian's colossal sepulchre on the banks of the Tiber (Fig. 111); in the mausoleum Constantine built for his daughter Costanza (Fig. 153), later rededicated as a church; and Theodoric's Tomb (below) 127. Theodoric's Tomb, Ravenna. *c.* 520. Base 45′ in diameter, dome 35′ in diameter.

(bottom) 128. Arian Baptistry, Ravenna, *c.* 520.

at Ravenna (Fig. 127). Dating from *c.*520, this tomb is built with blocks of hewn stone, the lower story being a ten-sided crypt, the upper part a circular chapel. The whole is surmounted by a shallow dome, a huge monolith 107 feet in circumference, carved from a single piece of Istrian marble. The ancient preference for the circular mausoleum can be explained partly by its symbolism. Immortality was frequently represented by the image of a serpent biting his tail—that is, a living creature whose end was joined to its beginning. Another ancestor is the round classical temple, such as the Temple of Vesta in Rome, and the Pantheon (Fig. 101).

The eight-sided Christian baptistry (Fig. 128) was taken over directly from the octagonal bathhouses found in ancient Roman villas. There the pool was usually octagonal and the structure around it assumed that shape. Early Christian baptisms involved total immersion, and the transition from bathhouse to baptistry was easy and natural. Since baptism is a personal and family affair, not calling for the presence of a congregation, baptistries usually are small. The Arian Baptistry (Fig. 128) was built in Theodoric's time in the same style as the earlier "Neonian" Baptistry for the Roman Christians. Both are domed structures with the chief interest centered on the fine interior mosaics. Both have similar representations of the baptism of Christ on the interior surfaces of their cupolas. That of the Arian Baptistry (Fig. 129) shows the ceremony being performed by St. John the Baptist, while the River Jordan is personified as an old man in the manner of the ancient pagan fluvial gods. Around this central scene are the twelve apostles who move processionally toward the throne of Christ. Just as the virgins and martyrs reenacted the offertory procession above the nave arcade of Sant' Apollinare Nuovo, so the apostles here mirror the baptismal rites on a more transcendental level. They group themselves around the center above where Christ is being baptized, just as the clergy, family, and sponsors gathered about the font below for the baptism of some Ravenna Christian. Here is yet another example of the *iconography* —the story being told—of the decorative scheme reflecting the liturgical activity that took place within the walls of the building.

The idea of a church built in the same form as a tomb is by no means as somber as it might seem. In the Christian sense, a church symbolized the Easter sepulchre, reminding all of the resurrection of Christ. In His memory, churches were dedicated to martyrs and saints who were believed to be partaking of the heavenly life with Him, just as the faithful hoped that they themselves (left) 129. *Baptism of Christ and Procession of Twelve Apostles. c.* 520. Dome mosaic. Arian Baptistry, Ravenna.

(above) 130. Dome construction: 1. pendentive; 2. drum; 3. cupola; 4. lantern.

131. Arched squinch.

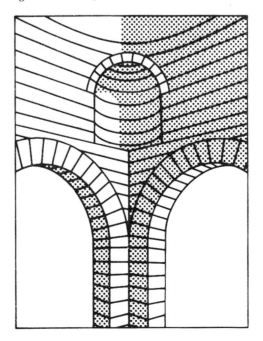

would one day be doing. The ancient Orphic cult had stressed the idea of the body being the tomb of the spirit. Hence, death and resurrection were aspects of one and the same idea, and the martyr's death was his mystical union with Christ. Indeed, the altar itself was a tomb or repository for the sacred relics of the saint to whom the church was dedicated. Early altars in the catacombs actually were sarcophagi that served also as communion tables. Thus, in the rites of the church, not only was the earthly past of Christ, His apostles, saints, and martyrs commemorated, but, at the same time, the glorious heavenly future was anticipated.

Balancing domes over square or octagonal supporting structures was a preoccupation of 6th-century architects. The Romans had found one solution in the case of the Pantheon—resting the dome on supporting cylindrical walls—but in Ravenna later builders found two other solutions. The exquisite little mausoleum of Galla Placidia (Fig. 113), which dates from about A.D. 425, was built in the form of an equal-winged Greek cross. Its dome rests on *pendentives* (Fig. 130)—that is, on four concave spherical triangles of masonry rising from the square corners and bending inward to form the circular base of the dome. The role of the pendentives is to encircle the square (left) 132. Interior, San Vitale, Ravenna. 526–547. Outer octagon 115′, inner octagon 54′ 9″. (Compare Plate 7.)

(bottom) 133. Interior, SS. Sergius and Bacchus, Istanbul (Constantinople). 527.

understructure and make the transition to the domed superstructure. The Ravenna baptistries exemplify the same pendentive solution, but in their cases the domes rest on octagonal understructures. Another solution stemming from the same early period is found in a baptistry in Naples in which a dome rests on an octagonal base by means of *squinches* (Fig. 131)—that is, a series of small apselike vaults placed across the angles of the octagonal walls. This was the method used for the doming of San Vitale. The eight piers of the arcaded central room below rise upward and culminate in an octagonal drum on which, by means of squinches, the dome rests. In order to keep the load as light as possible, the builders of San Vitale devised a most ingenious method of embedding hollow earthenware pots in the masonry.

Above the nave arcade and beneath the dome, the builders included a vaulted triforium gallery running around the church and opening into the nave (see Fig. 132; Plate 7). This gallery, which was called the *matroneum*, was for the use of women, who were more strictly segregated in the Byzantine than in the Roman rites.

The Eastern parallels of San Vitale are found in Justinian's churches at Constantinople—SS. Sergius and Bacchus (Fig. 133), known as "Little Hagia Sophia," and the great Hagia Sophia (Sancta Sophia, or Holy Wisdom), the foremost monument of the Byzantine style. As a combination of great art and daring engineering, Hagia Sophia has never been surpassed. Externally, as the view and floor plan (Figs. 134, 135) show, it is practically square with bulging buttresses and swelling half domes mounting to a full dome on top. Internally (Fig. 136) from the narthex entrance on the west, the space opens into a large nave, and the eye is led horizontally to the apse in the east. While the most ambitious Gothic cathedral nave never spanned a width of more than 50 feet, the architects of Hagia Sophia achieved here an open space 100 feet wide and 200 feet long.

Rising laterally on either side are colonnades that divide the nave from the side aisles and support a wide triforium matroneum. The forces then gather toward the four massive central piers from which spring powerful arches and tunnel vaults on two sides and two huge half domes on the others that soar to the base of the great dome

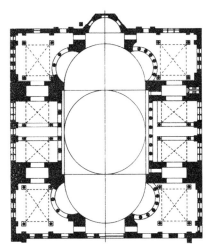

135. Hagia Sophia, plan.

(above) 134. ANTHEMIUS OF TRALLES and ISIDORUS OF MILETUS. Hagia Sophia, Istanbul (Constantinople). 532–537 (minarets after 1453). 308 × 236'.

(right) 136. Interior, Hagia Sophia. Dome 183' high.

137. *Emperor Justinian and Courtiers.* *c.* 547. Mosaic. San Vitale, Ravenna. (See also Plate 8.)

itself. Four pendentives—the concave spherical triangles originally decorated with mosaic images of winged seraphs—mediate between the square understructure and circular domed superstructure. Under the dome is a crown of forty windows that combine with those of the vaults below to bathe the interior with light, resulting in such ethereal effect that Justinian's historian Procopius was moved to say that the dome does not appear to rest on the masonry but to be suspended by a golden chain from heaven itself. The atmospheric effect of later medieval cathedrals relies on the mystery of darkness and dim light filtered through varicolored stained-glass windows. But at Hagia Sophia, it is the mystery of light itself through the many windows and that reflected with suffused radiance from the gold mosaic surfaces which line the interior. This light, as Procopius remarks, makes it seem that the church is "not merely illuminated from without by the sun, but that the radiance springs also from within it." Such spiritual illumination admirably realized the intent of the dedication, which is to Holy Wisdom and Christ as the Creative Word of God.

From this discussion it should be obvious that the dome of the central-type structure unifies the separate structural members, and that the eye perceives this unity at a glance. In the interior of San Vitale (Fig. 132) the dome and its supports are clearly visible and the structure is therefore self-explanatory. Psychologically, this equilibrium is important for it produces a restful effect, which is in direct contrast with the restless interiors of later Gothic cathedrals. There the dynamic surge depends partly on the fact that the exterior buttressing is not apparent. Indeed, the dome of

San Vitale is an interior fact only, because on the outside the octagonal base on which it rests has been continued upward and roofed over.

Centralized church plans have always conflicted with Christian liturgy. With the structural accent converging on the axial center beneath the dome, the logical spot for the altar is there, but, until our own times, tradition frowned upon placing the Christian congregation behind the altar. Consequently, at San Vitale as well as at Hagia Sophia, an apse was appended in the east for the altar, thus, in effect, dividing the architectural and liturgical climaxes of the edifice.

In the apse of San Vitale, facing the altar from opposite sides, are two panels in mosaic that portray the leading figures of the early Byzantine rule in Ravenna. On one, Emperor Justinian appears in the midst of his courtiers (Fig. 137) and on the other, facing him as an equal, is Empress Theodora in all her sovereign splendor (Plate 8). It is significant that the finest extant portrait of the great emperor should be in mosaic rather than in the form of a sculptured bust, a bronze effigy on horseback, or a colossal statue. It is just this medium that could best capture the unique spirit of his life and times. Concerned with the codification of Roman law, presiding at religious councils, and reconciling divergent political points of view, Justinian based his rule on the manipulation of legal and theological formulas as well as on naked military might. He is then represented as a symbol of unity between the spiritual force of the Church on one hand and the temporal power of the state on the other.

Preceding Justinian in the procession are the clergymen, among whom only Archbishop Maximian is specifically identified by name. His pectoral cross is held up as an assertion of his power as the spiritual and temporal lord of Ravenna. On the emperor's other side are his courtiers and honor guard holding their jeweled swords aloft. The shield with its Chrismon insignia points to the status of the soldiers as defenders of the faith. The Chrismon was a widely used monogram of the time, made up of the Greek letters Chi (X) and Rho (P), which together form the abbreviation of Christ. Somewhat more allegorically, the letters become a combination of the Cross and the shepherd's crook, which symbolize the Savior's death and pastoral mission. In the center stands Justinian, clothed in all his magnificence and crowned with the imperial diadem. The observer knows immediately that he is in the presence of no ordinary royal personage but rather one who could sign his name augustly to the preface of his *Digest of Laws* as the Emperor Caesar Flavius, Justinianus, Alamannicus, Francicus, Germanicus, Anticus, Alanicus, Vandalicus, Africanus, Pious, Happy, Renowned, Conqueror and Triumpher, ever Augustus.

On her side, the Empress Theodora (Plate 8), richly bejeweled and clad in the imperial purple, is seen as she is about to make her entry into the church from the narthex. Possibly because of her humble origin as the daughter of the feeder of the bears at the circus of Constantinople, Theodora appears more royal than the king. Her offering recalls another remark by Procopius, who said that she fed the geese of the devil while on the stage and the sheep of Christ when she sat on the throne. On the hem of her robe the offertory motif is carried out by the embroidered figures of the Three Wise Men, the first bearers of gifts to Christ. Since they also were from the East, this may have been a subtle attempt to gain the good graces of Ravenna for its Oriental rulers.

These two mosaic portraits are especially precious because they are among the few surviving visual representations of the vanished glories of Byzantine courtly ceremonials. The regal pair appear as if participating in the offertory procession at the dedication of the church, which took place in the year 547—though neither was actually present on that occasion. Such ceremonial entries were a part of the elaborate Byzantine liturgy, and both the emperor and empress are shown as the bearers of gifts. On his side, Justinian is carrying the gold paten, which was used to hold the communion bread at the altar, while Theodora is presenting the chalice that contains the wine. Since their munificence was responsible for the building, decoration, and endowment of San Vitale, the allusion is to gifts of gold as well.

In keeping with the rigid conventions of Byzantine art, all the heads appear in one plane. Those of Justinian and Theodora are distinguished by their halos, which in this case allude not only to their awesome power but to a carry-over of the semidivine status assumed by the earlier Roman emperors. Even though they are moving in a procession, they are portrayed frontally in the manner of imperial personages accustomed to receiving the homage of their subjects. In spite of the stylized medium, the eye can follow the solemn train as it moves in dignified cadence by means of the linear pattern made by the folds of the garments. The elegant costumes and other draperies add generally to the richness of the scene, emphasizing by their designs the lavish luxury of their Oriental origin.

In addition to the mosaics, the decorative design of San Vitale includes carved alabaster columns, polychrome marble wall panels, perforated marble choir screens (Fig. 138), and many other sculptural details. The capitals of the

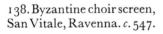

138. Byzantine choir screen, San Vitale, Ravenna. *c.* 547.

(left) 139. Byzantine capital, San Vitale, Ravenna. c. 547.

(bottom) 140. Byzantine capital, Hagia Sophia, Istanbul (Constantinople). c. 537.

(below) 141. Windblown acanthus capital, Sant' Apollinare in Classe.

columns are carved with a profusion of intricate patterns, such as the one seen in Figure 139, similar to the "basket-woven" capitals of Hagia Sophia (Fig. 140). The influence of San Vitale on subsequent Western European architecture dates from the time of Charlemagne's conquest. So impressed was he with this church that he not only carried off at least half of its original marble and mosaic decorations but also adopted its plan for his imperial chapel at Aachen (Figs. 142, 143). When the harmonious proportions of the building as a whole are compounded with the rich optical effects of the mosaics, polychrome marble, and ornamental sculptures, San Vitale, as the counterpart of Hagia Sophia, is the high point of Byzantine art in the West.

SCULPTURE

From its status as a major art in Greco-Roman times, sculpture declined to a relatively modest place in the hierarchy of early Christian arts. Instead of constituting a free and independ-

142. Capella Palatina, plan.

(right) 143. Interior, Capella Palatina (Charlemagne's Chapel), Aachen (Aix-la-Chapelle). 792–805. Diameter 48′.

ent medium, it became primarily an adjunct to the architectural and liturgical forms of the Church. Even its classical three-dimensionality was in eclipse, and sculpture tended to become increasingly pictorial and symbolic in early Christian usage. When it moved indoors, sculpture underwent a radical change in relation to light and shade. A statue in the round, for instance, was either placed against a wall or stood in a niche, which precluded its being seen from all sides. The close proximity in time and place to the pagan religions also served to channel Christian visual expression in other directions, and with the influence of such dictums as the First Commandment that forbade the making of "graven images," it is remarkable that the art survived as well as it did. A rare extant example of three-dimensional Early Roman Christian sculpture is the *Good Shepherd* (Fig. 144). Figures of peasants carrying calves or sheep to market are frequently found in ancient Greek and Roman genre sculpture. In the Christian interpretation, however, the shepherd is Christ, the sheep the congregation of the faithful, and, when a jug of milk is included, the whole refers to the Eucharist.

(right) 144. *Good Shepherd. c.* 350. Marble, 39″ high. Lateran Museum, Rome.

Sculpture, in general, proved adaptable to the new demands and purposes. In the new frame of reference, architectural sculpture—capitals of columns, decorative relief panels, carved wooden doors, and, to some extent, statues in niches—continued with appropriate modifications. The principal emphasis, however, shifted toward objects associated with the new form of worship, such as altars, pulpits, pierced marble screens, and carved ivory reliefs. Smaller items, such as precious metal boxes for relics, lamps, incense pots, communion chalices, jeweled book covers, and patens, all with delicately wrought designs, began to ally the former grand classical art more closely with that of the jeweler.

One of the strongest influences on early Christian design was the new orientation of thought in the direction of symbolism. As long as the religions of Greece and Rome were anthropomorphic, the sculptor could represent the gods as idealized human forms. But in Christian terms, how could he represent in concrete form such abstractions as the Trinity, the Holy Ghost, the salvation of the soul, or the idea of redemption through participation in the Eucharistic sacrifice? The solution could come only through use of parables and symbols. Thus the Christian idea of immortality could be rendered through Biblical scenes of deliverance—Noah from the flood, Moses from the land of Egypt, Job from his sufferings, Daniel from the lion's den, the men from the fiery furnace, and Lazarus from his tomb. One of the most often encountered was the story of Jonah (Fig. 145). Jesus had said: "For as Jonas was three days and three nights in the whale's belly; so shall the son of man be three days and three nights in the heart of the earth" (Matt. 12:40). Since a whale was beyond his ken, the sculptor illustrated this old Hebrew legend with the classical sea monster known as the hippogriff, which by now had become the symbol of the resurrection of Christ and frequently was carved on Christian sarcophagi. This is a typical example of the adaptation of ancient pictorial forms and ideas into new symbols.

In early Christian relief panels, flora and fauna were included less for naturalistic reasons than to convey symbolic meaning. The dove represented the Holy Spirit, the peacock stood for Paradise, and so on. The Cross is seldom found in early Christian art, since it recalled a punishment used for the lowest type of criminal. Instead, the Chrismon symbol already seen on the shield of Justinian's soldiers was used. A fish, or the Greek word for it, *Icthys*, is often found as a reference to Jesus making his disciples fishers of men. The letters of the word also constituted an abbreviation for Jesus Christ Son of God, Savior. Such symbols and lettered inscriptions caused sculpture to assume the aspect of engraved designs on stone surfaces, which carried special meaning and mystical significance to the initiated.

Capitals of columns departed from the unity and regularity of the classical orders and showed all sorts of variations. This tendency had begun with the early phases of Christian art, when materials for new churches had to be assembled from the parts of ancient buildings that had fallen into disrepair or disuse. Sant' Apollinare in Classe has a variation of the Corinthian order in its so-called "windblown acanthus" capitals (Fig. 141), while still another version is found at Sant' Apollinare Nuovo. Far greater complexity and variety appear, however, in the capitals of San Vitale and Hagia Sophia (Figs. 139, 140). These are more distinctly Byzantine in style and have intricate arabesque designs.

One of the chief forms of Early Roman Christian sculpture is the carved stone sarcophagus. The custom of burial above ground was carried over from late Roman times, and a special Christian impetus came from the desire for interment within the sacred precincts of the church. The relics of saints reposed in the altar; tombs of bishops and other dignitaries were housed in the church; while the sarcophagi of laymen were usually placed outside in the atrium. Survivals of this latter custom continue well into modern times with burials taking place in churchyards. A fine

145. *Jonah Sarcophagus*. 3rd century A.D. Marble, 7' 2" × 2' 3" × 2' 2". Lateran Museum, Rome.

(left) 146. Sarcophagus of Archbishop Theodore. 6th century. Marble, 3′3½″ × 6′9″. Sant' Apollinare in Classe.

(below) 147. Cathedra of Maximian (front view). *c.* 546–556. Ivory panels on wood frame, 59″ high, 23⅝″ wide. Archepiscopal Museum, Ravenna.

example is provided by the sarcophagus of Archbishop Theodore (Fig. 146). The front panel shows the combination of the Chrismon symbol with that of the first and last letters of the Greek alphabet, Alpha and Omega, another reference to Christ, taken from His statement that He was both the beginning and the end. Their inclusion here on a tomb indicates the end of earthly life and the beginning of the heavenly one. Flanking the symbols are two peacocks symbolizing Paradise and, on either side, a graceful vine pattern in which the small birds feeding on grapes refer symbolically to communion. The inscription reads in translation, "Here rests in peace Archbishop Theodore." On the lid are repetitions of the monogram below, here surrounded by the conventional laurel wreath symbolizing immortality. The end of the sarcophagus that shows in Figure 146 is carved to symbolize the trinity, with the urn from which springs the tree of life indicating the Father, the cross the Son, and the descending dove the Holy Spirit.

By far the most impressive single example of sculpture of this period is the chair which is thought to be that of Archbishop Maximian (Figs. 147–150), Justinian's viceroy who is portrayed beside him in the mosaic panel in San Vitale (Fig. 137). Such an episcopal throne is called a *cathedra*, and the church in which it is housed is called a *cathedral*. When a bishop addresses his congregation from it, he is said to be speaking *ex cathedra*. A cathedra may also be called a *sedes* (the Latin word for seat), from which word is derived the term *see*, which once meant the seat of a bishop but now means the territory or charge of a bishop. Originally *sedes* meant a chair denoting high position. Roman senators used such chairs on public occasions, and modern politicans still campaign for a "seat" in the senate or legislature. Both Jewish rabbis and Greek philosophers taught from a seated position; hence the reference in modern colleges to a "chair" of philosophy or history.

Maximian's cathedra has a wooden frame that originally was covered entirely with ivory panels. Since the sides and back are as elaborately covered as the front, the chair was meant to be seen from all angles. During the service, the bishop was seated in the east end of the church at the side or behind the altar in the section known as the presbytery or sanctuary. His words, however, would have been inaudible from this location, and his chair was brought forward at the proper time to a place where he could conveniently be both seen and heard.

The work here consists of a composition made up of ivory plaques, carefully joined together and

149. *Story of Joseph*, detail of Cathedra of Maximian.

150. *Story of Joseph*, detail of Cathedra of Maximian.

delicately carved. Originally, there were 39 different pictorial panels, some of which told the Old Testament story of Joseph and his brethren, and the others, the story of Jesus. The chair is thought to have been presented to Maximian by Justinian, and the different techniques employed in the various panels indicate collaboration of craftsmen from Anatolia, Syria, and Alexandria. On the front panel, below Maximian's monogram, is a representation of St. John the Baptist flanked on either side by the Evangelists (Fig. 147). The Baptist holds a medallion on which a lamb is carved in relief, while the Evangelists hold their traditional books. Three of the side panels that tell the story of Joseph are seen in Figures 148-150. The workmanship of the Joseph representations seems somewhat crude in comparison with that of the front panel. Due allowance, however, must be made not only for the difference in workshops, but also for artistic intentions and problems involved. The elegant Byzantine craftsmanship of the front panel—with its complex grapevine motif intertwined with birds and animals denoting the tree of eternal life, the peacocks symbolizing heaven, the symmetrically arranged saints, and the luxuriant linear pattern of their classical drapery—lends itself best to just such a static, formal, stylized design. In the Joseph story, however, the overriding concern is with an active narrative as related in a series of episodes. Content and vivid detail then rise above purely formal considerations. While sculpture is not the outstanding Byzantine art, such intricate tracery and arabesque patterns become highly important. Since ivory does not make monumentality either possible or desirable, such details as these, when handled with a jeweler's precision, are perhaps richer and more satisfying than the work as a whole.

At this formative phase, the Western and Eastern styles are not so separate and distinct as they tend to become in the later medieval period. The situation is also complicated by the fact that Roman artists could be summoned to work in Constantinople just as easily as Byzantine artists could be called to Rome or Ravenna. In general, however, one can conclude that the trend in the West was toward the oblong basilica, while the East developed the central-type structure. In mosaics and sculpture, the Early Roman Christian style stays closer to the heritage of classical naturalism, with figures modeled three dimensionally and appearing against landscape backgrounds, and shows a preference for simpler designs employing recognizable floral and faunal motifs. The Byzantine style, on the other hand, moves more in the direction of flat two-dimensional surfaces,

gold backgrounds, nonrepresentational designs, abstract geometrical forms, and luxurious arabesque patterns.

MUSIC

From the writings of Theodoric's learned ministers Boethius and Cassiodorus, some knowledge about the status of musical thought in 6th-century Ravenna can be gained. Like the writings of the Church fathers and other men of letters of the time, however, these reveal much about the theory of the art and little about its practice. Boethius was an indefatigable translator of Greek philosophical and scientific treatises into Latin, among which were no less than thirty books by Aristotle alone. When he fell from favor and was imprisoned, he wrote his *Consolations of Philosophy*, which became one of the most influential medieval books. Called by Gibbon "a golden volume not unworthy of the leisure of Plato or Tully [Cicero]," the *Consolations* later found its way into English via translations by Alfred the Great and Chaucer. Boethius' was a universal mind, capable of discoursing on anything from the mechanical principles of water clocks to astronomy.

Boethius' treatise on music became the common source of most medieval tracts on the subject, and thus, in transmitting the best of ancient Greek musical theory, it became the foundation stone of Western musical thinking. Like the ancients before him, Boethius believed that "all music is reasoning and speculation," and hence more closely allied with mathematics than with the auditory art that music is today. He divided music into three classes, the first of which was the "music of the universe," by which he meant the unheard astronomical "music" of planetary motion. The second was "human music," which referred to the attunement of the mind and body, or the rational and irrational elements of the human constitution, in the manner of a Greek harmony of opposites. The third was instrumental music and song, of which he had the philosopher's usual low opinion, considering only the theoretical aspects of the art as pursuits worthy of a gentleman and scholar. The only true "musician" in his opinion was one "who possesses the faculty of judging, according to speculation or reason, appropriate and suitable to music, of modes and rhythms and of the classes of melodies and their mixtures... and of the songs of the poets."

Cassiodorus also wrote in a similarly learned vein after he had retired from public life to the haven of his monastery at Vivarium. But while he was still embroiled in the affairs of Theodoric's kingdom, he was constantly called upon to solve every conceivable administrative problem. Among these was a request from Clovis, king of the Franks, for a *citharoedus*—that is, a singer who accompanied himself on the stringed instrument of the classical lyre type known as the cithara. In his search for such a musician, Cassiodorus turned to his fellow senator Boethius, who was in Rome at the time. His letter first launches into a flowery discourse on the nature of music, which he describes as the "Queen of the senses." It continues with interminable discussions about its curative powers, how David cast out the evil spirit from Saul, the nature of the modes, the structure of the Greek scale system, and the history of the art. Then he comes to the lyre, which he calls "the loom of the Muses," and after going off on a few more tangents, he finally gets to the point. "We have indulged ourselves in a pleasant digression," he says, making the understatement of the millennium, "because it is always agreeable to talk of learning with the learned; but be sure to get us that *Citharoedus*, who will go forth like another Orpheus to charm the beast-like hearts of the Barbarians. You will thus obey us and render yourself famous."

This rare document is the only source on the state of secular music in the Ravenna of the 6th century, and it tells little about the capacities and duties of such a musician. It is clear, however, that this type of bardic poet-singer still existed at that time, though apparently so scarce that Cassiodorus had to send to Rome and seek the advice of the most eminent musical authority of the time. Such professional poet-musicians must have been active at Theodoric's court, otherwise the request from Clovis would not have been addressed there. It is known that Theodoric's exploits, together with those of the other heroes of the migration period, found their way into the legends, fables, sagas, and songs of the Gothic peoples. Their transmission no doubt occurred through the medium of just such poet-musicians.

Knowledge about the church music of Ravenna at this time is also conjectural and must be gathered from a variety of sources. From the writings of the Church fathers, great importance evidently was attached to music in connection with divine worship. The problem was how to separate a proper body of church music from the rude folk musical idioms on one hand, and from the highly developed but pagan art music of Rome on the other. From St. Paul and Pliny the Younger, in the 1st and 2nd centuries respectively, it is known that the earliest Christian music sounded very much like the ancient Jewish singing

of psalms. A fragment of an early Christian hymn from the latter part of the 3rd century was recently found at Oxyrhynchos in North Africa. From the Greek text and ancient musical notation, it is possible to establish its stylistic connection with the late Hellenistic musical tradition. Hebrew, Greek, and Latin sources thus provided the basis for early Christian music, just as they had done in the cases of theology and the visual arts. Out of these diverse elements and with original ideas of their own, the Christians of the Eastern and Western churches over the centuries gradually worked out a synthesis that resulted in a musical art of great power and beauty. The 6th century witnessed the culmination of many early experimental phases; and at its close, the Western form of the art found official codification in the body of music known as Gregorian Chant. In its various transmutations and restorations, as well as in its theoretical aspects, this system has remained the official basis of Roman church music up to the present time. Closely related forms are still in use throughout Christendom, where free adaptations of its melodies have enriched the hymn books of nearly every denomination.

Knowledge about the Arian liturgy, such as that which was practiced at Sant' Apollinare Nuovo during Theodoric's reign, is very obscure, because all sources were destroyed when the orthodox Christians gained the upper hand and stamped out the Arian heresy. From a few derogatory comments, however, it is known that hymn and psalm singing by the congregation as a whole was among the practices. Arius, the founder of the Arian sect, was accused of insinuating his religious ideas into the minds of his followers by means of hymns that were sung to melodies derived from drinking songs and theatrical tunes. Such hymns were frowned upon in orthodox circles because they were too closely allied with popular music. Furthermore, the Arian way of singing them was described as loud and raucous, indicating that they must have grated on the ears of the more civilized Roman Christians.

The popularity of these musical practices, however, was such that the Arians were making too many converts. So in the spirit of fighting fire with fire, St. Ambrose, bishop of Milan, where the Arians were strong, compromised by introducing hymn and psalm singing into the Milanese church service. A first-hand account of it is contained in a passage from St. Augustine's *Confessions*. In the 4th century, when Bishop Ambrose was engaged in one of his doctrinal disputes with the Byzantine Empress Justina, he and his followers at one point had to barricade themselves in a church for protection. "The pious people kept guard in the

Aeterne rerum Conditor (hymn of St. Ambrose)   (after Dreves)

Ae - ter- ne re - rum Con - di - tor,   No - ctem di -em - que qui _ re - gis,

Et   tem-po- rum das tem - po-ra,   Ut   al - le-ves fa - sti - di - um ...

church, prepared to die with their bishop," wrote St. Augustine. "At the same time," he continues, "was it here first instituted after the manner of the eastern churches, that hymns and psalms should be sung, lest the people should wax faint through the tediousness of sorrow: which custom being retained from that day to this, is still imitated by divers, yea, almost by all thy congregations throughout other parts of the world." The practice spread widely and was incorporated into the Roman liturgy during the following century. Since Ravenna was the neighboring see to that of Milan, the musical practices there must have been quite similar.

Some half dozen hymns can be attributed to the authorship of St. Ambrose. Whether he also composed the melodies is not so certain, but they at least date from his time. From the example of *Aeterne rerum Conditor* (above), it can be seen that the extreme simplicity and metrical regularity of these vigorous Ambrosian hymns made them especially suitable for congregational singing. The mosaics of Sant' Apollinare Nuovo show files of male and female saints on opposite sides of the nave arcade. Below them, the men of the congregation were grouped on one side, while the women and children gathered on the other, thus forming two choirs. The psalms were sung in two ways: antiphonally and responsorially. When the two choruses sing alternate verses, then join together in a refrain on the word *alleluia* after each verse, the practice is referred to as *antiphonal psalmody*. When the celebrant chants one verse as a solo, and the choirs perform the next in unison, it is called *responsorial psalmody*. Both were widespread practices in the Western church, including Ravenna.

Since Sant' Apollinare Nuovo and San Vitale were designed for different purposes, it follows that their music must also have differed. As a part of the Byzantine liturgy, the music heard at San Vitale would have been like that of the cathedral in Constantinople. As in the West, congregational singing was included there at first, but, with the the abandonment of the offertory procession, congregational singing was gradually replaced by that of a professional choir. Music for congregational singing must always be kept relatively simple, but with a truly professional group all the rich potentialities of the art can be explored and developed.

Since San Vitale, like Hagia Sophia, was under the direct patronage of the emperor, and since both constituted a part of Justinian's grand design, provision for a group capable of performing the music of the Byzantine liturgy could hardly have been overlooked. The principal difference between the music of the Eastern and Western churches is that between a contemplative and an active attitude. The contemplative aspect of the Eastern liturgy is illustrated by a remark of St. John Chrysostom, who said that "one may also sing without voice, the mind resounding inwardly, for we sing not to men, but to God, who can hear our hearts and enter into the silences of the mind." This attitude contrasts strongly with that of St. Ambrose, who said in connection with the participation of the congregation in song: "If you praise the Lord and do not sing, you do not utter a hymn. ... A hymn, therefore, has these three things: song and praise and the Lord."

In a static form of worship, greater rhythmic freedom is possible, while the chant that accompanies a procession must have more metrical regularity. The singing of a virtuoso professional choir, furthermore, implies an elaborate and highly developed art, while the practice of congregational singing means the avoidance of technical difficulties. The difference, then, is the difference between the sturdy Ambrosian syllabic hymn (above)—that is, with a syllable allotted to each

Alleluia (Ambrosian chant of Byzantine origin)   (after Wellesz)

Hal - le - lu - jah.

note—and the melismatic alleluia of Byzantine origin (above)—that is, with each single syllable prolonged over many notes in the manner of a cadenza. Such Byzantine music had a distinctive style of its own, comparable in this respect to that of the visual arts. The elaborate melismas of the latter example would have been heard in San Vitale and in other Byzantine churches at the end of the 6th century. It was precisely such excessively florid alleluias that were ruled out by the Gregorian reform which was to occur in the early 7th century.

IDEAS

Since all the surviving monuments of early Christian art are religiously oriented, it follows that the various sources of patronage, the geographical locations, and the liturgical purposes are the qualifying factors in the forms of architecture, the iconography of mosaics, the designs of sculpture, and the performing practices of music. The Early Roman Christian and Byzantine styles were both Christian, and all the arts lived, moved, and had their being within the all-embracing arms of Mother Church. But her Western and Eastern arms pointed in different stylistic directions. The disintegrating Roman power in the West led to decentralization of authority and allowed wide latitude in local and regional styles, while the Byzantine emperors kept tight autocratic control of all phases of secular and religious life. Early Roman Christian art, on the one hand, was more an expression of the people;

it involved all social levels, its craftsmanship varied from crudity to excellence, and it was more simple and direct in its approach. Byzantine art, on the other hand, was under the personal patronage of a prosperous emperor who ruled both as a Caesar and a religious patriarch. Only the finest artists were employed; and the arts, like the vertical axis of a centralized church, directed attention to the highest level and tended to become more removed from the people and more purely symbolic. As the arts of both West and East pass by in review, two ideas seem to be the clues to their understanding: authoritarianism and mysticism.

Authoritarianism

Ravenna in the 6th century was the scene of a three-way struggle among a barbarian king, who was a champion of Roman culture; a Byzantine emperor, who claimed the prerogatives of the past golden age; and a Roman pontiff, who had little military might but a powerful influence based on the apostolic succession. As the conflict shaped up, it was among an enlightened secular liberalism, a theocratic traditionalism, and a new spiritual institution with a genius for compromise. In the course of the century, the Ostrogothic kingdom was vanquished by the Byzantine Empire. However, after a brief period of domination, Byzantine power in the West crumbled, and the political and military weakness that followed became the soil which nurtured the growth of the new Rome. By the end of the century, Gregory the Great had succeeded in establishing the papacy as the authority that eventually was to dominate the medieval period in the West, while the Eastern Empire continued in its traditional Byzantine forms of organization.

The principle of authority was by no means foreign to Christianity, which grew to maturity in the later days of the Roman Empire. With Christianity an official state religion under the protection of the emperors, Christian organization more and more reflected the authoritarian character of the imperial government. Roman Christian philosophers, such as Boethius and Cassiodorus, cited the authority of Plato and Aristotle on all matters. Theologians accepted the authority of the Scriptures and the commentaries on them by the early Church fathers. The thought of the period was expressed in constant quotations and requotations, interpretations and reinterpretations of ancient Hebrew, Greek, Latin, and early Christian authors. No one was willing or able to assume complete authority in his own right; on all issues, each had to cite ancient precedents for his position. The intellectual climate produced by this patristic type of thinking paved the way for the mighty struggle for political and spiritual authority. The only remaining question was what form the authority was to assume, and who would exercise it.

Justinian, who claimed the authority and semidivine status of the old Roman emperors, lived in an atmosphere so static and conservative that the words *originality* and *innovation* were used at his court only as terms of reproach. Despite the high price, Byzantine civilization purchased only a blanket uniformity. The principal creative energies of Byzantine man were channeled into aesthetic expression, largely because he had no other direction in which to move. Only in art was any variety and freedom to be found. Here again the art of both Church and state were under the sole patronage of the emperor. It was then all the more remarkable that such a flowering as that which produced Hagia Sophia in Constantinople and San Vitale in Ravenna could have taken place. In both of these instances, the methods of construction were experimental, and the solution developed in response to the architectural and decorative problems was strikingly uninhibited and daring.

The Byzantine concept of authority was embodied in the architectural and decorative plans of both Hagia Sophia and San Vitale. The central-type church, with its sharp hierarchical divisions that set aside places for men and women, clergy and laity, aristocrat and commoner, was admirably suited to convey the principle of imperial authority. The vertical axis culminated in a dome that overwhelmed Byzantine man by reminding him, when he was in the presence of the Supreme Authority, of his humble place in the scheme of things. The august imperial portraits in the sanctuary showed him that outside the clergy, only the emperor and empress and those who occupied the top rungs of the social ladder might approach the altar of God. He might not even presume to bring forward his gifts to the altar in the offertory procession. Since all material things came within the province of Caesar, the exalted duty of making the offering was his alone. Byzantine man, furthermore, was not even allowed to raise his voice with those of his fellowmen in God's praise, as it was also the emperor's prerogative to provide a chorus of qualified professional musicians whose privilege this was. The attitude of reverence was not only to God alone but also to His viceroys on earth. The imperial portraits left no doubt about that. The majesty of God was felt through the infinite power of government. Through the solemn rituals of sacred and courtly ceremonies, both spiritual and secular authority were imposed on Byzantine man from above. His place in this world was inexorably determined; and his human dignity was in proportion to the blandness of his acceptance of the unified ideal of one Christian empire with one church, one emperor, and one body of laws.

Sant' Apollinare Nuovo and its companion Sant' Apollinare in Classe (Figs. 151, 152) as typical Western forms of the basilica, on the other hand, indicated a contrasting conception of both God and man. As the twin rows of columns on either side of the nave marched forward, they carried the eyes and footsteps of the faithful with them. The approach to the sacred precincts was encouraged rather than forbidden, and even the gift of the widow's mite was acknowledged in one of the mosaic panels above. Just as the congregation had gone forth from the doors of their homes to the house of the Lord, the processions of saints in the mosaics likewise moved out of the gates of the twin cities of Classe and Ravenna. The rites they attended were not so incomprehensible and fearsome that they had, as in the Byzantine liturgy, to be enacted behind curtains and choir screens. In the West they took place in the open, and ordinary men and women enjoyed the privilege of ministering to the Lord. The spatial divisions of the oblong basilica, to be sure, still allowed for differences of status, such as that of men and women, choir and clergy. The allowance for all to participate in the sacred service, however, modified the authoritative concept, so that there was some religious freedom.

(above) 151. Apse, Sant'
Apollinare in Classe. *c.* 530.

(right) 152. Interior of apse,
Sant' Apollinare in Classe.
c. 530.

By exercising his power to offer gifts and by maintaining his active participation, Western man kept the concept of authority on a spiritual level, and he thus retained a certain individual freedom which Byzantine man had surrendered to his rulers. Sant' Apollinare Nuovo and San Vitale thus are reflections of two contrasting images of man. The oblong basilica was designed for active spatial and temporal movement, while the domed central-type church indicated Byzantine man's passive acceptance of the role of spectator. In the one case, the horizontal axis, by inviting forward movement, placed man in a progressive relation to space; in the other, the vertical axis, by pointing upward, tended to check physical movement and divert the energies toward stationary contemplation. The mosaics of Sant' Apollinare Nuovo, in addition to the processions, depict the life story of Christ in narrative form, while those in San Vitale are confined to individual representations of separate scenes without any sequential arrangement and are designed to dazzle by their splendor. The music of Sant' Apollinare Nuovo and other churches in the West was intended for congregational participation and had a metrical regularity conducive to marching, while that of San Vitale was highly complex, melismatic, and had an asymmetrical cadence that minimized bodily motion.

Mysticism

The art of the 6th century in Ravenna, like that of such other important centers as Constantinople and Rome, makes the transition from the classical Greco-Roman to the medieval world. While some of the ancient grandeur remained, the accent on symbolism laid the foundation for the coming medieval styles. The physical was replaced by the psychical, the rational road to knowledge by intuitive revelation. Many of the older art forms were carried over and reinterpreted in a new light. The Roman bathhouse became the Christian baptistry where the soul was cleansed of original sin, and the public basilica was redesigned for church mysteries. Mosaics, which were used for Hellenistic and Roman pavements, became the mural medium for mystical visions. The shepherd of classical genre sculpture became symbolically the Good Shepherd. Classical bird and animal motifs became symbols for the soul and the spiritual realm. Music became a reflection of the divine unity of God and man; and the classical lyre, because of its stretched strings on a wooden frame, was reinterpreted by St. Augustine as a symbol of the crucified flesh of Christ. Orpheus,

by means of its sounds, had descended into the underworld and overcome death. Christ is therefore frequently represented as playing on the lyre, and at Sant' Apollinare Nuovo he is seated on a lyre-backed throne.

The concept of space turned from the limited classical three-dimensional representation of the natural world to an infinite Christian two-dimensional symbolic world. Invisible things rose in importance above those that could be seen with the eyes. While classical man had regarded his world objectively from without, early Christian man contemplated his subjectively from within. Socrates once asked an artist whether he could represent the soul. The reply was: "How can it be imitated, since it has neither shape nor colour . . . and is not visible at all?" St. Augustine also observed that "beauty cannot be beheld in any bodily matter." Such mystical visions could be perceived only through symbolism. While natural science had been the foundation stone of ancient philosophy, symbolic theology became the foundation of Christian philosophy. Whereas Greek drama (which was a form of religious experience) had reached its climax step by step with remorseless logic, the Christian drama (as expressed in the liturgy) kindled the fires of faith and arrived at its mystical climax by intuitive means. The denial of the flesh and the conviction that only the soul can be beautiful doomed classical bodiliness and exalted abstract bodilessness. Instead of capturing and clothing the godlike image with flesh and blood, the new concern was with releasing the spirit from the bondage of the flesh.

What sometimes seems to be a crude technique in early Christian art, in contrast to the high quality of classical craftsmanship, is partly the result of the new orientation in which artists are no longer attempting to convey a natural image of the world. Elegance of linguistic as well as pictorial expression was considered too close to pagan aberrations for comfort. Civilized Roman men of letters, for example, chafed at the comparative roughness of the Hebrew Scriptures. St. Jerome, when he went into the wilderness to translate the Bible, took along with him a copy of his beloved Cicero. Such weakness, however, he attributed to his sinful nature. St. Augustine, as a grammarian, loved the noble Latin of Vergil and the beautiful classical melodies, but such "moral lapses" caused him bitter self-recrimination. The fervent congregational singing of the untutored faithful, no matter how unrefined it may have sounded, was morally preferable to the higher virtuosity of pagan musical sophistication. The Church fathers, who were among the highly educated few, had the difficult task of adapting

153. Interior, Santa Costanza, Rome. *c.* 350. Center 40′ in diameter.

154. Santa Costanza, plan.

the older theological, philosophical, artistic, and musical forms to the needs of their congregations, whose ranks included former slaves, artisans, and unlettered barbarians. The result was a technical decline from the high standards of classical craftsmanship in the arts and letters, owing to a lowering in the relative literacy of those to whom the new visual and verbal vocabularies were addressed. This was an age of transition from one cultural frame of reference to another. The fact that all the arts were adapted to the new religious orientation and in the process acquired an astonishing new vitality is all-important.

The great creation and the all-inclusive medium shaped during this period to convey this other-worldly vision was the liturgy. The thought, action, and sequence of the rites of Constantinople, Ravenna, Rome, and other centers determined to a large extent the architectural plans, the symbolism of the mosaics, and the forms of the sculpture and music. At this time, the fruits of generations of contemplative and active lives gradually ripened into mature structures. The content of centuries of theoretical speculation united with the practical efforts of countless generations of writers, builders, decorators, and musicians to produce the Byzantine liturgy in the East and the synthesis of Gregory the Great in the West. Removed from its primary religious association and seen in a more detached aesthetic light, the liturgy as a work of art embodies a profound and dramatic insight into the deepest longings and highest aspirations of the human spirit.

During the 6th century the controversy still raged as to whether Christ's nature was essentially human or divine. The more the Eastern view emphasized Christ's divinity, the more remote He became. One of the prayers of St. John Chrysostom begins: "O Lord, our God, Whose power is inconceivable and glory incomprehensible, Whose mercy is immeasurable and tenderness to man unspeakable...." Such a conception makes highly presumptuous any attempt to comprehend the divine essence by reason or by direct representation. Hence the mosaics of San Vitale weave such abstract symbols as that of the Chrismon into a rich arabesque of florid designs. Strict symmetry and other means were employed to raise the representation out of the plane of reality and thus to widen the immeasurable gulf between divinity and humanity. The dim lighting, the golden glow of the mosaics, the mysterious symbols whose meaning it was the privilege of Christians to contemplate—all helped conjure up this unfathomable and invisible divinity. The most sacred rites took place behind carved alabaster screens; the choirs sang softly in back of embroidered curtains. The words addressed from Maximian's carved ivory chair took on a superhuman impressiveness. All these in concert conveyed the mystical idea and awakened the vision of eternity in the minds of the beholders.

The Western position was eventually settled by a compromise upholding Christ's dual nature as both human and divine, but Western thought continued to accent His role as the sufferer for and Savior of humanity. The more this aspect was emphasized the more approachable and comprehensible the figure of Christ became. This is the side of His nature that finds expression in the mosaics of Sant' Apollinare Nuovo, especially in those that recount the parables and miracles as well as the passion, death, and resurrection of the historical Christ.

The Early Roman Christian and Byzantine styles were the responses to the need for new verbal, visual, and auditory modes of expression. In both cases, there was a shift from the forms designed to represent this world to those capable of conjuring up other-worldly visions. Through the poetry of language, the choreographic patterns of step and gesture, and the exalted melodies of the chant, the gripping drama of humanity embodied in the liturgy was enacted in sublime theaters that were furnished with a full panoply of stage settings, decor, costumes, and props created by the inspired hands of the finest craftsmen and artists of the time. The liturgy is, moreover, a continuous pageant lasting not only for a few hours but unfolding with constant variation during the continuous sequence of solemn and joyful feasts through the weeks, months, and seasons of the calendar year, the decades, centuries, and millennia.

5 - THE MONASTIC
ROMANESQUE STYLE

THE MONASTERY AT CLUNY, LATE 11TH AND EARLY 12TH CENTURIES

The most typical expression of the Romanesque period was the monastery. The life of ancient Athens and Pergamon had culminated in the constellations of their acropolis buildings, that of Rome had been realized in its forums and civil-engineering projects, while Constantinople and Ravenna had evolved the basilica and palace as the Church and state sides of a theocratic social order. In the Gothic period that succeeded the Romanesque it was to be the cathedral. As Christianity had spread northward after the fall of the West Roman Empire, southern classical forms had met and merged with those of the northern barbarian peoples. This union of the older settled Roman civilization, with its ideals of reason, restraint, and repose, and the newly awakened spirit of the north, with its restless energy and brooding imagination, resulted in the Romanesque, a style that reached its maturity between the years 1000 and 1150. Lacking the security of strong central governments, without the advantages of flourishing cities and towns, monastic man sought peace of mind in the abbey as a haven

from the storm-tossed seas of his anarchic social surroundings. Here in these centers off the beaten path he built a miniature world that contained a cross section of Romanesque life. Besides serving as a religious shrine where pilgrims could gather to revere sacred relics, the monastery was the manufacturing and agricultural center of its region as well as a seat of learning where the only libraries, schools, and hospitals of the time were found.

The largest and grandest of all Romanesque monasteries was the abbey at Cluny, and in Figure 156 Kenneth J. Conant reconstructs its plan at the pinnacle of its power and fame. Within its walls, men of contemplation were to be found beside men of action; those who were world-weary dwelled side by side with those who knew little of life beyond the cloister; saints brushed shoulders with criminals who sought refuge from the prosecution of secular authorities. Those who were drawn to the vocation of monk were firm believers in the seeming paradox in Christ's words: "For whosoever will save his life shall lose it: but whosoever will lose his life for my sake,

(above) *Medallion with Lamb*, from Third Abbey Church of Cluny. *c.* 1100. Ochier Museum, Cluny.

the same shall save it" (Luke 9:24). By taking the triple vows of poverty, chastity, and obedience, the monk automatically renounced such worldly pursuits as individual material rewards, the pleasures of the senses, the personal satisfactions of family life, and even the exercise of his own free will. According to the Rule of St. Benedict, the founder of European monasticism, a monk "should have absolutely not anything; neither a book, nor tablets, nor a pen—nothing at all. For indeed it is not allowed to the monks to have their own bodies or wills in their power." Through this renunciation of all worldly desires, the monk sought a higher life in the realm of the spirit, which can be summed up most completely in the words of St. Paul: "I live; yet not I, but Christ liveth in me" (Gal. 2:20). In order to realize such other-worldly aims, segregation from the secular world had to be effected, and a special way of life found.

The value of hard work was stressed in the Benedictine Rule, which prescribed an average of six or seven hours a day of manual labor. At first this meant literally toiling in the fields and tending the flocks, but with the growth in ranks and the accumulation of land and treasure, the monastic communities initiated something like a division of labor. At Cluny, the singing of psalms, reciting of prayers, the reading and copying of manuscripts had come to be construed as the proper "work" of a monk, and the actual agricultural pursuits were delegated to peasants and serfs who worked under the direction of lay brothers. Consequently, when Cluniac life had to be defended from the criticism of the stricter Cistercian order, Peter the Venerable, abbot of Cluny during the first part of the 12th century, wrote: "It is more noble to set one's hand to the pen than to the plow, to trace divine letters upon the page than furrows upon the fields. Sow on the page the seed of the word of God, and when the harvest is ripe, when your books are finished, the hungry readers shall be satisfied by an abundant harvest."

In order to provide such a life, a monastery had to be planned so that the monks would have all that was necessary for both their bodily subsistence and their spiritual sustenance. The objective was to be as independent of Caesar as possible so as to render their all unto God. The Benedictine Rule did not prescribe the exact form that a monastic building should take, and, nominally, each abbey was independent to solve its problems according to its needs, the contours of its site, and the extent of its resources. But tradition often operated as rigidly as rules, and with local variations most monasteries adhered to a common pattern. If one allows for the exceptional size and complexity due to its status as mother house of a great order, the plan of Cluny can be accepted as reasonably typical.

Since the life of a Cluniac monk was one of almost continuous religious observances alternating with periods set aside for contemplation, the soul of the monastery was in its abbey church, and its heart was in its cloister. The church served primarily as the scene of the constant devotional activities of the monks day and night throughout the year, and only secondarily as a shrine for the pilgrimages that were made to revere relics of saints. The monk's day was punctuated by the sequence of the Regular Hours that were sung in the abbey church. These holy offices consisted of prayers and canticles appropriate to each time of day and night together with the singing of entire psalms. Matins took place before dawn, with Prime coming just after sunrise and Tierce two hours later. Solemn high mass was celebrated after both Prime and Tierce, the latter being in commemoration of the dead and the mass that all brothers except those who were ill were expected to attend. Sext and None followed after Tierce at approximately three-hour intervals; Vespers came after sundown; Compline at nightfall; and both Nocturn and Vigils, in the course of the night. Since so much of the daily ritual took place at night or early in the morning in the unheated church, the monk had to dress in warm woolen robes, and in the winter he was provided with fur-lined boots. The Cluniac habit had a leather belt, heavy sleeves that could serve as hand muffs, a cowl that could become a hood, and a cape for extra warmth and protection from the elements.

Next in importance to facilities for the church services was the provision for the contemplative life that centered on the cloister. In the plan (Fig. 156), the cloister is found, typically, in the center of the abbey and south of the nave of the church, with the other monastic buildings clustering around it. The usual cloister was an open quadrangular garden plot that was enclosed by a covered arcade on all four sides. The somewhat irregular shape of the cloister at Cluny in the 12th century was owed to the ambitious building program necessitated by the rapid growth of the monastery. While the old 11th-century cloister of Abbot Odilo, next to the refectory, had been retained, once the abbey's great new third church was ready, the cloister was enlarged by demolishing the nave of the older second church. (The choir and narthex of this church can be seen in the plan on the east and west sides of the cloister garth.) It was here in this extended cloister that the monks sought the

General Events

480–	543	St. Benedict, founder of European monasticism; c.529 built abbey at Monte Cassino, Italy
768–	814	Charlemagne ruled at Aix-la-Chapelle (Aachen); Carolingian Period initiated.
c.792–	800	Centula monastery built by Charlemagne
c.796–	804	Palatine Chapel at Aix-la-Chapelle built
	800	Charlemagne crowned Holy Roman emperor in Rome by pope
	c.800	St. Gall (Switzerland) monastery begun
	910	Abbey of Cluny in Burgundy, France, founded
927–	942	Odo, abbot of Cluny, reputed author of musical treatises
	962	Otto the Great (936–973) crowned Holy Roman emperor
994–	1049	Odilo, abbot of Cluny
c.995–c.1050		Guido of Arezzo, author of musical treatises, inventor of staff notation
1000–	1150	Romanesque Period at height
1049–	1109	Hugh of Semur, abbot of Cluny
	1050	Holy Roman Empire at height; ascendancy of papal power
	1063	Pisa Cathedral begun
	1066	William, duke of Normandy, conquered England; reigned as king of England, 1066–1087
1071–	1112	Pilgrimage church at Santiago de Compostela, Spain, built
	1072	St. Peter Damian died
1073–	1085	Gregory VII (Hildebrande), pope
	1077	Emperor Henry IV bowed to Pope Gregory VII at Canossa; Abbot Hugh of Cluny was intermediary
c.1080		Church of Sant' Ambrogio begun at Milan
c.1080–	1160	Church of St. Sernin built at Toulouse, France
1088–	1099	Urban II, Cluniac pope
1088–	1130	Great third church at Cluny built (1088 Cluny III begun under Hugh of Semur by architect Hezelo; 1095 apse dedicated by Pope Urban II; 1120 church finished; 1125 nave vaults partially collapsed; 1131 church dedicated by Pope Innocent X)
	1095	Urban II preached the First Crusade
1096–	1120	Abbey Church of La Madeleine at Vézelay built (1096 church begun; 1104 original Romanesque choir and transept dedicated; 1110 nave finished; 1120 narthex begun and nave revaulted after fire; c.1130 tympanum over the central portal of narthex; 1132 dedicated)
	1098	Cistercian order founded; opposed Cluniac order; St. Bernard of Clairvaux was its principal spokesman
	1109	Pontius became abbot of Cluny
	1122	Peter the Venerable became abbot of Cluny
c.1130–	1135	Giselbertus carved sculptures at St. Lazare, Autun
1168–	1188	Matteo carved Pórtico de la Gloria at Cathedral of Santiago de Compostela, Spain

creative solitude they needed for the inward life as they walked to and fro in all kinds of weather, reading the Scriptures and other books from the adjacent library, pondering on the meaning of the symbolic sculptured capitals of the arcade, or carrying on their silent meditations. The rule of silence was rigidly maintained except for two periods of about half an hour each, one in the morning after the chapter was held and the other after Sext, when the monks were allowed to attend to their personal and domestic duties. The form of the cloister was undoubtedly derived from the atrium that stood before an Early Roman Christian basilica; and, like it, the cloister usually contained a fountain for ceremonial ablutions before entering the church. In the Cluny plan, a font labeled *Lavabo* can be seen before the entrance to the refectory, which was located typically on the south side of the cloister. Since this renowned marble-columned cloister no longer exists, the one of St. Trophîme at Arles (Fig. 155) will serve as an example. The columns and their outstanding Romanesque capitals date from the year 1100, when the abbey was one of the dependencies of Cluny.

At mealtimes, after washing their hands at the lavabo, the brethren entered the refectory where they ate in common. Here the silence was

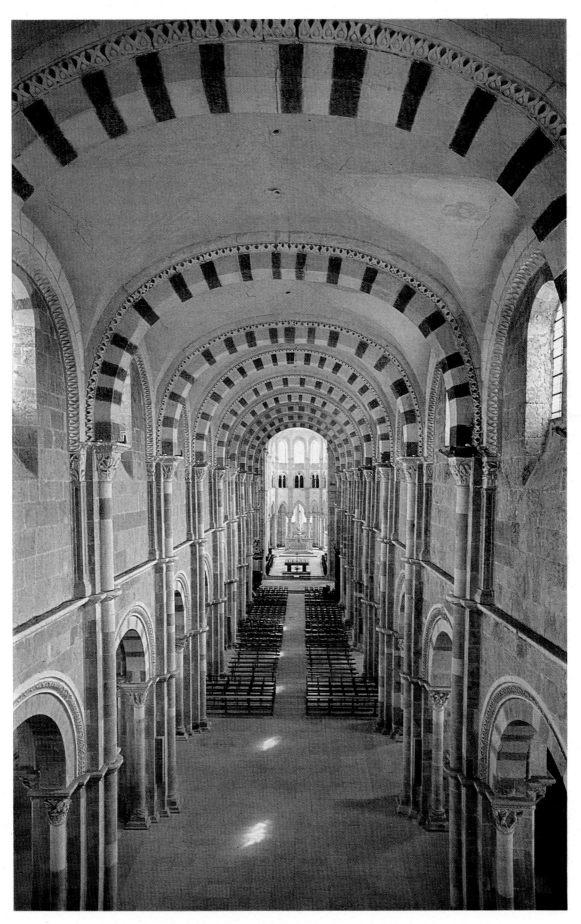

Plate 9. Nave interior from the east, Abbey Church of La Madeleine, Vézelay. 1104–1132. 33′ wide. (See p. 141.)

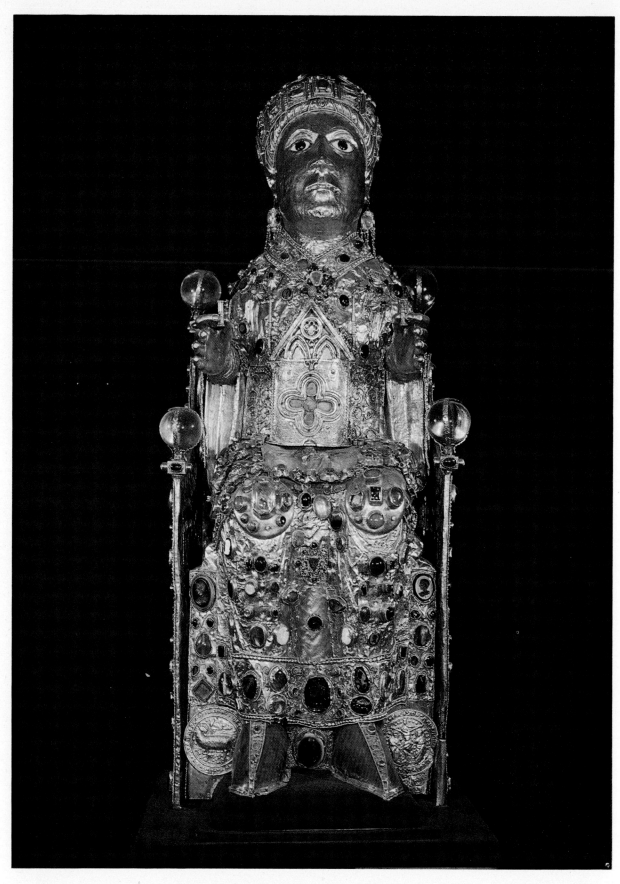

Plate 10. *Reliquary Statue of Ste. Foy.* 940–984.
Abbey of Conques, Aveyron, France. (See p. 146.)

155. Cloister, Abbey of St. Trophîme, Arles. *c.* 1100.

broken only by the lector who read aloud from the lives of the saints and the writings of the church fathers. The refectory shown in the plan is the one Hugh rebuilt to accommodate the ever-growing population of resident monks, which in his time numbered some 200, in contrast with the 70-odd during the abbacy of his predecessor. The refectory measured 112 feet in length and 67 feet in width, with a file of six pillars on either side. Besides the rows of tables for the monks, there were two tables on a raised platform, one for the grand prior of the order and one for the claustral prior. Fresco paintings of scenes from the Old and New Testaments decorated the walls, and a large picture of Christ in Majesty as at the Last Judgment was found at one end. Adjacent to the refectory were the kitchens, bakeries, and pantries; and opening out from the monks' kitchen and running along the west side of the cloister were the storerooms for food with cellars below. One of the rooms led into an outside court where alms were distributed to the poor.

The chapter house at Cluny opened off the east walk of the cloister. Here the monks gathered each morning following church service and breakfast. After a prayer and the reading of a chapter from the Rule of St. Benedict, the abbot from his throne presided over the meeting. At this time, the monks were given necessary information, received instruction, and participated in any business that properly might come before them. This might include anything from the admission of novices to the expulsion of an unworthy monk, from matters connected with the sale, purchase, or leasing of property to the acceptance of gifts. The most solemn business, however, came when a new abbot was chosen from among their ranks on the death of his predecessor.

Except for the church, cloister, refectory, chapter house, and the quarters for distinguished guests, the other monastic buildings were almost entirely utilitarian in character (see Fig. 157). Above the chapter house and the other large rooms adjoining it was the monks' dormitory.

156. Abbey of Cluny, plan. *c.* 1157. Reconstruction by Kenneth J. Conant.

Since services were held during the night as well as by day, the dormitory had to be located near one of the entrances to the church. As seen in the plan (Fig. 156), the monks at Cluny could go downstairs, move along the eastern walk of the cloister, and enter the church through the end of the greater transept. The dormitory itself, the wide barnlike building at the left center in Figure 157, was a long hall with tall narrow windows between which, on either side of a central aisle, were beds for the monks.

Such a complete abbey as Cluny had to provide for many other functions. To the east of the dormitory was the Chapel of Notre Dame. On one side was the small cloister where aged and infirm monks could meditate, on the other was the cemetery. Set at an oblique angle to the main axis of the abbey was the Great Infirmary Hall (Fig. 156, bottom left) with rows of beds in separate cubicles and small rooms for the laundry and servants' quarters. Adjacent to the infirmary was the Priory Group, a monastery within a monastery

157. Abbey of Cluny (bird's-eye view from southeast). *c.* 1157.
Reconstruction by Kenneth J. Conant.

for visiting monks and religiously inclined laymen who sought refuge from the world. On the south periphery (Fig. 156, left center) adjacent to the refectory were quarters for the training of novices before they were fully admitted to the order. Nearby to the west (Fig. 156, upper left) were workshops for such craftsmen as blacksmiths, carpenters, cobblers, and tailors. The location near the novices' quarters and outside the inner precincts of the Abbey indicates they were intended for lay workers rather than monks. The workers could then come and go without interfering with the routine of the monastery itself.

Also along the south and west sides were the stables for dairy cattle and other domestic animals, with sleeping quarters for lay brethren above. Hospices for poor pilgrims were located here, while across the court was St. Odilo's Guesthouse, a spacious room heated by an ornate fireplace, where distinguished guests were accommodated. Above it were separate dormitories for men and women with a common refectory in between. The abbot often entertained hundreds of guests, many of whom were of the aristocratic class who traveled with large retinues. Since donations for the new

church and support for the monastery came in part from such visitors, it was imperative that they gain the best possible impressions. Surrounding the monastery on all sides were thick walls to protect it from marauders, thieves, or armed bands in time of invasion. Outside the walls lay the gardens, groves, and farmlands under its control, which produced the necessities of life. As on the domain of a feudal lord, the soil was tilled by bound serfs working under the supervision of the lay brothers, and sometimes by tenant farmers who rented land from the monks on a crop-sharing basis. The buildings in this area included only such necessary structures as barns, granaries, and mills.

The plan of Cluny was thus a coherent system of adjoining quadrangles that embraced courts and cloisters of a size and importance which varied with the differing activities they were designed to accommodate. Altogether it was a highly complex and at the same time logical plan for a complete community, taking into account the ideals, aspirations, practices, and everyday activities of a group that gathered to work physically and spiritually toward a common end.

ARCHITECTURE

Hugh of Semur, greatest of the Cluniac abbots, succeeded Odilo in the year 1049. Under Hugh, Cluny was destined to attain a period of such resplendence that it could be described by an enthusiastic chronicler as "shining on the earth like a second sun." Taking as his model the accepted feudal organization of society, in which smaller and more dependent landowners swore allegiance to the larger and more powerful landlords in return for protection, Hugh began to bring many of the traditionally independent Benedictine monasteries into the Cluniac orbit. With the express approval of the popes, Hugh gradually concentrated the power of the whole order in his hands and transformed Cluny into a vast monastic empire over which he ruled benignly for sixty years. In the Church hierarchy he was outranked only by the pope, and in the secular world he was the peer of kings. He figured prominently in most of the historical events of his day, even to the extent of acting as intermediary between an emperor and a pope on the famous occasion at Canossa, when Henry IV came on bended knee to beseech Gregory VII for forgiveness. Hugh's greatest moment, however, came when Pope Urban II, who had received training as a monk and prior at Cluny under his personal guidance, was present to dedicate the high altar of his great new abbey church. Honor after honor was bestowed upon the monastery by this Cluniac pope, who was also the preacher of the First Crusade. On his deathbed he wrote to Hugh, his former master, saying that he "committed to him the care of his mother the Church, as Christ His mother to the beloved apostle."

In a period when cities were in eclipse, the influence of bishops and their ability to undertake new buildings were negligible. Kings, when they were constantly moving their courts from one city to another, had little opportunity or inclination to do any important building. Hence, with the consolidation of monastic life into a centralized system, and with the increasing concentration of wealth in the collective hands of the stable and growing religious orders, monasteries became the scenes of the most significant architectural and artistic developments of the time. Furthermore, the rise of the Cluniac star under the indomitable will of its great organizing genius and builder made Cluny itself the place where the most important and progressive developments occurred. As the influence of the mother house permeated the order, a characteristic touch became discernible, and a Cluniac style emerged that was synonymous with high Romanesque art.

Hugh had begun by undertaking many new monastic buildings to accommodate Cluny's ever-growing number of resident monks. Eventually the older second church also proved inadequate for the mother house of a great order, especially when delegations of monks from the priories far and wide assembled there for the chapters general. (Records show that on such an occasion in the year 1132, over 1,200 monks were in the processional line.) The growing importance of Cluny as a center for pilgrimages also added to the need for greater space in the abbey church. For these practical reasons, as well as his desire to crown his many achievements with a monument that would rival the legendary temple of Solomon, Hugh began the great new third abbey church. Even with all his power and influence, however, Hugh did not attempt it before the dominant position of Cluny in the scheme of things was completely consolidated, and before he was certain of generous financial support. The far-flung priories of the order, numbering at this time well over 1,000 and extending as far as Scotland in the north, Portugal in the west, and Jerusalem in the east, could all be counted on for contributions. In addition, offerings were received from people of all classes, from bishops to the humblest of their parishioners and from great lords

158. Surviving transept, Third Abbey Church of Cluny. 1088–1130.

down to the poorest pilgrims, who came to worship at the shrine. Thus in 1088, when he was past 65 and in his 40th year as abbot, Hugh of Semur, with an architect named Hezelo, began the monumental abbey church that in its magnitude and glory eclipsed all other churches in Western Christendom. Gilon, one of his earliest biographers, said that Hugh "began and erected such a church within twenty years that if an emperor had built it within so short a time, it would have been considered marvelous."

The Great Third Abbey Church at Cluny

Hugh's great church was dominated on the exterior by its imposing tower forms, one of which is still to be seen atop the single surviving transept (Fig. 158). The ground plan (Fig. 156) shows the unusual double transepts, the many apsidal chapels radiating outward from the choir, and its massive proportions. It was usual for large abbey churches to have an impressive lantern tower over the crossing of the nave and the transept. At Cluny, as with St. Sernin at Toulouse (Fig. 159), the immense size dominated the silhouette of the whole exterior, but Cluny's twin octagonal towers astride the transept wings were less common. The minor transept also had its central tower, thus making four on the east end, which, added to the two on either side of the narthex entrance, brought the total to six. Unlike later Gothic cathedrals, the exterior of the third church was unadorned by sculpture, all such embellishments being concentrated in the interior. Even the western façade was bare, since it was designed for an introspective, cloistered community and consequently had no need to extend sculptured invitations to the world outside, as did a city church. Rich façades as entrances to the nave did exist in abbey churches elsewhere, but they were masked by the narthex and hence essentially a part of the interior.

While on everyday occasions the monks entered the church from the cloister, high holidays, such as Easter, Pentecost, and the Feast of SS. Peter and Paul to whom the church was dedicated, called for a ceremonial entrance from the west end. Here the double portal between the towers led into a spacious three-aisled narthex, which was called the *minor nave*. In most churches, it was referred to symbolically as "the Galilee," because the celebrant (usually the abbot) who headed the procession going into the nave was likened to Jesus leading his disciples into the city of Galilee. At Cluny, however, the monks had their own Galilee portal, which can be seen in

159. Apse, Church of St. Sernin, Toulouse. *c.* 1080. Lantern tower 215′ high.

160. Church of St. Sernin, plan.

161. Nave, Third Abbey Church of Cluny. 1088–1130. Reconstruction by Kenneth J. Conant.

Figure 156 about halfway down the nave. The narthex, besides serving as the place where the grand procession could be marshaled, took care of the overflow of laymen who gathered at Cluny during the pilgrimage season. At Vézelay, the narthex was actually called the *ecclesia peregrinorum*, or church of the pilgrims (Fig. 166). When ceremonial entrance was made at Cluny, it was through three carved portals, the central one of which was 21 feet in height. Over the lintel and enclosed by the arch was an immense *tympanum*, the semicircular area enclosed by the arch, which contained a sculptured relief representing Christ in Glory surrounded by a heavenly host, the four symbolic evangelical beasts, and various apostles and elders.

On entering the nave (Fig. 161), the mighty proportions of the huge basilica loomed up. From the entrance portal to the end of the apse, it extended a distance of 415 feet, while the entire horizontal axis from front to back, including the narthex, reached an overall length of 615 feet. The nave itself had 11 bays that stretched forward a distance of 260 feet. Each bay was separated by a group of columns clustered around supporting piers, which, as the architectural counterpart of the monks, marched in solemn procession toward the climax of the building at the high altar. In width, the nave spread outward 118 feet and was divided into five aisles. This division was owing in part to the need to provide extra space for altars, since it was now the custom for each monk to say mass every day. The outside aisles, extending all the way around the church and choir, gave pilgrims access to these numerous altars and, more especially, to the smaller chapels in the choir without disturbing the monastic liturgy. These aisles also provided more room for the grand processionals that distinguished the Cluniac liturgy and that demanded ever more impressive and spacious settings. It can be seen in Figure 161 that a stone screen was placed across the nave to close off the space set aside for the monks' choir. The great height of the church was such that the unified impression of the whole was not broken by this screen, and the eye was drawn aloft to the tall columns around the high altar and above them, in turn, to the lofty figure of Christ, which, gazing downward as if in a vision, was painted in the fresco technique on the interior of the half dome of the apse.

Whereas the Early Roman Christian basilicas basically were horizontally directed, the Romanesque examples, because of the northern influence, raised the levels of the nave upward vertically. Gradually, this resulted in more and more accent being placed on the parts of the building above the nave arcade. At Cluny, a double row of windows was found, the lower of which was filled in with masonry, while the upper was left open and served as the clearstory. Though it had numerous windows, the church was criticized by later Gothic builders as being too dark. Its thick walls and massive proportions allowed little direct sunlight to penetrate into the church itself. This was not of great importance, because so much of the monastic liturgy took place at night when the interior was illuminated by candlelight. Churches designed for city people who worshiped by day naturally had to pay more attention to lighting problems.

As in the great Spanish pilgrimage church at Santiago de Compostela (Figs. 162, 163), the nave at Cluny was spanned by ribbed barrel vaulting, 32 feet in the clear, supported by slightly pointed transverse arches. Rising a full 98 feet above the pavement, the vaults were the highest achieved up to this time. But the emotional exuberance of attaining such height outran the engineering knowledge needed to maintain it, and a part of the Cluny vaulting soon collapsed. Out of this accident came experimentation with external buttressing so that when the vaults were rebuilt a range of rudimentary supports with open round arches was placed outside on the aisle roofs. Cluny thus achieved the distinction of being the first church to have external buttresses supporting its nave vaults, and, with its pointed arches, and high vaulting, Cluny combined for the first time in one structure three of the features that future builders would employ to make the unified system characteristic of the Gothic style.

The Romanesque basilica differed little from its Early Roman Christian counterpart except in size, vertical accents, and development of the transept and the parts beyond it. Monastic churches gravitated toward the eastern end

162. Cathedral of Santiago de Compostela, Spain. Nave interior from west. c. 1075–1150. Nave c. 164′ long, 65′ wide (including side aisles), 79′ high.

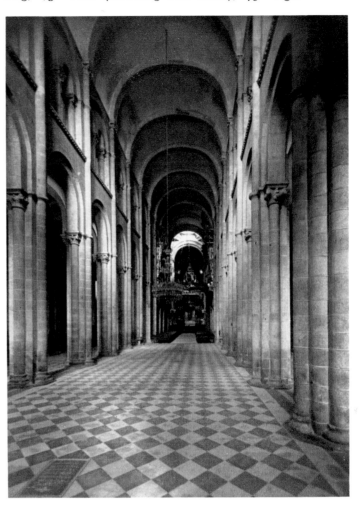

163. Santiago de Compostela, plan.

164. Third Abbey Church of Cluny, transverse section at transept. Restoration by Kenneth J. Conant.

(Fig. 164) where the choir assembled after the procession, and especially toward the high altar where the solemn rites were performed. In a city church, the nave had to provide space for a congregation, but in a monastic church the clergy, including the monks, numbered into the hundreds, and the lay congregation often was nonexistent. Logically, then, the space around the altar had to be extended so that all the monks who formed the choir could be seated. The enlarged apse and double transepts at Cluny were clearly developed to give the monks a sense of surrounding the high altar and to produce a spacious and resonant setting for the almost ceaseless chanting.

The high altar itself was set off from the surrounding ambulatory by eight columns of surpassing slenderness and beauty (Fig. 165). Crowning them were skillfully carved capitals (one of which is shown in Figs. 179–182), all that remains of the apse today. That these were as impressive in Romanesque times as they are now is attested to by Hildebert, bishop of Le Mans, who after a visit wrote: "If it were possible for those who dwell in heaven to take pleasure in a house made by hands, the ambulatory of Cluny would be a place where angels walked."

The decorative plan of the church was carried out on a scale comparable in quality to the grandeur of its spatial dimensions. More than 1,200 sculptured capitals surmounted the columns of the structure, while carved moldings outlined the graceful pointed arches of the nave arcade. Most of the sculpture was painted in rich colors

that gave an added glow to the splendor of the interior, and the whole church was paved with mosaic floors inlaid with images of saints and angels or with abstract designs.

All this magnificence did not go unchallenged. St. Bernard, the redoubtable opponent of the Cluniac order, disapproved violently of such extravagances, and in doing so in writing he unwittingly left a first-hand account of the glory of Hugh's church soon after it was finished. In a letter to one of the Cluniac abbots, he deplored (with Cluny in mind) "the vast height of your churches, their immoderate length, their superfluous breadth, the costly polishings, the curious carvings and paintings which attract the worshiper's gaze and hinder his attentions." His feeling was that "at the very sight of these costly yet marvelous vanities men are more kindled to offer gifts than to pray. ... Hence the church is adorned with gemmed crowns of light—nay, with lustres like cart-wheels, girt all round with lamps, but no less brilliant with precious stones that stud them. Moreover we see candelabra standing like trees of massive bronze, fashioned with marvelous subtlety of art, and glistening no less brightly with gems than with the lights they carry. What, think you, is the purpose of all this? The compunction of penitents, or the admiration of beholders?"

In spite of St. Bernard's diatribe, Cluny's third church became a model for many subsequent Cluniac abbey churches and spread the fame of

165. Apse arcade, Third Abbey Church of Cluny. Reconstruction by Kenneth J. Conant. Fogg Art Museum, Harvard University, Cambridge, Mass.

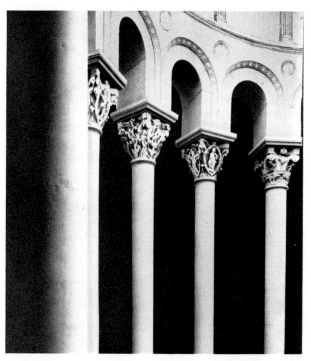

the Burgundian building art—and the taste for its pointed arches and other features that eventually were incorporated into Gothic cathedrals. As the most magnificent of all Romanesque churches, embodying as it did the most highly developed forms of the time, Hugh's church became the greatest single factor in the crystallization of the Romanesque style. Furthermore, it was destined to remain the largest and most magnificent edifice of its kind for a full five centuries—specifically until the new basilica of St. Peter was undertaken in Rome in the 16th century.

It stood proudly until the year 1798, when a wave of Revolutionary reaction in France caused it to be sacked and its very stones carried away. Before the romantic interest in things medieval had developed, and before the tourist traffic —that modern counterpart of the medieval pilgrimages—could intervene, Cluny was blown up by dynamite and the rubble sold as common building stone. All that now remains is a single transept with its tower still in place (Fig. 158), the ambulatory capitals (Figs. 165 and 179–182) and a number of fragments of its architectural sculptures (see p. 130). Thus other priories of

Hugh's time must be cited for clues to Cluny's architecture and sculpture. The great increase in the power and prestige of the order was reflected not only in the growth of the mother abbey but in the numbers who were attracted as monks and pilgrims to its priories and dependencies. At the same time that Hugh was engaged in his great building program, abbey churches were in the process of construction in more than a dozen other monasteries in France alone, including those of Moissac, Beaulieu, La Charité-sur-Loire, and Vézelay. Each in some way reflected directly the influence of Hugh's great basilica.

SCULPTURE

Some of the finest sculpture that dates from the period of Cluny's grandeur is in the abbey church of La Madeleine at Vézelay. The nave (Plate 9) and narthex (Fig. 166) are contemporary with Hugh's church at Cluny, and the intelligent restoration in the 19th century by the French medieval archeologist Viollet-le-Duc accounts for their present good condition. While its proportions are considerably smaller than the great basilica at

166. Central portal of narthex with tympanum, Abbey Church of La Madeleine, Vézelay. 1120–1132. 31′ 4″ wide, 35′ 6″ high.

167. Tympanum, Abbey Church of La Madeleine, Vézelay. *c.* 1120–1132

Cluny, La Madeleine today is the largest Romanesque abbey church in France. Rich in historical associations, it derived its principal fame in medieval times as the repository of the relics of St. Mary Magdalene. On the eve of her feast in the year 1120, after the completion of the nave, fire destroyed the wooden portions of the roof, and burning timbers fell on the assembled pilgrims. When the revaulting of the narthex was undertaken, the principle of the groin vault (see Fig. 94), which Romanesque builders had rediscovered, was used. In Figure 166 the *groins*, the sharp edges made by the intersecting vaults, do not show completely, but the principle is the same as that used in ancient Rome (see Fig. 96) as well as in later Romanesque and Gothic churches (see Figs. 207, 216). As at Cluny, strong transverse arches span the nave, but here the alternation of light

pink and darkish gray-brown stones results in an interesting color effect.

The principal interest at Vézelay, however, is the seemingly inexhaustible wealth of sculptured capitals and, above all, the relief compositions over its three portals leading from the narthex into the nave and side aisles (Fig. 166). For the first time since antiquity, monumental sculpture appears. In Romanesque churches it was used in the tympanums over the portals, the largest and most intricate sculpture being used in the tympanum over the central doorway.

The splendid tympanum over the central portal at Vézelay (Fig. 167) stems from the first quarter of the 12th century. In its iconography and workmanship, it is by far the most complex Romanesque tympanum, yet the logical division of space keeps the composition from seeming cluttered or confused. Here, as elsewhere, Romanesque designers and sculptors looked for their subjects and models in the drawings and miniature paintings that illustrated the texts of the Scriptures in monastic libraries. Such illuminated manuscripts provided convenient models that the monks could show to the sculptors who were to carry out the projects. At Vézelay, the robe of Christ, as well as those of the apostles, reveals a pattern of clear, sharp, swirling lines, which stems from pen drawings in manuscripts of the time.

The interpretation of the tympanum scene most often suggested is the commission of the apostles as found in the last chapter of Luke's Gospel, and the description of the Pentecost scene in the second chapter of the Acts of the Apostles. A more likely source, however, is the final vision of St. John from the last part of the Book of Revelation. Whether a single scene is intended or two or even three scenes are combined in a subtle Cluniac synthesis is a subject for scholarly speculation. If it is a single scene, the most convincing source is the first two verses of chapter 22 of the Book of Revelation: "And he shewed me a pure river of water of life, clear as crystal, proceeding out of the throne of God and of the Lamb. In the midst of the street of it, and on either side of the river, was there the tree of life, which bare twelve manner of fruits, and yielded her fruit every month: and the leaves of the tree were for the healing of nations."

Here again the figure of Christ dominates the composition, seated, as St. John says, on "a great white throne," but not so much to judge mankind as to redeem it. While the figure is supremely majestic, Christ is not crowned. The streams emanating from his fingers descend upon the barefooted apostles, the archetypes of the clergy, who bring spiritual understanding through the books they hold in their hands and physical healing through the divine mercy which they transmit to mankind. On one side of Christ's head, the water referred to in the quotation flows forth, while on the other are the branches of the tree. The 12 fruits, one for each month, are found among the 29 medallions in the middle band of *archivolts*—the series of arches that frame the tympanum. A figure treading grapes, for example, represents September; October is symbolized by a man gathering acorns for his pigs. The months themselves, besides being connected with these labors, are also symbolized by the signs of the zodiac that, in turn, remind man of the limited time he has in which to attain his salvation. A few of the other medallions picture strange exotic beasts taken from the *bestiaries*, those curious books of the time that recounted the lore about

animals actual and fabulous. A survival from antiquity can be noted in the fourth medallion from the lower right that depicts a centaur.

The inner band of the archivolt is divided into eight irregular compartments that contain figures representing the nations which the leaves of the tree of life are intended to heal. The one on the top left, next to the head of Christ, contains two dog-headed men, called in Isidore's *Etymologies* the Cynocephaloi, a tribe supposed to have inhabited India. The corresponding compartment on the right side shows the crippled and bent figure of a man and that of a blind woman taking a few halting steps as she is led forward. In the others, the lame on crutches are found along with lepers pointing to their sores.

Along the lintel below, a parade of the nations converges toward the center. While the compartments above picture those in physical distress, here are the pagans and heathens of the earth who need spiritual aid. Among these strange peoples who populate the remote regions of the earth are a man and woman (in the far right corner) with enormous ears and feathered bodies. Next to them is a group of dwarfs or pygmies, so small they have to mount a horse by means of a ladder. On the far left, half-naked savages are hunting with bows and arrows, while toward the left center some heathens are shown leading a bull to sacrifice. In the center stands St. John the Baptist holding a medallion with the image of the lamb on it. This is doubtless intended to convey the explanation that the "river of water of life" is baptism, which is the way to salvation that all must take if they want to enter into eternal life. It is a logical symbol with which to adorn the portal leading into the nave of the church, the interior of which with its glowing colors and jeweled decorations was often likened to the heavenly city, the new Jerusalem so eloquently described by St. John: "And the gates of it shall not be shut at all by day: for there shall be no night there. And they shall bring the glory and honour of the nations into it" (Rev. 21: 25–26). The open books of the apostles seated next to St. Peter on the left recall the following verse that states that all who enter it are the ones "which are written in the Lamb's book of life" (Rev. 21: 27). Futhermore, in a monastic church especially, the monks would have been conscious of the final reference to these gates: "Blessed are they that do his commandments, that they may have the right to the tree of life, and may enter in through the gates into the city" (Rev. 22:14). The awakened interest in foreign countries and peoples was doubtless owing to the influence of the early crusades, which were then being preached.

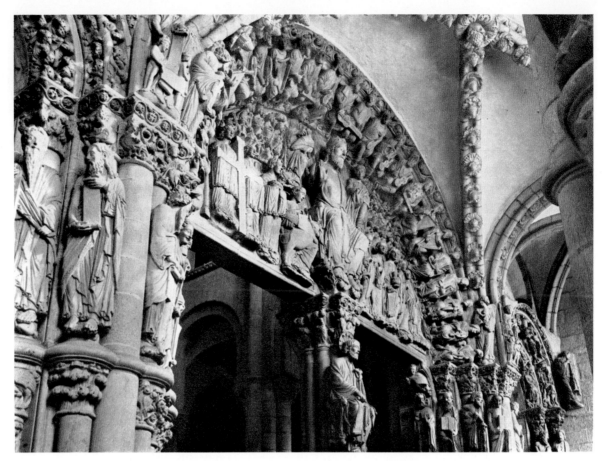

168. MASTER MATTEO. Tympanum, Pórtico de la Gloria, Cathedral of Santiago de Compostela, Spain. 1168–1188. 31' 2" high.

169. *Last Judgment*, tympanum at center portal of west façade, St. Lazare, Autun. Early 12th century. 21' wide.

Only a few fragments of the great tympanum at Cluny have survived, but at Santiago de Compostela there is a superb example (Fig. 168) carved by Matteo (Fig. 189), a late Romanesque master, showing Christ surrounded by apostles and the 24 elders of the Apocalypse holding musical instruments, which symbolize their praise according to the Revelation of St. John. Another sculptor, Giselbertus, executed a tremendous Last Judgment for Autun's cathedral (Fig. 169) with Christ appearing in an almond-shaped mandorla to judge the quick and the dead summoned from their graves by the trumpet blasts of angels. A similar composition in the Church of Ste. Foy at Conques dwells with horrendous emphasis on the tortures of hell.

At Vézelay, the imaginative scope displayed in the profusion of sculptured capitals is breathtaking. Biblical scenes, incidents from the lives of the saints, allegorical commentaries, and the play of pure fantasy are found throughout the narthex and the nave. One of the narthex capitals depicts the flight of the Angel Gabriel with his trumpet ready to sound the call to the Last Judgment (Fig. 170). Another in the nave shows the angel of death striking down the eldest son of Pharaoh (Fig. 171), and another shows a bearded figure pouring grain into a handmill that a barefooted man is turning (Fig. 172). The real meaning of this scene would be lost were it not for a chance remark in the writings of Suger, the abbot of St. Denis in Paris, who visited Cluny and Vézelay before beginning to rebuild his abbey church. He noted that the corn is the old law which is poured into the mystic mill by an ancient Hebrew prophet, probably Moses, and is being ground into the meal of the new law by St. Paul. Frequently depicted in other capitals are incidents from the lives of the two favorite Cluniac saints, Anthony and Paul, both hermits in the Egyptian desert. In one of the fearful temptations of St. Anthony, a demon symbolizing luxury (Fig. 173) appears in the guise of a ferocious monster, whose hair leaps upward like sulfurous flames and whose grimacing mouth opens to reveal his fangs. Other demons are seen combating for the souls of the unwary (Fig. 174).

170–172. Capital sculptures, Church of La Madeleine, Vézelay. *c.* 1130.

(top) 170. *Judgment Angel*, narthex capital.

(center) 171. *Angel of Death Killing Eldest Son of Pharaoh*, nave capital.

(right) 172. *Mystic Mill: Moses and St. Paul Grinding Corn*, nave capital.

173-174. Nave capitals, Church of La Madeleine, Vézelay. *c.* 1130.

(left) 173. *Demon of Luxury.*

(right) 174. *Combat of Two Demons.*

Unlike the statuary of antiquity that was made of marble or bronze, French Romanesque capitals are usually of soft sandstone and limestone. Their purpose was mainly to decorate interiors that did not have to resist the elements. The soft material, furthermore, was better adapted to the pictorial forms of Romanesque sculpture, and its plasticity responded more quickly to the imaginative demands made on it than a harder stone could have done.

While the examples discussed are stone carvings, the general category of Romanesque sculpture in this period should be broadened to include works in metal. Only a few examples of this kind have survived, owing to the fact that they were made of such precious materials as gold, silver, and copper, adorned with enamel work and studded with precious gems. Cluny, according to an early inventory, had a golden statue of the Virgin seated on a silver throne and wearing a jeweled crown. Such a work would have been similar to the reliquary statue of Ste. Foy at Conques (Plate 10). Churches also needed chalices, plates, and pitchers for the sacred services. On important feast days, books with ivory or metal covers encrusted with jewels (Fig. 175) were used on the high altar, where also reposed reliquaries

fashioned to contain the relics of saints (Fig. 176). Candelabras, incense burners, and metal choir screens added their beauty to the sacred precincts.

Romanesque sculpture always remained an integral part of the architectural design and is inseparable from the whole. The walls, ceiling, portals, columns, and capitals were not merely mute structural necessities; they were the places where the carved images communicated messages and meanings—the stones that spoke to monk and pilgrim alike in the eloquent visual language of form, line, and color.

PAINTING AND OTHER MONASTIC CRAFTS

Miniatures of modest proportions on the parchment pages of books and monumental murals in the apses of abbey churches were the two extremes of the art of painting in the Romanesque period. The one craft known definitely to have been consistently practiced by the monks themselves was the copying, illustrating, and binding of books, activities that took place in a large communal room called the *scriptorium*. This tradition, which dates from the time of Cassiodorus, was followed by all Benedictine houses, and those in the Cluniac order fostered it with both diligence and enthusiasm. While the Cluniac copyists were known for the beauty of their lettering and the accuracy of their texts, a monk skilled in his (left) 175. *Crucifixion*, cover of *Lindau Gospels*. Rheims or St. Denis, *c.* 870. Gold and jewels, 13¾ × 10½". Pierpont Morgan Library, New York.

(below) 176. Phylactery Reliquary of Tooth of St. Maclou. *c.* 1190. Gilded silver. St. Maclou, Bar-sur-Aube, France.

craft would certainly not have been content merely to copy letters all his life. A blank place in the manuscript provided him with both the space and the challenge to fill it in. At first, these spaces were filled with nothing more than fanciful little pen drawings or an elaborate initial letter at the beginning of a paragraph. Gradually, the drawings grew into miniature paintings, and the initial letters became highly complex designs. The luxurious development of this art of illuminating manuscripts seems to have been one compensation for the austerity of Benedictine life. As the practice became more widely accepted, specialists in the various phases began to be designated. A painter of small illuminated scenes, for instance, was called a *miniator*, while one who did initial letters was known as a *rubricator*.

Cluniac manuscripts were done with the utmost delicacy. Miniatures were painted in many colors, and halos of saints or crowns of kings were made with thin gold leaf. The letter Q (Fig. 177) in an evangeliary from St. Omer is an intricate example of the illuminator's art.

Such flourishes of the pen made by expert copyists on their parchment pages, and the gradual refinement of the painstaking miniature art of illumination, had effects far beyond the medium for which either was intended originally. They became the models for the large murals that decorated the walls and apses of churches and for the sculpture that embellished the spaces above portals and columns; later, they were the prototypes of designs for stained glass windows in Gothic cathedrals. The greater freedom provided by the pen and brush on the parchment page had to be developed before more monumental designs in stone and glass could be undertaken. Thus these miniature examples of the medieval painter's art were far more important than their size would indicate. Not only do they provide the few surviving examples of pictorial art in Western Europe from the 7th through the 10th centuries, but they were the source that gradually swelled

177. Page for Initial Q, from Evangeliary of Abbey at St. Omer. *c.* 1000. Illuminated manuscript. Pierpont Morgan Library, New York.

into the flood of monumental sculpture, mural painting, and stained glass of later centuries.

Contrasting with the diminutive art of illuminating manuscripts were the huge frescoes painted on the surfaces of barrel-vaulted ceilings, arches, and semidomed apses of churches of the Romanesque period. Here again, the most notable examples were found at Cluny and its satellite monasteries. The narthex at Vézelay still has one of these frescoes, showing Christ surrounded by the four evangelical beasts, though it is now so faded as to be barely visible. A monk visiting Cluny in 1063 sang the praises of the wall paintings in the great refectory. The most notable of all, however, was the colossal painting of Christ in Glory in the apse of Hugh's great church. From a study of the fragments that have been recovered, its style and technique are known to have been similar to that of an excellently preserved apsidal mural in the little chapel at Berzé-la-ville, less than ten miles from Cluny (Fig. 178). This small residence and chapel was built between the years 1100 and 1103 as a retreat for Hugh in the last years of his life. So close is the resemblance of the painting there to that in his great church at Cluny that it may have been done by the same artist.

In the Berzé-la-ville painting, the seated figure of Christ is enclosed in a many-hued mandorla, a form familiar from the relief sculptures over the portals of the churches. Here Christ is clothed in a robe of white over which is draped a red mantle. While blessing the sixteen surrounding apostles and saints with His right hand, He gives St. Peter a scroll containing the law with His left. The heavenly setting is suggested by the dark-blue background of the mandorla, which is studded with golden stars, and by the hand of God the Father, which hovers above Christ holding a crown. The term *fresco* is not used in the ordinary sense when it refers to this method of painting. A true fresco technique requires that color pigments mixed with water be applied directly to fresh plaster. The lime in the plaster then binds the pigments to the wall by chemical action, and a permanent though somewhat opaque surface is the result. This fresco technique seems to have been used only for the red ocher undercoats in the examples at Cluny and Berzé-la-ville. The undersurface was then coated with several layers of tempera—that is, pigments mixed with milk, egg, or glue—and finally glazed with wax over-painting to achieve the brighter and more transparent effect needed for the dark interiors. While their range was small, those colors the painters did develop had an extraordinary intensity well suited to their expressive needs. In the desire for brilliant color and strongly articulated outlines,

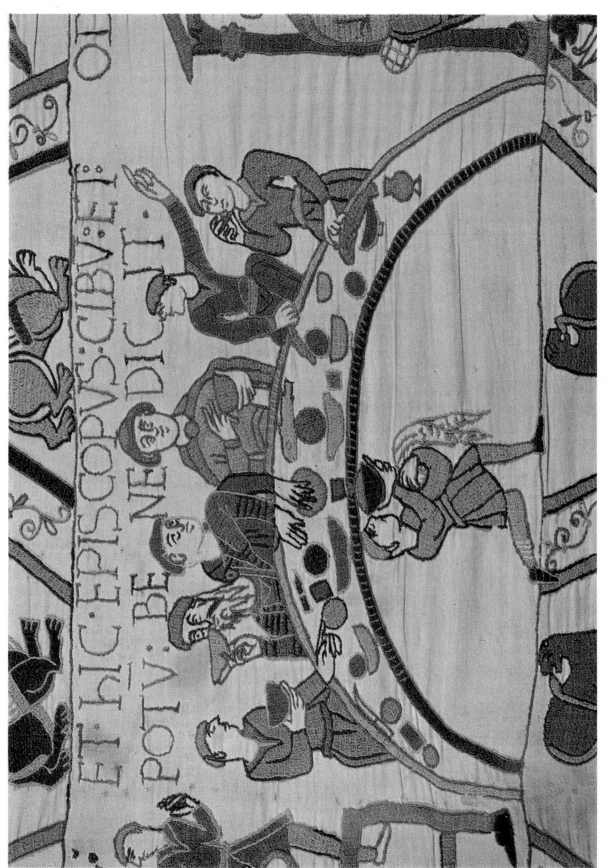

Plate 11. *William's Feast*, detail of Bayeux Tapestry. *c.* 1073–1088. Wool embroidery on linen. 20″ high, whole 321′ long. Town Hall, Bayeux. (See p. 166.)

Plate 12. *Heinrich Frauenlob Directing Minstrel Performance*. 14th century.
Manesse Manuscript of German Minnesingers. Heidelberg Library. (See p. 169.)

178. *Christ in Glory. c.* 1103. Fresco (apse mural), *c.* 13' high. Cluniac Chapel, Berzé-la-Ville, France.

these murals were undoubtedly influenced to some extent by Byzantine mosaics, especially by those of Ravenna.

Besides the arts of building, stone carving, and painting, many crafts were practiced in the workshops of Cluny and the other monasteries. These included embroidering altar cloths and vestments, weaving, ceramics, goldsmithing and other metal crafts, leather tooling, and the casting of bells. The constant experimentation and research carried on in these centers resulted in a continuous improvement in the methods employed, including better ways of manufacturing glass, and in the invention of chemical formulas for stained glass. Just how extensively the monks themselves took part in the actual production of such handicrafts at Cluny or elsewhere is not definitely known. There is no evidence, for instance, that a monk ever worked as a sculptor in stone. The capitals and relief sculpture were executed for the most part by journeymen carvers, who went from place to place in groups wherever building activity was in progress. Likewise, similar work in other media was probably performed by itinerant craftsmen or by lay workers from the region. The iconographic schemes, however, were always worked out under the direct supervision of the monks, some of whom may have possessed the necessary skills so that they could train the craftsmen working under them. The variety and subtle character of the work, therefore, often is as much the monks' as if they had taken the chisel or other tools into their own hands. Wherever a name has survived in connection with sculpture, painting, or other work, it is usually that of a monk who is said to have "made" it. But "made" could mean anything from donating the material or suggesting the subject to supervising the work in progress or even to doing the carving or painting itself.

The monastic attitude toward decorating a church is well summed up by Theophilus, a writer on the various crafts of this time, who addressed his fellow monks, saying: "... you have confidently approached the house of God, have decorated with utmost beauty ceilings or walls with various work, and showing forth with different colours a likeness of the paradise of God, glowing with various flowers, and verdant with herbs and leaves, and cherishing the lives of the saints with crowns of various merit, you have, after a fashion, shown the beholders everything in creation praising God, its creator, and have caused them to proclaim him admirable in all his works. Nor is the eye of man even able to decide upon which work it may first fix its glance; if it beholds the ceilings, they glow like draperies; if it regards the walls, there is the appearance of paradise; if it marks the abundance of light from the windows, it admires the inestimable beauty of the glass and the variety of the costly work. ..."

MUSIC

Odo of Cluny, abbot from 927 to 942, brought the monastery its earliest musical distinction through his active fostering of choral music. Documents tell of more than a hundred psalms being sung there daily in his time; and on his tours of inspection to other monasteries, he devoted much of his energies to the instruction of choirs. His great success made it necessary for his teaching methods to be written down, and from this fortunate circumstance something about the early status of music at Cluny can be ascertained.

Odo's great accomplishments include the arranging of the tones of the scale into an orderly progression from A to G; and by thus assigning to them a system of letters, he was responsible for the earliest effective system of Western musical notation. Odo's method, as expounded in his treatise, also included the mathematical measurement of spaces on the monochord, which made it possible to determine accurately the pitches and intervals of each of the Gregorian modes. Before Odo's time, the chants used in the sacred service had laboriously to be learned by rote; and if any degree of authenticity was to be achieved, they had to be taught by a graduate of the Schola Cantorum that Gregory the Great had established in Rome. By teaching the singers to read notes, the treatise declares that soon they "were singing at first sight and extempore and without a fault anything written in music, something which until now ordinary singers had never been able to do, many continuing to practice and study for fifty years without profit."

Refinements on Odo's method were made in the 11th century by another monk, Guido of Arezzo. His treatise, which was in the library of Cluny, made it clear that he embraced the Cluniac musical reforms. He also freely acknowledged his debt to the work of his great predecessor, the Abbot Odo, "from whose example," he said, "I have departed only in the forms of the notes." This slight departure by Guido was actually the invention of the basis for modern musical notation

on a staff of lines. As he explained it: "The sounds, then, are so arranged that each sound, however often it may be repeated in a melody, is always found in its own row. And in order that you may better distinguish these rows, lines are drawn close together, and some rows of rounds occur on the lines themselves, others in the intervening intervals or spaces. Then the sounds on one line or in one space all sound alike." Odo's work also led to Guido's system of *solmization*, which assigned certain syllables, derived from a hymn to St. John, to each degree of the scale:

C D F DED
Ut que-ant la - xis

D D C D E E
re - so - na - re fi - bris

EFG E D EC D
Mi- ra ge-sto - rum

F G a G FED D
fa - mu - li tu - o- rum,

GaG FE F G D
Sol - ve pol - lu - ti

a G a F Ga a
la - bi - i re - a - tum,

GF ED C E D
San - cte Jo - an - nes.

Later the syllable *si*, compounded from the first two letters of the Latin form of St. John (Sancte Ioannes), was added as the seventh scale degree. In France, these syllables are still used just as in Guido's time; in Italy and elsewhere, the first note *ut* is replaced by the more singable *do*.

The most remarkable fact about Odo's and Guido's treatises is that both champion music as an art designed to be performed in the praise of the Creator and to enhance the beauty and meaning of prayer. Previously, Boethius, along with most early writers on music, had considered music a branch of mathematics that could reveal the secrets of the universe. Guido, however, made a point of stating that the writings of Boethius were "useful to philosophers, but not to singers," and both Odo and he intentionally omitted heavenly speculations. Cluny, therefore, emerged as a center of practical music making rather than as a place where theoreticians pondered on music as an abstruse science.

The story of music at Cluny was also told visually with compelling beauty in two sculptured capitals that survive from the apse of Hugh's great church. In the sanctuary, the architectural climax of the whole edifice, was a series of columns grouped in a semicircle around the high altar, and the capitals of these pillars (see Fig. 165) constituted the apogee of late 11th-century sculptural skill. Here, capital by capital, were to be seen symbolic expressions of the highest ideals of the monk's life. One capital, for example, presented on its four faces the theological virtues; another, the cardinal virtues. On a third were pictured the cycles and labors of the monk's year in terms of the four seasons; and his hopes for the hereafter were portrayed by the four rivers and trees of Paradise. Finally, his praise for the Creator was expressed in a double quaternity with figures to symbolize the eight tones of sacred psalmody. This inclusion of music in the sacred precinct, next to the symbols of the highest human virtues and heavenly beauties, was further evidence of the high esteem in which the tonal art was held by the monks of Cluny.

On the first of the eight faces of these twin capitals (Fig. 179) is inscribed: "This tone is the first in the order of musical intonations," and the figure is that of a solemn-faced youth playing on a lute. Here the symbolism of the stringed instrument stems from the belief in the power of music to banish evil, as David had cast out Saul's evil spirit when he played to him. The second tone (Fig. 180) is represented by the figure of a young woman dancing and beating a small drum, the inscription reading, "There follows the tone which by number and law is second." Such percussion instruments are known to have been used to accompany medieval processions on joyful feast days in the manner described in the 68th Psalm: "The singers went before, the players on instruments followed after; among them were damsels playing with timbrels." The next inscription (Fig. 181) says: "The third strikes, and represents the resurrection of Christ." The instrument here is of the lyre type with a sounding board added, which is one of the 11th-century forms of the psaltery, the legendary instrument with which David accompanied himself as he sang the psalms. This instrument with its gut strings stretched over the wooden frame roughly resembles a cross and was used as a symbolic reference to Christ stretched on the Cross for the redemption of the world. The fourth figure (Fig. 182) is that of a young man playing a set of chime bells, and the accom-

179–182. Ambulatory capitals, Third Abbey Church of Cluny. 1088–1095. Ochier Museum, Cluny.

(left) 179. *First Tone of Plainsong.*

(right) 180. *Second Tone.*

(left) 181. *Third Tone.*

(right) 182. *Fourth Tone.*

panying inscription reads: "The fourth follows representing a lament in song." The Latin word *planctus* denotes a funeral dirge, and the practice of ringing bells at burials is pictured in the contemporary representation of the burial procession of Edward the Confessor (Fig. 195), where the figures accompanying the bier have small bells in their hands.

As a series, the eight inscriptions and symbolic figures reveal much about Cluniac musical practice. For example, in the second, fourth, fifth, and seventh tones, the figures are moving or standing, which seems to point to the processional chants; in the others, they are seated in a manner appropriate to the stationary chants. In those that have to do with action, the instruments are a small hand drum or cymbals, bells, and a horn of some type; all the seated figures play stringed instruments. This symbolism apparently points to some of the rhythmic and melodic differences in the two types of chant—the processional and the stationary—which, in turn, reflect the two aspects of life—the active and the contemplative.

The skillful chorus of Cluny was undoubtedly in the musical vanguard of that day, just as the third abbey church headed architecture and sculpture. Odo's teaching methods clearly indicated that a high degree of vocal culture was expected of his monastic choirs; and, since they sang most of the time, they got plenty of practice. They were thus able to perform chants of considerable complexity, and music was well on its way to becoming a highly developed art. While Gregorian plainsong was a purely melodic style and continued to be practiced as such, during the Romanesque period the choral responses began to show variations in the direction of singing in several parts. The 9th, 10th, and 11th centuries thus saw the tentative beginnings of the *polyphonic*, or many-voiced, style that was to flourish in the Gothic period and in the Renaissance.

Unfortunately, the polyphonic practice of the pre-Gothic period is known only through theoretical treatises. From the rules they give for the addition of voices to the traditional chant, however, some idea of the early forms of polyphony can be determined. As might be expected, the influence of mathematics and the Pythagorean number theory were found in the musical usages of the time. The perfect intervals of the octave, fifth, and fourth were preferred over all others, since their mathematical ratios indicated a closer correspondence with the divine order of the universe. In a treatise dating from the beginning of the 10th century, some years before Odo's time, the type of choral response known as *parallel organum* is discussed. The original Gregorian melody was maintained intact; and, as a variant in two parts, the principal voice was paralleled by an organum voice at the fifth below, so that there was a strict melodic and rhythmic concordance between the two parts. When sung in three parts, the organum was doubled at the octave above, so that the principal voice was embellished by the movement of parallel voices a fifth below and a fourth above. With the addition of the fourth part, both the principal and organal voices were doubled in octaves, thus making a composite intervalic texture that included the parallel movement of the three perfect intervals: the fourth, fifth, and octave.

Parallel organum, in effect, built a mighty fortress of choral sound around the traditional Gregorian line of plainsong. By thus enclosing it within the stark and gaunt but strong perfect intervals, a massive and solid style was achieved that was in the spirit of the other Romanesque arts.

The music of this time was yet another expression of the praise of God; and, when related to the great buildings, the richly carved sculpture, the illuminated manuscripts and painted murals,

Parallel Organum (10th century)   (from *Scholia enchiriadus*)

Sit   glo - ri - a   Do - mi - ni   in   sae - cu - la:

it fits into the picture as a whole. Consequently, when the choir section of a monastic church was being planned, every effort was made to provide resonant setting for the perpetual chant. Hugh's great church was especially renowned for its acoustics. The curved ceiling vaults and the great variety of angles in the wall surfaces of the broad transepts and cavernous nave gave the chant there a characteristic tone color that can be reproduced only in a similar setting. The effect of a monastic choir of several hundred voices performing jubilations with all its heart and soul must have been overwhelmingly impressive.

Cluny's sculptured capitals depicting the tones of plainsong represent an obvious synthesis of the arts of sculpture, music, and literature into an appropriate architectural setting. Their expressive intensity, moreover, bespeaks both the motion and emotion typical of the Romanesque style in general. As such, they are representative products of a people capable of the long and arduous pilgrimages and the fantastic effort associated with the organization of the First Crusade. These sculptures reveal something of that indomitable energy, and especially of a vigorous attitude toward the act of worship, that must have been channeled into a performance style which was emphatic in rhythm. They are, in fact, the embodiment of the spirit expressed by St. Augustine to "Sing with your voices, and with your hearts, and with all your moral convictions, sing the new songs, not only with your tongue but with your life." One of the other capitals suggests the representation of athletes with such figures as a boxer, a swimmer, and a tumbler. The whole Cluniac approach was aptly summed up by a friend of St. Hugh's, St. Peter Damian, who referred to Cluny as a "spiritual gymnasium."

IDEAS

The key to the understanding of the Romanesque as a living and active art is a knowledge of the opposing forces that created it. As the Roman Christian influence spread northward, it encountered the restless surging energies of the former barbarian tribes. In effect, a Church that venerated tradition and encouraged a static order was absorbing peoples with an urge for experimentation and action. The resulting innovations gave ancient forms new twists and turns. When the horizontal Early Roman Christian basilica, for example, was combined with the northern spire, the first step toward Romanesque architecture was taken. The further development of the style was the direct result of this union of southern horizontality and northern verticality, reflecting as it did the broad spirit of the late Roman humanism and the soaring northern aspirations. The musical counterpart is found in the joining together of southern monophony and northern polyphony, which occurred when the Mediterranean tradition of unison melody met the northern custom of singing in parts. The result was the experimentation with primitive forms of counterpoint and harmony that characterized the music of the Romanesque period. This meeting of southern unity with northern variety, and its slow maturation over the centuries, was thus responsible for the first truly European art style: the Romanesque. The ideas that underlie the monastic aspect of the style are an outgrowth of those that motivated the earlier period in Ravenna. The mysticism of the previous period moved into an other-worldly ascetic phase; and early Christian authoritarianism resulted in the rigid stratification of society into strict hierarchies. The two basic ideas, then, crystallize as asceticism and hierarchism.

Asceticism

The monastic way of life demanded the seclusion of the countryside as an escape from the distractions of the world. Since the monk conceived his earthly life to be but a steppingstone to life beyond, living required only the barest essentials. The very absence of physical luxury led to the development of a rich inner life, and the barren soil of rural isolation almost miraculously produced an important art movement. Poverty, chastity, and humility became virtues as the result of moral rather than aesthetic impulses, but the very severity of monastic life stimulated imaginative experience, and individual self-denial stimulated communal energies.

The attitude of turning away from the world found its architectural expression in the plain exteriors and rich interiors of monastic churches. Thus the net effect of asceticism was to increase the fervor of the spirit and to express this with great intensity. Two favorite Cluniac saints were the Paul and Anthony who had gone farthest into the forbidding African desert; it was they who had the most fantastic visions and the most horrendous temptations. The diffusion of social centers into widely scattered monastic communities likewise lent a peculiar intensity and a wide variety to the expressive forms of the Romanesque. The arts, consequently, were not intended to mirror the natural world or to decorate the dwelling place of an earthly ruler but, rather, to conjure up other-worldly visions of divine majesty. Thus all the arts found a common ground in their desire to depict the various aspects of the world beyond.

The monks developed an art of elaborate symbolism addressed to an educated cloistered community versed in sophisticated allegories. Such a symbolic language—whether in architecture, sculpture, painting, or music—could only have been fostered by an abbot like Hugh, whose learning was so universal that he succeeded in adding "philosophy to ornament and a meaning to beauty." By contrast, the later Gothic arts were directed toward the humble of the world and the unlettered people beyond the cloister. While the sculpture and stained glass of the Gothic cathedral were destined to become the Bible in stone and glass for the poor, in a monastic church the comparable forms were always aloof and aristocratic and at times intentionally subtle and enigmatic. This does not mean that Romanesque art was overly intellectualized and remote from the experience of those to whom it was addressed. On the contrary, it was very directly related to the intensity of the inner life and the visionary other-worldly focus of the religious communities that developed it.

Greco-Roman sculpture was successful in its way precisely because classical man had conceived his gods in human form, and as such they could be rendered so well in marble. When godhood was conceived as an abstract principle, a realistic representation of it became essentially impossible. Rational proportions were of no help to Romanesque man, who considered it impossible to understand God intellectually. God had to be felt through faith rather than comprehended by the mind. Only through the intuitive eye of faith could His essence be grasped. Hence He had to be portrayed symbolically, since a symbol could stand for something intangible rather than a literal representation. Visible physical substance was secondary, and soul stuff was primary; but the latter could be depicted only in the world of the imagination.

A life so metaphysically oriented and one motivated by such deep religious convictions could never have found its models in the natural world. The fantastic proportions of Romanesque architecture, the eccentric treatment and distortions of the human body in its sculpture, the unnecessarily elaborated initials in the manuscript illuminations, and the florid melismas added to the syllables of the chant were all evidence of a rejection of the natural order of things and its replacement by the supernatural. The book of the Bible most admired was Revelation, containing

183. *Isaiah*, on west portal, Church of Notre Dame, Souillac. *c.* 1110.

as it did the apocalyptical visions of St. John. The pictorial element in sculpture and painting in both large and small forms reflected Romanesque man's convictions with such intensity that the human figures seem to be consumed by the inner fires of their faith. Calm reason would seek to persuade by placid or serene attitudes, but such animated figures as those of the prophets at Souillac and Moissac (Figs. 183, 184) seem to be performing spiritual dances in which their slender forms stretch to unnatural lengths and their gestures are more convulsive than graceful.

Romanesque man thus dwelt in a dream world where the trees that grew in Paradise, the angels who populated the heavens, and the demons of hell were more real than anything or anybody he beheld in everyday life. Even though he had never seen such creatures, he never doubted their existence. Indeed, the monsters whose fearsome characteristics were described in the bestiaries, and which were represented in the manuscripts and sculptures, had a moral and symbolic function far more real to him than any animals of mere physical existence. All these imaginary creatures existed together in a kind of jungle of the imagination where the abnormal was the normal and the fabulous became the commonplace.

Hierarchism

A strict hierarchical structure of society prevailed throughout the Romanesque period, which was as rigid in its way inside the monastery as was the feudalism outside the cloistered walls. The thought of the time was based on the assumption of a divinely established order of the universe, and the authority to interpret it was vested in the Church. The majestic figure of Christ in Glory carved over the entrance portals of the Cluniac abbey churches, and echoed in the mural compositions painted on the interior of their half-domed apses, proclaimed this concept to the world at large. Christ was no longer the Good Shepherd of early Christian times but a mighty king, crowned and enthroned in the midst of His heavenly courtiers, sitting in judgment on the entire world. The keys to His heavenly kingdom, as seen in the Vézelay tympanum (Fig. 167) and the apse painting at Berzé-la-ville (Fig. 178), rest firmly in the grasp of St. Peter, the first of the popes according to the Roman tradition. As if to lend additional emphasis to this doctrine, St. Peter at Berzé-la-ville is seen receiving a scroll containing the divine statutes from the hands of Christ. The papacy of medieval days always found its most powerful support in the Cluniac order, and through such aid succeeded in establishing an all-powerful theocracy based on this mandate from on high.

The authority of the Church was nowhere better expressed than in these monumental sculptural and mural compositions that from their place of eminence warned those who entered that they were walking a road either to salvation or damnation. The milestones that marked the path were placed there by the Church, whose clergy alone could interpret them and assure the suppliant that he was on his way to the streets of gold instead of the caldrons of fire. The frequency with which the apocalyptic vision of St. John was represented, with apostles and elders surrounding the throne of Christ (Fig. 169, for example), was evidence of the veneration of the protective-father image in the form of the bearded patriarch. Like the clergy, these were the authorities who show the way by their willingness to offer their crowns to God, to praise Him by means of the musical instruments they hold in their hands, and to petition Him by means of the cups which contain their prayers.

In such a divine order, nothing could be left to chance; and all life had to be brought into an organizational plan that would conform to this cosmic scheme of things. The stream of authority, descending from Christ through St. Peter to his papal successors, flowed out from Rome in three main directions. The Holy Roman emperor received his crown from the hands of the Roman pontiff, and, in turn, all the kings of the Western

184. *Prophet*, doorjamb of narthex portal, St. Pierre, Moissac. Early 12th century.

world owed him homage, and on downward from the great lords to the humblest serf, all of whom had a preordained place in this great cosmic plan. Next, the archbishops and bishops received their mitres in Rome, and in their bishoprics they were feudal lords in their own right. Under them, the so-called "secular" clergy, from the parish priest to the deacon, owed their allegiance to the superiors from whom they received their orders. Finally, the monastic communities under their abbots also owed their allegiance to the pope; and through their loyal support of the papacy, the Cluniac order grew so strong that its abbot was, other than the pope, the most powerful churchman in Christendom.

Beginning as a small independent monastery, Cluny was from the first exempted from tribute to any power save that of the pope alone. But instead of remaining an independent unit like other Benedictine abbeys, Cluny adopted the feudal principle by expanding and absorbing other monasteries until it dominated the monastic movement. As the head of a monarchical system, the order was the most powerful unifying force of the time, not only in religious and political affairs but in architectural, artistic, and musical thought as well. Through this adherence to the feudal system, it became a great landowning institution, and in an economy where land was the sole source of wealth, the monasteries became the principal commissioners of works of art. In a world where faith triumphed over reason and where the sole road to salvation was through the Church, the Cluniac order acted as the mainstay of the Roman tradition and helped spread its authority, doctrines, and liturgy all over Christendom.

The ranks of the monks were drawn mainly from the aristocratic class, whose members were among the few who were free to choose their own way of life. All the higher Church offices were held principally by men from noble families, often by younger sons not eligible under the law of primogeniture to inherit the feudal estates. The vow of poverty applied only to individual ownership, and collectively a monastic community resembled a feudal manor. It was only in later times that the mendicant orders of monks attempted to interpret the vow of poverty literally. Hence, Romanesque art was also an aristocratic art, and it remained so throughout the period with the means of patronage concentrated in the hands of its abbots and bishops.

The Romanesque abbey church was organized according to a rigid hierarchical plan that mirrored the strict order of precedence in the processionals of the liturgy for which it was the setting. By its insistence on visible proportions, it bespoke the invisible plan of a divinely ordered world. The regularity of the monastic buildings that surrounded it likewise was designed to enclose those who expressed their willingness to conform to such a cosmic regularity of life, and thus to constitute a human reflection of the divinely established plan for the salvation of mankind. The very spaciousness of the abbey church was far in excess of anything that was needed to accommodate the few hundreds who normally worshiped there. It was, however, the monument that mirrored the unshakable religious convictions of Romanesque man; and, as the house of the Lord and Ruler of the universe, it became a palace surpassing the dreams of glory of any king on the face of the earth. In the insecurity of the feudalistic world, Romanesque man built a fortress for his faith and for his God, which was designed to withstand the onslaughts of heretics and heathens as well as to survive the more elemental forces of wind, weather, and fire. Furthermore, the abbey church was the place where the heavenly monarch held court, and where His subjects could pay Him their never-ceasing homage in the divine services that went on day and night, year in and year out.

This hierarchical principle, moreover, applied not only to the social and ecclesiastical stratifications but also to the basic thought processes. Authority for all things rested firmly on the

185. St. Front, Périgueux (view from southwest). 11th century. Main church 185 × 185', tower 215' high.

(left) 186. Interior, Monreale Cathedral, Sicily. 1174–1189.

(below) 187. Sant' Ambrogio, Milan (view from west). *c.* 1181. Length, including atrium, 390′, width 92′.

Scriptures and the interpretations of them by the early Church fathers. Rightness and fitness were determined by how ancient the tradition was, and scholarship consisted not so much in treading new intellectual paths as in the elucidation of the traditional sources. To the educated, this process took the form of learned commentaries; to the unlettered, it was expressed in the cult of relics. Thousands took to the dusty pilgrimage roads and traveled across France and Spain to touch the legendary tomb of the Apostle James at Compostela. In the arts, this veneration of the past made mandatory the continuance of such traditional forms as the Early Roman Christian basilica and the music of the Gregorian chant.

Yet this traditionalism, curiously enough, never led to stagnation or uniformity. In making learned commentaries on the Scriptures, the writers unconsciously, and sometimes quite consciously, interpreted them in the light of contemporary views. And as the untutored populace traveled about Europe on pilgrimages and later went to the Near East on the crusades, it absorbed new ideas that eventually were to jar the provincialism of feudal times into a more dynamic social structure.

All the arts, however, exhibited an extraordinary inventiveness and such a rich variety as to make the Romanesque one of the most spontaneous and original periods in history. Diversity rather than unity was the rule of Romanesque architecture. Regional building traditions and the availability of craftsmen and materials contributed to the varied pattern. At St. Mark's in Venice (Fig. 331) and St. Front at Périgueux in southern France (Fig. 185), the Romanesque combined the multidomed Byzantine style with Greek-cross ground plans. In Sicily at Cefalu and Monreale (Fig. 186), it revealed a mixture of stark Norman spired forms, Saracenic pointed arches, and rich Byzantine mosaic interiors. In Spain, the Moorish influence is felt; in northern Italy, Sant' Ambrogio at Milan (Fig. 187) has the rich red brickwork and square belfry towers typical of Lombardy; while in central Italy, the Romanesque is characterized by zebra-striped exteriors composed of alternating strips of dark-green and cream-colored marbles, as at the Baptistry of Florence (Fig. 263) and the Cathedral of Pisa (Fig. 188).

Romanesque structures never become types as Greek temples, Byzantine churches, and the later Gothic cathedrals did. Each building and each region sought its own solutions. Through constant experimentation, the Romanesque architects found the key to new structural principles, such as their vaulting techniques; and, by gradually achieving complete command of their medium, they were able to let their buildings grow from heavy fortresslike structures into edifices of considerable elegance. Meanwhile, the decorators groped their way toward the revival of monumental sculpture and mural painting. The need for larger and better choirs likewise led to the invention of notational systems, and the emotional exuberance in religious worship made many modifications of the traditional chant, which eventually culminated in the art of counterpoint. In all, the creative vitality exhibited in each art medium is a constant source of astonishment.

Within the formal framework provided by the abbey church, architectural detail, sculpture and other decorative arts, music, and liturgy combined as integral parts of the complete architectonic design. The vast nave and transepts of a church were designed as a resonant hall for the chant, just as the tympanum over the entrance portal and the semidomed interior of the apse were the settings for sculptural and painted mural embellishments. The sculptural representations of plainsong on the ambulatory capitals in the third abbey church at Cluny show a union of music and sculpture, while their inscriptions add a literary third dimension. All the arts converge into the unified structure of the liturgy, since all were created in the monastic concept for service in the glorification of God.

(above) 188. Pisa Cathedral. Begun 1063. 320 × 115', transept 230' wide.

(below) 189. MASTER MATTEO. *Self-portrait*. Detail from Pórtico de la Gloria, Cathedral of Santiago de Compostela, Spain. 1168–1188.

6 · THE FEUDAL ROMANESQUE STYLE

THE NORMAN CONQUEST AND THE BAYEUX TAPESTRY

While a monastery was a haven of peace, a feudal manor was an armed fortress. While the cloistered brothers were laying up treasures in heaven, the feudal lords were garnering theirs on earth. And while the monk was a man of prayer, the landed baron was a man of war.

Surviving examples of secular art from the Romanesque period are so rare that each is practically unique. The treasures of a monastery or cathedral were under the watchful eye of the clergy, and religious restraints against raiding Church property usually were strong enough to prevent wanton destruction. The same cannot be said for secular property. Feudal castles constantly were subject to siege, and those that survived frequently were remodeled in later centuries with the changing fortunes of their successive owners. Among the best preserved of these Romanesque residences are the Imperial Palace near Goslar, Germany (Fig. 190); the Wartburg Castle, where Tannhäuser's famous songfest took place (Fig. 200); and some parts of the Palace of the Normans in Sicily, notably the Dining Hall of Roger II (Figs. 191, 192).

Towns did grow up in the protective shadows of a castle, a monastery, or a cathedral, but only a few urban dwellings remain, such as those at Cluny (Fig. 193). Their arched doorways facing the street sometimes were decorated by sculptured hunting scenes or representations of an artisan's trade—a cobbler bending over his workbench, for example, or a merchant showing cloth to a client. Of interior decorations—mural paintings, wall hangings, furniture, and the like—almost nothing is left. And, since poetry and music were intended to be heard rather than read by these feudal people, little of either was written down.

History, however, is filled with accidents, and by coincidence a single large-scale example of secular pictorial art survives because it was designed for a church instead of a castle. The only French epic poem before the crusades owes its present existence to the hand of some monastic scribe who happened to write it down either for some minstrel with a poor memory or because he wanted to preserve it after it had ceased to be sung. The one authentic melody to which such poetry was chanted is extant because it was included as a jest in a 13th-century musical play.

(above) Oseberg Burial Ship, detail of prow. *c.* 825. Wood. University Museum of Antiquities, Oslo.

General Events

800	Charlemagne crowned Holy Roman emperor in Rome
805	Charlemagne's Chapel at Aix-la-Chapelle (Aachen) built in the style of San Vitale in Ravenna
841	Vikings invaded northern France and colonized French territory
911	Dukedom of Normandy ceded to Northmen by King Charles the Simple of France
c.1000	Leif Eriksen, Viking navigator, believed to have reached coast of North America
1000	Minstrels convened during Lenten season at Fécamp in Normandy
1035	William (c.1027–1087) succeeded his father Robert as duke of Normandy after the latter's death on pilgrimage to Jerusalem
1040	Abbey of Jumiège rebuilt in Norman style
1043	Imperial Palace of Holy Roman emperors built near Goslar (Germany)
1051	Duke William visited England; probably received promise of English succession from Edward the Confessor
1053	William married Matilda, daughter of Duke of Flanders, who traced ancestry from Alfred the Great
1056	Westminster Abbey (Church of Peter Apostle), in Norman style, dedicated by Edward the Confessor in London
1057	Normans began conquest of southern Italy
1059	Pope Nicholas II granted dispensation for marriage of William and Matilda; as expiation they founded abbeys of St. Stephen and Holy Trinity at Caen
1061	Duke Harold of England visited Normandy, apparently upholding William's claim to English throne
1061– 1091	Norman conquest of Sicily under Roger I (1031–1101)
c.1064	Church of St. Étienne (Abbaye-aux-hommes) begun at Caen under patronage of William
	Church of Ste. Trinité (Abbaye-aux-Dames) begun at Caen under patronage of Matilda
1066	Death of Edward the Confessor, king of England; Coronation of Harold as his successor; invasion of England by William the Conqueror; Battle of Hastings: English forces defeated; Harold killed; William crowned king of England
1078	Tower of London begun by William the Conqueror
1085	Domesday Survey, census and land survey of England, ordered by William as basis for taxation
c.1088	Bayeux Tapestry completed in an English embroidery workshop (probably)
1112– 1154	Roger II ruled Sicily
1132	Palace of Normans begun in Palermo, Sicily, containing Dining Hall of Roger II, and Capella Palatina
c.1237–c.1288	Adam de la Halle, author and composer of *Le Jeu de Robin et Marion* (c.1280), a pastoral play with music containing only authentic example of a *chanson de geste* melody

190. Imperial Palace at Goslar, Lower Saxony, Germany. Begun 1043, rebuilt 1132. (left) Chapel of St. Ulrich. 11th century.

191. Dining Hall of Roger II, Palace of the Norman Kings, Palermo. *c.* 1132.

192. Ceiling, Dining Hall of Roger II, Palermo. *c.* 1132.

And the keep, or fortress, that William the Conqueror constructed in London is still intact partly because of its later usefulness as a royal residence and prison and possibly because it housed an important chapel.

The single large-scale example of pictorial art is the so-called "Bayeux Tapestry," one of the most eloquent documents of this or any other time. Here, in visual form, is the story of the conquest of England by William the Conqueror recounted from the Norman point of view, in the course of which a vivid picture of the life and attitudes of feudal man unfolds. The term *tapestry* is a misnomer, justified in this case because of its function as a wall hanging. Since the design is applied in woolen yarn to a coarse linen surface rather than woven into the cloth itself, it is more accurately described as an embroidery. Such cloth decorations were used to cover the bare stone walls of castles, but in this case the extraordinary dimensions—20 inches wide and 231 feet long— and possession over the centuries by Bayeux Cathedral indicate that this tapestry or embroidery was intended to cover the plain strip of masonry over the nave arcade of that building. It was probably the product of one of the renowned

193. Romanesque house, Cluny. *c.* 1159.

English embroidery workshops and apparently was completed about 20 years after the great battle it describes. The central figure is, of course, William the Conqueror, who indelibly stamped his powerful personality on the north European scene throughout the latter half of the 11th century. The span of time is from the closing months of the reign of Edward the Confessor to that fateful day in 1066 when the Conqueror made good his claim to the throne by putting the English forces to rout at the Battle of Hastings.

The Bayeux Tapestry, in complete presentations, is divided into 79 panels, or scenes. The first part (panels 1–34) is concerned with William's reception of Harold, an English duke, whose mission to Normandy ostensibly was to tell William that he was to succeed Edward the Confessor as king of England. In one of these scenes, William and Harold are seen at Bayeux (Fig. 194), *where Harold took an oath to Duke William.* (The italics here and later are literal translations of the Latin inscriptions that run along the top of the Tapestry above the scenes they describe.) Placing his hands on the reliquaries that repose on the two altars, Harold apparently swears to uphold William's claim, although the exact nature of the oath is left vague. This is, however, the episode that later became the justification for the English campaign—because Harold, false to his supposed sworn word, had had himself crowned king. In these early panels, in the upper and lower borders, a running commentary on the

action continues a tradition begun in manuscript illuminations. Here the commentary is in the form of animal figures that were familiar to the people of the time from bestiaries and sculpture and the allusion is to certain fables of Aesop. The choice of the fox and crow, the wolf and stork, and the ewe, goat, and cow in the presence of the lion all have to do with treachery and violence and serve to point out the perfidious character of Harold.

William is seated serenely on his ducal throne, foreshadowing his future dignity as king. The scene, furthermore, actually is located in Bayeux Cathedral, the exterior of which is shown in the curious representation to the left of the seated William. Bayeux's bishop was none other than Odo, William's half brother, who in all probability commissioned the tapestry. If the visual evidence is taken literally, Odo's part in subsequent events was considerable. Although on this occasion his presence is only implied, Odo invariably turns up in every other important scene—giving William advice on the building of his fleet, blessing the meal after the landing in England, sitting in on the council of war, and exhorting the troops to greater deeds in the thick of battle. His participation is not at all improbable, since as a feudal bishop Odo was not only the master of manors and forests but the liege lord of more than a hundred knights. As if this were not enough, Odo is shown riding into battle swinging a huge mace, bearing out the medieval saying, "The bloodier the hand, the better the bishop." According to

194. *Harold Swearing Oath*, detail of Bayeux Tapestry. *c.* 1073–1088. Wool embroidery on linen. 20″ high, whole 231′ long. Town Hall, Bayeux.

195. *Death and Burial of Edward the Confessor*, detail of Bayeux Tapestry.

196. *Norman Ships Sailing toward English Coast*, detail of Bayeux Tapestry.

the curious convention of the time, however, his ecclesiastical position forbade his spilling the blood of the enemy with such worldly weapons as the sword and the spear. On this occasion, he seemed determined to keep pace with Archbishop Turpin in the *Song of Roland*, who delivered in the battle described in this literary epic "more than one thousand blows." Odo possibly intended that the tapestry be exhibited each year on the anniversary of William's conquest, and thus forever to commemorate the glory of that occasion—and, of course, the bravery of the bishop and builder of the church.

The main course of the action in the Bayeux Tapestry moves like the words on a printed page—that is, from left to right. At times, however, it was necessary to represent a pertinent episode apart from the principal action, whereupon the pictorial narrator simply reversed the usual order and moved his scene from right to left, thus, in effect, achieving a kind of visual parenthesis and avoiding any confusion with the flow of the main story. Such a reversal is employed in the scene depicting the death and burial of the Confessor (Fig. 195). On the right and side near the top is *King Edward in his bed* as he *addresses his faith-*

ful retainers. On one side of him is a priest; Harold is on the other; while the queen and her lady-in-waiting are mourning at the foot of the bed. Below, under the words *here he has died,* the body is being prepared for the last rites. Moving toward the left, the funeral procession approaches *the church of St. Peter the Apostle,* the Romanesque predecessor of Westminster Abbey in London, which Edward had built and dedicated but ten years before, while the hand of God descends in blessing. The procession includes a group of tonsured monks reading prayers and two acolytes ringing the funeral bells.

When William received word that Harold had been crowned, he immediately determined on invasion, and the second part of the Tapestry (panels 35–53) is concerned with the preparations for his revenge up to the eve of the battle. After all was in readiness, he set sail *and crossed the sea* (Fig. 196). The ships seen in the Tapestry are similar to those in which William's restless Viking ancestors invaded the French coast two centuries before (Fig. 197 and p. 159), and it was in just such ships that Leif Eriksen and his fellow mariners apparently reached the eastern coast of North America earlier in the same century.

After the landing, the grand finale begins with the assembling of forces for the great battle (panels 54–79). The Norman side has both archers on foot and knights on horseback, while the English fight in a solid phalanx with immense battleaxes, small spears, and clubs with stone heads. The Normans move in from left to right and the English from the opposite direction. The climax of the battle is reached in a wild scene at a ravine (Fig. 198), where men and horses are tumbling about while the *English and French fall together in battle.* Shortly after, Harold is killed, and the fighting concludes with the *English turned in flight.* The lower border in these scenes spares none of the horrors of warfare; dismembered limbs are strewn about, scavengers strip coats of

197. Oseberg Burial Ship. *c.* 825. Wood. University Museum of Antiquities, Oslo.

198. *Climax of Battle of Hastings*, detail of Bayeux Tapestry. (See also Plate 11.)

mail from the bodies of the fallen, and naked corpses are left on the field.

The design of the Bayeux Tapestry is dominantly linear and, like the illuminated manuscripts of the time, is rendered in two dimensions with no suggestion of spatial depth. The coarseness of the linen and the thickness of the wool, however, create interesting textural contrasts. The eight shades of woolen yarn—three blues, light and dark green, red, buff yellow, and gray—make for a vivid feeling of color, which is not used for natural representation but to enliven the design. Some men have blue hair, others green, and horses often have two blue and two red legs. Faces are merely outlined, though some attempt at portraiture is made in the various likenesses of William (Plate 11). Details, such as costumes, armor, mode of combat, and the deployment of troops in battle, however, are done with great accuracy. For this reason, the Tapestry is a never-ending source of amazement and one of the most important historical documents on the manner of life in the 11th century—so much so that its historical value is often allowed to overshadow its quality as a work of art. Admittedly crude and at times naïve, the Bayeux Tapestry does not elaborate details, for it is more concerned with telling its story, and the sweeping effect of the whole takes precedence over any one of its parts. As Hamlet advised his actors, the play is the thing—not the gesticulations, the declamation, or the ranting and roaring. So the Tapestry was addressed to men of action in a century in which deeds were admired more than words.

The Bayeux Tapestry is a thing of infinite variety. In the handling of the narration, after a slow beginning with frequent digressions, the designer went on in the middle panels to the rather feverish preparations that culminated in the breathless climax of the battle. In both tempo and organization, the Tapestry can stand comparison with the best works in narrative form, visual or verbal. The details, whether in the main panels or in the upper or lower borders, are handled so imaginatively that they not only embellish the design but add visual accents, comment on the action, and further the flow of the plot. Scenes are separated one from another by buildings that figure in the story and by such devices as the stylized trees that are mere conventions. So skillfully are these arranged that the continuity of the whole is never impeded, and the observer is hardly aware of their presence. All in all, a successful work of art designed for such a long and narrow space is a feat of visual virtuosity of no small order, and it leaves no doubt that it is the product of a master designer.

SONG OF ROLAND

A *chanson de geste* is a song of deeds, an action story in poetic form sung by a minstrel to the accompaniment of a viol or lyre, an epic poem in Old French, the medieval vernacular language of France, rather than in Latin. The *Chanson de Roland*, or *Song of Roland*, is narrated in an abrupt, direct manner, and transitions between episodes are sudden and unprepared. A martial atmosphere surrounds the characters, including the fighting Archbishop Turpin as well as the Archangels Gabriel and Michael who, like the Valkyries in the German epic *Song of the Nibelungs*, swoop down on the battlefield to bear the souls of fallen warriors to heaven. Though nominally set in an earlier time, the *Song of Roland* is, both in form and spirit, the product of the warlike feudalistic 11th century, and various chroniclers mention it in connection with the Battle of Hastings. Guy of Amiens, one of William and Matilda's courtiers, who died only ten years after the battle, was the author of a Latin poem about a jongleur by the name of Taillefer. This "minstrel whom a very brave heart ennobled," Guy relates, led William's forces into the battle throwing his sword in the air, catching it again, and singing a Song of Roland. William of Malmesbury, writing about fifty years after the battle, tells that William on that day started the *Song of Roland*, "in order that the warlike example of that hero might stimulate the soldiers." And one of the canons of the Bayeux Cathedral, who was the author of a history of the dukes of Normandy called the *Roman de Rou*, includes a verse which goes:

> Taillefer who was famed for song,
> Mounted on a charger strong,
> Rode on before the Duke, and sang
> Of Roland and of Charlemagne,
> Oliver and the vassals all
> Who fell in fight at Roncevals.

Taillefer, in the age-old tradition of minstrelsy, was a mime and singing actor, and his rendition of the epic was undoubtedly accompanied by skillful vocal declamation as well as with appropriate gestures and action.

The *Song of Roland* is thus a direct-action story, set in the time of Charlemagne and relating incidents from the campaign in northern Spain where that Emperor had been battling the pagan Saracens for seven long years. Roland, Charlemagne's favorite nephew, and the twelve peers, flower of French knighthood, had been left in charge of the rear guard, while Charles and the main body of the army were crossing the Pyrenees back into France. Betrayed by a false kinsman, strongly paralleling the episode of William and Harold in the Bayeux Tapestry, Roland is attacked near Roncevals by overwhelming pagan forces. The rear guard is cut to pieces, and Roland, before dying a hero's death, sounds his ivory horn summoning his uncle and his army from a great distance.

The third part of the poem has to do with the vengeance of Charlemagne, just as the cor-responding section of the Bayeux Tapestry related that of William. All is action and heroism, with swords flashing, helmets gleaming, drums beating, horns blowing, banners snapping, and steeds prancing. The battle unfolds in what amounts to a blow-by-blow account, echoing frequently with such phrases as "wondrous and fierce is the battle." (Quotations are from Isabel Butler's translation, published by Houghton Mifflin, 1904.) First one hears of the preparations in the camp of Charles. The poet, using a cumulative technique, describes the ten battalions one by one. Knight is added to knight, battle group to battle group, weapon to weapon, in order to build up the full monumentality of the occasion in the listeners' minds and imaginations. All the forces of Western Christendom are eventually drawn up on Charlemagne's side —the French, Normans, Bavarians, Germans, Bretons, and so on. The virtues of the men invariably are those of bravery, valiance, and hardiness; they have no fear of death; never do they flee the battlefield; and their horses are swift and good.

Then quite suddenly and without any transition we are in the midst of the pagan hordes. Ten Saracen battalions are described, and in order to show how the Christians were outnumbered, still another ten is added. The fearsomeness of the enemy, however, is not owed to numbers alone but to their ferocious character. The only admirable quality allowed them is that of being good fighters; otherwise they are hideous to behold, fierce and cruel, and love evil. Yet in spite of this they "ride on like goodly warriors." The physical appearance of the people from these strange parts is fantastically exaggerated. The men of Milciani, for instance, "have huge heads, and along the spine of their backs grow bristles like those of a wild boar." Of the warriors from the desert of Occiant, it is said that "their skins are hard like iron, wherefore they have no need of hauberks or helms [coats of mail and helmets]." Later, during the battle, these same men of Occiant "bray and neigh, and the men of Arguille yelp like dogs." Their religious life is just as much misunderstood as their appearance. The pagans are represented as polytheists who worship as strange an assortment of gods as was ever assembled—Apollo, Tervagant, and Mohamet. When things are not going well from their point of view, they upbraid these gods, take the statue of Apollo and "trod him under their feet"; Tervagant is robbed of his carbuncle; and Mohamet is cast "into a ditch, for the dogs and the pigs to worry and gnaw." Later, when Marsila, the king of Spain, dies, the listener hears that "eager devils seize upon his soul." Such descriptions could not have been written after the Crusades had brought Western warriors into contact with Moslem culture, and so, like the foreigners depicted on the Vézelay tympanum (Fig. 167), the imagery is filled with naïve wonder.

With the lines of battle thus drawn, the setting is described in a single line: "Vast is the plain and wide the fields." Then as the conflict begins, battalion falls on battalion, hewing and hacking away, Christian knights hurtle against pagan knights the whole day long until finally the battle is reduced to a personal encounter between Charlemagne and his opposite number, Baligant the Amiral (admiral). All the formidable fighting qualities of friend and foe are concentrated in these two contestants. Both are described as being older than the hills, and their beards are whiter than snow. The patriarchal image of society is consistently emphasized, just as it is in the representations of the elders of the Apocalypse found so frequently in Romanesque sculpture. Charles is called at times "the Emperor with the hoary beard," and at others "Charles the Old." Since all takes place in the present tense, he is by this time well on into his third century. But his adversary is not to be outdone in this respect, and Baligant is so old that he antedates Vergil and Homer. Charlemagne, of course, is the epitome of Christian virtue, but his opponent generously is allowed to be wise "according to his law, and in battle he is fierce and mighty." The combat of the centenarians is on, and in their initial clash their spears shiver against one another, their coats of mail are rent, the blows bring them both to the ground, and the battle continues on foot with bare swords. Each tries to convert the other between blows; and just when all seems blackest, with Charles sorely wounded, the Angel Gabriel appears beside him, and his strength miraculously returns. "He smites the Amiral with the sword of France, shatters the helmet which shines with precious stones, carves through the skull that the brains run out, and through the face even to the white beard, that the Amiral falls dead beyond all help." After this, the pagans flee and the day is won.

The lines of the original Old French proceed according to a rhyming scheme of crude assonance in which the final syllables of each line correspond roughly in sound. The last words of each line of one of the strophes will suffice to illustrate this principle of assonance: *magne, Espaigne, altaigne, remaigne, fraindre, muntaigne, m'enaimet, reclaimet, ataignet.* Much of the direct character and rugged strength of the poem is attributable to rigid avoidance of embellishment. This is observable in such minute details as the forward motion within such single lines as: *So sent Rollanz de tun tens ni ad plus.* Nothing is allowed to impede the progress of these sturdy military monosyllables. So consistently is this carried out all along the line that it even extends to the delineation of the characters themselves. Each is the embodiment of a single ideal and human type: Ganelon is all treachery and hatred; Roland, bravery to the point of rashness; Oliver, reason and caution; and Charles, preeminent in his solitary grandeur, represents the majesty of Church and state. Through each one of these devices separately and through all of them cumulatively, the poem as a whole rises to the heights of epic art. Its language, style, and form thus well become the brave deeds of the heroic men with which it is concerned.

THE ART OF MINSTRELSY

"A verse without music is a mill without water," said Folquet of Marseilles, the troubadour whom Dante immortalized in his *Paradise.* Poetry in medieval times was a popular art form in which verses were chanted by a *jongleur,* or minstrel, to the accompaniment of a viol or lyre. No festive occasion was complete without a minstrel who sang *chansons de geste,* lays, and romances, told tales and fables, played on a variety of musical instruments, performed dances, and astonished with juggling and sleight-of-hand tricks.

Records of these jongleurs go back many centuries. It is known that jongleurs convened at Fécamp in Normandy in the year 1000 and that they met together regularly during the slack season of Lent, when the Church forbade their public performances, to learn one another's tricks and techniques, and increase their repertories with new tales and songs. A lively account of their place in medieval society is contained in a description of a wedding feast in Provence, which says: "Then the *joglars* stood up, each one anxious to make himself heard; then you could hear instruments resounding in many a key. ... One played the Lay of the Honeysuckle, another that of Tintagel, another that of the Faithful Lovers, another the lay that Ivan made. ... Everyone performed at his best and the noise of the instrumentalists and the voices of the narrators made a considerable uproar in the hall."

The jongleurs of the 11th century were not of noble birth as were most of the later troubadours, trouvères, and minnesingers, but they were welcomed in every castle and abbey. Their importance in the creation of a secular literature in the vernacular languages of medieval times can hardly be overestimated. The feudal society of the

11th century was groping its way toward distinctive art forms of its own, as seen in the *chanson de geste*. The musical part of these epics was far more primitive than the poetry, but, crude as it was, it marked the beginning of secular art music, separated in style both from the church models and the lost folk music of that time. Under the patronage of the feudal nobility, this music was to bloom in the 12th and 13th centuries into the full-fledged art of the troubadours, trouvères, and minnesingers. Courtly tournaments, brave knights winning fair ladies (Fig. 199), and aristocratic poets making music with minstrels (Plate 12) enlivened the nobles' entertainments in the Gothic period. The practice of holding songfests also began at this time. The well-preserved Romanesque castle at Wartburg (Fig. 200), for instance, was the setting of a famous minstrels' contest in 1207—an incident that Richard Wagner later dramatized in his opera *Tannhäuser*.

Since the 11th-century secular music forms were just emerging, the models and prototypes undoubtedly were derived from certain formulas for church music. The simple repetitive melodies of the *chansons de geste*, together with the assonated verses and insistent rhythms of the poetry, had much in common with the litany— though, of course, the subject matter differed radically. It is greatly to be regretted that the

199. *Walther von Klungen in Tournament.* 14th century. Manesse Manuscript of German Minnesingers. Heidelberg Library. (See also Plate 12.)

200. Wartburg Castle, near Eisenach, Germany. *c.* 1175.

Chanson de geste melody (11th century)   ADAM DE LA HALLE (after Gennrich)

Au - di - gier, dit Raim - ber - ge, bou - se vous di.

Aucassin et Nicolette, strophe or *laisse* (13th century)   ADAM DE LA HALLE (after Gennrich)

Qui vau - roit bons vers o - ir ___ del de -
de deus biax en - fans pe - tis ___ Ni - co -

port du duel cai - tif
le - te Au cas - sins...

musical setting of the *Song of Roland* has not been preserved. While jongleurs could refresh their memories of longer epics from the manuscripts they carried in the leather pouches that they wore, these manuscripts included no musical parts. Hence it is safe to assume that the melodies were so simple there was no need to write them down.

The music of the *chansons de geste*, according to medieval sources, consisted of a short melody with one note to a syllable, repeated over and over for each verse in the manner of a litany or folk song. At the end of each strophe, or group of lines, was a melodic appendage, which served as a refrain much like the alleluias between the verses of psalms and hymns. In the manuscript of the *Chanson de Roland* the enigmatic letters AOI appear after each of the 321 strophes, while in the songs of troubadours and minnesingers the letters are EUOUAE or some variant. EUOUAE is an abbreviation of the last two words of the lesser Doxology, *saeculorum amen*, and thus is a link between the troubadour's refrain and a Gregorian melody. The AOI in the *Song of Roland* manuscript possibly refers to some similar liturgical cadence formula now lost. If so, either it refers to a repeated vocal cadenza at the end of each strophe, a kind of punctuation mark for the ear to relieve the audience's attention momentarily from the words (as with the "Fa la la's" of the later Renaissance madrigals), or it indicates a

place where a short instrumental interlude was performed on the viol or lyre. Whatever the explanation, the focus of attention in these epics was on the words of the poem itself, and the musical element was subordinate. In the closing formula, however, the purely musical element could have come to the fore with whatever special effects the jongleur had at his command.

The single authentic example of a *chanson de geste* melody that survives is found in a little pastoral play from the 13th century by Adam de la Halle, where it is quoted humorously by one of the characters. The two halves of this melody are repeated once for each line of the strophe, following which there would have been a short cadenza or refrain for either the voice or an instrument. The operation of this refrain principle is found in a song from *Aucassin et Nicolette*, a French *chante-fable*. Written about a century later, it is similar in style to that of the *chanson de geste*. The melody of the first eight measures is sung for each line of the strophe, each time to different words. The refrain in the final three bars is then either sung or played between each of the verses and again at the end. The extreme simplicity of these melodies indicates that the music alone would not have held the attention of an audience. The dominant interest was obviously epic poetry, and the minstrel's performance of it with appropriate action, gestures, and vocal inflection.

NORMAN ARCHITECTURE

The architecture of the Normans was sufficiently important to give one aspect of the Romanesque style the name of Norman. The building done in 11th-century Normandy not only had a lasting effect on that region of France but reached a logical conclusion in the keeps, castles, abbeys, and cathedrals that the Normans later built in England. Since the Romanesque style in England dates from the time of the conquest, it is still referred to there as the Norman style.

Norman architecture, like many other facets of Norman culture, resulted from the union of the rugged pagan spirit of the Vikings and the Gallic Christian remnants of the disintegrated Carolingian Empire. As a representative product of these people, their architecture reflects blunt strength and forthright character. Both the Carolingian and Viking societies were nomadic. Charlemagne and his successors as well as the dukes of Normandy down to William's time frequently shifted their residences, and the insecurity of the times discouraged building in general. But as the feudal system reached its mature stage and a more settled order became possible, the Norman conquerors turned to the assimilation and devel-

opment of the vast new lands they had acquired instead of seeking further conquests. William's policy thus shifted from offensive to defensive. Earlier he had discouraged the construction of castles and sanctioned only monasteries; now he proposed to impress his new subjects with solid and impregnable fortresses as well as feats of sword on the field of battle.

The Tower of London (Fig. 201), or more specifically the White Tower (Fig. 203), was begun by the Conqueror about 1078 and finished by his successor in order to defend and dominate the town. Its form was that of a Norman keep, and as such it was something new to England. The Tower is simply a massive, square, compact stone building, divided into four stories which rise 92 feet with a turret at each corner. A glance at the plan (Fig. 202) will show some of its many irregularities. Its four sides, for instance, are unequal in length, and its corners are therefore not right angles; three of its turrets are square, while one is round; the one on the west rises 107 feet, while that on the south is 118 feet high; the walls vary from 11 to 15 feet in thickness; and the interior is divided from top to bottom in two unequal parts by a wall running from north to south.

The barrenness of its exterior was well suited to the White Tower's function as a fortress, but

201. Tower of London (air view). 1078-1090.

THE AGE OF
VARIOUS PARTS
OF THE TOWER
OF LONDON

Roman

William I & II C. 1086-97

Richard I 1189-99

Henry III 1216-72

Edward I 1272-1307

Edward III & Richard II
C. 1350-99

Henry VIII 1509-1547

17th Century

18th Century

19th & 20th Centuries

0   50   100   150   200
SCALE OF FEET

202. Tower of London, plan.

203. White Tower, London.
c. 1081–1090. 92′ high.

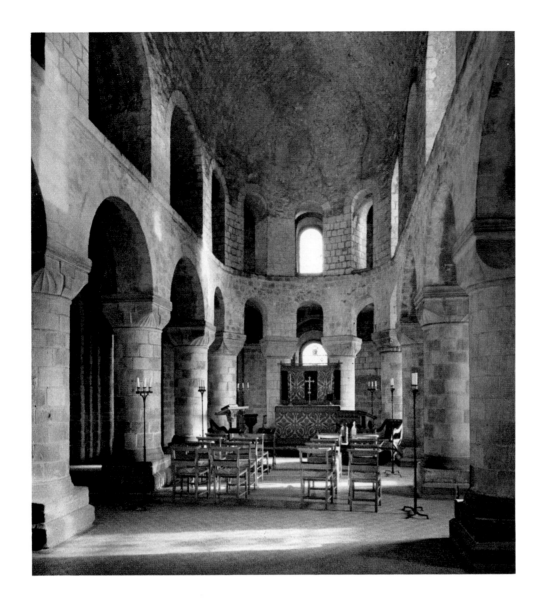

204. St. John's Chapel, Tower of London. 1078–1097.

the austerity of the interior was a commentary on the bleakness and general lack of physical comforts of medieval life. The Tower was divided into four stories by means of wooden floors, and its darkness was relieved only by narrow, slitted, glassless windows, which were more important as launching sites for arrows against an enemy than as sources of light and ventilation. After Norman times, other buildings were added until the whole became a concentric system of fortifications with the old Norman keep as its heart. From William's time to the present, the Tower has been in continuous use either as a fortress, palace, or prison.

From the plan, it will be seen that the main floor has three divisions: a large council chamber, which also doubled as a banqueting hall, a smaller presence chamber, and the well-preserved St. John's Chapel (Fig. 204). Like a miniature church, this chapel has a barrel-vaulted nave of four bays, with aisles on either side that command interest because of their early use of cross vaulting. The columns of the nave arcade are thick and stubby, and the cushionlike capitals have only the most rudimentary scalloped carving by way of decoration. Above is a triforium gallery, which was used by the queen and her ladies, with slitlike windows that serve as a clearstory.

At Caen in Normandy, two buildings were under the personal protection of William and Queen Matilda and designated as their respective burial places—St. Étienne, or Abbaye-aux-Hommes (Fig. 205), and Ste. Trinité, or Abbaye-aux-Dames (Fig. 208). Since both were abbey churches, they properly belong in a discussion of the monastic Romanesque style, but here they serve to complete the picture of the Norman style. Begun just prior to the conquest, St. Étienne has

205. Façade, St. Étienne (Abbaye-aux-Hommes), Caen. *c.* 1064–1135. Nave 157½′ × 32′ 10″, towers 295′ high.

206. St. Étienne, plan.

a well-proportioned façade (Fig. 205). Four prominent buttresses divide the section below the towers into three parts that correspond to the central nave and two side aisles of the interior. Vertically, the façade rises in three stories, with the portals matching the level of the nave arcade inside, while the two rows of windows above are at the triforium and clearstory levels, respectively. The windows are mere openings and in themselves are quite undistinguished. But the functional honesty in this correspondence of exterior design and interior plan was a Norman innovation that came into general use in the Gothic period.

The twin towers belong to the original design, but their spires are later additions. As with the usual Norman church, the towers are square and in three stories, thus repeating on a higher level the triple division of the façade below. The first story is of solid masonry; the second has alternate blind and open arches; while the greater open space of the third facilitates its function as a belfry and relieves the general heaviness. Otherwise the austerity and ponderousness of the façade in general is a fitting prelude to the gloomy grandeur of the interior (Fig. 207). The church as a whole is as thoroughly rugged and masculine in character as the personality of its founder and typifies the spirit of the Norman people and their forceful leader. Less gaunt and severe is the more lyrical façade of Matilda's church, the Abbaye-aux-Dames, with its graceful arches and arcaded staged towers (Fig. 208).

When the barren façade of St. Étienne is compared to the exterior of the Tower of London, it becomes apparent that the lack of decoration was a conscious part of the design. One façade impresses by its bold outlines, sturdiness, and straightforward honesty, and the other by its sheer strength and bluntness. Though it was to be replaced soon after the crusades by Saracenic innovations, the Norman accent on structure rather than embellishment did, however, lead to advances in the art of building. In their churches, the Normans achieved more adequate lighting than in previous Romanesque structures by increasing the space allotted to the clearstory, and more unified interiors by connecting the three levels of the nave arcade, triforium, and clearstory by single vertical shafts between the bays that ran from floor to ceiling. Both these features, as well as the harmonious spatial divisions of such a façade as that of St. Étienne, later were incorporated into the Gothic style. In spite of this, however, when the work of the Normans is placed alongside that of their more skillful Burgundian contemporaries, it seems crude by com-

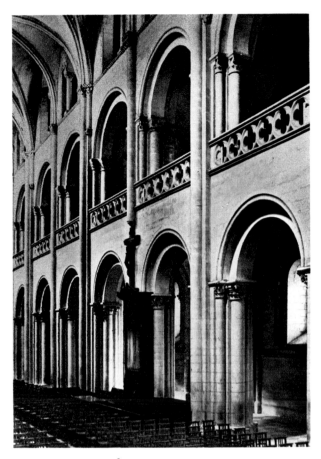

207. Interior, St. Étienne.

parison. The Normans were as blunt and brash as the Cluniacs were ingenious and subtle. The difference, in short, is that between men of action and men of contemplation.

IDEAS: FEUDALISM

The Bayeux Tapestry, the *Song of Roland*, the abbey churches at Caen, and the White Tower in London are representative examples of the Romanesque style and related in time, place, and content. Each was a high point in the development of Norman culture, falling between the dates of the Battle of Hastings in 1066 and the First Crusade in 1096. The *Song* was sung at the battle; the Tapestry was designed soon after the battle whose tale it tells (and both evidence the same form and spirit); and the building of the abbey churches and Tower coincided with the zenith of William's success and prosperity after the conquest. This relationship coincided with the climax of feudalism, and it is in the terms of this all-embracing concept that the individual works have their unity.

All the separate concepts of the Norman world were contained in the overpowering central idea of feudalism. Like the concentric rings of the inner and outer fortifications of the Tower of London (Figs. 201, 202) or the later Gothic castle complex at Carcassonne (Fig. 209), individuals in a feudal society were but tiny circles in an expanding cosmic scheme of things that determined their relations to their superiors, their peers, and their inferiors. It was a social system modeled on that of an army; and the ethic that bound the whole together was fealty, a kind of blind loyalty, with right and wrong being fixed by physical force rather than by reason and principle. The feudal system provided a proper place for every man in a strict hierarchy, with barons holding their power from their overlords, ecclesiastical or secular; dukes holding their realms from their king; and the king, emperor,

208. Façade, Ste. Trinité (Abbaye-aux-Dames), Caen. 1062–1066. Width 79′.

209. Carcassonne Castle. Gothic period, mainly 12th and 13th centuries; walls restored by Viollet-le-Duc 1855–1879.

and pope holding the earth as a fief from God. In the *Song of Roland*, for example, Charlemagne and his 12 peers were considered to be the secular counterparts of Christ and his 12 Apostles, the Apostles being vassals of Christ and Christ himself a vassal of God the Father.

The feudal virtues were faith, courage, and blind loyalty to peer and superior; any departure from this code was treachery and was dealt with by isolation and defeat. Defection had to be decided on the field of battle, with God awarding victory to the righteous cause. Enemies, however, provided their lineage was in order and their family trees properly pruned, were accorded the distinctions of honor and bravery; otherwise it would have been socially impossible to do battle with them. In the *Song of Roland* and in the Bayeux Tapestry, no one below the rank of baron figures with any degree of prominence; similarly, the abbeys of William and Matilda were intended primarily for persons of rank, and by their foundation the royal pair pledged their feudal oath to God.

In their subject matter, the *Song of Roland* and the Bayeux Tapestry have many points in common. As the song opens: "Charles the King ... has conquered all the high land down to the sea; not a castle holds out against him, not a wall or city is left unshattered, save Saragossa, which stands on a high mountain. King Marsila holds it, who loves not God, but serves Mahound, and worships Apollon; ill hap must in sooth befall him." If the simple substitution of William for Charles, England for Saragossa in Spain, the barrier of the sea for that of the mountain, and Harold for Marsila is made, the situation becomes the

contemporary one that the Tapestry so vividly portrays. Later, at the battle of Roncevals the dominant trio is Roland, Oliver, and the fighting Archbishop Turpin, in whom it is not difficult to recognize their parallels at Hastings: William and his half brothers Robert of Mortain and the irrepressible Bishop Odo.

In both *Song* and Tapestry, the cause for war ostensibly was religious. In one, it was Christianity versus paganism; in the other, the breaking of a sacred oath when Harold became king—and both causes were sanctioned by the pope. Again, in both, the enemy in the best feudal tradition was a worthy adversary, noble and brave but religiously misguided. In the *Song of Roland*, Marsila was crafty but at all times observed the rules of feudal warfare. The glory of Charlemagne's major pagan adversary, with his bright silks from Alexandria, gold of Arabia, carbuncle-studded sword, and bright gonfalons, is glowingly described in poetic language, just as Harold's knightly qualities are pictured repeatedly in visual form. In both, religious symbols figure prominently. Durendal, Roland's sword, is his most sacred possession, having within it a tooth of St. Peter, blood of St. Basil, hair of St. Denis, and a fragment of the Virgin's robe—all souvenirs of his pilgrimage to the Holy Land. The importance of such relics at this time was overwhelming. In the Tapestry, Harold's seizure of the kingly power was treacherous mainly because the oath had been sworn on the reliquaries in Bayeux Cathedral. Harold's perjury and breaking of a vow sworn under such sacrosanct conditions was sufficient cause for invasion.

Religious conviction is absolute in both *Song* and *Tapestry*. Such a sweeping statement as "Wrong the pagans, right the Christians are" leaves no room for lingering philosophical or theological doubts on the validity of the cause. In each, the importance and glorification of sheer strength and prowess at arms are apparent from the descriptive details of costume, armor, and weapons, which are dwelt upon with obvious pride. Both Tapestry and poem are set in a man's world based on clear-cut loyalties and moral and physical certainties. The chivalry in each is based on the ways of fighting men. The code of Roland and Oliver, and of William and Odo, was clearly that of "My soul to God, my life to the king, and honor for myself." It remained for the Gothic period to add: "My heart to the ladies." Roland's dying thoughts, for instance, are occupied with his family and lineage; his king, the great Charles; his country, the fair land of France; and his sword, Durendal. Significantly, he makes no mention of his betrothed, the Lady Aude. Earlier, the exasperated Oliver had reproached Roland for his rashness in not summoning aid sooner, and at that time he swore: "By this my beard, and I again see my sister, Aude the Fair, never shalt thou lie in her arms." No true or courtly love is this, only the feudal baron bestowing his female relatives like his goods and chattels on those whose faith and courage he has cause to admire. Later, after Charles returns to France, the poor Lady Aude inquires about the fate of her fiancé. The king tells her of his death and as a consolation prize offers her the hand of his son Louis, whereupon the lady expires at his feet. Whether she dies of grief for Roland or from the indelicacy of Charlemagne's suggestion is left open to conjecture. Since scarcely more than a dozen of the 4,000-odd lines of the poem are devoted to her, Henry Adams was well justified in his observation: "Never after the first crusade did any great poem rise to such heroism as to sustain itself without a heroine." Curiously enough, on the Saracen side Marsila's queen takes an important part in the affairs of state after her husband is incapacitated, while nowhere on the Christian side is a woman accorded anything like a similar status. And in the Bayeux Tapestry, the only place where a woman is mentioned by name is the enigmatic inscription *Where a cleric and Aelfgyva*, apparently introduced to give a motive for the minor episode describing an invasion of Brittany. While a few female figures are found in the borders and in attendance at the death of the Confessor, none figures with any prominence. Both works are thus as bold and direct as the poetry and art of the coming Gothic period was delicate and subtle.

Roland and his counterparts in the Tapestry fought the good fight for king and country, while the knightly heroes of the later period entered the lists for a loving glance from a pair of blue eyes, the fleeting smile on fair lips, or the fragrant petals of a rose tossed from a lady's bower.

Formal considerations of the *Song of Roland* and the Bayeux Tapestry are in keeping with their rugged character. The emphasis everywhere is on the concrete rather than the abstract, content rather than form, and narrative sequence over structure. The telling of the tale in both cases is almost completely unencumbered with either literary or visual flourishes. Just as deeds take precedence over poetic form in the *Chanson*, the narrative element in the Bayeux Tapestry is more important than the decorative detail. Every part of the Tapestry has some direct bearing on the story, and the action in the poem is so direct that it contains hardly a single figure of speech. In both, the attributes are fixed. In the Tapestry, the English always have moustaches and the Normans are clean shaven. In the poem, kings are always mighty no matter what side they may be on, and knights are invariably brave whatever their allegiance may be. Similarly, in the sculpture of the period, kings always have crowns on their heads, even if they are in bed, apostles always have bare feet, and so on. The curiously stylized trees in the Bayeux Tapestry come directly from manuscript drawings rather than from nature, and they function either as an indication that the action is taking place out of doors or as formal devices to divide one scene from another. In the epic, Roland always rests under a pine tree because he is French, while his enemies pause under olive trees because they are Saracens.

Symmetry seldom is considered. The lines of the poem, for example, are rough-hewn but heroic pentameters, which group themselves into irregular strophes averaging fourteen lines in length. Similarly, the space given to individual scenes in the Bayeux Tapestry, like the size of the compartments in the archivolt of the Vézelay tympanum (Fig. 167) and the unequal height of the arches in a Romanesque cathedral wall, such as at Pisa (Fig. 188), are disproportionate and asymmetrical.

Details in the *Chanson*, the Tapestry, St. Étienne, and the Tower of London thus remain crude and unpolished. The Romanesque in general and the Norman period in particular were an era of forming, building, experimenting, and reaching out toward new modes of expression rather than a time of crystallization, polished expression, and ultimate arrival. In architecture, the process of building was more important than what was built. The emphasis given in the Tapestry to representations of castles, fortifications, and specific buildings, such as Westminster Abbey and the abbey churches at Caen, suggests the image of a builder's world and a century of architectural activity and progress. The forthright and direct narration of deeds in the *Song* and Tapestry finds its architectural counterpart in the functional honesty of the style of the Tower and William's church at Caen. Just as the direct-action story of the *Chanson* and Tapestry takes precedence over literary form and decorative flourish, so the structural honesty of the building process, as exemplified in the Tower and St. Étienne, becomes the leading characteristic. The process of lengthening balladic poetry into the epic form of the *chanson de geste* capable of sustaining attention through the long Norman winter evenings or of extending a few pictorial panels into the heroic completeness of a tapestry depicting a major historical episode in its entirety was essentially the same as the process of piling up tall towers capable of piercing the gloomy northern skies.

The image of the Norman world as it thus builds up through the various arts is not essentially a complex one. There was little of the mystical about these clear-headed Viking adventurers. They caught on with alacrity to any progressive development of the time, whether it was the discarding of their rather inflexible mother tongue in favor of the more supple French or the adopting of many of the Cluniac moral and architectural reforms. A good example of their forthrightness is seen in the Bayeux Tapestry, where who a figure is and what he is doing are documented exactly with name and place. Whatever the Normans did, they did always with characteristic determination and energy. Thus the rugged man of action in William unites with the military monosyllables of the *Chanson*, the frank, almost comic-strip directness of the Bayeux Tapestry, and the rough-hewn stones of the Tower and abbeys to make a single monolithic structure. Each was concerned with forms of action, and whether in picture, word, or stone, the epical spirit is present. Deed on deed, syllable on syllable, stitch on stitch, image on image, stone on stone—each builds up into the great personality, heroic epic, impressive Tapestry, or gaunt Tower, and in the process reveals a Norman feudal structure of truly monumental proportions.

7 - THE GOTHIC STYLE

ILE-DE-FRANCE, LATE 12TH AND 13TH CENTURIES

In contrast to the shores of the Mediterranean, where such resplendent centers of culture as Athens, Alexandria, Antioch, Constantinople, and Rome flourished for centuries, northern Europe had been little more than a rural region with a few Roman provincial outposts and, later, a scattering of castles, monasteries, and villages. Before the 13th century not one medieval center north of the Alps could properly have been described as a city. Toward the end of the 12th century, however, Philip Augustus as king of France was promoting the destiny of Paris as his capital, enclosing it with walls and paving some of its streets with stone. The work was continued under his successors, and by the end of the 13th century Paris was the capital of a kingdom of growing importance. With its splendid Cathedral of Notre Dame, its university famed for the teaching of Abelard, Albertus Magnus, Thomas Aquinas, and Bonaventura, and with its flourishing mercantile trade capable of supporting about 150,000 inhabitants, Paris could well claim the status of a capital city. When it is remembered, however, that Constantinople was the hub of the rich East Roman Empire and had been a city of over 1,000,000 since Justinian's time, the status of this first transalpine urban center is seen in proper perspective.

The growth of Paris, while more rapid than other northern centers, was far from an isolated instance. For a full century, the town as a social unit had been gaining ascendancy over the manorial estate, and the literature of the time mentions Ghent with its turreted houses, Lille and its cloth, Tours and its grain, and how all were carrying on commerce with distant lands. With the exception of such occasional references, however, the life of medieval French towns would have remained a closed book had it not been for the visual record preserved in the castles of their feudal lords, in the monasteries, and, above all, in their cathedrals.

The prototype of the Gothic cathedral has been recognized in the Abbey Church of St. Denis just outside Paris (Fig. 210). This monastery was under the direct patronage of the French kings and was their traditional burial place. Around the middle of the 12th century its abbot was Suger, a man whose talents were as remarkable as his origin was obscure. The trusted confidant of

(above) *Visitation*, central portal, west façade, Rheims Cathedral. *c.* 1225–1245.

General Events

1096– 1291	Crusades: European Christians fought Moslems and Saracens; extended Christianity as well as opened up trade routes
1137	Louis VII began reign as king of France; married Eleanor of Aquitaine
1140	Abbey Church of St. Denis, prototype of Gothic cathedrals, begun by Abbot Suger
1142	Abelard, master of School of Notre Dame in Paris, died at Cluny
c.1150–c.1170	University of Paris founded
1163– 1235	Cathedral of Notre Dame in Paris built
c.1163	Oxford University founded; Cambridge University soon thereafter
1180	Philip Augustus crowned king of France; enclosed Paris with walls; promoted Paris as his capital city
1194– 1260	Chartres Cathedral begun after fire destroyed earlier structure; 1006 Fulbert appointed bishop of Chartres; 1020–1028 Romanesque cathedral built by Fulbert; 1134 Fulbert's cathedral destroyed by fire; 1145 Romanesque cathedral again rebuilt; 1194 fire destroyed Romanesque cathedral with exception of narthex, west portals, two towers, three stained glass windows; 1260 cathedral dedicated by Louis IX
1210	Rheims Cathedral rebuilt
1215	Magna Charta signed in England
1220	Amiens and Rouen cathedrals begun
1223	Louis VIII crowned king of France

1225	Beauvais Cathedral begun; choir finished in 1272
1226	Louis IX became king of France under regency of his mother, Blanche of Castile
1233	Chartres added to Crown territory of France
1236	Regency of Blanche of Castile ended
1240	Ste. Chapelle, royal chapel of French kings, begun in Paris
1250	Albertus Magnus taught at University of Paris
1274	Scholastic philosophy at height
	St. Bonaventura and St. Thomas Aquinas died

Philosophers

1079– 1142	Abelard
c.1193– 1280	Albertus Magnus
1221– 1274	Bonaventura
c.1225– 1274	Thomas Aquinas

Musicians

c.1122– 1192	Adam of St. Victor, joint author of hymns with St. Bernard of Clairvaux
c.1150	Leonin active at Cathedral of Notre Dame in Paris
c.1183	Perotin active at Cathedral of Notre Dame in Paris
c.1237–c.1288	Adam de la Halle, author and composer of *Le Jeu de Robin et Marion*, a pastoral play with music
c.1240	"Sumer is icumen in," oldest surviving piece of secular polyphony, written
c.1260	Franco of Cologne, musical theorist, active

two kings, he ruled France as regent while Louis VII was away on a crusade, and when he undertook the rebuilding of his abbey church, his great personal prestige, as well as its importance as the royal monastery, enabled him to call together the most expert craftsmen from all parts of the kingdom. Suger's church thus became a synthesis of all the ideas that had been tried and found successful by the best Romanesque builders. Posterity has had reason to rejoice that the abbot's enthusiasm for his project caused him to write extensively about it, and his book is an invaluable source of information about the architectural thought of the time. In 1130, when St. Denis was in the planning stage, as was mentioned, Abbot Suger had made a prolonged visit to Cluny to learn from first-hand observation about its recently completed church. His commentary on the iconography of St. Denis' windows and sculpture suggests that he took a personal hand in this part of the project, but of the architect who carried out the building no mention is made. St. Denis is notable not so much for its innovations as for its successful combining into a working relationship of such late Romanesque devices as the pointed arch, ribbed groin vault, and flying

Plate 13. North clearstory wall of nave, Chartres Cathedral.
c. 1194–1260. (See p. 186.)

Plate 14. *Blanche of Castile and St. Louis*, from *Moralized Apocalypse. c.* 1226–1234.
Illuminated manuscript. Pierpont Morgan Library, New York. (See p. 188.)

210. Façade, Abbey Church of St. Denis, near Paris. 1140–1144.

cathedral towns all. The loftiest expression of the medieval period is seen in these miracles of soaring stone—the crystalized expressions of community effort, religious exaltation, and emotional and intellectual forces of the people who created them. Gothic architecture, moreover, is a struggling, striving, dynamic urge that reaches upward to embrace infinity. Though the building process often spanned several centuries, there are no finished Gothic cathedrals. Completion can take place only in the imagination of the observer. The French medieval archeologist Viollet-le-Duc once projected such a complete cathedral with seven spires (Fig. 211)—one pair on the west façade, another on the north and on the south transept, and a climactic spire over the crossing.

Unlike an abbey church, a cathedral is located in a populated area where it comes under the jurisdiction of a bishop, whose official seat it is. A cathedral cannot rise from a plain like a

211. VIOLLET-LE-DUC. Drawing of a Gothic cathedral, complete with a full set of seven spires.

buttress. Many late Cluniac Romanesque churches had used these features separately, but not before Suger's church had they been grouped into a coherent structural system, and the abbot's position at the French court, as well as the proximity of his church to Paris, assured the widest possible currency of his ideas. Hence, St. Denis became the model for many of the Gothic cathedrals that were built in the region shortly afterward.

The Ile-de-France, the royal domain with Paris as its center, was the setting in which the Gothic style originated and where, over a period extending approximately from 1150 to 1300, it reached the climax of its development. The name of this region referred to the royal lands under the direct control of the French king, while the rest of what is now France was still under the dominion of various feudal lords. By heredity, marriage, conquest, and purchase, the Ile-de-France gradually had grown over the years into the nucleus of the future French nation, and, like a wheel with Paris as its hub, it radiated outward about 100 miles, with spokes extending toward Amiens, Beauvais, Rheims, Bourges, Rouen, and Chartres,

212. Chartres Cathedral (view from southeast).

monastic church; it needs the setting of a town where it can soar above the roofs and gables of the buildings that cluster around it. The barren exterior of an abbey forbids, while the intricate carving on the outside of a cathedral awakens curiosity and invites entrance. As the center of a cloistered life, a monastic church is richest in its dim interior, while the most elaborate decoration of a cathedral points toward the dwellings of the people. The tall towers of a Gothic cathedral need space from which to spring and room to cast their shadows. Their spires beckon the distant traveler to the shrine beneath and direct the weary steps of the toiling peasant homeward after a day in the fields, and the bells they enclose peal out to regulate the life of a whole town and its surrounding countryside. They tell of weddings and funerals and of the time for work and rest and prayer.

A cathedral is, of course, primarily a religious center, but in a time when spiritual and worldly affairs were interwoven, the religious and secular functions of a cathedral were intermingled. Its nave was not only the place for religious services but, on occasion, a town hall where the entire populace could gather for a meeting. The rich decorations that clothe the body of the cathedral told not only the story of Christianity but also the history of the town and of the activities of its people. The cathedral was thus a municipal museum on whose walls the living record of the town was carved. The iconography of a cathedral dedicated to Notre Dame was by no means concerned only with religious subjects. Since the Virgin Mary was also the patroness of the liberal arts, her cathedral was often a visual encyclopedia whose subjects ranged over the entire field of human knowledge. The pulpit was not only the place from which sermons were preached but also a podium for lectures and instruction. The sanctuary was the theater in which the constantly changing sequence of the religious drama was enacted; outside, the deep-set portals served as stage sets for the mystery plays appropriate to the season, and the porches became platforms from which minstrels and jugglers could entertain their audiences. The stone statues and stained glass were useful not only as illustrations for sermons but as picture galleries to stimulate the imagination. The choir was not only the setting for liturgical song but a concert hall or opera house, where intricate polyphonic motets were performed and the melodies of the religious dramas were chanted.

Chartres (Fig. 212), unlike Paris, was never a center of commerce but a small bishopric in the

213. Choir, Beauvais Cathedral. 1247–1272.

butchers, the bakers, and the candlestick makers, for all who practiced the same craft lived on the same street. As members of guilds, or associations, the townsmen had contributed their labor and products to the cathedral when it was being built, and as guilds they had donated windows and statuary. They also undertook to fill such continuous needs as candles for the altars and bread for the communion service.

The cathedral itself, toward which all eyes and steps were drawn, represented a composite effort of the stone cutters, masons, carpenters, and metalworkers, all of whom gave of their time, skill, and treasure to build it. It thus was the greatest single product a town and its craftsmen could produce. As a great civic monument, it was the pride of the community, and the ambitions and aspirations of its citizens determined its character and contours. In those days, the importance of a town was measured by the size and height of its cathedral as well as by the significance of the religious relics its cathedral housed. Consequently, civic rivalry was involved when the vaulting of Chartres rose 121 feet above the ground. Next came Amiens, which achieved a height of 140 feet, and finally Beauvais (Fig. 213) became the loftiest of all with the crowns of its vaulting soaring over 157 feet. At this time, the growth of town and cathedral were indistinguishable, and in the broader sense the cathedral with the buildings and dwellings that grouped themselves around it formed a single unit.

The extraordinary religious enthusiasm that prompted the undertaking and construction of these immense projects is well brought out in the accounts of several medieval writers. Allowing for the enthusiasm of a religious zealot, as well as for the probably symbolic participation of the nobles in manual labor, Abbot Haimon's words reflect the extraordinary spirit of these times. "Who has ever heard tell, in times past," he wrote after visiting Chartres, "that powerful princes of the world, that men brought up in honor and wealth, that nobles, men and women, have bent their proud and haughty necks to the harness of carts, and that, like beasts of burden, they have dragged to the abode of Christ these waggons, loaded with wines, grains, oil, stone, wood, and all that is necessary for the wants of life, or for the construction of the church? ... When they have reached the church, they arrange the waggons about it like a spiritual camp, and during the whole night they celebrate the watch by hymns and canticles. On each waggon they light tapers and lamps; they place there the infirm and sick, and bring them the precious relics of the Saints for their relief."

midst of a rural district well off the beaten path. Its greatest distinction came from its shrine of the Virgin Mary where annually thousands congregated from far and wide to celebrate the Feast of the Virgin, which was the grand climax of the usual sequence of Church festivals. Here, as elsewhere, the cathedral was not only the spiritual center of the lives of the townsfolk but the geographical center of the medieval town as well. Towering over all, its great shadow fell upon the clustering church buildings that included the bishop's palace, the cathedral school, a cloister, a hospice, and an almshouse. Its west façade constituted one side of the market place, and from the cathedral square radiated the narrow streets on which were located the houses and shops of the townspeople. Here were the streets of the

214. West façade, Chartres Cathedral. *c.* 1194–1260 (portals and lancet windows *c.* 1145; south tower *c.* 1180; north spire 1507–1513). Façade 157′ wide; cathedral 427′ long, south tower (right) 344′ high; north tower (left) 377′ high.

ARCHITECTURE OF CHARTRES CATHEDRAL

When the harmonious proportions of the west façade of the Cathedral of Notre Dame at Chartres (Fig. 214) are first observed, everything seems· as right as an immutable truth. Yet what seems so certain, so solid, so monumental is actually the end result of fire salvage, a long process of growth, and a goodly amount of improvisation. Four centuries, in fact, separate the earliest parts from the latest, and the interval between saw rapid construction in time of prosperity, lag in time of poverty, work inspired with religious ardor, and cruel destruction by fire.

The triple portal and lancet windows above first stood a full forty feet behind the twin towers; together they were all that remained of the previous Romanesque church after the conflagration of 1194. In the rebuilding, they were moved forward flush with the front towers. The large rose window was designed to fill the intervening space, and above it the arcade of kings and a gable were added to mask the apex of the wooden roof that protects the vaulting of the nave.

The stylistic difference between the two unsymmetrical spires is one of the most striking features of the Chartres façade. The supporting towers, as a part of the previous church, are approximately contemporary. The upper part and the spire of the one on the right, however, date from the time the later parts of the abbey church at Cluny were being finished; their counterparts on the left are contemporary with the laying of the foundations for St. Peter's basilica in Rome in the early 16th century. Close scrutiny will reveal such minor flaws as the discrepancy between the proportions of the portals and the scale of the façade as a whole, the rose window being set slightly off center; and the awkward joining of the gallery and arcade of kings above it with the tower on the left. In spite of these disparities the façade bears out the initial impression of unity surprisingly well, and its space is so logically divided as to become an external promise of the interior plan. Horizontally, the three entrance portals lead into the nave while the flanking towers face the aisles. Vertically, the portals correspond to the nave arcade within, the lancets to the triforium gallery, and the rose window to the clearstory level. By this means, its composition maintains an integral relationship between the inner and outer aspects of the structure.

Rising above the twin towers are the tall tapering spires that seem both a logical and necessary continuation of the vertical lines of the supporting buttresses below and a fitting expression of the Gothic spirit of aspiration generally. The façade of Chartres, however, is rare in having a pair of spires. In Paris, Rouen, Amiens, and elsewhere, spires were projected but never completed; and at Strasbourg, one tower has a spire while the other does not. The two at Chartres make an interesting contrast between the attitudes of the early and late architects. In the older one on the south (right), the builder felt that the junction between tower and spire should be made as smoothly as possible and did so by adding a story between the three levels of the tower below and the single shaft of the spire above. Here the eight dormerlike windows are each surmounted by alternating higher and lower miniature spire forms of their own that, in turn, overlap the base of the larger spire, break the line, and add to the rhythm of the vertical movement. The transition from the square supporting tower to the octagonal form of the spire, and the continuation of the straight lines rising from ground level to the receding sloping lines of the spire, which culminate 350 feet above, is accomplished with finesse. The later Gothic architect, whose task was to replace the old wooden spire that had burned, was more concerned with intricacy of design and with sending his slimmer and more elegant spire 27 feet higher than its neighbor. While both excel in terms of their separate stylistic frames of reference, it is the old south tower, still sound after seven centuries and almost as many fires, that connoisseurs admire.

When one enters Chartres through the central portal, the broad nave (Fig. 216) spreads out to a width of 53 feet, making it one of the most spacious of all Gothic naves. On either side are amply proportioned aisles with their stained-glass windows that allow a rich flood of light to enter. A look at the plan (Fig. 215) will show that, in comparison with the abbey church at Cluny (Fig. 156), the Gothic architect has practically dispensed with walls. Instead of running parallel to the nave, the supporting piers are now at right angles to it, and the area between is bridged over with vaults, thus allowing open space for glass to light the interior at both the ground and clearstory levels. The walls, instead of serving to bear the weight of the superstructure, now exist mainly to enclose the interior and as a framework for the glass. Through the language of form and color, the wall space communicates with the worshipers through representations of religious subjects; and on a sunny day the beams of filtered light transform the floor into a constantly changing mosaic of color. Together with the clearstory

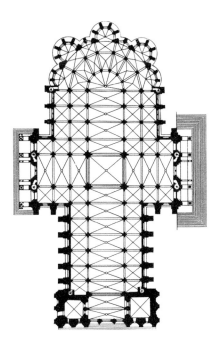

215. Chartres Cathedral, plan.

(right) 216. Nave and choir, Chartres Cathedral. *c.* 1194–1260. Nave, *c.* 130′ long, 53′ wide, 122′ high.

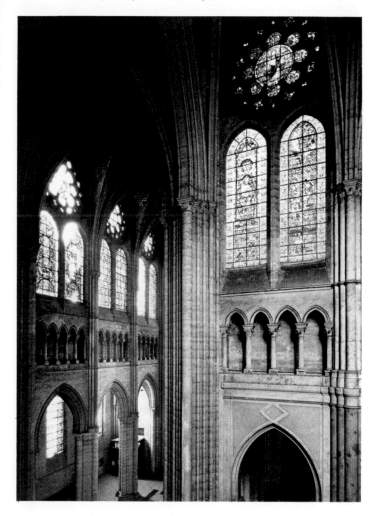

217. Interior at crossing, Chartres Cathedral. *c.* 1194–1260. (Compare Plate 13.)

The space above the graceful pointed arches of the nave arcade is filled by a series of smaller open arches that span the space between the bays. Behind them runs the triforium gallery, a passage utilizing the space above the internal roofing over the aisles and under the slanting external roof that extends outward from the base of the clearstory. Above the triforium runs the clearstory level, which now fully accomplishes its purpose. The triple pattern of two lancet windows below and a circular one above allots a maximum of space to the glass and a minimum to the masonry.

Covering the span of the nave is the triumph of the Gothic builders, the broad quadripartite vaulting (Figs. 216, 218), which at Chartres rises 122 feet above the ground level. It is this principle of vaulting that underlies all Gothic thinking and, in turn, explains all the supporting facts of shafts, colonettes, clustered columns, piers, and pointed arches—each of which comes into play to direct the descending weight of the intersecting ribs of the vaults toward the ground as efficiently as possible. The heavier transverse ribbing is carried past the clearstory and triforium levels by the large central shaft, while the smaller cross ribs are borne by the groups of slender colonettes that extend downward and cluster around the massive central piers of the nave arcade below. Chartres is about midway in the cumulative trial-and-error process by which the Gothic system was eventually perfected. The central piers of the nave arcade are still somewhat bulky, as though the architect could not entirely trust his own daring. Greater slenderness was achieved at Rheims and Amiens, and the tendency toward slimness and height continued until its limit was passed at Beauvais (Fig. 213).

Externally, there is an opposite number to each of these interior members (Fig. 220). The function of the flying buttress is to carry the thrust of the vaulting at specific points outward over the aisles to the piers that are set at right angles to the length of the nave. The function of flying buttress, pinnacle, and pier is now clarified. From the observer's point of view, just as in the interior the eye is drawn irresistibly upward by the rising vertical lines, so on the outside it follows the rising vertical piers to the pinnacles, along the rhythmic procession of the flying buttresses toward the gabled roof of the transepts, and on to the infinitude of space beyond.

The purpose of the pointed arch also becomes clear now. The Romanesque architects of Burgundy had used it at Cluny mainly as a decorative motif to promote a feeling of height and elegance. Gothic architects, however, pointed their arches

windows, the shafts of mysterious light serve also to accent the structural system of arches, piers, and vaults in such a way as to contribute to the illusion of infinite size and height. And since the eye is naturally drawn to light, the interior gives the impression of being all windows (Plate 13).

Returning to the center of the nave, one has his attention drawn next to the arcade of seven bays marching majestically toward the crossing of the transept (Fig. 217) and on to the choir beyond. The immense piers consist of a strong central column with four attached colonettes of more slender proportions clustered around them. As Figure 216 and Plate 13 plainly show, piers with cylindrical cores and engaged octagonal colonettes alternate with piers with octagonal cores and attached cylindrical colonettes. An interesting rhythm of procession and recession is set up, and a further variation is provided by the play of light on the alternating round and angular surfaces.

218. Chartres Cathedral, transverse section of nave (left) and diagram of vaulting (right). Drawing by Goubert.

to raise the crowns of the intersecting ribs of the vaulting to a uniform height so as to achieve greater structural stability (see Fig. 219). By the ever-increasing skill with which they used this device, they were able to achieve a constantly increasing height, which, in turn, led to loftier vaults and more ethereal effects.

When all these various devices—pointed arch, rib vault, flying buttress, triforium gallery, walls maintained by spacious arcades, window spaces maximized at all levels—came together in a

working relationship, Gothic architects were able to bring the inert masses of masonry into a resilient equilibrium of weights and balances. Gothic architecture is thus a complex system of opposing thrusts and counterthrusts (see Fig. 220) in which all parts exist in a logical relation to the whole. The weight and position of each stone had to be considered in terms of what was above and below it, so that its force could be properly transmitted along the various levels until that force eventually was grounded. If any part should give

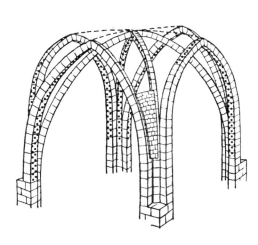

219. Romanesque vault (left) and Gothic vault (right).

way, the entire structure would be endangered. It is all the more remarkable when one remembers that Gothic builders used mortar and concrete in the joinings only as reinforcement and as a kind of structural insurance.

This logic of interior and exterior supports could not always take into account the irregularity of a cathedral's site. Over the years the ground might settle at certain points, or some of the piers and buttresses might be undermined by floods, thus putting the whole structure in danger. It also was impossible to make the vaults at high levels heavy enough to withstand wind and weather. At Chartres and elsewhere, the thin-webbed masonry had to be protected by the addition of wooden roofs, which at Chartres actually burned several times without, however, destroying the stone vaults underneath (see Fig. 221). The builder of Chartres achieved such stability that his structure has never had to be

reinforced, and it stands today substantially as it did seven centuries ago. Rheims Cathedral has fared equally well by surviving the centuries, two fires, and an artillery bombardment in World War I. Gothic cathedrals, in fact, have so far borne out the hopes of people who desired to raise buildings that "have nothing to fear from fire till the day of judgment."

At Chartres, the wings of the transepts terminate in triple portals (Fig. 222) that in size and magnificence surpass those of the western façade, which has survived from the previous church. The portals in the 13th-century style, however, are enframed by row upon row of richly sculptured receding archivolts that bring a maximum of light and shadow into play. Here also the plan (Fig. 215) will reveal that Gothic builders were not bound by the laws of symmetry, since the north and south porches are of different size and proportion. The shape of such sections was partly determined by the tastes of individual donors. The north transept with its portals, porch, and stained glass was the gift of the royal family of France, primarily Blanche of Castile and her son St. Louis (Plate 14), while its southern counterpart was donated by their arch-rival, the Duke of Brittany. When the cathedral was dedicated in the year 1260, Louis IX was present with such an assembly of bishops, canons, princes, and peasants as had rarely been seen.

Beyond the transepts extend the spacious choir and sanctuary, which are surrounded by a double-aisled ambulatory that gives easy access to the apse and its crown of radiating chapels. The increasingly elaborate Gothic liturgy demanded the participation of more and more clergymen, and the cavernous recesses of the huge structure were needed to accommodate an ever-growing number of choristers. The apsidal chapels are also a distinctive feature of a developed Gothic plan, so that pilgrims could have access to the various altars where the venerated relics of saints were kept. The Cathedral of Notre Dame at Chartres, as well as earlier churches that stood on the same site, was closely associated with the cult of the Virgin Mary. Its most renowned relic was the legendary veil of the Virgin which, by tradition, had been presented to Charlemagne by the Byzantine Empress Irene. Another chapel enshrined the skull of St. Anne, the Virgin's mother, which was brought back by crusaders and given to the church in 1205. This relic explains the many representations of St. Anne in statuary and stained glass and the pilgrimages in her honor, which were second only to those of the Virgin. The most important chapel in Gothic cathedrals was the *Notre Dame*, or Lady Chapel,

220. Nave exterior (south), Chartres Cathedral. *c.* 1194–1260.

(above) 221. Cross vaults, Chartres Cathedral. Drawing by Paul Durand after wooden roof burned in 1836.

(right) 222. South porch, Chartres Cathedral. 13th century.

devoted to Mary. It was usually placed on the main axis of the nave beyond the center of the apse, with chapels of other saints grouped on either side. All these considerations caused the parts beyond the transepts to expand to unprecedented proportions.

Gothic interiors need little more decorative detail than the vertical lines of the structural members, the variety of representations in stained glass, and above all, the flow of light. At Chartres, the lighting is so organized as to achieve a gradual crescendo from the dark violet and blue lancets and rose window in the west through the brighter tones of the aisle and clearstory windows of the nave, past the flaming reds of the transept rose windows to the high intensity of the five red and orange lancets in the apse, which soar above the altar and capture the rays of the morning sun. Romanesque abbey churches were lighted mainly from within by lamps and candles, while Gothic interiors are illuminated by sunlight transformed through stained glass into a myriad of mysterious prismatic colors. The interior masses and voids become activated and etherealized by the directional flow of light, and material and immaterial elements fuse into a glowing harmonious whole.

SCULPTURE OF CHARTRES CATHEDRAL

As important to the medieval mind as the structure itself was the choice and location of the sculptural and pictorial representations that were to give a church its significance and meaning. In a Romanesque monastic church, these were found in the carved tympanums over the narthex portals, on the capitals of the columns throughout the interior, and in wall paintings, especially in the apsidal end. Since such representations were designed for those leading cloistered lives, they gravitated toward the interior, and the variety and subtlety of their subjects make it clear they were meant to be pondered upon and carefully studied. Gothic sculpture was more popularly oriented and faced the outside world, where it clustered around and over the porches and entrance portals. Inside, the columns rose too high to make specific subjects distinguishable. The shafts with their colonettes made the surfaces of the capitals too irregular to permit unified pictorial designs, and the eye would have been distracted when viewing them against the complex lines of the vaulting. Hence, the interior capitals at Chartres and in other Gothic cathedrals are decorated mainly with generalized patterns of leaves, fruits, and flowers. Instead of fanciful Romanesque trees of Paradise, they came closer to patterns in nature. When one Gothic bishop was called upon to explain their symbolism, he could come up with nothing better than that they represented "the fruits of good works that grow from the works of virtue." So to dismiss the hundreds of Gothic capitals shows they conveyed little meaning. Except for these foliated capitals, at Chartres the only other interior sculpture was a series of relief panels on the choir screen that separated the sanctuary from the double-aisled ambulatory.

The intention of Gothic builders was to concentrate sculptural interest on the exterior where it was made an integral part of the architectural design. Both the proliferation of figures and the quality of their execution testify to the importance of sculpture in the art of the period. The exterior of Chartres has more than 2,000 carved figures, which are about evenly distributed among the west façade and the north and south porches of the transepts. Gothic sculpture, like the Romanesque, was done by journeymen craftsmen who gathered wherever a church was abuilding. From the enormous productivity of the period, it seems clear that the ranks of these craftsmen must have been numerous, and that the strokes of the sculptor's chisel on stone must have been a familiar sound. The Gothic sculptor had the advantage of excellent stone models to follow, where his Romanesque predecessors had had to translate the lines of illuminated manuscripts into the stone medium. While the Romanesque sculptor thought more in linear terms (see Figs. 167, 183, 184), his Gothic counterpart was more concerned with carving in depth; and the placement of the Gothic sculpture out of doors also made the play of light and shade more important. While the technique of the Gothic sculptor undoubtedly was superior, the iconography had become standardized in his time and did not allow him quite so much imaginative freedom as his predecessor had enjoyed. Both Romanesque and Gothic sculpture, however, shows the unevenness of workmanship associated with so-called "school sculpture," because some journeymen carvers were more skillful than others.

The profusion of sculpture in a Gothic cathedral might lead to considerable confusion were it not for the close relationship of the sculptured forms to the architectural framework. The Gothic structure was so complete, so overwhelming, that no amount of decorative license would have been able to overshadow it; but the Gothic carvers had no intentions of going their separate ways, and their work was always conceived and executed in terms of the architectural frame of reference. Even so, the enormous number of examples would be bewildering were it not for some attempt to unify the iconography. Since it is a people's church, the cathedral could not follow so consistent a system as that of an abbey, which was designed for a small group of people following a common ideal of life. Instead of single unified compositions, therefore, the Gothic cathedral went in for variety in order to provide something for every level of taste. At Chartres, most of the sculpture as well as the structure dates from the first half of the 13th century, and it is possible from the traditions and thought of that period to arrive at something of an overall iconographic plan.

A Gothic cathedral, with the all-embracing activities it housed and the all-encompassing subject matter of its sculpture and stained glass, has often been likened to the comprehensive compendiums of law, philosophy, and theology written by medieval scholars. Cathedrals have also been described as the Bible in stone and glass, or the books of the illiterate; but they should not be overlooked as visual encyclopedias for the educated as well.

The key to the iconography of Chartres is the encyclopedic character of medieval thought as found in the *Speculum Majus* of Vincent of Beauvais, who divided all learning into Mirrors of Nature, Instruction, History, and Morality. The Mirror of Nature is seen in the flora and fauna that are represented in comprehensive fashion; Instruction in the personifications of the seven liberal arts and the branches of learning taught in the universities; History in the story of mankind from Adam and Eve to the Last Judgment; and Morality in the figures depicting virtue and vice, the wise and foolish virgins, the saved and the damned in the Last Judgment, and in the hovering saints and angels and fleeing gargoyles and devils. There is also a recognizable sequence of presentation with a beginning on the west façade, where the story of Christ from His ancestors to the ascension is told; a middle on the north porch, where the history of Mary is traced along Old Testament lines from the creation of man to her death and heavenly coronation; and an end on the south porch, which takes up the drama of redemption from the New Testament, through the work of the Church, its saints, popes, abbots, and bishops, to the climax of the final day of the universe at the Last Judgment. Each of the three porches has some 700 carved figures clustered in the three tympanums over the portals, the archivolts that enframe them, and the columns below and galleries above. In addition to the Scriptural scenes and lives of the saints, the designers found a place for ancient lore and contemporary history, for prophecy and fact, for fabulous animals and beasts of burden, for old wives' tales and the latest scientific knowledge, for portraits of princes and those of tradesmen, for beautiful angels and grotesque gargoyles (some of which function as water spouts to drain the roof, others as decorative motifs symbolizing demons fleeing from the sacred precincts of the church).

The iconography at Chartres stems from three principal sources: the dedication of the cathedral to Our Lady, a church privilege that was shared with such other Notre Dame cathedrals as those at Paris, Rheims, Rouen, and Amiens; the presence of a cathedral school, an important center of learning, for Mary was also the patroness of the liberal arts; and the preferences of such patrons as the royal family, lesser nobility, and local guilds who donated miscellaneous representations.

It must also be borne in mind that sacred and secular elements in a medieval town and manor were so closely interwoven that every spiritual manifestation had a wordly counterpart. So the cathedral, as the court of Mary, Queen of Heaven, had to surpass in magnificence the grandeur that surrounded any mere earthly queen. Gothic chivalry and courtliness were rapidly replacing the might-makes-right code of Romanesque feudalism. And just as the clergy sang the praises of Notre Dame, so the knights of the castles lauded their ladies in particular and Our Lady in general. The high place of womanhood in secular circles is thus the courtly parallel of the religious cult of the Virgin. In poetry of the time, a knight's lady love is always the paragon of feminine virtue and charm. To woo and win her, he who aspired to her favor had to storm the fortress of her heart by techniques far more intricate and subtle than those needed to take a castle. When successful, he became the vassal of his mistress and she his liege lady to command him as she would. The concept of romantic love originated here in the Gothic period and came to full flower in the complex code of chivalry. With its exaltation of the position of women and its concern with the defense of the weak against the strong, chivalry established the Western code of manners that is valid to this day.

The favorite reading in aristocratic circles ranged from Ovid's *Art of Love* of ancient Roman days to the contemporary *Romance of the Rose*. Included also were such stories as Tristan and Iseult, Aucassin and Nicolette, and the legends

223. West portals, Chartres Cathedral. *c.* 1145–1170. 20′ 6″ high.

224. *Life of Virgin Mary*, tympanum of "Virgin Portal," west façade, Chartres Cathedral. 1145–1170.

of King Arthur's court. Since such works were addressed mainly to the knightly class, they usually began with extended lists of the ancestors of the hero and heroine, and at Chartres their visual counterpart is found in Biblical genealogies that showed the kings and queens of Judah as the ancestors of Mary and Jesus. A law of precedence as rigid as any courtly etiquette was observed in the order of presentation and the location of these figures. Because the Old Testament prophets, for example, lived before the Christian era, they are found in the shadows of the north porch, while the apostles and personalities of the New Testament are in the sunlit south porch. Christ and Mary, as King and Queen of Heaven, are found over the central portals, while lesser figures range outward from them according to their importance. Such a vast amount of statuary would take volumes to describe, and the discussion here is limited to parts of the 12th-century Virgin Portal on the west façade and its 13th-century counterpart on the north porch.

The central portal of the west façade (Fig. 223) is traditionally called the Royal Portal, and its tympanum encloses the figure of Christ in Majesty surrounded by the four symbolic beasts of the

Evangelists and the twenty-four elders of the Apocalypse. The tympanum over the left portal depicts the close of Christ's days on earth and ascension, while on the right is the tympanum of the Virgin Portal (Fig. 224), depicting the beginning of His earthly life. The story is told in the simplest possible terms in three rising panels. Starting in the lower left is the Annunciation, with just the figures of the Angel Gabriel and Mary; the next pair shows the Visitation; the Nativity is in the center; and the shepherds in the midst of their sheep are coming from the right for the Adoration, just as their successors came in from the fields near Chartres to worship at Mary's shrine. The middle panel depicts the presentation of the young Jesus in the temple. His position on the altar foreshadows His later sacrifice. Friends approach from both sides bearing gifts. In the top panel, the Virgin sits crowned and enthroned, holding her Divine Son and attended by a pair of archangels. She is shown frontally as a queen accepting the homage of the humble, who bow their heads as they enter her court through the portal below.

Of great interest are the figures in the archivolts that frame the tympanum. These symbolize Mary's attributes. Like Athena of old, the Virgin was the patroness of the arts and sciences. Albertus Magnus in his *Mariale* declared that the Virgin was perfect in the arts; and in his *Summa*, Thomas Aquinas included among his propositions the question of "Whether the Blessed Virgin Mary possessed perfectly the seven liberal arts"—which, of course, was triumphantly affirmed. These representations are also reminders that this was an age which produced great scholars, and that intellectual understanding as well as faith was now one of the paths to salvation. The fact that Chartres was the location of one of the great cathedral schools is also brought out; and before the founding of the University of Paris, it shared with Rheims the distinction of being the best-known center of learning in Europe. ⋅

The curriculum of the cathedral school was, of course, the seven liberal arts. These were divided into the Trivium, which dealt with the science of words in the three subjects of Grammar, Rhetoric, and Dialectic, and into the higher faculty of the Quadrivium, which was concerned with the science of numbers through the study of Arithmetic, Geometry, Astronomy, and Music.

On the archivolt, these seven arts are symbolized abstractly by female figures somewhat akin to the ancient muses, while below them are found their most renowned human exponents. Beginning with the lower left corner of the outside archivolt, Aristotle is seen dipping his pen into the inkwell. Above him is a thoughtful figure representing Dialectic. In one hand she holds a dragon-headed serpent symbolizing subtlety of thought, and in the other the torch of knowledge. Then

comes Cicero as the great orator, and over him the figure of Rhetoric making a characteristic oratorical gesture. The next pair are Euclid and Geometry, both of whom are deep in their calculations. In the same band, moving now from the top downward are Arithmetic and probably Boethius. Below them is the star-gazing figure of Astronomy, who holds a bushel basket which signifies the relationship of her science to the calendar, so important in a farming district like Chartres. Ptolemy, to whom the medievalists ascribed the invention of the calendar and clock, is her human representative.

The figures on the lowest level are Grammar and Donatus, the ancient Roman grammarian. Grammar (Fig. 225) holds an open book in one hand and the disciplinary switch in the other over the heads of two young pupils, one of whom is laughing and pulling the other's hair. The last pair in the series of seven are adjacent to those in the inner archivolt. Below is Pythagoras (Fig. 226), the reputed founder of music theory, who is shown writing in medieval fashion with a desk over his knees, while on the wall behind him is a shelf holding a supply of pens and sponges for erasures. Above him is the figure of Music surrounded by instruments (Fig. 227). At her back is a monochord, used to calculate the intervals and for accuracy of pitch; on her lap is a psaltery; on the wall hangs a three-stringed viol; and she is striking the set of three chime bells, an allusion to the Pythagorean discovery of the mathematical ratios of the perfect intervals—the octave, the fifth, and the fourth. Both Gerbert of Rheims and his pupil

225–227. Details, Virgin Portal Tympanum,
west façade, Chartres Cathedral. 1145–1170.

225. *Grammar.*   226. *Pythagoras.*   227. *Music.*

Bishop Fulbert of Chartres are known to have taken an active interest not only in the theory of music but in its performance, and the two figures, showing Pythagoras as the thinker and Music as the performer, symbolize that Chartres was an important center for both the theoretical as well as the practical aspects of music.

The liberal arts are also depicted on the north porch, and representations show how far intellectual inquiry had extended a century later. While the universities had absorbed the humanistic tradition of the arts as taught in the cathedral schools, they also included the study of theology, law, and medicine. So on the north porch are personifications of Philosophy (also by Aristotle); of Geometry, now coupled with Architecture and with Archimedes as their exponent; and of Medicine, represented by Hippocrates. In addition, there are some nonuniversity pursuits, such as Painting, personified by Apelles, Metalcrafts by Tubal-Cain, and Agriculture by a group made up of Adam, Abel, and Cain.

Far more elaborate in scope and less restrained in decorative detail than the west façade is the incomparable north porch, which, with its three portals, stretches out to a width of 120 feet, thus spanning the transept completely. A gift of the royal family of France, its construction and decora-

228. *Contemplative Life*, detail, north porch, Chartres Cathedral. 13th century.

tion extended from the reign of Louis VIII and the regency of his queen, Blanche of Castile, through that of their son St. Louis (Louis IX), or roughly the first three quarters of the 13th century. The north porch is dedicated to the Virgin and expands the theme of the Virgin Portal on the west façade to encyclopedic proportions. Her history from the annunciation and nativity through the childhood of Jesus is found on the left portal, while the scenes of her death and assumption are depicted on the lintel over the central door, and that of her enthronement and coronation in the tympanum above. Her attributes are revealed in the archivolts through series after series of cyclical representations, such as those of the 14 heavenly beatitudes and 12 feminine personifications of the active and contemplative life (Fig. 228). Especially fine is the single figure of her mother, St. Anne, holding the infant Mary in her arms, which adorns the *trumeau* that supports the tympanum of the central portal (Fig. 229). From the harmonious lines of the folds of her drapery to the dignified and matronly face, the work is one of the most satisfying realizations of the mature Gothic sculptural style.

It will be noted from the contours of the south porch (Fig. 222) that the arches of the portals are now more highly pointed, and their enclosure by triangular gables further emphasizes their verticality. The deep recession of the porch allows for a much greater play of light and shade in the statuary that covers every available space from the bases of the columns to the peak of the gable. The figures on both the north and south porches, in comparison with the earlier ones on the west façade, have bodies more naturally proportioned; their postures show greater variety and informality; and their facial expressions have far more mobility. The representations of plants and animals are considerably closer to nature; and in comparison with the impersonality of those on the west front, many of the human figures are so individualized that they seem like portraits of living persons. In the change of style, however, something of the previous symbolic meaning and monumentality has been lost as well as the closer identity with architecture.

THE STAINED GLASS OF CHARTRES

Time has taken its inevitable toll of Chartres' exterior sculptures. The flow of carved lines remains, and the varied play of light and shade relieves the present browns and grays. But only traces of polychrome and gilt are left to remind the observer that here was once a feast of color with

229. *St. Anne with Virgin*, trumeau of center portal, north porch, Chartres Cathedral. *c.* 1250.

an effect that now has to be imagined. In the interior, however, where the stained glass remains undimmed, the full color of medieval pageantry still exists. The wealth of pure color in the 175 surviving glass panels hypnotizes the senses, and through the medium of polychromatic light something of the emotional exaltation that inspired medieval man to create such a temple to the Queen of Heaven can still be felt.

Here, as elsewhere, the structural and decorative elements are closely tied together, and, just as with the sculpture, the glass does not exist separately but only as an integral part of the whole. The designer was always aware of the size, proportion, and placement of his window in relation to the architectural setting. Glass is not usually thought of as a building material until the 19th

and 20th centuries, but in medieval times and later it did have to fill a large architectural void while taking into account the pressure of wind and weather. This the designer accomplished mainly by dividing the space geometrically into smaller parts by the use of *mullions*, the vertical posts that divide the windows; by stone tracery to frame smaller glass panels, as in the great rose windows; by parallel iron bars across the open expanse; and, more minutely, by the fine strips of lead that hold the small pieces of glass in place. While Chartres must divide architectural and sculptural honors with its neighboring cities, the town was especially renowned as the center of glass making, and with the highest achievements of its glaziers exemplified in their own cathedral, Chartres is unsurpassed in this respect.

All the visual arts must come to terms in their separate ways with the problem of light. Architectural exteriors must take sunlight into account; sculpture, whether in relief or in the round, demands an expressive use of light and shade; and painting, whether fresco or panels, must be done with an eye toward the reflection of light. In each case, however, the observer receives his impression by means of light refracted from an opaque surface. Only in the case of stained glass is the direct ray the primary concern of the artist. In this medium, he transforms his light prismatically through his colored glass and thus achieves a greater variety and intensity than is possible in any other medium, which accounts for the immediate appeal of his art to layman and connoisseur alike. The use of stained glass as wall panels allies it to the earlier use of mosaics, fresco paintings, embroidered wall hangings and tapestries. While the glazier's art was developed in Romanesque times, not until the earliest Gothic structure was built by Abbot Suger did stained glass designs receive a place in the iconography on a par with that of sculpture and painting. With the virtual disappearance of the walls and the great height of the vaulting in Gothic buildings, mural and ceiling painting was out of the question. Pictorial decoration, however, was needed more than ever before, if the stony logic of the piers and vaults was not entirely to dominate the cavernous interior. The windows consequently became the only available space for such decoration, and much of the expressive impact of Gothic art depended on the effectiveness of these luminous and translucent tapestries.

The great variety of jewellike color was achieved chemically by the addition of certain minerals to the glass while it was in a molten state. When cool, the sheets were cut into smaller sections, and the designer fitted these into his previously prepared outline. Pieces of various sizes next were joined together by lead strips. Details, such as the features in the faces, were then applied in the form of metal oxides and made permanent by firing in a kiln. Finally, the individual panels making up the pattern of the whole window were fastened to the iron bars already imbedded in the masonry. When seen against the light the glass appears translucent, while the lead and iron become opaque black lines that serve to outline the figures as well as to separate the colors and prevent blurring when viewed at a distance. Reproductions can convey only the faintest idea of the brilliantly colored originals, and it should be noted especially that the black lines of the iron and lead become overaccented. It is nevertheless possible to observe from photographs the care with which the formal design and the details were executed.

The stained-glass artists shared with mosaicists and manuscript illuminators a distinct preference for two-dimensional designs. The dignified formality of their figures and the abstract patterns of the borders blended their work admirably into the architectural setting. By thus avoiding any hint of naturalistic effects, such as landscape backgrounds, and by concentrating on patterns of pure color and geometrical forms, they helped to promote the illusion of infinite space.

The iconographical plan of the glass at Chartres, like that of the exterior sculptures, is held together mainly by the dedication of the church as a shrine of the Virgin Mary. There is never any doubt on the part of those who enter that they are in the presence of the Queen of Heaven, who sits enthroned in majesty in the central panel of the apse over the high altar. Grouped around her in neighboring panels are the archangels, saints, and prophets, emblems of the noble donors, and symbols of the craftsmen and tradespeople, almost 4,000 figures in all, who honor her and make up her court. Below, on her feast days, were the crowds of living pilgrims who gathered in the nave and chapels at her feet, and who aspired to come into her eternal presence one day as they had come into her shrine.

An interesting commentary on the changing social conditions of the 13th century can be read in the records of the donors of the windows. In the lowest part of each one is a "signature" indicating the individual, family, or group who defrayed the great expense of the glass. Only a royal purse was equal to a large rose window, as evidenced by the fleur-de-lys insignia so prominent in the north rose (Fig. 233). Within the means of members of the aristocracy and the Church hierarchy, such as bishops and canons, were the lancet windows of the nave and choir. The status and prosperity of the medieval guilds of craftsmen and merchants, however, was such that the vast majority of the windows was donated by them. While the royal

230. *Bakers*, detail, stained glass window, Chartres Cathedral. *c.* 1250.

231. *Furriers*, detail, stained glass window, Chartres Cathedral. *c.* 1250.

Plate 15. *Notre Dame de Belle Verrière*. 12th century.
Stained glass window. Chartres Cathedral. (See p. 198.)

Plate 16. SIMONE MARTINI. *Annunciation.* 1333. Tempera on wood, 8′8″ × 10′. (Saints in side panels by LIPPO MEMMI.) Uffizi, Florence. (See p. 221.)

(below) 232. *Wheelwrights and Barrelmakers*, detail, stained glass window, Chartres Cathedral. *c.* 1250.

(above) 233. North rose window, Chartres Cathedral. 1223–1226. Diameter 44′.

family of France and the Duke of Brittany were content with windows in the transepts, the most prominent windows of all, the 47-foot-high center lancets of the apse, were given by the guilds; and the one over the high altar, toward which all eyes are drawn, was the gift of the bakers. Each guild had a patron saint, and a window under a guild's patronage was concerned with the life and miracles of its special saint. In the case of the nobility, the family coat of arms was sufficient to identify the donor; with a guild, the "signature" of the donor took the form of a craftsman engaged in some typical phase of his work. In the windows of Chartres some 19 different confraternities are represented, including the bakers (Fig. 230), the furriers (Fig. 231), and the wheelwrights and barrelmakers (Fig. 232).

The great rose window of the west façade dates from the early 13th century and thus is contemporary with the majority of examples in the rest of the church. The three lancets below it, however, like the portals and surrounding masonry on the exterior, originally were part of the previous church. Besides being the earliest of all the windows, they are, possibly, also the best. Their origin has been traced to the school that did the windows for Suger's church at St. Denis, and their work was on the whole much finer grained and more jewel-like, with infinite care lavished on the geometrical and arabesque patterns in the borders. They are dominated by their vibrant blue backgrounds, while the figures and abstract patterns are done in several shades of red, emerald green, yellow, sapphire, and white. Also dating from before the fire of 1194 is the central section of the regal and resplendent panel known as *Notre Dame de Belle Verrière*, Our Lady of the Beautiful Window (Plate 15).

The great rose window of the north transept (Fig. 233), like the sculpture on the porch outside, glorifies the Virgin Mary. Together with its lancets, the composition shares with the other glass of the 13th century a preference for red backgrounds instead of the earlier blue; the individual panes are larger; the borders are more conventionalized; and its greatest effect comes from the large splashes of warm color that contrast with the cool tones of the lancets of the west façade.

In the Gothic period the art of stained glass replaced the mosaics and mural paintings of the early Christian and Romanesque churches, and is the ultimate stage in the etherealization of interior space. (By giving form and meaning to light, the art of the glazier perhaps is better adapted to the expression of transcendental concepts than any other medium.) By the transformation of raw sunlight into a spectrum of brilliant prismatic color, the architect gained complete control over his interior lighting, which he could cause to flow in any manner he willed. This material control over an immaterial medium could then be placed at the disposal of the architects and iconographers to shape light to their structural, pictorial, and expressive needs. Something of the ecstasy felt by medieval man in the contemplation of the precious stones that adorned the altar and the jeweled glass of the windows is expressed in the following passage by Abbot Suger: "Thus, when—out of my delight in the beauty of the house of God— the loveliness of the many-colored gems has called me away from eternal cares, and worthy meditation has induced me to reflect, transferring that which is material to that which is immaterial, on the diversity of the sacred virtues: then it seems to me that I see myself dwelling, as it were, in some strange region of the universe which neither exists entirely in the slime of the earth nor entirely in the purity of Heaven; and that, by the grace of God, I can be transported from this inferior to that higher world in an anagogical manner."

GOTHIC MUSIC

Massive and magnificent as the Gothic cathedral is, it can be conceived as the highest achievement of Gothic man only if associated with the various activities it was designed to house. Most important, of course, is the liturgy. As the enclosed space increased, the cathedral grew into a vast auditorium that hummed with collective voices at communal prayer, resounded with readings and the spoken word from the pulpit, and reverberated with the chanting of solo and choral song from the choir.

Since no direct performance tradition links Gothic music with that of the present, it must be reconstructed from the meager signs on manuscript pages and from literary descriptions and visual representations of the period. Gothic music, therefore, is today something like a frame without a picture. Its approximate melodic and rhythmic structures are known; but because music comes to life only when performed, the melodic freedom, rhythmic flexibility, dynamic accentuation, as well as the parts known to have been improvised, have to be conjectured. One also has to take into consideration that, just as a statue or painting loses much of its significance when removed from its original architectural setting to a museum, so also does music suffer when transferred from the resonant spaces of a cathedral to a concert hall or recording studio. When heard in such modern settings, the stark intervals of the fifth and octave seem barren and hollow, and the dissonances somewhat harsh. The same works performed in a cathedral are alive and colorful. The long drawn-out tones reverberate against the irregular surfaces of the piers and vaults, resound through the cavernous vertical and horizontal expanses, and awaken the chants into a vibrant life all their own. In this way, Gothic music takes its place alongside the structural system, sculptural embellishments, and stained glass.

The Ile-de-France, site of the most significant developments in architecture of the 12th and 13th centuries, was also the scene of the most important musical innovations of the Gothic period. Specifically, these were the more sophisticated practices of *polyphonic*, or many-voiced, music and their relation with the still universally practiced monophonic, or unison, art of Gregorian Chant. Singing in parts was of northern origin in contrast to the prevailing Mediterranean style of singing in unison, and part singing in folk music apparently predates by several centuries its incorporation into church music. Just as the Gothic cathedral was the culmination in the long process of reconciling the northern urge for verticality with the southern horizontal basilica form, so Gothic music was the union of the northern tradition of many-voiced singing with the southern one-voice tradition.

The role of Chartres in these developments is obscure. John of Salisbury, the master of the cathedral school when the symbolic figure of Music was done for the west façade (Fig. 227), is known to have approved the theoretical study of music as a part of the Quadrivium as heartily as he disapproved of certain innovations in the music performed by the choir there. Scholarly discussions about the mathematical ratios of musical intervals had been going on ever since antiquity, and such abstract problems as how the music of the spheres or an angelic choir would sound had been on the academic agenda ever since Boethius' time. It is therefore probable that at this time the greater progress was being made in the field of practical music which John so despised. According to William of Malmesbury, who died about 1142, Chartres was celebrated for its "many musical modulations," and one of the greatest 13th-century musical theorists, Franco of Cologne, is supposed to have been educated at Chartres. From actual documents and the surviving manuscripts, however, it is evident that the greatest forward strides were being made in the Cathedral School of Paris, known after 1163 as the School of Notre Dame.

School of Notre Dame in Paris

It has already been noted that, in the construction of the first Gothic church, the builder of St. Denis brought together many principles that had been developed separately elsewhere and for the first time used them in a systematic whole. The same was true of music, and Paris as the growing capital of the French kingdom was the logical place for the pieces to be fitted into a whole. The contrapuntal forms and textures developed in such monasteries as Cluny and in such cathedral schools as Rheims and Chartres, as well as the tradition of folk singing in several parts, were organized systematically for the first time at the School of

Notre Dame in Paris. Again, as in the case of architecture, the man and the time can be fixed with certainty. The first great monument of Gothic music was the *Magnus Liber Organi* by Leonin, dating from *c.* 1163, which, as its name implies, was a great book bringing together a collection of music in two parts, arranged cyclically so as to spread over the entire calendar year.

In the traditional rendering of the Gregorian Chant, some parts were sung by a soloist and answered responsorially by a chorus singing in unison. In the Gothic period, the choir still chanted in the way it had done for centuries, but the solo parts began to be performed simultaneously by two or more individual singers. Notre Dame in Paris, for example, employed four such singers. The distinction between solo voice and choir hence was replaced by the opposition of a group of individual singers and a massed chorus. With several skilled soloists available, the way was open for an art of much greater complexity than heretofore. Since the music, however, was still intended for church performance, it was mandatory that one of the traditional sacred melodies be used; and a special part called the *tenor*, a term derived from the Latin *tenere*, meaning to hold, was reserved for it. This melody was also known as the *cantus firmus*, or fixed song, implying that it could not be changed. The development of Gothic music was that of taking this *cantus firmus* as an established basis, and adding one by one the voices called in ascending order, the *duplum*, *triplum*, and *quadruplum*. Since these voices were superimposed one above the other, a definite verticality of concept is implied, which contrasted strongly with the horizontal succession of tones that characterized the older monophonic chant.

The earliest forms of Gothic polyphony are almost as rigid in their way as the old parallel organum of the Romanesque period, but they are based on the new principle of *punctus contra punctum*, literally note against note, or point counter point. *Mira Lege* (below) illustrates one of the strictest applications of this idea. The Gregorian melody is in the lower part, while the counterpoint above moves as much in opposition to it as possible.

Mira Lege (12th-century discant)   (after Coussemaker)

Mi - ra le - ge, mi - ro mo - do, De - us for - mat_ho - mi - nem

While parallel movement is not against the rule, and from time to time does occur, contrary motion is preferred. A treatise written at the beginning of the 12th century declares: "If the main voice is ascending, the accompanying part should descend, and vice versa." The name given to this newly created melodic line was the *discantus*, or discant, referring to the practice of singing against the established melody, a practice that has continued in religious and secular music ever since.

In addition to such examples, Leonin's *Magnus Liber* contains another type of counterpoint known as *organum duplum*. The Gregorian *cantus firmus* is found in the lower voice, but the individual tones are stretched out to extraordinary lengths. The discanting, or duplum voice, moves now in free counterpoint consisting of florid melismas over what has in effect become a relatively fixed base.

The greater melodic and rhythmic freedom that the discant assumed called for expert solo singers, and much of the discanting of Gothic times is known to have been improvised. The practice of such a freely flowing melodic line over a relatively fixed bass points to a possible origin in one of the old types of folk singing. Survivals are found in the instrumental music of the Scottish bagpipers, where such a tune as "The Campbells Are Coming" is heard over a droning bass note. In performance, the slowly moving tenor, or *cantus firmus*, may have been sung by the choir, while the soloist sang his freely moving duplum part over it; or the tenor may have been played on the organ, as the instrument is known to have been in use at this time. The organ keyboard was a 13th-century Gothic innovation, and the many manuscript illustrations from the period point to the wide usage of organs. The term "organ point," furthermore, continues to be used to refer to a musical passage in which the bass tone remains static, while the other parts move freely over it.

Triplum (13th century)   (in Perotin's style; after Rokseth)

The next most significant development was the addition of a third part above the other two, which was known as the *triplum*, and from which the term treble is derived. This step is associated with the name of the first practicing musician in history to have the attribution of greatness attached to his name. He was Magister Perotinus Magnus, or Perotin the Great, active in Paris in the late 12th and probably in the early 13th century. In his revision of the work of his predecessor Leonin, Perotin moved away from polyphonic improvisational practices toward an art based on stricter melodic control and clearer rhythmic articulation. By thus achieving a surer command of his materials, and evolving a logical technique for manipulating them, he was able to add a third voice to the original two, and in two known instances even a fourth. The three-part motet, like its predecessors, still had its *cantus firmus* in the tenor, which was the lowest part and held the *mot*, or word, from which the term *motet* probably is derived. Over it the contrapuntal voices wove a web of two different strands, singing their independent melodic lines. In the hands of Perotin the three-part motet became the most favored and characteristic practice of 13th-century Gothic music.

Besides achieving ever-greater melodic independence, the two contrapuntal voices even had their own separate texts. A three-part motet thus had three distinct sets of words—the tenor, with its traditional line, and usually two contemporary hymnlike verses over and above it—which were sung simultaneously. Intended as they were for church performance, the words customarily were in Latin. However, around the middle of the 13th century, it was not uncommon for one of the contrapuntal voices to have its verses in French. With the entrance of the vernacular language came also popular melodies, so that above the stately tenor, it was possible to have a hymn to the Virgin in Latin and a secular love song in French going on at the same time. By the simple expedient of replacing the sacred melodies with secular tunes, a fully developed musical art independent of the Church was not only possible but by the end of the 13th century had become an accomplished fact.

Gothic music exists in such close unity with other manifestations of the Gothic style that it can scarcely be understood as a thing apart. The subjects of the new hymns, especially those with the words of St. Bernard and the melodies of Adam of St. Victor, were mainly devoted to the Virgin, as were most of the cathedrals and the iconography of the sculpture and stained glass. Instead of a monolithic choir chanting in unison or in parallel organum, the Gothic listener now heard a small group of professional singers. In the case of a three-part motet, he could choose, according to his temperament or mood, to follow either the solemn traditional tenor melody, the Latin commentary above it, or the French triplum in his own everyday mode of speech. This allowance for diversity of musical taste is a part of the general shift from the homogeneity of monastic life in the abbey to the heterogeneity of city life, of which the cathedral is the expression. The new melodic, rhythmic, and textual variety implies a congregation made up of people from all walks of life, just as had been the case with the diversified imagery of the sculpture and stained glass.

Since the individual voices were superimposed one above the other, a concept of verticality, similar to the architectural developments, is realized. The ear, like the eye, needs fixed points to measure rises and falls. In the *Mira Lege* example (p. 199), the intervals of the lower part established the point over which the discant moved in contrary motion. In the case of the *organum duplum* (p. 200), it was the long sustained tone in the tenor against which the soaring upward and plunging downward movement of the melody could be heard. In addition to this linear impulse, all types of counterpoint achieve a sense of rhythmical progress by having a relatively static point against which the more rapid mobility of the other voices can be measured. Together with the several opposing melodies, the clash of dissonant intervals, the simultaneous declamation of separate texts, as well as the progress of several independent rhythms, Gothic music was able to build up a sense of mounting tension that set it apart as a distinctive new style.

IDEAS

In the century between the dedication of the great Romanesque abbey church at Cluny (1095) and the beginning of Chartres cathedral (1194), much more than a change in artistic styles had occurred. A mighty shift in social and political institutions and in basic modes of thought had taken place, and the resulting changes in church, secular, and artistic life brought into the open sharp divisions of opinion. Old conflicts, long damped by the power of the medieval theocracy, now burst into flames, and new ones broke out, fanned by the breaths of new voices clamoring to be heard. Intellectual disputes grew hot and acrid as emotional tensions deepened. In this critical situation, the rational processes of scholasticism were brought to bear on these divisive forces, and the Gothic is best understood as a clashing and dissonant style in which opposite elements were maintained momentarily in a state of uneasy equilibrium. With the eventual dissolution of the scholastic synthesis in the following century, the basic oppositions became so irreconcilable that they led in some cases to the battlefield, in others to schisms within the Church, and generally to growing philosophical and artistic conflicts.

Gothic Dualism

Politically, the age-old struggle of Church and state, evidenced in Romanesque times by the interminable quarrels between popes and Holy Roman emperors, now shaped up as the conflict between traditional ecclesiastical authority and the growing power of northern European kingdoms, especially France and England. Simultaneously came the beginning of a split between the internationalism of the Church and Holy Roman Empire and rising nationalistic consciousness that produced centuries of rivalry between the south and north for the domination of Europe.

The prevailing monastic and feudal organizations of Romanesque times had tended to separate society into widely scattered units of cloister and manor, thereby isolating many of the causes of social strains. But as the towns began to grow into cities, the disparate elements were brought together in a common center where confrontation made problems more immediate. Tensions mounted between the landed aristocrats on the one hand and the volatile urban groups on the other, between the monastic orders and the growing secular clergy. And towns witnessed at close range the bitter rivalries between abbot and bishop, lord and burgher, clergy and laity. For the common people there was always the contrast between the squalor in which they existed and the luxury of their lords, bishops, and abbots; the poverty of their daily lives and glowing promises of heavenly glory in the beyond; between the strife of their world and the visions of serenity and peace in paradise. The arts were torn between expressing the aspirations of this world and those of the next, and the artist, between accepting a relatively anonymous status in the service of God and competing actively with his fellows in search of worldly recognition. Instead of the comparative unity of artistic patronage in the aristocratically oriented Romanesque period, patronage in the city was now divided between the social groups of aristocrats and clergy on the one hand and the increasingly important bourgeoisie and guilds on

234. Gothic half-timbered house, Rouen. 15th century.

the other. The rising power of the middle class is well illustrated by such dwelling places as one of the surviving Gothic half-timbered houses at Rouen (Fig. 234), and the splendid residence of the banker Jacques Cœur at Bourges (Fig. 235).

In architecture, be it the interior or exterior of the Gothic cathedral, one has an awareness of the opposition between the masses and voids, the interplay of thrust and counterthrust, and of the principle of attraction and repulsion that awaken dead weights into dynamic forces. In sculpture, the conflict of the particular and universal is seen in the remarkable feeling for human individuality in some of the separate figures and the iconographic necessity of molding them into the dignified impersonality required of a row of prophets and saints. In literature, the opposition between Latin and the vernacular languages becomes as evident as the growing distinction between the sacred and secular musical styles. Within the province of the tonal art are found such external disparities as the fruitless academic discussions about the hypothetical nature of the music of the spheres and the increasing importance of the actual sounds heard in the choirs of the churches; the abstract study of theoretical acoustics in the universities and the practical art of writing and making music. In music also there are such internal differences as the singing of monophonic choruses alternately with groups singing polyphonically, the contrast between voices and instruments, the flow of horizontally moving melodic lines versus their simultaneous vertical aspects, the juxtaposition of consonance and dissonance, the rhythmical opposition between the independent voices within a polyphonic motet, line against line, *cantus* versus *discantus*—in short all the inherent oppositions of an art based on the principle of point counter point.

The Scholastic Synthesis

In the face of so many disparities, it seems only a step short of the miraculous that the Gothic style was able to effect a synthesis at all. Such dualities, however, generated the need for some sort of *modus vivendi*, and that this was achieved is yet another proof of the remarkable intellectual ingenuity and creative vitality of this period. The method for achieving this coexistence was that devised by scholasticism: a kind of pro-and-con dialogue followed by a resolution. Its results shaped up in the form of the Gothic monarchy, university, encyclopedia, *summa*, and cathedral.

On entering Chartres Cathedral through the Virgin Portal, the worshiper was reminded by the personification of the seven liberal arts that faith needed to be enlightened by reason and knowledge. Architecture had to be a kind of logic in stone; sculpture and glass had to be encyclopedic in scope; and music had to be a form of mathematics in sound. All experience, in fact, had to be interpreted intellectually in contrast to the more intuitive and emotional orientation of the Romanesque. To the scholastic philosopher, God, as the Creator of a world based on principles of reason, was approachable through the logical power of the mind. Hence the key to the understanding of the universe was in the exercise of man's rational faculties. Philosophical truth or artistic value was determined by how logically a proposition fitted a rationally ordered sytem.

Abelard's *Sic et Non (Pro and Con)* was an early manifesto of Gothic dualistic thinking. With unprecedented audacity, Abelard posed one pertinent question after another, lined up unimpeachable authorities from the Scriptures and Church fathers for and against the propositions. His purpose was to bring out into the open some of the wide cleavages of thought among sanctioned authorities, and he made no attempt at reconciliation. His scholastic successors debated whether ultimate truth was to be found through faith or reason, blind acceptance of hallowed authorities or evidence of the senses, universals or particulars, causes or effects, theses or antitheses, determinism or freedom of the will, intuition or reason. Thomas Aquinas and his fellow scholastics found the answer in the dialectical method; and Aquinas' synthesis, as found in his *Summa Theologiae (Summation of Theology)*, was a comprehensive attempt to bring together all Christian articles of faith in a rational system. Abelard's pros and cons, and the divergent views of the previous 1,000 years of speculation, were reconciled by a subtlety of intellect that has never been surpassed. Such a *Summa* was as intricately constructed as a Gothic cathedral and had to embrace the totality of a subject, systematically divided into propositions and subpropositions, with inclusions deduced from major and minor premises. Every logical syllogism was fitted exactly into place like each stone in a Gothic vault; and if one of the premises were disproved, the whole structure would fall like an arch without its keystone. Thomas Aquinas' *Summa* mounted the heights of philosophical grandeur, just as the vaults and spires of the Gothic master builders soared skyward.

235. Courtyard, House of Jacques Cœur, Bourges. 1443–1451.

From this highly rationalistic viewpoint followed the scholastic definition of beauty, which, according to St. Thomas, rested on the criteria of completeness, proportion, harmony, and clarity —because, he said, the mind needed order and demanded unity above all other considerations. Mathematical calculation and symbolism therefore played an important part in the thought of the time, though it was sometimes more closely allied with the sort of Pythagorean number-magic now associated with numerology than with the purely logical processes of mathematics in the modern sense. The number 3 was especially favored because of its association with the Trinity; 4, to a lesser extent because it signified the material elements of fire, air, earth, and water; 7, as the sum of the two, indicated man, since his dual nature was composed of both spirit and matter; and their product pointed to such groups as the 12 apostles, 12 lesser prophets, and so on. Since

(above) 236. Façade, Rouen Cathedral. 13th–16th centuries.

(top) 237. Ulm Cathedral. 1377–1492. Tower, 528′ high.

the sacred number was 3, it was used by most of the overall formal divisions, with the encyclopedias and the *Summas* each having three divisions; the syllogism, in three parts; the façades of cathedrals, three portals and the sculptural tympanums above, three rising bands. Naves have a main and two side aisles; vertically, they ascend in the triple division of nave arcade, triforium gallery, and clearstory; and in the clearstory, each bay at Chartres had two lancets and one rose window, and so on. The triple rhyming plan of the Latin poetry as in the *Dies Irae* (Chapter 8, p. 224) and in the *terza rima* will serve as literary examples. In music, the favorite Gothic form was the three-part motet, and the prevailing rhythm was ternary, which was called *tempus perfectum* because of its Trinity symbolism, while binary rhythms were ruled out because they were considered too worldly.

In the cathedral schools and later in the universities, music was studied mainly as a branch of mathematics. Bishop Fulbert of Chartres emphasized theory in the training of singers, saying that without it "the songs are worthless." His view was generally held throughout the Gothic period, and as one theorist put it, a singer who is ignorant of theory is like "a drunkard who, while he is able to find his home, is completely ignorant of the way that took him home." Mathematical considerations, in fact, led composers to emphasize the perfect intervals of the octave, fifth, and fourth for theoretical reasons more than for the agreeableness of sound. The whole tendency was to suppress sensuous beauty of tone and emphasize the mathematical, theoretical, and symbolic aspects of the art.

The rise of national monarchies in France and England began to limit the international authority of the papacy, as well as to curb the provincial powers of the feudal lords domestically by increasing centralization of civil authority. In England, a political resolution between king and nobles, and between nobles and commoners, was made in the Magna Charta that became the basis for parliamentary government. In France, the establishment of a working relationship between the king and the urban middle class accomplished a similar purpose. King Louis IX of France was adroit enough to strengthen his own kingdom, while maintaining such good relations with the popes that he became a saint. In the cities the guilds brought patrons and craftsmen together; meanwhile, the system of apprenticeships and examinations insured a high standard of quality and workmanship.

The undertaking of the fantastic crusades was found to be a way of uniting many opposing European factions in a cause against a common enemy. The code of chivalry was an attempt to reconcile the opposition between idealistic love and the gratification of the senses, and, more broadly, to establish a standard of behavior between strong and weak, lord and peasant, rich and poor, oppressor and oppressed. The Gothic universities were set up as institutions to bring together all the diverse disciplines and controversial personalities and to fit all the various intellectual activities into a single universal framework. Scholasticism became the common mode of thought, and its dialectic the common method of solving intellectual problems.

The structural uniformity of Gothic vaulting and buttressing was, in effect, the Gothic builder's answer to Romanesque experimentalism. Ample allowance for urban heterogeneity was made in the iconography of the individual cathedral and in the differences of cathedrals from town to town, and country to country, where each had distinctive character (Figs. 236–238). Both internally and externally, Gothic architecture tried to synthesize the building with the space surrounding it. Externally, the eye follows the multiplicity of rising vertical lines to the spires and pinnacles

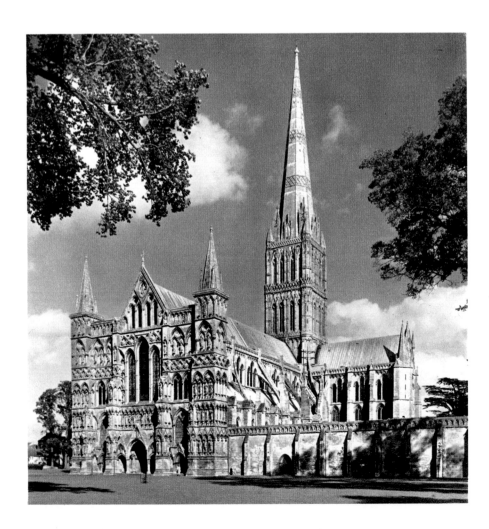

238. Salisbury Cathedral. 1220–1258.   473 × 230', spire 404' high.

and then to the sky. Inside, the experience is similar; the vertical lines rise to the window levels and thence through the glass to the space beyond. In contrast to the monastic church that was based on the notion of excluding the outside world, the Gothic cathedral attempted an architectural union of the inner and outer world as the exterior and interior flowed together through the glass-curtained walls. The thrust and counterthrust of the interior vaulting was paralleled on the outside by that of pier and flying buttress; the sculptural embellishments of the exterior were repeated in the iconography of the glass in the interior. Through the medium of stained glass, the iconographers endowed light with meaning by transforming physical light into metaphysical illumination.

The various European languages and dialects found a place for themselves in secular literature, but Latin was championed by the Church and universities as the universal language of scholarship. In music, the Latin and vernacular were reconciled in the polytextual motet; and when one language was used, the same form provided a highly ingenious method by which an authoritative text was declaimed, while at the same time one or more running commentaries upon it could be presented. Gothic music also represented a synthesis of theory and practice functioning together as equals. Through all these separate manifestations the Gothic spirit was revealed, whether in the systematic logic of St. Thomas, in the heightened sense of time and movement achieved by the musicians, or the visual aspirations and linear tensions of the builders.

No one of these resolutions was in any sense final, and the Gothic style must, in the last analysis, be viewed as a dynamic process rather than an end result. By contrast, a Greek temple or even a Romanesque abbey is a completed whole, and in both the observer's eye eventually can come to rest. The appeal of the Gothic lies in the very restlessness that prevents this sense of completion. The observer is caught and swept up in the general stream of movement, and from the initial impulse, he gets the desire to continue it. The completion, however, can only be in the imagination. There were, in fact, no finished cathedrals; each lacked something, from a set of spires in some cases to a nave as at Beauvais. Vincent's encyclopedia and St. Thomas' *Summa* were likewise never completed.

Gothic unity is therefore to be found mainly in such methods and procedures as its dialectic in philosophy, structural principles in architecture, and techniques of writing in literature and music. No more effective processes could have been devised to deal with the specific incongruities with which the Gothic mind had to contend. They were, in fact, the only ways to reconcile the seemingly irreconcilable, to arrive at the irrational by ingenious rational arguments, and to achieve the utmost in immateriality through material manifestations. The object of Gothic thought was thus to work out a method for comprehending the incomprehensible, for pondering on the imponderables, for dividing the indivisible. Gothic art as a whole was designed to bridge the impossible gap between matter and spirit, mass and void, natural and supernatural, inspiration and aspiration, the finite and the infinite.

239. NAUMBURG MASTER. *Uta.* *c.* 1250–1260. Naumburg Cathedral.

PART III
THE RENAISSANCE

8 - THE EARLY ITALIAN RENAISSANCE STYLE

ITALIAN PANORAMA, 14TH CENTURY

The oppositions that the Gothic 13th century had managed to maintain in a state of uneasy equilibrium by the application of scholastic logic and strict structurality broke out in the 14th century into open conflict. Like a stormy landscape, Italy was alternately chilled by the winds of a waning medieval winter and warmed by the first breaths of a waxing Renaissance spring. Gothic cathedrals were still being built in the north, while the dormant beauty of classical art was being revived in the south. Thunderous threats of fire and brimstone and fear of the Lord were hurled from church pulpits one day, to be followed the next by comforting Franciscan parables and assurance of divine love and mercy. Professors in universities still argued with the icy logic of scholastic philosophy, while the followers of St. Francis were persuading people with simple human truths. Some painters designed images of doomsday filled with warring angels and demons, while others portrayed Biblical stories as seen through the eyes of simple folk. And people wondered whether the world they lived in was a moral trap set by the devil to ensnare the unwary or a pleasant place a benign Creator meant them to enjoy.

For a drama of such sweeping scope, no single city or center could serve as the stage. All Europe, in fact, was the theater for this many-faceted performance in which men and their arts were in a state of creative ferment. The old Ghibelline and Guelph wars, which had started as a struggle between the forces loyal to the Holy Roman Empire and the partisans of the popes, assumed a new shape in the 14th century. People were moving from the country to the towns, where the entrenched landowning aristocrats rallied around the Ghibelline banner, and the growing ranks of city merchants and guilds of craftsmen raised the Guelph flag.

The new Franciscan and Dominican orders rarely kept to their cloisters but took to the highways and byways as preachers to all who would gather and listen. Internal Church dissensions were such that even the popes had fled their hereditary see in Rome to hold court in widely scattered residences, most notably at Avignon in southern France. Writers, such as Dante and Petrarch, became exiles from their native cities, and their words were written during extended sojourns in

(above) GIOTTO. *Scrovegni Family Donating Chapel*, detail of *Last Judgment*. c. 1305–1306. Fresco. Arena Chapel, Padua. (Compare Plate 17.)

General Events

	1140	Guelph and Ghibelline wars began
1182–	1226	St. Francis of Assisi; 1210 founded Franciscan order (confirmed by pope, 1223); 1225 wrote *Canticle of the Sun*; 1228 canonized
1198–	1216	Innocent III, pope; Church reached pinnacle of power
1228–	1253	Basilica of St. Francis built at Assisi
	1229	Thomas of Celano's first *Life of St. Francis*
	1247	Thomas of Celano's second *Life of St. Francis*
1252–	1273	Great Interregnum
	c.1260	Pulpit in Pisa Baptistry finished by Niccolo Pisano
	1262	St. Bonaventura's *Life of St. Francis*
1278–	1283	Campo Santo at Pisa built by Giovanni di Simone
c.1296–	1300	Frescoes on life of St. Francis painted at Assisi
c.1305–	1309	Giotto painted frescoes on history of the Virgin at Padua
1308–	1311	Duccio painted Maestà altarpiece, Siena Cathedral
1309–	1376	Popes resided at Avignon
	1310	First *Compagnie dei Laudesi* founded in Florence
1314–	1321	*Divine Comedy* written by Dante Alighieri
	1316	*Ars Nova*, musical treatise, by Philippe de Vitry
	c.1320	Giotto painted Bardi Chapel frescoes in Santa Croce, Florence
	1322	*Little Flowers of St. Francis*
1330–	1339	Bronze doors of Baptistry at Florence cast by Andrea Pisano
	c.1334	Andrea Pisano and Giotto collaborated on sculpture for Florence Campanile

	1348	Black Death swept Europe
1348–	1352	*Decameron* written by Boccaccio
	c.1350	*Triumph of Death* painted in Campo Santo at Pisa by Traini
	c.1354	*Triumph of Death* written by Petrarch
1378–	1417	Great Schism between rival popes

Philosophers

c.1214–	1294	Roger Bacon, Franciscan monk and scientist
c.1225–	1274	Thomas Aquinas, scholastic philosopher
c.1270–	1347	William of Occam, Franciscan monk and nominalist philosopher

Painters

1240–	c.1302	Giovanni Cimabue
c.1255–	1319	Duccio di Buoninsegna
c.1266–	c.1336	Giotto di Bondone
c.1285–	1344	Simone Martini
1305–	1348	Pietro Lorenzetti active
1323–	1348	Ambrogio Lorenzetti active
1321–	1363	Francesco Traini active

Sculptors

c.1205–	1278	Niccolo (d'Apulia) Pisano
c.1250–	c.1317	Giovanni Pisano
c.1270–	1349	Andrea Pisano

Writers

1265–	1321	Dante Alighieri
1304–	1374	Petrarch (Francesco Petrarca)
1312–	1353	Giovanni Boccaccio

Musicians

c.1200–	c.1255	Thomas of Celano
	1306	Jacopone da Todi died
1291–	1361	Philippe de Vitry
1325–	1397	Francesco Landini, organist-composer at Florence

half a dozen centers. Like them, the great painters were journeymen, traveling to wherever their commissions called them. Giotto, the leader of the Florentine school, did fresco cycles that occupied him several years each in Rome, Assisi, and Padua as well as in his home city. Simone Martini of Siena was active in Pisa and Naples before he painted a chapel of St. Francis' church in Assisi. Then he spent his last years at the papal court in Avignon. The great sculptors of Pisa worked also in Siena, Florence, Padua, and Arezzo. Musicians, likewise, sought their fortunes at various courts,

with French and Flemish influences and musical forms dominating the Italian musical scene. Artistic idioms in general showed wide variation, with local styles springing up in such centers as Venice, Pisa, Siena, and Florence, while an international style took shape in southern France at Avignon, where the papal court attracted the best talents from every country.

In this era of change, the little village of Assisi in the Umbrian hills of central Italy became more representative than a large center like Rome. A town of such small size would, of course, have been too insignificant to support a major art movement, and no important artist could have survived in this provincial location, had Assisi not been the birthplace of one of the most beloved of medieval saints. Consequently, after the completion in the mid-13th century of Assisi's great pilgrimage basilica, many of the outstanding artists of the age gathered there as journeymen to decorate its walls.

The town of Assisi was built upon a rocky hill in the midst of a countryside more austere than lush. A truly mountainous terrain might have nurtured a rugged spirit capable of bringing down some new commandments from above, but the gentle rolling green hills instead brought forth the most humble of Christian saints. A large city might have produced a great organizer of men, capable of moving the minds of the many with his clever speech to bring about a new social order. Francis of Assisi, however, recognized the dangers of bombastic oratory and the transient nature of all forms of social organization, and he accomplished his mission with the sweet persuasion of simple parables and the eloquence of his own exemplary life.

While the mature life of St. Francis fell within the 13th century, the collection of tales that made him a living legend, as well as the full development of the Franciscan movement, belongs to the 14th. The clergy who received their training in the universities and the scholarly orders of monks had never reached a broad segment of society. The Franciscans, however, found a way into the hearts and minds of the multitudes by preaching to them in their own vernacular and in the simplest terms, and Franciscan voices were heard more often in village squares than in the pulpits of the churches. The essence of the Franciscan idea is contained in the mystical marriage of the saint to Lady Poverty, the subject of one of the Assisi frescoes. When a young man had approached Christ and asked what he should do in order to have eternal life, the answer came, "... go and sell that thou hast, and give to the poor, and thou shalt have treasure in heaven: and come and follow me" (Matt. 19:21). St. Francis took this commandment literally, and in his last will and testament described his early life and that of his first followers. "They contented themselves," he wrote, "with a tunic, patched within and without, with the cord and breeches, and we desired to have nothing more. . . . We loved to live in poor and abandoned churches, and we were ignorant and submissive to all." He then asked his followers to "appropriate nothing to themselves, neither a house, nor a place, nor anything; but as pilgrims and strangers in this world, in poverty and humility serving God, they shall confidently go seeking for alms."

THE BASILICA OF ST. FRANCIS AT ASSISI

Had St. Francis' precept of complete poverty been followed strictly, no great art movement would have developed at Assisi. A building program involved the accumulation and expenditure of large sums, and immediately after Francis' death this matter created dissension among those who had been closest to him. Brother Elias wanted to build a great church as a fitting monument to his friend and master, while others felt that Francis should be honored by as close adherence as possible to his simple life pattern. The monument Brother

240. Franciscan monastery and town of Assisi.

Elias had in mind would take a vast treasure to erect, and many of his fellow friars were shocked when Elias set up a porphyry vase to collect offerings from pilgrims who came to Assisi to honor Francis. Yet only two years later, at the very time of his canonization, a great basilica and monastery (Fig. 240) was begun on the crest of the hill where St. Francis had wished to be buried.

Taking advantage of the natural contours of the site, the architects designed a structure that included two churches, a large one above for pilgrims (Fig. 241) and a smaller one below for the Franciscan monks. These twin churches seem to grow out of the hillside, the upper one resting like a crown on the brow of the hill, the lower one nestling on its bosom. It is this striking location rather than great architectural distinction that gives the Basilica of St. Francis at Assisi its unique character.

In spite of their comparatively large size, both churches are without side aisles, having just central naves terminating beyond transepts in polygonal apses. The large interior areas are spanned by spacious quadripartite groin vaults in the Lombard manner, which are partially supported by rows of columns set against the walls. Italian Gothic, contrary to the northern style, did not accent well-lighted interiors in which the walls were almost completely replaced with stained-glass windows. The southern sun made shade more welcome, and the interiors took on the character of cool retreats from the burning brightness of the world outside. The absence of a nave arcade and side aisles, and the small number of stained-glass windows, allowed ample wall space in both Assisi churches for the brightly colored fresco paintings that cover them. Lighted principally by the clearstory, the walls of the upper church glow in the dim interior with a mild inner light all their own, illuminated as they are by scenes from the life of St. Francis. More than anything else, it is these murals that bring the twin churches their most special distinction, and the names of the artists who worked on them read like a roster of the great painters of the period: Cimabue and Giotto of Florence and Simone Martini and Pietro Lorenzetti of the Sienese school.

THE LIFE OF ST. FRANCIS IN FRESCO

On entering the nave of the upper church at Assisi (Fig. 242), the observer encounters on its walls the series of frescoes on the life of St. Francis that tradition attributes to Giotto. His actual role as principal or part of a school of artists, his activity as designer or painter, are still matters of scholarly conjecture. The date generally assigned to the work is the four-year span just before the jubilee year of 1300. Knowing that pilgrims in unprecedented numbers would be traveling to Rome for the celebrations, the artists at Assisi

241. Upper Church of St. Francis, Assisi. 1228–1253.

Plate 17. GIOTTO. *Last Judgment. c.* 1305–1306. Fresco. Arena Chapel, Padua. (See p. 223.)

Plate 18. LORENZO GHIBERTI. *Gates of Paradise*, east doors of the Baptistry, Florence.
1425–1452. Gilt bronze, 18′6″ high. (See p. 241.)

242. Nave, Upper Church of St. Francis, Assisi. 1228–1253.

made every effort to cover the bare walls of the upper church in time. The frescoes for the friars' own lower church had to wait until the mid-14th century for completion.

Giotto, like other master artists of his period, had learned to work in a variety of techniques. In addition to frescoes, he did mosaics, painted altarpieces in tempera on wood, and was a sculptor. Several years before his death, he was named the chief architect of Florence, and in this capacity he designed the bell tower of the cathedral (Fig. 263), still popularly called Giotto's Tower. Some of the sculptured reliefs on the ground-floor level of this campanile may have been his, and others were presumably carried out from his designs by Andrea Pisano. Giotto's greatest fame, however, rests most securely on the three fresco cycles in Assisi, Padua, and Florence.

The fresco medium calls for the rapid and deft strokes of a sure hand and for designs that harmonize with the architectural scheme and awaken walls into a vibrant and colorful life. After first covering the entire wall with a layer of rough plaster and allowing it to dry thoroughly,

the artist makes a *cartoon*, a preliminary drawing in charcoal, on the surface. Then, taking an area he can finish in a single day, he smooths on a thin layer of wet plaster and retraces his original drawing. Next, earth pigments are mixed with water, combined with white of egg as a binder, and applied directly to the fresh plaster—hence the term *fresco*. The pigments and wet plaster combine chemically to produce a surface as permanent as that of any medium in painting. Artists sometimes paint over the surface after it is dry, but this repainting usually flakes off in time. If corrections are necessary, the entire section must be knocked out and redone. Fresco, then, is a medium that does not encourage overly subtle types of expression; and it is best adapted to a certain boldness of design and simplicity of composition. The emotional depth, the communicative value, and the masterly execution of Giotto's cycles rank them among the highest achievements in world art.

The first two panels of the series at Assisi are worthy of Giotto himself, but since Giotto worked with a corps of assistants, it is impossible to be completely certain these are actually his work. On (below) 243. GIOTTO(?). *Miracle of the Spring. c.* 1296–1300. Fresco. Upper Church of St. Francis, Assisi.

(right) 244. GIOTTO(?). *Sermon to the Birds. c.* 1296–1300. Fresco. Upper Church of St. Francis, Assisi.

the right, after one passes through the entrance portals, is the *Miracle of the Spring* (Fig. 243), while on the left is the well-known *Sermon to the Birds* (Fig. 244). The order of the scenes is psychological rather than chronological. The placing of this pair on either side of the entrance seems to have been done to impress pilgrims at the outset with the most popular Franciscan legends—those showing the saint ministering to the poor and humble on one side, and his kinship with all God's creatures, including his brothers the birds, on the other.

The literary source for the *Miracle of the Spring* is in the *Legend of the Three Companions*, which tells of Francis' journey to the monastery of Monte La Verna. A fellow friar, a peasant, and his donkey accompanied him, but the way was steep and the day hot. Overcome by thirst, the peasant cried out for water. Kneeling in prayer, the saint turned to him saying: "Hasten to that rock and thou shalt find a living water which in pity Christ has sent thee from the stone to drink." Pilgrims entering the church, like the peasant, were athirst for spiritual refreshment, and the placement of this picture assured them that they had arrived at a spiritual spring.

The composition is as simple as it is masterly. St. Francis is the focal center of two crisscrossing diagonal lines like the letter **X**. The descending light from the rocky peak in the upper right reveals the contours of the mountain in a series of planes and reaches its greatest intensity in its union with St. Francis' halo, diminishing in his shadow where his two companions and the donkey stand. The dark mountain at the upper left moves downward toward the shadowy figure of the drinking peasant at the lower right, as if to say he is still in spiritual darkness. But since St. Francis is also on this diagonal line, the way to enlightenment is suggested. Giotto's inimitable mountains are found in such other of his major compositions as *Joachim*

Returning to the Sheepfold (Fig. 259), the *Flight into Egypt*, and the great *Pietà* (Fig. 260), all in the Arena Chapel at Padua. Structurally, the mountains advance and recede to form niches for his figures, and their hardness and heaviness are complementary to the compassion and expressiveness of his human beings. The mountains, or architectural backgrounds, do not exist in their own right but become volumes and masses in Giotto's pictorial designs as well as inanimate extensions of human nature. Giotto's spatial proportions, furthermore, are psychologically rather than actually correct. Human beings, in keeping with their greater expressive importance, loom large against their mountain backgrounds; and his scattered trees are more spatial accents than natural trees.

The *Sermon to the Birds* (Fig. 244) on the other side of the entrance is less dramatic and more lyrical. The incident, taken from St. Bonaventura's life of St. Francis, is the one in which the birds hovered around the saint or perched in the bushes, inclining their heads as he spoke to them: "My brothers, the birds, much ought ye to praise your Creator, who hath clothed you with feathers and given you wings to fly, and hath made over unto you the pure air and careth for you without your taking thought of yourselves." The masterly touch is seen in the utter economy of means. Balanced by the massive stylized tree on the right, the two human figures contrast interestingly with each other. While St. Francis himself is intent on the birds, and his hands are raised in a gesture of blessing, those of his less-inspired companion are lifted as if he wished to shoo these little feathered brothers right out of the picture.

Perhaps the most dramatic of the series is *St. Francis Renouncing His Father* (Fig. 245) after a controversy involving worldly goods. In his haste to abandon the material world, Francis casts off his garments and stands naked before the townspeople saying: "Until this hour I have called thee my father upon earth; from henceforth, I may say confidently, my Father who art in Heaven, in whose hands I have laid up all my treasure, all my trust, and all my hope." The bishop covers Francis with his own cloak and receives him into the Church. The expressions of the various figures as revealed in their gestures and facial expressions

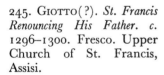

245. GIOTTO(?). *St. Francis Renouncing His Father. c.* 1296–1300. Fresco. Upper Church of St. Francis, Assisi.

make this fresco an interesting study of human attitudes. The angry father has to be physically restained from violence by a fellow townsman, yet his face shows the puzzled concern of a parent who cannot understand his son's actions. His counterpart on the other side is the bishop, who becomes the new father of the saint in the Church. Disliking such a scene, his glance shows both embarrassment and sympathy. These opposing figures are supported respectively by the group of townspeople and the apartment house and the clergymen and church buildings. An interesting pictorial geometry is used to unify the picture and resolve the tension. The two opposing groups, symbolizing material pursuits and spiritual aspirations, become the base of a triangle; between them the hand of St. Francis points upward toward the apex where the hand of God is coming through the clouds.

A notable example of Giotto's late style is found in the *Death of St. Francis* (Figs. 246, 247), the climax of a series of seven he did twenty years later for the Church of Santa Croce in Florence. The static horizontal lines of the recumbent body are relieved by the varied gestures of the surrounding groups, and with one exception all eyes concentrate on the head of St. Francis. The architectural framework echoes the disposition of the figures, with the horizontal line of the wall paralleling the body of St. Francis and the vertical lines, those of the standing figures. Within this setting a sense of depth is conveyed by color. The ermine collar and red robe of the figure kneeling at the saint's right hand project him into the foreground; the neutral grays and browns of the habits of the monks

246. GIOTTO. *Death of St. Francis* (with 19th-century restorations). *c.* 1318–1320. Bardi Chapel, Church of Santa Croce, Florence.

247. GIOTTO. *Death of St. Francis* (without 19th-century restorations).

216

248. GIOVANNI DI SIMONE. Campo Santo, Pisa. Begun 1277.

back of the bier place them in the middle ground; and the deep blue sky recedes into the background. Here again Giotto uses a triangular pattern in telling his story. According to St. Bonaventura's biography, at the moment of Francis' death one of the brothers beheld a vision of the saint's "soul under the likeness of a star exceeding bright borne on a dazzling cloudlet over many waters mounting in a straight curve unto Heaven...." In the fresco, the sides of the triangle are the line carried upward from the saint's head by the gesture of the disciple who sees the vision and the line formed by the inclining crucifix that meet at the apex where the heavenward journey is seen. Giotto thus ties the story content, emotional situation, and dramatic tension into a tight whole in his pictorial structure.

BEFORE AND AFTER THE BLACK DEATH

All went well in Italy during the first third of the 14th century. Townspeople prospered, life was good, the arts flourished. Beginning in 1340, however, a series of disasters befell the peninsula, starting with local crop failures and continuing with the miseries of famine and pestilence. The climax came in a fearful outbreak of bubonic plague in the catastrophic year of 1348. In this so-called "Black Death," more than half the populations of such cities as Florence, Siena, and Pisa perished. A chronicler of Siena, after burying five of his children with his own hands, said quite simply: "No one wept for the dead, because everyone expected death himself."

An event so cataclysmic, and one that spread over the entire continent, was bound to have a deep effect upon social and cultural trends. Many survivors found themselves suddenly impoverished or, through unexpected inheritances, vastly enriched. Thousands of residents in the relatively immune countryside flocked into the cities to take the place of those who had died. The lives of individuals underwent radical changes that quickened their normal instincts. For some, it was the "eat, drink, and be merry" philosophy, exemplified in Boccaccio's *Decameron*; for others, it was the moral recrimination and repentance, as seen in the purgatorial vision of the same author's later *Corbaccio*. Driven by fear and a sense of guilt, people felt that something had gone disastrously wrong and that the Black Death, like the Biblical plagues of old, must have been sent by an angry God to chastise mankind and turn him from his wicked ways. Both Boccaccio and Petrarch among the literary men turned to this view after their earlier more worldly writings, and what was true of literature was true also of painting.

The attitude before and after the Black Death is well illustrated at Pisa and Siena where important architectural, sculptural, and pictorial developments took place in the late 13th and early 14th centuries. The Cathedral of Pisa and its campanile (Fig. 188), the famous leaning tower, both date from Romanesque times. The Baptistry and Campo Santo, which complete the group, stem from the late 13th century. The Campo Santo (Fig. 248), a churchyard for burials, was designed and begun by Giovanni di Simone in the form of a Gothic cloister. The garth, or open courtyard, derived much fame at the time because its soil had been taken from Mt. Calvary and transported to Pisa by the shipload.

Giovanni Pisano and his father Niccolo were the two outstanding sculptors of their time. Niccolo Pisano, also known as Nicola d'Apulia from his southern Italian origin, designed a handsome pul-

249. NICCOLO PISANO. *Pulpit. c.* 1260. Alabaster and marble. Baptistry, Pisa.

pit with six religious panels for the Baptistry at Pisa (Fig. 249), and some years later Giovanni did one for the Cathedral. The panels of both depict scenes from the New Testament. The differing attitudes of the father's generation and of the son's are revealed when panels dealing with the same subject are placed side by side; together, their work represents the trend of sculpture before the Black Death.

Niccolo's panel of the *Annunciation and Nativity* (Fig. 250) clearly was influenced by the ancient sarcophagi the sculptor knew from his formative years spent near Rome. The Virgin appears as a dignified Roman matron reclining in a characteristic classical pose, while the angel at the left in the annunciation section is seen against a classical temple and is dressed in a Roman toga, as are many of the other figures. Niccolo employs the old simultaneous mode of narration, with the Virgin making three appearances on the same panel, and the relief as a whole is permeated by a monumental calm. Giovanni's work, as evidenced by his *Nativity and Annunciation to the Shepherds* (Fig. 251), moved away from his father's classicism into the French Gothic orbit. His figures are smaller in scale and more naturally proportioned to their surrounding space. Greater animation and agitation of line replace the serene repose of his father's style. The work of both father and son, however, has a sense of human warmth that closely resembles the spirit of Giotto's frescoes.

Nearby Siena, prior to the Black Death, was also enjoying a period of prosperity. Unlike its

250. NICCOLO PISANO. *Annunciation and Nativity.* 1259–1260. Detail of Fig. 249. Marble and alabaster, 33½ × 45¼ ". Baptistry, Pisa.

rival city Florence, which was a Guelph stronghold where power was held by the guilds and rich merchants, Siena was a staunch Ghibelline town dominated by landed aristocrats. These oppositions led Florence in a more progressive direction and kept Siena as a bastion of tradition. Cimabue, the leading Florentine artist of the late 13th century who brought the Gothic style to its apogee in his city, was succeeded by the formidable figure of Giotto whose painting points clearly to the coming Renaissance. In Siena, however, the great Duccio was followed by Simone Martini and the Lorenzetti brothers, who continued in the Byzantine tradition that had been introduced into Italy via such centers as Ravenna and Venice many centuries earlier. Despite this traditionalism, the Sienese school poured enough late-Gothic wine into the old medieval wine skins to bring about a brilliant, albeit final, flowering of Italo-Byzantine painting.

Three altarpieces for Florentine churches— similar in purpose, theme, and form but different in style—will illustrate this painterly trend. Cimabue's *Madonna Enthroned* (Fig. 252), designed for the high altar of Santa Trinità, has all the feeling of medieval majesty and monumentality. Gothic verticality governs the two-story composition with four solemn prophets below displaying their scrolls and the ascending deployment of the eight angels (below) 253. Duccio. *"Rucel-lai" Madonna.* 1285. Tempera on wood, 14′ 9″ × 9′ 6″. Uffizi, Florence.

(right) 254. Giotto. *Madonna Enthroned. c.* 1310. Tempera on wood, 10′ 8″ × 6′ 8″. Uffizi, Florence.

above. The Madonna sits frontally on a solid architectural throne of complexly inlaid wood. Her dark-blue mantle and rose-red robe are flecked with highlights of gold that combine with the rich folds to create a rhythmic linear pattern. The Christ Child conforms to the theological image of the miniature patriarch born knowing all things. Duccio's so-called *"Rucellai" Madonna* (Fig. 253), from the Church of Santa Maria Novella, is in a lighter, more buoyant and decorative vein. While Duccio undoubtedly knew Cimabue's monumental style, his kneeling angels are airier, as if gently settling down after a heavenly flight. The folds of the background drapery, liberal use of gold, Byzantine opulence of line, surpassing delicacy of the zigzag edges of the Madonna's robe, slight off-center angle of the throne, gauzy drapery of the Child whose mantle has slipped down—all achieve a maximum of grace and elegance.

The new direction of the early Renaissance, however, is manifest in Giotto's *Madonna Enthroned*

(Fig. 254), painted for the Church of Ognissanti about twenty years later than those of Cimabue and Duccio. Two angels kneel in the foreground, while the angels of the heavenly choir are placed one in front of the other so as to expand the sense of space and to create a recession in depth toward the back row where six grave saints are depicted. The drawing is simplified, thus parting company with its predecessors, the Madonna's gaze meets that of her beholders, her figure is heavier, the breasts prominent, the Child in a more natural posture, and her robe is modeled in light and shadow so as to delineate the flesh beneath.

In the *Annunciation* (Plate 16) by Duccio's Sienese disciple and Giotto's contemporary, Simone Martini, aristocratic aloofness prevails. The Gothic setting is courtly with the elegant vase of lilies and the regal Madonna draped in a French style blue gown rendered in powdered lapis lazuli. Disturbed in her reading by the sudden appearance of the Archangel Gabriel, his robes and wings aflutter, the startled Virgin recoils in fear and astonishment as she hears the words that appear in relief: "Hail Mary... the Lord is with thee." The composition is a masterly combination of color and curvilinear design.

Ambrogio Lorenzetti's *Good Government* is one of several large-scale murals that decorate a room in the Palazzo Pubblico (Town Hall) at Siena. The subject is an allegory in which a noble king is enthroned amid such virtues as Justice, Wisdom, Concord, and Peace. In the detail (Fig. 255), one sees Siena where citizens are dancing in the streets (foreground center), peasants are bringing produce to market (lower right), and the winding streets lead the eye above where workmen are completing the roof of a building. Borrowing much from Giotto but without his sense of drama, Ambrogio Lorenzetti's crowded scenes are more spacious than earlier Gothic paintings, but his whole composition still retains the gaily colored decorative quality of Gothic tapestries.

When Ambrogio and Pietro Lorenzetti perished in the Black Death of 1348, Sienese art declined. The reaction to the great plague is well illustrated in the series of frescoes on the inner walls of the Campo Santo at Pisa. The theme is the Last Judgment, and Traini's *Triumph of Death* (Fig. 256) took its name from a poem by Petrarch. While no cause-and-effect relationship between picture and poem can be proved, both were reactions to the plague, both shared common attitudes of the time, and both were based on a similar theme.

Triumph of Death is a grandiose utterance, with so much detail crowded into every square inch of space that something in it was bound to appeal to everybody. Like the sermons of the time, each part warned of the imminence of death, the terrors of hell if the soul were claimed by the devil, or the bliss of being carried off by the angels. The latter process, however, seems anything but peaceful, since the devils contend furiously with the angels for the spirits of the dead that appear as nude forms. The tug of war over the soul of the paunchy monk on the right side above the scene in the pleasure garden is a typical example. When the

255. AMBROGIO LORENZETTI. *Good Government* (detail). 1338–1340. Fresco. Palazzo Pubblico, Siena.

256. FRANCESCO TRAINI. *Triumph of Death*. c. 1350 (partially destroyed 1944). Fresco. Campo Santo, Pisa.

demons win, they cast their victims into the flames of the open volcano at the top. What happens to the souls saved by the angels is left to the imagination.

Death is beheld in the guise of a hideous blonde woman flying on enormous bat's wings and carrying a scythe like Father Time. She passes over the miserable creatures in the lower center who cry out to be relieved of their intolerable sufferings. Instead she is about to swoop down on the group of ten figures in the prime of their lives, who are reading, conversing, and enjoying the delights of the world. Everything dies in her wake, as seen in the piles of corpses beneath her; and the next two victims are being pointed out by the black-winged angels of death who hover above the pair on the left of the group. One is a youth holding a falcon and the other a maiden fondling a dog in her lap. In Petrarch's poem, Death is also represented by a feminine form and the scene is similar.

A lady clothed in black, whose stern looks were
With horror fill'd, and did like hell appear,
Advanced, and said, "You who are proud to be
So fair and young, yet have no eyes to see

How near you are your end; behold, I am
She whom they fierce and blind and cruel name,
Who meet untimely deaths;...

The likeness of the group in the pleasure garden to that in Boccacio's *Decameron* seems too close to be a coincidence. The book tells of ten well-to-do young Florentines who escape from the plague, which is ravaging their city, to a country villa where they entertain themselves with lively tales, music, and dancing. As in the *Decameron*, the group in the fresco is composed of seven women and three men; all are animated by a vivacious spirit; and, as the description in Boccaccio's introduction goes: "Breakfast done, the tables were removed, and the queen bade fetch instruments of music; for all, ladies and young men alike, knew how to tread a measure, and some of them played and sang with great skill. So, at her command, Dioneo having taken a lute, and Fiametta a viol, they struck up a dance in sweet concert ...." The similarity of the group, even to those on the far right who are playing the musical instruments, indicates that the painter may well have had the *Decameron* in mind when he designed his fresco.

In the lower left, a group of mounted nobles are equipped for the chase, but instead of the quarry they are pursuing, they find only the prey of death. Inside the three open coffins serpents are consuming the corpses of the onetime great of the earth. Petrarch also speaks of death as the great leveler when he asks "the Popes, Emperors, nor Kings, no enseigns wore of their past hight but naked show'd and poor. Where be their riches, where their precious gems? Their miters, scepters, robes and diadems?" Hard by is a bearded Anchorite monk unfolding a prophetic scroll that warns them to repent before it is too late. The only relief from this scene of horror and desolation is found in the upper left where some monks are gathered around a chapel busying themselves with the usual monastic duties. Apparently only those who renounce the world can find respite from its general turmoil and terror of death.

In his *Last Judgment* (Plate 17) at Padua, Giotto's emphasis on the tortures of hell is minimal, while in Traini's mural and in other doomsday pictures done after the Black Death, the stark horror is relieved only by such occasional tranquil scenes as the monastery chapel. The attitude is the reverse of the milder, more humanistic spirit of Giotto. Traini's designs, furthermore, are as complex and burdened with detail as Giotto's are simple. Traini also included allegories that go beyond the pictorial medium. The two angels behind the figure of Death, for example, unfold a scroll; the miserable ones petition Death in writing as well as in gesture; and the monk warning the hunting party does so with an inscription. Such details weigh down the picture with a heaviness quite foreign to Giotto's buoyant work and are apt to obscure the picture's meaning.

MUSIC AND LITERATURE

The *Dies Irae* and the *Canticle of the Sun*

The contrast between the dour, threatening medieval world view and the benign, joyful Franciscan spirit is illustrated by two 13th-century hymns. The facts of their composition alone are sufficient to point out the ideational cleavage of the period. The *Dies Irae*, which so admirably reflects the prevailing medieval spirit, was written

Di - es i - rae, di - es il - la   Sol - vet __ saec - lum __
Quan-tus tre - mor est fu - tu - rus, Quan- do __ ju - dex __

in fa - vil - la,   Te - ste __   Da - vid __ cum Si - byl - la.
est ven - tu - rus,   Cunc -ta __   stri - cte __ dis - cus - su - rus.

by the great Latin stylist Thomas of Celano a few years before he met St. Francis and became one of his friars. The second, the *Canticle of the Sun*, is by St. Francis himself. Thomas of Celano entered the Franciscan order about the year 1215, enjoyed the friendship of St. Francis for several years, and was entrusted by Pope Gregory IX with the official biography that was written shortly after Francis' canonization in 1228.

In the triple stanzas and 57 lines of the *Dies Irae*, the medieval Latin poetic style reaches a high point. Its content invokes the vision of the final dissolution of the universe, the sounding of the angelic trumpets calling the dead forth from their tombs, and the overwhelming majesty of the coming of Christ as king to judge the quick and the dead. The grandeur of its language and the perfection of its poetic form are in every way equal to this solemn and awesome theme. The images and moods run a gamut from anger and terror to hope and bliss before coming to a close with a final supplication for eternal rest. A sampling of its 19 vivid verses reads:

Day of Wrath! O day of mourning!
See fulfilled the prophets' warning,
Heaven and earth in ashes burning!

Wondrous sound the trumpet flingeth;
Through earth's sepulchres it ringeth;
All before the Throne it bringeth.

Guilty, now I pour my moaning,
All my shame with anguish owning;
Spare, O God, Thy suppliant groaning!

While the wicked are confounded,
Doomed to flames of woe unbounded,
Call me, with Thy saints surrounded.

Although the colorful alliterations and verbal rhythms of the Latin original have a music all their own, the *Dies Irae* is inseparable from a melodic setting in the mixed Dorian mode. While the melody cannot with certainty be attributed to Thomas of Celano, the close correspondence of tone and word makes it definite that they were at least from the same time. Both the poem and its melody found their way into the liturgy as a sequence that is still an indispensable part of the requiem mass for the dead. Sequences are so named because they follow the gradual and alleluia in the part of the mass between the reading of the epistle and the gospel. They attained wide popularity during this period and usually were sung by both congregation and choir.

The most characteristic Franciscan contribution to poetry and music is found in a body of informal spontaneous hymns called *laudi spirituali*—songs of praise or, simply, lauds—traceable directly to St. Francis and his immediate circle. The practice of spontaneous hymn singing continued from his time onward and in the 14th century was firmly established as the most popular form of religious music. Singing societies known as *Compagnie dei Laudesi*, companies of laudists, have existed up to the present time, mainly in Italy. Besides Provençal French, Francis had learned the songs of Provence from his mother, who was of an old family of that region, and the biography known as the *Legend of the Three Companions* recounts how he sang aloud the lauds and canticles while praying and how during his travels "the holy man sang praises in French with a voice loud and clear." Since this was the great period of the troubadours, when many of the best known of these lyric poets visited Italy, St. Francis certainly was well acquainted with their lyrics and music. By his knowledge of the forms of these Provençal poets and by his practice of bursting into rhapsodic verse in his own vernacular Umbrian Italian, he played a leading role in the new poetic movement. Significantly, he called himself and his companions who sang the lauds with him *jongleurs de Dieu*, minstrels of God. St. Francis thereby identified himself with the performing musicians of the people rather than with the aristocratic writers of amorous verse.

In music, as in his religious work, St. Francis drew together the sacred, courtly, and popular traditions. The lauds were thus a poetic bridge between the traditional music of the Church, the music of the castle, and the music of the streets. The words always had a religious theme; often they were mere paraphrases of psalms and litanies sung to popular airs, but, above all, they were music and poetry that the people could both sing and feel with their hearts. Contrapuntal choral music, whether it was in the form of a church motet or a secular madrigal, was a sophisticated musical medium that needed the voices of skilled professionals. By contrast, the lauds were folklike in spirit, simple and direct in their appeal, and sung either as solos or jointly with others in unison. Just as the highly trained monastic choir was characteristic of the Cluniac movement and the contrapuntal chorus the musical counterpart of the northern Gothic spirit, the lauds became the special and characteristic expression of the Franciscans.

The *Canticle of the Sun,* known definitely to be by St. Francis, is at once the most sublime of all the lauds as well as the most original. The legend goes that when St. Francis was recovering from an illness in a hut outside the convent of St. Clare, the nuns heard from his lips this rapturous new song. The informality, even casualness, of its composition and its rambling rhythms and rhymes make it as simple and unaffected in its form as the Umbrian dialect in which it is written. It is thus characteristically opposed to the canons of scholarly Latin on one hand and to the erotic courtly utterances of the troubadours on the other. Sincerity and deep human feeling dominate the unequal strophes of St. Francis' songs of praise, rather than any attempt at learned communication or poetic elegance.

Altissimu, onnipotente, bon signore, tue so' le laude la gloria e l'onore, et onne benedizione a te solu, altissimu, se konfanno a nullu homo ene dignu to mentovare!

O most high, almighty, good Lord God, to Thee belong praise, glory, honor, and all blessing!

Praised be my Lord God with all his creatures, and especially our brother the sun, who brings us the day and who brings us the light; fair is he and shines with very great splendor; O Lord, he signifies to us Thee!

Praised be my Lord for our sister the moon, and for the stars, the which He has set clear and lovely in heaven.

Praised be my Lord for our sister water, who is very serviceable unto us and humble and precious and clean.

Praised be my Lord for our brother fire, through whom thou givest us light in the darkness; and he is bright and pleasant and very mighty and strong.

Praised be my Lord for our mother the earth, the which doth sustain us and keep us, and bringeth forth divers fruits and flowers of many colors, and grass.

The Assisi manuscript that contains the words of the *Canticle of the Sun* in its purest form also provided space for musical notation, which is, alas, blank. While the original melody seems to have been lost forever, countless lauds do survive, some of which date back to shortly after St. Francis' time. A Franciscan monk by the name of Jacopone da Todi, who died in 1306, was one of the most prolific producers of lauds. His most famous hymn is the *Stabat Mater Dolorosa,* which was officially incorporated in the liturgy in the 18th century to be sung for the feast of the Seven Dolours. This remarkable man, like St. Francis before him, was of Umbrian origin, and, after a succession of such diverse careers as lawyer, hermit, and Franciscan preacher, he turned poet and composer. His hymns readily found their way into the texts of the early miracle plays, and his music became the foundation of the laudistic tradition. The example below is a part of one of his lauds, which continues in the form of a dialogue. Its emotional intensity and stylistic character mark it as typical of the early Franciscan movement.

Lauda (late 13th century)   JACOPONE DA TODI (after Liuzzi)

O Chri-sto' ni-po-ten-te, Do-ve sie-te_ in-vi-a-to, Che si po-ve-ra-men-te_____ Gi-te_ pel-le-gri-na-to?

Dante's *Divine Comedy*

In the early years of the 14th century, a synthesis of divergent philosophical, political, and religious world views was achieved by Dante Alighieri in his *Divine Comedy*—at once the greatest book of the medieval past and a prophecy of Renaissance things to come. In one stroke, Dante established vernacular Italian as a modern literary language and endowed his country with its most enduring literary masterpiece. The *Divine Comedy* is not only a synthesis of scholastic and Franciscan philosophies but of the whole thought of the medieval period and of Greco-Roman antiquity as its author knew it. Classical figures, such as Aristotle, Vergil, Ovid, and Cicero, rub shoulders across its pages with Boethius, St. Thomas Aquinas, St. Francis, and Giotto who, as tradition has it, portrayed Dante in a *Paradiso* of

his own painted in the Chapel of the Bargello at Florence (Fig. 257).

The form of the poem is laden with medieval mathematical symbolism, the mystical number 3 serving as a kind of trinitarian motif. Each stanza has three verses; the rhyming scheme is the melodious *terza rima*—*aba, bcb,* etc.; one time after another, Dante is terrified by three animals; in each case he is saved by the mediation of three holy women; he is piloted on his travels by three guides. The whole poem is divided into three parts—Hell, Purgatory, and Heaven; each section contains 33 cantos, the number of Christ's years on earth; and, finally, the introductory canto, added to the three times 33 others, brings the total to an even 100, that number having the quality of wholeness or completion.

In spite of the heavy burden of number theory and other scholastic baggage—discourses on the laws of planetary motion, civil and canon law, medieval science, dialectical argumentation, and allegorical meanings, such as that of Vergil representing reason and Beatrice inspiration—Dante is far from an orthodox scholastic thinker. If he were, he would have written a treatise in the learned Latin instead of a poem in Tuscan Italian. No scholarly discourse ever began with the announcement: "The style is careless and humble, because it is in the vulgar tongue, in which even housewives hold converse." The revolutionary nature of this linguistic departure is almost impossible for the modern reader to understand, for in Dante's time literature was a possession of the learned few who possessed an adequate knowledge of Latin. All those who read poetry, philosophy, or history in effect had to do so in a foreign language. But even to an Italian, Dante's progress through the Inferno, Purgatory, and Paradise is not an easy one to follow. The path is hard and rough, and its obscurity comes from the doubts and conflicts that clouded the time. Since lecturers in Italian universities offered commentaries on it soon after the poet's death, the *Divine Comedy* must also have been difficult for those close to Dante's own time.

For all its carefully worked out form, and in spite of its inclusion of a cross section of the medieval scientific knowledge, the *Divine Comedy* is neither learned, elegant, nor aristocratic. It is obscure, unpolished, and abrupt. It is also so complex that no key, whether that of theology, metaphysics, philosophy, or politics, will open the door to understanding. In contrast to the philosophical writings of that day, it mixes its subjects at times to the point of confusion. References to local politics are found side by side with glimpses into the beauty of Paradise; names of unremembered inhabitants of the towns Dante visited are placed beside those of the immortals; crude gossip and old wives' tales keep company with the scientific knowledge of the period. Hell and Heaven, faith and reason, events of the past and present, history and prophecy, paganism and Christianity, and the Greco-Roman and medieval worlds are all present in its pages. The mass of detail is kept from marring the greatness of the poem only by the vast conception of the whole and by the tight formal framework which tend to throw the multiplicity of its parts into proper perspective. Compensation for the confusion is found in the incomparable beauty of its language, so much of which is lost in translation. Dante, like Giotto, possessed the gift of making his characters live by just a few deft strokes. Like St. Francis', his allegories are not mere riddles for the learned doctors but lively tales for the untutored.

Dante has a true musician's ear for sound, and his verses have a music all their own. He also has the expert painter's eye for the minute details of appearances, and his images are a feast for the inner eye of the imagination as well. One instance of this imagery is his sensitivity to the medium of light. Primarily it is a spiritual light that concerns him, but he conjures up its vision in familiar everyday impressions filtered through the mind's eye of a great poet. He sings of sunlight, firelight, starlight; the sparkle of precious stones; the gleaming rays of a lamp in the darkness; the translucent effects of light filtered through water, glass, and jewels; rainbows and the colored reflections from clouds; the ruddy glow of infernal flames and the pure unearthly radiance of Paradise; the light of the human eye and that of the halos surrounding the heads of the saints; and finally each one of the three sections of the poem closes on the word "stars."

In spite of the preponderance of so many medieval elements, Dante achieves much that is associated with the Renaissance viewpoint. For all its mathematical structure, the *Divine Comedy* is full of violent human storms, passionate outbursts on the unnecessary wickedness of those in high places, and a general reassertion of the role of emotion in human affairs. For all his austerity, remoteness, and unapproachability, Dante does not pronounce a stern and final judgment. The very title would preclude this, because in his conception, "Comedy, indeed, beginneth with some adverse circumstances, but its theme hath a happy termination. . . ." Dante further specifically states that the didactic purpose of his poem is "to remove those living in this life from a state of misery and to guide them to a state of happiness." He writes with an unbounded faith in humanity, and when he relates the punishments meted out to those who suffer in his Inferno, he does so with the practical moral purpose of correcting such worldly evils as simony, usury, and avarice that he saw being practiced in the world as he knew it. It is important to point out that Dante did not write only the Inferno—a general impression derived from the romantic 19th-century writers who practically took this part to be the whole. His Purgatory and his Heaven, line for line, are equal in space with his Hell.

While the *Divine Comedy* is subtitled the *Vision of Dante Alighieri*, and the scene is laid in Hell, Purgatory, and Paradise, Dante's vision was not concerned only with life after death. By inference, he is describing the spiritual course of human life from birth in original sin through the purgation process of experience to a knowledge of ideal goodness. This dynamic spiritual journey is full of quite unmedieval emotions. After plunging with Dante into the bowels of the earth, the reader makes an upward ascent through the infernal regions on the back of Satan to the mountain of Purgatory, and, finally, into the metaphysical stratosphere of the various stages of Heaven. Civilization likewise, as Dante saw it, had struggled upward from the pagan world of Greece and Rome to the theocratic foundations of the medieval world, which had rested on an all-powerful Church and its secular counterpart, the Holy Roman Empire. It is a vertical and dynamic concept representing the ascent of humanity from the depths to the heights, from darkness into the light.

IDEAS

The 14th century in Italy had one foot in the Middle Ages and the other in the Renaissance. The opposing world views are reflected in the great Church schism; the social struggle between the old landed aristocracy and the growing cities; the incompatibility of Gothic architecture and the sunny landscape of Italy; the presence of medieval devils and genuine human types in Giotto's frescoes; the opposing visions of the Inferno and Paradise in the *Divine Comedy*; the attitudes expressed in poetry and painting before and after the Black Death.

The backward and forward directions are illustrated also in the struggle within the minds and consciences of individual men. The life of St. Francis, to cite one example, combined an other-worldly self-denial with an obvious this-worldly love of natural beauty. Fire for him was not created so much for the purpose of roasting the souls of sinners in Hell as to give light in the darkness and warmth on a cold night. The Romanesque St. Peter Damian had said: "The world is so filthy with vices the holy mind is befouled by even thinking of it." In contrast, the Gothic encyclopedist Vincent of Beauvais exclaimed: "How great is even the humblest beauty of this world!" St. Francis in his *Canticle of the Sun* found evidence of God's goodness everywhere—in the radiance of the sun, in the eternal miracle of springtime. He saw all nature as a revelation of divinity and, seeing thus, foreshadowed a departure from the divisive medieval dualism based on opposition of flesh and spirit. After a lifetime of self-mortification, he humbly begged pardon of his brother the body.

The two great Italian writers of the 14th century—Petrarch and Boccaccio—reveal a similar inner conflict. Boccaccio, in his youth, wrote the worldly and joyous *Decameron* and reveled in the rediscovery of classical Greco-Roman literature. In his old age, however, he recanted by disavowing the *Decameron* and disposing of his library because it contained so many pagan books. Petrarch's poetry was a curious blend of Gothic chivalry and revival of ancient Roman forms; he wondered whether it was better to write in classical Latin or in vernacular Italian; and his early sensuous sonnets to Laura contrast strongly with his later *Secret*, a moralistic dialogue with the ghost of St. Augustine.

The 14th century thus straddles the medieval and the Renaissance worlds. Looking backward, it represents a culmination of certain aspects of later medievalism; looking forward, it anticipates many of the ideas of the Renaissance. The breakdown of medieval symbolism is seen in the growth of naturalism in painting, and the shift from an other-worldly focus to a this-worldly approach is apparent in the rise of humanitarianism. It is most important, however, to distinguish between the 14th-century naturalism, which is largely an outgrowth of late Gothic ideas, and its more scientific equivalent in the 15th century and between Franciscan humanitarianism and the more classically oriented humanism of the later Renaissance.

Late Medieval Naturalism

The abstractions of the scholastic mind found a new challenge in the concretions of the philosophers who called themselves nominalists. Late scholasticism had, in fact, become more and more a strained exercise in logical gymnastics, and its forms all too often disregarded the real world and the facts necessary to give substance to thought. The nominalists simply turned the scholastic processes of thought completely upside down. They insisted that generalities are built up from the grouping of individual objects, whereas scholastics, by beginning with a hypothetical proposition or eternal Platonic idea, derived the facts of the phenomenal world from their proposition. To use the language of the schoolmen themselves, the scholastics reasoned *a priori*, while the nominalists did so *a posteriori*; one started from premises *ante rem*, and the other from propositions *in re*; or, to put it more simply, one reasoned *before* and the other *after* the fact. These systems approximate the difference between deductive and inductive thought, the latter leading to the experimental method of modern science.

The nominalist viewpoint, as it gained a foothold, weakened medieval authoritarianism, in which the world of Aristotle and the Church fathers was accepted without question, and initiated the modern practice of finding facts from firsthand observation. Particular things became more important than universal forms. A plant, now, was a vegetable or flower that grew in a garden rather than the manifestation of an *a priori* universal idea of a plant existing in the mind of God. The result of this new mental orientation was a renewed interest in a tangible reality that was to have as important consequences in art as it did in the realm of scientific inquiry. In the next century, it was to lead to the representation of figures amid natural surroundings, the rendering of the body with anatomical accuracy of bone and muscle, the modeling of figures three dimensionally by means of light and shadow, and the working out of laws of linear perspective for foreground and background effects.

While opposing systems of logic were being argued in the universities, the friars of St. Francis were bringing his message to town and country folk. With them, religious devotion became a voluntary, spontaneous relationship between man and God rather than an imposed obligation, an act based on love rather than on fear. The Franciscans also sought to establish a common bond between a man, whatever his station in life, and his fellowmen—an important shift from the vertical feudal organization of society, in which men were related to those above and below them by a hierarchical authority, to a horizontally oriented ethical relationship that bound man to his fellowmen. St. Francis everywhere saw evidence of God's love in everything, from the fruits and flowers of the earth to the winds and the clouds in the sky—a concept that was to have great consequences for the course of art. The birds to

Plate 19. FRA FILIPPO LIPPI. *Nativity. c.* 1459.
Tempera on wood, 50 × 46″. State Museums, Berlin. (See p. 248.)

Plate 20. SANDRO BOTTICELLI. *Venus and Mars. c.* 1485. Oil on wood, 26 ¾ × 67 ¾".
National Gallery, London (reproduced by courtesy of the Trustees). (See p. 251.)

which St. Francis preached (see Fig. 244), for instance, were the birds that were heard chirping and singing every day, not the symbolic dove of the Holy Ghost or the apocalyptical eagle of St. John. While this tendency toward naturalism was already noticeable in the 13th-century sculpture of Chartres and elsewhere, it became widespread in the 14th century. As this view of the natural world gained ascendance over the supernatural, based as it was on concrete observation rather than on metaphysical speculation, it released the visual arts from the perplexing problems of how to represent the unseen. The love of St. Francis for his fellowmen and for such simple things as grass and trees, which could be represented as seen in nature, opened up new vistas for artists to explore.

St. Francis' message was taught in parables and simple images of life that all could understand, and Giotto succeeded in translating these into pictorial form. In this favorable naturalistic climate, he found his balance between the abstract and the concrete, between divine essence and human reality. By refraining from placing his accent on symbolism, Giotto moved away from medieval mysticism and in his pictures portrayed understandable human situations. To him, the saints were not remote transcendental spirits but human beings, who felt all the usual emotions from joy to despair; just as did the people in the Italian towns he knew so well. Now that he no longer had to be concerned mainly with allegories but could reproduce the world of objects and actions as he saw it, a new pathway was opened. Even his contemporaries could see that Giotto was blazing new trails. Yet when they extolled him for his faithfulness to nature, their praise must be measured by the art that had preceded his time rather than by 15th-century or later standards. While Giotto undoubtedly showed a love of nature as such, he never accented it to the point where it might weaken his primary human emphasis. His interest was less in nature for its own sake than in its meaning in the lives of his subjects.

In viewing a Giotto picture, one does well to begin with his people and be concerned only secondarily with their natural surroundings, because his pictures are in psychological rather than in linear perspective. His subjects seem to create their own environment by their expressive attitudes and dramatic deployment. While his work shows an increasing preoccupation with problems of natural space, this space remains subordinate to his expressive intentions, and his use of color and shading gives his human figures the sense of depth and volume that brings them to life. In this way, both human nature and nature as such attains an intimate and distinctive identity in Giotto's pictorial conceptions.

Franciscan Humanitarianism

Long before, Cluny had changed the character of monasticism by uniting cloistered life with feudalism. Now the new orientation of the Franciscan order was no less revolutionary. St. Francis did not confine his monks in cloisters but sent them forth as fishers of men. The idea of evangelical poverty, humility, and love for mankind expressed through living and working with simple people resulted in a union with, rather than a withdrawal from, society. The Franciscans did not shun the world so much as they shunned worldly pursuits, and, as G.K. Chesterton has remarked, what St. Benedict had stored, St. Francis scattered. The Cluniacs were, in the proper sense of the word, an order—that is, a strict hierarchical organization. The Franciscans by contrast were, in every sense of the word, a movement.

The icy intellectualism of the medieval universities was bound to thaw in the warmth of Franciscan emotionalism. Asceticism and self-denial held little appeal for an increasingly prosperous urban middle class. The mathematical elegance of Gothic structurality began to yield to more informal types of buildings. The logical linear patterns of the surviving Byzantine pictorial style gave way to the expressive warmth of Giotto's figures, and the vacuous stylized faces of Byzantine saints pale in the light of the human tenderness found in a smiling mouth or tearful eye in a Giotto picture. The formal architectural sculpture and abstract patterns of Gothic stained glass were replaced by the colorful informality of mural paintings in fresco. St. Francis in his music, as in his religious work, drew the sacred and popular traditions closer together, and in the lauds he encouraged people to sing; he gave them a music that they could feel in their hearts without having to understand with their brains.

St. Francis, son of a village merchant, was not an aristocratic saint. Although his company and counsel were sought by bishops, popes, and King Louis IX of France, he ministered primarily to the poor and humble of town and country alike. The painter Simone Martini of Siena, unlike St. Francis and Giotto, was a member of the knightly class. Martini's fresco in the lower church at Assisi, *St. Martin before Emperor Julian* (Fig. 258), shows a preoccupation with social stratification in his concern with protocol and his emphasis on such details as the emperor's orb and scepter and (below) 258. SIMONE MARTINI. *St. Martin before Emperor Julian. c.* 1326. Fresco. Lower Church of St. Francis, Assisi.

(bottom) 259. GIOTTO. *Joachim Returning to the Sheepfold.* 1305–1306. Fresco. Arena Chapel, Padua.

the elegant costuming. Martini's painting harks back to the courtly Gothic tradition, while in the same basilica the work of Giotto, a commoner, appears by comparison strikingly modern. Giotto's art was frankly addressed toward the new middle class, and his figures are simply human beings in all their warmth, frailty, and dignity. In such pictures as his *Joachim Returning to the Sheepfold* (Fig. 259) and *Death of St. Francis* (Fig. 246), Giotto's work attains something of the Franciscan humanitarian spirit. St. Francis and his successors preferred the simple folk songs of the jongleurs to the more aristocratic troubadour music or the more formal Gothic counterpoint. Since his mission was preaching to the common people as they paused from their labors in the fields or market place, he communicated with them in simple, unsophisticated language.

When Dante declared that Giotto's fame outshone that of Cimabue, and when Boccaccio proclaimed that Giotto revived painting after it had "been in the grave" for centuries, Giotto's contemporaries were recognizing in his art the presence of a new spirit and style. These are also apparent in the *Decameron*, where the ten city dwellers satirize the manners and foibles of Gothic knights, abbots, and monks and the outmoded feudal ideal to which they clung. And they were also apparent in music. In France, Philippe de Vitry published a musical treatise *c.*1316 with the title *Ars Nova*, or new art, which he opposed to the *ars antiqua*, or old art, of the Gothic 13th century. The new movement of which he was the spokesman, especially in its ardent championship of the new secular rhythms, was deemed sufficiently important to warrant censure in a vigorous bull issued by Pope John XXII at Avignon in 1325.

A new spirit of freedom was in the air, a freedom from tradition. St. Francis earlier had struck out in a new religious direction, and Giotto, by translating the saint's life into pictures, avoided the traditional Biblical subjects and their traditional stylized treatment. Actually he was working on an almost contemporary subject as well as rendering it in a new manner. Subjects that came within the iconographical tradition, such as *Joachim Returning to the Sheepfold* (Fig. 259) and the *Pietà*, or *Lamentation* (Fig. 260), were done far more dramatically than previously. In general, Giotto's figures moved about in the space he created for them with greater suppleness than heretofore. His world was marked by a new and intelligible relationship between man and his fellowmen, between man and nature, and between man and God. Giotto's moving *Pietà* and Duccio's more reserved rendering of the same scene (Fig. 261) make for an interesting contrast of temperament. Both can

260. GIOTTO. *Pietà (Lamentation)*. 1305–1306. Fresco, 7′ 7″ × 7′ 9″. Arena Chapel, Padua.

be traced to a common Byzantine iconographical source.

Representations of Christ as an infant in arms began to replace the mature image in divine majesty of the Gothic period, and along with the growing interest in the cycle of Christ's infancy, legends of Mary's life became more and more prominent. The emotional element in the Passion was largely conveyed through compassion for the Virgin as the mother of sorrows. This was as true for Giotto's cycle in Padua as it was for Jacopone da Todi's *Stabat Mater Dolorosa*. The adoption of the vernacular tongue in literature, the informal treatment of fresco painting, and the folk spirit in the music—all make it apparent that the works of art were being addressed to a new group of patrons. Furthermore, one of Giotto's recorded sayings reveals the artist's new conception of himself. Each man, he said, "should save his soul as best he can. As for me, I intend to serve painting in my own way and only so far as it serves me, for the sake of the lovely moments it gives at the price of an agreeable fatigue." Even the Black Death had some beneficial effects for the artists after Giotto's time, because the younger masters could assert their independence and develop new ideas and techniques with fewer restrictions from their conservative guilds.

261. DUCCIO. *Pietà*, detail from *Maestà*. 1308–1311. Tempera on wood. Cathedral Museum, Siena.

What appears to be a renewed interest in classical antiquity began to be seen, heard, and read in the works of the artists and writers of the 14th century. The panels of Niccolo Pisano's pulpit show the classical Roman influence of such narrative reliefs as Trajan's Column (Figs. 106–108). His son Giovanni, in spite of the Gothic orientation of his own work, placed ancient Roman sarcophagi alongside contemporary examples in the arcade of the Campo Santo in Pisa. The Roman poet Vergil appears prominently in Dante's *Divine Comedy*. All these phenomena, however, can be explained much more logically as the continuation of a tradition that had, in fact, never really died out. If Niccolo's sculpture is placed chronologically after a group of French Gothic examples, it certainly seems to be closer to the art of ancient Rome than to the Gothic. But since Roman sculpture was present everywhere in Italy, any Italian sculptor with his eyes open could not miss seeing it. Simple as it may sound, the explanation is a geographical rather than a chronological or psychological one: central Italy is closer to Rome than to northern France. Since Dante was writing an epic poem, the obvious antecedent was the *Aeneid*, which had never ceased to be read. While a growing consciousness of the classical in the works of Dante and his contemporaries is not to be overlooked, it must be seen from the 14th-century point of view as a continuation of a cultural tradition rather than as a rebirth of classicism. The influence of the classic authors and classical art had never been quite so neglected or dead as many historians have supposed. Vergil, Cicero, and certain works of Aristotle were as widely read in medieval times as they were in the 14th and 15th centuries.

This is not to deny the fact that a new spirit of curiosity enlivened the search, instituted by Petrarch and Boccaccio, in monastic libraries for manuscripts by other Greek and Roman authors than those who bore the hallowed approval of Church tradition. This probing also went hand in hand with the discovery in Rome of some long-buried antique sculpture and with the study of Roman building methods. Even though Petrarch amid much classical fanfare was crowned in Rome with the laurel wreath, that ancient token of immortal fame, and even though he wrote his cycle of Triumphs with the Roman triumphal arch form in mind, it is doubtful that he or Dante or Boccaccio did more than bring the ancient world a little closer to their own time. They certainly had no such admiration for pagan antiquity for its own sake as did the 15th-century Florentines. Even though Giotto spent some time in Rome, the joyous humanistic spirit that permeates his work is much closer to the new Franciscan outlook and the continuous tradition of Roman relief sculpture and fresco painting than to any conscious reappraisal of classical culture as such. It is necessary, then, to dissociate the spontaneous 14th-century Franciscan humanitarianism from the more self-conscious revival of antiquity that characterized developments in 15th-century Florentine and early 16th-century Roman humanism.

The 14th-century conflict of opposing ideas and forward-backward trends has variously been designated as the post-Gothic, proto-Renaissance, or pre-Renaissance period. But any period that contains the magic names of St. Francis, Dante, Petrarch, Boccaccio, Giotto, Duccio, and Simone Martini and that exhibits such a high degree of originality and creativity can well stand on its own rather than be a postlude or a prelude to another. In style as well as ideas it is indeed the Early Renaissance.

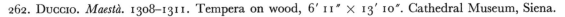

262. DUCCIO. *Maestà*. 1308–1311. Tempera on wood, 6' 11" × 13' 10". Cathedral Museum, Siena.

9 - THE FLORENTINE RENAISSANCE STYLE

FLORENCE, 15TH CENTURY

Colorful festivals were the delight of all Florentines, but March 25, 1436, was a special occasion that was to linger long in the memory of these prosperous and pleasure-loving people. The dedication of Florence's newly completed cathedral (Fig. 263) brought together an unprecedented number of Church dignitaries, statesmen, and diplomats, and in their entourages were famous artists, men of letters, and musicians. The white-robed pontiff Eugene IV, crowned with the triple tiara, attended by 7 cardinals in bright red and no less than 37 bishops and archbishops in purple vestments, made a triumphal progress through the banner-lined streets, accompanied by city officials and heads of the guilds with their honor guards. Appropriately enough, the cathedral was christened Santa Maria del Fiore (Mary of the Flower), since Florence (derived from *flora*) was indeed the city of flowers. March 25 was also the Feast of the Annunciation, the beginning of new life nine months before Christ's birth, and both the Annunciation and Nativity were favorite subjects of Florentine painting.

The eyes and thoughts of all Florentines that day were directed upward to the mighty cupola that crowned the crossing of their cathedral and gave their city its characteristic profile. Though the building had been begun in the late 13th century, construction had languished because no architect had the necessary knowledge to dome such an enormous, gaping, 140-foot-wide octagonal space. But Filippo Brunelleschi, after studying the Pantheon and other ancient monuments in Rome, had returned and undertaken the gigantic task now at the point of completion. Starting at a level some 180 feet above ground, he sent eight massive ribs soaring skyward from the angles of the supporting octagon to a point almost 100 feet higher where they converged at the base of a lantern tower (Fig. 265). Concealing them from external view, he added two minor radial ribs between each major one, twenty-four in all, to make his inner shell. Reinforcing these by wooden beams and iron clasps at key points, he then had the necessary support for the masonry of his inner and outer shells. The structure is, in effect, an eight-sided Gothic vault. But by concealing the functional elements and shaping a smooth external silhouette, Brunelleschi crossed the bridge into Renaissance architecture.

(above) LUCA DELLA ROBBIA. *Choristers*, detail of *Cantoria (Singing Gallery)*. *c.* 1435. Marble, *c.* 38 × 24″. Cathedral Museum, Florence.

General Events

1401	Competition for Baptistry north doors
1403– 1424	Ghiberti worked on Baptistry north doors
1406	Pisa under Florentine rule
1421	Giovanni de' Medici elected magistrate
1425– 1452	Ghiberti worked on Baptistry east doors
c.1429	Pazzi Chapel begun by Brunelleschi
1434	Pro-Medici government elected; Cosimo de' Medici (1389–1464) began rule
1434– 1444	Pope Eugene IV resided in Florence
1436	Cathedral dedicated (begun 1298; dome by Brunelleschi)
1439– 1442	Council of Florence brought nominal union of Eastern and Western Churches
1444– 1459	Medici-Riccardi Palace built by Michelozzo
1447	Parentucelli, Florentine humanist, elected Pope Nicholas V
1464– 1469	Piero de' Medici ruled after Cosimo's death
1469– 1492	Lorenzo de' Medici ruled
1476	Portinari Altarpiece by van der Goes of Flanders brought to Florence
1478	Pazzi family led unsuccessful revolt against Medici; Giuliano de' Medici assassinated; Lorenzo consolidated political power
c.1480	Heinrich Isaac succeeded Squarcialupi as organist at Cathedral; court composer to Lorenzo
1482	Marsilio Ficino's translations of Plato's dialogues printed
c.1485	Alberti's treatise *On Architecture* printed; *On Painting* (1436), *On Sculpture* (1464) also printed c.1485
1489	Savonarola (1452–1498) preached moral reform
	Michelangelo apprenticed to Ghirlandaio
c.1490	Aldine Press founded in Venice; began publishing works of Plato and Aristotle
1492	Lorenzo de' Medici died
1494	Medici exiled from Florence; government dominated by Savonarola
1497	Burning of books, pictures, and all "vanities"
1498	Savonarola burned at stake

Architects

1377– 1446	Filippo Brunelleschi
1391– 1473	Michelozzo di Bartolommeo
1404– 1472	Leone Battista Alberti

Painters

1387– 1455	Fra Angelico
1397– 1475	Paolo Uccello
c.1400– 1461	Domenico Veneziano
1401– 1428	Masaccio
c.1406– 1469	Filippo Lippi
c.1416– 1492	Piero della Francesca
1420– 1497	Benozzo Gozzoli
1423– 1457	Andrea del Castagno
c.1429– 1498	Antonio Pollaiuolo
1444– 1510	Sandro Botticelli
1449– 1494	Domenico Ghirlandaio
1452– 1519	Leonardo da Vinci
1458– 1504	Filippino Lippi

Sculptors

1371– 1438	Jacopo della Quercia
1378– 1455	Lorenzo Ghiberti
1386– 1466	Donatello
1400– 1482	Luca della Robbia
c.1429– 1498	Antonio Pollaiuolo
1435– 1488	Andrea del Verrocchio
1475– 1564	Michelangelo Buonarroti

Musicians

1400– 1474	Guillaume Dufay
1430– 1495	Jean de Ockeghem
1436– 1475	Antonio Squarcialupi
c.1450– 1517	Heinrich Isaac
1450– 1505	Jacob Obrecht
c.1460– 1521	Josquin des Prez

Writers and Philosophers

1304– 1374	Petrarch (Francesco Petrarca)
1313– 1375	Giovanni Boccaccio
1433– 1499	Marsilio Ficino
1449– 1492	Lorenzo de' Medici
1454– 1494	Angelo Poliziano
1463– 1494	Pico della Mirandola
1469– 1527	Niccolo Machiavelli
1478– 1529	Baldassare Castiglione

(above) 263. Florence Cathedral group. Cathedral begun by ARNOLFO DI CAMBIO, 1296; dome by FILIPPO BRUNELLESCHI, 1420–1436; present façade 1875–1887. Cathedral 508' long, dome 367' high. Campanile ("Giotto's Tower") begun 1334 by GIOTTO; continued by ANDREA PISANO, 1336–1348; 269' high. Baptistry (right) 1060–1150.

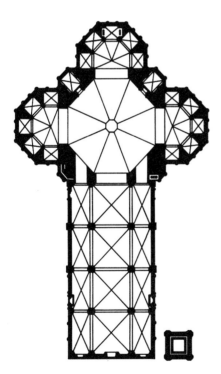

(above) 264. Florence Cathedral, plan.

(right) 265. FILIPPO BRUNELLESCHI. Dome, Florence Cathedral. 1420–1436. 367' high.

Opposite the façade of the cathedral is the old Romanesque baptistry (Fig. 263, lower right), which was feeling new Renaissance life with Ghiberti's gilded bronze doors. Already in place were the handsome north doors, and the sculptor was well on his way to completing the east doors (Plate 18), which Michelangelo was later to hail as worthy of being the Gates of Paradise. Helping him cast these doors in his workshop at various times were the architect Michelozzo, the sculptor Donatello, and the painters Paolo Uccello and Benozzo Gozzoli. Donatello, at the same time, was working on a series of statues of prophets for niches on the exterior of both the cathedral and the campanile, known as Giotto's Tower.

In Pope Eugene's entourage were some of the leading Florentine humanists, including the artist-scholar Leone Battista Alberti, who had just completed his book *On Painting* and was at work on his influential treatise *On Architecture*. On hand to provide music for the occasion was the papal choir, whose ranks included the foremost musician of his generation, Guillaume Dufay, who composed the commemorative motet for the occasion. Antonio Squarcialupi, regular organist of the cathedral and private master of music in the Medici household, is thought to have composed the solemn high mass. According to an eyewitness, the magnificent pontifical procession was preceded by a great band of wind players, "each carrying his instrument in hand, and arrayed in gorgeous cloth of gold garments." After them came the combined choirs that "sang at times with such mighty harmonies that the songs seemed to the listeners to be coming from the angels themselves."

Lining the streets for the grand procession and crowding their way into the vast nave of the cathedral were the colorfully costumed citizens of this prosperous Tuscan town. In contrast with northern countries, in this region city life had come of age. At a time when many feudal aristocrats still inhabited their dank fortresslike castles, the Florentine patrician families lived in a style that could well have been the envy of kings. The working members of the population belonged to the various guilds and trade organizations, the most important of which were those dealing with the carding, weaving, and dyeing of wool and silk for the famous Florentine textile industry. Metalcrafts and stonework followed in importance, and so on down to the butchers and bakers. The masters of the principal guilds were the influential citizens from whose ranks the members of the Signory, or city council, were chosen and from which the merchant and banking families emerged.

The most renowned of these was the Medici family, whose head at this time was Cosimo. By a combination of political sagacity and financial acumen in manipulating his large fortune, he dominated the government of the city. Knowing his fellow townsmen's passion for equality, Cosimo never assumed a title or other outward sign of authority but, instead, was the benign political boss, ruling from behind the scenes with the support of the guilds, which knew that a stable government and peaceful relations with their neighbors were the best safeguards of their prosperity. The Medicis were also the papal bankers who received on deposit Church funds from England, France, and Flanders; and from their branch offices in London, Lyon, and Antwerp, they lent the money at fantastic rates of interest to foreign heads of state. With the papal revenues, they also bought English wool, had it processed in the Netherlands, shipped it to Florence to be woven into fine fabrics, and exported these at a handsome profit. It was Cosimo who made the florin the soundest currency in Europe. But political power and high finance were not the only pursuits of this ambitious banker.

Cosimo's other accomplishments were unusual for a Renaissance merchant capitalist. As a diligent student of Plato, he became one of the founders of the Neoplatonic Academy, an institution that had enormous intellectual influence. From all the parts of Europe where his financial interests extended, he commissioned works of art, while at home he gathered a library of rare manuscripts for scholars to study and translate. Through his generosity, a group of Dominican monks had just moved into the monastery of San Marco, which was being rebuilt for them by his personal architect Michelozzo. Among the monks was Fra Angelico, whom Cosimo encouraged to decorate the monastery walls with his famous frescoes. Although Masaccio, one of the century's most original painters, had been dead for six years, Filippo Lippi, the future teacher of Botticelli, was active and looking to Cosimo for commissions. Cosimo took Donatello's advice, collected antique statuary, placed it in his gardens, and encouraged young sculptors to work there. Small wonder, then, that after his death in 1464, the Signory voted him the posthumous title *Pater Patriae*, father of his country.

For such solemn ceremonies as dedications and coronations, it was the custom to perform a motet especially written for the occasion. Dufay, a musician educated in the Burgundian French tradition, had been a member of the papal choir since 1428 and had composed such an occasional motet for the ceremonies at the conclusion of peace between Pope Eugene and the Emperor Sigismund in 1433. The motet, coming as it does outside the normal liturgical music of the mass, lent itself well to the purposes of an occasional piece that could be composed for a specific ceremony to a text which contained topical allusions. The words in this case begin: *Nuper rosarum flores ex dono pontificis*—Flower of roses, gift of the pontiff. The cathedral is referred to as this "most spacious temple," and Brunelleschi's dome is praised as a "mighty artifice," a "marvel of art." The text appropriately concludes with a supplication to the Virgin Mary on behalf of the people of Florence: "O Virgin, the glory of virgins, thy devoted people of Florence beseech thee that he who prays . . . may deserve to receive thy gracious benefits. . . ." Since such motets were composed for official occasions, their style tended toward traditional practices rather than experimentation. Dufay therefore built his formal structure on the severe isorhythmic principles developed by the 14th-century French composers. Such a method is governed by certain rules of musical logic, and the forms are compounded of sections that are unified by an identity of rhythmic relationships but not necessarily of melodic patterns. Such music was never intended primarily to please the ear or stir the emotions but to mirror the hidden harmonies of the universe and thus to constitute a worthy offering to its Creator. In Dufay's conception, however, the universe is no mere structure but is populated with shapely melodies, warm harmonic colors, and a variety of rhythmic forms.

This dedicatory scene of Santa Maria del Fiore has often been cited, both by those who witnessed it and by later historians, as the beginning of a new era. There was, of course, a new spirit in the air, but at the same time it was never clearer that no sharp break with the medieval past was being made. The cathedral itself was late Gothic in style; Brunelleschi's dome was constructed by Gothic vaulting methods; and Dufay's isorhythmic motet was a late Gothic musical form. The Italian Gothic, however, had never had either the dynamic verticality or the aspiring force of its northern counterpart. Brunelleschi's dome was, to be sure, the first of such magnitude to be constructed since antiquity, but smaller domes over the crossing were not unusual in Tuscany, as a glance at the cathedral of nearby Pisa (Fig. 188) will show. But while the construction of Brunelleschi's dome fell within the scope of the Gothic, the new emphasis was on smoother lines and the shapeliness of the external silhouette. Dufay's motet, for its part, showed an increasing secular feeling in church music, since the composer was apparently much less concerned with making a pious setting of his text than he was with making his mathematical proportions fit smoothly into his musical structure. While such mental gymnastics were late Gothic in conception, the Italian sense of melodic contour, the increased emphasis on secular duple time, the softening of the dissonant passing tones, and the pliancy of the contrapuntal texture, all point in the direction of the Renaissance. Dufay's special contribution was in clothing the austere skeletal structure of such a composition with skillful voice leading and a fluency of sound that made it a joy to the ear as well as to the mind.

PAZZI CHAPEL AND MEDICI-RICCARDI PALACE

Impressive as is the immense cupola of Florence's cathedral, the new architectural spirit is more readily grasped in Brunelleschi's smaller Pazzi Chapel (Fig. 266). Here, in a building of diminutive proportions, the architect could give

(left) 266. FILIPPO BRUNELLESCHI. Façade, Pazzi Chapel, Cloister of Church of Santa Croce, Florence. *c.* 1429–1433. 59′9″ × 35′8″.

(below) 267. Pazzi Chapel, plan.

(below) 268. FILIPPO BRUNELLESCHI. Pazzi Chapel, detail of façade. Church of Santa Croce, Florence.

(bottom) 269. FILIPPO BRUNELLESCHI. Interior, Pazzi Chapel.

his full attention to design without having to be absorbed in complex construction problems. The fruits of his studies of ancient Roman buildings are more in evidence, and the break with the Gothic tradition is complete. The harmonious spacing of the columns of the portico, the treatment of the walls as flat surfaces, and the just balance of horizontal and vertical elements make Brunelleschi's design the prototype of the Renaissance architectural style. The entablature (Fig. 268) gives still further evidence of the classical influence. The curved pattern above comes directly from ancient Roman sarcophagi, while the elegant carving of the Corinthian capitals, the Composite pilasters, and other design details reveal Brunelleschi's early training as a silversmith as well as his study of authentic Roman originals that were then known to artists.

The interior (Fig. 269) fully bears out the initial promise of the façade and shows a Roman classical concern with the logical molding of interior space. Without a trace of Gothic mystery and indefiniteness, the pilastered walls give a cool, crisp impression. Frames of dark-colored stone divide the surfaces into geometric forms easily assimilated by the eye. Mystery and infinity have yielded to geometrical clarity. Overhead the rectangular room is covered by transverse barrel vaults, with a low dome on pendentives rising in the center at the point of intersection. Somewhat hesitantly to be sure, this interior indicated a new concept of space without, however, realizing its full implications. The clear-cut simplicity of its design made the Pazzi Chapel a highly influential model throughout the Renaissance, and the unity of its centralized organization under a dome became the point of departure for the church plans of Alberti, Bramante, and Michelangelo.

When Cosimo de' Medici decided to build himself a new house, he is said to have rejected a palatial plan submitted by Brunelleschi, with the observation that envy was a plant that should not be watered. For the Medici-Riccardi Palace (Fig. 270) he chose instead a less ostentatious design submitted by Brunelleschi's disciple Michelozzo. (The palace has a dual name because it was acquired in the 17th century by the Riccardi family.) As the design materialized, the building turned out to be an appropriately solid structure, eminently suited to the taste of a man of such considerable substance as Cosimo. As a type, such buildings were actually a continuation, rather than a revival, of the multistoried Roman city apartment house, such as the one at Ostia (Fig. 100). Here the dominance of solid mass over the space allotted to the windows, plus the heavily rusticated masonry of the first story (many of the stones protrude more than a foot) still has something of the forbidding aspect of a medieval fortress. But as the eye moves upward, the second and third floors present an increasingly urbane appearance. The accent on horizontal lines, seen in the molding strips that separate the three stories and in the boldly projecting cornice at the roof level, are quite unmedieval. An allusion to the classical tradition can be seen in the semicircular arches

that frame the windows (the pediments over those on the lower story are a somewhat later addition). Details, such as the colonettes of the windows on the second and third floors as well as the egg-and-tongue pattern and the dentil range that appear in the cornice frieze, are definitely Renaissance in style.

In the interior (Fig. 271) the classical interest is even more apparent. The various rooms are

(above) 270. MICHELOZZO. Façade, Medici-Riccardi Palace, Florence. 1444–1459. c. 225′ long, 80′ high.

(left) 271. MICHELOZZO. Courtyard, Medici-Riccardi Palace.

272. FILIPPO BRUNELLESCHI. *Sacrifice of Isaac.* 1401. Gilt bronze, 21 × 17½″ (without molding). National Museum, Florence.

273. LORENZO GHIBERTI. *Sacrifice of Isaac.* 1401. Gilt bronze, 21 × 17½″ (without molding). National Museum, Florence.

grouped around the court as in a Pompeian columned interior courtyard, and a staircase connects the various parts of the house as in a Roman atrium. An interesting detail is the use in the frieze of the Medici coat of arms, which is also observable in a corner of the exterior (Fig. 270). These are the *palle*, or red balls, on a field of gold. The Medici, with a classical flourish, said the balls represented the golden apples of the Hesperides. The townspeople, however, interpreted them more prosaically—either as the pills (*palle*) or palliatives of the medicos, physicians, who were the family founders; or as the trademark of the Medici banks, which, then as now, was used as a pawnbroker's emblem.

Cosimo's sense of austerity stopped with the palace's exterior, and inside the doors everything was on a princely scale. With the frescoes of Benozzo Gozzoli and an altarpiece by Filippo Lippi decorating its second floor chapel, easel paintings by Uccello and Botticelli hanging on salon walls, antique and contemporary bronze and marble statues standing in the courtyard and gardens, collections of ancient and medieval carved gems and coins in its cabinets, and precious metal vessels and figurines standing on its tables, a library with priceless manuscripts including the works of Dante, Petrarch, and Boccaccio, the Medici-Riccardi Palace was, in fact, one of the first and richest museums in Europe.

SCULPTURE

In the year 1401, the Signory of Florence together with the Guild of Merchants had held a competition to determine who should be awarded the contract for the projected north doors of the Baptistry. Like the earlier pair by Andrea Pisano, the material was to be bronze, and the individual panels were to be enclosed in the quatrefoil pattern. The subject, for the purpose of the contest, was to be the Sacrifice of Isaac. Some half dozen sculptors were invited to submit models, among them Brunelleschi and Lorenzo Ghiberti. Both men were in their early twenties; both were skilled workers in metal and members in good standing of the Goldsmiths' Guild. A comparison of their panels (Figs. 272, 273), however, reveals many significant differences of viewpoint and technique. Brunelleschi's composition shows the influence of Gothic verticality in the way the design is built in three rising planes; Ghiberti's composition is almost horizontal, and his two scenes are divided diagonally by a Giotto-like mountain. Brunelleschi's panel is crowded, and his figures spill out over their frame; Ghiberti's is uncluttered, and all his figures and details converge toward a center of interest in the upper right formed by the heads of the principal figures. Brunelleschi accents dramatic tension, with Abraham seizing the screaming Isaac by the neck and the angel staying his hand at the last moment; Ghiberti sacrifices intensity for poise and decorative elegance. Brunelleschi shapes Isaac's awkward body with Gothic angularity; Ghiberti models it with smooth lines and the impersonal grace of a Hellenistic statue. (Ghiberti's *Commentaries* mention the discovery near Florence of the torso of an ancient classical statue after which he modeled his Isaac.) Finally, Brunelleschi cast his relief in separate sections, mounting these on the bronze background plate; Ghiberti, with greater technical command, cast his in a single mold. The decision in Ghiberti's favor showed the way the aesthetic winds were blowing in 1401. Ghiberti then set to work on the 20 panels of the north doors, which were to occupy the major part of his time for the next 24 years, while Brunelleschi, accompanied by his friend Donatello, went off to Rome to study architecture.

Ghiberti's north doors were no sooner in place than he was commissioned, this time without competition, to execute another set. The famous east doors (Plate 18), on which he worked from 1425 to 1452, tell their own tale. The Gothic quatrefoil frames were now a thing of the past, and, while his north doors were conceived in terms of their architectural function, the east doors served largely as a convenient framework for decoration. They even show some disregard for techniques appropriate to the two-dimensional medium of relief sculpture and in effect became pictures painted in gilded bronze. Ghiberti attempts daring perspectives far in advance of the painting of the period; and some figures, such as those in the center panel of the left door, are in such high relief as to be almost completely in the round. In the Adam and Eve panel (Fig. 274) at the top of the left door, he uses three receding planes: the high relief in the lower foreground is employed to tell the creation of Adam (left) and Eve (center) and the expulsion (right) in the present tense; the immediate past is seen in the half relief of the middle ground showing the Garden of Eden; and the low relief in the background is such that the figure of God and his accompanying cloud of angels seem to be dissolving into the thin air of the remote past.

On either side of the pictorial panels, Ghiberti included a series of full-length figurines that alternate with heads which recall Roman portrait busts, one of them being a self-portrait (Fig. 275). Hebrew prophets on the outer sides are set opposite pagan sibyls, all of whom were supposed to have foretold the coming of Christ. The figure beside the second panel from the top on the right door is that of the Biblical strong man Samson, but his stance and musculature are those of a Hel-

(below) 274. LORENZO GHIBERTI. *Story of Adam and Eve*, detail of east doors, Baptistry, Florence. *c.* 1435. Gilt bronze, 31¼″ square. (Compare Plate 18.)

(bottom) 275. LORENZO GHIBERTI. *Self-portrait*, detail of east doors, Baptistry, Florence. 1425–1452. Gilt bronze.

lenistic Hercules (see Fig. 62). Ghiberti mentions in his *Commentaries* how he sought to imitate nature in the manner of the ancient Greeks when molding the flora and fauna of these door frames. The care and delicate craftsmanship he lavished on these and other details make the east doors a high point in the metalworker's art. Ghiberti, as was said, belonged to the Goldsmiths' Guild, and its influence is felt in many aspects of Florentine art. It is to be seen not only in such door moldings but in pulpits, wall panels, window brackets, columns, pilasters, cornices—all of which were wrought with a wealth of fine detail lovingly dwelt upon.

Donatello's personality and career contrast strongly with Ghiberti's. A man of fiery temperament and bold imagination, Donatello scorned the fussy details which allied Ghiberti's work with that of the jeweler, and his sculpture has a rugged grandeur that makes Ghiberti's appear precious by comparison. While Ghiberti studied local examples of antique sculpture and read Vitruvius' treatises, Donatello had gone to Rome with Brunelleschi to see the finest surviving classical statuary. While Ghiberti remained a specialist in bronze, Donatello was at home with all materials—marble, wood, painted terracotta, gilded bronze; in all mediums —relief and in the round, small scale and heroic size, architectural embellishment and independent figure; in all subjects—sacred and secular, historical scene and portraiture. While Ghiberti had a single style, Donatello had many. His power of epical expression, enormous energies, vehemence, and impetuosity make him the representative sculptor of his period and the immediate artistic ancestor of Michelangelo.

Lo Zuccone, or *Baldpate* (Fig. 276), is one of a series of marble statues that Donatello was commissioned to do for the Florence Cathedral and its campanile in 1424. Designed for a third-story niche of the campanile, it was intended to be seen about 55 feet above ground level. The deep-cut drapery and lines of the face consequently took into account this angle of vision and lighting. By the boniness of the huge frame, the powerful musculature of the arms, the convulsive gesture of the right wrist, the tension of the sinews of the neck, and the intensity of the face, Donatello sought to produce a powerfully expressive rather than a handsome figure. Representing an Old Testament prophet (either Habakkuk or Jeremiah), the figure is full of inner fire and fear of the Lord, a seer capable of fasting in the desert, dwelling alone on a mountaintop, or haranguing an unheeding multitude from his niche and exhorting men to penitence. The classical influence is discernible in the drapery, an adaptation of the toga, and in the rugged features and baldness,

276. DONATELLO. *Prophet (Lo Zuccone)*, detail of Campanile, Florence Cathedral. 1423–1425. Marble, 6' 5" high. Original in Cathedral Museum, Florence.

which recall realistic Roman portraiture. With *Lo Zuccone*, Donatello created a unique figure of strong individuality, not one of the traditional iconographical types. The nickname the Florentines gave the statue shows that it was accepted as such.

In his bronze *David* (Fig. 277), Donatello works in a more lyrical vein. As a figure meant to be seen from all angles, the *David* is definitely a departure from the Gothic tradition of sculpture in niches and as architectural embellishment; and as the first lifesize bronze since antiquity, it marks the revival of classical nude statuary. David stands alone in the confident attitude of the victor over the vanquished, a sword in his right hand, a stone in his left. The serenity of the classical profile and the stance and modeling of the youthful body show Hellenistic influence. A local touch is provided by the Tuscan shepherd's hat, which throws the face into strong shadow and serves to accent the somewhat gawky lines of the adolescent body. The opposite end of Donatello's emotional range is seen in the spectral statue of the *Repentant Magdelene* (Fig. 278). The emaciated, cadaverous figure stands in the Florence Baptistry as a

279. DONATELLO. *Equestrian Monument of Gattamelata.*
1445-1450. Bronze, *c.* 13' high, 11' long. Piazza del
Santo, Padua.

of the horseflesh, saddle leather, and metal armor
are handled with assurance and telling effect.

Quite another attitude is revealed in the
work of the succeeding generation, of which
Antonio Pollaiuolo and Verrocchio are the leading
representatives. The work of Pollaiuolo is dominated by scientific curiosity, especially in regard to
human anatomy. (He is known to have dissected
cadavers in order to study the muscle and bone
structure at first hand.) Trained with his brothers
in his father's goldsmith shop, he is known for
such muscular figures in bronze as *Hercules
Strangling Antaeus*, of which he made both painted
and sculptural versions (Figs. 280, 281). The
legends of the strong man of antiquity were
excellent subjects that permitted the artist to
bring out the musculature of the male figure in
action. In this instance, Hercules overcomes his
adversary, the Lybian giant, by raising him off the
earth that was the source of his strength, while
Antaeus struggles desperately to release the strangle-
hold Hercules has upon him. The sinews in Hercules' legs as they bear the weight of both bodies
should be noted. Pollaiuolo also painted a series
of pictures on the Labors of Hercules. Like his
work in bronze, they are studies of muscular tension, full of athletic energy and quite unrelieved
by gracefulness.

Verrocchio, a contemporary of Pollaiuolo's,
was the official sculptor of the Medici. For this
family he designed everything from tournament
trophies and parade paraphernalia to portraits and
tombs. Like Donatello, he occasionally worked
outside Florence, and at the time of his death in
1488, he was just completing the monument to
Bartolommeo Colleoni (Fig. 282), a condottiere
who left his entire fortune to the Venetian Republic
in return for an equestrian statue to stand in the
city he had served so long. Verrocchio portrays
him as the stern 15th-century man of action he
was. With arrogant mien he dominates his mount,
just as he would the troops under his command.
Donatello's rider and mount are generalized, while
Verrocchio's are more individually and literally
treated. Bartolommeo's steed, a warhorse capable
of bearing the fully armored figure on his back,
stands with one foot unsupported, impatient to
be off. Details of the saddle and armor definitely
belong to the 15th century, and they are richly
wrought with all the silversmith's skill that
Verrocchio possessed.

Verrocchio, like Antonio Pollaiuolo, was also
a painter at a time when sculpture led the field
in experiments with perspective, anatomy, and
light and shadow. When they painted or made
engravings (see Fig. 298), the sharp outlines and
hard contours of their figures reveal them primarily

reminder to the participants in the baptismal
ceremony of the original sin that is washed away,
and of the universal presence of death among the
living.

Donatello's *Gattamelata* (Fig. 279), a statue of
Erasmo da Narni, condottiere of the Venetian
Republic, was the first heroic bronze equestrian
monument to be executed since the days of the
Roman Empire. It stands in Padua where the
sculptor worked during the decade 1443-1453.
The work was undoubtedly inspired by the equestrian portrait of Marcus Aurelius (Fig. 86) that
Donatello had observed in Rome, and the horse
was possibly modeled after one of those above the
portals of St. Mark's in nearby Venice (Fig. 333),
which date from the time of Nero. Other classical
touches are found in the short-skirted Roman
armor worn by the rider and the general poise of
the composition. The anatomy of the horse has
been well observed, and the contrasting textures

(below) 280. ANTONIO POLLAIUOLO. *Hercules Strangling Antaeus. c.* 1470. Tempera on wood, 6¼ × 3½". Uffizi, Florence.

(bottom) 281. ANTONIO POLLAIUOLO. *Hercules Strangling Antaeus. c.* 1475. Bronze, 17¾" high. National Museum, Florence.

282. ANDREA DEL VERROCCHIO. *Equestrian Monument of Bartolommeo Colleoni.* 1485–1488. Bronze, *c.* 13' high. Campo SS. Giovanni e Paolo, Venice.

as workers in metal, especially bronze. Unlike the classical orientation of Ghiberti and Donatello, Pollaiuolo and Verrocchio were primarily scientifically minded, and it was in Verrocchio's workshop that Leonardo da Vinci got his training. It was Leonardo who carried on the unquenchable scientific curiosity of his master, while it remained for Michelangelo, under the stimulus of Donatello's art, to carry on the humanistic ideal into the next century.

PAINTING

With Brunelleschi and Donatello, the third member of the triumvirate of early 15th-century innovators was Masaccio, the only one born within the century. The importance of his series of frescoes in the Brancacci Chapel of the Church of Santa Maria del Carmine can hardly be over-

283. MASACCIO. *Expulsion from the Garden.*
c. 1427. Fresco, 6' 6" × 2' 9". Brancacci
Chapel, Church of Santa Maria del
Carmine, Florence.

estimated. In the *Expulsion from the Garden* (Fig. 283), he chose one of the few subjects in the iconographical tradition in which the nude human body could be portrayed in churches without raising ecclesiastical eyebrows. By defining the source of light as coming diagonally from the right and by having Adam and Eve approach it, Masaccio was able to represent them as casting natural shadows. In addition, by surrounding his figures with light and air, by relating them to the space they occupy, by modeling them in light and shadow like a sculptor would so that they appear as if seen in the round with all the weight and

volume of living forms, Masaccio achieved one of the great innovations in painting—*atmospheric perspective.* Masaccio, moreover, was well aware of the drama of the situation. The full force of man's first moral crisis is expressed by the human body alone with almost no reliance on surrounding details. Eve, aware of her nakedness, cries aloud, while Adam, ashamed to face the light, expresses his remorse by covering his face. Even the avenging angel who drives them out of the garden reflects the tragedy of the fall of man by an expression of human concern and solicitude. Adam's right leg was apparently drawn so as to show the motion of the expulsion; but the proportions of his arms, and the drawing of Eve's lower hand, are definitely incorrect. Such flaws, however, are minor in comparison with the momentous step in painting that puts man in an entirely new relationship to his spatial environment.

The *Tribute Money* (Fig. 284), another of the Brancacci Chapel frescoes, further illustrates the principle of atmospheric perspective. When approached by the collector, Jesus tells Peter that the first fish he catches will have a coin in its mouth. The old simultaneous mode of presentation is employed with St. Peter appearing first in the center, then at the left fishing, and finally at the right paying the debt. Masaccio's premature death at the age of 27 prevented a more complete realization of his discoveries, and it remained for Leonardo da Vinci and Michelangelo to work out their full implications.

Spiritually, Fra Angelico was in many respects a late-Gothic artist, who never painted anything but religious subjects. While he dwelt lovingly on the older forms, he did, however, often treat them within the new frame of reference. The *Annunciation* (Fig. 285) that he painted for the upper corridor of his own monastery of San Marco is a remarkable blend of these old and new elements. A mystic by temperament, Fra Angelico found angels as real as his fellow human beings. But while he always paints with the deepest religious sentiment, his figures in this case appear within the new conception of space. The perspective and the 15th-century architectural details are so exact that the event could well be taking place in a corner of the San Marco cloister that Michelozzo recently had rebuilt. Furthermore, the native Tuscan flowers seen in the garden are well enough observed to satisfy a botanical expert. The lighting, however, is far from the natural illumination of Masaccio; Fra Angelico makes it seem that the figure of Gabriel and the ineffable purity of Mary are beheld as if in a vision.

Unlike the eyes of Fra Angelico, those of his favorite pupil Benozzo Gozzoli were focused firmly

284. MASACCIO. *Tribute Money*. c. 1427. Fresco, 19′ 8″ × 8′ 4″. Brancacci Chapel, Church of Santa Maria del Carmine, Florence.

285. FRA ANGELICO. *Annunciation*. c. 1445–1450. Fresco, 7′ 6″ × 10′ 5″. San Marco, Florence.

on this world. With Cosimo's son Piero as his patron, Benozzo painted the fresco cycle of the *Journey of the Magi* that covers three walls of the chapel in the Medici Palace. A favorite subject for pomp and pageantry, Benozzo's talents were more than equal to their task. In the detail (Fig. 286), a sumptuously attired and caparisoned young Wise Man sits astride his splendid steed. At the head of the retinue that follows in his wake Benozzo portrays three generations of the Medici family. From right to left, Piero de' Medici (in profile) appears at the head of the procession. Emblazoned on the lower part of the harness of his white horse is the motto *Semper* (Forever), a part of the Medici coat of arms, each letter being in the center of one of the jeweled rings that make a continuous chain. Beside him is the elderly Cosimo (also in profile) on a gray mule with a blackamoor groom at his side. The youthful Giuliano and his older brother, the future Lorenzo the Magnificent, are at the extreme left. Bringing up the rear are various intimates and retainers of the Medici court, with the artist himself in the second row back identified by a cap band that reads *Opus Benotii* (Work of Benozzo). Other faces are thought to be those of the philosopher Pico della Mirandola, the poet Poliziano, and Fra Angelico.

The procession winds around through the mountains and valleys of the lovely Tuscan landscape punctuated by tall parasol pines and needle cypresses toward the niched altar where Fra Filippo Lippi's *Nativity* (Plate 19) was seen. Lippo's frank, joyous acceptance of the festive Renaissance spirit is akin to the art of Fra Angelico and the sculptor Luca della Robbia (see p. 233). His Madonnas are lithe and girlish, his babies plump and childlike, his saints benign and patriarchal. The linear emphasis of his drawing, softened by his lush palette of pastel hues, had a decisive influence on the art of his pupil Botticelli. In the *Nativity*, the pictorial space is bisected symmetrically by the Trinity with God the Father imparting a blessing on His Son through the descending rays of the Holy Spirit, which find an earthly echo in the rising vertical lines of the tree trunks. Niches are thus created for the figures of the Madonna, St. John, and St. Joseph.

To decorate one of the salons of the Medici Palace, Cosimo called upon Paolo Uccello. As a student of spatial science, Uccello was trying to solve the problem of *linear perspective*—the formula of arranging lines on a two-dimensional surface so that they converge at a vanishing point on the horizon and promote the illusion of recession in depth. One of his three scenes depicting the *Battle of San Romano* (Fig. 287), a skirmish of 1432 in which the Florentines put the Sienese army to flight, shows his pioneering effort in applying Euclidean geometry to pictorial mechanics. As a scientific experiment, Uccello lays his lances and banners out on the ground as if on a chessboard. He was evidently so absorbed with his lines that his bloodless battle is staged more in the manner of a dress parade than a clashing conflict. He also did not develop the element of light and shade, so that his merry-go-roundlike horses, despite the

286. BENOZZO GOZZOLI. *Journey of the Magi* (detail). *c.* 1459–1463. Fresco, *c.* 12' 4¼" long. Chapel, Medici-Riccardi Palace, Florence.

variety of their postures, remain as flat as cardboard. For all this intellectual effort, the solution of the linear problem eluded him, and in this respect he was always a pupil and never a master.

Present in Florence during the 1440's was Piero della Francesca. As an assistant to Domenico Veneziano, he absorbed the richness of Venetian color; studying Masaccio, he learned about atmospheric perspective and how to model figures in light and shade; and associating with Ghiberti, Brunelleschi, Alberti, and Paolo Uccello, he eventually became a master of linear perspective and later wrote a treatise on the subject. His *Resurrection* (Fig. 288), painted for the chapel of the town hall of his native Umbrian town of Borgo San Sepolchro, is one of his most sophis-

(above) 287. PAOLO UC-CELLO. *Battle of San Romano.* *c.* 1455. Tempera on wood, 6′ × 10′ 5″. Uffizi, Florence.

(left) 288. PIERO DELLA FRANCESCA. *Resurrection. c.* 1460. Fresco, 9′ 6″ × 8′ 4″. Gallery, Palazzo del Comune, Borgo San Sepolcro.

289. SANDRO BOTTICELLI. *Adoration of the Magi. c.* 1475. Tempera on wood, 43½ × 52¾". Uffizi, Florence.

ticated works. His geometrical clarity of design is seen at once in the compact pyramidal composition that builds up from the sleeping soldiers (the second from the left is generally thought to be a self-portrait) and sarcophagus to the figure of Christ modeled like a classical statue and holding the triumphant banner. Color contrasts, as well as light and shade, play appointed roles both in the pictorial mechanics and in the symbolism. The somber tones of the soldiers' costumes are offset by the diaphanous pink of Christ's robe. Furthermore, the dark-clad soldiers, paralleled by the shadowy earth, set up an alternating rhythm with the glowing figure of Christ against the Easter dawn. The barren earth on the left yields to the springtime regeneration of the fields on the right; and the effect of the brightening sky above, together with the radiant spirit of Christ with the piercing, almost hypnotic gaze, is reflected in the disturbed soldiers below, who, though still asleep, are yet dimly aware of the dawn.

Painting in the first part of the 15th century must reckon with many different trends and diverse personalities. Sandro Botticelli, however, rose above the majority of his contemporaries and became the most representative artist of the humanistic thought that dominated the latter half of the century. Botticelli enjoyed the patronage of the Medici family, and his *Adoration of the Magi* (Fig. 289) portrays the clan as had his predecessor Benozzo Gozzoli (Fig. 286). Among the

admirably arranged figures, one finds the elderly Cosimo kneeling at the feet of the Christ Child; also kneeling are his two sons Piero and Giovanni; behind them, standing against the ruined wall, is the profiled figure of Giuliano, who was the handsome grandson of Cosimo and the younger brother of Lorenzo the Magnificent, who is to be found in the extreme left foreground. His opposite number at the right usually is identified as Botticelli himself. Though the coloring is bright—ranging from the cool azure of the Virgin's robe and the dark-green and gold embroidery of Cosimo's costume to the ermine-lined crimson cloak of the kneeling Piero and the bright orange of Botticelli's mantle—it falls into a harmonious pattern. Attention should also be called to the classical touch provided by the ancient Roman ruin in the left background.

Botticelli was not a popular painter of pageants like Benozzo Gozzoli and his contemporary Ghirlandaio but a member of the sophisticated group of humanists who gathered around his Medici patrons. In this circle, which included the poet Angelo Poliziano and the philosophers Marsilio Ficino and Pico della Mirandola, Lorenzo the Magnificient, and his cousin Pierfrancesco di Lorenzo de' Medici, classical myths were constantly discussed and interpreted. The dialogues of Plato, the *Enneads* of Plotinus, and Greek musical theory were all thoroughly explored. With the Florentine interest in the pictorial arts, the ancient references to sculpture and painting were not neglected. This neopagan atmosphere with its Christian concordances is reflected in many of Botticelli's paintings.

Venus and Mars (Plate 20) is one of Botticelli's allegorical pictures inspired by the humanistic speculations of the Florentine Neo-Platonists. Commissioned apparently for a marriage in the famous Vespucci family, the unusual shape of the panel suggests that its prototype was a classical sarcophagus, and that it was intended either for a wedding chest or a bed board. Venus and Mars were, of course, the mythological lovers of antiquity; and Marsilio Ficino, in his commentary on Plato's *Symposium*, mentioned that "Mars is outstanding in strength among planets because he makes men stronger, but Venus masters him...." The wealthy Vespucci family, close associates of the Medici, numbered several celebrated members, among them Simonetta Cattaneo, wife of one Marco Vespucci, and Amerigo Vespucci, the Florentine geographer and explorer whose claim that he had discovered an unknown continent gave his name to the new world. The fair Simonetta was elevated into a Platonic personification

of ideal beauty and goodness. As such she was enshrined by Poliziano and Lorenzo the Magnificent in a poetic niche, much as Beatrice had been by Dante and Laura by Petrarch. She is also thought to have inspired the ideal Venus type that appears in many of Botticelli's masterpieces.

The *Birth of Venus* (Fig. 290) and its companion piece the famous *Primavera*, or *Allegory of Spring*, were both painted for the Magnificent's young cousin Pierfrancesco di Lorenzo de' Medici to decorate a newly purchased country villa. The picture may have been inspired by a literary description of a lost painting from antiquity—*Aphrodite Anadyomene* (Venus rising from the sea) by Alexander the Great's court painter Apelles. The historian E. H. Gombrich suggests that the immediate source for Botticelli's painting may have been the 1469 Roman printing of Apuleius' *Golden Ass*. In this ancient novel the character Lucius recounts his dream: "... from the midst of the sea there emerged a divine face of an appearance worthy of veneration even by the Gods: then gradually I saw a whole shining figure rising out of the sea... her hair, most abundant in its richness, flowed

290. SANDRO BOTTICELLI. *Birth of Venus.* c. 1480.
Tempera on canvas, 6′ 7″ × 9′ 2″. Uffizi, Florence.

yieldingly around her divine neck in slight curves, fluttering luxuriously. . . ."

Botticelli depicts the goddess vividly as she floats across the green sea on a pink shell gently blown by Zephyrs. On the shore ready to clothe her in a flowery mantle is one of the Horae, or Hours. The pose of the body is that of the *Venus de' Medici*, an antique marble statue belonging to that family and now in the Uffizi Gallery (Fig. 291). The coloring of the picture is as cool as called for by a classical subject. The fluttering drapery of the side figures imparts a sense of lightness and movement and leads the eye toward the head of Venus, which is surrounded by an aura of golden hair. The incisiveness of outline, the balletlike choreography of dancing lines, and the varied pattern of linear rhythms recall the technique of relief sculpture.

Botticelli's penchant for intellectualized interpretations of antiquity reaches record proportions in his later picture called *Calumny* (Fig. 292). This is yet another attempt to reconstruct a lost painting by Apelles. A literary description by the Roman author Lucian was known to Botticelli in a translation by Alberti, and the subject was undoubtedly discussed at length by the group of scholars around Lorenzo. Moving from right to left in this elaborate allegory on justice, the observer notes that the seat of judgment is occupied by a wicked prince. On either side of him are his advisers, Ignorance and Superstition, who whisper evil counsel into his long donkeylike ears. Before him in tattered clothing stands the plaintiff, Envy, who is leading

(above) 291. *Venus de' Medici*. 3rd century B.C. Marble, 5′ high. Uffizi, Florence.

(right) 292. SANDRO BOTTICELLI. *"Calumny" of Apelles.* c. 1485–1490. Tempera on wood, 24 × 35³/₈″. Uffizi, Florence.

Calumny, the holder of the flaming torch, before the judge. She, in turn, is dragging by the hair the innocent victim, who raises his hands in a gesture of supplication. Treachery and Deceit, personified by two feminine figures, are entwining Calumny's hair with precious ornaments. The dark-hooded figure in mourning garments to their left is Remorse, whose hands point to the accused and whose face is turned toward the naked Truth, who, in turn, raises her hand to high heaven.

In spite of the heavy allegorical burden it has to carry, the picture is a success. The painting has a smooth surface finish, and the colors, even after the passage of almost 500 years, are still of enamel-like clarity and brilliance. The placement of the figures in relation to the architectural setting makes pictorial as well as allegorical sense. The movement of the draperies expresses extreme agitation, but the turbulence of the human drama is kept within bounds by Botticelli's mastery of composition. The finely proportioned and spacious building, though it was intended to represent a Roman basilica, is completely in the Florentine Renaissance style. Even the relief sculptures and statuary in niches, in spite of their classical intentions, are far more Florentine than antique in feeling.

With Lorenzo's death in 1492, just about the time *Calumny* was finished, Botticelli's career and the arts generally underwent a period of eclipse. Under the influence of the monk Savonarola, a fiery preacher and prophet of doom, all sorts of apocalyptical visions were conjured up. His maledictions and deprecations gathered around him all the anti-Medici factions, which succeeded in driving the ruling family out of Florence only two years after the death of the Magnificent. Botticelli, always an introspective personality, repented of his paganism, reputedly burned as many of his pictures of nude subjects as he could lay his hands on, and became a follower of Savonarola. His late work reflects this religious preoccupation. The beautiful pagan dream of Lorenzo's time, however, had burst like a bubble, and with it Botticelli's inspiration which he never succeeded in recapturing.

Medici patronage reached out beyond Florence to all the European centers where the family had branch banks—Milan, Venice, Lyon, London, and especially Bruges, where two Medici representatives figured prominently in Flemish painting. *Giovanni Arnolfini and His Wife* (Plate 21) by Jan van Eyck is a masterly portrait of the shrewd calculating Medici banker. Bright light suffuses the entire space and illuminates every object evenly and naturally. Each detail is described with the keenest observation from the more subdued tones and textures of the wooden floor and shoes, the

293. Jan van Eyck. *Giovanni Arnolfini and His Wife* (detail). 1434. Oil on wood. National Gallery, London (reproduced by courtesy of the Trustees). (Compare Plate 21.)

furry dog, and the cloth of costumes and bed to the higher gloss of the metal chandelier and the mirror (Fig. 293), itself a picture in miniature containing a wedding certificate and a self-portrait of the artist as witness to the ceremony.

In the latter half of the 15th century, Tommaso Portinari, another Medici representative in Bruges, commissioned an altarpiece (Fig. 294) for the hospital of Santa Maria Nuova in Florence. Hugo van der Goes, the artistic heir of van Eyck, painted the donor, his wife and children, and their patron saints Thomas and Margaret in the wide folding wings of the triptych. In the central panel, depicting the Adoration of the Shepherds, one sees the same close observation of naturalistic detail as van Eyck's—from the weather-beaten faces of the shepherds to the brocaded cloth of the angel's robes. But van der Goes is also concerned with symbolism—the harp in the tympanum of the background building indicates that Mary and the Child stem from the house of David; the sheaf of wheat signifies Bethlehem; and the flowers, the future sorrows of Mary. The artist also makes use of some spatial distortion to achieve expressive effect—the floor tipping slightly upward to project the figures forward; the relative sizes of the figures in relation to the picture plane, with Joseph, Mary, and the shepherds in the middle ground looming larger than the angels in the foreground.

294. HUGO VAN DER GOES. *Portinari Altarpiece. c.* 1476.
Oil on wood, 9′ 2½″ × 21′ 8½″. Uffizi, Florence.

The arrival of this triptych in Florence in 1476 created a sensation, for it provided the first opportunity local painters had to observe a large-scale product by one of their northern contemporaries. Clearly it influenced Ghirlandaio and Botticelli. Their special interest was in the new oil medium perfected by Jan van Eyck. In Italy, such panels traditionally were done with water-soluble pigments in the process known as tempera. The Flemish painters, however, were now using oil to suspend pigments. The boards on which they painted were first built up with a fine white cementlike substance called gesso, and on this a cartoon of the picture was drawn with ink and modeled in light and shade. After the painting had been made in opaque oil colors, a translucent glaze with varnishlike brightness was then applied. This glaze, also in an oil medium, could be worked with the brush to give iridescent effects, so that the colors seemed to glow from within the picture. Gradually, the deeper colors and brilliant enamellike finish of this oil medium supplanted the brighter colored but duller surfaces of Italian tempera painting.

POETRY AND MUSIC

The principal poets of the Florentine Renaissance were Lorenzo de' Medici and Poliziano. Lorenzo's title *Il Magnifico*, in retrospect, seems fitting recognition of his activities as poet, humanist, philosopher, discoverer of genius, patron of the arts and sciences, and adviser to writers, sculptors, painters, and musicians. The terracotta

bust from Verrocchio's workshop (Fig. 295), suggests that Lorenzo's contemporaries apparently saw a different side of the man, that of the forceful statesman, the victor in the Pazzi family conspiracy, the averter of war with Naples, the holder of the balance of power in Italy, the sponsor of lavish civic celebrations—in short, the personification of the Machiavellian prince. There is little in Verrocchio's portrait to suggest that behind the impassive face of the shrewd professional diplomat, which shows so well a will to power, was the soul of a poet, the contemplative mind of a philosopher, and a heart

295. ANDREA DEL VERROCCHIO. *Lorenzo de' Medici. c.* 1480. Painted terracotta, 25⅞″ high. National Gallery, Washington.

and spirit capable of the warmest human understanding. For a portrait of this other side of a complex personality, we must turn to his creative interests that led a contemporary historian to conclude in 1530 that Florence could not have had a better or more delightful tyrant.

Under the wise guidance of his grandfather Cosimo, *Pater Patriae*, Lorenzo had been educated by Pico della Mirandola and other Latin and Greek scholars of the highest repute to be the type of philosopher-ruler that Plato had expounded upon in his *Republic*. Social conditions, however, had changed considerably since Cosimo's time, and while his grandfather had been a banker with intellectual and artistic tastes, Lorenzo became a prince whose power rested on philosophical prestige and leadership in matters of taste as well as on his banking fortune. Lorenzo maintained embassies at all the principal courts to which he made loans, but while he was willing to finance foreign conflicts, provided he saw a substantial profit for himself, he preferred to fight his own wars with words. By having the services of the greatest humanists under his command, he never ran out of ammunition in the form of elegantly turned phrases, apt epithets, veiled threats, and invectives. Changes in the status of the arts had also come about as the 15th century progressed. In the early decades Ghiberti had been employed by the Signory, and his work was intended for public view. Later the major commissions came from a few families, and under Lorenzo the arts took on more of a courtly character, and the audiences grew correspondingly more restricted. Some painters were able to remain outside the charmed circle and to make careers depicting social scenes of births and marriages for an upper middle-class clientele. Botticelli's pictures, however, were done mainly for the group of humanistic connoisseurs.

Lorenzo himself, though the leader of this exclusive group, had the instincts of a popular ruler and did not neglect the common touch. He participated actively in the gay Florentine festivals by composing new verses for the traditional folk tunes, by encouraging others in his circle to do the same, and by holding competitions among composers for better musical settings of the songs. Lorenzo thus gave new impetus to popular literature in the vernacular. In a commentary on four of his own sonnets, he went to considerable lengths to defend the expressive possibilities of Tuscan Italian; and, after comparing it with Hebrew, Greek, and Latin, he found that its harmoniousness and sweetness outdid all the others. While he continued to write sophisticated sonnets, Lorenzo also wrote popular verses that have, in addition to their beauty and literary polish, all the spontaneous freshness, humor, and charm of folk poetry. In some of his pastoral poems he even uses the rustic dialogue of true country folk. Few poets could rival the lyricism of his *canti carnascialeschi*, or carnival songs, one of which contains the oft-quoted lines:

> Quanto è bella giovinezza,
> Che si fugge tuttavia!
> Chi vuol esser lieto, sia:
> Di doman non c' è certezza.

> Fair is youth and free of sorrow,
> Yet how soon its joys we bury!
> Let who would be, now be merry:
> Sure is no one of tomorrow.

In order to flourish, popular poetry of this kind needed appropriate musical settings. As a young man of 18, Lorenzo was in search of a composer to set his lyrics, and a letter he wrote at that time (1467) requests the "venerable Gugliemo Dufay," who by this time was approaching 70, to compose music for his verses. This was the same Guillaume Dufay who some 30 years earlier had composed the dedicatory motet for the cathedral.

Popular music making in Florence and other Italian cities was as much a part of the good life as any of the other arts. But it was mainly an art of performance, and little music was ever written down. The Franciscan tradition of singing lauds during Advent, Lent, and especially Holy Week continued throughout the 15th century, and both Lorenzo and his mother wrote lauds for performance by members of their family and households. Antonio Squarcialupi, music master to the Medici, enjoyed a high reputation for his skill on the organ and lute, but as a composer he was a minor figure in comparison with his great contemporaries from Burgundy or the Netherlands—Dufay, Ockeghem, Obrecht, and Agricola—each of whom was active in Florence at one time or another. When the time came to appoint a successor to Squarcialupi after his death in 1475, Lorenzo's choice fell on Heinrich Isaac, a native of Flanders and a rapid and prolific composer. Florence immediately became a second home to this truly cosmopolitan figure, and native Italian idioms soon were combined with those of his own background and training.

Isaac's duties included those of organist and choirmaster at the Florence Cathedral as well as at the Medici Palace, where Lorenzo is known to have had no less than five organs. Together with the poet Angelo Poliziano, he was also the teacher of Lorenzo's sons, one of whom was destined to be the music- and art-loving Pope Leo X. But most important, Isaac collaborated with Lorenzo on

A-mor a tal___ fol-li - a M'in - dus-se al - lor___ ch'-i' rup-pi

the songs written for popular festivals. He thus became cocreator of one of the popular genres of secular choral music that eventually led to the madrigal. Dufay's settings of Lorenzo's verses are now lost, but many by Isaac are extant. In one of these, he shows the tendency away from complex counterpoint and toward simple harmonic, or chordal, texture. Its style is that of a Florentine *frottola*, a carnival song for dancing as well as singing, and its lilting rhythm freely shifts its meter, as in the fourth bar.

As the setting stands, it could be performed for three-part chorus; as a solo song with the two lower parts taken by the lute or two viols; or as a vocal duet with the soprano and any one of the two other voices. The collaboration of Lorenzo and Isaac thus resulted both in a meeting of minds and a merging of poetic and musical forms. Lorenzo's verses were a union of the courtly *ballata* and popular poetry while Isaac succeeded in Italianizing the Burgundian *chanson*, or song —Italianizing in this case means simplifying, omitting all artificiality, and enlivening a rather stiff form with the graceful Florentine folk melodies and rhythms. It can be seen that such a movement worked both ways by raising the level of popular poetry on the one hand, and at the same time rejuvenating the more sophisticated poetic and musical forms by contact with popular idioms.

IDEAS

The dominating ideas of the Florentine Renaissance cluster around three concepts—classical humanism, scientific naturalism, and Renaissance individualism. In their broadest meaning, humanism, naturalism, and individualism were far from new. Humanism in the humanitarian Franciscan sense was a carryover from the 13th and 14th centuries; naturalism stemmed from late Gothic times; and some form of individualism is always present in any period. The term *Renais-*

sance, implying as it does a rebirth, is a source of some confusion. To the early 16th-century historians, it meant an awakening to the values of ancient classical arts and letters after the long medieval night. But just what, if anything, was *reborn* has never been satisfactorily explained. Since all the principal ideas were present in the Gothic period, one might do better to speak of a maturation of certain tendencies present in late medieval times. Yet there was a specific drive that gave an extraordinary impetus and color to the creative life and thought of this small Tuscan city-state in the 15th century. It is important, therefore, to discover just what it was, and what it was not, that gave Florence its special flavor.

That the Renaissance meant a secularization of life as opposed to the predominantly religious outlook of the medieval period has often been asserted. The secular spirit may indeed have been stronger during the Renaissance, but in medieval times there was a secular tradition in the architecture of castles, guild halls, and market buildings, in such pictorial works as the Bayeux Tapestry, in such epics as the *Chanson de Roland*, in Goliardic folk verse, in the aristocratic poetry of the troubadours, and in the music of the minstrels. The fact that so little of this has survived too often has led to the conclusion that secular works did not exist. And a look at the record of the 15th century will reveal that the great majority of the statuary, paintings, and music were religious works intended for placement or performance in churches. Such works as Antonio Pollaiuolo's Hercules series, Botticelli's mythological pictures, and Isaac's and Lorenzo's carnival songs were conspicuous exceptions rather than the rule. On the other hand, the 15th century did have Dufay's dedicatory motet *Nuper Rosarum* and Benozzo Gozzoli's *Journey of the Magi*, which, though nominally religious, have contemporary implications. Lorenzo's sacred drama *San Giovanni e Paolo*, with music by Isaac, was a family affair performed at the Medici Palace, and Botticelli's *Adoration of the Magi* is in reality a family portrait. Although the pure piety of Fra Angelico was becoming increasingly rare, there is no reason to assume that the 15th century in Florence was antireligious or even irreligious. Religious motivation was still a powerful force, as the career of Savonarola proved, but its expression simply assumed another form.

Though Florentine humanism evolved from the Franciscan spirit, it did take on a consciously classical coloration. Here again, however, a word of caution is necessary when speaking of a "rebirth" of the spirit of antiquity. In Italy, much more than in northern Europe, the classical tradition had been more or less continuous. Roman remains were everywhere in evidence. Many Roman arches, aqueducts, bridges, and roads were still in use, while fragments of ancient buildings, such as columns, were used and reused as building materials. In the late 13th century, Niccolo Pisano's sculptural models were the Roman remains he saw all around him, and the revival of the classical male nude as an instrument of expression is seen in the work of Ghiberti, Donatello, Pollaiuolo, and Verrocchio. At the end of the century Michelangelo had developed such a formidable sculptural technique that his *David* (Fig. 296) not only rivaled the work of such ancient craftsmen as Praxiteles (see Fig. 32) but actually surpassed them. Aristotle was still the official philosopher of the Church, and ancient musical theory was still studied. What was new to Florence was the study of the Greek language, the setting up of Ciceronian rather than medieval Latin as a standard, and a passionate interest in Plato. In spite of a certain antiquarianism, however, the net result was less a revival of things past than a step forward. It was—as such movements usually are—a search for past precedents to justify present practices.

Much has been said also about the pagan aspect of this interest in antiquity. Here again it was less anti-Christian than appears on the surface. Florentine Neo-Platonism was certainly anti-scholastic, but it was mainly a substitution of the authority of Plato for that of Aristotle. Marsilio Ficino, as the high priest of the movement, in his interpretation of the *Republic* and *Laws*, speaks of Plato as the Attic "Moses." He is also known to have added "Saint" Socrates to the litany and to have burned a candle before the bust of Plato. In this light, his thought appears more as a reinterpretation of Christianity in Platonic terms than paganism as such. There was also a certain amount of anticlericalism in Florence, as there was elsewhere at this time. Lorenzo, however, as the papal banker and as a father who chose the Church for his son Giovanni's career, was not so

296. MICHELANGELO. *David.* 1501–1504. Marble, 18' high. Academy, Florence.

much a religious skeptic as he was a political realist. It is important to keep in mind that the Florentine humanists were a small band of learned men, whose Platonic disputations have made much more noise in the corridors of history than they did in their own time. Actually, they never had, nor did they seek, a large audience. In the first quarter of the following century, however, the humanists had the international forum of Rome. The artistic expression of Neo-Platonism came to its climax in the works of Michelangelo, and the full discussion of the movement—which must include the art of Botticelli and Raphael, the patronage of Julius II and the Medici popes Leo X and Clement VII, as well as the Neo-Platonic philosophers—will be discussed in the next chapter.

Naturalism, in the sense of fidelity to nature, appears in a well-developed form both in the northern Gothic sculpture and in the poetry of St. Francis, who had died as long before as 1226. By the 14th century, representations of man and nature alike had pretty well lost their value as other-worldly symbols. But rather than remaining a generalized interest in this world, Florentine 15th-century naturalism took a noticeably scientific turn. Careful observation of natural phenomena and the will to reproduce objects as the eye sees them was evidence of an empirical attitude; dissection of cadavers in order to see the structure of the human body revealed a spirit of free inquiry; and the study of mathematics so as to put objects into proper perspective involved a new concept of space. Thus, while Fra Angelico's religious and Botticelli's pagan dreams are ample evidence that the visionary element was still present, clearly a new scientific spirit was now afoot.

297. *Burning of Savonarola, 1498.* Old engraving. Uffizi, Florence.

While individualism as such is practically universal, the distinctive feature of its Florentine expression was that conditions in this small city-state were almost ideal for artists to come into immediate and fruitful contact with their patrons and audience. Competition was keen; desire for personal fame was intense; and a high regard for personality is seen in the portraiture, biographies, and autobiographies.

It should therefore be clear that the Florentine Renaissance was characterized by no sharp cleavage with the past, and that the special savor of this period lies in the quality of its humanism, in the tendency of its naturalism, and in its particular regard for individualism.

Scientific Naturalism

The two basic directions taken by the naturalism of the 15th century led to a new experimental attitude and a new concept of space. A close partnership between art and science developed, with architects becoming mathematicians, sculptors anatomists, painters geometricians, and musicians acousticians. The spirit of free inquiry was by no means confined to the arts alone. It permeated all the progressive aspects of the life of the time from a reexamination of the forms of secular government to Machiavelli's observations on how men behave in a certain given set of political circumstances. This searching curiosity reached its full fruition in the early years of the next century in Machiavelli's political handbook *The Prince*; in the same author's attempt to apply the Thucydidean method of rational historical analysis in his *History of Florence*; and in the scientific observations in Leonardo's notebooks, which cover everything from astronomy to hydraulics. Well within the 15th century, however, the same spirit manifested itself. Ghiberti's *Commentaries* took up the mathematical proportions of the human body as the basis of its beauty, and he wrote the first treatise in Italian on optics. Brunelleschi, as a diligent student of Vitruvius, was concerned with the mathematical proportions of his buildings. Alberti, in his books on painting, sculpture, and architecture, stressed the study of mathematics as the underlying principle of all the arts.

The sculptors and painters who followed the leadership of Antonio Pollaiuolo and Verrocchio were animated by the desire to express the structural forms of the body beneath its external appearance, and their anatomical studies opened the way to the modeling of the movements and gestures of the human body, ranging from Verrocchio's realization of incipient muscular move-

(left) 298. ANTONIO POLLAI-UOLO. *Battle of Ten Nude Men.* c. 1465–1470. Engraving. Uffizi, Florence.

(below) 299. LEONARDO DA VINCI. *Adoration of the Magi* (detail). 1481–1482. Tempera on wood, 7′ 11⅝″ × 8′ ⅞″ (area shown 24 × 30″). Uffizi, Florence.

ment to Pollaiuolo's energetic athleticism (Fig. 298). The result was the reaffirmation of the expressive power of the nude. In painting, naturalism meant a more faithful representation of the world of appearances and one based on detailed and accurate observation. Even Fra Angelico showed an interest in the exact reproduction of Tuscan botanical specimens in the garden of his *Annunciation*; and Botticelli, under the influence of Pollaiuolo and Verrocchio, combined objective techniques with his highly imaginative subject matter. The culmination of this line of thought was reached in Verrocchio's pupil Leonardo da Vinci, who considered painting a science and sculpture a mechanical art. Leonardo's scientific probing extended far beyond the physical and anatomical into the metaphysical and psychological aspects of human nature. A detail from his early, unfinished *Adoration of the Magi* (Fig. 299), for instance, reveals through turbulent gesticulations and quizzical facial expressions the bewilderment and emotional turmoil of the Wise Men as they try to comprehend the miraculous meaning of the Messiah's coming. In music there was a continued interest in Greek theory, coupled, however, with attempts to experiment with acoustical problems. The compositions of Dufay and others of the northern school were characterized by extreme erudition; and mathematical laws were strictly applied to such aspects of composition as rhythmical progressions, formal proportions, and the development of elaborate technical devices.

Highly dramatic was the conquest of geographical space that began with the voyages of Columbus, leading to the development of trade routes and commerce and the tapping of new and distant sources of wealth. In architecture, this breakthrough in space is reflected in the raising

of Brunelleschi's cupola almost 400 feet into the air. In painting, it is seen in the placing of figures in more normal relationship to the space they occupy, and in landscape settings; in Masaccio's development of atmospheric perspective, in which figures are modeled in light and shade; in working out the rules of linear perspective whereby the illusion of depth on a two-dimensional surface is achieved by defining a point at which lines converge; and by *foreshortening*, the diminishing of size of figures and objects in direct ratio to their distance from the picture plane.

Since the subject matter of medieval art was drawn from the other world, it was outside the scope of naturalistic representation and had to be rendered symbolically. Art now entered a new phase of self-awareness as Renaissance artists began to think less in terms of allegory, symbolism, and moral lessons and more in terms of aesthetic problems, modes of presentation, and pictorial mechanics. In medieval music, the emphasis had been on perfect intervals and mathematical rhythmic ratios in order to please the ear of God. Renaissance musicians now reversed the process by concentrating on sounds that would delight the human ear. The new spirit was also heard in the extension of the range of musical instruments in both higher and lower registers, to broaden the scope of tonal space. Thus the development of pleasant harmonic textures, the softening of dissonant passing tones, and the writing of singable melodies and danceable rhythms are all related phenomena.

In this trend toward scientific naturalism, the arts of painting and sculpture became firmly allied with geometrical and scientific laws, a union that lasted until 20th-century expressionism. The 15th-century Florentine artists literally reveled in the perspective, optical, and anatomical discoveries of their day. And when all the basic research, experiments, and discoveries had been made, it was left for their successors—Leonardo da Vinci, Michelangelo, and Raphael—to explore their full expressive possibilities.

Renaissance Individualism

Whether one considers the Renaissance patrons' reasons for commissioning artists, the forms and techniques employed in the various arts, the regard for human personality seen in portraiture, the desire for personal prestige through art, or the social status of the artist, one finds evidence everywhere of a special attitude of Renaissance man toward himself, his fellowmen, and his place in the world. The religious nature of the vast majority of the works of art has already been pointed out, but personal patronage was in the ascendancy. Brunelleschi built the Pazzi Chapel, Masolino and Masaccio decorated the Brancacci Chapel, and Benozzo Gozzoli and Filippo Lippi did the paintings for the Medici Chapel on commission from private donors as memorials to themselves and their families. San Lorenzo, the parish church of the Medici, was rebuilt and redecorated by Brunelleschi and Donatello—but the money came from Cosimo and not from the Church. Fra Angelico decorated the corridors of the monastery of San Marco, which was under the protection of the Medici family, and Squarcialupi and Isaac were on the payroll of the Medici when they played the organ in the cathedral, in a church, or in the family palace. Piousness and the desire for spiritual salvation were not the only motives for such munificence; a knowledge that the donor's present and posthumous fame depended on his building of monuments and his choice of artists to decorate them was also present.

In addition to the circumstances of patronage, certain technical considerations within the arts themselves point in the same individualistic direction. The development of perspective drawing, for example, implied that the subject in the picture —whether a Madonna, a saint, or an angel—was definitely placed in this world rather than symbolically in the next, and hence was more on a par with the observer. The unification of space by having all the lines converge at one point on the horizon tended to flatter the spectator. By such clear organization of lines and planes, linear perspective presupposes that everything is seen from a single optical vantage point. While it is actually that of the artist, he makes it seem as if it were also that of the observer. By closing his form, the artist further implies that nothing of importance lies outside, and the whole of the picture can then be taken in at a glance. Since nothing, then, is beyond the grasp of the viewer, and all can be comprehended with relatively little effort, the eye and mind of the onlooker are reassured. The central-type church that Alberti, Bramante, and later Michelangelo and Palladio preferred to design, in which the space is unified under a dome, is the architectural expression of the same idea. The Gothic cathedral purposely led the eye and imagination outward into the transcendental beyond, while the central-type church revolves around man himself. Standing under the cupola, the observer is aware that the axis of the building is not objectively outside or transcendentally beyond but subjectively in himself. He is, for the moment at least, the center of the architectural space. The center of the universe is not therefore at some remote point beyond the horizon; rather, it is within man himself.

Human figures, whether intended as prophets or portraits, tended to become more personal and individual. Each statue by Donatello, be it *Lo Zuccone*, *David*, or the *Gattamelata*, was a human individuality who made a powerful and unique impression. Even Fra Angelico's Madonna was a personality more than an abstraction, and his figure of the Angel Gabriel possessed genuine human dignity. Whether the medium was marble,

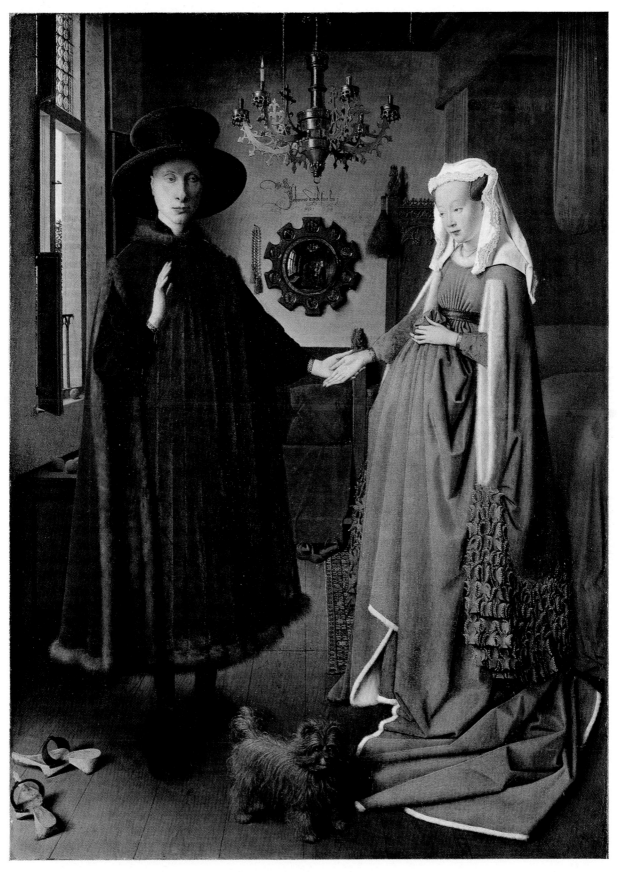

Plate 21. JAN VAN EYCK. *Giovanni Arnolfini and His Wife.* 1434.
Oil on wood, 33 × 22 ½″.
National Gallery, London (reproduced by courtesy of the Trustees). (See p. 253.)

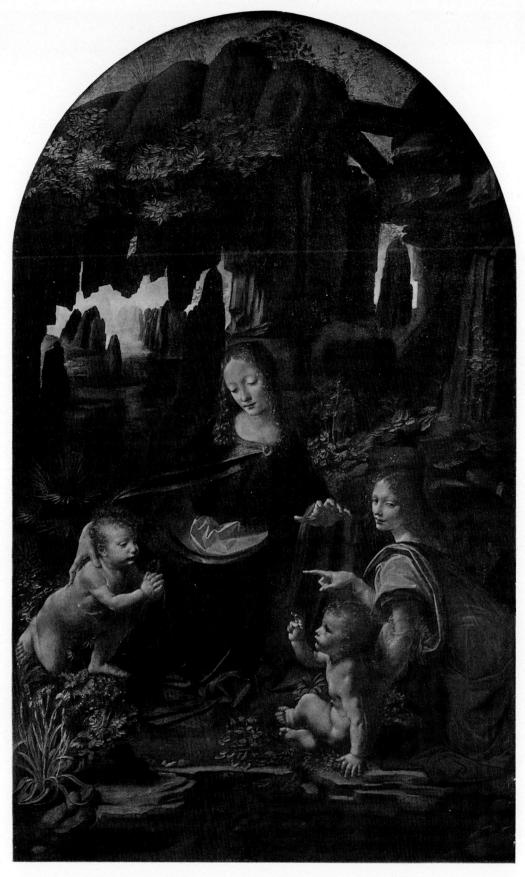

Plate 22. LEONARDO DA VINCI. *Madonna of the Rocks*. *c.* 1485.
Oil on wood, 75 × 43 ½″. Louvre, Paris. (See p. 266.)

terracotta, paint, words, or tones, there was evidence of the new value placed on human individuality. Whether the picture was a disguised family group, as Botticelli's *Adoration of the Magi*, or a personal portrait, as Verrocchio's bust of Lorenzo, the figures were authentic personages rather than stylized abstractions; even though Lorenzo de' Medici was the most powerful political figure of Florence, Verrocchio saw him as a man, not as an institution.

The higher social status accorded Florentine artists was evidenced by the inclusion of self-portraits in such paintings as that of Benozzo Gozzoli in his *Journey of the Magi* and the prominent position Botticelli accorded himself in his *Adoration of the Magi*. Ghiberti's personal reminiscences in his *Commentaries* were probably the first autobiography of an artist in history; his inclusion of the lives and legends of his famous 14th-century predecessors were the first biographies of individual artists. Signatures of artists on their works became the rule, not the exception; and the culmination came when Michelangelo realized that his work was so highly individual that he no longer needed to sign it. The desire for personal fame grew to such an extent that Benvenuto Cellini no longer was content to let his works speak for him but wrote a voluminous autobiography filled with self-praise. The painter Giorgio Vasari likewise took up the pen to record the lives of the artists he knew personally and by reputation. More broadly, such works as Pico della Mirandola's essay on the *Dignity of Man*, Machiavelli's *The Prince*, and Castiglione's *The Courtier* were written to enhance the intellectual, political, and social status of man in general and the scholar, politician, courtier, and artist in particular.

In late medieval and early Renaissance times, artists were content with their status as craftsmen. They were trained as apprentices to grind pigments, carve wooden chests, make engravings, and prepare wall surfaces for frescoes as well as to carve marble reliefs and paint pictures. In the late 15th and early 16th centuries, however, it was not enough for an artist to create works of art. He had to know the theory of art and the place of art in the intellectual atmosphere of his period. The quality most admired in Renaissance man was *virtù* (the word comes closer in the modern sense to *virtuoso* than *virtuous*). *Virtù* revealed itself in the boundless vitality and extraordinary ability that led to the achievements of a Lorenzo the Magnificent or the breathtaking conceptions of a Michelangelo. With *virtù*, the Renaissance artist could no longer confine himself to a single specialty but sought to become the *homo universale*, the universal man. Brunelleschi was a goldsmith, sculptor, en-

gineer, and mathematician as well as one of the leading lights of Renaissance architecture. Alberti was an athlete, horseman, brilliant wit, Latin stylist, mathematician, architect, musician, and playwright as well as the founder of Renaissance theory of art. For Leonardo da Vinci, it is more difficult to find a field in which he was not proficient than one in which he excelled.

From Lorenzo's time through the early 16th century, the greatest artists were intellectuals. Alberti was a scholar-architect who wrote books on the subject, designed buildings on paper, and left the actual construction to a master mason. Botticelli associated with men of letters and worked elaborate allegories into his pictures. Leonardo da Vinci thought sculpture inferior to painting because of the physical labor involved, and in his later years devoted himself more to science than to painting. Bramante and Raphael were to be artist-scholars as well as architects and painters. Michelangelo hated the workshop, even though the realization of his grandiose designs depended on the work of many hands. He was to become the ideal of the modern individualistic artist, consciously an intellectual, dealing with popes and princes as equals, insisting that he painted with his brains not with his hands, and rejecting all offers of noble titles. When people began calling him "the divine," the cycle was complete.

300. LEONE BATTISTA ALBERTI. Rucellai Palace, Florence. 1451–1455. 69' high.

IO - THE ROMAN RENAISSANCE STYLE

ROME, EARLY 16TH CENTURY

On April 18, 1506, when the foundation stone of the new Basilica of St. Peter (Fig. 324) was laid, Rome was well on its way to becoming the undisputed artistic and intellectual capital of the Western world. Pope Julius II was gathering about him the foremost living artists in all fields, and together they continued the transformation of the Eternal City from the darkness of its medieval past into the resplendent Rome of today. Donato Bramante, originally from Umbria but educated in Lombardy, was the architect at work on the plans for the central church of Christendom. Michelangelo Buonarroti from Florence was collecting the marble for a monumental papal tomb and was about to begin the painting of the Sistine Chapel ceiling. Raffaelo Sanzio from Umbria was soon to be summoned from Florence to decorate the walls of the Vatican Palace. The Florentine Andrea Sansovino was carving a cardinal's tomb in one of Julius II's favorite Roman churches, Santa Maria del Popolo, where the Umbrian Pinturicchio was covering its choir vaults with a series of frescoes. The singer-composer Josquin des Prez, who had been a member of the papal choir for eight years, had left to become choirmaster to the king of France. The papal court under Julius II and his successor Leo X was such a powerful magnet

that for three years the three greatest figures of the Renaissance—Leonardo da Vinci, Michelangelo, and Raphael— were at the Vatican. In 1517, however, the aged Leonardo abandoned the artistic field of honor there to become a courtier of Francis I of France.

The flight of the Medici from Florence in 1494 had signaled a general exodus of artists. Many had found temporary havens in the ducal courts of Italy, but the magnet of attraction had been the papal court at Rome. Hence, during the days of the two great Renaissance popes, Julius II (della Rovere) and Leo X (de' Medici), the cultural capital shifted from Florence to Rome. And, since Leonardo, Andrea Sansovino, Michelangelo, and Pope Leo were from Florence, and since Bramante and Raphael had absorbed the Florentine style and ideas in extended sojourns there, the cultural continuity was unbroken. It was, in fact, like a smooth transplantation from the confines of a nursery to an open field—a move that gave artists the opportunity to branch out from local styles in the universal air of Rome. Such projects

(above) MICHELANGELO. Study for the *Libyan Sibyl* (detail). *c.* 1508. Red chalk, 11 ³/₈ × 8 ¹/₂″. Metropolitan Museum of Art, New York (purchase, 1924, Joseph Pulitzer Bequest).

as the building of the world's largest church, the construction of Julius II's tomb, the painting of the Sistine ceiling, and the Vatican Palace murals could be found only in Rome. Nowhere else were monuments of such proportions or commissions of such magnitudes possible. In Rome also were the cardinals in residence, who maintained palaces and princely retinues that rivaled the brilliance of the papal court.

The Eternal City, though it was the artistic heir of all the ages, curiously enough lacked a Renaissance style of its own. It had, in fact, no native artists of major stature; and during the 15th century, architects, sculptors, painters, and musicians had been imported from various European centers. When their projects were completed, they departed. The plans of the 16th-century popes, however, were on such a colossal scale that they were able to absorb the major creative energies of the giants of their age. Furthermore, the popes were determined to regenerate the authority and glory of the Holy See—as well as to insure their own immortality—through their patronage of the arts. While Lorenzo de' Medici had remained more or less a local Tuscan figure, his son Leo X became a *magnifico* on an international scale that made his pontificate a golden age for the arts.

The interest in antiquity had animated many other Italian centers, but when the Renaissance got under way in Rome, it was, so to speak, on home soil. When antique statues were excavated elsewhere, they caused a considerable stir. In Rome, however, many of the ancient monuments were still standing, and when the archeological shovels probed the proper places, a veritable treasure trove was waiting. One by one the *Apollo Belvedere* (Fig. 78), the *Venus of the Vatican*, and the *Laocoön Group* (Fig. 75) came to light to give new impetus to the work of Michelangelo and other sculptors. The frescoes from Nero's Domus Aureus and the Baths of Titus provided the first important specimens of ancient painting. While the art of working in tempera on fresh plaster had never died out, these ancient Roman fragments gave fresco painting a new impetus in the Renaissance vocabulary.

Julius II had received most of his training in diplomacy and statecraft from his uncle Pope Sixtus IV, and fortunately, a passionate love of the arts was included in this education. It was Sixtus who had built the chapel that has subsequently borne his name, and who had installed there the group of papal singers that have ever since been known as the *Capella Sixtina*, or the Sistine Chapel Choir. It remained for Julius to establish a chorus to perform in St. Peter's—one

that still bears his name, the *Cappella Giulia*, or Julian Choir. This latter group corresponded to the ancient Schola Cantorum and prepared the singers for the Sistine Choir. Both have always received strong pontifical support, and both are still flourishing institutions.

Essentially a man of action, Julius II was an expert wielder of the sword as well as the crozier. He met his age on its own terms, and the spectacle of *il papa terribile* riding a fiery steel into the smoke of battle had a remarkably demoralizing effect on his enemies. As one of the principal architects of the modern papacy, he also saw the need of a setting in keeping with the magnificence of the apostolic Church and made it a matter of policy to command artists as well as soldiers. At the end of his career, his volcanic energies spent, Julius II became the subject of one of Raphael's most penetrating portraits (Fig. 301).

When Leo X ascended the papal throne, one of the eulogies ran: "Venus has had her day, and Mars his, now comes the turn of Minerva." Venus symbolized the reign of the Borgia pope, Alexander VI; Mars, of course, referred to Julius II; and Minerva, the Roman equivalent of

301. Raphael. *Julius II*. 1512. Oil on wood, 42½ × 31½". Uffizi, Florence.

General Events

1471–	1527	Roman Renaissance art and humanism reached climax
1471–	1484	Sixtus IV (della Rovere), pope
1473–	1480	Sistine Chapel built
1481–	1482	Sistine Chapel side-wall frescoes painted by Rosselli, Ghirlandaio, Botticelli, Perugino, Signorelli, Pinturicchio, Piero di Cosimo
1484–	1492	Innocent VIII (Cibò), pope
1486–	1492	Josquin des Prez in Sistine Chapel Choir
1492–	1503	Alexander VI (Borgia), pope
1493–	1506	Excavations uncovered ancient Roman frescoes and statues: *Apollo Belvedere, Laocoön Group*
1496–	1501	Michelangelo in Rome, working on *Bacchus* and *Pietà*
1503–	1513	Julius II (della Rovere), pope
	1505	Michelangelo began Julius II's tomb
	1506	New Basilica of St. Peter begun by Bramante; Old St. Peter's razed
1508–	1512	Michelangelo painted Sistine Chapel ceiling
		Raphael painted frescoes in Vatican Palace
	1512	Capella Giulia Choir founded
1513–	1516	Leonardo da Vinci in Rome
1513–	1521	Leo X (de' Medici), pope
	1515	Ariosto wrote *Orlando Furioso (Madness of Roland)*
	1517	Protestant Reformation began in Germany with Luther's 95 Theses
	1521	Luther excommunicated
1523–	1534	Clement VII (de' Medici), pope
	1523	Michelangelo worked on Medici tombs in Florence
	1527	Rome sacked by Emperor Charles V; Clement VII imprisoned
	1528	Castiglione's *The Courtier* published
	1532	Machiavelli's *The Prince* published
1534–	1549	Paul III (Farnese), pope
	1534	Church of England separated from Rome
		Reaction to Renaissance humanism began
1535–	1541	Michelangelo painted *Last Judgment* in Sistine Chapel
	1542	Michelangelo painted frescoes in Pauline Chapel
	1547	Michelangelo named architect of St. Peter's
	1550	Vasari's *Lives of Most Eminent Painters, Sculptors, and Architects* published
	*c.*1550	Philippe de Monte in Rome; published first book of madrigals 1554
	1551	Orlando Lassus in Rome
	1564	Michelangelo died

Architects

*c.*1444–	1514	Donato Bramante
1475–	1564	Michelangelo Buonarroti
1556–	1629	Carlo Maderno

Sculptors

1460–	1529	Andrea Sansovino
1475–	1564	Michelangelo Buonarroti
1500–	1571	Benvenuto Cellini
*c.*1524–	1608	Giovanni da Bologna

Painters

*c.*1441–	1523	Luca Signorelli
*c.*1450–	1523	Perugino
1452–	1519	Leonardo da Vinci
1454–	1513	Bernardino Pinturicchio
1475–	1564	Michelangelo Buonarroti
1483–	1520	Raphael Sanzio

Writers

1474–	1533	Ludovico Ariosto
1478–	1529	Baldassare Castiglione
1483–	1531	Martin Luther
1511–	1574	Giorgio Vasari
1544–	1595	Torquato Tasso
1548–	1600	Giordano Bruno

Musicians

*c.*1445–	1521	Josquin des Prez
*c.*1521–	1603	Philippe de Monte
1525–	1594	Giovanni da Palestrina
*c.*1532–	1594	Orlando di Lasso

302. RAPHAEL. *Leo X with Two Cardinals.* c. 1518. Oil on wood, 60⁵/₈ × 46⁷/₈". Uffizi, Florence.

Athena, was Leo who, as the son of Lorenzo the Magnificent, brought with him to Rome the spirit of Florence, that latter-day Athens. Michelangelo, whom Leo had known since his childhood at the Medici palace, was unfortunately bound by the terms of his contract to serve the heirs of Pope Julius, but the suave and worldly Raphael was available—and more congenial to the personal taste of Pope Leo than the gruff titan. Once again Raphael served as papal portraitist in the unusually fine study of *Leo X with Two Cardinals* (Fig. 302).

Heinrich Isaac, Leo's old music teacher, wrote the six-part motet that commemorated his accession, and Isaac's pupil became one of the most liberal of all Renaissance patrons of music. Other princes of Europe had difficulty in keeping their musicians, because the pope's love of the tonal art was so well known. Leo collected lute and viol players, organists, and the finest singers; chamber music was avidly cultivated at the pontifical palace; and a wind ensemble performed at papal dinners.

Leo's encouragement of music to the point of putting it on a par with literary pursuits caused considerable murmurings among men of letters. As a competent composer in his own right, he knew the art from the inside as few patrons have ever known it. As a philosopher, writer, connoisseur, and collector, his patronage, like that of his father, was accompanied by an active participation in many of the pursuits that he sponsored.

The luster of the papal court is recorded in the *Horatian Epistles* by Ludovico Ariosto, a friend from Leo's university days. Ariosto, author of the great Italian epic poem *Orlando Furioso (Madness of Roland)*, described some of the distinguished artistic events he witnessed. Among these was the presentation of his *Suppositi*, with scenery painted by Raphael. This poetic comedy called for a solo singer, a chorus, and an orchestra of fifes, viols, cornets, bagpipes, lute, and organ. A later English adaptation of Ariosto's play with the title *Taming of the Shrew* led to Shakespeare's play of that name.

As one of the leading representatives of Renaissance humanism, Leo X brought a lofty intellectual tone to Rome. Even more than his father, Leo aspired to be a Platonic philosopher-king. He envisaged the papacy as a great civilizing force, and under him the visual arts, letters, music, and the theater entered a period of rare florescence. Other aspects of his pontificate appear, by comparison, somewhat less lustrous. Ominous rumblings of the Protestant Reformation reverberated across the Alps, and the papal treasury approached bankruptcy. But rarely has Athena been served so well, and Leo's reign might indeed be called a carnival of culture. The Renaissance historian Jacob Burkhardt put it well when he wrote that Rome "possessed in the unique court of Leo X a society to which the history of the world offers no parallel."

303. MICHELANGELO. *Bacchus*. 1496–1497. Marble, 6′ 8″ high. National Museum, Florence.

SCULPTURE

In spite of his many masterpieces in other media, Michelangelo always thought of himself first and foremost as a sculptor. Other projects were undertaken reluctantly, and on the contract for the painting of the Sistine Chapel ceiling he pointedly signed Michelangelo *scultore*—Michelangelo the sculptor—as a protest. His first visit to Rome at the age of 21 coincided with the discovery of some ancient statuary, including the *Apollo Belvedere* (Fig. 78), that proved a powerful stimulant to his own productivity. His most important statues from this early period are a *Bacchus* (Fig. 303) and a *Pietà*, which illustrate the conflicting pagan and Christian ideals that were to affect his aesthetic thought throughout his long career.

The *Pietà* (Fig. 304), now in St. Peter's, was commissioned in 1498 by Cardinal Villiers, the French ambassador to the Holy See. Its beauty of execution, delicacy of detail, and poignancy of expression reveal that Michelangelo was still under the spell of the Florentine Renaissance. In its pyramidal composition, a type worked out by Piero della Francesca (Fig. 288) and by Leonardo da Vinci, as exemplified in his drawing for *Madonna and Child with St. Anne* (Fig. 305) and in the *Madonna of the Rocks* (Plate 22). Michelangelo uses the voluminous folds of the Madonna's drapery as the base of the pyramid and her head as the apex. The figure of Christ is cast in the perfect form of a Greek god, while the Madonna, though overwhelmed by grief, maintains a classical composure. No tears, no outcry, no gesture mar this conception of Mary as the matronly mother of sorrows. Yet Michelangelo allows himself many liberties with the proportions of his figures in order to heighten their expressive effect and enhance the harmony of his design. The excessive drapery exists to provide a multiplication of folds and sweeping lines. The horizontal body of Christ is far shorter than the vertical Madonna, but the disproportion serves to make the composition more compact. The triangular shape, as a self-sufficient form, holds the attention within the composition and obviates the necessity for such external considerations as niches or architectural backgrounds. As such, the *Pietà* is a kind of sculptural declaration of independence, and it bears the unique distinction of being the only work Michelangelo ever signed.

After finishing the *Pietà*, Michelangelo went home to Florence, where he worked on the *Bruges Madonna* and the *David* (Fig. 296). In 1505, however, he was summoned back to Rome by the imperious Julius to discuss a project for a colossal tomb. In the inception of this gigantic composition, (left) 304. MICHELANGELO. *Pietà.* 1498–1499. Marble, 5′ 9″ high. St. Peter's, Vatican, Rome.

(below) 305. LEONARDO DA VINCI. Cartoon for *Madonna and Child with St. Anne.* 1497–1499. Charcoal and white chalk on paper, 54¾ × 39¾″. National Gallery, London (reproduced by courtesy of the Trustees).

the artist's imagination for once met its match in his patron's ambitions. Julius' monument was conceived as a small temple within the great new temple—St. Peter's—that was abuilding. It was to rise pyramidally from a massive quadrangular base visible from all four sides (Fig. 306), and it was to include more than 40 statues. Consequently, the entire marble quarries of Carrara had to be placed at Michelangelo's disposal. But, like all such challenges to the gods, fate proved stronger than human will power. Floods on the Tiber prevented the marble from reaching Rome; wars and rumors of wars distracted the attention of the pontiff; and the monumental dream soon turned into a nightmare. In exasperation, Michelangelo defied papal authority and temporarily fled from the Eternal City. "If I were to remain in Rome," he wrote to a friend, "my own tomb would be prepared before that of the Pope. This is the reason for my sudden departure."

When Julius died in 1513, only a few parts of the project had been finished and a new contract with his heirs had to be negotiated. Further revi-

306. MICHELANGELO. Projected Tomb of Julius II. Drawing. Uffizi, Florence.

sions were made later, each reducing the proportions of the project and eliminating more of the unfinished statues. In its final form of 1545, the magnificent temple had shrunk to the relatively modest wall tomb to be seen today in the aisle of the Church of San Pietro in Vincoli (Fig. 311). Thus it is that Michelangelo's biographers have referred to this unfinished chapter in his life as the "Tragedy of the Tomb." As with all great art, however, the grandeur and idealism of the original conception outweigh the later compromises and ultimate realization.

Tombs of the popes, like the triple tiaras with which they are crowned, were traditionally in three rising zones, symbolizing earthly existence, death, and salvation. For the original project, Michelangelo translated these divisions into Neo-Platonic terms representing the successive stages of the liberation of the soul from its bodily prison. For the final project, the monument lapsed into more traditional stratifications. In the original scheme, the lowest level was to have figures symbolizing those who are crushed by the burden of life and

those who rise above the bonds of matter. This idea was retained in some of the later revisions, and some six of the so-called "Slaves" or "Captives" and one Victory survive in various stages of completion.

On the second level of the original project were to have been placed heroic figures of the leaders of mankind, those individuals who pointed the way toward the divine goal of humanity—reunion with God. Moses and St. Paul were to represent the old and new law, while Rachel and Leah were to personify the active and contemplative ways of life. Of these, only the Moses was finished by Michelangelo. The figures of Rachel and Leah (see Fig. 311), begun by the master but finished by assistants, now stand on either side of Moses in the finished tomb, though whether they are in the form intended for the initial project is questionable. The third and highest level was to have represented the gates of heaven, with angels receiving the soul of Pope Julius. None of these was even begun by Michelangelo.

The three figures that date from the years 1513 to 1516, when Leo X was pope, are the two

"Slaves" now in the Louvre and the *Moses*. The "*Bound Slave*" (Fig. 307) is the more nearly finished of the two, and it seems to represent a sleeping adolescent tormented by a dream rather than the "dying captive" it is sometimes called. The imprisoned soul, tortured by the memory of its divine origin, has found momentary respite in sleep. The cloth bands by which the figure is bound are only symbolic, since Michelangelo is not concerned with the external aspect of captivity but rather with the internal torment. Its companion piece, the so-called "*Rebellious Slave*" (Fig. 308), represents the violent though vain struggle of a wide-awake, enormously muscular figure. The implied power of the strong bodies in both figures only emphasizes their ineffectiveness and makes their attempts at escape seem all the more futile. In both is the same grappling with fate; in both, the battle is hopeless. It is the tragedy of man, limited by time but troubled by the knowledge of eternity; mortal but with a vision of immortality; bound by the weight of his own body yet dreaming of a boundless freedom. This tragedy of the tomb was understood only too well by Michelangelo himself, who had the conception of his great project in mind but was doomed to see only a few fragments of his dream completed. Figures, such as the "Slaves" and "Victory" that Michelangelo envisaged, were associated with the triumphal arches as well as with the mausoleums and sarcophagi of ancient Rome. Models for the "Slaves" can be traced to the Hellenistic Marsyas figures (Fig. 70), and the similarity between the "*Bound Slave*" (Fig. 307) and the younger son in the 2nd century B.C. *Laocoön Group* (Fig. 75, figure on the left) has aptly been pointed out.

307. MICHELANGELO. "*Bound Slave*." 1513–1516. Marble, 7′ 5″ high. Louvre, Paris.

308. MICHELANGELO. "*Rebellious Slave*." 1513–1516. Marble, 6′ 10½″ high. Louvre, Paris.

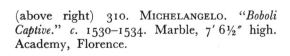

(above right) 310. MICHELANGELO. *"Boboli Captive."* c. 1530–1534. Marble, 7′ 6½″ high. Academy, Florence.

(right) 311. MICHELANGELO. Tomb of Julius II. 1506–1545. San Pietro in Vincoli, Rome.

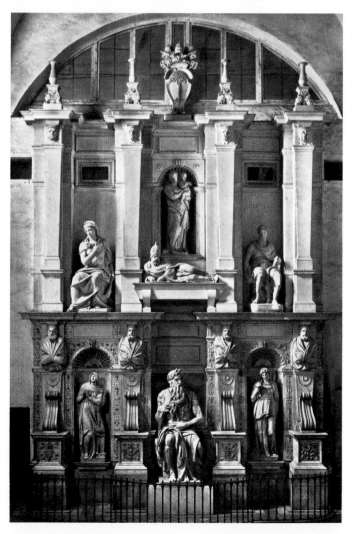

The Platonic idea of man's soul confined in the bonds of the flesh was continued in a later version of the tomb. The four so-called "Boboli Captives," one of which is seen in Figure 310, were part of the revised plan of 1532, but they were eventually given by Michelangelo to Duke Cosimo de' Medici, who placed them in a grotto of the Boboli Gardens in Florence. In contrast to the buoyant *Victory* (Fig. 309), the imprisonment of the spirit by matter in these "*Captives*" is all but complete. Unconscious, locked in their stone wombs, they struggle and writhe to be born out of their material medium. Their unfinished state gives an interesting glimpse into Michelangelo's methods, which were similar to that of relief sculpture. The statue to Michelangelo was a potential form hidden in the block of marble awaiting the hand of the master sculptor to be born. "The greatest artist has no single concept which a rough marble block does not contain already in its core...," wrote Michelangelo in a sonnet, and the artist-creator must discover, "concealed in the hard marble of the North, the living figure one has to bring forth (The less of stone remains, the more that grows)." The Neo-Platonic implication is that the soul of man is still entombed in the body and can only be perfected into pure being by the hand of a higher creative power.

Moses (Fig. 312) is the only statue completed entirely by Michelangelo's hand to find its place in the completed tomb (Fig. 311). Both Julius II and Michelangelo possessed the quality of *terribilità* that is incarnated in this figure. Julius was known as *il papa terribile*, meaning the forceful or powerful pope, imbued with the fear of the Lord. Michelangelo conceives his *Moses* as the personification of a powerful will, and partially as an idealized portrait of the indomitable Julius who, as the codifier of canon law, had something in common with the ancient Hebrew lawgiver. Moses is further portrayed as the personification of the elemental forces—the human volcano about to erupt with righteous wrath, the calm before a storm of moral indignation, the dead center of a hurricane of emotional fury, the author of those thunderous Thou Shalt Nots of the Ten Commandments, the man capable of ascending Mt. Sinai to discourse with God and coming back down to review all humanity from the seat of judgment.

Medieval rather than classical precedents are to be cited here, with Moses' immediate ancestors found in Donatello's seated *St. John the Evangelist*. Details, such as the stone tablets of the law and the long beard, are according to the iconographical tradition. The horns are also traditional for Moses, although they stemmed from a medieval mistranslation of the Bible. (After Moses descended from Mt. Sinai where he had heard the voice of the Lord, the children of Israel beheld two *rays* of light [not horns] issuing from his head.) Rodin once made the observation that the statue could be rolled down hill without any essential part being broken off. This compactness reinforces its expressive power by holding it in check. The smoldering agitation revealed through the drapery, the powerful musculature of the arms, the dominating intellectuality of the face, the fiery mood, and the torsions of the body as it twists in the act of rising are characteristic of Michelangelo's style. An interesting detail is the carved irises of the eyes, also done earlier in his *David* (Fig. 296), which Michelangelo did to express a look of fixed determination. When he wanted to convey the qualities of dreaminess, gentleness, and resignation, as in his Madonnas, he left the eyes untouched.

312. MICHELANGELO. *Moses. c.* 1513–1515. Marble, 8′ 4″ high. San Pietro in Vincoli, Rome.

313. MICHELANGELO. Tomb of Giuliano de' Medici, duke of Nemours. 1524–1534. Marble, *c.* 20′ high. Central figure 5′ 11″ high. New Sacristy, San Lorenzo, Florence.

From 1521 to 1534, Michelangelo again worked in Florence on various sculptural projects, the most outstanding of these being the Medici tombs (Fig. 313). Thereafter he was in Rome, occupied with fresco painting and architectural projects. Only in the spare moments of the last 30 years of his long life, and without specific commissions, did he work on several *Pietàs*. One of them was intended for his own tomb; like all the others, it was unfinished when he died.

Michelangelo worked at the time when many of the most outstanding examples of antique statuary were being unearthed and admired. Inevitably this led to critical comparisons. Michelangelo, like the Greco-Roman artists, saw man as the lord of creation, but man's natural environment was always a matter of indifference to him. His early art especially was an affirmation of man's supreme place in the universal scheme of things. That world was populated by godlike beings at the peak of their physical power, full of vitality, creatively active, and buoyantly self-confident. As his art matured, his men and women were beset with quite unclassical tensions, doubts, and conflicts. Unlike the statues of antiquity, his figures, when they come to grips with fate, are armed with mental and moral powers that imply the hope of ultimate victory. Having thus surpassed the art of the ancients as well as that of his own time, not only by his technical mastery but by his expressive power, he came to be regarded by his contemporaries with awe. Vasari, his biographer, wrote: "The man who bears the palm of all ages, transcending and eclipsing all the rest, is the divine M. Buonarroti, who is supreme not in one art only but in all three at once." History has had no reason to reverse this judgment.

THE SISTINE CEILING

When Michelangelo fled from Rome because of accumulated frustrations with plans for Julius II's tomb, the Pope resorted to every means from force to diplomacy to get him to return. Knowing he had a restless genius on his hands, Julius conceived two interim projects to keep Michelangelo busy until all the problems with his tomb were solved. The first was a colossal bronze statue of himself, sword in hand, for the newly conquered city of Bologna; the statue was destroyed after the pontifical army was routed a few years later. The second was the painting of the ceiling of the Sistine Chapel (Fig. 314). The building itself, the roof of which can be seen paralleling the nave on the right of St. Peter's in Figure 324, was built by and named for Julius' uncle, Sixtus IV, as the private chapel of the popes. The interior consists of a single rectangular room 44 by 132 feet. Around the walls were frescoes painted by the foremost 15th-century artists, including the Florentines Ghirlandaio (who was one of Michelangelo's teachers), Botticelli, and Perugino (teacher of Raphael). Above the frescoes were six windows high up on the side walls, and overhead was a barrel-vaulted ceiling 68 feet above the floor with 700 square yards of surface stretching before Michelangelo.

Julius apparently had in mind a series showing the twelve apostles, but, according to a letter of 1523, Michelangelo was given a free hand. "Then he [Pope Julius]," wrote the sculptor, "gave me a new commission to make what I wanted, whatever pleased me." The design and details of the iconography evolved slowly from the mind of the artist as he worked. As the time for this "interim project" extended from months to years, the pope's impatience increased correspondingly. On his periodic visits of inspection,

314. Sistine Chapel (view from rear), Vatican, Rome. 1473–1480. 132' long, 44' wide, 68' high.

273

315. MICHELANGELO. Ceiling, Sistine Chapel. 1508–1512. Fresco, 44 × 128'. Vatican, Rome. (See also Plate 23.)

the scenes between them mounted in violence with threats being hurled from below and above the scaffolding. Julius knew Michelangelo's temperament as only one volcano can know another, and his eruptions alternated with periods of quiescence and generosity, with the result that the job finally got done—though it took four years to do it.

The entire Sistine ceiling (Fig. 315) was conceived as an organic composition motivated by a single unifying philosophical as well as artistic design, as has so convincingly been pointed out by Charles de Tolnay in the second volume of his monumental monographs on Michelangelo. As with the initial project for the Julius tomb and in the later Medici tombs, the iconography is a fusion of the traditional Hebrew-Christian theology and the Neo-Platonic philosophy that Michelangelo knew from his days in the Medici household, where he came into daily conversation with Lorenzo himself, Poliziano, Marsilio Ficino, and Pico della Mirandola. His space is divided into geometrical forms, such as the triangle, circle, and square, which were regarded in Plato's philosophy as the eternal forms that furnish clues to the true nature of the universe. Next is a three-way division into zones in which the varying intensity of the lighting plays a part. The lowest and darkest comprises the eight triangular spandrels and the four corner penden-

tive-shaped spandrels (Fig. 314). The second is the intermediate zone that includes all the space outside the spandrels except that allotted to the nine center panels, which in turn constitute the third and brightest zone.

Symbolically these divisions correspond to the three Platonic stages—the world of matter, the world of becoming, and the world of being. Analogies to such triple divisions run as an undercurrent through all aspects of Plato's thought. Plato divided society, for instance, into three classes: workers, free men, and philosophers, which he symbolized by the metals brass, silver, and gold. Each stratum had its characteristic goal: the love of gain, the development of ambition, and the pursuit of truth. Learning was similarly broken down into the three stages of ignorance, opinion, and knowledge. Plato's theory of the human soul was also tripartite in nature, consisting of the appetitive, emotional, and rational faculties, located in the abdomen, breast, and head, respectively. Of these only the rational or intellective part could aspire to immortality. Man, by reason of his intellect, said Plato at the end of his *Timaeus*, "is like a tree with its root not in the earth but in the sky." It is then the rational element of the soul which "raises us from earth to our kindred who are in heaven."

Michelangelo's image of man agreed in all essentials with that of Pico della Mirandola, who considered man "the intermediary between creatures." In his address on *The Dignity of Man*, Pico declared that it was possible for man "to descend among lower forms of beings, which are brute beasts" or be "reborn out of the judgment of your own soul into the higher beings which are divine." Michelangelo thus places uninspired man on the low level of the spandrels. In the intermediate area are the inspired Old Testament prophets and pagan sibyls who have knowledge of the divine and mediate between man and God. In the central section are the panels that tell the story of man in his direct relationship to God, and they are seen through the architectural divisions as if taking place beyond on a more cosmic plane. In Michelangelo's time, the chapel was separated into two parts by a screen with the section near the altar reserved for the clergy and the other for laymen. The central space of the ceiling is divided lengthwise into nine panels, with the part over the lay section telling the story of man and that over the altar, the story of God. Instead of starting at the beginning and proceeding chronologically as in the Book of Genesis, Michelangelo conceives the story of creation in reverse order, or as the Platonic ascent of man from his lowest estate back to his divine origin. In this return to God, the soul in its bodily prison gradually becomes aware of God and moves from finiteness to infinity, from material bondage to spiritual freedom. Immortality, in this sense, is not the reward for a passive and pious existence but the ultimate achievement of a tremendous effort of the soul as it struggles out of the darkness of ignorance into the blinding light of truth.

The eight spandrels, one of which is seen in Figure 316, tell the dismal tale of humanity without vision—"and Ezekias begat Manasses; and Manasses begat Amon; and Amon begat Josias." So reads the genealogy of the ancestors of Christ at the beginning of St. Matthew's Gospel. Endless generations of humdrum humanity, whose sole purpose is to reproduce themselves and hand the spark of life down to their children; as St. Luke says, they "sit in darkness and in the shadow of death," awaiting the light that will come when the Savior is born. In Gothic iconography, the ancestors were the kings of Judah starting with Jesse, David, and Solomon. Here in this spandrel, the child is the future King Josias, but Michelangelo represents him and all the others as a succession of common people dwelling in darkness. The mixture of good and evil is implied by the beauty of the mother on the child's right and the unenlightened form of his father Amon, who adored idols, on his left. The families huddled within these triangular prisons are but dimly aware of the words of the prophets above them and are quite unconscious of the divine happenings in the central ideal region. In the four corner spandrels are the heroic men and women whose active deeds secured temporal deliverance for their people. David's slaying of Goliath, Judith's decapitation of Holophernes, and Haman's punishment through Esther—all have to do with the victory of the weak over the strong with the aid of God. A note of prophecy and ultimate hope is sounded by the episode of Moses and the brazen serpent, an incident in the delivery of the children of Israel from their Egyptian bondage. The allusion comes from the Gospel of St. John: "And as Moses lifted up the serpent in the wilderness, even so must the Son of man be lifted up: that whosoever believeth in him should not perish, but have eternal life" (3: 14–15).

This serves as an introduction to the representations of the seven Hebrew prophets, who alternate with five pagan sibyls like a chorus prophesying salvation. These are the inspired men and women who, through the exercise of their minds and imaginations, become the mediators between the human and divine spheres. They are placed, consequently, outside the confines of the dark spandrels and in a zone where the lighting approaches that of the central panels.

The *Delphic Sibyl* (Fig. 316) is the first of the series. In the Greek tradition and in Plato, she

(above) 316. MICHELANGELO. *Delphic Sibyl*, detail of Sistine Ceiling. 1509. Vatican, Rome.
(below) 317. MICHELANGELO. *Ancestor of Christ (Josias)*, detail of Sistine Ceiling. 1509. Vatican, Rome.

Plate 23. MICHELANGELO. *Creation of Adam*, detail of Sistine Ceiling. 1511. Vatican, Rome. (See p. 279.)

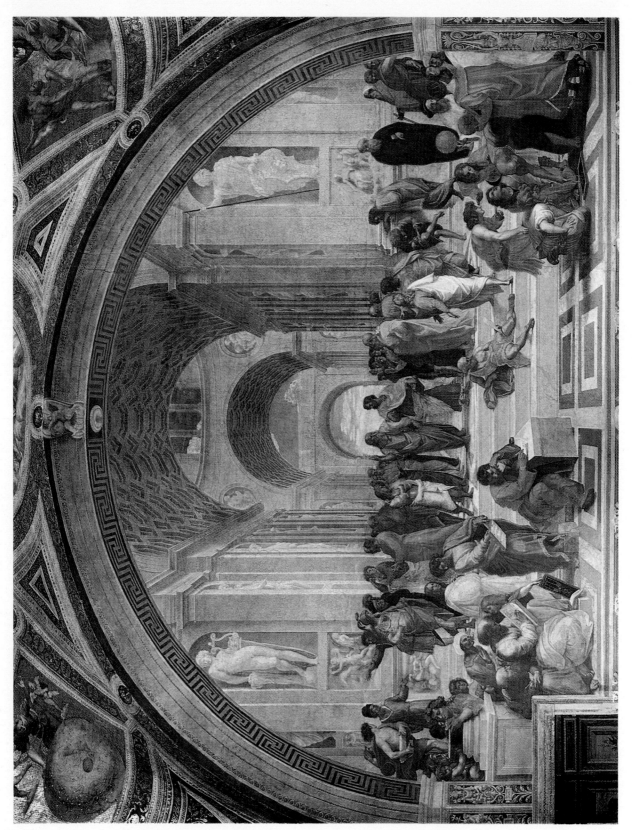

Plate 24. RAPHAEL. *School of Athens*. 1510–1511. Fresco, *c.* 26 × 18'.
Stanza della Segnatura, Vatican, Rome. (See p. 280.)

318. MICHELANGELO. *Drunkenness of Noah*, detail of Sistine Ceiling. 1508–1509. Vatican, Rome.

was the priestess of Apollo at Delphi. In Vergil's *Aeneid*, Book VI, she is described as a young woman possessed by the spirit of prophecy. In the grip of divine fury, she turns her head toward the voice of her inspiration. Though clothed in Greek garments, her beauty is similar to that of Michelangelo's early Madonnas. On either side of her throne are pairs of caryatidlike figures that are a part of the painted architectural pattern. In the shadow below the tablet, the head of a figure that symbolizes her corporeal nature can be seen. Diagonally behind her are a pair of nude figures that symbolize her inspiration. According to Plato, the soul, when concerned with the truth, is borne aloft on two wings. Neo-Platonic philosophers interpreted these either as the mind and will or as the active and contemplative aspects of life, both of which are necessary for salvation. Above each of the prophets and sibyls and enframing the central panels are *ignudi*, or nude youths, as seen in Figure 321. In the Christian tradition, these figures would have been represented as angels, but in the Platonic theory, they personify the rational faculties of the sibyls and prophets by which man rises to the contemplation of divine truth, and by which he is able to bridge the gap between the physical and spiritual, or earthly

and heavenly regions. Thus all the prophets and sibyls have a single figure below to denote the body, a pair of nudes behind them to signify the will, and a heroic *ignudo* to personify the immortal soul. These three levels correspond to Plato's tripartite conception of the soul—the appetitive, the emotional, and the intellective. These symbolic figures also play an aesthetic part in the softening of the harsh contours of the architectural design. The nude adolescents function ostensibly as the bearers of the garland that runs around the central panels and from which the painted bronze medallions are suspended. By covering the corners of the frames, and by their postures, they contribute a needed diagonal accent and bring a welcome variety to the design as a whole.

The first of the histories in the nine central panels is the *Drunkenness of Noah* (Fig. 318). As in the "Slave" figures of the Julius monument, the picture of Noah shows man in his most abysmal condition as the victim of his own bodily appetites. His servitude is symbolized at the left, where he is seen tilling the parched soil. Though still strong physically, his spirit is overwhelmed by the flesh. His sons, young adolescents in their physical prime, do not seem to be discovering their father's (above) 319. MICHELANGELO. *Fall of Man and Expulsion from Paradise*, detail of Sistine Ceiling. 1508–1509. Vatican, Rome.

(below) 320. MICHELANGELO. *Creation of the Sun and the Moon*, detail of Sistine Ceiling. 1511. Vatican, Rome.

nakedness, as related in the Bible, but the tragic fate of man himself, who must work, grow old, and die. Noah's reclining posture recalls that of the ancient Roman river gods, and in this case the head has sunk forward on his chest in what seems to be a premonition of death. After this picture of Noah as the prisoner of his own baser nature, the next panel pictures the *Deluge*, which shows the plight of man when beset by the elemental forces of nature beyond his control. In the third panel, *Noah's Sacrifice*, man's dependence on God is first implied.

Fall of Man and Expulsion from Paradise (Fig. 319) follows next. Temptation here is no mere passive affair but a willful, greedy act of man. Adam eagerly reaches out for the fruit—again the

victim of his appetites but with the power of making decisions. Eve, contrary to the Biblical story, is seen as the more passive of the two. Adam's hulking body is almost subhuman, while that of Eve is soft and sensuous. The motif of her uplifted arm is repeated by the branch springing out of the tree trunk in the background. The serpent with the torso of a woman recalls that of the ancient sirens or maenads. The pairing of the serpent and the avenging angel on the expulsion side probably implies that sin and retribution, like cause and effect, are the twin aspects of evil. Masaccio's fresco in the Brancacci Chapel (Fig. 283) was clearly the model for Michelangelo's Adam and Eve on this side. Adam's body, however, has undergone a significant change from the temptation side, and he now appears morally aware of his action, while Eve cringes and attempts to hide in his shadow. On one side, the concern was with blind desire; on the other, it is a matter of knowledge and remorse.

The last five panels are concerned with the various aspects of God's nature. In the *Creation of Eve*, He appears as a patriarchal figure closed within the folds of His mantle, His head bent forward as if in deep thought. As in the Gospel according to St. John: "In the beginning was the Word, and the Word was with God, and the Word was God." The implication in Michelangelo's Neo-Platonic conception is that the creative process is a rational one. In the *Creation of Adam* (Plate 23), God appears in the skies, His mantle surrounding Him like a cloud, as He moves toward the earth and the inert body of Adam. The creative force is here the divine fire that flashes like lightning from the cloud to the earth. Adam's body is one with the rock on which he lies, not unlike the unfinished "Slaves" of the Julius tomb. In keeping with the Platonic idea of life as a burden and imprisonment, Adam is awakening to life reluctantly rather than eagerly. With His other arm, God embraces Eve, who again resembles Michelangelo's Madonna types, and who looks with fear and awe on this act of creation; His fingers point to the coming Christ Child, while behind Him are the heads of unborn generations of mankind.

In the *Creation of the Sun and the Moon* (Fig. 320), the representation of God becomes a personification of the creative principle. Like one of the celestial bodies, He moves in an orbit throwing off stars and planets, which continue in the courses He sets for them. This flight through the firmament implies the omnipresent aspect of God. The progressive minimizing of the subject matter as the story unfolds shows that Michelangelo was concentrating progressively on God's creative power rather than on the things created.

In *God Dividing the Light from Darkness* (Fig. 321), the final panel of the series, the climax and the realm of pure being are attained. Here is clarity coming out of chaos, order from the void, existence from nothingness, the idea from unconsciousness. You shall know the truth and the truth shall make you free, according to the Scriptures; or know thyself, as the Delphic oracle told Socrates. The conception of God has progressed from the patriarchal human figure of the *Creation of Eve* to that of a cosmic spirit in the intervening panels, and now He is seen as a swirling abstraction in the realm of pure being. The Neo-Platonic objective of the union of the soul with God has been achieved by the gradual progress from the bondage of the

spandrels, through the prophetic visions of the seers, and finally, by ascending the ladder of the histories into the pure light of knowledge, to the point of dissolution into the freedom of infinity. In the words of Pico della Mirandola, man "withdraws into the center of his own oneness, his spirit made one with God."

The weight of expression, story content, and philosophical meaning is carried entirely by Michelangelo's disposition and treatment of the 300-odd human figures in a seemingly infinite variety of postures. The colors are limited by the medium, and as the work progressed Michelangelo's preference was more and more in the direction of shades of gray, which accented the three-dimensional, sculpturesque quality of the figures. Such large projects are almost always school jobs, but internal evidence of the frescoes and documentary sources suggest that Michelangelo did all the painting himself, with assistants doing the preparatory work only.

Owing to the very awkward nature of ceiling painting, Michelangelo had to lie on his back most of the time—a fact that gave rise to one of his most eloquent sonnets, which goes in part:

321. MICHELANGELO. *God Dividing the Light from Darkness*, detail of Sistine Ceiling. 1511. Vatican, Rome.

322. RAPHAEL. *School of Athens* (detail). 1510–1511. Fresco. Stanza della Segnatura, Vatican, Rome. BRAMANTE as ARCHIMEDES (figure bending over slate); ZOROASTER (bearded figure) and PTOLEMY (with crown); RAPHAEL (in profile) and SODOMA at extreme right. (Compare Plate 24.)

My beard turns up to heaven; my nape falls in,
Fixed on my spine: my breast-bone visibly
Grows like a harp: a rich embroidery
Bedews my face from brush-drops thick and thin.

Though he later returned to the Sistine Chapel to paint the *Last Judgment* on the altar wall (Figs. 314, 366) and worked on another group for the Pauline Chapel in the Vatican, Michelangelo never recaptured the buoyant optimism and creative force of the earlier series. The impact of the Sistine Chapel ceiling today, as it was on Michelangelo's contemporaries, is like a revelation of one of the eternal verities. Coming as this stupendous work did at the height of the artist's creative powers, the composition as a whole is among the highest peaks in the mountain range of Western art.

At the same time that Michelangelo was painting the Sistine ceiling, Raphael, a younger contemporary, was at work on the murals of the Vatican Palace. In *School of Athens* (Plate 24), Raphael presents such a complete visual philosophy that it places him, along with Michelangelo,

in the rarified ranks of artist-scholars. Raphael's fresco is full of intellectual as well as pictorial complexities. Yet by the expanding space of the setting and the skillful deployment of the figures, as well as their relationships to each other and the architecture, it is clear and uncluttered. As members of a philosophical circle intent on reconciling the views of Plato and Aristotle, Raphael and his friends held that any point in Plato could be translated into a proposition of Aristotle and vice versa—the principal difference being that Plato wrote in poetic images, while Aristotle used the language of rational analysis. The two philosophers, "who agree in substance while they disagree in words," are placed on either side of the central axis of the fresco with the vanishing point between them. The book Plato holds in his hands is his *Timaeus*, and he points skyward to indicate his idealistic world view; Aristotle carries a copy of his *Ethics* and indicates by his earthward gesture his greater concern with the real and practical world.

In the spacious hall, which recalls the Roman poet Lucretius' remark on "temples raised by philosophy," the various schools of thought argue or ponder on the ideas propounded by the two central figures. On Plato's side a niche contains a statue of Apollo, patron of poetry; on Aristotle's is one of Athena, goddess of reason. This division of the central figures equates the entire picture, with the metaphysical philosophers ranked on Plato's side and the physical scientists pursuing their various researches on Aristotle's. Spreading outward are groups corresponding to the divergent schools of thought within the two major divisions, and which carry the various arguments to their logical conclusion. The figure of Plato is thought to be an idealized portrait of the aged Leonardo da Vinci, and in the group at the lower right (Fig. 322) Raphael portrayed his architect friend Bramante as Archimedes demonstrating on his slate a geometrical proposition. At the extreme right, Raphael paints a self-portrait in profile next to his friend and collaborator, the painter Sodoma. In *School of Athens* as a whole, Raphael captured the intellectual atmosphere and the zest with which Renaissance ideas were argued. By his grouping and placement of figures, and by their attitudes, attributes, and gestures, he provides a far clearer commentary on the complex thought of his time than did the more tortuous philosophical treatises of the period. To paint such metaphysical abstractions at all, and clothe them with plastic form, is a triumph of clear thinking and logical organization; and posterity is fortunate to have this summation of Renaissance humanism as seen through the eyes of such a profound artist.

THE DOME OF ST. PETERS

The religious and intellectual atmosphere of Rome was a far cry from what it had been in the days of Julius II and Leo X when in the 1540's Michelangelo completed his series of frescoes on SS. Peter and Paul in the Pauline Chapel of the Vatican. The Protestant Reformation was an established fact, and the Council of Trent was beginning the deliberations that set the forces of the Counter Reformation in motion. Ignatius Loyola had already been in Rome, and the Jesuit order had received papal approval. The Congregation of the Inquisition and the censorship of printed matter promised restrictions on the expression of ideas. Artists were given a less free hand with their pictures and had to accept the advice of ecclesiastical authorities. And Michelangelo, now in his seventies, was under attack for the nudes and pagan elements of his recently completed *Last Judgment* mural in the Sistine Chapel.

This and other considerations weighed heavily on Michelangelo and to a certain extent influenced his decision to devote himself mainly to architecture during the remainder of his life. Consequently, it was not difficult for his friend Pope Paul III, for whom he had painted the Pauline Chapel frescoes, to persuade Michelangelo to finish the Farnese Palace in 1546 (Fig. 323) and then to become chief architect of St. Peter's (Fig. 324), the project that absorbed most of his energies thereafter.

(above) 323. ANTONIO DA SANGALLO THE YOUNGER and MICHELANGELO. Farnese Palace, Rome. Façade completed by Michelangelo 1547. Façade 185' wide, 96' 6" high.

(right) 325. St. Peter's. Plans of BRAMANTE, MICHELANGELO, and present complex.

(below) 324. St. Peter's Basilica and the Vatican, Rome. Apse and dome by MICHELANGELO, 1547–1564; dome completed by GIACOMO DELLA PORTA, 1588–1592; nave and façade by CARLO MADERNO, 1606–1626 (façade 147' high, 374' wide); colonnades by GIANLORENZO BERNINI, 1656–1663.

326. MICHELANGELO. Apse and dome, St. Peter's. Begun 1547. Dome 452′ high.

While the foundations of the new St. Peter's had been laid as early as 1506, when Michelangelo was starting plans for Pope Julius' tomb, comparatively little progress had been made in the tempestuous years that followed, in spite of the succession of brilliant architects. Michelangelo favored the centralized church plans of Brunelleschi and Alberti just as his predecessor Bramante had done. The latter's design, however, was to have culminated in a low dome, modeled after that of the Pantheon but with a peristyle base and a lantern on top. Michelangelo accepted Bramante's Greek-cross ground plan with a few alterations of his own (Fig. 325), but he envisaged a loftier canopy rising over the legendary site of St. Peter's tomb. This dome was to be of such monumental proportions that it would unify not only the interior spaces and exterior masses of the building but would serve also as the climax of the liturgical, religious, and artistic forces of the Catholic world and as a symbol of the center of Christendom.

Michelangelo's first problem was an engineering one—to find out if the masonry was strong enough to support such a dome. It was not, and he had to reinforce the four main piers until each was a massive 60 feet square. Pendentives became the means by which the square understructure was encircled, and then the drum was ready to rise. Meanwhile he made a large model of the dome itself, so that it could be built by others if necessary. All the preparatory work was thus completed, and Michelangelo lived just long enough to see the drum finished. The dome (Fig. 326) was completed after his death by two of his associates without substantial alterations. But for the aftermath of the Council of Trent and the Counter Reformation, Michelangelo's centralized church might also have been finished. The new spirit of orthodoxy, however, frowned on anything that might be considered a pagan form, and a reactionary wave was started in favor of a return to the traditional Latin-cross plan. In the early 17th century, Carlo Maderno undertook the lengthening of the nave (Fig. 325), and the design of the façade (see Fig. 324). Liturgically, the new nave provided more space for the grandiose processions; practically, it provided room for larger congregations; historically, it absorbed all the area formerly occupied by Constantine's basilica, which had been demolished to make way for the new structure; but, aesthetically, the proportions suffered, and the climactic effect of the great dome was diminished. The scale of the interior (Fig. 327), however, was already set by Michelangelo's huge piers beneath the dome, and Maderno had to continue the same proportions. The vaulting thus rises a little over 150 feet above the pavement, while the enormous interior covers more than 25,000 square yards in area.

The exterior of the church Michelangelo planned can best be seen from the apse, and the interior from beneath the dome where it appears as the compact unified structure he wanted. From the apse of the completed church (Fig. 326), where the lengthened nave does not detract, the effect is still substantially as Michelangelo intended it to be. From this vantage point the building itself appears as a great podium for the support of the vast superstructure; and from the ground level to the base of the dome there is a rise of about 250 feet. The cupola then continues upward to the top of the lantern, where an ultimate height of 452 feet above the ground level is attained. Until the advent of the Eiffel Tower and the 20th-century skyscrapers, St. Peter's was at once the world's tallest and largest building. Coming as it did with the spread of the Counter Reformation and the commercial exploitation and colonization of the New World, St. Peter's and its great dome had enormous influence on future church architecture (see Figs. 385, 453, 472) and on such secular structures as the capitol in Washington, D.C., and on a number of the American state capitols.

JOSQUIN DES PREZ AND THE SISTINE CHAPEL CHOIR

"I am well aware that in his day Ockeghem was as it were the first to rediscover music, then as good as dead, just as Donatello discovered sculpture in his; and that of Josquin, Ockeghem's pupil, one might say that he was a natural prodigy in music, just as our own Michelangelo Buonarroti has been in architecture, painting, and sculpture; for just as Josquin has still to be surpassed in his compositions, so Michelangelo stands alone and without a peer among all who have practiced his arts; and the one and the other have opened the eyes of all who delight in these arts, now and in the future." So wrote a Florentine literary historian in a book on Dante published in 1567. Josquin des Prez, to whom he referred, was thus still regarded almost half a century after his death as a figure comparable to that of Michelangelo. A Florentine could bestow no higher praise. The same opinion, moreover, was held by musicians. The distinguished theorist Glareanus wrote that the work of Josquin was "the perfect art to which nothing can be added, after which nothing but decline can be expected."

The so-called *ars perfecta*, or perfect art, rested on the typical Renaissance historical assumption of the great development of the arts in antiquity, which had been lost in medieval days and subsequently rediscovered in the then-modern times. The quotation above is a critical application of this doctrine of perfection regained to the art of music. Italians, whether at home or abroad, took the greatest pride in the achievements of their own architects, sculptors, and painters, but universally they acknowledged the supremacy of the northern composers. The spread of the northern polyphonic art dated from the time the popes had become acquainted with it at Avignon. Later, it led to the establishment of the *Cappella Sixtina* in 1473, which was dominated by Flemish, Burgundian, and French musicians, whose influence from there spread over the entire Christian world. From this time forward, the mastery of these artists in contrapuntal writing became the standard of perfection.

Under Pope Sixtus IV, church music had moved from its status as the modest handmaiden of the liturgy to a position of major importance. The grandeur of the Roman liturgical displays called for music of comparable magnificence. Owing to the prevailing taste of the time, musicians from the great singing centers of Antwerp, Liège, and Cambrai flocked to Rome to seek their fortunes. The highest honor of all was an appointment to the Sistine Choir, whose privilege it was to perform on the occasions when the pope officiated. Membership was highly selective, totaling from 16 to 24 singers except during the time of the musical Leo when it was increased to 36. These singers were divided into four parts: boy sopranos, male altos, tenors, and basses; normally they sang *a cappella*—that is, without instrumental

accompaniment—a practice that was exceptional rather than usual at the time. The quality of the choir can be deduced from the roster of distinguished men who made their reputations in its ranks. Dufay, the first composer to view the mass as an organic work of art, entered the choir in 1428. In its archives are numerous masses, motets, and psalm settings by Josquin des Prez, who served from 1486 to 1494. Palestrina, who learned contrapuntal fluency from Josquin, first became a member in 1551 and later brought the organization to a pinnacle of technical perfection.

Josquin's attitude on the dignity of the art of composition is most revealing. When the Duke of Ferrara needed a composer, he hesitated between Isaac and Josquin. He was advised in a letter from a friend who knew them both to choose Isaac, "because he is able to get along with his colleagues and composes new pieces quicker. It is true, Josquin composes better, but he does it only when it suits him and not when he is requested. More than this Josquin asks 200 ducats while Isaac is pleased with 120." Like Michelangelo, then, Josquin behaved very much as the modern independent artist with high standards of proficiency, rather than as a craftsman who produced works on order regardless of quality.

In Josquin's compositions, the stark barren intervals of Gothic polyphony and all traces of harshness in the voice leading are eliminated. He allows dissonances to occur only on weak beats or as suspensions on the stronger ones. His rhythms and forms are based on strict symmetry and mathematically regular proportions. His writing is characterized by the usual northern fondness for canonic imitations and other complicated contrapuntal constructions. Such devices, however, are managed with complete mastery, and his tremendous technique in composition never intrudes upon his expressive design. He was at home in all Renaissance musical forms, excelling perhaps in his motets and in his solo and choral chansons. In Rome, where his unique abilities were combined with the warmth and fluidity of Italian lyricism, his art mellowed into a style of incomparable beauty, formal clarity, and the purest expressivity.

Josquin's four-part motet *Ave Maria* will serve as an admirable illustration of his art. Like Michelangelo's early *Pietà*, it is in a perfectly self-contained form, emotionally restrained, and full of luxuriantly flowing lines. Even such a short excerpt as this shows his penchant for canonic imitation between the voices and the smoothness of contour that comes with stepwise melodic motion. He treats all four voices with balanced impartiality but prefers to group them in pairs, as in this example, in order to achieve a transparency of texture and an ineffable purity of sound. Darker sides of Josquin's emotional spectrum can be found in his Requiem masses and in his setting of the psalm *De Profundis*.

Later periods saw in Michelangelo both a summing up of the Renaissance and the beginning of the baroque style. Josquin's place was more limited; and while he was universally acknowledged as the greatest musical mind of the early 16th century, the very perfection of his art implied that it was on the verge of becoming archaic. His mantle was inherited by a number of composers in the succeeding generation, who carried his art to its logical conclusion. Palestrina's music has been held to be better adapted to religious purposes, though he remains Josquin's inferior in invention, inspiration, and depth of expression. Victoria carried the style to Spain, William Byrd to England; and through Philippe de Monte and Orlando di Lasso, it spread throughout France and Germany. In the 17th century, though the art was still studied, it became known as the "antique style" in contrast to the baroque music, which was called the "modern style." Within its limitations the art has never been surpassed. Even today it is considered the ideal for church music, and no conservatory curriculum is complete without a course in 16th-century counterpoint.

IDEAS: HUMANISM

Florentine humanism and its Roman aftermath were motivated by a reappraisal of the values of Greco-Roman antiquity, by an attempt to reconcile pagan forms with Christian practices, by a desire to reinstate the philosophy of Plato and reinterpret that of Aristotle, and, above all, by a rediscovery of the world and man. The Renaissance humanist was not primarily religious- or scientific-minded. He tended to substitute the authority of respected classical writers for that of the Bible and Church dogma. In looking forward, he found more convenient and convincing precedents in the civilizations of Greece and Rome than in the immediate medieval past. Lorenzo de' Medici, for instance, found a new orientation for secular government in Plato's *Republic*;

Machiavelli, a new method for writing history in Thucydides; and Bramante, a new adaptation of the Greco-Roman temple for Christian worship.

Bramante's Tempietto (Fig. 328) was a conscious revival of the rounded commemorative structures of antiquity (see Figs. 16, 47). This temple in miniature, coming as it did just at the beginning of the 16th century, became the architectural manifesto of the Roman Renaissance, just as Brunelleschi's Pazzi Chapel (Figs. 266–269) had been in the 15th-century Florentine Renaissance. Placed in the cloistered courtyard of the Church of San Pietro in Montorio, the little temple, like a sculptured reliquary, rests on the site where St. Peter is supposed to have been crucified. For his architectural order Bramante chose the simple yet monumental Roman Doric. He adhered to the classical principle of the module whereby all parts of the building are either mul-

328. Donato Bramante. Tempietto, San Pietro in Montorio, Rome. 1504. Marble, 46′ high, diameter of colonnade 29′.

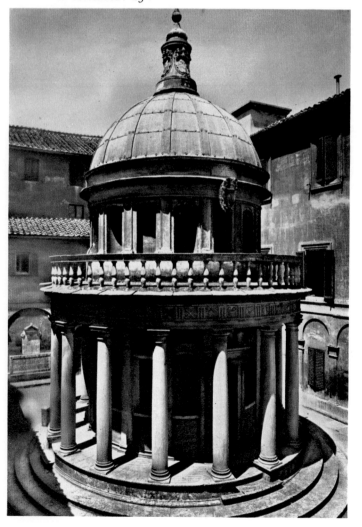

tiples or fractions of the basic unit of measure. He also promoted the feeling of balance and proportion by making the height and width of the lower floor equal to that of the upper story. Spare of ornament, the only formal decorative element is in the Doric frieze with the regular triglyphs alternating with metopes that employ a shell motif. Above all, Bramante wished to demonstrate the cohesiveness and compactness of the centralized plan under the unifying crown of a cupola. Later when Pope Julius entrusted him with the design of the new St. Peter's, Bramante had his chance to build on a monumental scale (see Fig. 325). Here again he turned to the ancient world for inspiration and is reputed to have declared: "I shall place the Pantheon on top of the Basilica of Constantine."

The humanists preferred purer versions of classical art forms to the adaptations that had been made in the thousand-year period between the fall of Rome and their own time. The members of the Florentine humanistic circle learned to read and speak ancient Greek under native tutors. Ficino translated the dialogues of Plato, while Poliziano translated Homer from the original Greek into Italian and wrote treatises in Latin on Greek poetic and musical theory. Other scholars catalogued and edited books for the Medici library, while Squarcialupi compiled the musical compositions of the preceding century. The interest in cataloguing, editing, translating, and commenting was pursued with such enthusiasm that it all but blotted out the production of live literature. The Latin of Renaissance scholars was Ciceronian rather than medieval Latin, which they considered corrupt. The architects read Vitruvius and preferred central-type churches modeled on the Pantheon to the oblong-basilica form that had been evolved over the centuries. They revived the classical orders and architectural proportions in a more authentic form. Decorative motifs were derived directly from ancient sarcophagi, reliefs, and carved gems. Sculptors reaffirmed the expressive possibilities of the nude, and with Michelangelo it became the chief expressive vehicle of his art. Painters, lacking tangible survivals, used mythological subjects and the literary descriptions of ancient masterpieces.

Musicians reinterpreted Greek musical thought, and some made concrete attempts to put into practice the theories expounded in Euclid's musical treatise. The Greek assertion that art imitates nature was universally acknowledged, but in architecture and music this had to be applied in the general sense of nature as an orderly and regular system conforming to mathematical proportions and laws. Josquin des Prez was hailed as

329. LEONARDO DA VINCI. *Last Supper.* 1495–1498. Fresco, 14′ 5″ × 28′ ¼″. Santa Maria delle Grazie, Milan.

a modern Orpheus who had regained the lost perfect art of the ancients—though the Greeks would have been bewildered by his musical style. Josquin's less-enthusiastic admirers pointed out that the trees and stones still showed some reluctance to follow him as they had not in the case of the original Orpheus. His art, however, like that of Michelangelo, was thought by the humanists to be a path back to a lost classical paradise.

Both Botticelli and Michelangelo set out to produce works in the Neo-Platonic spirit. The literary ancestry of Botticelli's *Allegory of Spring* (the famous *Primavera*), *Birth of Venus* (Fig. 290), and *Venus and Mars* (Plate 20) has been traced through the poetry of his contemporary Poliziano back to the Roman poets Lucretius and Horace. Their philosophical forebear, however, is the Plato of the *Symposium*, which deals with the nature of love and beauty. Man, according to Plato's theory, has drunk of the waters of oblivion and forgotten his divine origin. Falling in love with a beautiful person reminds him of his natural affinity for beauty. From physical attraction and ephemeral loveliness, he is led to thoughts of the lasting beauty of truth and, finally, to the contemplation of the eternal verities of absolute beauty, truth, and goodness. Venus is, of course, the image of this transcendent beauty, and the way to approach it is through love. The eternal feminine, as Goethe later said in the closing lines of *Faust*, draws us ever onward. Michelangelo's Plato, however, was the Plato of the *Timaeus*, which discourses on the creation of the

world by the Demiurge, the metaphysical nature of the human soul, and the return to God. Unlike Botticelli's fragile dream of beauty, Michelangelo had a virile vision of the creative process itself. When Botticelli came under the influence of the fiery Savonarola with his resurgence of medievalism, he repented of his paganism and turned exclusively to religious pictures. Botticelli never tried to combine his paganism and Christianity as did Michelangelo, and for him they remained in separate compartments and on an either/or basis. Michelangelo, however, had the mind to assimilate Platonic abstractions, the overwhelming urge to express his ideas, and the technical equipment to translate them into dramatic visual form. But the voice of Savonarola spoke loudly to him, too, and in his rugged mind Michelangelo was destined to wrestle with the two essentially irreconcilable philosophies for the rest of his life. Leonardo da Vinci, contrariwise, kept the religious themes of his paintings (see Fig. 329) and his scientific inquiries in separate intellectual compartments.

To Michelangelo, a work of art always had to participate in the world of ideas, and all of his works are philosophical as well as aesthetic creations. On the concordance of earthly loveliness and divine beauty, of transient charm and eternal truth, he wrote:

Sculpture, the first of arts, delights a taste
Still strong and sound: each act, each limb, each bone
Are given life and, lo, man's body is raised,
Breathing, alive, in wax or clay or stone.
But oh, if time's inclement rage should waste,

Or maim, the statue that man builds alone,
Its beauty still remains, and can be traced
Back to the source that claims it as its own.

O my dear Lord, who give and take away,
And with your Blood alone can heal and cleanse
Man's every action and his fault immense.

In his early *Bacchus* he wholeheartedly embraced paganism, a fact that made the *Pietà* that followed it no less a sincere declaration of religious faith. Then came the synthesis of the Sistine ceiling, in which pagan sibyls sit side by side with Hebrew prophets, and the Platonic theory of the return to God is reconciled with the Christian doctrine of salvation. Even with the apocalyptical fury of the *Last Judgment,* mythological characters are juxtaposed with those from the Old and New Testaments. In his old age he was still musing on the pagan-Platonic and Judaic-Christian themes of his youth. A long series of poems that he intended to publish in his lifetime concludes thus:

Through mortal beauty, thus, I can behold
And know my God; and I am free to love
Whatever so superbly mirrors Him.

Yet on another occasion he can pray:

Michelangelo's Madonnas reveal the unity between bodily beauty and eternal beauty; his *Moses* links human moral power and eternal goodness; and his organic compositions connect temporal with eternal truth. His triple divisions symbolizing the stages of the soul as it progresses from its bodily tomb to its liberation and reunion with God are a constantly recurring preoccupation. Even in his abstract architectural forms of St. Peter's, the pilasters are the "slaves" imprisoned by the weight of the material burden they must carry, while overhead soars the lofty dome in the geometrical perfection of the circular form, symbolizing the paradise that man has lost and that he must somehow regain. The whole building is thus conceived as an organic system of pressures and tensions leading upward and culminating in a cupola that ascends toward the divine realm and finally dissolves into the freedom of infinity.

330. MICHELANGELO. Dome interior, St. Peter's, Vatican, Rome.

PART IV

THE BAROQUE PERIOD

II - VENETIAN MANNERISM AND EARLY BAROQUE

VENICE, 16TH CENTURY

A glimpse of Venice as it was at the threshold of the 16th century can be seen through the eyes of the painter Gentile Bellini. His faithful reporting in *Procession in St. Mark's Square* (Fig. 331)—so accurate that architectural historians can make reconstructions of buildings long since razed; that researchers can study the mosaics and sculptures of St. Mark's Basilica as they were before later restorations; that historians of liturgy, musical performance, and costume find it prime source material—belongs to Renaissance naturalism. When compared with the forthcoming flights of mannerist and early baroque imaginations, the stateliness and stability of Bellini's painting are all the more striking. Hence, the subject matter of the *Procession in St. Mark's Square*, its story content, mode of representation, formal orgànization, and the circumstances of its commission reveal much about the life of Venice and the unique developments in the arts during a period of transition.

Surrounding St. Mark's Square, Venice's spacious piazza (Fig. 332), are buildings from many periods and in several styles, reflecting the history of the city—the domed Church of St. Mark (middle left) and Campanile (right) were begun in Romanesque times; the Doge's Palace (upper left and cen-

ter) is mainly 14th-century Gothic; the Library of St. Mark (behind the Campanile) was constructed by Sansovino in 1536 and later continued, with an additional story, by Scamozzi around the inner side of the square (extreme right). St. Mark's (Fig. 331) at once proclaims Venice the meeting place of Orient and Occident. Begun in the 10th century, it is the product of centuries of community effort. Indeed an early law required every Venetian ship to bring back materials for the construction or decoration of the church. As a result, fragments from every Mediterranean country can be found somewhere in its fabric—from the four Roman bronze horses of the first century A.D. that stand over the central portal (Fig. 333), the Alexandrian polychrome marble columns and Greek alabaster windows, to the present-day additions and alterations. The plan is that of a Greek cross with domes covering each of the four wings and a 42-foot cupola in the center.

Above the narthex entrance, stretching the full width of the façade, is an open gallery on which, in Bellini's picture, several figures can be seen. Above the gallery is a row of five 13th-century Gothic ogee gables that frame the upper tier of mosaics. On

(above) TINTORETTO. *Paradise* (detail of orchestra). Oil sketch. Louvre, Paris.

General Events

	1453	Fall of Constantinople to Turks; Venetian commerce challenged
	1492	Geographical discoveries by Spanish and Portuguese navigators weakened Venetian maritime trade
	1495	Aldine Press began publishing inexpensive editions of Greco-Roman classics
	1501	*Odhecaton*, anthology of vocal and instrumental works by Josquin des Prez, Obrecht, Isaac, and others printed in Venice by Petrucci
	1517	Protestant Reformation began
1527–	1562	Willaert choirmaster of St. Mark's
	1536	Library of St. Mark built by J. Sansovino
	1540	Loggietta at base of Campanile built by Sansovino
1545–	1563	Council of Trent initiated Counter Reformation
	1549	Basilica at Vicenza built by Palladio
	1550	Villa Rotonda near Vicenza begun by Palladio
	1565	Church of San Giorgio Maggiore, Venice, built by Palladio
	1570	Palladio published *Four Books of Architecture*
	1571	Naval Battle of Lepanto; Venice and Spain defeated Turks
	1573	Veronese called before Inquisition
1576–	1578	Church of Il Redentore, Venice, built by Palladio
1579–	1580	Olympic Theater, Vicenza, built by Palladio
	1584	Procuratie Nuove, continuation of Sansovino's Library of St. Mark design, built by Scamozzi
1585–	1612	Giovanni Gabrieli choirmaster of St. Mark's
	1589	Olympic Theater at Vicenza dedicated with performance of Sophocles' *Oedipus* (music by A. Gabrieli)
1613–	1643	Monteverdi choirmaster of St. Mark's
	1631	Santa Maria della Salute begun by Longhena

Architects

1486–	1586	Jacopo Sansovino
1508–	1580	Andrea Palladio
1552–	1616	Vincenzo Scamozzi
1604–	1675	Baldassare Longhena

Painters

1429–	1507	Gentile Bellini
*c.*1430–	1516	Giovanni Bellini
*c.*1455–*c.*1526		Vittore Carpaccio
*c.*1490–	1576	Titian (Tiziano Vecelli)
1478–	1510	Giorgione
1510–	1592	Jacopo Bassano
1518–	1594	Jacopo Tintoretto
1528–	1588	Paolo Veronese

Musicians

*c.*1480–	1562	Adriano Willaert
1510–	1586	Andrea Gabrieli
1516–	1565	Cipriano de Rore
1517–	1590	Gioseffo Zarlino
1557–	1612	Giovanni Gabrieli
1567–	1643	Claudio Monteverdi
1602–	1676	Francesco Cavalli

Italian and International Mannerists

*c.*1492–	1546	Giulio Romano
1494–	1540	Rosso Fiorentino
1494–	1556	Jacopo Pontormo
1500–	1571	Benvenuto Cellini
1503–	1540	Francesco Parmigianino
1503–	1572	Angelo Bronzino
1511–	1574	Giorgio Vasari
1529–	1600	Giovanni da Bologna
*c.*1540–	1609	Federigo Zuccaro
1555–	1619	Ludovico Carracci
1560–	1609	Annibale Carracci

the crest of the central gable is the winged lion of St. Mark, one of the four beasts that symbolize the Evangelists, placed here to honor him as the city's patron saint. To the right is a corner of the Doge's Palace where the ruler and his guests are seated on the second-story arcade. This bizarre variation of a Gothic town hall rises in two stories of open pointed arches surmounted by a third story notable for its diamond-shaped design in bright pink marble tiling. On the extreme left is the old library from which many spectators are watching the activities in the square below. The building with its castellated roof and odd-shaped chimney pots also dates from medieval times.

More remarkable than its architecture, however, is the institution of the library itself. In lieu of outstanding literary figures, Venice treasured the collections of books that had been left her by the

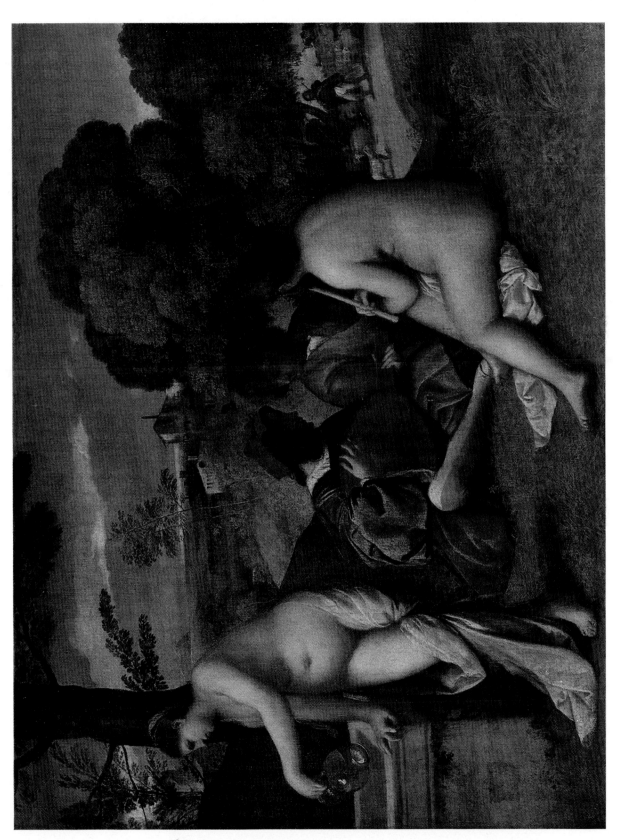

Plate 25. GIORGIONE. *Concert Champêtre* (*Pastoral Concert*). *c*. 1510.
Oil on canvas, 43 ¼ × 54 ⅜″. Louvre, Paris. (See p. 304.)

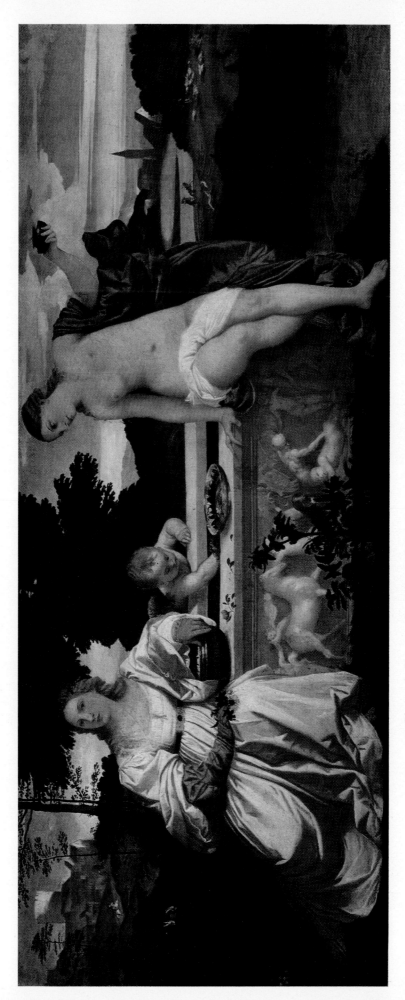

Plate 26. TITIAN. *Sacred and Profane Love. c.* 1514. Oil on canvas, 3′6″ × 8′7″. Borghese Gallery, Rome. (See p. 304.)

331. GENTILE BELLINI. *Procession in St. Mark's Square.* 1496. Oil on canvas, 12 × 24'. Academy, Venice.

332. Venice. St. Mark's (middle left); Doge's Palace (upper left and center); Library of St. Mark (opposite palace); Campanile (right); Procuratie Nuove (extreme right).

333. Four Horses of 1st century A.D. St. Mark's Basilica, Venice. Lifesize, gilt bronze.

poet Petrarch, the Greek scholar Cardinal Bessarion, and other donors, because in this watery city the danger of fire was less than elsewhere. In addition to these collections, the library housed all the specimens of the city's elegant printing and book-making industry, which included fine but inexpensive editions of classics published here for the first time by the famous Aldine Press, and which gave such great momentum to the spread of learning throughout the educated world. In the 16th century, these collections were transferred to the handsome building across the square designed by Sansovino especially to house them (Fig. 334). In Bellini's *Procession in St. Mark's Square*, after the ceremony in the church, the procession files out of the basilica through a passageway between St. Mark's and the Doge's Palace in the right background and moves around the square to the opposite side where all the separate groups gather.

Since it was commissioned by the organization known as the *Gran Scuola di San Giovanni Evangelista* as a mural for its chapter house, and since it is a collective portrait of the *Scuola's* membership, Bellini's painting is technically a corporation picture. Aristocrats and commoners, priests and laymen, men and women—all in all about two thirds of Venice's population—were members of some 200-odd *scuole*. These fraternal bodies combined the activities of a social club, lodge, professional society, charitable institution, and insurance company as well as the patronage of the arts. On the annual feast days of their patron saints, they sponsored grand public ceremonies such as that depicted.

While Bellini's picture narrates an event in the history of the school, one has to look hard to find the main character in the kneeling figure (behind canopy, center foreground) of a visitor from Brescia. That morning he had heard that his son had been injured in a hunting accident, and he drops to his knees imploring divine aid as the reliquary containing a splinter of the true Cross passes by. Later he learns that his son was restored to health at that very moment. The miraculous incident is obviously subordinated by Bellini to the construction of a large picture in skillful perspective, to the portraiture of members of the *scuola* in their ceremonial robes, and to the splendor of the colorful pageant. Such detachment foreshadows the break from the tyranny of subject matter that is to come in the pastoral themes and elusive moods of Giorgione and Titian, and the establishment of formal controls that is to result from the academic approach of Palladio and Veronese. Bellini's picture also stands in direct opposition to the turbulent treatment and feverish illusionism a similar scene is to receive at the hands of such free mannerist and early baroque figures as Tintoretto and El Greco.

In the procession scene, a feeling of open public life and freedom of social movement can be sensed in both the participants and the bystanders. The independence of Venice and the prosperity of her citizenry were owing in many respects to the city's unusual situation. Built on a group of island lagoons at the head of the Adriatic, Venice was truly what a Florentine poet described as "a city in the water without walls." Secure from attack by land and by sea by possession of the largest navy then in existence, Venice carried on an active commerce between Orient and Occident that afforded her citizens a manner of life unrivaled in its time for comfort and luxury. Lacking the ups and downs of other medieval and Renaissance cities, such as Pisa and Siena with their brief periods of florescence, Venice developed slowly and consistently from the glow of its Byzantine dawn, through a Renaissance high noon and a brief thunderstorm of mannerism, to its florid baroque sunset.

Here lived no literary giant such as Dante, no magnifico with the vision of a Lorenzo, no political philosopher of the caliber of Machiavelli, no thundering religious reformer like Savonarola. In fact, without great men of letters, without outstanding individual art patrons, without inspired religious leaders—in short, without experiencing the heights and depths of the human spirit known in Florence or Rome—Venice built up in its architecture, painting, and music a culture uniquely its own.

Though the Venetian government was dominated by a coalition of wealthy merchant families, a measure of political freedom was maintained under the doges, who were elected rather than hereditary rulers. Some religious freedom was also achieved by isolation from Rome and by such a strategic device as the designation of immense St. Mark's as the "private chapel of the doges," since heads of state could always control the appointment of clergy, choirmasters, and singers in their personal establishments. But while this island city-state in Bellini's time could still justify its chosen title of Most Serene Republic, storm clouds were gathering on the horizon.

The fall of Constantinople to the Turks and the rising power of the Ottoman Empire spelled competition for Venice's commercial empire, and sporadic warfare had already begun. While Venice had given birth to one great explorer, Marco Polo, the voyages of the 16th-century Spanish, Portuguese, Dutch, and English navigators were being exploited to enrich rival countries, thereby upsetting the traditional economy in which Venice had flourished. Italy was soon to become a battleground in the European power struggle between the Holy Roman Empire and France. Charles V, Titian's great patron, became emperor in 1519, and in addition to Spain his dominions included the Low Countries, Germany, and Austria. Francis I of France, feeling his country caught in a giant pincers, tried to fortify his position by invading Italy. But one by one each Italian kingdom, principality, dukedom, and republic fell to Charles V. Finally, by sacking and pillaging Rome itself with his ruthless mercenaries and imprisoning Pope Clement VII, Charles achieved the surrender of the papacy.

334. Jacopo Sansovino. Library of St. Mark, Venice. Begun 1536. *c.* 290′ long, 60′ high.

The religious crisis brought on by opposing forces of the Reformation and Counter Reformation likewise unsettled Venice's trade and cultural relations with northern Europe. Though the Universal Inquisition was felt more mildly in Venice than elsewhere, Roman Catholic censorship of printed matter and assertion of the clergy's control of art proved more than a threat to Venice's publishing industry and artistic freedom. Venetians, to be sure, were no strangers to insecurity as fabulous fortunes were made overnight when their ships came in, and financial ruin and debtor's prison followed shipwrecks, seizure by pirates, or sinkings in naval battles.

This Pandora's box of troubles created a crisis in the literal sense of a split, with East and West divided, the Ottoman Turkish Empire on one side and an alliance of Christian European states on the other; with Christendom itself rent asunder by the Reformation and the Counter Reformation; with Italy under siege by both the Holy Roman Emperor and the King of France. Such a critical state, with its accompanying inner anxieties and complicated contradictions, was bound to find expression in the arts.

One road out of the crisis was to lead to a freezing of Renaissance conventions, formal logic, and balanced symmetry in a conservative academic *mannerism*—art "in the manner" of the great masters of the immediate past, such as Michelangelo and Raphael. The other was to lead to the search for a new style in a free mannerism with its deliberate violations of Renaissance proportions, experimental forms, capricious eccentricities, unresolved tensions, and restless imbalances. A reconciliation of these opposites was eventually to resolve itself into the synthesis of the baroque style, which developed in the 17th century.

ARCHITECTURE

As did all the other arts, Venetian architecture reached out toward new forms. Although begun as early as 1536 and still within the Renaissance tradition, the Library of St. Mark (Fig. 334) by Jacopo Sansovino already had enough new ideas to qualify it as a transition to the coming baroque style. Standing out boldly from the façade are the rich decorative details the Venetians loved. Instead of the solid, flat surfaces of a Renaissance façade with a rusticated ground floor (see Figs. 270, 300), Sansovino has an open arcade, paralleled above by the row of deeply indented windows. This projection in depth makes for an effective play of light and shadow, an element hitherto associated more with sculpture and painting than with architecture.

It would seem far from accidental that the origins of baroque architecture can be traced to Michelangelo, Sansovino, and Palladio, who were first trained as sculptors. This transfer of sculptural thought to architecture is also responsible for the ascendancy of embellishment over architectural function that characterizes the baroque. In the case of the Library of St. Mark, however, Sansovino's design can hardly be characterized as florid (Fig. 335). The dignified arcade of the lower story serves as a base for the increasingly rich adornment of the upper parts. The deeply arched windows of the second floor are unified by the regularity of the Ionic columns, while the poses of the sculptured nudes in the spandrels provide variety. Above runs a frieze of cherubs in high relief holding garlands that alternate with small, deep-set windows. Over this rises a balustrade that goes all the way around the roof and supports a row of statues silhouetted against the skyline, with obelisks accenting the corners. The proportion of the upper entablature is noteworthy in that it is over one third the height of the supporting order itself.

Sansovino's love of lavish detail is expressed in the Loggietta (Fig. 336) at the base of the Campanile. The prototype is the triumphal Arch of Titus in Rome, here expanded into a triple-arch design. The sculptural panels depict mythological scenes, and the ornate bronze gates lead into a meeting hall used on ceremonial occasions.

Sansovino's designs influenced Andrea Palladio, the greatest architect associated with the Venetian style. As the author of the highly influential *Four Books of Architecture*, first published in Venice in 1570, Palladio has left a detailed exposition of his philosophy. In his Preface he paid eloquent tribute to his ancient Roman mentor Vitruvius, whose writings stimulated his study of the classical buildings in Rome. "Finding that they deserved a much more diligent Observation than I thought at first Sight," he noted, "I began with the utmost Accuracy to measure every minutest part by itself." Palladio's ideas thus were based on a thorough grounding in traditional design. He likewise paid tribute to his immediate predecessor Sansovino, whose Library he praised as "perhaps the most sumptuous and the most beautiful Edifice that has been erected since the time of the Ancients."

Palladio's architecture can be studied more fully in Vicenza than in Venice itself. The winged lion of St. Mark is as prominent a feature there as it is in the corresponding main square in Venice some forty miles away, since Vicenza was at that time a part of the Venetian Republic's extensive holdings on the mainland of Italy. The most imposing building of the central piazza at Vicenza is

(left) 335. Jacopo Sanso-
vino. Library of St. Mark
(detail), Venice. Begun
1536.

(below) 336. Jacopo Sansovino. Loggietta of Campa-
nile, Venice. 1536.

(right) 337. ANDREA PAL-
LADIO. Basilica, Vicenza.
c. 1550. 232 × 124′.

(below) 338. ANDREA PAL-
LADIO. Basilica (detail),
Vicenza.

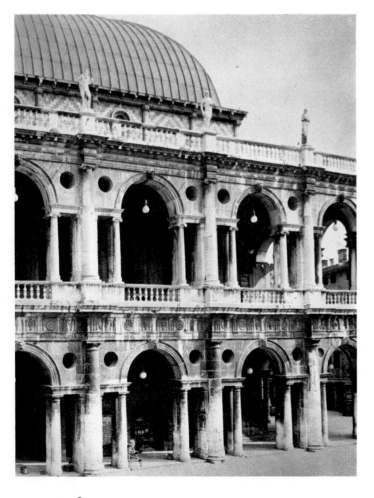

Palladio's Basilica (Figs. 337, 338). Explaining his
intentions, he stated: "As the Ancients made their
Basilicas after such a manner, that in the Spring
and Summer People might come together there, to
treat of their affairs, and to carry on their Lawsuits; so in our times every City, both in *Italy* and
out of it, do erect certain spacious public Halls,
which may deservedly be termed *Basilicas.*" While
the nucleus of his building was an old Gothic public
hall, the surrounding porticoes, arcades, and galleries are his own. Like Sansovino, Palladio used
the Doric order on the ground floor with the Ionic
above. In both cases, balustrades separate the
stories, while another is found above outlining the
roof and supporting a row of statues. But Palladio
goes a step farther than his predecessor by including spacious galleries on both floors, by using more
slender supporting piers with open spaces on either
side, and by piercing the spandrels on each level
with the round portholelike openings that promote
a sense of deep space and achieve a greater surface
play of light and shade.

Just outside Vicenza is the Villa Rotonda
(Figs. 339, 340), a country villa in the grand style
and the prototype of many later buildings. Geometrically, it is a cube enclosing a cylindrical core and
topped by a low saucer dome. The villa rests on
a hill from which it dominates the surrounding
countryside. Facing the four points of the compass,
grand flights of steps lead up to Ionic porticoes that

(top) 339. ANDREA PALLADIO. Villa Rotonda, near Vicenza. Begun 1550. 80 × 80', dome 70' high.

(below) 340. ANDREA PALLADIO. Villa Rotonda, plan.

project 14 feet forward and spread 40 feet outward. The pediments are in the manner of a classical temple, with statues placed on either side and above. Each portico provides entrance into the imposing reception room that gives the villa the name *rotonda*. This central salon is as high as the house itself and culminates in the cupola above. Alcoves left over from the parts between the round central hall and the square sides of the building allow space for four winding staircases and for no less than 32 rooms in the adjoining corners—all excellently lighted both from the outside and from the eight round windows at the base of the cupola. At the corners of the main floor are four large reception rooms, each 20 by 30 feet, and four smaller ones—eight in all on this floor alone. Below, a basement includes storerooms, servants' quarters, and kitchens. Palladio's achievement here is a house that is spacious but simple in plan. Such villas were built for a formal style of living, and Palladio observes that when an architect "builds for Persons of Quality, and more especially for those that are in public Employment, he must built their Palaces with Portico's, Galleries, and large stately Halls richly adorned: that those who come for business, or to pay their respects to the Owner, may be received commodiously, and delighted and amused whilst they wait for him."

When advancing years curtailed Sansovino's activities, Palladio was called to Venice to construct several buildings, among them the churches of San Giorgio Maggiore with its picturesque island setting (Fig. 341) and Il Redentore (Figs. 342–345). Palladio set himself the problem of reconciling the Greco-Roman temple with the traditional oblong Christian basilica plan. Since a classical temple is of uniform height with a simple shed roof, and a Christian basilica has a Latin-cross ground plan with a central nave rising high above two side aisles, his solution shows great ingenuity. The central part of the façade of Il Redentore (Fig. 344) becomes the portico of a classical temple complete with columns and pediment to face the high central nave within, while the acute angles of a fragmentary second pediment face the side aisles. The pediment idea is repeated in the small triangle above the entrance and in the side angles at the roof level, to make in all two complete and two incomplete pediments. This broken-pediment motif was later incorporated into the baroque vocabulary. To create the feeling of deep space, Palladio alternated square pilasters with round attached columns and arranged the pediments in a complex intersecting design. The interior (Fig. 345) is a model of geometrical clarity; and in order to create a feeling of spatial depth, he eliminated the traditional walled apse that closes the space around the altar and replaced

(above) 341. ANDREA PALLADIO. San Giorgio Maggiore, Venice. 1560–1580.

(below) 344. ANDREA PALLADIO. Façade, Il Redentore, Venice. 1576–1592.

(above) 343. ANDREA PALLADIO. Il Redentore, plan.

(left) 342. ANDREA PALLADIO. Il Redentore, Venice. Drawing. Façade begun 1577.

345. ANDREA PALLADIO.
Interior, Il Redentore,
Venice. 1576–1592.

(left) 346. ANDREA PALLA-
DIO. Interior, Olympic The-
ater, Vicenza. 1580–1584.
Stage 230′ wide.

(below) 347. ANDREA PAL-
LADIO. Olympic Theater,
plan.

it by a semicircular open colonnade against clear glass windows, so that the eye is led past the altar into the distance.

The last building Palladio undertook was the Olympic Theater at Vicenza (Figs. 346, 347). It was begun the year of his death and finished later from his designs by Scamozzi. An ingenious device to create the feeling of deep space is seen through the central arch from which actors made their entrances—a rising ramp flanked by building façades, which recedes only about fifty feet but creates the illusion of a long avenue leading to an open city square in the distance. Clearly inspired by ancient Roman amphitheaters, the Olympic has, in turn, been the inspiration for many later theaters, such as the Palladium in London.

In any comparison of the works of Sansovino and Palladio, the materials these architects used deserves mention. As architect of large public edifices, Sansovino had his choice of rare marbles and the finest stone; Palladio, working so frequently on private dwellings and buildings in the more provincial and less wealthy Vicenza, had to content himself largely with brick, stucco, and terracotta. Palladio comments many times on the importance of design over materials, and his achievement of richness and monumentality with baser materials proves that architectural grandeur lies more in conception of form than in content. Reasoned proportion of the whole and logical disposition of the parts are two prime characteristics of his art. His love of symmetry and his systematic use of the five architectural orders—the Tuscan, Doric, Ionic, Corinthian, and Composite—were transmitted to the succeeding age. His skillful use of the principle

of dualism and opposition—both in the winged organization of his palace façades and in his allowance for the reflection of façades in the water as in his Venetian buildings—is also noteworthy. The use of water as an element of architecture was absorbed into the later baroque vocabulary. But, whereas the ripple of water was natural to Venice, artificial reflecting pools had to be designed to set off the façades of buildings in other locations (see Figs. 383, 406).

Scamozzi, the younger collaborator of both Sansovino and Palladio, was commissioned in 1584 to add a wing to Sansovino's Library on the side toward St. Mark's Square (Fig. 348), to house the Procuratie Nuove, the new civic agencies. His design shows the usual Palladian angularity, but he turned to Michelangelo for the alternation of semicircular and angular window brackets (see Fig. 323). A touch of manneristic caprice is found

348. VINCENZO SCAMOZZI. Façade (detail), Procuratie Nuove, Venice. 1584.

349. GIULIO ROMANO. Courtyard (detail), Palazzo del Tè, Mantua. 1525–1535.

302

(left) 350. FEDERIGO ZUCCARO. Garden gate, Palazzo Zuccari, Rome. *c.* 1593.

(below) 351. BALDASSARE LONGHENA. Santa Maria della Salute, Venice. 1631–1656. *c.* 200 × 155'.

in the precariously perched nudes atop the third-story window brackets. Here again, architecture is borrowing the materials of sculpture. The figures are variations of those on Michelangelo's Medici Tombs (Fig. 313), but at their height, Scamozzi's nudes seem even more in danger of slipping down the sloping sides than do those on Michelangelo's sarcophagi.

Similar mannerist shock techniques are seen in the Palazzo del Tè, or Tea Palace (Fig. 349), that Giulio Romano built for the ruling family of the neighboring duchy of Mantua. To enclose this small pleasure garden, he built a wall of heavily rusticated masonry much too massive for its function, and Doric columns far larger than necessary to support the frieze. This dramatic overstatement, however, pales in comparison with the syncopated effect of the frieze itself in which every third triglyph slips downward a notch. Still another startling example is provided by the Roman mannerist painter and architect Federigo Zuccaro in his design for the monstrous garden gate (Fig. 350) and similarly gruesome windows of the Palazzo Zuccari.

It remained for Longhena in the early years of the 17th century to make the break from the brittle rectilinear style of Palladio and Scamozzi and carry Venetian architecture over into the exuberant baroque spirit with his Church of Santa Maria della Salute (Figs. 351, 352). From the octagonal base, each side of which is treated like a Roman triumphal arch and surmounted by a triangular pediment pierced by a Palladian "porthole," the structure culminates in the high-pitched main dome and the smaller echoing one at the rear. Buttressing the cupola and mediating between it and the octagonal mass below are striking

352. BALDASSARE LONGHENA. Santa Maria della Salute, plan.

ornamental scrolls. The elaborately decorated exterior is held together by the good composition of the design as a whole. This building was far more to the taste of the Venetians than the restrained and academic Palladian style, and it is one of the finest examples of the early baroque.

Palladio, however, emerges as the most influential architect of his period. Throughout the succeeding century, the classical temple façade was accepted as a norm for Roman Catholic church buildings, but with later architects it became structurally weaker and increasingly the basis for the elaborate ornamentation characteristic of the florid baroque (see Figs. 387–389). To counteract this tendency, Palladio's academicism was also carried over into the new style, and his objectivity and exactness operated as a balance to the more exuberant tendencies of the new style. One of his remarks that must have been frequently pondered by later generations was: "But as for what concerns the ornaments, that is, the Bases, Columns, Capitels, Cornishes, and such like things, I have intermixed nothing of my own; but they were measured by me with the utmost care and exactness, from divers fragments found in the very places where stood the Temples themselves."

And, finally, Palladio's thought as expressed in his *Four Books of Architecture* with their sketches and drawings had an even wider influence in France, England, Ireland, and America than did his buildings. The English translation, published with notes by his disciple Inigo Jones, did much to establish the Georgian tradition both in England and in America, where it was carried on by Thomas Jefferson. The latter's staunch Palladianism is seen in his designs for his residence at Monticello and the Rotunda of the University of Virginia (Fig. 501), both of which are adaptations of the Villa Rotonda. Jefferson also wanted to build the White House at Washington, D.C., on the same plan, but his design, submitted anonymously, was not the chosen one. However, even in its present form the White House has Palladio's winged design on either side of a classical temple portico.

PAINTING

Venetian painting in the course of the 16th century ran a gamut of styles—from the transitional late-Renaissance work of Giorgione and Titian with its partial emancipation from traditional subject matter and story content to the mannerist and early baroque pictures of Tintoretto and Veronese with their illusionism and flights of imagination. Technically, Venetian painting is marked by the refinement and perfection of painting with oil on canvas, since the methods of tempera on wood panels and fresco were unsuited to the damp Venetian climate. Venetian painters also developed rich color palettes and used high intensities of light by which the principal figures are dramatically spotlighted and subordinate ones thrown into various degrees of shadow.

Giorgione's *Concert Champêtre,* or *Pastoral Concert* (Plate 25), impresses with its spaciousness and its distribution of interest from foreground to background. The eye first is arrested by the four figures of the picture plane, then is led leisurely toward the middle ground where the shepherd is tending his flock, and finally comes to rest on the gleaming water of the distant horizon. This pastoral idyll is enlivened by such oppositions as the clothed male figures and feminine nudes; the pairing of the urbane courtier and stately lady at the left with the rustic shepherd and shepherdess on the right; the attitudes of the two women—one intent upon her lover, the other turning away; and by the lute symbolizing lyric poetry and the flute, pastoral poetry.

Giorgione's so-called *Tempest* (Fig. 353) is even less concerned with storytelling than *Concert Champêtre* and more with pictorial mechanics. The sunny foreground and human figures define the picture plane, while the eye is led in receding planes to deep space and the threatening sky in the distance. Stability is maintained by judicious balance of vertical (the standing figure, broken columns, trees, and buildings) and horizontal lines (the unfinished parapet and bridge). In both the *Pastoral Concert* and the *Tempest*, Giorgione creates a mood rather than tells a story, builds a picture rather than communicates concrete meaning. A puzzle to his contemporaries who were accustomed to the usual iconographical subjects, Giorgione is understandable to the modern observer who is used to separating subject matter from pictorial form and seeing a picture as a composition complete within itself rather than as an illustration of a religious or literary theme.

A similar reconciliation of opposites is found in Titian's *Venus and the Organ Player* (Fig. 354), one of the many versions of a theme the artist did in his later years. The young man at the organ seems torn between the sacred pursuits symbolized by that instrument and the sensual pleasures implied by Venus. In addition to this major one, several minor contrasts are present, such as the foreground interior against the receding landscape, the clothed organist and the undraped Venus, the immature Cupid beside the mature Venus, and the tactile quality of the nude flesh against the velvet couch cover. These oppositions are harmonized by Titian's warm colors and brilliance of surface treatment.

A more complex handling of this theme is found in *Sacred and Profane Love* (Plate 26). The (left) 353. GIORGIONE. *Tempest.* c. 1505. Oil on canvas, 32¼ × 28¾". Academy, Venice.

(below) 354. TITIAN. *Venus and the Organ Player.* c. 1545. Oil on canvas, 4'6" × 7'6". Prado, Madrid.

(left) 355. TITIAN. *Assumption of the Virgin.* 1516–1518. Oil on canvas, 22′6″ × 11′8″. Frari Church, Venice.

templative mood, while the playful Cupid swishing the water of the fountain suggests that their thoughts have turned to love. This is supported by the resemblance of the nude figure to Renaissance Venus types. The first rays of the sun come from the goddess' side and have just touched the tower on the left, and the opposition of divinity and mortality is reinforced by the light-bathed open landscape behind Venus and the shadowy confined space between the clothed figure and the castled hill behind her. The warmth of the right side is further supported by the red mantle of Venus, while the shadows of the left are supported by the cool steel-gray costume of her counterpart. The dimension of time is suggested by the wreath of flowers in the hand of the clothed figure and the rose petals strewn on the edge of the fountain, which like her beauty will fade. Under her arm is a brazier, filled with the dying embers of coals, which Venetian ladies customarily carried with them for warmth. On the other side, one sees the timeless beauty of the goddess holding in her hand the brightly burning lamp that points to the sky. For continuity, the eye is quietly led from the darkness at the lower left by the lines of the drapery and the inclining attitude of the clothed figure, past the loving Cupid, diagonally to the nude figure and upward by her extended arm to the eternal sea and sky at the right. This quiet and dignified action fits well with the Platonic theory of earthly love as the means by which the thoughts of time-bound mortals are led to the contemplation of the eternal aspects of things, or from physical beauty to the ideal form of divine beauty. The Platonic concept of time is also present in the contrast of the changing world of appearances, and the unchangeable world of forms beyond. These were frequently the subjects for the Neo-Platonic dialogues of the Renaissance and seem to fit the intent of this picture better than any of the other interpretations.

An entirely different pictorial organization is found in Titian's altarpiece *Assumption of the Virgin* (Fig. 355). In this dramatic composition, heavenly and earthly spheres converge momentarily. Below in deep shadow are the apostles, whose uplifted arms point to the intermediate zone and the ascending Madonna, whose gesture, in turn, raises the eye to the dazzling brightness above. The upward motion then is arrested by the descending figure of God the Father surrounded by His seraphs. Linear movement and gradations of light, as well as transitions of color from somber shades to light pastel hues, are skillfully adapted by Titian to carry out his theme of the soaring human spirit triumphant

title is not Titian's but one of many advanced to solve the riddle of the picture. Since this is not the place to go into the complex philosophical interpretations of this work, here it will suffice to call attention to the facial resemblance of the clothed (profane or worldly love) and unclothed (ideal or sacred love) figures—close enough to make them alter egos—and to the secluded setting at dawn with the awakening life of a new day—the rabbits and butterflies on the meadow, the shepherd tending his flock, and the hunters going forth to the chase. The attitudes of the two women set a conover the gravitational pull of material considerations. Titian herewith created a new pictorial type that was to have profound influence on El Greco (see Fig. 391), Bernini, and the whole of Counter Reformation baroque art.

Titian's sumptuous coloring became the model for such later Venetians as Tintoretto, as well as for such baroque masters as Rubens and Velázquez. A fine example occurs in his *Bacchus and Ariadne* (Fig. 356), which depicts the mythological incident of the god's return from India accompanied by his motley band of revelers. On seeing the deserted and lovelorn Ariadne, he leaps from his panther-drawn chariot, his rose-colored drapery aflutter, to embrace her in wedlock. Titian devises a slashing diagonal direction for the precipitous downward plunge of Bacchus, a device to be emulated often in the baroque period. A subtle touch of visual counterpoint can be observed in the sky where the incident is reenacted by the clouds whose shapes echo the drapery and gestures of the principals, and where the starry crown of immortality awaits Ariadne. In spite of Titian's compositional innovations and great influence on later periods, his art as a whole remains within the scope of the late Renaissance. The painting of his younger colleague Tintoretto, however, crosses the stylistic bridge and probes the expressive possibilities of free mannerism.

The drawing of Michelangelo and the color of Titian were the twin ideals of Tintoretto. His violent contrasts of light and dark; his off-center diagonal directions; his interplay of the natural and supernatural, earthly and unearthly light, human and divine figures; and his placement of principal figures on the periphery of the action, from whence he created lines that lead the eye in several different directions, all combine to make his art both dy-

356. TITIAN. *Bacchus and Ariadne. c.* 1520. Oil on canvas, 5′8″ × 6′ 7/8″. National Gallery, London (reproduced by courtesy of the Trustees).

357. Tintoretto. *Last Supper.* 1592–1594. Oil on canvas, 12′ × 18′8″.
San Giorgio Maggiore, Venice.

namic and dramatic. His *Finding St. Mark's Body* (Plate 27), one of a series he painted for the *Scuola di San Marco*, tells the tale of the Venetian search in Alexandria for the body of their patron saint. Because the men do not know which of the several corpses is the correct one, St. Mark (left foreground) appears to stay the hands of those in the upper right and confirm that the body in the lower right is his. The gesticulating figures in the foreground set up a complex series of criss-crossing diagonals, while the eye is led along the spiraling lines of the vaulting with its phosphorescent lighting into the deep space of the background. Even here the eye does not come to rest, because through the strange half-open wall, the space continues into the mysterious distance. Lacking a natural source, light apparently can come only from the apparition of St. Mark, but it emanates from no single source and falls capriciously on the several figures.

In his *Last Supper* (Fig. 357), Tintoretto represents the miraculous moment when Jesus offers the bread and wine as the sacrificial body and blood of man's redemption. To illuminate this unfathomable mystery of faith, Tintoretto bathes his canvas in a supernatural luminosity that emanates partly from the figure of Christ and partly from the flickering flames of the oil lamp, the smoke of which is trans-

formed into an angelic choir hovering around the head of Christ. The drastic diagonals of the floor are paralleled by those of the table, but instead of directing the eye to the head of Christ, they lead to an indefinite point in the upper right and to space beyond the picture.

Of all subjects, the most congenial to Veronese's art was festivity. Painted with the primary object of delighting the eye, his canvases nevertheless captured an important aspect of Venetian life—the conviviality of large social gatherings and the love of sumptuous surroundings embellished with fruits, flowers, animals, furniture, draperies, and jesters in bizarre costumes. Veronese seems never to have refused a commission to do a feast, and a note on the back of one of his drawings, believed to be in his own handwriting, bears this out. "If I ever have time," he wrote, "I want to represent a sumptuous banquet in a superb hall, at which will be present the Virgin, the Saviour, and St. Joseph. They will be served by the most brilliant retinue of angels which one can imagine, busied in offering them the daintiest viands and an abundance of splendid fruit in dishes of silver and gold. Other angels will hand them precious wines in transparent crystal glasses and gilded goblets, in order to show with what zeal blessed spirits serve the Lord."

Plate 27. TINTORETTO. *Finding St. Mark's Body. c.* 1562.
Oil on canvas, 13′3 ½″ square. Brera Gallery, Milan. (See p. 308.)

Plate 28. PAOLO VERONESE. *Marriage at Cana. c.* 1560. Oil on canvas, 21'10" × 32'5".
Louvre, Paris. (See p. 309.)

358. PAOLO VERONESE. *Marriage at Cana*, detail.
Portraits of VERONESE (left foreground), TINTORETTO (whispering to VERONESE), JACOPO BASSANO
(playing flute), TITIAN (right foreground). (Compare Plate 28.)

Marriage at Cana (Plate 28) is truly a complete picture in that Veronese paints a historical-religious subject, includes portraiture, works in genre scenes, delights in still-life detail, and puts everything in an outdoor urban setting in lieu of a landscape. The meaning of the picture, moreover, can be read on many different levels, from the surface to a deep allegorical interpretation. In his consummate rendering of the world of appearances Veronese most completely realizes himself, and in so doing the Verona-born artist succeeds in being more Venetian than the Venetians. The scene, except for the central figures of Jesus and Mary, is that of a rich wedding feast in Venice, drawn from his observations and imagination.

The guests are a portrait gallery of the great personages of the 16th century. The black-bearded groom, dressed in purple and gold and seated at the extreme left, is Alfonso d'Avalos, a contemporary Spanish grandee. Next to him as the bride is Eleanor of Austria, sister of Charles V and in real life the second wife of Francis I of France. Other royal portraits include those of Francis I, Charles V, Suleiman I, sultan of Turkey, and Queen Mary of England. Monks, cardinals, and the artist's personal friends are also depicted. The major interest

in portraiture is concentrated on the orchestra (Fig. 358) in the center foreground, which is made up of the leading Venetian painters of the day. To the right, in this large canvas, the figure holding the cup in his left hand is the artist's brother Benedetto Cagliari, who collaborated with him by adding architectural backgrounds to this and other of Veronese's large paintings. Less important figures are everywhere. Over Christ's head behind, a butcher chops meat with a cleaver, while bustling servants prepare food or rush to and fro to serve it on smoking gold and silver platters.

For unity in composition, Veronese's picture relies principally on the horizontal and vertical linear patterns beginning with the table, back through the balustrade and the rich Corinthian columns on either side, to the Sansovinian-Palladian architecture against the bright sky. The rigidity of such a plan is softened by the series of intricate curves that carry the eye to the head of Christ. A fine balance is contained in the opposition of the crowded scene below to the serene architectural order and the spaciousness of the open sky above.

Beyond its sumptuous surface, Veronese's *Marriage at Cana* probes for the deeper philosophical

359. PAOLO VERONESE. *Feast in the House of Levi.* 1573.
Oil on canvas, 18′2″ × 42′. Academy, Venice.

meaning of the miracle. The hourglass and musical score on the table were often used in Renaissance art as symbols of the passage of time. The painter-musicians, moreover, are to be interpreted as representations of the three ages of man, a traditional humanistic theme. In a period when great artists enjoyed the favors of princes—Titian, for instance, was ennobled by Emperor Charles V and highly honored by his son Philip II of Spain—famous painters would never have been depicted as mere public entertainers. The ages-of-man idea was often the subject of poetry, and Giorgione's *Three Philosophers* and *Concert* (Fig. 363) show youth, maturity, and old age as corresponding to the Neo-Platonic stages of learning—ignorance, opinion, and knowledge or wisdom. The bearded Titian is portrayed as the patriarch of Venetian artists, clothed in a red damask robe and playing the bass viol; Veronese in a brilliant yellow cloak sits opposite, with Tintoretto whispering in his ear. Both are in their middle years and both have violas da braccia. The young flute player in back is thought to be Jacopo Bassano, placed behind the other musicians since wind instruments had been ranked lower by Plato and Aristotle.

In Christian thought, the marriage at Cana, the first of Christ's miracles in which water was changed to wine, is considered as a prophecy of the Last Supper, in which He transubstantiated the bread and wine into His body and blood to be shed for the remission of sins. The Scriptural passage

describing the wedding feast reveals Jesus as being reluctant to comply with Mary's request, answering "...mine hour is not yet come" (John 2:4). The picture on this level then becomes an allegory of time, which Plato had so eloquently described as being the moving image of eternity.

Another of Veronese's colossal canvases is the *Feast in the House of Levi* (Fig. 359), painted as a Last Supper for a Venetian monastery. The spacious design is appropriate to its huge size, for originally the canvas covered an entire wall of the refectory, where its architectural background and open sky seen through the three arches gave the cloistered monks the illusion of the out-of-doors. Questions were soon raised, however, about the propriety of its content. By tradition a *Last Supper* portrayed only Christ and the twelve apostles, but Veronese had included some fifty figures, and this departure from tradition brought him before the Inquisition.

In one of the most remarkable documents in the history of painting—a summary of the painter's actual testimony—much about this picture in particular and about Veronese's conception of art in general is revealed. The inquisitors were disturbed not only by the number of figures but by the presence of a dog and cat, which Veronese had painted in the foreground. Even more disquieting was the inclusion of German soldiers, sitting on the staircase at the extreme right, at the very time when the Roman Catholic Church was having such trouble in Germany with the Lutheran Reformation.

Question. Did anyone commission you to paint Germans, buffoons, and similar things in that picture?
Answer. No, milords, but I received the commission to decorate the picture as I saw fit. It is large and, it seemed to me, it could hold many figures.

Q. Are not the decorations which you painters are accustomed to add to paintings or pictures supposed to be suitable and proper to the subject and the principal figures or are they just for pleasure— simply what comes to your imagination without any discretion or judiciousness?

A. I paint pictures as I see fit and as well as my talent permits.

Q. Does it seem fitting at the Last Supper of the Lord to paint buffoons, drunkards, Germans, dwarfs and similar vulgarities?

A. No, milords.

Q. Do you not know that in Germany and in other places infected with heresy it is customary with various pictures full of scurrilousness and similar inventions to mock, vituperate, and scorn the things of the Holy Catholic Church in order to teach bad doctrines to foolish and ignorant people?

A. Yes, that is wrong; but I return to what I have said, that I am obliged to follow what my superiors have done.

Q. What have your superiors done? Have they perhaps done similar things?

A. Michelangelo in Rome in the Pontifical Chapel painted Our Lord, Jesus Christ, His Mother, St. John, St. Peter, and the Heavenly Host. These are all represented in the nude—even the Virgin Mary—and in poses with little reverence.

The figures seated with Jesus at the damask-covered table should be the twelve apostles, but only two could be specifically identified by the artist— St. Peter, on His right, in robes of rose and gray, who according to the painter is "carving the lamb in order to pass it to the other end of the table"; and St. John, on His left. When questioned about the other figures, Veronese was evasive and pled that he could not recall them as he had "painted the picture some months ago." Since but ten months had passed, a faulty memory was his convenient way of avoiding explanation of the portraits of Titian and Michelangelo seated at the table directly under the left and right arches, respectively.

The verdict required Veronese to make certain changes in the picture. Instead, he simply changed its title from the *Last Supper* to *Feast in the House of Levi*, a subject outside iconographical tradition. So

that there would be no future misunderstanding, he took the unusual step of painting the title on the stair railing at the left, while on the staircase railing at the right he cites chapter and verse—Luke 5:29–31. This passage reads in part: "And Levi made him a great feast in his own house: and there was a great company of publicans and of others that sat down with them. But their scribes and Pharisees murmured against his disciples, saying, why do ye eat and drink with publicans and sinners? And Jesus answering said unto them, They that are whole need not a physician; but they that are sick." Thus there was a place here even for the German halberdiers. The buffoon seated below the host, a dwarf with a bird on his wrist being teased by a young Negro, and the dog intently eyeing the cat under the table all remained in the picture. This altercation with the Inquisition is a landmark in art history. By defending his artistic code and seeing that his picture remained intact, Veronese raises a monument to the ascendancy of aesthetic and formal considerations over the traditional religious viewpoint. The picture also proclaims that laws of space, color, form, and composition are more important than subject-matter considerations.

In the *Feast in the House of Levi*, Veronese departs from the Renaissance pictorial tradition and reveals some traits of mannerism. His triple archway, possibly inspired by Sansovino's Loggietta at the base of the Campanile in St. Mark's Square (Fig. 336), automatically centers his composition with Christ as the central figure. But instead of drawing all the lines so that the focus is on the head of Christ, as Leonardo da Vinci had done in his famous *Last Supper* (Fig. 329), Veronese sets up several different converging points. The floor tiles run slightly to the oblique; the lines of the architectural background meet not at one but several points in the sky above; and the prominent diagonals of the stairs lead the eye not to Jesus but to the self-portrait of Veronese greeting the guests on the left and to the corresponding figure of the steward supervising the feast on the right. The cavalier treatment of the iconographic tradition, the strict academic control of pictorial structure, the liberties with linear perspective, the disregard for normal diminution in the size of figures in relation to their distance from the picture plane are distortions that make for manneristic restlessness rather than Renaissance repose. In his wall and ceiling paintings for various villas, and in the *Triumph of Venice* (Fig. 360) for the Doge's Palace, Veronese goes a step farther and produces surprising illusions by his bold foreshortening effects. Such manneristic devices, as well as the grandiose size of his pictures, were to become part of the baroque vocabulary.

360. PAOLO VERONESE. *Triumph of Venice. c.* 1585. Oil on canvas. Ceiling, Doge's Palace, Venice.

MUSIC

The frequent representation of musical subjects in painting is evidence of the importance of music in the life of Venice. Angelic choirs with complex orchestras were often represented in Venetian Renaissance paintings, and keyboard instruments were included in 16th-century canvases at the time when the organists of St. Mark's were among the most progressive composers on the European scene. Critics frequently have turned to musical analogies when discussing Venetian painting. When referring to the composition of a painting, one 17th-century writer used such terms as *orchestrale* and *concertare*; and a present-day historian still speaks of Giorgione's plastic *orchestration*. Significantly, Giorgione, Titian, Tintoretto, and Veronese actually played musical instruments, frequently employed small house orchestras to perform while they were painting, and took a lively interest in their city's musical life.

The high peak of Renaissance musical development was the polyphonic style of the Netherland composers. The general admiration for this art at the beginning of the 16th century was summed up by the Venetian ambassador to the court of Burgundy, who, in effect, said that three things were of the highest excellence: first, the finest, most exquisite linen of Holland; second, the tapestries of Brabant, most beautiful in design; and third, the music, which certainly could be said to be perfect. With such sentiments being expressed in official circles, it is not surprising to find that a Netherlander, Adrian Willaert, was appointed in the year 1527 to the highest musical position in Venice: that of choirmaster of St. Mark's.

Adoption of the northern musical ideal is but another instance of the cosmopolitanism of the Venetians; and under Willaert, a leading representative of the polyphonic art, and his successors, Venice became a center of musical progress, while Rome remained the bastion of tradition. The measure of its religious freedom also predisposed Venice to new developments, and a number of new musical forms and modifications of older ones were the results. In vocal music, this meant the development of the madrigal, the modification of the church motet, and the development of the polychoral style that made simultaneous use of two, three, and sometimes four choirs. Instrumental music found a new idiom in the organ *intonazione*, *ricercare*, and *toccata* for keyboard solo, and in the *sinfonia*, and early *concertato* and *concerto* forms for orchestra. Here the Venetian school spoke in a new voice and in tones of individual character. During the late 16th century, as it gradually lost favor, the old *ars perfecta* became known as the *stile antico* in contrast to the *stile moderno*, which was associated with Giovanni Gabrieli in Venice and his organ music, early orchestral writing, and the development of the polychoral style, with Vincenzo Galilei, Peri, and Caccini in Florence and their solo songs, and early opera experiments; with Frescobaldi in Rome and his virtuoso organ works; and with Claudio Monteverdi in Mantua and Venice, whose madrigals and operas became the cornerstone of baroque music.

The culmination of the musical development that Willaert began was reached in the work of Giovanni Gabrieli, who held the position of first organist at St. Mark's from the year 1585 until his death. His principal works were published under the title of *Symphoniae Sacrae* in 1597 and 1615. The domed Greek-cross plan of St. Mark's, with its choir lofts placed in the transept wings, seems to have suggested some unusual acoustical possibilities to composers. When a choir is concentrated in the more compact space at the end of a long nave, as in the traditional Latin-cross church, it is more unified. When placed in two or more widely separated groups, as at St. Mark's, the interplay of sound led to experiments that resulted in the so-called "polychoral style." In effect, it dissolved the unified choruses of the Netherland tradition and heralded a new development in the choral art. These *chori spezzati*—literally, broken choruses—as they were called, added the element of spatial contrast to Venetian music and new color effects were created. These included the echo nuance, so important in the entire baroque tradition; the alternation of two contrasting bodies of sound, such as chorus against chorus, a single choral line over a full choir, solo voice opposing full choir, instruments versus voices, and contrasting instrumental groups; the alternation of high and low voices; a soft dynamic level alternated with a loud one; the fragmentary versus the continuous; massive chords on one side with contrapuntal weaving together of many melodies on the other; and blocked chords contrasting with flowing counterpoint. The resultant principle of duality is the basis for the *concertato* or *concerting* style, both words being derived from *concertare*, meaning to compete with or to strive against. The word appears in the title of some works Giovanni published jointly with his uncle Andrea Gabrieli in 1587: *Concerti...per voci et stromenti* (Concertos...for voices and instruments). The term later came to be widely used, with such titles as *Concerti Ecclesiastici* appearing frequently.

Giovanni Gabrieli was one of the first to develop a distinction between a vocal and instrumental style of writing, and the precise instrumentation directions given in his later works clearly show that he was thinking in terms of the color of the various instruments at his command. His precision is in contrast to the custom of his predecessors to specify only the range of the instrumental parts and leave the choice of instrument up to the performer. When Gabrieli called for such combinations as violins, bass viols, cornetti (trumpets of wood), trombones, and bassoons, one can begin to speak of specific orchestration, and his work is one of the foundation stones of the modern orchestra.

The motet *In ecclesiis* (p. 316), written as the second part of the *Symphoniae Sacrae,* is an example of Gabrieli's mature style. It is a nonliturgical motet in the sense that it was not intended for use in the regular service, and in such an occasional piece, the composer was able to relax the strong though unwritten rules of tradition. An astonishing instance of the liturgical independence of Venice occurred just about the time Gabrieli wrote this motet some eight years before his death. Under the influence of the English ambassador Sir Henry Wotton, Venice adopted and for a time followed the Anglican ritual. The fury of Rome was heard by the Venetians in Pope Paul V's subsequent threat of excommunication. Though the specific occasion for which it was intended is unknown, Gabrieli's motet is of the processional type and as such appropriate music for ceremonies similar to that depicted in Bellini's picture (Fig. 331). And the choirs he deployed in groups, as well as a brass ensemble, are similar to Bellini's details (Figs. 361, 362). Since

361. GENTILE BELLINI. *Brass Ensemble,* detail of Fig. 331.

362. GENTILE BELLINI. *Choristers,* detail of Fig. 331.

Bellini's setting was in St. Mark's Square, all the Venetian love of civic pomp and splendor are in evidence, and Gabrieli's music was in every respect quite able to fulfill the similar demands of any such later outdoor ceremonial. His art was as typical of its time and place as that of his colleagues in the other arts—Titian, Veronese, Sansovino, and Palladio.

The text of *In ecclesiis,* with an English translation after each verse, is as follows:

In ecclesiis benedicite Domino,
Alleluia, alleluia, alleluia.

Praise the Lord in the congregation,
Alleluia, alleluia, alleluia.

In omni loco dominationis benedic, anima mea,
   Dominum.
Alleluia, alleluia, alleluia.

In every place of worship praise the Lord, O my soul.
Alleluia, alleluia, alleluia.

In Deo, salutari meo et gloria mea.
Deus auxilium meum et spes mea in Deo est.
Alleluia, alleluia, alleluia.

In God, who is my salvation and glory, my help, and
   my hope is in God.
Alleluia, alleluia, alleluia.

Deus, te invocamus, te adoramus,
Libera nos, salva nos, vivifica nos.
Alleluia, alleluia, alleluia.

O God, we invoke thee, we adore thee,
Deliver us, save us, enliven us.
Alleluia, alleluia, alleluia.

Deus, Deus, adjutor noster aeternam.
Alleluia, alleluia, alleluia.

O God, my God, our eternal judge.
Alleluia, alleluia, alleluia.

The structure of Gabrieli's motet is based on the recurring word *alleluia,* which functions as a refrain and acts as a divider between the verses. The alleluias also are set in the static triple meter suggesting a pause in the procession, while the stanzas have the more active beat of march time. The work opens with the sopranos of Chorus I singing the first verse with organ accompaniment. The first Alleluia refrain (measures 6–12) is taken by the sopranos of Chorus I, all of Chorus II, and the organ (the numbering of the bars follows the edition published by G. Schirmer, Inc., New York). The tenors of Chorus I then sing the second verse with organ accompaniment (measures 13–31), while the Alleluia following this verse is the same as at first. Now come the blazing chords of the instrumental Sinfonia (32–43) with their strange, almost barbaric dissonances. The third verse is sung in two-part

counterpoint by the altos and tenors of Chorus I supported now by the six-part instrumental group without organ. The Alleluia after this verse (93–99) is taken by the same two voices of Chorus I, with the full Chorus II and organ but without the brass ensemble. The fifth verse is for full double choir, instruments, and organ, making a total of 14 independent parts. The gradual build-up of volume can be heard in the sequence of sopranos and full chorus; tenors and full chorus; the instrumental Sinfonia first alone, then in combination with tenors and altos; and the instrumental color against the chorus with organ support. The cumulative climax is then brought about by the final grandiose union of all vocal and instrumental forces, ending in a solid cadence radiating with color and producing the huge sonority necessary to bring the mighty work to its close. The brassy magnificence of these massive sounds seems determined to fill the out-of-doors, just as they had filled the vast interior of St. Mark's.

Giovanni Gabrieli's music foreshadows the baroque by setting up such oppositions as chorus against chorus, solo and choir, voices versus instruments, strings alternating with wind ensembles; the interplay of harmonic and contrapuntal textures; diatonic and chromatic harmony; the polarities of soprano and bass lines, loud and soft dynamics; and the distinction of sacred and secular styles.

While Gabrieli's vast tonal murals became the precedent for the later "colossal baroque," it remained for his great successor Claudio Monteverdi to divine the inner spirit of the new style. With Monteverdi in music, as with Longhena in architecture, the transition to the baroque is complete. Appointed master of music of the Most Serene Republic in 1613 after serving as court composer at Mantua for 23 years, Monteverdi achieved a working synthesis of Renaissance counterpoint and all the experimental techniques of his own time. The new emotional orientation is stated in the Foreword to his *Eighth Book of Madrigals* (1638): "I have reflected that the principal passions or affections of our mind are three, namely, anger, moderation, and humility or supplication; so the best philosophers declare, and the very nature of our voice indicates this in having high, low, and middle registers. The art of music also points clearly to these three in its terms 'agitated,' 'soft,' and 'moderate' [*concitato, molle,* and *temperato*]." The collection has the significant subtitle, "Madrigals of War and Love," and Monteverdi says he intends to depict anger, warfare, entreaty, and death as well as the accents of brave men engaged in battle. According to Monteverdi, vocal music of this type should be "a simulation of the passions of the words." Descriptive melodies in this *representative*

In ecclesiis (processional motet)

GIOVANNI GABRIELI

Zefiro torna (Return, O Zephyr)

MONTEVERDI

l'on - - - - - - - - de

e da mon-ti da mon-ti e da val-li da val-li i -me e pro-fon- de style reflected the imagery of the poetic text. In Monteverdi's madrigal *Zefiro torna* (Return, O Zephyr), the word *l'onde* (waves) is expressed by a rippling melody while *da monti e da valli ime e profonde* (from mountains and valleys high and deep) is rendered by precipitously rising and falling lines.

A striking instance of Monteverdi's "agitated" style occurs in his short theater piece *The Combat of Tancred and Clorinda*, the text of which comes from the 12th canto of *Jerusalem Delivered* by the Italian baroque poet Torquato Tasso. In his Preface, Monteverdi requests the singers and instrumentalists to play their parts "in imitation of the passions of the words." The score includes a rhythmic figure representing the galloping of horses and a *tremolando* on the strings to simulate trembling or shuddering. At Mantua, Monteverdi had already written his *Orfeo* (1607), the first full-length and complete opera in music history. At Venice, where the first public opera house was established in 1637, he continued with a series of lyrical dramas of which only the last two survive: *Return of Ulysses* (1641) and the *Coronation of Poppea* (1642).

IDEAS: MANNERISM

Venetian architecture, painting, and music—with their recurring themes, attitudes, qualities, shapes, and ideas—transcend a merely local style.

All three are sufficiently representative not only to embrace a significant phase of mannerism but to mark the beginning of baroque art.

Venetian space is never in repose but is restless and teeming with action. Sansovino's and Palladio's buildings with their open loggias, recessed portals and windows, and pierced deep-cut masonry invite entrance; and inside, their capacious interiors allow for freedom of movement. Action is also felt in the lively contrasts of structural elements and decorative details, rectangularity juxtaposed with rotundity, and complete and broken intersecting pediments. Palladio's churches, with their open semicircular colonnades around the altar and windows in the apse, allow the eye to continue into deep space beyond. The reflection of façades in the rippling waters of the canals and the use of mirrored interior walls serve to activate the static masses of masonry and to increase the perception of light and space.

The compositional decentralization of Venetian painting is a similar manifestation in two dimensions. Dynamic space is felt in the winged balance of opposites on the picture plane, as in Titian's *Venus and the Organ Player;* the receding planes of a composition in depth that let the eye travel from fore- to middle- and background with points of interest in each succeeding plane, as in Giorgione's *Concert Champêtre* and *Tempest;* in the rising planes of a vertical organization, as in

363. GIORGIONE and TITIAN. *Concert. c.* 1510. Oil on canvas, 40 × 48″. Pitti Palace, Florence.

Titian's *Assumption;* in the giddy heights reached by Veronese in his *Triumph of Venice;* and in the wheellike rotary movement Tintoretto sets up in his *Bacchus and Ariadne* (Fig. 364). The diagonal accent is found both in the gentle movement from lower left to upper right in Titian's *Sacred and Profane Love* and in the slashing zigzag lines of Tintoretto's *Finding of St. Mark's Body.* Breaking up the unity of central perspective in the pictures of Tintoretto and Veronese produces a fragmentation that leads the eye simultaneously in several directions.

A similar expression is heard in music. In Gabrieli's "broken" choirs, parts of one group are contrasted with the full sound of a whole chorus, and the sequence of contrasting sonorities progressively builds up ever-larger volumes until the climax is reached in the union of them all. The tossing back and forth of contrasting or unequal sound masses in the concerting style, the alternation of loud and soft dynamic levels of opposing groups as well as in the Venetian echo nuance, and the polarization of high and low parts—all are devices to intensify the motional and emotional effects of music.

Each of the Venetian arts also shows an affinity for the reconciliation of opposites with the notion of heightening the sense of drama and involving the observer and listener on as many levels as possible. Especially is this evident in the case of textures— with architects contrasting smooth with rough or rusticated materials; painters contrasting clothed and nude figures or metal and glass objects against rustling silks and satins; and composers alternating voices and instruments, large and small ensembles.

The increased dimension in all the arts is also striking. Palladio's interiors are designed for large gatherings and to impress visitors by their spaciousness so necessary to the grand manner of living to which his clients aspired. His preference for central plans in such private dwellings as the Villa Rotonda and for church buildings as well is, as he says, because "none is more capacious than the round." The growth in the size of paintings by Titian, Veronese, and Tintoretto is a phenomenon in itself. The dimensions alone predispose them to the monumental. (The finished version of Tintoretto's colossal *Paradise* mural in the Doge's Palace has more than 500 figures and measures about 72 by 23 feet.) The grandeur of sound produced by the vast musical resources that Gabrieli marshaled for his polychoral motets also exceeded anything before their time. The Venetian ideal of the human figure is likewise large and ample. Womanhood, draped and undraped, approaches the monumentality of the spacious façades, the large canvases, and the huge sonorities of polychoruses. All point in the direction of the grandiose.

While mannerism had its inception in Florence early in the 16th century and subsequently flourished elsewhere, it was the Venetian adapta-

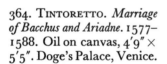

364. TINTORETTO. *Marriage of Bacchus and Ariadne.* 1577–1588. Oil on canvas, 4′9″ × 5′5″. Doge's Palace, Venice.

tion of the style that was most readily assimilated into the baroque.

Living in the shadow of such universal masters of the immediate past as Leonardo da Vinci, Michelangelo, and Raphael created a dilemma for the younger generation of painters. Quite aware that a golden age had preceded them, and that there was no possibility of improving on the craftsmanship of their illustrious forebears, these young artists found themselves at a crossroads. Following the old paths would mean selecting certain ideas and techniques of their predecessors and reducing them to workable formulas. Striking out in new directions would imply taking for granted such perfected technical achievements as linear and atmospheric perspective, mathematical principles of foreshortening, and correct rendering of anatomy and then deliberately breaking the rules with daring and telling effect.

The first course meant working "in the manner" of the giants of the past, and academies sprang up to transmit the traditional techniques to young artists. The second course led to bold dramatic departures from past precedents. It was this revolutionary aspect that partisans of the Renaissance saw as the dissolution of an ideal order and the adoption of an "affected manner" by highly individual artists. Either course eventually led in new directions, and some present-day historians separate the period from *c.* 1520 to 1600 from the dying Renaissance and the baroque that was aborning. To encompass and characterize much of the art of these years, they propose a period and style called *mannerism.* Since mannerism was born of crisis, it is a style facing in two different directions. The more conservative artists linked themselves with tradition and consequently can be classified as academic mannerists; the more liberal group can be termed free mannerists.

Academic Mannerism

When Vasari, the disciple of Michelangelo, used the term *de maniera,* he meant working in the manner of Leonardo, Michelangelo, and Raphael. By reducing their art to a system of rules, he could work fast and efficiently; and his boast was that before his time it took a Michelangelo six years to finish one work, while he had made it possible to do six works in one year. The experimental stage was over; the era of fulfillment was at hand. No more eccentric geniuses and soul-searching prophets, only competent craftsmen. Such was the course taken by Vasari, Palladio, and Veronese. Vasari, in Florence, was instrumental in founding an Academy of Design in 1561. Some 36 distinguished artists were selected as members, and while it was not a teaching organization in the modern sense, its members bore the title of professor and were expected to advise younger artists. At Bologna in 1585, the Caracci family established an institute with the significant word *academy* in its name, and there courses in the theory and practice of art were offered.

Such academic mannerist artists did not go to nature as Leonardo had done but studied masterpieces with the thought of assimilating systematically the vocabularies of the late Renaissance giants. Art, in other words, did not hold up a mirror to nature but rather to art. At the lowest level, this implied well-schooled craftsmen and a style based on stereotypes; an eclectic borrowing and reassembling without the birth pangs of the original creative synthesis. At its highest, this approach could lead to virtuosity of execution. In no way did it rule out inspiration—that intangible essence that could be caught but not taught.

With Palladio, academic mannerism came to terms with the classical orders of his ancient Roman mentor Vitruvius. By adapting Roman architectural forms to contemporary needs, he contained the Venetian love of lavishness and curbed the excesses of overdecoration. Veronese, by the symmetry of his designs, his closed forms, and the organizing function of his architectural backgrounds, was able to handle large crowds and bustling movement without impairing his pictorial unity. And while Gabrieli's music broke up the unity of the Renaissance choir—encompassing and increasing the scope of musical space—his adherence to the traditional Renaissance polyphonic methods kept his work under strict academic control.

Free Mannerism

Mannerism also includes the "mannered" art of highly individual artists who, in their revolt against Renaissance ideals, cultivated eccentricity and reveled in inner conflicts. This generation of painters could no longer be thrilled by the mathematics of linear perspective or by finding the proper relationship of figures to their surrounding space. Instead, they found excitement in breaking established rules with dash and daring and in violating Renaissance assumptions for the sheer shock effect. Under such capricious conditions, naturalism gave way to the free play of the imagination; classical composure yielded to nervous movement; clear definition of space became a jumble of picture plane crowded with contorted figures; symmetry and focus on the central figure were replaced by off-balance diagonals that made it difficult to

365. BENVENUTO CELLINI.
Saltcellar of Francis I. 1539–
1543. Gold, 10¼ × 13″.
Kunsthistorisches Museum,
Vienna.

find the protagonist of the drama amid the multiplicity of directional lines; backgrounds no longer contained the picture but were nebulous or nonexistent; the canon of body proportion was distorted by the unnatural elongation of figures; chiaroscuro served no more to model figures but to create optical illusions, violent contrasts, and theatrical lighting effects; and strong deep color and rich costumes faded to pastel hues and gauzy fluttering drapery. In short, the Renaissance dream of clarity and order became the mannerist nightmare of haunted space, and art was in danger of becoming artifice.

Some of these tendencies were already present in the late Renaissance. Giorgione's enigmatic pictures that broke with the iconographical tradition puzzled his contemporaries. In Leonardo's *Madonna and Child with St. Anne* (Fig. 305), the figures are uncomfortably superimposed on each other; how St. Anne supports the weight of the Madonna and what they are sitting on is left to the imagination. The unstable figures of Day and Night in Michelangelo's Medici tombs (Fig. 313) seem to be sliding down the sides of the sarcophagus, and the gaunt figures bear no relation to classical bodily forms. In the black terror and bleak despair of his *Last Judgment* (Fig. 366), clarity of space no longer exists—there are crowded parts and bare spaces; the size of figures is disproportionate; and one cannot even be sure who are the saved and the damned.

The exception in the late Renaissance, however, became the rule under mannerism, which quickly, albeit briefly, became an international style. Such Florentine mannerists as Rosso Fiorentino and Benvenuto Cellini were summoned to Paris to become court artists of Francis I, and Raphael's pupil Giulio Romano was the official architect of the Duke of Mantua. The languid figures and Michelangelesque postures of Cellini's gold saltcellar (Fig. 365) illustrate this aristocratic phase of international mannerism. In spite of their desire to dazzle and their capriciously contrived tricks, these men had no intention to deceive, since this art was addressed to the sophisticated few. Only those well aware of the rules could enjoy the witty turns and startling twists by which they were broken. This courtly phase of the mannerist style, however, was too much restricted to a single class and too refined and self-conscious in its aestheticism to endure long. In the more cosmopolitan, middle-class atmosphere of Venice, where the group patronage of the *scuole* broadened its base, mannerism gained vitality and virility. It was these aspects that were transmitted almost intact to the baroque.

ROADS TO THE BAROQUE

From Venice, as well as from Rome and the centers where international mannerism flourished, the roads to the baroque fanned out in all directions. The thriving printing industry assured currency for Venetian ideas in every civilized country. The writings of Palladio, as translated into English with commentary by Inigo Jones, led to the architecture of Christopher Wren and the Georgian styles and thence to the colonial and federal styles in America. The printing of musical scores assured Venetian composers of general prominence. Venetian diplomacy, by avoiding commitments to either extreme, paved the way for the acceptance of certain aspects of the Venetian style in both Reformation and Counter Reformation countries. Venetian innovations in architecture and painting were eagerly adopted in Church and court circles of Spain and France. Both the Church hierarchy and the aristocracy needed the impressive splendor of the arts to enhance their exalted positions. The more monumental the buildings, the more lavish the decorations, the more grandiose the musical entertainments, the better the arts served their purpose. Hence it was natural for both to seek out the richest expression of this ideal, which was to be found in Venice.

El Greco, after studying in Titian's workshop and absorbing Tintoretto's mannerism, found his way to Church and court circles in Spain, where his art left an indelible impression. Rubens spent eight years in Italy, much of the time making copies of Titian's pictures, then took the Venetian techniques with him to the Low Countries and France. Rubens and his pupil van Dyck, in turn, transmitted them to England, and eventually they reached America. In the Counter Reformation countries, church music remained more constant to the Roman tradition, but Venetian music was readily accepted in secular circles. However, for the Reformation centers—Holland, Scandinavia, and particularly northern Germany—the greater liturgical freedom of Venetian musical forms proved more adaptable to Protestant church purposes precisely because of their deviation from orthodox Roman models. Sweelinck, who studied in Venice with Andrea Gabrieli and Zarlino, carried the Venetian keyboard style to Amsterdam, where his great reputation brought him organ students from Germany who later taught the generation of Pachelbel and Buxtehude, both major influences on the style of Bach and Handel. Cavalli, Monteverdi's successor at the Venetian opera, was called to Paris to write the music for the wedding festivities of Louis XIV. Heinrich Schütz, the greatest German composer before Johann Sebastian Bach and George Frederick Handel and another force in determining their art, was a pupil of both Giovanni Gabrieli and Claudio Monteverdi. In sum, the Venetian style became a part of the basic vocabulary of the larger baroque language.

12 - THE COUNTER REFORMATION BAROQUE STYLE

ROME, LATE 16TH AND EARLY 17TH CENTURIES

The cataclysmic events that convulsed Rome and all Europe in the course of the 16th century awakened the Eternal City from its Renaissance dream of harmony and confronted it with the stark reality of contradiction and conflict. Subsequently, every aspect of life—religious, scientific, political, social, economic, and aesthetic—was destined to undergo reexamination and radical change. A succession of disturbing visitors proved to be harbingers of developments to come. Martin Luther had been in Rome at the turn of the century, and his observations had added fuel to the fire of his moral indignation. The reform movement he initiated, along with Zwingli and John Calvin, was to sever the unity of the Universal Church and divide Europe into Reformation and Counter Reformation camps.

The next visitor, the Holy Roman Emperor Charles V, was even less welcome. Previously, the voyages of the great navigators and the exploits of the conquistadors who followed in their wake had brought most of North, Central, and South America under the Spanish crown. With the monopoly of the spice trade of the Orient and with the gold and silver mines of the New World pouring fabulous riches into its treasury, Spain was rapidly becoming the most powerful country in the world. By a combination of heredity, marriage, and high finance, Charles I of Spain had become Charles V of the Holy Roman Empire. With the Low Countries, the Germanies, and Austria firmly in his grasp, the ambitious emperor turned his attention next to Italy, and, one by one, the formerly independent duchies and city-states came under his domination. Opposition from any quarter proved intolerable, and in 1527 His Catholic Majesty's mercenaries marched on Rome, sacking and plundering. Eight days later the great city was a smoking ruin, the Vatican a barracks, St. Peter's a stable, and Pope Clement VII a prisoner at Castel Sant' Angelo. Thereafter, the papacy had no choice but to acquiesce in Spanish policy; a Spanish viceroy ruled in Naples, and a Spanish government was installed in Milan. Through the Gonzagas in Mantua, the Estes in Ferrara, the Medici in Florence, the Spaniards controlled all important centers; and with Spanish rule came Spanish austerity and religiosity, etiquette and courtly elegance.

With the Holy Roman Emperor destroying the center of Christendom and threatening the life of the pope, with the Universal Church split asunder by

(above) GUARINO GUARINI. Dome interior, Santa Sidone, Turin. 1667–1690.

reformers, with once-proud independent states reduced to puppet regimes, with rampant inflation and speculation bringing sudden wealth to some and total ruin to others, with the shift of economic power from old centers to new ones depriving Italy of her primary position in commerce and banking, a sense of crisis prevailed throughout Europe.

Another visitor was the astronomer Copernicus, whose book on the *Revolution of the Planets in their Orbits* was destined to change the conception of the cosmos from an earth-centered to a sun-centered world. A shock reaction followed as baroque man began to realize he inhabited a minor planet whirling through space, and that he was no longer at the center of creation. Later, when his observations tended to prove the Copernican theory, Galileo was tried for heresy, sentenced to prison, and released only when he recanted. The cumulative effect of these and other scientific discoveries began to weaken the belief in miracles and divine intervention in human affairs.

Then came the theologians, during the sessions of the Council of Trent that undertook the reform of the Church from within. When the test came, bold humanistic thinking was transformed into violent reaction; Neo-Platonic philosophy was succeeded by a reversion to Aristotelian scholasticism; the distant but seductive voices of pagan antiquity were drowned out by the roar of rekindled medieval fire and brimstone; the reveling in sensuous beauty was followed by bitter self-reproach; promises of liberal religious attitudes were inundated by a return to strict orthodoxy; new access to literature and knowledge through the printing press and scientific discoveries was suppressed through the Universal Inquisition and of the *Index Expurgatorius;* God appeared not as the Loving Father but as a terrifying Judge, Christ not as the Good Shepherd but as the Great Avenger.

The founders of the new Counter Reformation religious orders, which were to shape the course of Roman Catholicism in the 17th century, were in Rome at various times. Philip Neri brought together laymen of all classes, from aristocrats to street urchins, in his Congregation of the Oratory for informal meetings and encouraged them to pray or preach as the spirit moved them. By dramatizing and setting to music familiar Biblical stories and parables (prototypes of the baroque oratorios), he generated a cheerful devotional spirit that stirred the hearts of the poor and humble. Ignatius Loyola came from Spain to obtain papal sanction for his Society of Jesus, a militant order dedicated to foreign missionary work, education, and active participation in worldly affairs. There were also the mystics Teresa of Avila and John of the Cross, whose abilities to combine the contemplative and active ways of life resulted in a significant literary expression of the period and in the reorganization and redirection of the Carmelite orders; and there was Carlo Borromeo, the young energetic archbishop of Milan, who wrote manuals for artists as well as for the students and teachers in the many seminaries he founded. At a single grand ceremony in the newly completed Basilica of St. Peter on the 22nd of May, 1622, Ignatius Loyola, Francis Xavier, Teresa of Avila, and Philip Neri were canonized and admitted to the honors of the altar. Thereupon, Giacomo Vignola, Giacomo della Porta, Carlo Maderno, Gianlorenzo Bernini, and Francesco Borromini were called upon to build churches and chapels dedicated to them.

In this floodtide of reform, the classical harmony, stability, and poise of Renaissance art were not hardy enough to survive, nor could the over-refined, overly dramatic art of mannerism adapt itself to the new religious climate. Gaiety gave way to sobriety, Venuses reverted to Virgins, Bacchuses and Apollos to bearded Christs. The organic form and unity of Michelangelo's Sistine ceiling was succeeded by the calculated shapelessness of his fearful *Last Judgment* (Fig. 366). Palestrina was conscience

366. MICHELANGELO. *Last Judgment*, detail (self-portrait on flayed skin in lower right). 1534–1541. Fresco, 48 × 44'. Sistine Chapel, Vatican, Rome.

General Events : Rome

1527	Charles V's mercenaries sacked Rome
	Protestant Reformation in progress under Luther in Germany, Zwingli and Calvin in Switzerland
	Reaction to Renaissance humanism began
1534	Counter Reformation began
1540	Society of Jesus (Jesuit order) founded by Ignatius Loyola
1542	Universal Inquisition established
1543	Copernicus' *De Revolutionibus Orbium Coelestorum* published
	Censorship of printed matter began
1545	Council of Trent (1545–1563) undertook reform within Church; reaffirmed dogma
1547	Michelangelo named architect of St. Peter's
1555	Volterra ordered to paint drapery on "offending" nudes in Michelangelo's *Last Judgment*
c.1562	Teresa of Avila and John of the Cross reformed Carmelite orders
1575	Congregation of the Oratory (founded by Philip Neri) approved
1616	Galileo enjoined by pope not to "teach or defend" researches confirming Copernican theory; called before Inquisition in 1633
1622	Canonization of Ignatius Loyola, Teresa of Avila, Philip Neri, Francis Xavier

General Events : Spain

1474– 1516	Ferdinand and Isabella reigned; West Indies discovered by Columbus (1492); South America (1498); expulsion of Moors and Jews from Spain
1516– 1556	Charles I, king of Spain; became Holy Roman Emperor Charles V in 1519
1556– 1598	Philip II, king of Spain; Spanish empire reached greatest extent
1561	Madrid chosen as capital
1563– 1584	Escorial Palace built
1583	Victoria published *Missarum libri duo*, book of masses dedicated to Philip II
1588	Spanish Armada sunk by English navy
1598– 1621	Philip III, king of Spain; decline of Spanish power
1600	Victoria published collection of masses, motets, psalms, hymns, dedicated to Philip III
1604	Cervantes' *Don Quixote*, Part I published in Madrid (Part II, 1615)
1621– 1665	Philip IV, king of Spain
1623	Velázquez appointed court painter
1648	Treaty of Westphalia; Spanish power in Europe checked

Architects and Sculptors

?	– 1567	Juan Bautista de Toledo
1507–	1573	Giacomo Vignola
1530–	1597	Juan de Herrera
1531–	1621	Juan Bautista Monegro
c.1540–	1604	Giacomo della Porta
1556–	1629	Carlo Maderno
c.1580–	1648	Gomez de Mora
1598–	1680	Gianlorenzo Bernini
1599–	1667	Francesco Borromini
1665–	1725	José de Churriguera
c.1683–	1742	Pedro de Ribera

Painters

1498–	1578	Giulio Clovio
c.1541–	1614	El Greco (Domenicos Theotocopoulos)
1573–	1610	Michelangelo Merisi da Caravaggio
1599–	1660	Diego Velázquez
1617–	1682	Bartolomé Murillo
1642–	1709	Fra Andrea Pozzo

Musicians

c.1500–	1553	Cristobal Morales
c.1500–	1566	Antonio de Cabezón
1524–	1594	Giovanni da Palestrina
c.1548–	1611	Tomás Luis de Victoria

Writers

1491–	1556	Ignatius Loyola
1515–	1582	Teresa of Avila
1538–	1584	Charles Borromeo
1542–	1591	John of the Cross
1547–	1616	Miguel de Cervantes
1562–	1635	Lope da Vega
1600–	1681	Pedro Calderón

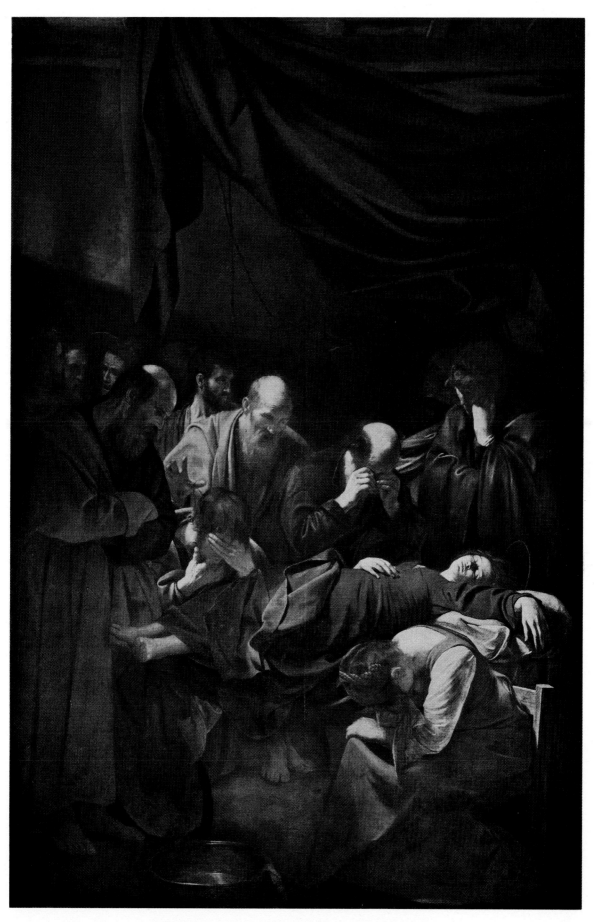

Plate 29. CARAVAGGIO. *Death of the Virgin. c.* 1605.
Oil on canvas, 12′1″ × 8′5″. Louvre, Paris. (See p. 329.)

Plate 30. GIANLORENZO BERNINI. *Baldacchino* and *Cathedra Petri*. St. Peter's, Vatican, Rome.
Baldacchino, 1624–1633; bronze (partly gilt), 93′ high. *Cathedra Petri*, 1657–1666;
marble, bronze (partly gilt), colored glass, and gilt stucco. (See p. 331.)

stricken for having written madrigals and henceforth wrote only masses. Under the rulings of the Council of Trent, Church art was firmly realigned with religion, and the clergy had to assume responsibility for the way artists rendered religious subjects.

The lives and attitudes of Counter Reformation artists were profoundly affected by the new religious climate. Michelangelo's *Last Judgment* was censured because his Apollo-type Christ was unbearded and because such pagan classical details as Charon, the sepulchral boatman, rowing souls across the river Styx had been included. Drapery was ordered to cover his "offending nudes," and only the timely intervention of a group of artists saved the *Last Judgment* from complete obliteration. The great man became a recluse in his last years, gave up figurative art for the abstractions of architecture, and devoted himself to the building of St. Peter's, a project for which he would accept no fee. In the privacy of his own studio, he worked intermittently at sculpture and brooded over his last *Pietàs*, one of them intended for his own tomb. Palestrina was banished from his post as leader of the Sistine Choir because he refused to take the priestly vow of celibacy and give up his wife. Later he was reinstated and entrusted with the reforms of Church music.

Gianlorenzo Bernini, busiest and most successful sculptor-architect of the Counter Reformation baroque, was closely associated with the Jesuits and regularly practiced St. Ignatius' *Spiritual Exercises*. Andrea Pozzo, who painted the illusionistic ceiling of the Church of Sant'Ignazio, was a member of the Jesuit order. El Greco, Spain's greatest representative of Counter Reformation art, was a religious mystic in whose last visionary canvases physical matter practically ceases to exist, his figures more spirit than flesh, his settings more heavenly than earthly.

As matters shaped up, the Counter Reformation baroque style had its inception in Rome where it reached its apogee in the 50-year period from *c.*1620 to 1670; its reverberations were felt simultaneously in Spain, the strong secular arm of the Church militant. Thereafter the impetus spread throughout the Roman Catholic countries of Europe and traveled with the missionary orders to the Americas and the far-flung colonies of Spain and Portugal.

ROMAN
COUNTER REFORMATION ART

Architecture

As the central monument of the Jesuit order, the Church of Il Gesù in Rome (Figs. 367–369) became the prototype for many Counter Reformation churches. Indeed, so many different versions and variants have since appeared that with justifi-

(left) 367. Giacomo Vignola and Giacomo della Porta. Façade, Il Gesù, Rome. *c.* 1575–1584. 105′ high, 115′ wide.

(below) 368. Il Gesù, plan.

369. ANDREA SACCHI and JAN MIEL. *Urban VIII Visiting Il Gesù.* 1639–1641. National Gallery, Rome.

cation it has been called the most influential church design of the past four centuries. Commissioned in 1564, Il Gesù combines classical motifs from the Renaissance heritage with some of the new elements that were to identify Counter Reformation architecture. The nucleus of the structure—the domed crossing of the nave and the short transepts (Fig. 368)—are derived from Michelangelo's and Palladio's centralized plans. But the short longitudinal nave reaching forward from the crossing repeats the compromise reached in St. Peter's when Bramante's and Michelangelo's plans were combined with the appendage of Carlo Maderno's long nave. Giacomo Vignola's façade design (Fig. 367), somewhat revised after his death by his successor Giacomo della Porta, recalls a Roman triumphal arch on the ground floor, but the lean-to roofing over the side chapels is masked with graceful scrolls that swirl upward toward the triangular templelike pediment.

The full force of the baroque power to mold space into astonishing new forms was not felt until the 17th century was well under way. By that time, Counter Reformation churches had become theaters where a concert of all the arts was played. Biblical stories were dramatized in miracle plays, painting of the barrel-vaulted naves and inner surfaces of domes produced the visionary illusions of

(above) 370. FRANCESCO BORROMINI. Façade, San Carlo alle Quattro Fontane, Rome. Begun 1635, façade 1667. Church 52 × 34'; façade 38' wide.

(below) 371. FRANCESCO BORROMINI. San Carlo alle Quattro Fontane, plan.

formed by two equilateral triangles joined at the base to make a diamond-shaped rhomboid, which was then softened with curved lines. Like a rippling stage curtain, the undulating walls rise upward toward an oval dome (Fig. 372), the inner surface of which is encrusted with coffering of octagons and elongated hexagons that join to produce Greek crosses in the intervening spaces. These shapes diminish in size toward the top to suggest greater height. Partially concealed openings allow light to filter in and give the honeycomblike pattern a gleaming brightness. The façade (Fig. 370), like that of Sant' Agnese in the Piazza Navona (Fig. 373), is set into swaying motion by the alternating concave and convex walls and the flow of curvilinear forms, which allow a maximum play of light and shade over the irregular surface.

souls wafting heavenward on wings of seraphic choirs, sculptured saints and angels floating aloft on marble or stucco clouds, and earthly choirs being echoed by unseen angelic voices of choristers concealed around the domes.

Borromini's San Carlo alle Quattro Fontane (Figs. 370–372) is one of the most ingenious expressions of the period. Turning to full advantage the small site at the intersection of two streets with a fountain at each of the four corners, the architect devised a plan that embraced a complex interplay of geometrical shapes. The plan (Fig. 371) is

(top) 372. FRANCESCO BORROMINI. Interior of dome, San Carlo alle Quattro Fontane, Rome. *c.* 1638.

(left) 373. FRANCESCO BORROMINI. Sant' Agnese, Piazza Navona, Rome. Begun 1652. Façade. *c.* 160' wide.

(above) 374. GIANLORENZO BERNINI. Fountain of Four Rivers, Piazza Navona, Rome. 1648–1651.

327

375. CARAVAGGIO. *Calling of St. Matthew. c.* 1597–1598. Oil on canvas, 11′1″ × 11′5″. Contarelli Chapel, San Luigi dei Francesi, Rome.

Painting and Sculpture

Of all the painters and sculptors active in late 16th-century Rome, two tower above all others—Caravaggio and Bernini. Taking his name from his native town, Caravaggio brought the northern Italian and Venetian tradition of free mannerism with him to Rome; while the sculptor-architect-designer-painter Bernini synthesized Renaissance, Michelangelesque, mannerist, and baroque elements and brought the baroque to its expressive climax in the Eternal City. Restless and rebellious, Caravaggio was always at odds with society and his patrons. Bernini, despite his passionate temperament, was nevertheless a suave courtier. "It is your good luck," Bernini was told by the newly elected Pope Urban VIII, "to see Maffeo Barberini pope; but we are even luckier that Cavaliere Bernini lives at the time of our pontificate." Both artists were destined to have far-reaching effects on future developments—Caravaggio with his bold chiaroscuro on later Italian and French baroque painters, as well as on Rubens and Rembrandt; Bernini with

his twisted columns and visionary illusionism on the course of baroque sculpture and architecture.

Caravaggio, who painted in Rome from *c.*1590 to 1606, scorned Renaissance decorum, dignity, and elegance and set out to depict religious subjects in a vivid, down-to-earth way. His *Calling of St. Matthew* (Fig. 375) shows the future Evangelist among a group at a public tavern. A significant darkness hovers over the table where tax money is being counted; and as Jesus enters, a shaft of light illuminates the bearded face of St. Matthew and the countenances of the young men in the center. As the light strikes each figure and object with varying degrees of intensity, it becomes the means by which Caravaggio penetrates the surface of events and reveals the inner spirit of the subjects he depicts. The *Calling of St. Matthew* was at first refused by the clergy of the church for which it had been painted, because it showed the saint in a too-worldly situation, even though the story is told by the Evangelist himself.

In the *Conversion of St. Paul* (Fig. 376), Caravaggio creates a blinding, lightninglike flash to highlight the saint's inner illumination. "And suddenly there shined round about him a light from heaven," reads the New Testament passage, "and he fell to earth, and heard a voice saying unto him, Saul, Saul, why persecutest thou me?" (Acts 9:4–5). As the observer beholds St. Paul's prone body from an extremely foreshortened angle, with arms flung out as if to embrace the new light that has dawned, he is caught up in the event and shares the wonderment and concern of the attendant and the huge horse.

The *Death of the Virgin* (Plate 29) departed radically from the usual way of depicting that subject in order to bring the meaning of the event more immediately and forcefully into the lives of the worshipers. Caravaggio's Madonna is no ethereal figure awaiting her assumption into heaven but, as one of his early biographers put it, "the swollen corpse of an ordinary dead woman." The apostles also are not transcendental beings but men of the people, earthy peasants in humble garb and with dirty feet. They betray a gamut of emotion from deep concern to tearful outbursts. Caravaggio goes

far beyond Renaissance chiaroscuro and tells his story with the dynamics of his dramatic lighting. Under the luxurious folds of the dark-red curtain the light descends diagonally along the row of bald heads, past the foreshortened body of the Virgin lying at an oblique angle to the picture plane, onto the shoulders of the sorrowing Mary Magdelene.

Caravaggio's efforts to create a truly popular religious art as seen through the eyes of the common man met with a mixed reception, and, paradoxically, it was only the sophisticated few who grasped its originality and significance. The *Death of the Virgin*, for instance, was originally painted as an altarpiece for a Roman church, but the fathers were shocked because the Madonna was bare-legged and "resembled a courtesan." The picture was taken down, sold to the Duke of Mantua on Rubens' recommendation, and later found its way into the collections of Charles I of England and Louis XIV. Both the Roman priests and public preferred more conventional elegance and illusionism, and it was the work of Pozzo and Bernini that this audience found more congenial to its taste.

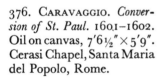

376. CARAVAGGIO. *Conversion of St. Paul.* 1601–1602. Oil on canvas, 7′6½″×5′9″. Cerasi Chapel, Santa Maria del Popolo, Rome.

377. Fra Andrea Pozzo. *St. Ignatius in Glory. c.* 1691. Fresco, nave ceiling. Sant' Ignazio, Rome.

(right) 378. FRA ANDREA POZZO. *America,* detail of Fig. 377.

(below) 379. *Cornaro Chapel, Santa Maria della Vittoria, Rome.* 18th-century painting. Museum, Schwerin, Germany.

Andrea Pozzo succeeded in capturing the new spirit in his extraordinary painting on the barrel-vaulted ceiling of the Church of Sant' Ignazio (Fig. 377), dedicated to the founder of the Jesuit order. Above the clearstory windows, the walls of the building seem to soar upward so that the vaulting of the nave becomes that of heaven itself. In a series of remarkable foreshortenings, St. Ignatius is borne aloft by a heavenly host, ascending in ever-winding spirals toward figures symbolizing the Trinity. Here all the lines converge and beams of light radiate outward to illuminate the four corners of the world—personified by allegorical representations of Europe, Asia, Africa, and America (Fig. 378)—where missionary work of the Society of Jesus was carried on. Pozzo was also the author of a definitive book on perspective, in which he advised artists "to draw all points thereof to that true point, the Glory of God."

In Gianlorenzo Bernini, the impetuous and versatile architect-sculptor-painter, the Roman Counter Reformation baroque found its most representative and prolific exponent. Designer of the piazza of St. Peter's (Fig. 324) that begins with the trapezoidal *piazza obliqua* in front of the façade and opens out into the mighty elliptical area enframed by massive four-fold Doric colonnades; sculptor of the gigantic bronze canopy over the high altar of St. Peter's (Fig. 327; Plate 30) whose four spiraling columns soar 100 feet upward toward Michelangelo's great dome; sculptor of many of the basilica's key chapels, notably the one in the apse with the Chair of St. Peter; designer of such monuments as the Fountain of Four Rivers in Piazza Navona (Fig. 374) in which allegorical river gods and rock and shell forms join with the lively movement of gushing springs to form a revolutionary design—Bernini, even more than Michelangelo, is responsible for lifting the face of modern Rome.

Of all his many works, the Cornaro Chapel (Fig. 379), dedicated to the *Mistica Dottora* St. Teresa, is most typical of this phase of the baroque. In the central sculptured group over the altar (Fig. 380), Bernini portrays the saint in a state of ecstasy, his source being one of Teresa's poems in which she graphically describes her mystical union with God:

When that sweet Huntsman from above
First wounded me and left me prone,
Into the very arms of Love
My stricken soul forthwith was thrown.
Since then my life's no more my own...
And all my lot so changed is
That my Beloved One is mine
And I at last am surely His.

The dart wherewith He wounded me
Was all embarbed round with love,
And thus my spirit came to be
One with its Maker, God above.
No love but this I need to prove:
My life to God surrender'd is
And my Beloved One is mine
And I at last am surely His.

St. Teresa, as revealed by the undulating folds of her deep-cut drapery, seems to be rising and falling in voluptuous rapture, and the angel (closely resembling Cupid with his dart) is about to pierce her heart. The polished white-marble group is framed by dark marble columns and set in a niche of varicolored marbles of brown, red, pink, green, and amber hues. Gleaming gilded-bronze rays descend from above, and the whole is lighted magically by a concealed window glazed with yellow glass. On either side are groups in relief portraying members of the Cornaro family, donors of the chapel, who are watching the miraculous proceedings as if from stage boxes at the theater.

The chapel begs the question—"Is it architecture, sculpture, painting, stage design? Is it sculpture in the round, in relief?" The answers in each case must be "yes"—but combined not separated, in fusion not isolation. The sculptured center group is surrounded by actual and simulated architecture; the painted sky above and the theatrical lighting effects are all part of a single conception in which the real and visionary elements are blended into one; in which metal, marble and pigments, forms, colors, and light are harmonized into a concert of the arts.

380. GIANLORENZO BERNINI. *St. Teresa in Ecstasy.* 1645–1652. Marble and gilt bronze, lifesize. Cornaro Chapel, Santa Maria della Vittoria, Rome.

SPANISH
COUNTER REFORMATION ART

The close alliance of Italy and Spain that had begun with the invasion of Charles V continued throughout the baroque period. Politically and economically the Spanish crown controlled all major Italian regions by viceroys and puppet regimes. Papal sanction of the Jesuit order made the influence of its militant missionaries worldwide and brought sainthood to two of its Spanish founding members, Ignatius Loyola and Francis Xavier. And the words of two great Spaniards, St. Teresa of Avila and San Juan de la Cruz (St. John of the Cross), perhaps most completely captured the Counter Reformation spirit in literature and became the most widely read in the Roman Catholic world.

The personal tastes of that morose monarch Philip II, who succeeded his father Charles V, were austere to the point of severity. His worldly position and ambitions, however, made it mandatory that he surround himself with the necessary magnificence to command awe and respect. To unify his kingdom, wrest local authority from his feudal lords, and vest himself with all the power of an absolute monarch, Philip selected as his capital the then-obscure but centrally located town of Madrid. Consequently, an enormous building program had to be undertaken in order to house the court and provide city palaces for the aristocracy.

With the riches of the Old World and the unlimited resources of the New at his command, Philip summoned the leading artists of Europe to help build and embellish his chosen capital, and his ambassadors were under instruction to buy any available masterpiece of painting and sculpture. While they remained in their native cities, Titian and other Italian artists continued to paint for Philip as they had for his father. But Domenicos Theotocopoulos, the Greek-born artist who had been trained in the Venetian mannerist style and had studied the work of Michelangelo and Raphael in Rome, settled in Spain, where he became known as the foreigner El Greco (the Greek). The Spanish composer Victoria, though he was fully established in Rome, dedicated a book of masses to Philip in the hope of receiving a court commission. Attracted by the glitter of Spanish gold, other artists from all parts of Europe, known and unknown, flocked to Madrid in search of fame and fortune. Thus, while Spain's power and prestige were to decline in the 17th century, the precedent set by Charles V and Philip II as patrons of the arts continued through the reigns of Philip III and Philip IV to round out a full century of brilliant artistic activity.

Architecture

Bound by the terms of his father's will to build Charles V a tomb, bound by his own solemn oath to found a monastery dedicated to the Spanish martyr St. Lawrence, on whose day he gained his great military victory over the French, and bound also by his intense religious fervor and his consciousness of his royal prerogatives, Philip II envisioned a vast architectural project that would coordinate these diverse objectives and resolve some of his own inner conflicts. As the plan matured in his mind, this monument was to be at once a temple to God, a mausoleum for his ancestors and descendants, a national archive of arts and letters, a dwelling place for the Hieronomite monks, a college and seminary, a place of pilgrimage with a hospice for the reception of strangers, a royal residence, and, in general, a symbol of the glory of the Spanish monarchy.

A site in the barren foothills of the Guadarrama Mountains about thirty miles from Madrid was chosen for the undertaking, which took its name from the near-by village of Escorial. The original plans were drawn up by Juan Bautista de Toledo, who had studied with Jacopo Sansovino and Palladio and worked on St. Peter's in Rome under the direction of Michelangelo. Subsequently, the work was completed by Juan Bautista's collaborator, Juan de Herrera.

According to Philip's instructions, the monument had to embody the ideals of "nobility without arrogance, majesty without ostentation." Both Philip and his father, as pillars of the Church and as international rulers, were conscious of the reincarnation of Roman power in their empire and kingdoms. The Roman classical style, as formulated by Palladio and others, seemed best to symbolize their international position and prestige. The simplicity and severity of the Escorial were therefore in keeping with Philip's personal taste; and the hard, unyielding, tawny yellow granite of which it was built exercised a still further restraining influence on the architects and decorators. As it stands, the Escorial is a vast quadrangle of almost 500,000 square feet, which is subdivided into a symmetrical system of courts and cloisters (Fig. 381). The form symbolically refers to the gridiron of St. Lawrence on which he met his martyrdom. The corner towers can be said to represent the legs of the iron grill, while the palace, which projects from the east end, forms its handle. Elsewhere in the building the grill is widely used as a decorative motif.

The Escorial strikes a note of gloomy grandeur and stark magnificence in keeping at once with the Spanish spirit as well as with the dour personality of Philip II. Each side (Fig. 382) presents a long expanse of wall, entirely devoid of decoration, its monotony broken only by the endless rows of seriate windows. The principal entrance, found on the west front (Fig. 383), is carried out in the strict Doric order with only the royal coat of arms and a colossal statue of St. Lawrence holding his gridiron to relieve the general austerity. The portal leads into the Patio of the Kings (Fig. 384), which takes its name from the statues of David, Solomon, and the other kings of Israel over the entrance to the imposing church located on the central axis. The plan of this church, as well as many of the interior and exterior details, was adapted from Michelangelo's original design for St. Peter's (Fig. 325). It is a centralized structure, following the form of a Greek cross and culminating in a dome that rises more than 300 feet above the floor. The main body is conceived in the strong and dignified Doric style, relieved by a series of chapels, numerous altars with

(above) 381. J. B. DE TOLEDO and JUAN DE HERRERA. Escorial Palace, near Madrid. 1563–1584. 675 × 685'. Towers 200' high, dome 312' high.

(right) 382. Escorial Palace (side view).

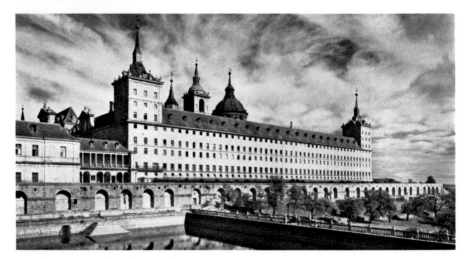

383. J.B. DE TOLEDO and JUAN DE HERRERA. Escorial Palace. Engraving after elevation by HERRERA.

painted altarpieces, and ornate organ lofts. Below the high altar is the burial crypt known as the Royal Chapel of the Pantheon, finished during the reign of Philip IV, in which the kings and queens of Spain repose in baroque coffins arranged in strict order of protocol.

Much of the Escorial's area is devoted to the monastery and seminary of the Order of St. Jerome. The heart of this section is the handsomely designed enclosed double-decked cloister known as the Court of the Evangelists (Fig. 385), which faces one wing of the church. The walk below is again in the Doric order with its simple frieze punctuated by the rhythmical triglyphs. Still more space for monastic meditations is provided by the Ionic gallery, which, in turn, is surmounted by a balustrade in the Palladian manner. In the center of the garth is a small structure of polychrome marble that functions as an echo of the great dome of the church which soars above it. Statues by Monegro of each of the four Evangelists look outward from their niches toward their respective pools, which are watered from spouts in the forms of the symbolic evangelical beasts.

In the palace section of the Escorial are the reception halls, the impressive galleries, and the state dining rooms that go with the grandeur of the proud Spanish monarchy. The only departure from the prevailing air of splendor is the monastic severity of Philip's own apartment. Elsewhere there are the quarters of the majordomos, the secretaries of state, the lords of the bedchamber, lodgings for ambassadors, and apartments for members of the royal family. To awe friends and warn foes, pictures of Spain's sea and land victories line the walls of the ambassadorial waiting rooms. Other halls are hung with rich Flemish tapestries depicting Biblical, mythological, and literary subjects. The picture galleries contain a vast number of the paintings that were purchased so liberally over the centuries by the Spanish kings. The Escorial still houses many of Philip's own collection of the Venetian masters he so much admired. Other Italian schools, as well as Flemish and native Spanish artists, are represented by outstanding examples. Of interest also is the library, a barrel-vaulted structure with its east and west windows arranged according to the maxims of Vitruvius. Drawings for its decoration with detailed notes of instruction to the artists show that Herrera kept a firm hand on every aspect of the design of his building

(above) 384. JUAN DE HERRERA. Patio of Kings, Escorial Palace. 1563–1584.

(below) 385. JUAN DE HERRERA. Court of Evangelists, Escorial Palace. 1563–1584. 210 × 207'.

386. JUAN DE HERRERA. Design for the Decoration of the Escorial Library. Drawing, 11³/₄ × 19″. British Museum, London.

(Fig. 386). Many rare medieval manuscripts and codices are housed in this library as well as the royal collection of medals, coins, and bronzes. Among its treasures are the manuscripts of the books of St. Teresa of Avila, that pillar of the Counter Reformation who was once Philip's guest at the Escorial. In Philip's time, works of the great Arabic and Jewish authors were placed in a special enclosure where they could have been seen but not read or touched.

So vast is the whole Escorial that it has been estimated one would have to walk ten miles to see every room. On it Philip lavished the energies of nearly forty years of his leisure, and it was his fondest wish to see it completed during his lifetime. Most of the work actually was done before his death, but the Pantheon and many details of the complex structure remained for his successors to carry to completion. The fact that the building was conceived and built mainly under one patron in less than half a century gives it a closer unity than such palaces as the Vatican and the Louvre, which evolved over many centuries and constantly were changing with the varying tastes and fortunes of their proprietors. For this reason too, the Escorial appears to be dominated by the restless melancholy spirit of its founder, which seems to have crystallized here into the rigidity and majesty of death. The Escorial nevertheless remains unique among the buildings of the world, combining as it does in a single structure the functions of a royal residence, military fortress, colossal church, national art gallery, state archives and library, monastery, theological college, pantheon of Spanish kings, and sepulchre of princes.

The Escorial, by reaching out to bring all the functions of an absolute monarch within a single structure, is baroque in the grandeur of its conception. However, the restraint of Philip's taste, as well as the discipline of his architects, kept decorative exuberance well within academic bounds. Exercising the prerogatives of an absolute monarch, Philip insisted on the right to pass on the suitability and style of every public building that was undertaken during his reign. Herrera, as the court architect, was commissioned to inspect all such plans and, as a consequence, became an artistic dictator who enforced the restricted preferences of his royal master on the nation. Not until after Philip's death was Spain free to develop the florid style that is now such a prominent feature of the face of its large cities. And some of the florid baroque's emotional exuberance and excesses came as a direct reaction to the formal severity of Philip's time. Daring designs, fantastic forms, curved lines, the spiral twist of corkscrew columns replaced the severe façades and classical orders enforced by Herrera.

Architectural developments at Salamanca and Madrid will dramatize the situation. The Casa de las Conchas, or House of the Shells (Fig. 387, right), is a Renaissance structure built in 1514, well before Philip's time. It nevertheless shows the tendency toward applied decoration that was popularly known as the *plateresque style*, a name derived from the Spanish word *platero* (silversmith). Across the street is the church of the Jesuit college of La Clérica (Fig. 387, left), which was begun after the period of Philip and Herrera. The lower part dates from the early 17th century and was designed by Juan Gomez de Mora. Even though it still adheres (below) 387. GOMEZ DE MORA. Façade, La Clérica (left). 1617. Casa de las Conchas (House of Shells, right). 1514. Salamanca.

(bottom) 388. JOSÉ DE CHURRIGUERA. Altarpiece, San Esteban, Salamanca. 1693.

nominally to the classical orders, the decorative urge is seen clearly in the attached Composite columns and in the baroque triglyphs above them, as well as in many of the other details. The towers and gable belong to the latter part of the 17th century and were executed by Churriguera, whose name is associated with the more florid aspects of Spanish baroque, the *Churrigueresque* style.

Churriguera's ornate altarpiece for the Church of San Esteban (Fig. 388) is an architectural-sculptural-pictorial extravaganza. More than ninety feet high, it combines the Composite order with gilded and garlanded twisted columns, set at various depths, that writhe upward in rhythmic profusion. Churriguera's followers, however, usually went far beyond their master, as seen in the former Hospicio de San Fernando, now the Municipal Museum of Madrid. The daringly imaginative portal (Fig. 389), like an open-air baroque altarpiece, develops fantastic forms with telling theatrical effect.

(right) 389. PEDRO DE RIBERA. Façade, Hospicio de San Fernando, Madrid. 1722.

(left) 390. EL GRECO. *Martyrdom of St. Maurice and Theban Legion.* 1581–1584. Oil on canvas, 14′6″ × 9′10″. Escorial Palace.

the worship of false idols is another matter. The line is thus clearly drawn, and a choice has to be made between duty to the state and duty to the Church, between the city of man and the city of God. For St. Maurice there is but one possible decision, and his hand points upward.

El Greco's spiral composition is well adapted to convey the tension between the material and spiritual realms, the natural and supernatural, the terrestrial and celestial. It can be sensed in the twitching muscles, flamelike fingers, taut faces, and swirling upward motion of the composition itself. In serpentine fashion, it winds around to the left middle ground where St. Maurice is seen again, this time giving comfort to the men as they await their turn for decapitation. The tempo is accelerated toward the background where the nude figures of the soldiers seem already to have parted company with corporeality and are drawn into the spiritual vortex that bears them aloft on a Dantesque whirlwind. The eye is led upward by the constantly increasing light and the transition of color from the darker hues below to the vaporous pink and white clouds above. There a visionary vista in the heavens is beheld, where some of the floating angelic figures hover and hold crowns for those who suffer and die below, while others produce the strains of celestial harmony.

In spite of the grimness of the subject, the light transparent-color palette El Greco uses gives the work an almost festive air, with the rose-colored banners, steel-blue and lemon-yellow costumes set against a background of silvery gray. The originality of the work, with its daring color dissonances and the lavish use of costly ultramarine blue, forfeited for El Greco the favor of King Philip, whose tastes ran to the more conservative Italian style. El Greco made only one other attempt to interest the royal patron: a study for a picture later called the *Dream of Philip II.* The commission for its execution on a large scale, however, was not forthcoming.

If the doors to the Escorial were closed, the gates to Toledo, see of the archbishop primate, always remained open to El Greco. His reputation there had been securely established by the series of paintings he had done for the Church of San Domingo el Antiguo. Most renowned of these was the *Assumption of the Virgin* (Fig. 391) for the high altar. El Greco's model was the picture Titian had painted on the same subject some sixty years earlier (Fig. 355). El Greco's version, however, reveals the baroque preference for open space, while Titian

Painting

While the Escorial was still abuilding, Philip II commissioned El Greco to paint an altarpiece for the Chapel of St. Maurice. The subject of El Greco's early masterpiece, the *Martyrdom of St. Maurice* (Fig. 390), is typical of the Counter Reformation in that it has to do with the dilemma of the individual who is caught between conflicting loyalties. St. Maurice, the figure in the right foreground, was the commander of the Theban Legion, a unit of Christians serving in the Roman imperial army. An order has just arrived commanding all members of the unit to acknowledge the orthodox Roman deities or be put to death. In the expressive gestures of their hands, St. Maurice and his staff officers reveal their positions. Christ, it is true, has sanctioned by his own example the rendering unto Caesar the material things that are Caesar's, but (left) 391. EL GRECO. *Assumption of the Virgin. c.* 1577. Oil on canvas, 13′2″ × 7′6″. Art Institute, Chicago.

peries as the soul of the count is borne heavenward on angelic wings to be received by the radiant figure of Christ. The row of mourners include portraits of the Toledo clergy and gentry, among them a self-portrait of the artist directly above the head of St. Stephen. A note of subtle humor is struck in the portrait of El Greco's eight-year-old son Jorge Manuel as the acolyte in the lower left. The boy points to the encircled white-and-gold rose embroidered on St. Stephen's vestment—the circle being the symbol of immortality, the rose of love. On his son's pocket handkerchief El Greco signs the painting in Greek: "Domenicos Theotocopoulos made it, 1578." But the date is not that of the picture; it is the year of his son's birth.

The driving out of the money changers from the temple is the only incident in the Gospels where Christ assumes an attitude of righteous anger and the only time when He resorted to physical action

contains all action within his picture. By dividing his composition into three planes, Titian starts a vertical ascending motion in the lower two but arrests it by the descending figure of God above. By combining the acute receding diagonal lines of the sarcophagus with the circular groupings of the apostles, El Greco in his *Assumption* forms a conelike base from which the Madonna soars aloft in a spiraling movement that leads the eye upward out of the picture into the open space above.

Also for Toledo, El Greco painted his masterpiece, the *Burial of Count Orgaz* (Plate 31), for his own parish church of San Tomé. The count, who rebuilt and endowed the church, was legendarily honored in 1323 by the miraculous appearance of SS. Stephen and Augustine, who gently lower him into his tomb just below the picture (Fig. 392). The vivid terrestrial and visionary celestial spheres are separated by the flickering torches and swirling dra-

392. EL GRECO. Chapel with *Burial of Count Orgaz.* 1586. San Tomé, Toledo, Spain. (Compare Plate 31.)

(right) 393. EL GRECO. *Expulsion from the Temple. c.* 1572–1574. Oil on canvas, 4′8″ × 4′11″. Minneapolis Institute of Arts (Dunwoody Fund).

(below) 394. EL GRECO. *Cardinal de Guevara. c.* 1596–1601. Oil on canvas, 67¼ × 42½″. Metropolitan Museum of Art, New York (bequest of Mrs. H.O. Havemeyer, 1929).

and corporeal punishment. Consequently, the subject had been rare in Christian iconography, but it was revived during the Counter Reformation when the Roman Catholic Church was undergoing just such a purgation. El Greco painted no less than six versions of it. In *Expulsion from the Temple* (Fig. 393) Christ appears in the role of the refining fire as prophesied by Isaiah, and His mood of fiery anger is reflected in El Greco's clashing colors of crimson red, pink, orange, and greenish yellow. While Christ's gesture bespeaks violence, His face is serene in the knowledge that what He does is for the good of those whom He chastises. The atmosphere recalls that of a Last Judgment with the figure of Christ separating the two groups. The side toward which His lash is directed is full of turbulence and confusion as the traders cringe under the accusing eye, yet try to save their wares. On the other side, all is calm as the disciples ponder the meaning of the event. A personal touch is contributed by the four heads in the lower right where El Greco acknowledges his artistic mentors Titian, Michelangelo, Giulio Clovio, and Raphael.

In his penetrating portrait of Cardinal Don Fernando Niño de Guevara (Fig. 394), El Greco has produced a personification of the spirit of the Counter Reformation. At the time it was painted, the cardinal was about to leave his post as archbishop of Toledo to assume the office of Grand Inquisitor at Seville, a position that gave him the

Plate 31. EL GRECO. *Burial of Count Orgaz*. 1586.
Oil on canvas, 16′ × 11′10″. San Tomé, Toledo. (See p. 339 and Fig. 392.)

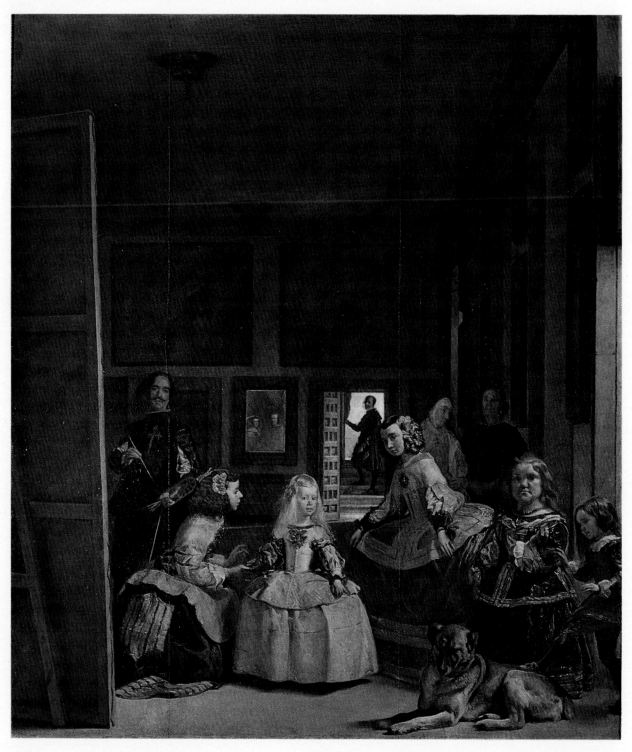

Plate 32. Diego Velázquez. *Las Meninas (Maids of Honor)*. 1656.
Oil on canvas, 10′5 ¼″ × 9′ ¾″. Prado, Madrid. (See p. 341.)

leadership of the dread Spanish Inquisition. His bearded face betrays an attitude of uncompromising righteousness. The piercing eyes, magnified by thick lenses, are those of a religious zealot combining fanaticism with pitiless logic. The tense pose of the body, with one hand relaxed and the other gripping the arm of the chair, is that of a prosecutor and the practitioner of a rigid spiritual discipline. The generally austere impression is relieved only by the obvious delight El Greco took in the brilliant carmine red and the contrasting white lace of the cardinal's robes, which are sumptuously painted.

To understand El Greco's vocabulary, his origin and education as well as the geographical and religious environment of his adopted Spain must be taken into account. His use of bright colors, for instance, undoubtedly had something to do with the dark Spanish churches for which his pictures were painted. The lengthening of the bodies as well as the hands and heads of his figures are related to the artist's Byzantine background and to the distortions of Italian mannerism. As an expressive device, his verticality and elongations produce the illusion of figures on a higher level, somewhat like statues seen from a kneeling position. But, more important, El Greco's figures are animated by inner fires and are caught up in spiritual whirlwinds as they behold mystical visions. El Greco was concerned with the translation of such miracles into convincing visual terms, reinforced by a heightened emotionalism and an exploration of mystical experience. Within this frame of reference naturalistic and logical explanations simply do not apply; but his inner world does not for this reason lack either coherence or consistency. When El Greco is accepted on his own terms, his world responds to its own laws, and its forms then become communicable patterns of the utmost expressivity.

Spain's other great baroque master, Diego Velázquez, had spent his early years in his native Seville painting casual genre pictures in the vein of the well-known *Water Carrier of Seville* (Fig. 395). Less than a decade after El Greco's death, the new monarch Philip IV appointed Velázquez his court painter. Velázquez' art, consequently, comes within the category of the aristocratic baroque, which is treated in the next chapter, but as a complete contrast to El Greco and as an equally great contribution to the high Spanish period, it is more appropriately discussed here.

While El Greco concerned himself almost exclusively with religious subjects, Velázquez, with few exceptions, painted scenes of courtly life. In contrast to El Greco's personal involvement in his pictorial content, Velázquez sees his world with cool detachment and an objective eye. His work is admirably summed up in his masterpiece *Las Meni-*

395. DIEGO VELÁZQUEZ. *Water Carrier of Seville.* c. 1619–1621. Oil on canvas, 41½ × 31½". Wellington Museum, London (Crown copyright reserved).

nas, or the *Maids of Honor* (Plate 32). With it, the painter combines the formality of a group portrait with the informality of a genre scene in his studio. Attention is about evenly distributed among the various groups. In the foreground, the Infanta Margarita dressed in a gown of white satin is standing in the center. On the left, a maid of honor is offering her a drink of water from a red cup on a gold tray. At the right is a group made up of a second maid of honor and two of the court dwarfs, one of whom is poking the sleepy mastiff with his foot. In the middle ground, on the left, is Velázquez himself wearing the cross of the Order of Santiago, which was conferred on him by his friend and patron, the king. He stands before a canvas which, by reason of its large dimensions, seems to be *Las Meninas* itself. He is looking at King Philip IV and Queen Mariana, whose faces are reflected in the mirror at the back of the room. As a balance for his own figure, Velázquez paints the conversing lady-in-waiting and courtier in the right middle ground. In the rear of the room, a court attendant stands in the open doorway pulling back a curtain, possibly to adjust the light for the painter.

Velázquez is a virtuoso in the handling of space and light. With the utmost precision, he has organized the picture into a series of receding planes, and by so doing, he gives the figures their spatial relationships. The first plane is in front of the picture itself where the king and queen and, by inference, the observer are standing. Next comes that in which the principal group stands in the light of the window at the right, which again is outside the picture but which provides the brilliant illumination that falls on the blonde hair of the princess. The light here is balanced by that from the door at the rear, which defines the plane in the background. In between is the intermediate plane with the figures of Velázquez and the attendants, who are shown in more subdued light. Otherwise the space is broken up geometrically into a pattern of rectangles, such as the floor, ceiling, the easel, the pictures hanging on the wall, the mirror, and the door at the back.

In such a precise analytical study of space and light, which lacks both the spiritual mysticism of El Greco and the worldly grandiosity of the Venetian painters, the baroque qualities are not immediately apparent. Velázquez, however, is a virtuoso of external rather than internal vision, and therefore his baroque qualities are found in such things as the intricate play of light and shadow, the complex spatial arrangements, the fact that much lies outside the picture space itself, and the subtle relationships of the subjects to each other. Proof of the latter is evidenced by the fact that Velázquez experts still cannot agree on what is actually going on. Is Velázquez painting the king and queen, and have the infanta and her ladies wandered in to look around? Or is Velázquez looking into a mirror as he paints the infanta, and have her parents dropped in to watch the proceedings?

Just as Spanish architecture showed a reaction when the restraints of the earlier period were lifted, Spanish painting moved away from the austerity and intensity of the previous century. No painter could sustain the spiritual insight and emotional power of El Greco. The relaxation into sentimentality is clearly seen in Murillo's *Immaculate Conception* (Fig. 396). The subject was one in particular favor with the Spanish church, and Murillo and his workshop are known to have turned out some twenty versions of it. According to Roman Catholic belief, Mary was conceived miraculously without original sin. Artistically she is represented as in St. John's vision: "And there appeared a great wonder in heaven; a woman clothed with the sun, and the moon under her feet, and upon her head a crown of twelve stars" (Rev. 12:1). In this instance she is borne aloft by cherubs holding the lily, olive branch, and palm leaf—symbols of purity, peace, and martyrdom.

396. BARTOLOMÉ MURILLO. *Immaculate Conception.* c. 1666–1670. Oil on canvas, 6′9″ × 4′8 ⅝″. Prado, Madrid.

Music

The Roman zeal for reform predisposed Church music to look more to the past than the future, to traditional rather than experimental forms. "The Antiphoners, Graduals, and Psalters have been filled to overflowing with barbarisms, obscurities, contrarieties, and superfluities as the result of clumsiness or negligence or even wickedness of the composers, scribes, and printers," read the papal brief authorizing Giovanni da Palestrina to undertake the reform of Church music along lines laid down by the Council of Trent. An ardent advocate of the Flemish contrapuntal style of Josquin des Prez and Heinrich Isaac, Palestrina, together with

Si   est do - lor   do   -   lor   si - mi - lis

his great contemporaries Orlando di Lasso and Tomás Luis de Victoria, brought that art to its final fruition. Palestrina's prayers in song achieved a fluidity and transparency of texture, a balance of melody and harmony, a spiritual and organic unity worthy of the closing years of the *ars perfecta*, or perfect art. The music of his younger colleague Victoria, however, has a darker mood, a brooding emotional fervor, and a deeper concern with the dramatic meaning of his texts. After serving thirty years as a chaplain, singer, and composer in the German College in Rome, an institution founded by his fellow Spaniard Ignatius Loyola, Victoria returned to his native country as choirmaster in court circles.

The music at the court of Philip II, like the architecture, painting, and sculpture, was religiously oriented, and the records of the period, as well as the design of the church at the Escorial, testify to the important place accorded the tonal art there. The choir at the Escorial was established even before the whole building was completed and in 1586 numbered in its ranks 150 monks. The choir section of the church is divided into two parts, since Philip's musical preferences were for the Venetian double-choral style he had heard in his youth. Besides the two organs in the choir, there are two others on either side of the nave, both large double-manual concert instruments of Flemish manufacture, 50 feet wide and 40 feet high. The same maker also built three portable organs for processions, which were placed in the galleries, thus making it possible on high feast days to hear seven organs pealing forth.

Since his patron's taste embraced both the traditional counterpoint and the new developments of the Venetian style, Victoria was able to bridge the gap between Renaissance polyphony and the baroque polychoral style. The book of masses he published in 1600 is in the massive Venetian polychoral style with an independent organ part. The vocal demands are of such complexity that it must be assumed these masses were composed for the skilled chorus of the Escorial. Certain idioms recur

often enough in Victoria's writing to give clues to his expressive purposes. Among these are the characteristic descent along the line of the minor triad and the use of the dissonant minor second to symbolize sorrow and pain. At times, he also breaks up the normal continuity of contrapuntal lines into a succession of short phrases to produce a sobbing effect.

Victoria's settings of the *Offices for Holy Week* have become an established tradition for performance in the Sistine Chapel. One of these is the four-part motet *O vos omnes*, the text of which comes from Jeremiah and the mood of which is one of lamentation. The passage above shows the characteristic grief motive in the descending tenor voice in measure 4, as well as the dissonance created by the dip of the minor second by the same voice in measure 5, both of which intensify the meaning of the word *dolor*, or sorrow.

Victoria never wrote a single note of secular music. As he stated in one of his dedications, he was led by some inner impulse to devote himself solely to church music. In his motets and masses, he even avoided the secular *cantus firmus* themes that were customarily employed by his contemporaries. Instead, he chose his motives and melodies from his own religious works or from the traditional plain song. In his later compositions after his return to Spain, his work took on an even greater fervor and passionate intensity. With its ascetic quality, religious ardor, and devotional spirit, his music rises in its way to the same heights of mystical grandeur as the writings of St. Teresa of Avila, the architecture of Herrera, and the pictures of El Greco.

IDEAS: MILITANT MYSTICISM

The Counter Reformation was accompanied by a vigorous reassertion of the mystical world view. In keeping with the spirit of the times, however, it was a practical mysticism of this world as well as the next, a realistic blending of the active as well as contemplative life, a religious experience not limited to future saints but broadened to include all those faithful to the Church as the mystical body of Christ. The new mysticism was socially oriented to enlist laymen as well as clergy, those active in wordly affairs as well as those behind convent walls. It was a rekindling of the fires of faith at a time when the foundations of faith were threatened by new scientific discoveries; a call to arms for all those willing to fight for their convictions in a war to the finish against doctrines the Roman Catholic Church considered heretical; a military mysticism of a Church militant on the march.

The enemy was made up of the various Protestant movements at home; the pagan religions of Africa, Asia, and the Americas abroad; the materialistic world view that went with growing nationalism and colonial expansion; and the forces of rampant rationalism unleashed by free scientific inquiry. The Counter Reformation was just as much a resurgence of spiritual and moral values in the face of growing scientific materialism as it was an anti-Protestant movement. The Church plainly saw that if the mechanistic image of the world as "matter in motion" were generally accepted, the belief in miracles would be undermined, the notion of divine intervention in worldly affairs would be destroyed, and the sense of mystery would be drained out of the cosmos.

The new psychology was not so much concerned with abstract theological speculation as with concrete religious experience through vivid imagery. The mysticism of St. Teresa and St. John of the Cross differed from medieval mysticism in its rational control and written documentation of each stage of the soul's ascent from the abyss of sin to the ecstasy of union with the divine. As expressed by St. John of the Cross:

> O happy night and blest!
> Secretly speeding, screen'd from mortal gaze,
> Unseeing, on I prest,
> Lit by no earthly rays,
> Nay, only by heart's inmost fire ablaze.

> When from the turret's height,
> Scattering his locks, the breezes play'd around,
> With touch serene and light
> He dealt me love's sweet wound,
> And with the joyful pain thereof I swoon'd.

The most typical expression of the Church militant, however, was the Society of Jesus, founded by that soldier and man of action St. Ignatius Loyola. His Jesuits helped adapt Church doctrine to modern conditions, faced the moral and political realities of the century, and took an active part in education,

public affairs, as well as missionary work. Under the director general, a Jesuit enlisted as a "warrior of God under the banner of the Cross" and stood ready to go for the "propagation of the faith to the Turks or other infidels even in India or to heretics, schismatics or some of the faithful." The whole world, for missionary purposes, was divided into Jesuit provinces, and the priestly army of occupation followed in the wake of the navigators and conquistadors.

The spiritual side of the Jesuit military organization is reflected in St. Ignatius' *Spiritual Exercises*, a precise, disciplined exploration of the mysteries of faith through the medium of the senses. As part of the Jesuit system of education, St. Ignatius worked out a four-week series of meditations leading to a purgation and purification of the soul. All faculties are brought into play so that the experience becomes a vividly personal one. Sin is the subject of the first week, and its consequences are felt through each of the senses in turn. In the "Torment of Sight," the student visualizes the terrible words engraved on the gates of Hell—*Ever, Never*—and sees the flames spring up around him. In the "Torment of Sound," he listens to the groans of millions of the damned, the howls of demons, the crackle of flames that devour the victims. With the "Torment of Smell," he is reminded that the bodies of the doomed retain in Hell the corruption of the grave. Their "stink shall come up out of their carcases," prophesied Isaiah (Isa. 34:3). For the "Torment of Taste," the condemned shall suffer hunger like dogs; "they shall eat every man the flesh of his own arm" (Isa. 9:20), and their wine shall be the "poison of dragons, and the cruel venom of asps" (Deut. 32:33). And in the "Torment of Touch," the damned will be enveloped in flames that boil the blood in the veins and the marrow in the bones but do not consume the victim. Both flames and flesh are forever renewed so that pain is eternal. In the final phases, the progress leads up to the suffering, resurrection, and ascension of Christ, and it closes with the contemplation of heavenly bliss. By proclaiming that man could influence his own spiritual destiny, Jesuit optimism held a ready appeal for men of action.

Such a strong accent on sense experience as the means to excite religious feeling was bound to have repercussions in the arts. Through architectural, sculptural, pictorial, literary, and musical illusions, miracles and transcendental ideas could be made to seem real to the senses, and the mystical world view could be reasserted through aesthetic imagery. The increasing complexity of life, the proliferation of new knowledge, the deepening of psychological insights—all shaped the course of baroque art. As religious, social, and economic pres-

397. Mexico City Cathedral. 1656–1791.

sures mounted, people were increasingly inclined to resolve their insecurities by turning to the cults of visionary saints or to the power of the absolute state. Artists were enthusiastically enlisted to enhance the power and glory of both Church and state. Counter Reformation churches were spacious, light, and cheerful; and visual artists, dramatists, and composers joined forces to make them like theaters where a concert of the arts played a prelude in an optimistic tonality to the delights of future heavenly bliss. In Counter Reformation churches, the arts, which had remained independent media in the Renaissance, became fused into one grand ensemble to make the religious experience as complete as possible. Artists had, of course, to conform to the requirements of Church dogma; otherwise their imagination could soar without hindrance.

Renaissance clarity of definition and the compartmentalization of space into clearly perceived patterns gave way to an intricate baroque geometry that took fluidity of movement into account. Neat Renaissance lines, circles, triangles, and rectangles became the intertwining spirals, parabolas, ovals, elongated lozenges, rhomboids, and irregular polygons of the baroque. With Borromini, horizontal and vertical surfaces were set into waves of rippling rhythms; balance and symmetry yielded to restless, unsettled movement; walls were molded sculpturally; surfaces treated with a rich play of color, light, and shadow. Pictures escaped from their ver-

tical walls and settled upon spherical triangular pendentives and spandrels, concave and convex moldings, and the inner surfaces of ceilings, vaults, and domes. With Pozzo's paintings, solid walls, vaulted ceilings, and domes dissolved into nebulous, illusionistic vistas of the great beyond. With Bernini, marble saints and angels floated freely in space. With El Greco, corporeal being almost ceased to exist, and his figures are more spirit than flesh, his landscape backgrounds more heavenly than earthly. St. Teresa recorded and published her ecstatic visions in sparkling Spanish prose and poetry so that a wide public could experience them vicariously. Palestrina and Victoria illuminated the hymns of the liturgical year with the clarity of their counterpoint, and their moving melodies made them glow with new mystical meaning.

By adopting the baroque style as their own and helping shape the artistic vocabulary of the time, the Jesuits not only brought baroque art down from the exclusive aristocratic level but carried the new idioms with them wherever they went, thus broadening the baroque into an international style. Counter Reformation baroque churches are found as far afield as Mexico (Fig. 397), South America, and the Philippines. The extraordinary vigor of the Church militant thus succeeded in tapping new spiritual sources and invigorating Roman Catholicism to such an extent that it emerged once more as a popular religious movement.

I3 · THE ARISTOCRATIC BAROQUE STYLE

FRANCE IN THE TIME OF LOUIS XIV

Everything about Louis XIV suggested grandeur. His concept of kingship assured him of the designation of *le grand roi*; his code of etiquette created the grand manner; he was in every sense the *grand seigneur*; a splendid avenue in Paris is named *Rue Louis le Grand*; and his reign gave his century the name of *le grand siècle*. At the time his portrait (Fig. 398) was painted by Hyacinthe Rigaud in 1701, Louis had been king in name for well over half a century and a king in fact for a full forty of those years. Dressed in his ermine-lined coronation robes, with the collar of the Grand Master of the Order of the Holy Ghost draped about his regal neck, Louis XIV might actually be uttering the very words for which he was so famous: *L'état c'est moi*—I am the state. Since he was in fact the personification of France, his portrait, appropriately enough, was that of an institution; and his figure was as much a pillar holding up the state as is the column that supports the building in the background. Pompous though the portrait is, it was part and parcel of the illusionism of a period that strove to make such transcendental abstractions as the divine right of kings seem real to the senses.

Absolute monarchy, accompanied by the cult of majesty, did not lack a rational basis. Louis' favorite image was provided, possibly, by the astronomer Copernicus, who proclaimed in his famous treatise that "the sun, as if sitting on a royal throne, governs the family of stars which move around it." Louis was indeed the center of a solar system that included among its satellites innumerable ministers and mistresses as well as a somewhat more select company of poets and artists. Descartes, in like vein, built his philosophy on the premise that the universe was an orderly system, whose parts were derived from the whole and where all the forces emanated from a single center. The philosopher believed that the things he clearly and distinctly perceived were true, and in this connection often cited the image of sunlight. Political theorists hastened to point out that, since the sun was the center of the solar system and the source of light, the king was the logical center of the state, the apex of the social pyramid, the head of the civil service, the army, the police, and so on. In this frame of reference, Louis' exalted place in the scheme of things was not quite so arbitrary as it appears today, and it would certainly have been impossible even in his own time had it not enjoyed the support of the most

(above) Sun King Medallion. 1674.

346

astute French politicians of the century, Henry IV, the Cardinal prime ministers Richelieu and Mazarin, and the finance minister of Louis' own reign, Jean Baptiste Colbert.

The success of this system of centralization is seen in the list of positive accomplishments of a reign in which the feudal power of the provincial nobles was broken; the Church became a part of the state instead of the state a part of the Church; Paris became the intellectual and artistic capital of the world; and France attained the dominant position among European nations. For the arts, the alliance with absolutism meant that they were of value as instruments of propaganda, factors in the assertion of national power and prestige and the means of enhancing the glory of the court, impressing visiting dignitaries, and stimulating export trade. All this led, of course, toward the concept of art as an adjunct to the cult of majesty and as the perpetuator of the myth. With the king as principal patron, art inevitably became a department of the government, and Louis was surrounded with a system of cultural satellites each of whom was supreme in his own field. The foundation of the Academy of Language and Literature in 1635, the Royal Academy of Painting and Sculpture in 1648, and the others which followed later, made it possible for Boileau to dominate the field of letters, Lebrun that of the visual arts, and Lully the art of music. Absolutism in this sense meant standardization, since no artist could receive a commission or even employment except through official channels. Louis, however, was quite aware of what he was doing, and in an address to the Academy he once remarked: "Gentlemen, I entrust to you the most precious thing on earth, my fame." Knowing this, he defended his writers and artists, supported them generously, and above all exercised that most noble attribute any patron can possess—good taste.

The outward and visible sign of this absolutism was to be seen in the dramatization of the personal and social life of this *roi du soleil*, or Sun King. The adoption of the sun as his symbol was natural enough, and such motifs as the sunburst were widely used in the decor of his palaces. As patron of the arts, Louis could identify himself freely with Apollo, the sun god, who was also the Olympian protector of the muses. In the morning, when it was time for the Sun King to rise and shine, the *lever du roi* was as dazzling in its way as a second sunrise. This special dawn was accompanied by a cloud of attendants who flocked into the royal bedchamber precisely at 8 A.M. in order to hand the king the various parts of his royal apparel. A similarly colorful ceremony accompanied the *coucher du roi*, when the Sun King in a golden glow of candlelight finally set at 10 P.M. Louis' life was one continuous pageant

in which each hour had its appropriate activity, costume, cast, and audience. Less frequent events, such as a christening, a wedding, or a coronation, had their special ceremonies. Even the royal births called for an audience so as to assure the country of the legitimacy of any future sovereign. In the present day of prosaic cabinet officers and drab parliamentary bodies, it is difficult to imagine the overwhelming effect of the formal pomp and circumstance surrounding an absolute monarch's court. If his peers and subjects beheld a sufficiently majestic spectacle or grandiose procession, a ruler apparently could get by with anything.

Throughout a reign of 72 years, Louis XIV played the leading role in this incessant court drama with all the effortless technique and consummate self-assurance of an accomplished actor. His play was a success from the opening night, his press notices invariably extravagant, and the ambition of every aristocrat in the world was to get into the act if possible—or at the very least to receive a bid to the performance. Such a great actor needed, of course, a great audience; and such a dramatic spectacle demanded an appropriate stage setting. Architects therefore were called upon to plan the endless series

398. Hyacinthe Rigaud. *Louis XIV*. 1701. Oil on canvas, 9′1½″ × 6′2⅝″. Louvre, Paris.

General Events

1598–	1610	Henry IV, king of France
1610–	1643	Louis XIII, king of France with his mother Maria de' Medici (1573–1642) as regent during his minority
1615–	1624	Luxembourg Palace built for queen mother by Salomon de Brosse
1618–	1648	Thirty Years' War. Spain and Austria defeated, France became dominant European nation
	1621	Rubens commissioned to paint murals in Luxembourg Palace
1624–	1642	Cardinal Richelieu (1585–1642), prime minister
	1635	French Academy of Language and Literature established
	1636	Mersenne's *Traité de l'Harmonie Universelle (Treatise on Universal Harmony)* published
	1640	Poussin returned from Rome to decorate the Louvre Palace
1643–	1661	Cardinal Mazarin (1602–1661), prime minister
1643–	1715	Louis XIV, king of France; ruled without prime minister from 1661
	1648	Royal Academy of Painting and Sculpture founded
1661–	1688	Versailles Palace built by Louis Le Vau and J. Hardouin-Mansart; chapel added 1699–1708
1665–	1683	Colbert (1619–1683), minister of finance
	1665	Bernini came to Paris to rebuild the Louvre Palace
		French Academy in Rome established
	1666	Academy of Sciences established
1667–	1674	East façade of the Louvre Palace built by Perrault
	1669	Royal Academy of Music (Paris Opera) established under Lully
	1671	Academy of Architecture established
	1674	*Alceste*, lyrical tragedy by Quinault and Lully, performed at Versailles
		Boileau's *L'Art Poétique (Art of Poetry)* published
	1683	Government and ministries of France installed at Versailles

Architects

1552–	1626	Salomon de Brosse
1598–	1680	Gianlorenzo Bernini
1612–	1670	Louis Le Vau
1613–	1688	Claude Perrault
1613–	1700	André Le Nôtre
1646–	1708	J. Hardouin-Mansart

Painters

1577–	1640	Peter Paul Rubens
1594–	1665	Nicolas Poussin
1600–	1682	Claude Gelée Lorrain
1619–	1690	Charles Lebrun
1659–	1743	Hyacinthe Rigaud

Writers and Philosophers

1596–	1650	René Descartes
1606–	1684	Pierre Corneille
1621–	1695	Jean de La Fontaine
1622–	1673	Molière (J. B. Poquelin)
1623–	1662	Blaise Pascal
1635–	1688	Philippe Quinault
1636–	1711	Nicolas Boileau
1639–	1699	Jean Racine

Sculptors

1598–	1680	Gianlorenzo Bernini
1622–	1694	Pierre Puget
1628–	1715	François Girardon
1640–	1720	Antoine Coysevox

Musicians

1602–	1676	Francesco Cavalli, Venetian opera composer
c.1602–	1672	Jacques de Chambonnières, organist and clavecinist
1632–	1687	Jean-Baptiste Lully
1668–	1733	Couperin le Grand, clavecinist
1683–	1764	Jean-Philippe Rameau

399. GIANLORENZO BERNINI. First drawing for Louvre, east front. 1664.

400. GIANLORENZO BERNINI. Second drawing for Louvre, east front. 1665.

of communicating salons as impressive backdrops for the triumphal entries; landscape designers to fashion the grand avenues for the open-air processions; painters to decorate the ceilings with pink clouds and classical deities so that the monarch could descend the long flights of stairs as if from the Olympian skies; and musicians to sound the ruffles and flourishes that accompanied the grand entrances. It was therefore no accident that the Louvre and Versailles palaces resembled vast theaters, that the paintings and tapestries of Lebrun seemed like curtains and backdrops, that Bernini's, Puget's, and Coysevox' sculptural adornments took on the aspect of stage props, that the most important literary expression should be the tragedies of Racine and the comedies of Molière, and that the characteristic musical forms should be Lully's court ballets and operas.

ARCHITECTURE

In 1665, at the insistence of his minister Colbert, Louis XIV requested the pope to permit his principal architect Gianlorenzo Bernini to come to Paris to supervise the rebuilding of the Louvre Palace. When he arrived on French soil, Bernini was received with all the honor due him as the ranking artist of his day. The design he made for the Louvre was radical in many ways. It would have necessitated the replacement of the existing parts of the building by a grandiose baroque city palace of the Italian type (Figs. 399, 400). Colbert conceded that Bernini's palace with its ballrooms and monumental staircases was truly grand in style, but it actually left the king housed no better than before. After a round of festivities, Bernini returned allows for the rich play of light and shadow that was so much a part of the baroque ideal. The frieze of garlands adds a florid touch, while the central pediment as well as the classical orders of the columns and pilasters act as a restraining influence. Only in the scuptural details (see Fig. 402) is a livelier note struck in this architectonic composition, but even here the animation of the figures is tempered by a dignified formality.

Even before Bernini came to Paris and long before the Louvre was completed, Louis XIV had conceived the idea of a royal residence outside Paris where he could escape from the restrictions of the city, take nature into partnership, and design a new way of life. Colbert, who felt that a king's place was in his capital, advised against it, and Louis allowed the Louvre to be completed as a concession to Paris. But his real capital was destined to be Versailles. This project was sufficiently awe-inspiring to serve as a symbol of the supremacy of the young absolute monarch as he asserted his power over rival nations, the landed aristocracy of his own country, the parliament, the provincial governments, the town councils, and the middle-class merchants. Away from Paris there would be a minimum of distraction and a maximum of concentration on his own person. In a wooded site almost half the size of Paris, which belonged entirely to the crown, everything could be planned from the beginning, nothing need be left to chance, and an entirely new manner of living could be organized.

The grand axis of the Versailles Palace starts with the *Avenue de Paris* (Figs. 403, top center; 405, top right), bisects the palace building itself, and runs along the grand canal toward the horizon where it trails off into infinity (Fig. 404). As the avenue enters the palace grounds (Fig. 404), the barracks for the honor guard, coach houses, stables, kennels, and orangeries are found on either side. The latter building caused an ambassador from a foreign country to remark that Louis XIV must

to Rome; his plan was scrapped; and a French architect, Claude Perrault, was appointed to finish the job. This little episode proved to be a turning point in cultural history. It marked the weakening of Italian artistic influence in France, and it also indicated that Louis XIV had certain plans of his own.

Perrault's façade (Fig. 401) incorporated some parts of Bernini's project, such as the flat roof concealed behind a Palladian balustrade and the long straight front with the wings extending laterally instead of projecting forward to enclose a court in the traditional French manner. Perrault's own contributions can be seen in the solid ground floor, which is relieved only by the seriate windows. This story functions as a platform for the classically proportioned Corinthian colonnade, with its rhythmic row of paired columns marching majestically across the broad expanse of the façade. The space between the colonnade and the wall of the building

403. Versailles Palace, view toward Paris. Engraving by PERELLE. Bibliothèque Nationale, Paris.

(left) 404. Versailles Palace, view toward gardens. Engraving by PERELLE. Bibliothèque Nationale, Paris.

(below) 405. Versailles Palace (aerial view). 1661–1688. Palace 1,935′ wide.

indeed be the most magnificent of beings since he had a palace for his orange trees more beautiful than the residences of other monarchs. The wide avenue narrows progressively with the parade grounds toward the marble court of honor (Fig. 422) above which is found the heart of the plan —the state bedroom of Louis XIV (Fig. 407). The whole grand design is so logical, so symmetrical, that it becomes a study in absolute space composition and makes Versailles an all-embracing universal structure which encompasses a vast segment of external as well as internal space. No one building or any part of it is a law unto itself, and together they are inconceivable without their natural environment. The gardens, parks, avenues, and radiating pathways are just as much an integral part of the whole as the halls, salons, and communicating corridors of the palace itself.

As Louis XIV's power expanded, the palace grew like a living organism capable of adapting itself to changing conditions. With the victories over Spain and Franche-Comté, the palace sprouted

(top) 406. LOUIS LE VAU and JULES HARDOUIN-MAN-SART. Garden façade, Versailles Palace. 1669–1685.

(left) 407. Louis XIV's state bedchamber, Versailles Palace.

(above) 408. Queen's bedchamber, Versailles Palace.

new wings as if to symbolize the triumphs. For well over a quarter of a century, the place hummed with the activities of architects, sculptors, painters, decorators, woodcarvers, masons, and carpenters. It has been estimated that altogether more than 30,000 men, including practically all the trained artists and craftsmen in the country, were employed at one time or another in the various building activities. Finally, in 1683, the palace was proclaimed Louis' official residence, and all the ministries of France were installed in the new wing designed for them. Versailles thus became a royal residence, the court with all its attendant social activities, and the administrative center of the French government. The roofed area of the palace covered 17 acres and housed a population of around 10,000 people, including the royal family, the lords and ladies of the court, the priests and clergy, and the military guard of honor, plus the armies of servants, gardeners, and grooms.

Jules Hardouin-Mansart was the architect of the two wings that extend the main building to a width of over a quarter of a mile. His design is noteworthy for the horizontal accent attained by the uniform level of the roof line, broken only by the roof of the chapel, which was added in the early 18th century. The simplicity and elegance of these long, straight lines, in contrast to the irregular profile of a medieval building, proclaim the new feeling for space. From every room vistas of the garden are a part of the interior design and tell of a new awareness of nature. A detail of the garden façade

(Fig. 406) reveals how freely Mansart treated the classical orders, and how the levels become increasingly ornate from the podiumlike base below to the attic and balustrade with the silhouetted statuary above. As a whole the building is a commanding example of baroque exuberance tempered by Palladian restraint.

Some of the interior rooms have been preserved or restored in the style of Louis XIV. All the heavy ornateness of the period can be seen in Louis' state bedroom (Fig. 407). Above the bed is a gilded stucco relief depicting France between two figures representing Fame. Elsewhere tapestries, paintings, carved wood, and mirrors cover every available inch of space. On the mantelpiece is a marble bust of the Duchess of Burgundy by Coysevox. Since comfort was considered a purely private matter, it seems to have been given hardly a thought. In the queen's apartments (Fig. 408) and the Salon de la Guerre (Plate 33), the baroque interior style is seen again in the heavily decorated ceilings, the painted murals with caryatids supporting fanciful scroll frames, the large Gobelin tapestries on the walls, the sculptured details, the furnishings of carved wood, bronze, polychrome marble, and rich fabrics.

The grandest room of the palace, however, was the famous Hall of Mirrors (Fig. 409) stretching across the main axis of the building and looking out toward the spacious gardens. Designed by Mansart and decorated by Lebrun, it was the scene of the most important state ceremonies and a kind of apotheosis of the absolute monarchy. Corinthian

409. JULES HARDOUIN-MANSART and CHARLES LEBRUN. Hall of Mirrors, Versailles Palace. Begun 1676. 240' long, 34' wide, 43' high.

410. ANDRÉ LE NÔTRE.
Gardens of Versailles, plan.
1662–1688.

pilasters of green marble support the ornate vault that is covered with paintings by Lebrun and inscriptions by Boileau and Racine—all to the greater glorification of the Sun King. The room was originally decorated sumptuously with brocaded damask curtains, chairs of enameled silver, orange trees reposing in silver urns, mirrors framed with chased copper, and chandeliers of crystal and gold. Clear geometrical divisions prevented the elaborate details from getting out of hand yet allowed full scope for the general magnificent effect of the composition.

The gardens, which were laid out by André Le Nôtre (Fig. 410), are not just a frame for the buildings but are incorporated into the whole spatial design. Their formality and geometrical organization symbolized the dominance of man over nature, but with the idea of embracing nature rather than keeping it at arm's length. The square pools across the garden side, so liberally populated with goldfish and swans, reflected the contours of the building like an external echo of the mirrored halls within. The statues of river gods and nymphs, which are found at the angles, were executed from sketches by Lebrun and personify the rivers and streams of France. The gardens and park form a logical system of terraces, broad avenues, and path-

ways radiating outward from clearings. They are liberally embellished by fountains, pools, canals, pavilions, and grottos, all of which are richly decorated with statuary. More than 1,200 fountains were installed by skilled engineers of waterworks, and with their jets spouting water into the air in many different patterns, they were marvels of their craft. Each had its name, and each was adorned with an appropriate sculptural group.

The great fetes that took place at Versailles served the purpose of distracting the unemployed nobility and compensating them for the loss of their power. Since royal favors were obtainable only at court and since the entertainment there was on such a lavish scale, the proud nobles were inevitably drawn into Louis' orbit, thus relinquishing their local privileges in exchange for an opportunity to participate in the festivities. This shift of the aristocrats from their country castles to the ultraurbane surroundings of Versailles sometimes necessitated a hasty and hectic education in the social graces for many of the courtiers. Lessons in courtly deportment, dancing, and the elegant use of language were obligatory in a place where one of the worst disasters that could befall a man was to make a *faux pas*, literally a false step, in the minuet. It might even necessitate his withdrawal from courtly life for an indefinite period. The gardens, parks, and canals provided endless opportunities for strolling, picnicking, lovemaking, hunting, fireworks displays, boating, and water pageants. The various salons in the palace provided the setting for card games, gambling, masquerade balls, theatrical entertainments, concerts, ballets, and opera performances.

Versailles Palace, therefore, was not so much a monument to the vanity of Louis XIV as it was a symbol of the absolute monarchy and the outstanding example of aristocratic baroque architecture. It represented a movement away from a feudal decentralized government toward a modern centralized state. As a vast advertising project it was a highly influential factor in the international diplomacy of the time. By urbanizing the country aristocracy and promoting court activities, Versailles built up for the arts a larger and more discriminating audience. It assured the shift of the artistic center of gravity from Italy to France. The court also functioned as a center of style and dress and, as a school for the training of skilled craftsmen, it virtually assured the status of France as a continuous center of elegant workmanship and fashion to this day. By combining all the activities of a court in a single structure, Versailles pointed the way toward the concept of architecture as a means of creating a new pattern of life. At Versailles a large housing development the size of a town was constructed so as to encompass rather than escape from nature. Details of Le Nôtre's garden plan, such as the radiating pathways, were the acknowledged basis for the laying out of new sections of Paris; and the city plan of Washington, D. C., for instance, was a direct descendant of the parks of Versailles. Modern city planners and housing developers have hailed Versailles as the prototype of the contemporary ideal of placing large residential units in close contact with nature. Finally, by starting with a grand design, Versailles pointed the way to the planning of whole cities from the start without the vicissitudes of haphazard growth and change. In this light, Versailles is seen as one of the earliest examples of modern urbanism and city planning on a large scale.

SCULPTURE

While Gianlorenzo Bernini was working on the Loúvre plans, he was besieged by requests from would-be patrons to design everything from fountains for their gardens to tombs for their ancestors. The king as usual came first in such matters, and Bernini received a commission from Louis XIV for a portrait bust (Fig. 411). This minor by-product

411. GIANLORENZO BERNINI. *Louis XIV*. 1665. Marble, 33¹/₈″ high. Versailles Palace.

of the artist's Paris sojourn ultimately turned out to be far more successful than his major mission. The recorded conversations of the artist and the accounts of his contemporaries make this portrait one of the most amply documented works in art history.

Dispensing with the usual formal sittings, Bernini made rapid pencil sketches while Louis was playing tennis or presiding at cabinet meetings, so that he could observe his subject in action. He was convinced that movement was the medium that best defined the personality and brought out the unique characteristics of his subjects, and the informal sketches were made, as he said, "to steep myself in, and imbue myself with, the King's features." After he had captured the individuality he was to portray, his next step was to decide on the general ideas—nobility, majesty, and the optimistic pride of youth. Here all the accessories, such as the costume, drapery, position of the head, and so on, would play their part. After the preliminaries were over and the particular as well as the general aspects were settled, the king sat thirteen times, while Bernini, working directly on the marble now, made the finishing touches.

Bernini's expressed intention was to paint in marble, but the problem was always that of transferring the impression of color to the white material. He said that if a man's hair and face were completely whitened, "even those who see him daily would have difficulty in recognizing him." His solution was to use shadow for the features, even if this meant altering them somewhat, and to make strong contrasts in textures, such as those of the soft hair, starched lace collar, metallic armor, and silken drapery. To liven the static medium, Bernini thought "the best moment to choose is when the model is about to speak, and I have tried to catch that moment." It will be seen that the lips are slightly parted as if about to give a command. The eyes were of great importance to Bernini, who at the sittings marked in the irises with black chalk. Only after many changes was he ready to use the chisel, and the proper look of determination was thus achieved. The complex folds of the deep-cut drapery were done with great care to appear as if blown by the wind and so bring a spontaneous movement into the otherwise static form.

Like most other works of the period, the bust has its allegorical allusions. Bernini noted in his conversations the resemblance of Louis XIV to Alexander the Great, whose countenance he knew from ancient coins. Courtly flattery was partially responsible, of course; but according to the conventions of the time, if the king were to appear as a military hero, it would be as a Roman emperor on horseback; or, if he were to be the *roi soleil*, it would be in the guise of Apollo. Since Bernini's intention here was to convey grandeur and majesty, Alexander, as the personification of kingly character, was the logical choice.

After his return to Rome, Bernini did one more sculptural work for Versailles—an equestrian statue of Louis XIV in marble. It was so fiery and turbulent and met with so much disfavor that the king ordered its removal to a remote part of the garden where the features were altered and it was renamed for the ancient Roman hero Martius Curtius. Bernini's original conception, however, has been preserved in his clay model (Fig. 412).

In addition to such portraits, Bernini's fame as a sculptor rested more broadly on religious statues, such as his *St. Teresa in Ecstasy* (Fig. 380), on the many fountains he designed for Rome (Fig. 374), and on mythological groups such as his *Apollo and Daphne* (Fig. 413), to embellish aristocratic residences. This youthful work is full of motion and tense excitement. According to the myth, Apollo, as the patron of the muses, was in pursuit of ideal beauty, symbolized here by the nymph Daphne. The sculptor chose to make permanent the pregnant moment from which the previous and forthcoming action may be inferred. As Daphne flees from Apollo's ardent embrace, she

412. GIANLORENZO BERNINI. *Model for Equestrian Statue of Louis XIV.* 1670. Terracotta, 30″ high. Borghese Gallery, Rome.

413. GIANLORENZO BERNINI. *Apollo and Daphne.* 1622–1625. Marble, lifesize. Borghese Gallery, Rome.

Plate 33. JULES HARDOUIN-MANSART and CHARLES LEBRUN. Salon de la Guerre, Versailles Palace. Begun 1678. Relief of Louis XIV on horseback by ANTOINE COYSEVOX. (See p. 353.)

Plate 34. PETER PAUL RUBENS. *Disembarkation of Maria de' Medici at Marseilles.* 1622–1625.
Oil on canvas, 13′ × 9′8″. Louvre, Paris. (See p. 358.)

These replicas were then sent back and placed on
pedestals along the various walks at Versailles.
Other sculptors, like Girardon, made variants of
Bernini's fountains and incorporated the movement of the water into their designs as he had done.
Most of the statuary at Versailles, however, is
effective mainly as part of the general setting, and
only a few works have survived the test of time to
emerge as individual masterpieces. Notable among
these sculptures were such works of Puget as his
Milo of Crotona (Fig. 414). This statue shows the
ancient Olympic wrestling champion who had
challenged Apollo himself to a match being
accorded the inevitable punishment meted out to
any mortal who competes with an immortal god.
Coysevox, who lived and worked at Versailles,
likewise was influenced by Bernini. Such examples
as his oval relief in the Hall of War (Plate 33) and
his numerous portrait busts helped establish the
tradition of French academic sculpture.

PAINTING

Patronage of the arts on a lavish and international scale had been a royal prerogative ever since
Francis I's time, and the procession of distinguished
figures to the French court, which in the 16th century had included Benvenuto Cellini and Leonardo
da Vinci, had continued. Foremost among the new-
comers was that great cosmopolitan Fleming,
Peter Paul Rubens (Fig. 415). Though loyal to
Flanders and Antwerp where he maintained his
studio, Rubens had studied the works of Titian and
Tintoretto in Venice as well as those of Michel-

cries aloud to the gods, who hear her plea and
change her into a laurel tree. Though root-bound
and with bark already enclosing her limbs, she
seems to be in quivering motion. The diagonal line
from Apollo's hand to Daphne's leafy fingers leads
the eye upward and outward. The complex surfaces are handled so as to give maximum play to
light and shadow. The sculptor has carefully delineated the various textures, such as the smooth
flesh, flowing drapery, floating hair, the bark,
leaves, and branches, in keeping with his objective
of painting in marble. But above all Bernini has
realized his express intention, which was to achieve
emotion and movement at all costs and to make
marble seem to float in space.

The Versailles gardens provided French sculptors with an inexhaustible outlet for their wares.
Many went to Italy to copy such admired antiques
as the *Laocoön Group* (Fig. 75), the *"Farnese" Hercules*
(Fig. 62), and *Marsyas and the Slave* (Figs. 69, 70).

angelo and Raphael in Rome. Never lacking aristocratic favor, he passed long periods in Spain and, particularly, in Italy at Mantua. During Louis XIII's reign, when the Luxembourg Palace was being completed for the Queen Mother Maria de' Medici, her expressed desire was for a painter who could decorate the walls of its Festival Gallery in a manner matching the Italian baroque style of its architecture. Maria's career as Henry IV's queen and as Louis XIII's regent was as lacking in luster as her own mediocre endowments could possibly have made it. Nevertheless, as the direct descendant of Lorenzo the Magnificent, she seemed to sense that the posthumous reputations of princes often depended more on their choice of poets and painters than on their skill in statecraft. The famous Flemish artist was brought to her attention by her sister, the Duchess of Mantua, at whose court Rubens had spent eight of his youthful years. Since then he had achieved a formidable reputation for his accomplishments as a courtier and diplomat as well as for his pictures, which were eagerly sought after by popes, kings, and cardinals.

Rubens' cycle of 21 large canvases gave the needed imaginary apotheosis to Maria's unimaginative life, and the success of this visual biography belonged more truly to the man who painted it than to the lady who lived it. The remarkable thing was how Rubens could exercise so much individual freedom within the confines of courtly officialdom and succeed so well in pleasing both himself and his royal mistress. In his grandiose conception, the ancient gods had deserted the rarified regions of Mt. Olympus and taken up their abode in the vastly more exhilarating atmosphere of Paris. Even before Maria's birth, Juno and Jupiter had cajoled the Three Fates into spinning a brilliant web of destiny for her. The governess who taught her to read was none other than Minerva, while her music teacher was Apollo himself. Her mythical eloquence came from the lips of Mercury, and every possible feminine fascination was imparted to her by the Three Graces. When this paragon of brilliance and virtue reached the apex of her grace and beauty, the Capitoline Triad themselves presided over the scene of *Henry IV Receiving the Portrait of Maria de' Medici* (Fig. 416). Minerva, as goddess of peace and war, whispers words of wisdom into the king's ear, while a whimsical touch is provided by the cupids who playfully try to lift the heavy helmet and shield of the king's armor. The celestial scene above assures everyone concerned that marriages are indeed made in heaven, where Jupiter with his eagle and Juno with her peacocks are seen bestowing their Olympian blessing.

When the royal marriage was solemnized at Florence in 1600, the accompanying festivities included the performance of Peri's *Euridice*, the earliest extant opera. This great event, however, was much too incidental for inclusion in such a cosmic conception, and the observer is next privileged to witness the *Disembarkation of Maria de' Medici at Marseilles* (Plate 34). As she steps ashore, a personification of France makes a low bow of welcome, while figures representing Fame sound the triumphal trumpets to announce the arrival. The denizens of the deep are overjoyed at the safe conclusion of the voyage, and Neptune himself issues the command to moor the galley, while tritons and sea nymphs disport themselves in the rippling rhythms of the water and playfully tug at the ropes. From the accentuated lighting and undulating movement, it is obvious that the painter was most concerned with this part of his picture. Authorities have also established that the voluptuous water nymphs were done by Rubens' own hand. All his love of the robust female form is present in these opulent figures. He was painting large surfaces—in this instance the mural is 13 by almost 10 feet—and his concept of space demanded feminine forms capable of filling both the canvas and the eye.

The demand for Rubens' work was such that he employed sometimes as many as 200 apprentices and assistants. This series for the Luxembourg Palace was executed in his studio in Antwerp beginning in 1622. As was his custom in such a project, Rubens sketched out the composition of each picture, then delegated the preparatory work to one assistant, an architectural background to another, landscape and animal figures to other specialists, and for himself reserved certain choice parts. When the pictures were installed in 1625, Rubens was on hand to put in the finishing touches, while Queen Maria watched him at work and, from reports, took pleasure in his conversation.

The baroque ideal of richness and lavishness is seen once again in a picture from Rubens' later years, the *Garden of Love* (Fig. 417). The actual setting for this allegory was the garden of his palatial home at Antwerp, and the ornate doorway in the background still exists. The bacchanalian theme unfolds in a diagonal line beginning with the chubby cherub in the lower left. Rubens himself is seen urging his second wife Helena Fourment, who appeared in so many of his later pictures, to join the others in the garden of love. The rest of the picture unfolds in a series of spirals mounting upward toward the figure of Venus who, as a part of the fountain, presides over the festivities. The use of large areas of strong primary colors—reds, blues, yellows—enlivens the scene and enhances the pictorial structure.

Rubens succeeded in combining the rich color of Titian and the dramatic tension of Tintoretto

(left) 416. PETER PAUL RUBENS.
*Henry IV Receiving the Portrait of
Maria de' Medici.* 1622–1625. Oil
on canvas, 13′ × 9′8″. Louvre,
Paris. (See also Plate 34.)

(below) 417. PETER PAUL RUBENS.
Garden of Love. c. 1632–1634. Oil
on canvas, 6′6″ × 9′3½″. Prado,
Madrid.

418. Peter Paul Rubens. *Rape of Daughters of Leucippus. c.* 1618. Oil on canvas, 7′3″ × 6′10″. Alte Pinakothek, Munich.

with an unbounded energy and physical exuberance of his own. His conceptions have something of the heroic sweep of Michelangelo, though they lack the latter's introspection and restraint. His complex organization of space and freedom of movement recall El Greco, but his figures are as round and robust as the latter's were tall and emaciated. His success in religious pictures, hunting scenes, and landscapes, as well as the mythological paintings that suited his temperament so well, shows the enormous sweep of his pictorial powers. For sheer imaginative invention and bravura with a brush he has rarely, if ever, been equaled.

While Rubens was executing his murals for the Festival Hall, an obscure French painter named Nicolas Poussin, who had been working on minor decorations, left the Luxembourg Palace for the less confining atmosphere of Rome. There he soon built a solid reputation that came to the attention of Cardinal Richelieu, who bought many of Poussin's paintings and became determined to bring the artist back to Paris. In 1640, Poussin did return to decorate the grand gallery of the Louvre —and receive from Louis XIII a shower of favors and the coveted title of First Painter to the King. The inevitable courtly intrigues that followed such marked attention made Poussin so miserable that

after two years he returned to Rome. There he acted as the artistic ambassador of France and supervised the French painters sent under government subsidies to study and copy Italian masterpieces for the decoration of the Louvre. And there, for the rest of his life, Poussin had the freedom to pursue his classical studies, the independence to work out his own principles and ideals, and the time to paint pictures ranging from mythological and religious subjects to historical canvases and architectural landscapes.

Two paintings depicting the same story, that of the rape of the Sabine women (Figs. 418, 419) provide a lively comparison of the temperamental differences between Rubens and his younger French contemporary. The subject alludes to the legendary foundation of Rome according to the historians Livy and Plutarch. Romulus, having been unsuccessful in negotiating marriages for his warriors, has arranged a religious celebration with games and festivities as a stratagem to bring families from the neighboring town of Sabina to the Roman Forum. For Rubens, the affair is one of robust personal passion with Romulus and Remus who, as Aldous Huxley puts it, "fairly dived into the sea of female flesh that splashed and wildly undulated around them." The more studious Poussin, in his efforts to

(above) 419. NICOLAS POUSSIN. *Rape of Sabine Women.*
c. 1636–1637. Oil on canvas, 5′1″ × 6′10½″. Metropolitan Museum of Art, New York (Dick Fund, 1946).

re-create the classical past, turned to Roman
museums for models of many of his figures, and to
Vitruvius for his architectural setting. From his
position of prominence on the portico of the temple
at the left, Romulus is giving the prearranged
signal of unfolding his mantle, whereupon every
Roman seizes a Sabine girl and makes off with her.
Though the subject is one of passion and violence,
Poussin manages to temper his picture by a judicious juxtaposition of opposites. The anger of the
outraged victims contrasts with the impassive calm
of Romulus and his attendants. As a ruler, Romulus
knows that the future of his city rests on the foundation of families, and that in this case the end justifies
the means. The turbulent human action is counter-
balanced also by the ordered repose of the architectural and landscape background. The smooth
marblelike flesh of the women contrasts with the
bulging musculature beneath the bronzed skins of
the Romans, and the contours of the figures generally are clearly defined as if they had been chiseled
out of stone. Poussin's constant preoccupation with
antique sculpture is readily seen when the group

in the right foreground is compared with the Hellenistic *Gaul and His Wife* (Fig. 54). While such direct
derivations are comparatively rare, this group is
indicative of the close study the artist made of the
antique statuary in the Roman museums. The
building at the right, a reconstruction Poussin made
from a description of a Roman basilica by Vitruvius, is further evidence of Poussin's desire for accuracy of detail.

Et in Arcadia Ego (Plate 35) shows Poussin in a
quieter and more lyrical mood. The rustic figures
of the shepherds might well have stepped out of one
of Vergil's pastoral poems, while the shepherdess
could be the tragic muse in one of Corneille's dramas. As they trace out the letters of the Latin
inscription on the sarcophagus, "I Too Once
Dwelled in Arcady," their mood becomes pensive.
The thought that the shepherd in the tomb once
lived and loved as they, casts a spell of gentle
melancholy over the group. In this meditative
study in spatial composition, the feminine figure
parallels the trunk of the tree to define the vertical
axis, while the arm of the shepherd on the left rests
on the sarcophagus to supply the horizontal balance. Each gesture, each line, follows inevitably
from this initial premise with all the cool logic of
a geometrical theorem. The subject is obviously a

sympathetic one to Poussin, for he had found his own Arcadia in Italy and took a lifelong delight in the monuments of antiquity and the voices from the past that spoke through just such inscriptions. Like the ancients he tried to conduct his own search for truth and beauty in a stately tempo and with a graceful gesture. Like them, too, he sought for the permanent in the transient, the type in the individual, the universal in the particular, and the one in the many.

Claude Gelée, better known as Claude Lorrain, like his countryman Poussin, also preferred life in Italy to that in his native France. His lifelong interest was landscape, but the convention of the time demanded that pictures have personages in them as well as titles for them. Claude solved the problem by painting his landscapes, letting his assistants put in a few incidental figures, and giving the pictures obscure names, such as *Embarkation of the Queen of Sheba, Expulsion of Hagar,* or *David at the Cave of Adullam.* With tongue in cheek, he once remarked that he sold his figures and gave away his landscapes. Harbor scenes like the one entitled *Disembarkation of Cleopatra at Tarsus* (Fig. 420) were his special delight. In them, he could concentrate on limitless space and the soft atmospheric effect of sunlight on misty air. His usual procedure was to balance his compositions on either side of the foreground with buildings or trees, which are treated in considerable detail. Then the eye is drawn deeper into the intervening space with long vistas over land or sea toward the indefinite horizon. Formal values dominate, and nothing arbitrary or accidental intrudes to mar their stately quality.

Charles Lebrun was one of the painters who came under Poussin's influence when he was in Rome. Though a friend and ardent admirer of Poussin, Lebrun preferred the fuss and feathers of life at Versailles. An opportunist of the first magnitude, he ingratiated himself there by designing the costumes for Louis XIV's pageants, fountains for the parks, and tapestries for the salons. His facile painting technique and his talent for courtly flattery hastened his rapid rise to the position of leader of the Academy, First Painter to the King, head of the royal tapestry and furniture studios, and artistic arbiter of the reign. His *Alexander the Great Entering Babylon* (Fig. 421), like most of his other pictures, was one of a series of huge canvases designed for the pompous interiors of the Versailles Palace. Since Louis XIV spent much of his time and energy cultivating the art of Mars, and since his courtiers invariably hailed the returning victor as a second Alexander, the significance of the central figure was not likely to be overlooked by anyone. Lebrun left the victorious army discreetly outside his picture, so that Alexander could dominate the scene in lonely triumph from his elephant-drawn chariot. While he thought he was carrying out Poussin's theories, Lebrun's pictures illustrate what happens when an artist allows the letter to crowd out the spirit. In all fairness, however, it must be said that Lebrun was a better decorator than he was a painter; consequently, his pictures usually make better sense in the context of their original surroundings than as separate entities.

The acquisition of paintings by the crown was begun under Colbert on a massive scale. The purchases reveal the gradual veering away from an international toward a national viewpoint. Rubens and the Italian artists were liberally represented, but, on Lebrun's advice, the systematic buying of

420. CLAUDE LORRAIN. *Disembarkation of Cleopatra at Tarsus. c.* 1647. Oil on canvas, 46¾ × 66½″. Louvre, Paris.

Poussin's pictures and those by French artists exhibiting in the annual salons was begun. By 1709 the collection of Louis XIV numbered over 2,400 pictures, including 29 Poussins. While their primary purpose was to decorate the royal galleries, they were available to French painters for study and were the subjects of discussion at sessions of the Academy. The stylistic differences of Rubens and Poussin admirably illustrate the free and academic sides of the baroque coin. Both painters were well versed in the classics, both reflected the spirit of the Counter Reformation, and both in their way represented the aristocratic tradition. But while Rubens' impetuosity knew no bounds, Poussin remained aloof and reserved; while Rubens cast restraint to the winds and filled his pictures with violent movement, Poussin was austerely pursuing his formal values; while Rubens' figures are soft and fleshy, Poussin's are hard and statuesque; while Rubens sweeps up his spectators in the tidal wave of his volcanic energy, Poussin's pictures are more conducive to quiet meditation. The Academy's championship of Poussin made clear the distinction between academic and free baroque. In the late 17th and 18th centuries, painters were divided into camps labeling themselves either Poussinist or Rubenist, and well into the 19th century echoes were still to be heard in the classic versus romantic controversy.

MUSIC

The musical and dramatic productions at the court of Louis XIV were as lavish in scale as the other arts. Three groups of musicians were main-

tained, the first of which was the *chambre* group, which included the famous *Vingt-quatre Violons*, or Twenty-four Viols, the first permanent stringed orchestra in Europe. This was the string ensemble that played for balls, dinners, concerts, and the opera. Lutenists and clavecinists also were found in this group. Next came the *chapelle*, the chorus that sang for religious services, and the organists. The *Grande Écurie* formed the third category, which consisted mainly of the wind ensemble that was available for military processions, outdoor fetes, and hunting parties.

The favored form of entertainment during the early years of Louis XIV's reign was the *ballet de cour*, an elaborate form of the ballet that began with an instrumental overture and, in addition to the dancing, included a sequence of sung recitatives, choruses, and songs as well as instrumental interludes. Louis XIV, who was an excellent dancer, took an active interest in these court ballets and frequently appeared at the climactic moment in the role of Apollo, the sun god. He was serious enough about his acting to rehearse diligently under the supervision of Lully and Molière.

During the years of Louis' minority, the popularity of the court ballet had been challenged by Italian opera, the "spectacle of princes" that Cardinal Mazarin sought to introduce from his native land. In 1660, Cavalli, who had brought the Venetian lyric drama to a high point of development, was invited to Paris to write and produce an opera. It met with a mixed reception, but two years later Cavalli was again on hand to write another, this time for Louis' wedding celebration. Another challenge to the court ballet came from Molière, who united the elements of comedy, music, and the

421. CHARLES LEBRUN. *Alexander the Great Entering Babylon. c.* 1666. Oil on canvas, 14′9″ × 23′. Louvre, Paris.

dance into a form he called the *comédie-ballet*. The best known of these is the perennially popular *Le Bourgeois Gentilhomme (The Would-be Gentleman)* which was first performed at the court in 1670. A full decade of these brilliant entertainments was brought to a close by the death of the great dramatist.

The ever-resourceful Jean-Baptiste Lully, however, was biding his time on the sidelines until he could spring some surprises of his own. A Florentine by birth and French by education, he was fiddling away at the early age of seventeen as a violinist in the *Vingt-quatre Violons*. When Cavalli produced his two operas, it was Lully who wrote the ballet sequences that, incidentally, proved more popular than the operas themselves. It was Lully again who collaborated with Molière by supplying the musical portions of the *comédie-ballets*. And when the propitious moment arrived, it was Lully who came up with a French form of opera that he called *tragédie lyrique*, or lyrical tragedy. One of the earliest of these was the performance of *Alceste* in the Marble Court at Versailles on July 4, 1674 (Fig. 422). With a genius for organization, Lully used the *Vingt-quatre Violons* as the nucleus of his orchestra, supplementing them with wind instruments from the *Grande Écurie* for fanfares as well as for the hunting, battle, and climactic transformation scenes. The *chapelle* was also drafted into the operatic service, and the generous dance sequences Lully included assured the ballet group plenty of activity. Lully could have had the collaboration of the great dramatist Racine for the texts, but he deliberately chose Quinault, a poet of less distinction, but one who would be more pliable to his demands and who could be counted upon not to claim too much of the credit.

The form of these lyrical tragedies crystallized early and changed relatively little in the following years. Each begins with an instrumental number of the type known as the French Overture. The first part is a ponderous dignified march with dotted notes, massive sonorities, and chains of resolving dissonances as in the Ritornel on page 365. The second half is livelier in tempo and more contrapuntal in texture. Next came the prologue, and that of *Alceste* is quite typical. The setting is the garden of the Tuileries, the palace in Paris that was still the official royal residence at this time, where the Nymph of the Seine is discovered. Declaiming her lines in recitative style, she makes some topical allusions to the current war, couched in flowery mythological terms. Glory now enters to the tune of a triumphal march, and a duet and solo air ensue. The two are joined eventually by a chorus of naiads and pastoral divinities, whose songs and dances give assurance that France will be ever victorious under the leadership of a great hero, whose identity is never for a moment in doubt. The overture is then repeated, and the five acts of a classical tragedy follow with much the same formal pattern as that of the prologue.

Two excerpts from Act III, Scene 5, of *Alceste* will illustrate Lully's style. After the death of Alceste, a long instrumental ritornel provides the pompous elegiac strains for the entrance of the mourning chorus. One of the grief-stricken women comes forward, indicating her sorrow by her gestures and facial expressions. Her Air (p. 365) is in the recitative style which J. J. Rousseau considered Lully's chief "title to glory." The composer always insisted that the music as well as the other elements

422. LOUIS LE VAU. Marble Court, Versailles Palace (during a performance of Lully's *Alceste*, 1674). Engraving by LEPAUTRE. Metropolitan Museum of Art, New York.

La mort, la mort bar - ba - re De - truit au-jourd' huy   mille ap - pas.

of the opera were the servants of drama and poetry, and he always counseled his singers to emulate the noble and expansive intonations of the actors trained by Racine. A Lully air consequently is never so set as an Italian aria but follows instead the elastic speech rhythms and the natural declamation of French baroque poetry and prose. The mourning chorus takes up where the Air leaves off with a variant of the opening Ritornel, and the scene closes with a long cadential passage alternately for orchestra and chorus based on a continuation of the Ritornel.

Since the hero was so closely identified with the monarch, a tragic ending was quite impossible. A *deus ex machina*, therefore, invariably appeared in the fourth act, just when all seemed darkest, and the fifth act always brought the lyrical tragedy to a triumphant and glorious conclusion.

By exploiting the success of his operas and through clever diplomatic strategy, Lully became by royal warrant the founder and head of the *Académie Royale de Musique*. With the substitution of the word *Nationale* for *Royale*, this is still the official title of the Paris grand opera company. With incredible energy, this musical monopolist of the regime produced an opera every year; and in addition to writing the score, he conducted the orchestra, trained the choir, coached the singers and dancers in their parts, and directed the staging. He ruled his musical and dramatic forces with the iron hand of an absolutist, allowing nothing arbitrary or capricious

to creep in anywhere. As a consequence Lully developed the best-disciplined group of singers, dancers, and instrumentalists in Europe. Their fame spread far and wide, and from contemporary accounts his orchestra was especially noted for the purity of its intonation, uniform bowing of the strings, accuracy of tempo and measure, and the elegance of its trills and melodic ornaments that were compared to the "sparkling of precious stones."

Practically singlehanded, Lully unified the ballet and founded French opera. His standardization of the sequence of dances became known as the French suite; his form of the overture, the French overture; and his organization of the opera remained standard practice for almost two centuries. Even though Quinault wrote the texts, Lully's operas may be considered the musical reflection of Racine's tragedies. In them are found the same observance of classical proprieties, the same dignified declamation, the same polished correctness. Their limitations were the inevitable outgrowth of the circumstances of their creation. By being addressed so exclusively to a single social group, they neglected to provide the more resonant human sounding board needed for survival in the repertory. Like Poussin, they remained aloof, restrained, and aristocratic. Opera, however, by its combination of grandiloquent language, emotional appeal, sonorous splendor, majestic movement, and visual elegance, emerges as one of the most magnificent creations of the baroque era.

IDEAS

The many manifestations of the aristocratic baroque style crystallize mainly around two distinct but interrelated ideas—absolutism and academicism.

Absolutism

The concept of the modern unified state, which first emerged in the Spain of Philip II, was adapted to French political purposes by Cardinal Richelieu and ultimately reached its triumphant consummation under Louis XIV. "It is the respect which absolute power demands, that none should question when a king commands," was the way Corneille stated the doctrine in 1637 in his heroic drama *The Cid*. As the principal exponent of monarchical absolutism and the centralized state, Louis XIV, the Sun King, assumed the authority to replace natural and human disorderliness with a reasonable facsimile of cosmic law and order. All human and social activities came under his protectorship, and by taking the arts under his paternal wing, he saw that they served as useful adjuncts to the cult of majesty. Versailles thus became the symbol of his absolutism, the seat of the absolute monarchy, and the personal apotheosis of the king.

Just as political absolutism meant the unification of all social and governmental institutions under one head, its aesthetic counterpart implied the bringing together of all the separate arts into a single rational plan. While *le grand siècle* produced some buildings, statuary, paintings, literature, and music that command attention in their own right, they spoke out most impressively in their combined forms. It is impossible to think of Versailles except as a combination of all art forms woven together into a unified pattern and as a reflection of the life and institutions of the absolute monarchy. The parks, gardens, fountains, statuary, buildings, courtyards, halls, murals, tapestries, furnishings, and recreational activities are all parts of a single coordinated design. As such, Versailles accomplished the daring feat of unifying all visible space and all units of time into a spatio-temporal setting for the aristocratic way of life. Indoor and outdoor space are inseparable, even music and the theater went outdoors. Sculpture was an embellishment of the landscape; painting became the handmaiden of interior design; comedy was allied with ballet; and tragedy was absorbed into opera. All the arts, in fact, were mirrored in the operatic form with its literary lyricism, orchestral rhetoric, dramatic declamation, instrumental interludes, statuesque dancing, architectural stage settings, mechanical marvels, and picturesque posturings. In Lully's hands opera became a kind of microcosm of court life, an absolute art form in which all the separate parts existed in the closest possible relation to the whole. None was allowed to dominate, nothing was disproportionate.

The spirit of absolutism was also directly revealed in the drama surrounding the life of the monarch. All the arts took the cue, became theatrical, and sought to surprise and astonish. The purely human element was buried under an avalanche of palatial scenery, pompous wigs, props, and protocol. Only in Molière's satires, La Fontaine's fables, and the secret memoirs of the period is it possible to catch glimpses of a more truthful version of the actualities behind the scenes of courtly life. Otherwise the architecture of Versailles, the statuary of Bernini and Coysevox, the triumphal murals of Lebrun, the tragedies of Racine, and the operas of Lully were all designed to promote the illusion that Louis XIV and his courtiers were beings of heroic stature, powerful will, and grandiose utterance.

Academicism

While the academic movement began formally with the first French academy during the reign of Louis XIII, it was not until later in the century that the implications of academicism were completely realized and its force fully mobilized. Both Louis XIV and his minister Colbert believed that art was much too important to be left exclusively in the hands of artists. The various academies, therefore, became branches of the government and the arts a part of the civil service. An administrative organization was instituted, topped by the king and director through professors, members, and associates, to the students. Approved principles were taught, and theoretical and practical knowledge communicated by lectures, demonstrations, and discussions. Boileau as the head of the Academy of Language and Literature, Lebrun of the Academy of Painting and Sculpture, Mansart of the Academy of Architecture, and Lully of the Academy of Music were subject directly to the king and were absolute dictators in their respective fields. As such, they were the principal advisers to the king and his ministers, and, in turn, they were responsible for carrying out the royal will. Complete control of patronage was centered in their hands; theirs was the final word in determining those who would receive commissions, appointments, titles, licenses, degrees, pensions, prizes, entrance to art schools, and the privilege of exhibiting in the annual salons.

The academies were thus the means of transmitting the absolute idea into the aesthetic sphere. Academicism invariably implied a patriarchal principle, whereby regularly constituted arbiters of taste placed their stamp of approval on the products in the various art media. These interpreters of the official point of view inevitably tended to become highly conservative. Aristocratic baroque art was the superpersonal expression of a class whose code of behavior was based on etiquette, politeness, and cultivation of good taste. All intimate personal feeling, capriciousness, and eccentricity had to yield to self-discipline, urbanity, correctness, and accepted standards of good form. The academies were therefore charged with the making of aesthetic definitions, artistic codes, and technical formulas valid for their respective fields. They functioned as a kind of board of directors who decided what was best for the stockholders. They had, moreover, the power to enforce their decisions, which meant that academicism could, at best, establish and maintain a high level of creative quality and, at worst, degenerate into conventionalism and downright regimentation, with varying degrees of standardization in between. What artists stood to gain in official recognition was liable to be matched by a corresponding loss of artistic freedom.

One example will show how academicism worked. Under Lebrun, the Academy of Painting and Sculpture favored the restrained style of Poussin over the passionate exuberance of Rubens. It thereby set up an academic subdivision of the baroque style as opposed to the expression of the free baroque. Many reasons for the choice can, of course, be advanced. Poussin's pictorialism, for instance, may—readily and demonstrably—be reduced to a system of formal values based on geometrical principles, while Rubens' style is so personal, impetuous, voluptuous, and violently emotional that it always remains a bit beyond the grasp. Academicism in this case was trying to tame baroque exuberance and reduce it to formulas and rules. Nothing eccentric, nothing unpredictable was allowed to creep in and destroy the general impression of orderliness. The Academy always remained somewhat skeptical of emotion just as it did of color, since neither was subject to scientific

laws. The pictorial standards of the Academy were therefore based on formal purity, demonstrable mathematical relationships, logical definition, and rational analysis. These were the qualities that brought academic art the designation of *classic*, a term that was defined at the time as "belonging to the highest class" and hence approved as a model. Since similar standards were generally to be found in Roman antiquity, classic art and Roman art inevitably became associated. The 17th-century adaptation of Greco-Roman models, however, was quite in the spirit of the time, and hence must not be confused with the archeological exactitude that was set up as the standard for neoclassicism in the late 18th century and the Napoleonic period.

French academicism was from the start an unqualified practical success. Under the academies, the artistic hegemony of Europe passed from Italy to France where it has effectively remained up to recent times. The hundreds of skilled artists and artisans who were trained on the vast projects of Louis XIV became the founders and teachers of a tradition of high technical excellence. French painting alone, to use the most obvious example, continued its unbroken supremacy from the foundation of the Academy to the 20th century. In Spain, by way of contrast, the only successor to El Greco, Velázquez, and Murillo was the lonely figure of Goya; in Flanders there were no outstanding followers of Rubens and van Dyck except Watteau, who to all intents and purposes was French; in Holland there was no one to take up where Rembrandt and Vermeer had left off. In France, however, painting continued on a high level throughout the 18th and 19th centuries; and, by setting high technical standards, academicism was a determining force even in nonacademic circles. The work of Perrault and Mansart in architecture, Boileau in criticism, Molière in comedy, Racine in tragedy, Lully in opera was also absorbed directly into a tradition that succeeded in setting up measuring sticks of symmetry, order, regularity, dignity, reserve, and clarity, which to this day still have a certain validity even if only as points of departure.

I4 - THE BOURGEOIS BAROQUE STYLE

AMSTERDAM, 17TH CENTURY

If a visitor to 17th-century Amsterdam—or any of the other sturdy Dutch towns for that matter—looked about for triumphal arches, pretentious palaces, or military monuments, he was doomed to disappointment. In fact, if there was anything grand at all about life in the Low Countries, it was its complete commonplaceness. After they had achieved their cherished independence by wresting their country town by town and province by province from the grasp of the Spanish despots, the people organized themselves and their government with a minimum of unity and a maximum of diversity. The Netherlanders had no intention whatsoever of substituting one brand of tyranny for another, much less a domestic variety; and so the land became the United Provinces under a *stadtholder*, or governor. Let their English rivals call them the "united bogs"; their muddy swamps and marshlands were poor things, but at least they were their own. Their wars of independence, geographical isolation, constant struggle against the encroachments of the sea, dour climate, seafaring economy, Calvinist Protestantism, and individualistic temperaments conspired with all the other circumstances of Dutch life to focus the center of interest in the home. A Dutchman's home was not even his castle; it was just his solid, comfortable,

plain, brick house. Instead of the cult of majesty, his was the cult of the home.

When Jakob van Ruisdael painted the *Quay at Amsterdam* (Fig. 423), he was painting more than just a view of the old fish market at the end of the broad canal known as the Damrak. In this local variant of the international academic style (compare with Fig. 420), he was in fact picturing the bourgeois way of life in a scene where thrifty housewives were gathering up provisions for their dinner tables; where a part of the fishing fleet that gave the Dutch a monopoly of the pickled and salted herring industry was moored; where, lying at anchor in the distance, there were some of the merchant vessels that helped the Dutch create an efficient modern commerce by plying the seven seas, trading their clay pipes, glazed tiles, Delft pottery, and cured herrings for Russian furs, West Indian sugar, tobacco, and other raw materials; where the spice trade of the Indies had led to the formation of corporations whose shares were traded on a modern stock exchange—complete with booms (like that in the stock of the Dutch West India Company in 1628 after it had declared a 50 percent dividend) and busts (like that of the tulip crash a decade later when more of the treasured bulbs had been sold

(above) REMBRANDT. *Landscape with Three Gabled Cottages*. Etching, 6¼ × 9". Rijksmuseum, Amsterdam.

(left) 423. Jakob van Ruisdael. *Quay at Amsterdam.* c. 1669. Oil on canvas, 20¾ × 26″. Frick Collection, New York (copyright).

(below) 424. Jan van der Heyden. *City Hall at Amsterdam.* 1668. Oil on canvas, 28½ × 34″. Louvre, Paris.

than could be delivered). In short, Ruisdael was painting the scene of the active mercantilism that had spread the base of prosperity so widely that every industrious citizen could aspire toward having at least some share of the good things of life for his home.

In such a situation, some families inevitably accumulated more than others, and by means of the wealth that was concentrated in their hands, they became a ruling oligarchy. These so-called "regent" families were the ones from whose ranks the members of the town councils and mayors were selected. They were, however, an upper-middle-class group rather than an aristocracy, and there was safety in their numbers. Their power, together with that of the professional and mercantile societies known as guilds, depended upon the retention of a maximum of local authority. This decentralization favored the growth of universities—those at Leyden and Utrecht became the most distinguished in Europe—and promoted the careers of such eminent native humanists as Constantijn Huygens, friend and patron of Rembrandt, and Hugo Grotius, founder of the new discipline of international law. The freedom to think and work attracted such foreigners as the French philosopher René Descartes (Fig. 438), who resided in Holland for almost twenty years, and the parents of Baruch Spinoza— one of the profoundest human intellects of all time—

who found refuge in Amsterdam after the persecution of the Jews had made life intolerable for them in their native Portugal.

The architectural expression of this bourgeois way of life is found in the various town halls, of which that of Amsterdam is a good example (Fig. 424); in such mercantile structures as ware-

General Events

	1517	Protestant Reformation began in Germany
	1535	*Institution of Christian Religion* published by John Calvin (1509–1564); Dutch Reformed Church established later along Calvinist lines
	1566	Revolt of Netherlands against Spain began
	1575	University of Leyden, first of the Dutch universities, founded by William the Silent, prince of Orange
	1602	Dutch East India Company organized
1618–	1648	Thirty Years' War; 1609 Low Countries given virtual independence in truce with Spain; full independence under Treaty of Westphalia (1648)
	1621	Dutch West India Company founded
	1624	*Tablatura Nova* by Samuel Scheidt
1629–	1648	René Descartes resided in Holland
1630–	1687	Limited public art patronage dispensed through Constantijn Huygens
	1631	Rembrandt settled in Amsterdam
	1637	*Discourse on Method* published in Leyden by Descartes
	1642	Dutch explorer Tasman discovered New Zealand
	1644	*Principles of Philosophy* published by Descartes in Amsterdam
	1648	Independence of Netherlands recognized by Treaty of Westphalia
1652–	1674	Anglo-Dutch commercial wars
	1670	Spinoza published *Tractatus theologica-politicus*

Painters

c.1580–	1666	Frans Hals
1606–	1669	Rembrandt van Rijn
c.1617–	1681	Gerhardt Terborch
c.1619–	1662	Jan van de Velde
c.1628–	1682	Jakob van Ruisdael

c.1629–	1679	Jan Steen
c.1629–	1683	Pieter de Hooch
1632–	1675	Jan Vermeer van Delft
1637–	1712	Jan van der Heyden

Philosophers and Scientists

1467–	1536	Desiderius Erasmus
1583–	1645	Hugo Grotius, founder of international law
1596–	1650	René Descartes
1629–	1695	Christian Huygens
1632–	1677	Baruch Spinoza

Writers

1587–	1679	Joost van den Vondel, Dutch dramatist and author of *Lucifer*, poem similar to Milton's *Paradise Lost*
1596–	1687	Constantijn Huygens, poet, humanist, diplomat

Musicians

1562–	1621	Jan Pieterszoon Sweelinck
		English School
c.1542–	1623	William Byrd
c.1562–	1628	John Bull, organist of the Cathedral of Antwerp (1617–1628), friend of Sweelinck
c.1562–	1638	Francis Pilkington
c.1576–	1643	Henry Peacham, author of *Compleat Gentleman*, teacher and composer
1583–	1625	Orlando Gibbons
		German School
1587–	1654	Samuel Scheidt, pupil of Sweelinck
1596–	1663	Heinrich Scheidemann, pupil of Sweelinck
1623–	1722	J. A. Reinken, successor of Scheidemann as organist at Hamburg, and influencer of J. S. Bach
1685–	1750	Johann Sebastian Bach
1685–	1759	George Frederick Handel

houses, countinghouses, and the market building, seen on the extreme right in Figure 423; and, above all, in the long rows of gabled brick houses like those seen on either side of the canal in the same picture. Dating from former times were such ecclesiastical buildings as the Oudekerk, or Old Church, whose Gothic tower is silhouetted against the sky in the right background; originally Roman Catholic, it had been taken over by the Dutch Reformed Church after the Reformation. As organized under the precepts of John Calvin, the Reformed Church held that religious truth was not the monopoly of any individual or any group, and that the word of God was available to all without the mediation of priestly authority. Through the development of the printing press, every family could have its own Bible, and by means of the high degree of literacy that prevailed almost everyone could read it. As in government, the Dutch people were wary of authority in religion; and as confirmed Protestants, they took rather literally the words of Christ to go into their closets and pray. Thus through family devotions, hymn singing, and Bible reading, much of the important religious activity took place in the home. According to the teaching of Calvin, the reason for going to church was to hear a sermon and sing the praises of the Lord. No architectural embellishments, statuary, paintings, and professional choirs or orchestras should distract the worshipers' attention. Since commissions were no longer forthcoming from church and aristocratic sources, the artist, more and more, had to conceive his work in terms of the house.

The prosperous Dutch families fortunately felt the need of an art that would reflect their healthy materialism and reveal their outlook, their institutions, and their country just as they were—solid, matter-of-fact, and without airs. In this happy state of affairs, patronage was spread on a broad-enough basis so that almost every home had at least a small collection of pictures. In spite of the turbulent times, Dutch art avoided heroic battle scenes just as it did grandiose mythological allegories and complex symbolism. Landscape had a strong attraction, since the Dutch had fought for every inch of their soil, and paintings of their fields, mills, and cottages appealed to their sense of proprietorship. Genre scenes were likewise popular, because such casualness and informality harmonized with their domestic surroundings. The severe simplicity of still-life compositions (Fig. 425) also found favor, since quiet arrangements of fruit, flowers, oysters, herrings, ceramics, and textiles were visible evidences of the good life. As men of affairs, the Dutch liked corporation pictures where they were depicted among their fellow directors or board members in a group portrait designed to perpetuate their memory on the walls of some guild hall, professional society, officers' club, or charitable trust. Above all, the Dutch burgher wanted family portraits for his living room—commemorative pictures of such family festivals as christenings and weddings; paintings of quiet interiors with his wife or daughter dutifully doing some household chore or, if one of them showed special talent, perhaps playing a musical instrument; and for himself, he liked to be portrayed at his work, surrounded by the perquisites of his wordly position (Fig. 426).

Under Calvinistic austerity, the only professional musicians to survive were the church organists, the hired groups of singers and instrumentalists who performed for weddings, banquets, and parades, and the band of music teachers who taught the younger members of the family to sing and to play the lute, viola da gamba, and keyboard instruments, such as the virginals and spinet. Music,

(top) 425. JAN JANSZ. VAN DE VELDE. *Still Life: Fruit Piece*. 1657. Oil on wood, 15 × 12¾″. Frans Hals Museum, Haarlem.

(below) 426. REMBRANDT. *Portrait of Jan Uytenbogaert, Receiver General (The Gold-Weigher)*. 1639. Etching, 9¾ × 8″. Rijksmuseum, Amsterdam.

therefore, like all the other aspects of Dutch life, was centered largely in the home. During the Renaissance, the Low Countries had dominated European music with the polyphonic glories of their distinguished composers. Owing to the fact, however, that the artistic and material rewards were so much greater elsewhere, such a lively export trade in musicians developed that it eventually depleted the home ranks. Only one musical genius of universal stature was left in the Amsterdam of the early 17th century: Jan Pieterszoon Sweelinck, whose career brought to a brilliant close the radiant chapter of Netherlands music that had dominated the Renaissance.

All the arts were thus centered in the home. The simple and unpretentious Dutch dwelling with its polished tiled floors, tidy interiors, and window boxes for the tulips was the modest framework for this bourgeois way of life. Unless ceramics are included, there was little sculpture other than a few figurines on the mantelpiece and an occasional statuette. The primary aesthetic indulgences of the Dutch were their pictures and domestic music-making, while such objects as their Delft pottery jugs, tablecloths, laces, and draperies enriched their world of qualities. The reality of daily life was made up of the routine of the business establishment, the market place, and the household. It was a reality of simple truths in which nothing was too small to be overlooked. All things, even the most insignificant, were considered to be gifts of God; and, as such, they were studied in the Holland of the 17th century in the minutest detail.

PAINTING

Towering above all other Dutch painters, because of the breadth of his vision, the power of his characterizations, and the uncompromising integrity of his ideals, stands the figure of Rembrandt van Rijn in lonely eminence. Like his contemporaries, Rembrandt painted portraits, genre scenes, historical subjects, and landscapes, but unlike them he refused to specialize and succeeded magnificently in all. Furthermore, he brought a new psychological profundity to his portraiture, an unaccustomed animation to his genre scenes, a greater dramatic intensity to his religious pictures, and a broader sweep to his landscapes than had been achieved before in the northern tradition. His discoveries of the power of light, in all its varying degrees, to illuminate character both from without and from within, to define space by the interpenetration of light, and to animate that space by the flowing movement of shadows identify him as one of the prime movers in the establishment of the northern baroque pictorial style. Rembrandt's art as a whole reveals a consistent growth from his early to his late years in the power to penetrate the world of appearances, to lay bare the quickening spiritual forces that lie beneath.

Soon after he settled in Amsterdam, the 26-year-old painter received his first important assignment from the local Guild of Surgeons and Physicians. The result was *Dr. Tulp's Anatomy Lesson* (Fig. 427), a composition that combines group portraiture of the so-called "corporation type" with the anatomy pictures of the medieval and Renaissance tradition. The subjects in this case were the heads of the guild and other prominent citizens, whose names are duly recorded on the sheet of paper held by the figure in the center. Anatomy pictures appeared regularly as drawn or engraved illustrations in medical books and less frequently as paintings. Since vivisection was forbidden by church law or otherwise strictly regulated, such occasions were comparatively rare. The guild, however, had official permission from the Amsterdam authorities to hold once a year a public dissection of a newly executed criminal. Indeed this was considered part of his punishment. Staged in an amphitheater seating more than 200 persons, such an anatomy lecture was looked upon as a scientific event for the dissemination of knowledge and, less loftily, as a garish form of public entertainment.

In his painting, Rembrandt's grouping of figures and placement of the heads on different levels impart a certain freedom and informality to the composition. By the use of light, the artist develops the inherent drama of the situation, and by the expression on each of the faces shows reactions that vary from intense concentration to casual indifference. The fullest light is focused on the cadaver and on the hands of Dr. Nicholas Tulp, the professor of anatomy who is giving the lecture. The large open book at the feet of the corpse is quite possibly a recent edition of Vesalius' *Anatomy*. This universally recognized authority was the work of the Dutch scientist Andries van Wesel (1514–1564), who had taught and held just such demonstrations at the University of Padua. Since Dr. Tulp styled himself *Vesalius redivivus* (Vesalius revived), the allusion is appropriate. In sum, Rembrandt's dramatization of the spirit of scientific inquiry is a vivid product of a period that has quite accurately been called the Age of Observation.

Exactly a decade elapsed between the *Anatomy Lesson* and the *Sortie of Captain Banning Cocq's Company* (Plate 36), Rembrandt's masterpiece of the corporation type. Group portraits of such military units that had fought against the Spaniards were common enough at the time to have the designation of "musketeer pictures" (see Plate 37).

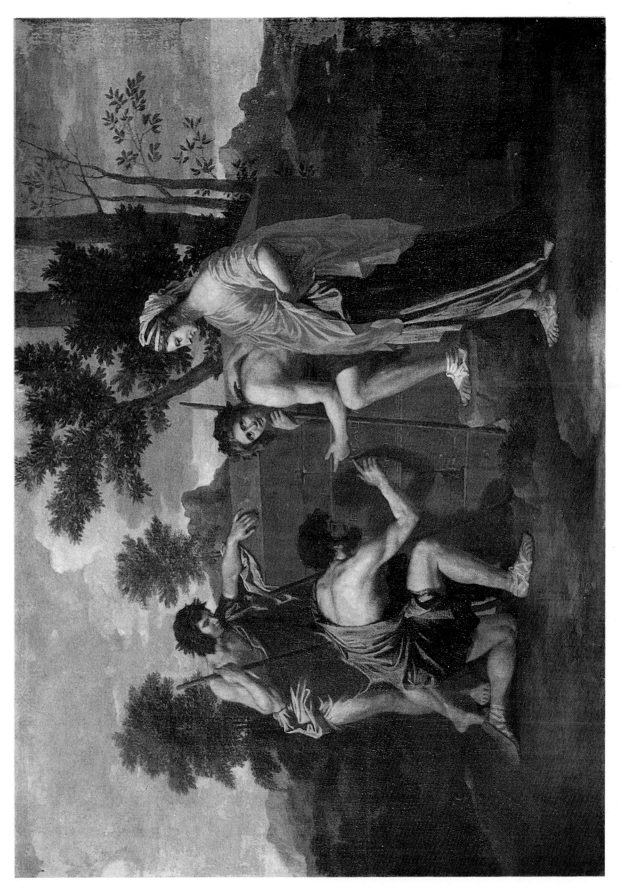

Plate 35. NICOLAS POUSSIN. *Et in Arcadia Ego.* 1638–1639.
Oil on canvas, 33 ½ × 47 ⅝". Louvre, Paris. (See p. 361.)

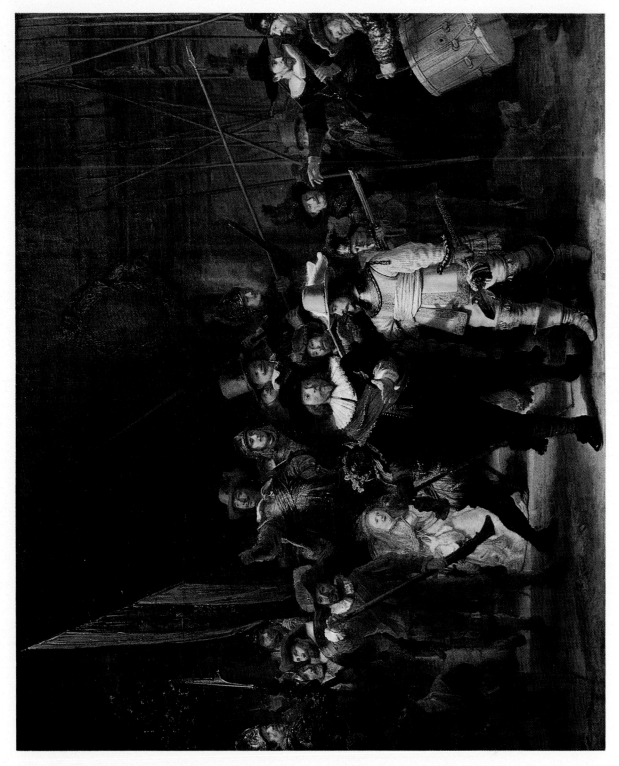

Plate 36. REMBRANDT. *Sortie of Captain Banning Cocq's Company of the Civic Guard.* 1642.
Oil on canvas, 12′2″ × 14′7″. Rijksmuseum, Amsterdam. (See p. 372.)

427. REMBRANDT. *Dr. Tulp's Anatomy Lesson.* 1632.
Oil on canvas, 5'3 ³/₈" × 7'1 ¹/₄". Mauritshuis, The Hague.

Once their original purpose in the struggle for independence was gone, many of these companies continued as parts of the civic guard and as officers' clubs, available as the occasion warranted for anything from emergency duty to a parade. By 1642, most members had become prosperous shopkeepers, who hugely enjoyed dressing up now and then in their dashing uniforms, polishing their shooting irons, and posing as warriors in processions or civic celebrations. In "musketeer pictures," they were usually shown in convivial situations, such as gathered around a banquet table, but in order to get life and movement into his picture, Rembrandt discarded this rather stilted pose and chose to show Captain Cocq's company in action, as if responding to a call to arms. The lifesize figures are therefore seen moving out of the city gate before falling into formation.

Popularly known as *The Night Watch*, the painting, thanks to a recent cleaning, has proved to be a "Day Watch" instead. The varnish that had darkened in the course of time and the original placement near a large fireplace were responsible for the general gloom. Now the free flow of light can be seen moving rhythmically throughout the whole composition, pervading every corner with dynamic gradations ranging from dark to bright. The light is most intense in the center, where Captain Cocq is explaining the plans to his lieutenant, whose uniform catches the rays of the morning sun. As a counterbalance, Rembrandt places the whimsical figure of a young girl in gleaming cream-colored satin at the captain's other side. Strung from her belt are a powder horn and a white cockerel, possibly a Rembrandtian pun on the captain's name. The shadow of Captain Cocq's hand falling across the lieutenant's uniform defines the source of light, that, in turn, blends together and relates all the other figures to the central pair by the degree of illumination that falls upon them. Such virtuosity in the handling of light and shadow for dramatic purposes was one of Rembrandt's unique achievements.

Contrary to popular legend, the picture was not a failure. It hung proudly in the company's quarters until its removal to the Amsterdam City

428. ANONYMOUS. *Night Watch*. Watercolor from album of Banning Cocq family. *c.* 1660–1665. 5¾ × 7″. Rijksmuseum, Amsterdam. (Compare Plate 36.)

429. REMBRANDT. *Christ Healing the Sick (Hundred Guilder Print). c.* 1649. Etching, 10⅞ × 15⅜″. Metropolitan Museum of Art, New York (H. O. Havemeyer Collection, 1929).

Hall in 1715. Then, so as to fit into the available space, the picture was cut down on all sides, most drastically on the left where three figures on the bridge and part of the canal are known to be missing. An unpretentious, informal watercolor from the Cocq family album (Fig. 428) shows the picture in its original proportions. The cutting has had the unfortunate effect of making the composition symmetrical, whereas the artist had intended the principal figures to be off-center to the right.

The etching *Christ Healing the Sick* (Fig. 429), familiarly known as the "Hundred Guilder Print," is an example of Rembrandt's several hundred works in what was then a popular medium (see p. 368; Figs. 447, 449). Financially, the relatively modest price of an etching assured Rembrandt of some income—and a fairly wide distribution of his work—at those times when his paintings piled up unsold in his studio. (The price in the case of this etching was a record rather than a rule.) Technically, the medium of etching gave Rembrandt the opportunity to explore the qualities of light in simple line patterns independent of pigments and colors. By scratching a coated metal plate with a stylus, an artist makes a linear pattern that is etched, or bitten, into the metal upon immersion in an acid solution. When the coating is removed and the plate inked, an etching is made by transferring the inked impression on the metal plate to paper. In this example, the gradations of light and dark run from such inky blackness as that behind the figure of Christ to the whiteness of the untouched paper as that of the rock in the extreme left. Rembrandt's true artistic stature is revealed in the way his art scales the heights of moral grandeur within severe limitations. The expressive power of *Christ Healing the Sick* is as great as the material medium is small.

Rembrandt was brought up in a family of Anabaptists who tried to live according to strict Biblical precepts. His religious subjects are seen from a Protestant point of view and, as such, show an intimate personal knowledge of the Scriptures. Since he was not painting for churches, and thus was under no compulsion to conform to the usual iconographical tradition of Madonnas and Child, Crucifixions, and so on, he was free to develop new themes and new points of view. Much of the intimacy and effectiveness of such free works is owed to the fact that they were not conceived as public showpieces. Rembrandt also loved to explore the Amsterdam ghetto and found stimulation as well as many of the types for his religious pictures among the descendants of the people who created the Old Testament.

Rembrandt is known to have painted at least 62 self-portraits, surely a record number. The motivation, however, came more from a deep introspective tendency than from personal vanity. Besides, no model was more readily available. Extending from young manhood to his last year, his likenesses of himself read like a pictorial autobiography. At the age of 23, while still living in his native Leyden, he appears in one (Fig. 430) as a rustic, uncouth, grinning fellow with an unkempt stubble beard; in the other (Fig. 431) as a proud, aspiring, self-confident young artist. After successfully establishing himself in Amsterdam and after his marriage to Saskia van Uylenburch, daughter of a wealthy family, Rembrandt enjoyed a period of material prosperity. In cavalier costume and exuberant mood, he paints himself with his attractive young wife sitting on his knee as he lifts his glass in a toast (Fig. 432).

From 1640 on, Rembrandt sustained a series of sorrows, beginning with his mother's death which was followed two years later by that of

(below) 430. REMBRANDT. *Self-portrait. c.* 1629. Oil on wood, 15¾ × 13″. Rijksmuseum, Amsterdam.

(bottom) 431. REMBRANDT. *Self-portrait. c.* 1629. Oil on wood, 14¾ × 11½″. Mauritshuis, The Hague.

432. REMBRANDT. *Self-portrait with Saskia.* c. 1634. Oil on canvas, 63½ × 51½". Gemäldegalerie, Dresden.

Saskia shortly after the birth of their son Titus. By 1650 artistic tastes had changed, but Rembrandt (Fig. 433) resolutely followed his own genius, making no concessions to fickle fashions. The penetrating look, glowing with an internal light, peers into the depths of his own character and seems to be asking, "Whither now?" From this time onward, Rembrandt realized more and more that his mission was to explore the world of the imagination and leave the world of appearances to others. Consequently, his countenance bespeaks the serenity of a man who, having chosen his course, knows there is no turning back. Financial troubles increased as debts piled up, and from 1656 to 1660 the artist went through bankruptcy. His fine house with its furnishings, his personal collections of paintings, prints, armor, and artistic props all were sold to satisfy creditors. At this point (Figs. 434, 435), the searching gaze of the luminous eyes begins to turn inward in self-appraisal as he forthrightly assesses

his moral and artistic progress. The last years were saddened by the deaths of his faithful friend and housekeeper Hendrickje Stoeffels (1662) and his son Titus (1668). Still working incessantly, Rembrandt in his last self-portrait (Fig. 436) shows the familiar face marked by illness and resignation but still full of the deep human compassion that marked his life and art.

Between the polar extremes of the introspective Rembrandt and the detached Vermeer is the gamut of subjects and moods projected by their contemporaries. While Rembrandt sought to portray the spirit of the whole man, Frans Hals was content to capture human individuality in a fleeting glance or a casual gesture. In his early work he was more interested in appearances than essences. Later, when he came under the influence of Rembrandt's soul-searching, he gave up his vivid colors and light touch for somber hues and serious subjects. The infectious gaiety of his *Merry Lute Player*

433. REMBRANDT. *Self-portrait*. 1650. Oil on canvas, 34¾ × 28″. National Gallery of Art, Washington (Widener Collection, 1942).

434. REMBRANDT. *Self-portrait*. *c.* 1656–1658. Oil on wood, 20 × 16″. Kunsthistorisches Museum, Vienna.

435. REMBRANDT. *Self-portrait at Easel*. 1660. Oil on canvas, 44 × 34″. Louvre, Paris.

436. REMBRANDT. *Old Self-portrait*. 1669. Oil on canvas, 23¼ × 20¾″. Mauritshuis, The Hague.

(Fig. 437) is typical of Hals' carefree early period. With tousled hair and cap cocked at a jaunty angle, the subject might well be an entertainer at a public tavern. The way the glass of sparkling wine is held reveals the source of light, which strikes both face and instrument. In similar pictures the people of Hals' native Haarlem—quarreling fishwives, carousing officers, and tipsy merrymakers—live again with all their animal vitality and capacity for life. While he found inspiration in the lighter moments of his slightly disreputable fellow towns-people, Hals also painted commissioned portraits, such as that of the philosopher Descartes (Fig. 438) with its dignified demeanor.

Throughout Hals' career, commissions for corporation pictures were forthcoming, and the bril-liant color palette and convivial mood of the *Company of St. George* (Plate 37) is one early example. It contrasts strongly, however, with the sobriety of the pictures of his old age, such as the group portrait of the governors of the old men's almshouse at Haarlem (Fig. 439) from which the artist received a small subsidy in his destitute years. Although he was in his eighties, Hals' grasp of character (note the dissolute gentleman fourth from the left), his eye for revealing detail, and his deftness of touch had never been surer.

Pieter de Hooch's *Mother and Child* (Fig. 440) is a quiet study of domestic life in a proper household. Like his fellow painters, de Hooch knew that light was the magnet which attracted the eye and that its vibrations gave such an interior its share of life

(above left) 437. FRANS HALS. *Merry Lute Player.* c. 1627. Oil on canvas, 35½ × 29½″. Private collection.

(above right) 438. FRANS HALS. *René Descartes.* 1649. Oil on canvas, 30 × 26 ¾″. Louvre, Paris.

(right) 439. FRANS HALS. *Governors of Old Men's Home at Haarlem.* 1664. Oil on canvas, 5′8″×8′5″. Frans Hals Museum, Haarlem.

(left) 440. PIETER DE HOOCH. *Mother and Child. c.* 1660. Oil on canvas, 20¾ × 24″. Rijksmuseum, Amsterdam.

441. JAKOB VAN RUISDAEL. *The Jewish Graveyard. c.* 1660. Oil on canvas, 4′8″ × 6′2¼″. Detroit Institute of Arts.

and movement. But de Hooch works with a subdued light that matches the tranquility of his subject matter. Sunlight streams inward from the open Dutch door at the back and the window at the upper right. By this means the artist separates his three receding planes without ambiguity; explores the contrasting textures of the tile flooring, transparent glass, varnished wood surfaces, soft textiles, and metallic brilliance of the copper bedwarmer; as well as reveals the figures of mother, daughter, and dog. De Hooch's world is more static than Rembrandt's, his figures less animated than Hals', and his pictorial geometry more casual than Ver-

meer's. Yet each of his interiors has the timeless tranquility of a still life, with figures and objects blending together in their Dutch domestic surroundings.

Jakob van Ruisdael's somber study of a cemetery belongs to the category of the landscapes that meant so much to the Dutch people who had fought persistently for their country against the Spanish oppressors. While his *Quay at Amsterdam* (Fig. 423) is a forthright cityscape, exact in its descriptive detail, Ruisdael in *The Jewish Graveyard* (Fig. 441) seems to be searching for deeper symbolic values. The setting was the Jewish graveyard

442. JAN VERMEER. *Street in Delft. c.* 1658. Oil on canvas, 21¼ × 17¾". Rijksmuseum, Amsterdam.

In his *View of Delft* (Plate 38) Jan Vermeer van Delft paints the profile of his native city. From the people strolling in the lower left foreground, the artist carries the eye across the canal, along the line of mercantile buildings and houses behind the city wall on the left, past the stone bridge in the center with the steeple of the church rising in the background, to the moored boats and drawbridge on the extreme right. Vermeer's treatment of space is seen in this horizontal sweep, which makes no attempt to draw the eye into deep background space. The effectiveness of the picture is greatly enhanced by the subtle treatment of light and color. As the sunshine filters through the broken clouds, the light falls unevenly over the landscape, varying from the shadowy foreground and the dull red of the brick buildings, through the flame and orange tones in the sunny distance, to the brilliant gleam of the church tower. More than half the area of the picture is allotted to the ever-changing Dutch sky, where patches of blue alternate with the silvery and leaden grays of the clouds, while the waters below reflect the mirror image of the town.

In *Street in Delft* (Fig. 442) Vermeer again uses the warm red color of brick, tempered by the cool gray tints of a cloudy sky. Contrast is provided by the brown pavement, the green shutters, and the yellows and blues of the women's dresses. More important than the color this time, however, is Vermeer's meticulous geometrical organization in which each part is related to the whole. The picture can be broken down into a system of sharply defined rectangular surfaces—the pavement, open doorways, shuttered and unshuttered windows, and stepped gables of the houses. Highly selective rather than literal, Vermeer has eliminated everything that is not germane to his picture. Nothing extraneous is allowed to clutter up the tidiness of the composition, and each element of texture and surface is worked out to the minutest detail and presented with crystal clarity.

The same meticulousness and economy of means are found in such an interior scene as *Officer and Laughing Girl* (Fig. 443). Here Vermeer's logical organization of rectangles and intersecting surfaces is somewhat softened by the prominence given to the conversing figures. The daring cameralike perspective projects the figure of the officer forward and gives greater size to his large slouch hat and head than to that of the girl. His red coat and sash also contrast noticeably with the cooler colors of the girl's white cap, black and yellow bodice, and blue apron that allow her figure to recede. The map on the wall is painted with the greatest care in relation to the light and angle of the wall. Its Latin title is quite clear, and reads: "New and Accurate Map of all Holland and West Friesland." The warm,

at the Oudekerk in Amsterdam, but to heighten the mood of his picture the painter invents many imaginary picturesque details. The abandoned ruins of the old castle and the skeletonlike trunks of two dead trees, which were not in the actual scene, unite with the white stone slabs of the tombs to permeate the picture with thoughts of death. The inscriptions on the headstones—several of which are still there— remind the viewer that the religious toleration of the Netherlands made the country the haven for the Jewish refugees from the Spanish and Portuguese inquisitions. Under one of them a Dr. Montalto, physician to Henry IV of France, was buried in 1615. Another grave contains the remains of Chaicham Usiel, head rabbi of Amsterdam, who was a native of Fez in Morocco. Ruisdael projects a depth of feeling as well as of space into this landscape. With the waterfall and gnarled trees groping toward the threatening sky, he captures something of the sublimity of nature that sweeps both man and all his works before it. His eye for the picturesque anticipates in a remarkable way certain aspects of 19th-century romanticism.

rich, natural light that streams in from the open casement window gives both unity and life to the severe division of planes. It bathes every object and pervades every corner of the room, starting with the maximum intensity of the area adjacent to the source and tapering off by degrees into the cool bluish tones of the shadows in the lower right.

Almost always content to let objects and situations speak for themselves, Vermeer, on rare occasions, ventures into the realm of symbolism. *Artist in his Studio* (Fig. 444) is, to be sure, a self-portrait, and the studio is his own. The lady, however, personifies Fame, and the artist is starting his picture with her laurel wreath to indicate his pursuit of beauty and immortality. The trumpet, as if to sound a fanfare for a famous person, is one of Fame's attributes; and the book in her arm and the volumes and death mask on the table add a literary and sculptural dimension to this allegory of the arts.

The contrast between Rembrandt's restless searching spirit and Vermeer's sober objective detachment is fully as great as that between El Greco and Velázquez, or Rubens and Poussin. Rembrandt's light is the glow of the burning

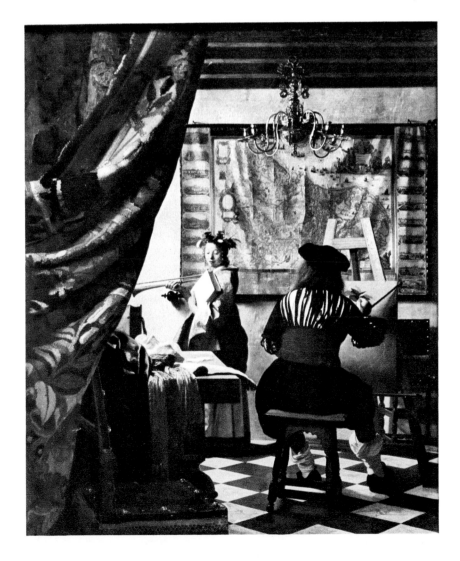

(above) 443. JAN VERMEER. *Officer and Laughing Girl.* c. 1656. Oil on canvas, 20 × 18″. Frick Collection, New York (copyright).

(left) 444. JAN VERMEER. *Artist in His Studio.* c. 1665–1670. Oil on canvas, 52×44″. Kunsthistorisches Museum, Vienna.

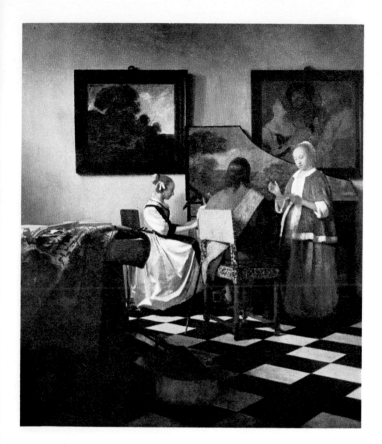

445. JAN VERMEER. *Concert. c.* 1660. Oil on canvas, 28 × 24¾". Isabella Stewart Gardner Museum, Boston.

human spirit, Vermeer's that from the open casement window. Rembrandt tries to penetrate the
world of appearances, Vermeer is content with the
visual image. With his warm personal quality,
Rembrandt embraces humanity as completely as
Vermeer's cool impersonality encompasses space.
Rembrandt is concerned at all times with moral
beauty, Vermeer with physical perfection. Rembrandt's inner dramas need only the monochro-
matic crescendo of a single color from deep brown
to golden yellow or in an etching from black to
white, while Vermeer's absence of drama demands
the entire chromatic spectrum. Like a philosopher,
Rembrandt lays the soul bare in his moving characterizations, while Vermeer, like a jeweler, delights
the eye with his unique perception of the quality
and texture of things. Thus in Holland, as well as
in both Spain and France, the 17th century, like
a stormy March, had been swept in on the leonine
gusts of free baroque flamboyance and had gone
out on a gentle lamblike academic breeze.

MUSIC

The one great musician of 17th-century Holland was Jan Pieterszoon Sweelinck, who succeeded
his father and was, in turn, succeeded by his son as
organist at the Oudekerk, so that the family rounded out a century of music making there. Under the
strict tenets of Calvinism, church music consisted
mainly of the congregational singing of psalms and
hymns, preferably unaccompanied. As such, the
development of music as an art would have been
ruled out were it not for the fact that Dutch tradition favored the organ, and the organist was
allowed to play preludes and postludes on sacred
themes before and after the service. On special
occasions, choral settings of the psalms with some
degree of elaboration were performed. Sweelinck's
viewpoint, like that of the other Dutch composers
of the century, was international in scope. He apparently had studied in Venice with Zarlino and
Andrea Gabrieli and was a colleague of the famous
Giovanni Gabrieli. He had also visited England
and was thoroughly familiar with the English keyboard school and choral-composing tradition. His
official title was Organist of Amsterdam, and as
such his duties included the giving of public concerts. The Oudekerk, according to contemporary
accounts, was always crowded on these occasions,
and large audiences consistently took delight in his
improvisations and variations on sacred and secular
themes; the baroque flourishes of his Venetian toc-
catas; his fantasies "in the manner of an echo," a
keyboard adaptation of the Venetian double-
choral style; and the choral preludes and fugues
that he built on Protestant hymn tunes.

The other public Dutch music was of the occasional type, given by choral groups and instrumental ensembles that, for a modest price, would furnish anything from the madrigals sung at weddings
to the dances played at receptions. All available
evidence points to the home as the center of the
major part of the musical life of the time. Most of
the extant compositions from this period are found
in the numerous manuscript copies that were made
for home use. Printed scores, however, were obtainable from Venice and London, and early in the
17th century music printing began to flourish in
Antwerp, Leyden, and Amsterdam. Holland also
became noted as a center for the manufacture of
musical instruments. The musical practices of the
time can be vividly reconstructed by combining the
surviving scores and musical instruments with the
rich visual evidence available in the paintings of
the period. Vermeer's *The Concert* (Fig. 445), for
one, shows a typical musical situation in the home.
The trio is made up of a young woman, who
reads her song part from the score she holds in her
hand; a seated man, who supplies the harmonic
background on his theorbo, a species of the lute;
and a girl at the spinet, the winged version of the
virginals, who plays the keyboard part. A viola da

gamba, which corresponds to the modern 'cello, is seen on the floor; and, ordinarily, if a player were available, it would be used to duplicate the bass line of the keyboard part in the instrumental combination known as the *continuo*.

The widespread custom of domestic music making resulted in a large body of literature that was designed for home rather than public performance. Since such music always had a friendly, sociable basis, it was mainly for two or more participants. Even the solo pieces were written for amateurs and purposely avoided any complexities that might imply showing off. The attitude is well summed up in *The Compleat Gentleman*, published in London in 1622 by the English schoolmaster Henry Peacham. "I desire no more in you," he said, "than to sing your part at first sight; withal to play the same upon your Viol, or the exercise of the Lute, privately to yourself."

An example of the type of music Mr. Peacham's gentlemen or Vermeer's ladies were prepared to perform is "Now Peep, Boe Peep," by Francis Pilkington, a number from that composer's *First Booke of Ayres*, published in 1605. The score was arranged and printed so that the participants could be seated comfortably around a table (see Fig. 446). On the left side, the words and melody of the Canto, in this case the soprano part, appear above the lute tablature. To their right sits the tenor opposite the alto, with the bass in between.

A transcription of the beginning of the piece is given above.

One of the interesting things about such a work is the great number of ways it can be performed. In its complete form, it is a vocal quartet with a lute accompaniment that duplicates the three lower parts. It also can be performed as a soprano solo with lute accompaniment, as given on the left half on page 384; a cappella—that is, for four voices without the lute; as a duet for soprano and any one of the other voices; as a lute solo; as an instrumental piece with viols instead of voices; as a combination of voices and viols; as an instrumental ensemble with doublings of the parts; or with wind instruments substituting for the voices and viols; and so on practically ad infinitum. Such music had to be adaptable to the size and skill of any group that might gather together for an evening of musical pleasure in the home.

While Italian and French influences were far from negligible in the Dutch visual arts, such painters as Frans Hals, Rembrandt, Vermeer, and their contemporaries were identified with a distinct national style. In music, English influences were strong, especially in the keyboard style, and as the century progressed Italian influences gradually would become dominant in the Netherlands, just as they did in France and England. But at this time, the music of the Netherlands was much more international in scope and character than was Dutch

Ow peep, boe peep, thrife happie bleft mine eies, For I haue found faire Phillis, for I haue found faire Phillis where fhe lies, Vpon her bed, with armes vnfpred, all faft a fleepe, Vnmaskt her face, thrife happie grace, fare-well, fare-well my Sheepe, Looke to your felues, new charge I muft ap-proue, Phillis doth fleepe, Phillis doth fleepe, And I muft guard my Loue. Looke.

2 Now peep boe peep, mine eyes to fee your bliffe,
Phillis clofd eyes atrackts you, hers to kiffe :
Oh may I now performe my vow, loues ioy t'impart,
Affay the while, how to be-guile, farewell faint hart.
Taken fhe is, new ioyes I muft approue,
Phillis doth fleep, and I will kiffe my Loue.

3 Now peep, boe peep, be not too bould my hand,
Wake not thy Phillis, feare fhee doe with-ftand :
Shee ftirs alas, alas, alas I faint in fpright,
Shee opes her eie, vnhappie I, farewell delight.
Awakt fhee is, new woes I muft approue,
Phillis awakes, and I muft leaue my Loue.

446. FRANCIS PILKINGTON. *First Booke of Songs or Ayres of 4 Parts:*
With Tablature for Lute or Orpherian with violl de gamba. London, 1605.
Henry E. Huntington Library, San Marino, California.

painting. In the decade before 1650, Dutch composers were publishing instrumental ensemble pieces in the Netherlands just as they did in France and England. In the decade before 1650, Dutch composers were publishing instrumental ensemble pieces called sinfonias for from two-stringed to five-stringed instruments. These corresponded closely to the fantasies for the same combinations that were written in England by such composers as William Byrd and Orlando Gibbons. After the middle of the century, however, Italian trio sonatas for two treble instruments (usually violins or flutes) and continuo began to be heard. Eventually this became the standard form of chamber music here as elsewhere. Such trio sonatas came to be written by French, German, and Dutch composers as well as by Italians, but the form was essentially international in style.

Keyboard music—for organ, virginals, spinet, clavichord, and harpsichord—was distinctively northern in character. Sweelinck had absorbed both the Venetian and English traditions, and his organ playing attracted to Amsterdam students from all over northern Europe. Through them his influence was widely extended, especially over the Protestant parts of Germany. His most noted pupil here was Samuel Scheidt of Halle, whose *Tablatura Nova*, published in 1624, did much to crystallize the German Protestant organ and choral style. In this book, all the technical procedures he had learned from Sweelinck were brought together and worked out with characteristic Germanic thoroughness. Happily, however, they were coupled with a considerable degree of creative imagination as well as technical invention. In its pages are found compositions intended for home performance, mainly in the form of variations. French and Flemish secular songs as well as dances, like the *allemande*, *paduan*, *courant*, and *gaillard*, appear with variants that are full of the complexities which so intrigued the baroque mind. The first two parts of Scheidt's book also contain fugues, echo fantasies, and chorales, while the third is concerned with harmonizations of Lutheran hymns and Protestant chorales with ornamental commentaries in the form of variations. Scheidt's work became a landmark in organ literature, since it assimilated and systematized the ornate Venetian manner, the English keyboard variation style, and Sweelinck's contrapuntal ingenuity. It brought together for the first time a collection of pieces admirably adapted for Protestant church purposes, and a number of musical models for other composers to emulate. A direct line thus extended from Sweelinck, who coordinated the Venetian and English schools, through such pupils as Scheidt, who transmitted the tradition to northern Germany, down to the time of Johann Sebastian Bach and George Frederick Handel, both of whom were born there in the year 1685.

IDEAS: DOMESTICITY

The various aspects of the bourgeois baroque style find a common undercurrent in the idea of domesticity. Many related ideas, such as mercantilism, Protestantism, anti-authoritarianism, nationalism, individualism, the ardent championship of individual rights and liberties, and the practical application of scientific discoveries, converge on this central concept, but the unity lies in the cult of the home. Bourgeois house comforts, for instance, were never so highly cultivated in the warmer, friendlier south where so much recreational activity can take place in the open air, while the northern climate was conducive to the concentration of communal pleasures in the home.

The spirit of commerce led to navigational adventure on the high seas and to the exploration of distant lands. The Dutch conquests, however, were mainly those of the businessman; their empire was based on corporate enterprise; and their personal kingdoms were those of the banking houses and holding companies, which were often under the dynastic control of a single family. All was undertaken with the thought of ultimately enriching and enlivening home and family life. The success of Calvinistic Protestantism was owed in no small part to the sanctioning of business activity and the regarding of success as a sign of divine favor. The Calvinist could charge interest with good conscience and without the fear of bringing down priestly maledictions on the practice of usury. Hard work and industriousness coupled with frugality led to a widespread accumulation of wealth in the hands of the middle class. No riotous living or public displays of luxury were possible when the church allowed no embellishment in its buildings and no musical elaboration in its services. While both the Anglican and Lutheran reform movements preserved much of the beauty of the traditional Roman Catholic liturgy in a modified form, Calvinistic Protestantism was marked by its extreme austerity. A strict interpretation of Calvinism would lead directly to a gloomy form of asceticism, but the innate good sense and honest enjoyment of material pleasures saved the Dutch from the bleaker aspects of this doctrine. But the principal outlet for their prosperity and desire for aesthetic enjoyment was their homes.

The wealthy burgher, however, did not build a palace—though he certainly had the means to do so. He was content with a comfortable house that was functionally suited to his needs. Fighting the Spanish crown for their independence, and resisting the growing menace of Louis XIV's absolute state, made the Dutch look with disfavor on any form of courtly pomp and ostentation. The Protestant movement also fortified their hostility to authority and intensified their nationalist consciousness. The middle-class merchant particularly resented the draining off of his province's wealth in the direction of Rome, and the resentment was equally strong against the secular arm of the Roman Catholic Church: the Holy Roman Empire. Protestantism thus took root and became identified in the Dutch mind with patriotism. The protection of their national and provincial rights, together with their individual freedoms, further focused their attention on their homes where they were their own lords and masters.

Philosophy, philology, social theory, and the natural sciences flourished in the Dutch universities. These intellectual pursuits speculated on the existence of an ordered and regulated universe in which everything could be measured and understood. The solid citizen instinctively distrusted the physical and emotional forces that could render his world chaotic and unpredictable. Hence, an ideal universe had considerable appeal for a bourgeoisie whose security and comforts could be perpetuated in such a world order. Descartes' rationalistic cosmology and psychology and Spinoza's mathematically demonstrable ethical system paralleled the concept of art as a form of reasoned organization, but it took a Rembrandt to illuminate this age of reason with an inner glow and to warm this rational world with the fire of human feeling.

Human anatomy was of consuming interest, and with Vesalius' *Anatomy* as a point of departure, dissection was carried over analogously into other fields. Books appeared with such titles as *Anatomy of Melancholy, Anatomy of Wit, Anatomy of Abuses, Anatomy of the World.* In this Age of Observation, the restless human eye extended by the lens could explore a plurality of worlds, and more things were seen in heaven and earth than were ever dreamed of before. Optical instruments were developed by the skilled lens makers of Holland, who numbered Spinoza among their ranks. An astronomical observatory was constructed at the University of Leyden, where the telescope could scan the skies. Conversely, the microscope opened up a new world in miniature. Though their eyes were on the heavens, Dutch savants did not neglect earthly applications of their discoveries. Astronomical calculations led to the discovery of triangulation and the spiral balance, both of vast value to navigation. The pendulum was applied to the keeping of time, and the pocket watch gave punctuality to daily life.

447. REMBRANDT. *Beggars Receiving Alms.* Etching, 6½ × 5". Rijksmuseum, Amsterdam.

The circumstances of the Dutch state of mind and material prosperity led to the placement of artistic patronage in the hands of a well-to-do middle class. Outside such necessary public buildings as the town halls, churches, and mercantile structures, Dutch architecture was, for all intents and purposes, domestic architecture. Since the houses were about the same size as middle-class homes today, there was no place in the scheme of things for monumental sculpture. The major domestic aesthetic expressions, therefore, were painting and music, together with all the minor decorative arts that added to the comfort and beauty of the home. Since pictures were destined for living-room walls, their sizes were correspondingly smaller than those painted for palaces and public halls. Easel pictures rather than murals became the norm for Dutch painting. There was a seemingly insatiable demand for pictures and the output was prodigious. The number of professional artists multiplied with the demand and led to a corresponding degree of specialization. In portraiture there were the painters of the decorous *pater familias* types, of the winebibbers in public taverns, and of corporation pictures. There were landscapists, seascapists, skyscapists, and even those whose specialty was cows. Painters also gravitated to the various social levels, with Jan Steen painting ribald tavern scenes and such boisterous gatherings as the *Merry* (right) 448. JAN STEEN. *Merry Family*. 1668. Oil on canvas, 43¼ × 55½". Rijksmuseum, Amsterdam.

(below) 449. REMBRANDT. *Three Trees*. 1643. Etching, 8¼ × 11". British Museum, London.

Family (Fig. 448) with himself playing the bagpipes; Frans Hals finding his subjects among fishwives and fruit peddlers; de Hooch and Vermeer depicting scenes in proper middle-class homes; and Terborch delighting in upper-class manners and elegant society portraiture.

The character of music was likewise molded by bourgeois patronage. In free cities, the organist and other municipal musicians were chosen by committees of the town councils, which supervised the musical life of the community as diligently as any of its other aspects. Auditions were held and competition encouraged. Public employment from the musician's point of view meant freedom from the arbitrary whims of a single aristocratic patron, and this was generally preferred because of the security it implied. When the tastes of the many

had to be taken into consideration, however, experimentation tended to be suppressed and standardization often was promoted. This was balanced to a considerable extent by the vast opportunities for private music making in the home, where musical expression took on a distinct domestic coloration.

The home was thus the factor that determined the art forms and imparted to them such an intimate character and quality. Dutch domestic architecture, painting, and music were all designed to be lived with and enjoyed by middle-class people who frankly took delight in their physical comforts and the arts that enriched their lives. Large canvases designed for altarpieces or to cover palace ceilings, colossal choral compositions for cathedrals, and operatic performances for palaces were productive of grandiose oratorical utterances but had no place in the home. The more modest dimensions of a painting or an etching designed for a living-room wall or of a chamber sonata or solo keyboard piece meant to be played in the same room were conducive to a more intimate and personal form of communication. The choice of medium is analogous to a composer's selection of the modern symphony orchestra for his epical pronouncements and of a chamber-music group or a piano sonata for his more confidential statements. The home was the dominant architectural form as well as the place where the pictures were hung, the books read, and the music played. In Holland and the northern countries generally, the baroque style was adapted both to Protestantism and to the tastes of the middle class. The bourgeois aspect of baroque art finds its unity in the cult of the home, and domesticity is the key to the understanding of the style.

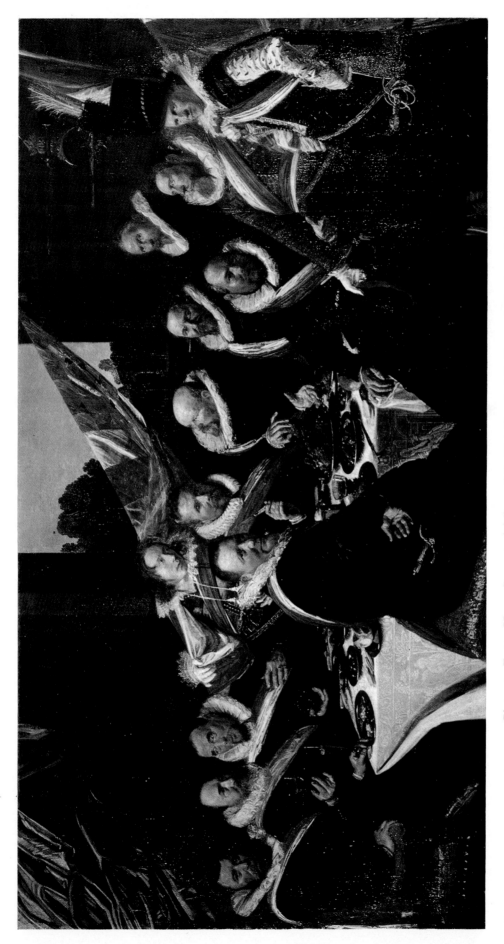

Plate 37. FRANS HALS. *Banquet of Officers of the Civic Guard of St. George at Haarlem.* 1616. Oil on canvas, 5′9 ½″ × 10′ 7 ½″. Frans Hals Museum, Haarlem. (See p. 378.)

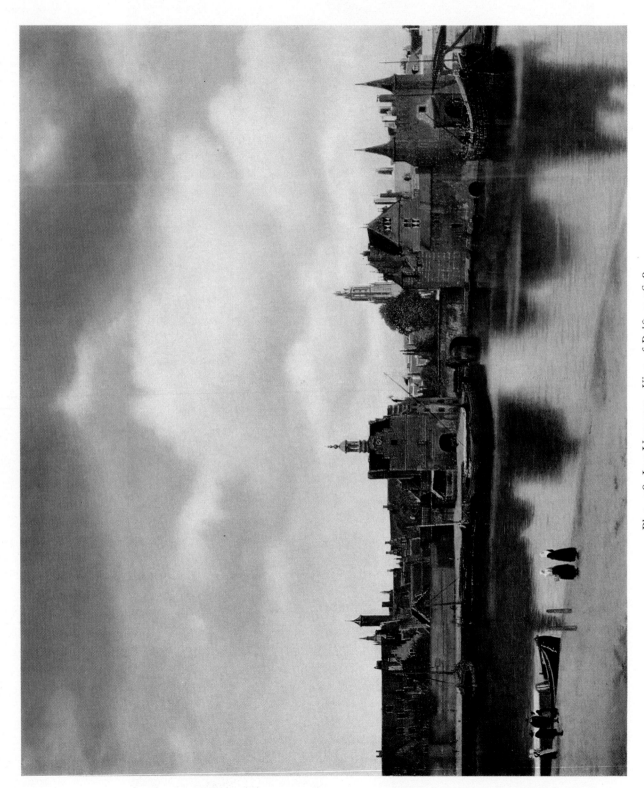

Plate 38. JAN VERMEER. *View of Delft. c.* 1658.
Oil on canvas, 38 ¾ × 46 ¼″. Mauritshuis, The Hague. (See p. 380.)

I5 - THE BAROQUE SYNTHESIS

LONDON DURING
THE RESTORATION

That day in the year of our Lord 1661, as Charles II made his triumphal progress to Westminster Abbey for his coronation, the sounds of Mr. Matthew Locke's march music for the sackbuts and cornets mingled with the cordial cheers of Charles' subjects. They were the cheers of a people wearied by a generation of civil strife and the effort of conforming to the rigors of puritanical idealism. They were the cheers of a people who hoped and prayed that the Restoration would bring them peace and normalcy. They were the cheers of a people who did not know that a few years hence their numbers would be decimated by an outbreak of the dreaded bubonic plague; that their city would be leveled by the Great Fire of London; and that the Restoration, which was supposed to be bringing back the old order, was actually ushering in the new.

The picture of a period embellished by a merry monarch, libertine lords, licentious ladies, and amorous adventurers has been painted all too often. That of a time which vibrated to the thunder of John Milton's poetry, spoke with the polished rhetoric of John Dryden, wondered at the mathematical ingenuity of Isaac Newton's equations, marveled at the majesty of Christopher Wren's architecture, and heard the harmonies of Henry Purcell's music has received much less attention. Even the merry monarch had a serious side, developed through the trials and tribulations of a troubled youth (during which his father's stormy reign had led to Charles I's losing his head) and throughout his exile in France where his most formative and impressionable years were spent. Charles II was an amateur astronomer, whose enthusiasm led to the founding of the Greenwich Observatory; a patron of the theater, whose interest played an important role in the development of the Restoration drama; a connoisseur of the arts, whose support of Christopher Wren led to an architectural rebirth in England; and a music lover, who took pride now and then in lifting his voice in song in what has been described politely as a "plump bass." Thus, in 1661, Charles II's years at Louis XIV's court were about to pay off handsomely, because in addition to some questionable absolutistic political ideas and some doubtful French courtly morals, he had brought back with him a goodly measure of Continental enthusiasm for the arts. During his reign, London was to become as much a cultural

(above) INIGO JONES. Banqueting House, Whitehall, London. Detail of cornice. 1619–1622.

General Events

1603–	1625	James I (Stuart) reigned
	1604	*Advancement of Learning* by Francis Bacon
	1611	King James' authorized English translation of Bible completed
1619–	1621	Banqueting House, Whitehall, built by Inigo Jones
	1620	*Novum Organum* by Francis Bacon
1625–	1649	Charles I reigned; after 1629 ruled without Parliament
	1628	*Treatise on Terrestrial Magnetism and Electricity* by William Gilbert (1540–1603) published in English edition
		Circulation of blood discovered by Harvey (1578–1657)
1642–	1660	English Civil Wars
	1643	Theaters closed by Parliament
	1649	Charles I executed, England proclaimed Commonwealth
	1651	*Leviathan; or the Matter, Form, and Power of a Commonwealth, Ecclesiastical and Civil* by Hobbes
1653–	1658	Oliver Cromwell (1599–1658) ruled
	1660	Restoration of monarchy
1660–	1685	Charles II reigned
	1661	*The Sceptical Chymist* by Robert Boyle (1627–1691)
	1662	Royal Society of London for Improving Natural Knowledge founded; Christopher Wren, Robert Boyle, John Dryden, charter members
	1662	Christopher Wren appointed deputy surveyor-general to king; 1665 in Paris to observe remodeling of Louvre; met Bernini, Perrault, Hardouin-Mansart
1664–	1665	Black Death bubonic plague swept London
	1666	Great Fire of London
	1667	*Paradise Lost* by Milton
	1669	Wren appointed surveyor-general to king
	1670	John Dryden appointed poet laureate and royal historiographer
1671–	1680	St. Mary-le-Bow and other London parish churches built by Wren
1675–	1710	St. Paul's Cathedral built
	1678	*Pilgrim's Progress*, Part I, by Bunyan; Part II, 1684
	1680	Purcell appointed organist at Westminster Abbey; named composer-in-ordinary to king (1683)
	1682	*Venus and Adonis*, chamber opera by John Blow, performed at court
	1685	*Albion and Albanius*, opera by Dryden and Purcell, performed in London
1685–	1688	James II reigned
	1687	*Philosophiae Naturalis Principia Mathematica* (Mathematical Principles of Natural Philosophy) by Newton (1642–1727)
	1688	Glorious Revolution. James II deposed; William of Orange and Mary (Stuart) became parliamentary rulers
1689–	1702	William and Mary reigned
	c.1689	*Dido and Aeneas*, opera, composed by Purcell
	1690	Wing of Hampton Court Palace built by Wren; *Essay Concerning Human Understanding* by John Locke
	1691	*King Arthur . . . A Dramatick Opera* by Dryden and Purcell performed
	1692	Nahum Tate appointed poet laureate
	1704	*Opticks* by Isaac Newton
1722–	1726	St. Martin-in-the-Fields built by Gibbs

Writers

1561–	1626	Francis Bacon
1563–	1593	Christopher Marlowe
1564–	1616	William Shakespeare
1572–	1631	John Donne
1573–	1637	Ben Jonson
1588–	1679	Thomas Hobbes
1608–	1674	John Milton
1628–	1688	John Bunyan
1631–	1700	John Dryden
1632–	1704	John Locke
1633–	1703	Samuel Pepys
1652–	1715	Nahum Tate

Architects

1573–	1652	Inigo Jones
1632–	1723	Christopher Wren
1682–	1754	James Gibbs

Painters

1577–	1640	Peter Paul Rubens
1599–	1641	Anthony van Dyck

Composers

1606–	1668	William Davenant
c.1647–	1674	Pelham Humfrey
c.1648–	1708	John Blow
1658–	1695	Henry Purcell
1685–	1759	George Frederick Handel

450. Inigo Jones. Banqueting House, Whitehall, London. 1619–1622. 120' long, 75' high.

suburb of Versailles as the common sense of his subjects would bear.

London had caught a brief glimpse of Continental elegance under James I, Charles II's grandfather, who had commissioned Inigo Jones to build the Banqueting House at Whitehall (Fig. 450) as the first unit of a projected royal palace. Modeled on Palladian principles, this structure marked a new departure in English architecture. When the great Peter Paul Rubens arrived in England on a diplomatic mission, he was persuaded by Charles I to paint the Banqueting Hall ceiling designs (Fig. 451). Anthony van Dyck, Rubens' most famous pupil, was appointed by Charles to paint a series of family portraits (Plate 39, Fig. 452). Now under Charles II the gates were about to be flung wide open.

Nicholas Laniere was dispatched to Italy to purchase pictures for the royal collection. William Davenant, who had been a guest in Paris of Charles and his mother and had closely observed Lully's musical methods, was summoned to become England's first opera manager. When the French opera composer Robert Cambert was outmaneuvered at home by the wily Lully, he found a ready welcome at the English court. Pelham Humfrey, a promising young composer of 17 and later the teacher of Purcell, was sent to Paris by Charles to see how Lully managed his orchestra and ballet. Since Louis XIV

451. Inigo Jones. Interior, Banqueting House, Whitehall, London. Ceiling paintings by Peter Paul Rubens, 1629–1634.

had his *Vingt-quatre Violons*, Charles II would have his Four-and-twenty Fiddles. When the monarch was looking around for a poet laureate, the choice fell to Dryden, who was most familiar with Boileau and the French baroque drama. And when Charles heard that King Louis and Colbert were getting ready to remodel the Louvre, he saw to it that Wren was on the spot to study the plans and to meet Bernini and Perrault.

The stage on which the Restoration scene was to be played, however, had a distinctive character of its own. The City of London was a mercantile center under the domination of neither Church nor monarchy. To this day, the Greater London Council does not have jurisdiction over the City of London, and the British sovereign must—theoretically at least—request the permission of the Lord Mayor to enter its territorial limits. In the 17th century, the City of London, with its population of about 500,000, was London. The aristocracy maintained their country houses elsewhere, leaving London to the merchants and clerks who worked in their shops and countinghouses and lived upstairs. To change anything in this conservative middle-class stronghold took one of those decisive events that are defined legally as acts of God. In 1666, one came in the form of the fire which, according to the diary of Samuel Pepys, destroyed 13,000 houses, 400 streets, and 90 churches, including much of Old St. Paul's Cathedral that dated from shortly after the Norman conquest. Before the charred ruins had stopped smoking, Christopher Wren was sketching a plan for the rebuilding of the entire city. The fire gave him the greatest opportunity ever afforded an English architect; and even though his plan was not to be carried out completely, enough of it was realized to determine the architectural course of late 17th-century London and to give that city its superb skyline (see Fig. 464).

The collision between the staunch middle-class citizenry and their foreign-bred king brought further tangible proof of the English genius for compromise. The Stuarts from the beginning had tried to impose the Continental concept of absolutism on their reluctant subjects. The extremes of Charles I and his failure to come to terms with the middle-class merchants and their official body, the House of Commons, had brought about the Cromwellian Commonwealth. The uncompromising Oliver Cromwell on his side had alienated the still-powerful aristocracy. Charles II had some success in trying to find a middle ground. His successor James II, however, again overstepped his prerogatives, and it took still another revolution—this time the bloodless Glorious Revolution—to bring about the alliance between the sovereign and the middle class under the compromise formula of a limited monarchy.

Much the same struggle is mirrored in the arts. The French aristocratic baroque, just like the absolute monarchy, was too rich for the English diet. When it came time to build a new cathedral, Charles and his principal architect, Sir Christopher Wren, thought in terms of the richly embellished classical orders, the splendor and spaciousness of the Louvre and Versailles, and the central-church plans of Palladio and Michelangelo. The Church of England clergy and their lay advisors, however, still thought of a cathedral as a tall, imposing Gothic structure. Wren wanted it to be crowned with a dome; the churchmen thought it should have a spire. So Wren built his dome and put a high lantern tower on top of it. Charles wanted the London parish churches to be free of Gothic gauntness and gloom, but the parishioners insisted on belfries with tall-spired steeples. So Wren gave them their steeples, but with classical geometrical flourishes. Charles wanted Lullian opera, but London theatergoers showed remarkable resistance toward sung recitative. So they got a hybrid form of spoken dialogue interspersed with some songs and punctuated with instrumental interludes.

With political authority divided between the monarch and parliament, literary precedents between the classical and Elizabethan traditions, architectural ideas between the French baroque and English Gothic, and musical expression between the latest continental developments and native preferences, the British genius for compromise effected a synthesis of aristocratic and middle-class institutions, Roman Catholicism and Protestantism, as well as the Continental and English traditions. Through the efforts and genius of three men—Wren in architecture, Dryden in literature, and Purcell in music—the Continental influences were absorbed, adapted, mingled with native traditions, and finally synthesized into a distinctive Restoration style.

ARCHITECTURE

In the crypt beneath St. Paul's Cathedral in London a Latin inscription on a stone slab reads: "Beneath is laid the builder of this church and city, Christopher Wren, who lived more than 90 years, not for himself but for the good of the state. If you seek a monument, look around you." As the observer studies the structure, he will first be struck by the unity of St. Paul's (Fig. 453), for this is the

453. CHRISTOPHER WREN. Façade, St. Paul's Cathedral, London. 1675–1710. 514 × 250', dome 366' high.

(left) 454. Christopher Wren. St. Paul's Cathedral, perspective view of great model design. Engraving by John Soane, 1726.

(right) 455. St. Paul's Cathedral, plan as executed.

only major cathedral in Europe to be built by one architect, by one master mason, and during the episcopate of one bishop. In contrast it took 13 architects, 20 popes, and more than a century to build St. Peter's in Rome (Fig. 324). The last stone on the lantern tower above the dome of St. Paul's was put in place in 1710 by one of Wren's sons in the presence of the 78-year-old builder, and for another 8 years Wren continued to supervise the completion of the last decorative details.

Even before the Great Fire, Wren was a member of a commission charged with the remodeling of Old St. Paul's. The plan had to be scrapped when a survey after the fire showed the building beyond repair. It was this that gave Wren his great opportunity. Like Bramante and Michelangelo before him, Wren envisaged a centralized area of great spaciousness surrounded radially by subsidiary spatial units. Like his eminent predecessors, he too preferred a central-church plan based on the Greek cross. In this way, a building of such monumental proportions could have both its exterior mass and interior space dominated by the all-embracing, unifying force of a dome. From a practical point of view, Wren was also aware that he was designing a Protestant cathedral which should permit as many people as possible to be within earshot of the pulpit so as to hear the sermon-centered service of the Anglican Church of his day.

The conservative members of the clergy, with thoughts of the ancient Catholic processional liturgy in mind, wanted a long nave with aisles on either side. Wren, therefore, without sacrificing the heart of his plan, lengthened the edifice by adding an apse in the east and a domed vestibule with an extended porch in the west. His model (Fig. 454), however, brought further objections from the clergy, necessitating still other revisions. All Wren's diplomacy, versatility, ingenuity, and, above all,

patience were called into play to effect a workable compromise (Fig. 455) that would satisfy his difficult clients and yet save the essence of his cherished conception. He gave the clergy their aisled nave and transepts and their deep choir, but these he grouped around the central plan of his original design. In this way, he could still concentrate great space under the dome. Wren thus was actually building two churches, the clergy's and his own, a procedure that was bound to produce some architectural dissonances but for which he was able to find a satisfactory if somewhat uneasy resolution in the cathedral that was finally completed.

Wren's practical problems with St. Paul's were as numerous as his difficulties with the authorities. Funds for construction were limited; the site demanded engineering ingenuity, for there, as in much of London, solid ground was buried beneath forty feet of clay and sand that could not bear excessive weight. Long before his cathedral was completed, he had had to abandon his hopes for an unimpeded view and an axial approach to his façade (Fig. 453) up Ludgate Hill on which St. Paul's rests. In the eagerness to rebuild after the fire, the vicinity had become a clutter of shops and houses, and it took the German air force in World War II to clear the land around the south side and the choir (Fig. 456). And when no quarry could supply stone of the necessary lengths for the great columns of his original façade, Wren had had to separate the façade into two separate stories of the Corinthian and Composite orders. His use of paired columns recalls Perrault's colonnade on the east front of the Louvre (Fig. 401). The side turrets were designed after 1700, and it is of more than passing interest that for some time one of them was left hollow except for a circular staircase, so that Wren and his fellow astronomers could use it temporarily for an observatory.

Externally, the proportions of St. Paul's needed a massive dome, while internally one of lesser size would suffice. With the foundations demanding as little weight as possible, Wren's solution was a double dome with the smaller inner shell of brick ingeniously supporting the larger outer sheath of lead-coated timber which rises over 275 feet above the ground. The colonnade around the outer part of the drum functions practically to absorb the lateral thrust of the masonry and decoratively to complete the rhythm of the classical orders that mount upward from below. But the clergy still longed for a lofty spire that would dominate the city's skyline as that of Old St. Paul's had done. Wren therefore added a tall lantern tower that soared upward a full 90 feet above the top of his dome.

The effect of Wren's preferred plan is felt most strongly in the rotunda beneath the dome (Fig. 457). Geometrically, the space is bounded by a gigantic octagon, punctuated at the angles by the eight piers on which the cupola rests. These are bridged over by a ring of contiguous Roman triumphal arches, which, in turn, are crowned by the great dome, the culmination of the entire composition. From this central area, the arches open outward into eight spatial subdivisions that give the interior such constant variety and interest. The centralization under the lofty dome, the complex divisions and subdivisions of space, the imaginative design and Roman detail reveal Wren's affinity for the baroque. The restraining influences of the conservative clergy, the lack of unlimited funds, and

456. CHRISTOPHER WREN. St. Paul's Cathedral (view from southeast). 1675–1710.

457. CHRISTOPHER WREN. Rotunda, St. Paul's Cathedral. Aquatint by THOMAS MALTON, 1798.

458. CHRISTOPHER WREN. Plan for City of London after Great Fire of 1666.

Wren's rationalistic viewpoint demonstrate his remarkable achievement in making the style palatable to British taste.

Wren's plan for the rebuilding of London met with even stiffer resistance than his project for St. Paul's. It included the laying out of a series of new streets that radiated outward starlike from central squares and that took the main traffic routes into consideration (Fig. 458). Certain public buildings were to be oriented on an axis involving the new cathedral and the Royal Exchange. The spires of the various parish churches were to punctuate the silhouette at certain points and by degrees lead up to the grand climax of St. Paul's dome. The plan, if it had been carried out, would have gone far beyond Versailles (see Fig. 410). But Wren's king was not an absolute monarch with the power to condemn property and the money to buy it. Time also ran against Wren, because the shopkeepers throughout London were in a hurry to rebuild and start their business concerns again. About all he was able to rescue were the steeples of the parish churches he was called upon to design.

As London's principal architect, Wren was commissioned to build more than fifty of these new parish churches. Consultations had to be held with the churchwardens on the problems and needs of each church. Owing to the limited funds at his disposal, the churches of necessity had to be rather modest affairs. Wren, in keeping with the spirit of the time, wanted to build them in the restrained baroque style based on the classical orders. His clients and the Gothic tradition still demanded the spires that not only had the force of symbols but the practical purpose of housing the bell tower, which was still a functional unit of a church. Wren's problem, therefore, was to balance the vertical tendency of the steeple with the horizontality of his classical temple façades—once more, the reconciliation of northern and southern building traditions. Wren's solution, which can be counted

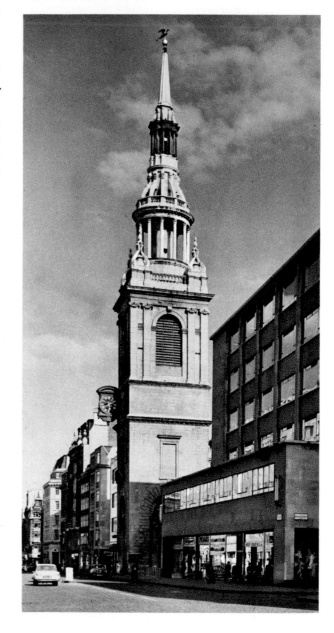

459. CHRISTOPHER WREN. St. Mary-le-Bow, London. 1671–1680. Total height 216′1″, steeple 104′6″.

460. JAMES GIBBS. St. Martin-in-the-Fields, London. 1721–1726.

among his minor miracles, can only be understood through an actual example.

The steeple of St. Mary-le-Bow (Fig. 459), where the famous Bow Bells once rang out, shows the mathematician's obvious delight in a free play of geometrical forms. From a solid square base it moves through several circular phases and terminates finally in an octagonal pyramid. By the judicious use of baroque scrolls and twists at various points, this is achieved without a hint of abruptness. Knowing that the churches themselves were bound to be hidden by the surrounding buildings, Wren lavished most of his skill on their spires. The continuation of the Wren tradition into the next century is seen in James Gibbs' Church of St. Martin-in-the-Fields (Fig. 460). Wren had always planted his steeples firmly in the ground, so to speak, so that they seemed to grow in an organic relation to the whole composition. Gibbs' spire, by contrast, appears to sprout unexpectedly out of the roof. The memory of these churches and their steeples was carried to the American colonies by the founding fathers; and when they came to build their own churches in new cities, it was to the designs of Christopher Wren and James Gibbs that they turned for their models.

Despite his many responsibilities, Wren found the time to design some commodious houses for well-to-do middle-class clients. During the reign of William and Mary, he was also commissioned to complete the unfinished Royal Hospital at Greenwich (Fig. 461) begun earlier by Inigo Jones, and to add a new wing for Hampton Court Palace. His patron, William of Orange, remembered the good red brick of his native Holland, while Wren recalled the grandeur of the Louvre and Versailles palaces. Another of Wren's famous designs was effected in

461. CHRISTOPHER WREN. Greenwich Royal Hospital. 1696–1705. 150′ high.

his design for the Fountain Court (Fig. 462) and the garden façade at Hampton Court Palace (Fig. 463).

Thus it was that Wren, the professor of astronomy at London and Oxford, left off probing the mysteries of the heavens with his telescope and equations and became the engineer and architect who penetrated that segment of the sky above London with the majestic spires and domes that gave the city its characteristic profile and skyline (Fig. 464).

DRAMA AND MUSIC

On the gala occasion of the formal opening of the King's Theatre in 1674, His Majesty and London's most distinguished audience gathered there for the evening's entertainment. John Dryden, that cold, aristocratic but brilliant author, took advantage of the situation afforded by the Prologue to express his sentiments in some well-chosen words, which went in part:

'Twere folly now a stately pile to raise,
To build a playhouse while you throw down plays;
Whilst scenes, machines and empty Operas reign,
And for the Pencil you the Pen disdain;
While Troops of famished Frenchmen hither drive,
And laugh at those upon whose Alms they live:
Our English Authors vanish, and give place
To these new Conquerors of the Norman race.

Dryden was thus making the valiant effort of an exasperated man of letters to stem the tide toward the foreign forms of opera, which, in his opinion, threatened to engulf reason with rhyme. The course of events, however, was flowing far too strongly; and, to keep from being inundated, he soon was collaborating with one of those fashionable Frenchmen and writing some very fancy "scenes and machines" himself.

With all the adaptability of a thoroughly equipped professional writer, Dryden honestly tried to squeeze some content into those "empty Operas." To help acclimate this exotic form to its new surroundings, he fell back on the tradition of the

462. CHRISTOPHER WREN. Fountain Court, Hampton Court Palace, near London. c. 1690.

463. CHRISTOPHER WREN. Garden façade, Hampton Court Palace. c. 1690.

464. CANALETTO. *London. c.* 1750. Oil on canvas, 42 × 73″. Reproduced by gracious permission of Her Majesty Queen Elizabeth II (Crown copyright).

English court masque, a native equivalent of the French *ballet de cour*, which had set the precedent for the development of opera at the court of Louis XIV. The masque was a hybrid that included poems, songs, dances, spoken dialogue, and scenic spectacle. In the reign of James I, court masques were produced on a lavish scale and enlisted the efforts of the foremost talents. In a performance of Ben Jonson's *Masque of Blackness* at Whitehall in 1605, the dancers included the queen and her ladies, and the designer of the scenic spectacle was none other than the famous architect Inigo Jones (Fig. 465), who is credited with the invention of modern movable scenery. Ludlow Castle was the setting in 1634 for Milton's *Comus*, with music by Henry Lawes.

When Dryden came to write his *Albion and Albanius*, he had to summon all his tactical skill to balance these opposing elements and try to keep them in proper proportion. In his Preface, he was more than a little apologetic about having to write so as "to please the hearing rather than gratify the understanding"; and, he continued, "it appears, indeed, preposterous at first sight, that rhyme, on any consideration, should take the place of reason." His solution was to use spoken dialogue for the ordinary mortals in the play but to include what he called a "songish part" for such supernatural characters as gods and goddesses, spirits and sprites. Their behavior, he observed, "being extended beyond the limits of human nature, admits of that

sort of marvelous and surprising conduct, which is rejected in other plays."

This opera of Dryden contains many remarkable scenes and machines. In one, "Mercury descends in a chariot drawn by ravens"; in another, "the clouds divide, and Juno appears in a Machine drawn by Peacocks; while a Symphony is playing"; in yet another, Venus and Albanius rise out of the sea in a great scallop shell drawn by dolphins to a symphony of "flutes-doux." The stage directions for the final scene read: "Whilst a Symphony is

465. INIGO JONES. Drawing for Scene 5 of WILLIAM DAVENANT's masque *Salmacida Spolia.* 1640. Pen and ink, 12 1/8 × 16 1/2″. Devonshire Collection, Chatsworth Library, Derbyshire, England.

playing, a very large, and very glorious Machine descends; the figure of it oval, all the clouds shining with gold, abundance of Angels and Cherubins flying about them, and playing in them; in the midst of it sits Apollo on a throne of gold; he comes from the machine to Albion."

In spite of the gaudy machines, Dryden's attempt in this instance was a failure—possibly because it was not sufficiently distinguished from the court masque to be a true opera, but more probably because the music provided by Monsieur Grabu was mediocre. Though Henry Purcell was already 26 years old, England had to wait almost a decade before it was to have the collaboration of a poet and musician comparable in stature to Molière and Lully in France.

While awaiting the invitation from Dryden to collaborate on *King Arthur*, England's greatest composer had to content himself with writing incidental music to dozens of undistinguished plays. The best of them were such Shakespearean adaptations as *The Tempest* and *The Fairy Queen* (from *A Midsummer Night's Dream*), which bear only a remote resemblance to the originals. For his one great opportunity in the operatic field, *Dido and Aeneas*, he had to get along with a book by Nahum Tate, whose stature in English letters is several notches below that of his French counterpart Quinault, who was Lully's chief librettist. But there is not a shred of evidence to show that Purcell was unhappy about the situation. The picture of his career is simply that of a professional composer, diligently active at all times, and technically capable of fulfilling any commission which came his way, whether from church, court, or independent sources.

It was through Josias Priest, a dancing master in one of the London theaters, that Purcell received the invitation to write a short opera to be performed at his boarding school for young gentlewomen at Chelsea. Thus it was that about 1689, Purcell came to write his little operatic masterpiece for a group of schoolgirls. As such it is a true *chamber*

opera, designed for a limited space and restricted to a limited cast of characters and a small orchestra. Though small in scale, it is large in emotional scope; and while it falls within the province of amateur performance, it is filled with the utmost musical sophistication. Its immediate antecedent was *Venus and Adonis*, a three-act chamber opera written a few years earlier by Purcell's teacher John Blow. This charming intimate work had been performed for the entertainment of Charles II and his court circle shortly before the monarch's death. It was one of the few existing through-composed operas (that is, with the entire text set to music) in English; otherwise, for local precedents there was only the masque tradition and the Dryden-Grabu experiments to guide him. Purcell, however, was conversant with the latest Continental developments in the operatic field, and it is the piquant blend of these native and foreign elements that gives his work its characteristic color and variety.

Dido and Aeneas opens with a dignified overture in the Lully style, marked by the halting rhythms and harmonic suspensions of a slow beginning, and the fugal imitations of a lively conclusion. All the orchestral sections seem to have been scored only for strings with the usual keyboard support. For his recitatives and airs, he turns to the models developed by Monteverdi and his successor at the Venetian opera, Cavalli. Purcell makes particularly bold use of the so-called "representative style," a type of word-painting, by which the descriptive imagery of the text is reflected in the shape and turn of the melodic line. This prosody of the representative style can be illustrated by the first word in the opera, "Shake" (a), and the menacing movement of the line for "storms" (b). When speaking of Aeneas' parentage, the valor of his father Anchises is characterized by a martial rhythm (c); while immediately afterward a modulation to the minor mode and a caressing chromaticism express the voluptuousness of Venus' charms (d); and when Aeneas' entrance is announced, Belinda's words take on the shape of a trumpet fanfare (e).

my fate, Re-mem-ber me, but ah!_____ for-get my_ fate!

The airs show a considerable variety as to type. Dido's opening and closing songs are built over a short repeated bass pattern as in the Italian *ostinato aria*. The melody of "Oft She Visits" is written over a continuously flowing bass line in the manner of an Italian *continuo aria*; while the three-part melodic form of "Pursue Thy Conquest, Love," in which the final section is a repetition of the beginning, identifies it as a *da capo aria*.

The emphasis on the choruses and dances is in the English court masque tradition, but both are handled by Purcell with a highly ingenious blend of native and Continental elements. In the palace scenes, the courtiers function as a true Greek chorus by making solemn comments in unison on the action. The final number, "With Drooping Wings," is a typical French mourning chorus straight out of Lullian opera. The witches, however, sing in the English madrigal style with the amusing substitution of some malicious "Ho, ho, ho's" for the jollier "Fa la la's," to signify their sinister purposes. Highly interesting is Purcell's introduction of a Venetian echo chorus in these solemn surroundings. While the witches sing "In Our Deep Vaulted Cell," an offstage chorus softly echoes "-ed cell." By thus increasing the perception of space, Purcell is able to add the necessary uncanny touch as the witches start to prepare their mysterious charms. The spell is further carried out in the Echo Dance of Furies, in which an offstage instrumental ensemble echoes the principal orchestra with telling effect. The dances show much of the same stylistic mixture as the choruses. Scene 1 concludes with the courtiers doing a Triumphing Dance, which is a vigorous version of a Lully *chaconne* treated as a set of instrumental variations over a ground bass. During Act III, when Aeneas is preparing to sail away from Carthage, Purcell paints a typical English seaport scene in which the swinging sailors' dances mingle with the salty comments of a chorus of common people. The angularity of such native rhythms is a distinct contrast to the more formal *courantes* and *chaconnes* that are danced by the courtiers.

Purcell's logic and fine dramatic perception do not permit him to soften his opera toward the end by allowing a *deus ex machina* to bring it to a happy ending in the manner of the French court style of Lully. The human will when contending with the gods is always doomed, and the plot must move inexorably onward. The tragedy is therefore carried through to its predestined conclusion with growing eloquence and mounting emotion. As a consequence, "Dido's Farewell" (p. 401) becomes one of the most moving moments in all music, combining as it does the most passionate feeling with the dignified restraint demanded of a tragic heroine out of Vergil's *Aeneid*. It is cast in the form of an *ostinato aria* with an obstinately repetitive bass figure, which descends chromatically to the rhythm of the stately *passacaglia*. Dido's inner struggle is expressed by the tension between the free obbligato melodic line that she sings and the inflexible bass, and she contends with this fixed force as with her tragic fate. Vainly she tries to bend it to her will, as seen in some of the asymmetrical diagonal shifts of her phrases off their center, but in the end she must resign herself to it while the orchestra carries the aria onward to its tragic conclusion.

Within the limitations of this short opera, which takes but little more than an hour to perform, Purcell produced a major work of art. Though it is his only through-composed piece for the lyric stage, it reveals the sure touch of one who knows every aspect of his dramatic business. The extensive emotional range and the variety of technical devices are all the more astonishing in view of the meager resources he had at his disposal. Purcell possesses, first of all, the rare power to delineate and create believable human characters by musical means, a gift he shares with Gluck and Mozart. He is also one of the few composers who know how to convert the dry academic techniques of counterpoint into lively dramatic devices, a characteristic he shares with Bach and Handel. This is apparent, for example, in Dido's first air, "Ah, Belinda." Her melody is like a series of descending sighs over a ground bass that, like destiny, is relentless and unyielding. At the words "Peace and I are strangers grown," the parting of the ways is depicted by a canon at the octave; and on the word "strangers," the predominant four-bar pattern begins to wander and is stretched out into five bars. Again, after Aeneas declares he will defy destiny itself in order to remain with Dido, the chorus makes contrapuntal comments that graphically give expression to their disturbed and conflicting emotions. When Purcell wants to depict the hustle and bustle around the departing ships in the scene at the dockside in Act III, the independent lines of the fugal introduction, with their imitative thematic entries and exits, humorously describe the coming and going of the people. When such skillful means as these are combined with his fanciful orchestration, colorful use of chromaticism, and deep poetic feeling, they are sure to lead to

significant ends—as indeed, in this case, they did.

One more opportunity to write an English opera was presented to Purcell when Dryden, the literary arbiter of Restoration drama, invited him to collaborate on *King Arthur* in 1691. Dryden, in this case, was trying to breathe something of the grandiloquence of the French baroque theater into a patriotic English drama. His Preface shows that he was still groping for a formula to adapt music and poetry to the English lyric stage, and his sincere misgivings are apparent when he complains: "I have been obliged to cramp my Verses, and make them rugged to the Reader, that they may be harmonious to the Hearer." Like a good rationalist, he was also worried about writing a play "principally designed for the Ear and Eye" rather than for the mind. He still felt that the human characters should speak and that only the superhuman ones should sing. In this parenthetical way, the music could be made to sound more plausible and thus not seem like an intrusion into the course of the main dramatic sequence. Fortunately for Purcell, there were so many superhuman characters that his score assumed very ample proportions. *King Arthur* was a truly distinguished attempt to solve the problem of English opera. In its way, it was another typically English compromise, since it was neither an opera nor a play but a compound of elements drawn from both. If this collaboration between Dryden and Purcell had continued, it eventually might have led to a distinctive English form of the music drama. As *King Arthur* stands, it remains a noble but somewhat inconclusive experiment.

In spite of Purcell's sparing but convincing use of the sung recitative, and his efforts to extract the essence out of Monteverdi's representative style by removing some of the Italian bombast in order to render it palatable to London audiences, recitative simply did not take root. Through-composed opera was destined to remain an exotic plant on English soil. As the *Gentlemen's Journal* of January, 1692, put it, "Experience hath taught us that our English genius will not rellish that perpetual singing."

A judicious comparison between the three great figures of the Restoration style—Wren, Dryden, and Purcell—can be highly illuminating. Each in his way was trying to bring his country up to date on the latest Continental developments, just as each was trying to inject something of the grandeur of the baroque style into an English art form. In order to do so, each was willing to make the necessary compromises to avoid parting company with English audiences. When Wren was designing his preferred models on his drawing board, when Dryden was writing solely for his readers, and when Purcell was composing experimentally for amateurs, each could be as free as he chose. But when it came to building a cathedral, mounting a play, and composing music for the theater, many subtle and even drastic adjustments had to be made. Each man had sufficient mastery in his field and each was sufficiently versatile and inventive to make those adjustments. Each preferred and developed an aristocratic style but never neglected the common touch. Each, in his turn, had an effect on posterity that lasted well into the next century. Wren's buildings became the backbone of the Georgian style; Dryden's works, the background for 18th-century classicism in English letters; and the fact that many of Purcell's works until recently have been thought to be by Bach and Handel is proof enough that they were absorbed directly into the sacred and secular music of the succeeding generation.

IDEAS

Baroque Rationalism

Stimulated by the explorations of navigators of the globe, the scanning of the skies by astronomers, and the ingenuity of inventors, baroque man came to have a new concept of himself and his place in the universe. Galileo's telescope confirmed and popularized Copernicus' theory of a solar system in which the earth revolved around the sun rather than vice versa. The concept of the static Aristotelian universe thus had to yield to one that was full of whirling motion. Since the earth was no longer considered as a fixed point located at the nerve center of the cosmos, man could hardly be regarded any longer as the sole purpose of creation. It was some consolation, however, to know that this strange new moving universe at least was subject to mechanical and mathematical laws, and therefore to a considerable extent predictable. Copernicus and Kepler as well as the other scientists were convinced of its unity, proportion, and harmony; and the fact that man had the privilege of probing into the secrets of nature—if his intellect proved equal to the task—was a highly exhilarating thought. The rationalism of the 17th century, then, was based on the view that the universe could at last be understood in logical, mathematical, and mechanical terms. As a philosophy and semireligion, this world view had far-reaching consequences by preparing the pathway for the theories of positivism and materialism, the doctrines of deism and atheism, and the mechanical and industrial revolutions.

While Greek rationalism had been based on the perception and measurement of a static world, baroque rationalism had to come to terms with a dynamic universe. Scientific thought was concerned with movement in space and time. The need for a mathematics capable of comprehending a world of matter in motion led Descartes to his analytical geometry, Pascal to a study of cycloid curves, and both Leibniz and Newton to the simultaneous but independent discovery of integral and differential calculus. Baroque invention led to refinements in navigation, to improvements in the telescope and microscope for the exploration of distant and minute regions of space, the barometer for the measurement of air pressure, the thermometer for the recording of temperature changes, and the anemometer for the calculation of the force of winds. Astronomers were occupied with the study of planetary motion; William Harvey discovered the circulation of the blood in the human body; and physicists were making speculations in the field of thermodynamics and gravitation.

Newton's preoccupation with mass, force, and momentum, his speculations on the principles of attraction and repulsion, and his calculations on terrestrial and celestial mechanics led him to a monumental synthesis that he presented to the British Royal Society in 1686 and published in London a year later. Newton's *Principia* embraced a complete and systematic view of an orderly world based on mechanical principles, capable of mathematical proof, and demonstrable by accurate prediction. His work was, in fact, a scientific *summa* that established the intellectual architecture of the new view of the universe.

Such a changed world view was bound to have important consequences for the arts, which responded in this case with a ringing reassertion of man's supremacy and a joyous acceptance of this new understanding of the universe. The application of rationalistic principles to aesthetic expression is by no means accidental or casual. Before he became an architect, Christopher Wren was a mechanical inventor, an experimental scientist, and a professor of astronomy at London and Oxford. As one of the founders of the Royal Society, he was in close communication with such men as Robert Boyle and Isaac Newton. The fellows of the Royal Society appointed John Dryden to a committee whose purpose was to study the English language with a view toward linguistic reforms. They recommended that English prose should have both purity and brevity, so that verbal communication could be brought as close to mathematical plainness and precision as possible. Dryden's embarrassment in writing an opera that was designed to please the ear rather than gratify the understanding was therefore quite understandable. Purcell's music likewise was based on a system of intricate contrapuntal principles and tonal logic in which certain given premises, such as sequences or repeated ground basses are followed by predictable conclusions. His music, moreover, is characterized by intellectual discipline, symmetry, clarity, and a sure sense of direction. His forms are models of brevity in which each part has its proper place, no loose ends are left dangling, and the cadences bring everything to a positive conclusion. Together with Wren's architecture and Dryden's poetic drama, Purcell's music reflects a buoyant self-confidence, an inventive spirit that gave birth to new forms, an exploration of novel optical and acoustical ideas, and a conviction that a work of art should in its way be a reflection of an orderly and lawful universe.

BAROQUE SYNTHESIS AND CONCLUSION

While the baroque period is mainly centered in the 17th century, its extreme temporal limits extend all the way from the mid-16th to the mid-18th centuries, from Michelangelo to Johann Sebastian Bach. During this span of time the concept of the world had moved from a terracentric to a heliocentric universe; philosophical speculation had turned from a supernatural to a natural world view; the fundamental processes of thought had shifted from the acceptance of authority on faith to scientific experimentation; the unity of Christianity symbolized by one universal Church had been opposed by a number of Protestant sects; and the theoretical political unity of the Holy Roman Empire had given way to the practical fact of a balance of power distributed among a family of nations. The baroque period was one in which irresistible modern forces met immovable traditional objects. Out of the resulting theological disputations, philosophical discussions, scientific arguments, social tensions, political strife, warring nations, and artistic creation, both the baroque style and the modern age were born.

The baroque world was one in which irreconcilable oppositions had to find a way of coexistence. The rise of rationalism was accompanied by the march of militant mysticism; the aristocratic cult of majesty was echoed by the bourgeois cult of domesticity; the internationalism of Roman Catholicism was in conflict with the nationalism of the Protestant sects; religious orthodoxy had to contend with freedom of thought; the Jesuits brought all the arts into their churches, while Calvin did his utmost to exclude the arts as vanities; Philip II built a palatial mausoleum and monastery, while Louis XIV erected a pleasure palace and theater; Charles I tried to force an absolute monarchy on England, and Cromwell's answer was a republican commonwealth; the printing press made books available, while suppression by censorship took them away; the boldest scientific speculation took place alongside a reassertion of the belief in miracles and a renewal of religious fundamentalism; Newton's *Principia* and the final part of Bunyan's *Pilgrim's Progress* appeared in London within two years of each other. In Spain, the emotional involvement of El Greco was succeeded by the optical detachment of Velázquez; in France the spontaneity of Rubens was followed by the academic formalism of Poussin; in Holland, the broad humanity of Rembrandt led to the specialization and precision of Vermeer.

Such oppositions could hardly be expected to resolve themselves into a single uniform style. At best, they could achieve a temporary resolution and a fusion of forms, such as those found in a Counter Reformation church, the Versailles Palace, Rembrandt's visual dramatization of the Bible, and Purcell's operatic synthesis. In them, forceful striving and restless motion are more characteristic than serenity and repose. Baroque art thus emerges from these tensions and speaks in eloquent accents of the expanding range of human activities, grandiose achievements, and a ceaseless search for new and more powerful means of expression.

All this took place within the expanse of a tremendously enlarged sense of space. The astronomers told of remote regions populated by an infinite number of stars. Pascal speculated on the mathematical implications of infinity. The gardens and avenues of Versailles were laid out in keeping with this vastly extended conception of space. The vistas led the eye toward the horizon and invited the imagination to continue beyond. The unification of the vast buildings and gardens there placed baroque man wholly within the scope of nature and declared him to be a part of the new measurable universe. Wren's attempt to bring his cathedral, parish churches, and public buildings into one all-embracing scheme was also in keeping with this image of the comprehensive baroque universe. Painters likewise delighted in leading the eye outside their pictures and attempted to convey the impression of infinity through the bold use of light and exaggerated perspective effects. The Dutch landscapists tried to capture atmospheric perspective, and Rembrandt was concerned with the infinite gradations of light. Through use of illusionistic effects, ceilings of Counter Reformation churches opened the skies and tried to promote the feeling of a world without end.

In music there was a corresponding expansion of tonal space. The organs and other keyboard instruments were built to encompass a wider range from bass to soprano. Both the wind and the

Plate 39. ANTHONY VAN DYCK. *Charles I of England. c.* 1635.
Oil on canvas, 8′11″ × 6′11″. Louvre, Paris. (See p. 391.)

Plate 40. JEAN-HONORÉ FRAGONARD. *The Swing. c.* 1766–1769.
Oil on canvas, 32 × 25 ½″. Wallace Collection, London. (See p. 414.)

stringed instruments were constructed in families, ranging all the way from what Orlando Gibbons called the "Great Dooble Base" to the high soprano register of the violin. Louis XIV and Charles II incorporated this string family into ensembles of twenty-four viols, thus increasing both the resonance and volume of sound through the doubling process. The coming into use of chromatic harmony with all the half-tone divisions of the octave was the internal extension of the same idea. Purcell's opposition of ground basses and soprano melodies emphasized the baroque love of a spacious distribution of sonorities. His adoption of the Venetian double chorus and his dramatic use of the echo effect in *Dido and Aeneas* were still further evidence of the desire to increase the perception of space through sound and to use their aural breadth for expressive purposes.

Above all, the baroque universe was in ceaseless movement. Whether a rationalist thought of it in terms of whirling particles or a mystic as full of swirling spirits, both saw their world as a vortex of spheres and spirals describing infinitely complex patterns of motion. Kepler's planets revolved in elliptical orbits; Counter Reformation churches were built over undulating floor plans; their walls rippled like stage curtains; the decorative profusion of their façades further activated the static masses and increased their rhythmic pulsation; under their domes terra-cotta angels flew in parabolas; the unyielding stone of the statuary finally rose off the ground and melted into a myriad of fluid forms; paintings escaped from flat wall spaces up to the more congenial concave surfaces of the ceilings, where they could soar skyward and where more daring perspective effects were possible. Baroque music also mirrored a moving universe. Its restless forms took on the color of this dynamic age, and its sound patterns floated freely through their tonal spaces unencumbered by gravitational laws. No longer in bondage to religious ritual, to the dance, or to poetry, its emancipation was now complete. Of such ideas and materials was the image of this brave new baroque world constructed.

466. Antonio Gherardi. Cupola, Auila Chapel, Santa Maria in Trastevere, Rome. *c.* 1686.

16 · THE 18TH-CENTURY STYLES

THE 18TH-CENTURY PANORAMA

The momentum of the baroque style was sufficient to propel it well into the 18th century. New social dynamics, new springs of ideas, new aesthetic currents came together to bring about, in some cases, a confluence of the main baroque streams and, in others, the formation of new ones. With the death of Louis XIV in 1715, the aristocratic baroque style moved into its final rococo phase. The regent for his young successor closed the majestic Versailles Palace and reestablished the royal residence in Paris. Artistic patronage was no longer the monopoly of the court, and the painter Watteau, arriving in Paris the same year the Sun King died, had to look for his patrons among a broad group drawn from the ranks of both the nobility and the middle class. Throughout the century, the operas of Rameau, Gluck, and Mozart were composed for public opera houses where aristocrats rubbed shoulders with the bourgeoisie. The arts, in effect, moved out of the marble halls into the elegant salons, where finesse and charm were considered higher aesthetic virtues than impressiveness and grandeur.

The rococo, that latter-day manifestation of the aristocratic baroque style, was by no means confined to Paris. All European courts assumed in some degree the character of cultural suburbs of Versailles. French fashions in architecture, painting, furniture, costume, and manners were echoed in such far-off corners as the courts of Catherine the Great of Russia and of Maria Theresa in Vienna. Whether a prince ruled a province in Poland or a duchy in Denmark, French was spoken in his household more naturally than the language of his native country. In Prussia, Frederick the Great built a rococo palace at Potsdam and called it *Sans-souci*; the king of Saxony commissioned the jewellike Zwinger pleasure pavilion in Dresden; and the Prince-Bishop erected a handsome residence in Würzburg. Such French authors as Voltaire and Jean Jacques Rousseau found an international reading public; French dances dominated the balls and French plays the theaters. In southern Germany and Austria, however, Italian influence was still strong. At the court in Vienna an Italian architect finished the Schönbrunn Palace for Maria Theresa; Italian paintings decorated its walls; Metastasio was the poet laureate, playwright, and opera librettist; and only plays and operas in Italian could be performed in the royal theaters.

(above) BENDEL. *Rococo Angel.* 1737. Augustiner-Chorherren-Stiftskirche, Diessen, Germany.

406

The missionary zeal of the Jesuits working outward from Rome spread and popularized the ecclesiastical counterpart of the aristocratic style throughout the Counter Reformation countries.

Baroque rationalism had remained restricted to a relatively few eminent minds. In the 18th century, however, as the scientific knowledge of Newton and the social theories of John Locke became the common property of the educated classes, rationalism broadened into the movement known as the *Enlightenment*, a term—like the *rococo*—that generally refers to the period between 1715 and 1789. As the streams of rationalism and academicism converged, the most characteristic expression of the Enlightenment become the 35-volume *Encyclopédie*, edited by Denis Diderot. In this *Classified Dictionary of the Sciences, Arts, and Trades*, some 180 outstanding intellects of the time collected and made available in clear language all the knowledge that had heretofore existed only in difficult scientific tracts. Trade secrets that for centuries had been the closely guarded property of the guilds and a few master craftsmen now appeared in print. Knowledge that in the 17th century had remained largely in the realm of pure science began to be applied to the solution of practical problems. Middle-class manufacturers saw the commercial usefulness of baroque inventiveness and turned it toward the production of new wealth.

While the fruits of rationalism became the common property of the middle class, *reason*, in the vocabulary of the 18th century, by no means implied only cold intellectuality. Reason was considered to be a mental faculty shared by all who chose to cultivate it. Among its implications were common sense, exercise of good judgment, and the development of taste—all of which were accompanied by a healthy involvement in active human pursuits. As applied to the arts, reason meant the search for expressive forms and sentiments of sufficient universality and validity to be accepted by all who subscribed to the principles of good taste and judgment. With the broadening of the bases of wealth and education, the middle class was able to rise and challenge the ancient authority and prerogatives of the aristocracy. Through the power of knowledge released by the Enlightenment, the age-old shackles of superstition, intolerance, and fear began to be thrown off. The ideals of freedom championed by men of reason were eventually written into the American Declaration of Independence and Bill of Rights and became the moving force behind the French Revolution. More and more, it was now the middle class who wrote and read the books, who constructed and lived in the buildings, who painted and bought the pictures, and who composed and listened to the music.

The philosophy of the Enlightenment did not, however, go unchallenged, and undercurrents of irrationalism were found in movements that presaged 19th-century romanticism. Just as the more emotional approaches to religion emphasized revelation, so literature and the other arts came to consider intuition a higher human faculty than reason. In England, such novelists as Fielding told their tales in the first person, a device designed to promote greater subjectivity of feeling on the part of readers and a break with the Enlightenment ideal of viewing events with objective detachment. The opposition of reason and intuition is mirrored in the title and two heroines of Jane Austen's novel *Sense and Sensibility*. Rousseau gave sensibility a deeper emotional tone, and in France generally *sensibilité* meant tugging at the heart strings of readers, observers, and listeners. In sensibility literature, the poor were always nature's noblemen in proud possession of a few paternal acres, living by the honest sweat of their brows, constantly having their peace of mind disturbed by the intrusion of material progress, which usually appeared in the guise of a sophisticated man about town. In Germany, emotionalism burst out in the more violent form of the so-called "Storm-and-Stress" movement that made a rather personal interpretation of Rousseau's initial statement in his *Social Contract*: "Man is born free, and everywhere he is in chains." Goethe's characterizations of Faust and Prometheus and Mozart's Don Giovanni were independent human beings, who defied the gods of convention and demanded a gamut of inner and outer experience, even if they had to pay the penalty of eternal torment. The truth they sought was one of feeling rather than logic, and their curiosity was insatiable. By bursting the bonds of civilized restraints, they were in full rebellion against hereditary aristocratic privilege as well as stern middle-class morality. Their freedom was far from that of the Enlightenment; it was in fact an antirationalistic, antiuniversal, powerfully proindividualistic freedom that bordered on self-destruction and anarchy.

The 18th century as a whole was marked by a quickening of the pulse in human affairs. The flood of material from the printing presses alone made it all but impossible to keep up with the pace set in philosophy, literature, and music. The spread of wealth led to the development of urban centers and widespread building projects. Writers, painters, and musicians no longer aimed their output exclusively at one social group. While it is often called the Age of Reason, the 18th century gave birth to some of the most bizarre and irrational beings, real or imaginary, ever to populate the mind or imagination. The passionate disputes begun

General Events

	1715	Louis XIV died
1715–	1774	Louis XV, king of France
	1724	Belvedere Palace, Vienna, finished, Hildebrandt architect
	1726	*Gulliver's Travels* by Swift
	1728	*Beggar's Opera* by John Gay (1685–1732) performed in London
	1732	Hôtel de Soubise, Paris, begun; Boffrand, architect
1740–	1780	Maria Theresa, empress of Austria
1740–	1786	Frederick the Great, king of Prussia
	1744	Schönbrunn Palace built in Vienna (begun in 1696 by Fischer von Erlach)
	1748	*Spirit of Laws* by Condorcet
		Excavations at Pompeii begun
1751–	1772	*Encyclopédie,* or *A Classified Dictionary of Sciences, Arts and Trades* published by Diderot
	1752	Pergolesi's *Serva Padrona* performed in Paris
		Guerre des Bouffons, "war" in Paris over serious *versus* comic opera
	1759	*Candide* by Voltaire
	1762	*Social Contract* by J. J. Rousseau
		Gluck's *Orpheus* performed in Vienna
1762–	1768	Petit Trianon, Versailles, built by Louis XV for Mme Dubarry; Gabriel, architect
1762–	1796	Catherine the Great, empress of Russia
1774–	1792	Louis XVI, king of France
	1774	Gluck's *Orpheus* and *Iphigenia in Aulis* performed in Paris
	1775	Beaumarchais' *Barber of Seville* presented in Paris
	1776	American Declaration of Independence
		Sturm und Drang (Storm and Stress), play by Maximilian Klinger (1752–1831), gave name to art movement
1780–	1790	Joseph II, emperor of Austria
	1781	Mozart settled in Vienna
		Critique of Pure Reason by Kant
	1784	Beaumarchais' play *Marriage of Figaro* presented; 1786 Mozart's *Marriage of Figaro* performed in Vienna
	1787	Mozart's *Don Giovanni* performed in Prague; in Vienna 1788
	1789	French Revolution begun
	1790	*Faust, A Fragment,* by Goethe published in Leipzig
	1794	*Progress of the Human Spirit* by Condorcet
	1797	*Sense and Sensibility* written by Jane Austen; published in 1811

Architects

1650–	1723	Johann Fischer von Erlach
*c.*1660–	1726	Jakob Prandtauer
1667–	1754	Germain Boffrand
1668–	1745	Lukas von Hildebrandt
1698–	1782	Ange-Jacques Gabriel

Painters

1684–	1721	Antoine Watteau
1697–	1764	William Hogarth
1699–	1779	J. B. S. Chardin
1703–	1770	François Boucher
1725–	1805	Jean-Baptiste Greuze
1732–	1806	Jean-Honoré Fragonard

Sculptors

1714–	1785	Jean-Baptiste Pigalle
1716–	1791	Étienne Falconet
1738–	1814	Clodion (Claude Michel)
1741–	1828	Jean-Antoine Houdon

Composers

1668–	1733	François Couperin (Le Grand)
1683–	1764	Jean-Philippe Rameau
1714–	1787	C. W. Gluck
1714–	1788	C. P. E. Bach
1732–	1809	Joseph Haydn
1756–	1791	W. A. Mozart

Writers and Philosophers

1667–	1745	Jonathan Swift
1689–	1761	Samuel Richardson
1694–	1778	Voltaire (F. M. Arouet)
1698–	1782	Pietro Metastasio
1707–	1754	Henry Fielding
1712–	1778	J. J. Rousseau
1713–	1784	Denis Diderot
1724–	1804	Emmanuel Kant
1728–	1774	Oliver Goldsmith
1729–	1781	G. E. Lessing
1732–	1799	Caron de Beaumarchais
1744–	1803	J. G. von Herder
1749–	1832	Wolfgang Goethe
1749–	1838	Lorenzo da Ponte
1759–	1805	Friedrich Schiller
1775–	1817	Jane Austen

in the 17th century continued, but on the surface at least the divisions did not appear to be so sharp. The irreconcilable oppositions of the baroque were softened into sarcastic satires, gentle ironies, witty repartee, and wistful melancholies. What appeared as a period of comparative quiescence, however, was but the calm before the storm, the prelude to a social explosion that brought the aristocratic rococo to a violent, revolutionary end, and catapulted into the next century the forces of reason and emotion it had generated.

THE ROCOCO

The word *rococo* apparently was a pun on *barocco*, the Italian word for baroque, and on *rocailles* and *coquilles*, the French words for rocks and shells, which were so widely used as decorative motifs in the rococo style. As such, the rococo must be considered as a modification or variation of the baroque rather than as a style in opposition to baroque. Its effect is that of a domesticated baroque, better suited to fashionable town houses than palace halls, though the rococo was used in both. If the baroque may be said to be built from the outside in, the rococo reversed the process by building from the inside out.

The rococo was mainly an interior style adapted to the small salons where intimate groups could gather tête à tête and match wits in the subtle art of conversation. But the rococo was not confined to the major arts and could apply to any interior feature, from the graceful curves of a table

leg to the gilded scroll tracery of a ceiling design. Quite typical of the time is a drawing by Watteau (Fig. 467) that makes prominent use of the shell motif. It is seen here as an engraving, but the design could have been used for the paneling of a room, a stage curtain, a wall paper, a terracotta relief finished in white and gold, a tapestry, a mantlepiece, a needlepoint piece for the back of a chair, and so on. When a rococo interior like that in the Hofburg Palace in Vienna (Fig. 468) is compared with one from the time of Louis XIV (Plate 33), the difference becomes apparent at once. Where the baroque was ponderous, massive, and overwhelming, the rococo is delicate, light, and charm-

(above) 469. JOHANN FISCHER VON ERLACH and PICASSI. Grand Gallery, Schönbrunn Palace, Vienna. 1760–1780.

(right) 470. LUKAS VON HILDE-BRANDT. Façade, Belvedere Palace, Vienna. 1724.

ing. Even the Grand Gallery at the Schönbrunn Palace (Fig. 469) in Vienna, with its inlaid parquet floors, walls all cream and gold, and glistening crystal chandeliers, seems intimate when compared with the grandeur of the Hall of Mirrors at Versailles (Fig. 409). Monumentality is succeeded by finesse, stateliness by elegance, the pompous purples and golds by modulated pastel shades.

In the Belvedere Palace in Vienna (Fig. 470), the decorative impulse can be seen as the rococo bursts out-of-doors into a lavish exterior design. Details (Fig. 471) that the French architects had

for the most part confined to interiors are found here on the garden façade of a summer palace begun in 1713 by Lukas von Hildebrandt for Prince Eugene of Savoy. Palladian academic restraint has been cast to the four winds. On either side of the center windows, highly ornate double Composite pilasters can be found, and over the entrance some grotesque caryatid figures are grouped in a ballet-like formation. Otherwise the architectural orders as points of reference have all but disappeared. The triangular repose of the temple pediments and window brackets of the academic style has dissolved into a flowing pattern of undulating curves and broken rhythms.

Austrian Counter Reformation churches evolved in much the same way as Austrian palaces. Johann Fischer von Erlach, who had studied in Rome with Bernini and who was the architect of the Schönbrunn Palace, exercised considerable restraint in his design for the Karlskirche in Vienna (Figs. 472, 473). Fischer was influenced in his project by Borromini's Roman baroque churches—Sant' Agnese in Piazza Navona (Fig. 373) and San Carlo alle Quattro Fontane (Fig. 370), which is dedicated to the same saint, Charles Borromeo, as is the Karlskirche. His façade shows the same tendency as do the two by Borromini to break up flat surfaces and allow for a sculpturesque play of light and shadow at various times of day. The walls of the Karlskirche seem to be in full motion. From side to side there is a swelling of the convex and concave masses—forward and backward from the Corinthian portico to the depth of the elongated oval dome, and upward and downward with the spiral lines of the twin bell towers in the form of Trajanesque columns. As a man of profound learning and the author of one of the first modern histories of architecture, Fischer von Erlach must have taken

(right) 471. LUKAS VON HILDEBRANDT. Façade detail, Belvedere Palace, Vienna. 1724.

(left) 472. JOHANN FISCHER VON ERLACH. Façade, Karlskirche, Vienna. 1716–1727.

(above) 473. Karlskirche, plan.

411

(above) 474. JOHANN FISCHER VON ERLACH. Great Hall, Austrian National Library, Vienna. 1726.

(below) 475. JAKOB PRANDTAUER. Abbey Church, Melk-on-the-Danube. 1702–1738.

special delight in his splendid design for the Austrian National Library in Vienna (Fig. 474).

The Counter Reformation fusion of the arts in order to produce mystical-emotional excitement is well exemplified by the Benedictine abbey church at Melk (Fig. 475), built in a commanding position on a rocky ledge overlooking the Danube. In its colorful interior, designed by the Viennese theater architect Jakob Prandtauer, red marble columns and pilasters rise upward toward the flowing lines, undulating curves, and visionary vistas of the heavens that enliven the vaulting (Fig. 476). All the other decorative details combine to carry out this sense of heightened motion. A climax is reached in the choir loft and ceiling at the back (Fig. 477), where the tones of the organ mingle with the concealed chorus and float upward past the terracotta angels perching precariously on stucco clouds to a point where the eye is lost in the vast atmospheric perspective of the painted vaulting.

The rococo painter par excellence was Antoine Watteau. A quick comparison of the *Music Party* (Fig. 478), an example of his *fêtes galantes* or elegant entertainment style, with a bombastic Lebrun canvas (Fig. 421) or the sensuous *Garden of Love* by Rubens (Fig. 417) will reveal the hallmarks of the new idiom. The dimensions of the pictures alone tell their story, since Watteau did small easel paintings for the drawing room rather than murals for a grand gallery. Watteau was both a fellow countryman of Rubens and an ardent admirer of his art. In Watteau's pictures, however, Rubens' massive (below) 476. Jakob Prandtauer. Interior toward altar, Abbey Church, Melk-on-the-Danube. *c.* 1738.

(right) 477. Jakob Prandtauer. Choir loft and organ, Abbey Church, Melk-on-the-Danube. *c.* 1738.

figures are reduced to lithe and slender proportions. They are animated, but Rubens' bacchanalian furies now dance the graceful minuet. With Watteau the effect is capricious rather than monumental, and the spirit vivacious rather than voluptuous.

In the *Music Party*, a group has gathered on a terrace for a pleasant afternoon of musical instruction. The 'cello has been laid aside, the score is still open, and the lady who has just had her lesson lets her elbow rest on her guitar. The music master is tuning his theorbo before beginning to play, and a gentle melancholy mood settles over the company in anticipation. The music master was an established character in 18th-century life. Bazile in Beaumarchais' *Barber of Seville* was helpful to the

478. Antoine Watteau. *Music Party. c.* 1719. Oil on canvas, 25½ × 36¼". Wallace Collection, London.

413

(top) 479. FRANÇOIS BOUCHER. *Toilet of Venus*. 1746. Oil on canvas, 42 ⅝ × 33 ½″. Metropolitan Museum of Art, New York.

(below) 480. ÉTIENNE-MAURICE FALCONET. *L'Amour Menaçant (Mischievous Cupid)*. 1755–1756. Marble, 13 × 18″. Rijksmuseum, Amsterdam.

young ladies in carrying on their amorous intrigues and always stood by considerately to console them with sweet music when things turned out badly.

As in the *Music Party*, misty langorous landscapes are very important in conveying Watteau's elusive moods. As in the pastoral novels of the time, elegant ladies and their equally elegant lovers stroll at their leisure through lush gardens in fancied emulation of the life of Arcadian shepherds. Watteau handles such scenes with a characteristic lightness of touch, jewellike color, and a delicacy of nuance that set the tone for the later development of the rococo style.

François Boucher, the favorite painter of Mme de Pompadour, worked in a gayer vein than Watteau. The *Toilet of Venus* (Fig. 479) shows the 18th-century boudoir ideal of feminine charm in all its artificiality. Love is no longer the robust passion it was with Rubens but a sophisticated flirtation. Voluptuous mature womanhood is replaced by slender girlish forms.

Jean Honoré Fragonard was Boucher's successor as the leading exponent of the French rococo. *The Swing* (Plate 40), which was commissioned for the young aristocrat depicted in the lower left, portrays the frivolous, pleasure-seeking pursuits of his class. He has bribed the servant (lower right) to conceal him in the shrubbery while his lady love disports herself. The Cupid, who gestures for secrecy and silence, is taken directly from Falconet's *L'Amour Menaçant*, or *Mischievous Cupid* (Fig. 480). The artist's fine feeling for color and the masterly draftsmanship with which he handles his diagonal composition save it from the twin perils of preciousness and triviality.

Much the same spirit of elegance and charm animates the sculpture of Falconet and Clodion, of which the *Clock of the Three Graces* (Fig. 481) is a fascinating example. Terracotta can be modeled quickly, and so it was a fine medium in which to capture the fleeting rhythms of a Bacchic dance, as in the *Nymph and Satyr* (Fig. 482). These rococo figurines were replete with subtle classical allusions and were even franker in their eroticism than the paintings of the period.

THE BOURGEOIS INFLUENCE

While the aristocrats were still powerful as leaders of fashion and arbiters of taste, their influence on the arts was on the wane. Not only did wealth put the means of patronage in the pockets of a rising bourgeoisie, but education let the middle class speak more and more in cultured accents. In France, many of Watteau's pictures were painted for bourgeois walls, and in England, the clientele for Hogarth's drawings and engravings came mostly from middle-class ranks. The vast majority of Voltaire's and Rousseau's readers were members of the middle class, while the novels of Richardson, Fielding, and Goldsmith were aimed at this growing reading public. Lessing's *Miss Sara Sampson* (1755) and Diderot's *The Natural Son* (1757) established the German and French bourgeois drama. The collective patronage of the concert hall replaced that of the restricted court circle. Instead of aiming to please one patron, the composer and virtuoso now tried to win the favor of the many. Mozart, for one, felt strong enough to break with his tyrannical archbishop and strike out as an independent composer; and it is far from an accident that his great opera *Don Giovanni* was commissioned for the municipality of Prague rather than for the royal capital of Vienna.

One of Watteau's most significant pictures was painted for a Paris art dealer by the name of Gersaint, who had suggested that the painter fill a period of inactivity by doing a signboard for his shop (Plate 41). Watteau idealized his sponsor to the extent of showing him as the proprietor of a gallerylike showroom filled with the fashionable élite of Parisian society—though that was not the case at the time. On the right, Gersaint is extolling the virtues of a Watteau-like painting to a lady and gentleman who view it through their lorgnettes; on the left, the packing of pictures after the sale is in progress. (Sometime after the middle of the century the painting was cut in half.)

Genre pictures with casual everyday subjects are to be reckoned among 18th-century middle-class reactions to aristocratic posturing, similar to those in 17th-century Holland. A master in this category was Chardin, whose sensitive painting revealed visual poetry in the lives of ordinary people going about their daily routines or indulging in quiet pleasures (Fig. 483). His many still-life

(top) 481. ÉTIENNE-MAURICE FALCONET. *Clock of the Three Graces. c.* 1760. Marble, 31 ½" high. Louvre, Paris.

(below) 482. CLODION. *Nymph and Satyr. c.* 1775. Terracotta, 23 ¼" high. Metropolitan Museum of Art, New York (bequest of Benjamin Altman, 1913).

(right) 483. JEAN-BAPTISTE SIMÉON CHARDIN. *Boy Spinning Top.* 1741. Oil on canvas, 26 ½ × 28¾". Louvre, Paris.

compositions (Plate 42) are veritable glorifications of commonplace things familiar in every household —bottles, cups, jugs, kitchen utensils, fruit and vegetables for the dinner table. But beyond Chardin's modest subject matter and deceptive simplicity, a thoughtful relationship between these objects is discernible. By his careful arrangements, textural contrasts, and subtle coloration, these become symbols of the good life. Chardin's geometrical clarity and pictorial harmony became the model for many modern masters, notably Manet (see Plate 49), Cézanne (see Plate 54), and Matisse. With Greuze, such family scenes and subjects had more sentimental than artistic value, but they satisfied Diderot's demand that art should praise virtue and condemn vice. In the melodrama and theatrical gesticulations of the *Village Bride* (Fig. 484) and the *Return of the Prodigal Son*, however, this earnestness of Greuze crosses the borderline where moral uplift ends and hypocrisy begins.

The English painter William Hogarth must be reckoned among the distinguished company of 18th-century social satirists. Like Swift's *Gulliver's Travels*, John Gay's *Beggar's Opera*, and Voltaire's *Candide*, Hogarth's series of six pictures entitled *Marriage à-la-Mode* was a merciless exposé of the conditions and customs of his time, tempered by the saving grace of a brilliant wit. As Dickens and Zola, Goya and Daumier were to do in the less-humorous 19th century, Hogarth dramatized the conditions he saw and issued a challenge to society to do something about them. In this case it is the evil of putting human beings on the auction block of

marriage. The *Marriage Contract* (Fig. 485) introduces the characters as in the first scene of a play. The gouty nobleman points with pride to the family pedigree as he is about to sell his social standing in the person of his son to pay off the mortgage on his ancestral estate. The merchant, who is marrying off his daughter, scrutinizes the settlement through his spectacles just as he would any other hard-driven bargain. The pawns in this game, the future bride and groom, sit with their backs to each other. The lawyer, Counselor Silvertongue, beginning a flirtation, flatters the future Lady Squanderfield, while her fiancé consoles himself with a pinch of snuff.

The other five scenes show the unhappy consequences of this loveless union as it progresses from boredom and frivolity to infidelities, a duel, and death. In the *Countess' Levee* (Fig. 486), Lady Squanderfield entertains some of her fine-feathered friends as she makes her morning toilet. Counselor Silvertongue, now her lover, shows her tickets for a masked ball that evening, while an Italian barber dresses her hair, a servant passes cups of chocolate, a fencing master snores, a little Moorish slave points gleefully to the horns of a doll, and a grotesquely fat singer and his lean flute-playing accompanist add to the general din. The singer is considered to be Carestini, the famous castrato, who sang the feminine leads in Handel's Italian operas. The story takes a melodramatic turn after the masked ball in the scene at an inn where milady has had a tryst with her lover (Fig. 487). Her husband has been run through in

484. JEAN-BAPTISTE GREUZE. *Village Bride*. 1761. Oil on canvas, 36 × 46½″. Louvre, Paris.

485. WILLIAM HOGARTH. *Marriage Contract* (Scene I from *Marriage à-la-Mode*). 1744. Oil on canvas, 27 × 35″. National Gallery, London (reproduced by courtesy of the Trustees).

486. WILLIAM HOGARTH. *Countess' Levee* (Scene IV from *Marriage à-la-Mode*). 1744. Oil on canvas, 27 × 35″. National Gallery, London (reproduced by courtesy of the Trustees).

487. WILLIAM HOGARTH. *Death of the Earl* (Scene V from *Marriage à-la-Mode*). 1744. Oil on canvas, 27 × 35″. National Gallery, London (reproduced by courtesy of the Trustees).

a duel defending his honor, and Silvertongue is escaping through the window.

This and such other series as the *Harlot's Progress* and the *Rake's Progress* were first made as paintings and then copied in the form of copper engravings. The prints were widely sold by subscription, and this type of group patronage made them financially successful. Horace Walpole likened them to Molière's plays, and Charles Lamb said: "Other pictures we see, Hogarth's we read." The series were indeed managed in the manner of chapters in a novel; and, since they were done for a public whose primary responses were literary, Hogarth knew that his audience expected a picture to have narrative content. Based as they are on an intimate knowledge of London, the stories are told with a zest for life that saves them from cynicism. Every detail in his crowded rooms is a commentary on both the action and the taste of his time. In addition to their biting satire, Hogarth's pictures are works of art in their own right by virtue of his draftsmanship and sense of composition.

As might be expected, bourgeois sculptural expression was at home in the domain of portraiture. Houdon's fine feeling for the delineation of character assures him a place among the foremost portraitists of Western art. His bust of Voltaire (Fig. 488) is one of several portraits he did of the famous French philosopher and dramatist. By the tilt of the head and the humorous gleam of the eye, Houdon captures the bemused look of the philosopher as he ponders and discourses on the foibles and follies of his fellow mortals. To chisel a glance of amiable skepticism in marble is no small feat. By leaving a rough edge in the outline of the pupil of the eye, the artist is able to produce a special glint that gives just the desired effect. By such means Houdon achieved a speaking likeness in which, during a fleeting moment of animated conversation, the philosopher might just have coined one of his famous epigrams.

Houdon's gallery also embraced many eminent Americans, including Thomas Jefferson, John Paul Jones, Robert Fulton, and Benjamin Franklin (Fig. 489), while he was ambassador to the court of Louis XVI. In 1785, on the invitation of Jefferson, he crossed the Atlantic with Franklin and spent several weeks at Mount Vernon making studies for the statue of George Washington now at the Virginia state capitol at Richmond.

(above) 488. JEAN-ANTOINE HOUDON. *Voltaire*. 1781. Marble, 20″ high. Victoria and Albert Museum, London (Crown copyright reserved).

(right) 489. JEAN-ANTOINE HOUDON. *Benjamin Franklin*. 1778. Terracotta, 16 1/8″ high. Louvre, Paris.

THE MOZARTIAN SYNTHESIS

Wolfgang Amadeus Mozart's most mature music was written during the last decade of his life as a resident of Vienna. While he continued to compose chamber music for aristocratic salons, an occasional chamber opera for the Schönbrunn Palace, and German *Singspiele* (comic operas) for the popular musical theater, his art attains its most universal expression in the works he created for the public opera houses and concert halls, where noblemen and commoners gathered together for their mutual recreation. It was here that Mozart's musical cosmopolitanism found its widest scope, here that he could explore the endless variety of tragic and comic situations that give his operas their boundless humanity, and here that his dramatic power could make its greatest impact. It is also these qualities that were carried over into the less direct and more abstract form of his symphonies and concertos and that give them their particular dramatic intensity.

As a highly impressionable child, guided by a wise father, Mozart had been piloted around the important musical centers, met the most eminent composers, and absorbed all the current ideas. In London, he came under the sway of Christian Bach, one of the sons of the prolific Johann Sebastian. Mozart's generation had reacted to that of J. S. Bach and Handel much as the French painters had to Rubens and Lebrun, and their music spoke in the gentler accents of the gallant style rather than in the muscular rhythms and massive sonorities of the baroque. In Paris, Mozart was introduced to the rococo keyboard style, that art of the elegant trifle expressed in tinkling bon-bons for the ear. There he also made his first contact with the operas of Gluck, from which he learned his deep regard for dramatic truth and elimination of everything except what was germane to the unfolding of the plot. In Italy, he came to know the full beauty of the human voice and the all-persuasive quality of Latin lyricism. In Mannheim, he heard the finest orchestra in Europe and was struck by the lightning of its dynamic crescendos and diminuendos as well as the brilliance of its wind instruments. In Vienna, he learned from Joseph Haydn how to divine the soul of the orchestra and to explore the full expressive possibilities of the symphonic form. From first-hand contact he had discovered the idioms of the Neapolitan *opera seria*, Pergolesi's *opera buffa*, Rousseau's pastoral opera, and the German *Singspiel*. The spirit of the Enlightenment can be seen in the logical clarity and constructive unity of his forms; his letters show his enthusiasm for Rousseauian naturalness; and from his knowledge of literature, the explosive energy of the Storm-and-Stress movement finds its way into his music. Everything in his epoch was assayed in the laboratory of his brilliant mind, sifted through his creative consciousness and eventually refined into pure musical gold. In opera, he found the form in which he could combine all these ideas, idioms, and styles into one grand kaleidoscopic pattern, and for him the lyric theater was always his most natural medium of expression.

Mozart's power of characterization is akin to that of Shakespeare, though his dramas are made with musical materials. No composer understood better than Mozart that an opera is not a drama *with* music but a drama *in* music, or knew better that a character has no existence apart from the melody he sings; he *is* the melody. As the supreme musical dramatist, Mozart can awaken a character to life by a phrase or a rhythmical pattern, carry him through living situations by the direction of a melodic line, and develop the most complex interactions with the others in a scene by harmonic modulations and contrapuntal intricacies. His emotional range is enormous. Within but a short span of time, Mozart can be both gay and profound, serene and agitated, cheerful and serious, calm and turbulent, ethical and diabolical, yet all takes place within an ordered framework and nothing ever gets out of hand. His *Marriage of Figaro*, an adaptation of Beaumarchais' play, is one vast human panorama in which all the characters, whether master or servant, nobleman or knave, appear as equal partners in the dance of life. Every possible amorous situation is explored with objectivity, deep psychological insight, good humor, and warm understanding. From Cherubino's adolescent awakening to the fascinations of the opposite sex and the mature love of Figaro and Susanna, he moves on to the Count and Countess as the philandering husband and neglected wife, and finally to a pair of scheming blackmailers. The situations meanwhile run a gamut from intrigue, coquetry, and lust to infidelity, forgiveness, and tender reconciliation. Much of Beaumarchais' political satire is missing, but every nuance of human feeling is explored and exploited to the utmost. By contrast, when Mozart had to perform the duties of a court composer and write an opera on a stilted Metastasio libretto in connection with the emperor's coronation, the work was a failure. When, however, the invitation to write a new opera came from the provincial but highly musical city of Prague, he had both the ideas and the audience he needed, and the result was the operatic masterpiece *Don Giovanni*.

Don Giovanni

For *Don Giovanni*, Mozart was fortunate in having the collaboration of Lorenzo da Ponte, a skillful writer and facile adapter with a real theatrical and histrionic flair. On hand at the final rehearsals of this saga of the world's greatest lover, and helping put a few finishing touches on the text, was none other than Giacomo Casanova, a man who had done enough research on the subject to qualify him as an authority. The Don Juan story was far from a novelty, and like the Faust legend, it went all the way back to the medieval morality drama. In literature, the earliest known version is by a Spanish playwright, and in Italy, the tale was frequently dramatized in Jesuit churches under the title of *Atheisto Fulminato*, or the *Blaspheming Atheist*. Molière made a prose comedy out of the Don Juan story, in which the satirical element replaced the moralizing tone. Many passages and phrases from his play found their way into da Ponte's libretto. Donna Elvira, a lady whom Don Juan had kidnapped from a convent and later deserted, as well as the pastoral pair, Zerlina and Masetto, also stem from Molière. An English version called *The Libertine* by Thomas Shadwell, with incidental music by Purcell, was mounted in London in 1676; and as late as 1817 a play called *Don Giovanni, or A Spectre on Horseback*, inspired Byron's poem on the subject. The direct ancestor of da Ponte's book, however, was an Italian libretto by Bertati, though elements from all the known Italian, French, and German plays made their contribution.

Both the subject matter and Mozart's marvelous music led to the adoption and deification of *Don Giovanni* by the following generation, who saw in it the prototype of the romantic opera. In one of his late conversations, Goethe remarked rather wistfully that Mozart should have composed a *Faust*. What the venerable poet overlooked was that Mozart had already done so, since the Faustian concept completely permeates the character of Don Giovanni, who was a Mephistopheles and Faust rolled into one. Stylistically, the opera incorporates the spirit of the Storm-and-Stress drama and led directly to Spohr's opera *Faust*, E. T. A. Hoffmann's *Undine*, and Weber's *Freischütz*. The 19th century unfortunately burdened *Don Giovanni* with all kinds of interpretations. To the partisans of the French Revolution, Don Giovanni was the dissolute nobleman bent like an arch-criminal on bringing about the destruction of the moral law. If so, he was certainly the most beloved villain in all melodrama, with the sympathies of the audience enlisted for once on the side opposite law and order. The philosopher Kierkegaard regarded him as the incarnation of Desire, which by its very nature can never admit of satisfaction. He thus became a Nietzschean superman, or personification of the Dionysian life force. How then is it that in the opera each love affair either ends in frustration or leaves

him in some ridiculous situation? To the classical enthusiasts, Don Giovanni was the mortal who dared to defy the very gods themselves and by so doing brought about his own destruction. To the romantics, he was the towering tragic hero who, like Faust, was the victim of his own insatiable lusts. To others, he was the uncompromising idealist always in pursuit of perfect beauty.

To find Mozart's real meaning, one must blow off the accumulation of 19th-century moral and philosophical dust and appraise it anew. Is it a tragedy or a comedy? Even today performances tend to emphasize one aspect or the other. Mozart's subtitle *dramma giocosa* suggests a combination of both. In the thematic catalogue of his own works, he also refers to it as an "opera buffa in two acts." Bearing in mind that Mozart was entirely capable of leaving it as a subtle enigma, that his inspired music raises it to the status of a unique masterpiece, and that it was originally composed for a small theater, one may decide that the best approach to it is as a high-spirited 18th-century comedy of manners, in which Molièrian satire is mixed with some Storm-and-Stress demonic elements.

The pace of the opera is breathtaking. In the first scene alone there is an attempted rape, a challenge and duel, the dying gasps of an outraged father, blasphemy, the escape of the culprits, and oaths of vengeance. In all this the absolute dramatic center is Don Giovanni, who bursts the bonds of civilized restraint, defies all social conventions, sweeps aside every barrier in his way, and stands alone against the world. In the *Marriage of Figaro* all the characters interacted with each other; here the figures, like the spokes of a wheel, exist only in their relation to the hub, Don Giovanni. Opposite him are the three feminine leads, each of equal importance—Donna Anna, Donna Elvira, and Zerlina, in the order of their appearance.

Chronologically, Donna Elvira comes first, since she has been seduced and deserted before the curtain rises. Hers is the fury of a woman scorned, joined with the desire to forgive and forget and to save Don Giovanni from perdition. Her character is most clearly revealed in Aria No. 8, "*In qual eccessi*," where she advises the lightheaded young Zerlina of the pitfalls of life with the dashing Don. Mozart writes it as a typical Handelian baroque rage aria. By so doing, he implies that Elvira's moral preachments are somewhat archaic, and the dignified form makes it an effective contrast to the prevailing frivolity.

The emotional life of Donna Anna, whose screams are heard at the beginning of the opera, is no less complicated. Full of righteous wrath, possibly mixed with some unconscious admiration for Don Giovanni, and tempered with filial affection

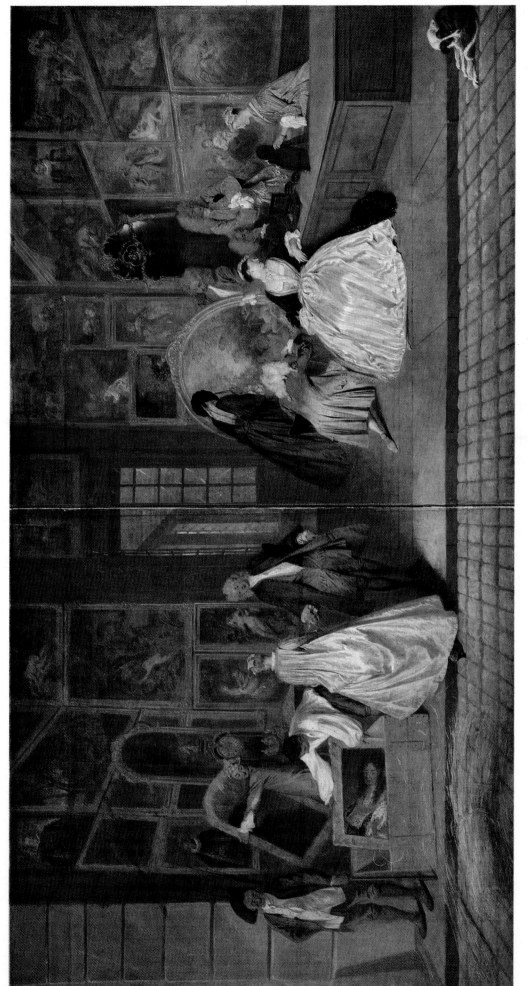

Plate 41. ANTOINE WATTEAU. *Gersaint's Signboard.* 1720–1721. Oil on canvas, 5′3 7/8″ × 9′11 1/8″. State Museums, Berlin. (See p. 415.)

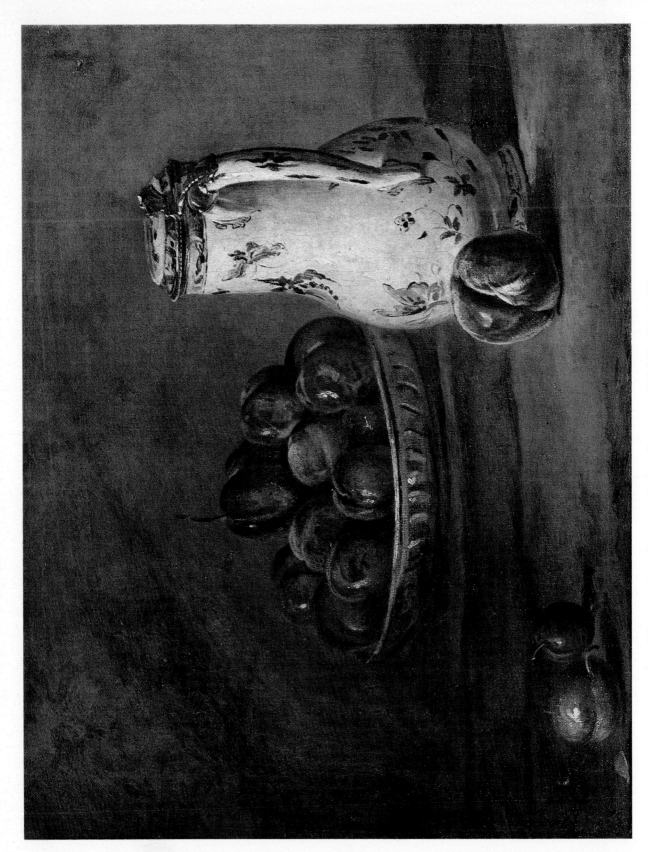

Plate 42. JEAN-BAPTISTE SIMÉON CHARDIN. *Still Life : Bowl of Plums.* 1759.
Oil on canvas, 17 ¾ × 22 ½". Phillips Collection, Washington, D.C. (See p. 416.)

for her murdered father, she swears vengeance on his assassin. She is joined in this resolve by her gentlemanly fiancé, Don Ottavio, and together they constitute the serious couple usual in Italian opera buffa. Since Don Ottavio is the lonely champion of lawful love versus licentiousness, he is bound to appear somewhat pale in these highly charged surroundings. His two tenor arias, *"Dalla sua pace"* and *"Il mio tesoro"* (Nos. 10B and 21), contain lovely lyricism but are parenthetical rather than part of the main action. Donna Anna, on the contrary, rises to truly tragic stature in *"Or sai chi l'onore"* (Aria No. 10); where, outraged but yet attracted to Don Giovanni, she intermingles hatred with passion.

Third in this list is the naïve but flirtatious Zerlina, torn between loyalty to her rustic bridegroom and the flattering attentions of the dashing Don. The duet *"La ci darem la mano"* (No. 7) is a subtle piece of musical characterization in which the division of the melody between the voices and the minute melodic variants point up their respective attitudes. The Don is tender, yet always the imperious aristocrat, accustomed to having his own way; Zerlina is very feminine, hesitant, doubtful of his good intentions, but thoroughly enjoying every moment. Later, in a reconciliation scene with her young peasant husband, the aria *"Vedrai carino"*

(No. 18) brings out all her maternal impulses toward him.

On the male side, Don Giovanni has no romantic competition, only a very substantial shadow in the form of Leporello, the comic manservant who plays Sancho Panza to his Don Quixote. Leporello is a stock opera-buffa character, who expresses his rather earthy cynicism in some chattering patter songs based on a running series of rapidly repeated syllables and notes. He introduces himself in the first aria of the opera; and in the famous Catalogue Aria (No. 4), he enumerates the list of his master's amorous conquests in what must surely be the most hilarious set of statistics in history.

The two scenes in which all the characters are on stage are the Finales to Acts I and II. In the first, Don Giovanni is entertaining a lively peasant wedding party in the hope of winning the bride Zerlina for himself. Fine dramatic contrast is provided in Don Giovanni's gay drinking song (No. 11) that sparkles like the wine he is ordering, and the sullen resentment of Masetto when he senses that his bride's head is being turned by this glamorous member of the privileged class. The scene reaches its brilliant climax when the dance music strikes up. There are no less than three ensembles on stage in addition to the main orchestra in the pit. Everyone at the time would have recognized this as a typical Viennese public ballroom scene for which Mozart frequently composed music. So that there would be dances that appealed to everybody, minuets were customarily played in one room, waltzes in another, and so on. Here the three groups also play different dances. The first, consisting of two oboes, two horns, and strings, plays the best known of all minuets. On the repetition of the last part, the second stage orchestra, made up of violins and a bass, does a type of square dance known as a *contredanse*; while a third ensemble, also of stringed instruments, plays an old-fashioned German waltz. An obvious stratification of social levels is implied, with the masked figures of Donna Anna and Don Ottavio doing the aristocratic minuet; the peasants stamping out the vigorous, laendlerlike meter of the waltz, with strong accentuation on the beats of three and one, while Don Giovanni and Zerlina meet on the middle-class ground of the bourgeois contre-danse. Each social group is thus expressed through a characteristic rhythm. With the stage bands playing against the main orchestra below, all the plots and subplots boiling merrily away, and all the characters conversing and commenting on the action, the resulting rhythmic complexity and dramatic tension make this scene one of the major miracles of musical literature.

In the cemetery scene, which precedes the Finale to Act II, Don Giovanni as a fugitive from justice is confronted with the equestrian statue of the Commendatore whom he has murdered at the beginning of the opera. The stentorian tones of the voice from the tomb reproach him for his wickedness; and Don Giovanni, always the courteous host, responds by inviting the statue to a midnight meal. The final scene opens with the preparations for the banquet, while the trumpets and drums sound the proper note of aristocratic hospitality. Like all noblemen of his time, Don Giovanni has his own liveried house orchestra standing by to play dinner music. This wind ensemble plays snatches from two popular Italian operas by Mozart's rivals; and a delightful bit of humor is introduced when they quote the "*Non più andrai*" from his own *Marriage of Figaro*, which happened to be a hit tune of that season, not a classic as now.

Donna Elvira, ever the kill-joy, now enters to play her trump card, which is the announcement that she is returning to her convent where life under the veil will presumably be more peaceful. As she reaches the door, her shriek heralds the arrival of the statue. With ominously heavy footsteps, the monument sings a long melodic line as rigid in its way as rigor mortis itself, reinforced by the sepulchral sounds of the trombones, instruments which were then associated with solemn church festivals and funerals. The contrast between the quick and the dead is brought out by the static pedal point of the statue's melody, around which the other characters react in ways varying from farce to tragedy. When Don Giovanni takes the hand of his marble guest, the horror music that had been foreshadowed in the overture is heard. Strings play spine-tingling scale figures upward and downward, alternately soft and loud. Claps of thunder are heard, a chorus of demons shouts from below, flames mount upward; and Don Giovanni, unrepentant to the last, goes to his predestined doom singing the descending scale of D major. Breathlessly the other characters arrive too late for the excitement but in the nick of time to sing a quintet to the following words before the curtain falls:

> Sinner, pause, and ponder well,
> Mark the end of Don Juan!
> Are you going to Heaven or Hell?

IDEAS

The 18th-century styles either continued, modified, or departed from the high baroque. The shift of audience from a declining aristocracy to the rising bourgeoisie was accelerated, and the final phase of the aristocratic baroque style was reflected in the rococo; the continuation of 17th-century rationalism was found in the Enlightenment; voices of a classical revival began to be heard; new emotional outbursts were felt in the emphasis on sensibility and in the Storm-and-Stress movement. Besides neoclassicism, discussed in Chapter 17, the ideas that weave the arts of the 18th-century into a coherent pattern are the rococo, the Enlightenment, and the emotional reaction to them known as the Storm and Stress.

The Rococo

The rococo is the last Western style that can lay claim to universality and the last to adhere strictly to the canons of beauty. The cosmopolitan rococo is a reflection of an aristocracy that still retained dominant control of artistic patronage. This was an international upper class who freely intermarried with the nobility of all parts of Europe, who spoke French and Italian better than the native tongues of their respective countries, who read French philosophers, attended French plays, and collected French art. This was, moreover, an educated group who cultivated wit, charm, social polish, and refinement of taste as a way of life. After the French Revolution and the Napoleonic

490. ANGE-JACQUES GABRIEL.
Grand Gallery, Petit Trianon, Versailles. 1762–1768.

wars, the power of nationalism grew so strong that the arts appeared more and more in local frames of reference.

The Renaissance cult of the beautiful likewise finds its terminal point in the rococo, where beauty comes perilously close to mere prettiness and over-refinement. Fischer von Erlach, Lukas von Hilde-brandt, Watteau, Boucher, Fragonard, Falconet, and Clodion never overstep the boundaries of beauty. Mozart, in spite of his extraordinary emotional power, makes his aesthetic views on this quite clear in a letter to his father: "Passions, whether violent or not," he wrote, "must never be expressed in such a way as to excite disgust, and as music, even in the most terrible situations, must never offend the ear, but please the hearer, or in other words must never cease to be *music*."

Examples of the rococo are found in all countries where the aristocracy possessed the means to follow the fashionable style, and where the Counter Reformationists undertook the building of churches. The hallmarks of the style are found in details of such salons as those in the Hôtel de Soubise (Plate 43) and the Petit Trianon (Fig. 490); the paintings of Watteau, Boucher, and Fragonard; the sculptures of Falconet and Clodion; and in such moments in Mozart as the exquisite aria sung by the Countess at the beginning of Act II of the *Marriage of Figaro*.

The Enlightenment

The *Enlightenment* is a blanket term under which it is possible to group such tendencies as the inventive spirit, scientific inquiry, the encyclopedic movement, the optimistic world view, and the belief in progress, turning the light of intelligence on life's problems, substituting reason for custom and tradition, and questioning everything. The impetus that the Enlightenment gave to scientific invention was applied by middle-class manufacturers and businessmen to the production of wealth. Pure science and nature in this case were less important than technology and artifact. The new social order is mirrored most directly in the shift of artistic patronage in the direction of the middle-class audience. For the first time, it is possible to speak of the bourgeois novel and drama. Watteau painted one of his most important pictures for an art dealer; Chardin, Greuze, and Hogarth found their clientele among the same social segment. And Mozart, by turning the social tables upside down, making the Count the villain and the servant the hero, was certainly bolstering the ego of the bourgeoisie and blasting the aristocracy.

The Enlightenment spirit of free scientific inquiry, which grew out of 17th-century rationalism, was so distinctly anticlerical that it almost developed into a substitute religion. To the deists, God was a kind of cosmic clockmaker who created a mechanical universe, wound it up for all eternity, and let it go. The experimental method of science became the liturgy of this pseudoreligion, the encyclopedia its bible, nature its church, and all men of reason, the congregation. One of the most productive impulses of this aspect of the Enlightenment resulted in the encyclopedic movement. All the important intellects made their contributions to Diderot's *Encyclopédie*, with Voltaire writing the historical parts, Rousseau the sections on music, and so on. The same intellectual spirit, though in different religious circumstances, is observable in the comprehensive musical output of J. S. Bach. In *The Art of the Fugue* he applied the scientific method to musical composition. By keeping his themes constant, he carefully controlled the variables of form and thus systematized all possible fugal types. His extant cantatas add up to four for each Sunday of the year. His keyboard compositions were conceived encyclopedically and comprise examples in every possible form. His 48 preludes and fugues, known as the *Well-Tempered Clavier*, were written as a double cycle, two for each possible tonality; and his Brandenburg concertos explore every possible instrumental combination. His entire works thus emerge as a comprehensive design consciously planned to survey and sum up all the musical practices known to him.

The Enlightenment image of the cool man of reason inhabiting a world governed by purely rational principles was the object of Voltaire's satirical pen in the novel *Candide*. While maintaining his staunch belief that he lives in the Leibnizian "best of all possible worlds," the hero experiences every disaster known on the planet, including the great earthquake of Lisbon in 1745. The use of satire as a social weapon takes visual form in Hogarth's *Marriage à-la-Mode*. A certain amount of Voltairean skepticism can also be found in the character of Don Giovanni, who fears neither the supernatural nor the hereafter. When the statue talks in the cemetery scene, the unenlightened Leporello cowers with superstitious fear; but Don Giovanni assumes the role of an art critic, sees that the statue is really nothing more than a typical cemetery monument, and addresses it: "*O vecchio buffonissimo*" (ridiculous old gentleman). The Enlightenment spirit finds an even clearer statement and takes a more constructive form in Mozart's last opera, *The Magic Flute*, an allegory of Freemasonry in which the forces of reason are lined up squarely against those of superstition and fear.

The Enlightenment was accompanied by a spirit of optimism and by a belief in progress and the perfectibility of man. Theologically, the Hebraic and Christian viewpoints were based on the fall of man and the doctrine of original sin dating from the expulsion of Adam and Eve from the Garden of Eden. Philosophically, Plato's theory of knowledge was also founded on a doctrine of prenatal perfection and the subsequent acquisition of knowledge by the process of remembrance. Humanists, such as Gibbon and Winckelmann, believed in the intellectual and artistic paradise of ancient Greece and Rome and as a consequence wrote their declines and falls. Without denying the greatness of Greece, the exponents of the Enlightenment were well aware that they had gone far beyond classical science and believed that, if the rational processes could be properly applied, they could eventually surpass the ancients in all fields. Kant, for instance, enthusiastically hailed Rousseau as the Newton of the moral world, and Condorcet in his *Progress of the Human Spirit* enumerated the ten stages by which man had raised himself from savagery to the threshold of perfection. Material progress was certainly an observable fact; and since nature held all the secrets that a man needed to know, and reason could unlock them, eventually man could control his environment. If he therefore would only use his mental and moral powers to their fullest extent, the argument ran, man could go in one direction only, onward and upward. The full force of this optimism is felt in the American and French revolutions, and in the painting of David and the music of Beethoven, which will be discussed in the next chapter.

"Storm and Stress"

In the latter half of the 18th century, various irrational tendencies came about as reactions to both the rococo cult of the beautiful and the Enlightenment's emphasis on reason. As early as 1756, Burke's *Essay on the Sublime and the Beautiful* insisted that in literature and art there is an element more important than beauty. This is the Sublime, which transcends mere beauty and can even admit of the ugly. "Whatever is fitted in any sort to excite the ideas of pain and danger," he said, "whatever is in any sort terrible, or conversant about terrible objects, is the source of the Sublime." The free exercise of the emotions and the imagination, even if it meant experiencing the painful, the astonishing, the horrible, was therefore legitimate territory for art to explore. This idea led to a renewed interest in Shakespeare; reveled in Rousseau's descriptions of alpine scenery, accompanied as they were by avalanches and storms; and delighted in the Rousseauian revolt against the restraints of civilization. This line of thought also constituted the background of the Storm-and-Stress movement in Germany. While the Enlightenment was trying to tame nature and bring it under man's control, the *Sturm und Drang* authors were reveling in how nature imposed her obscure and unfathomable will on man. In Goethe's early drama, Faust was the rebel against all accepted forms of wisdom, especially those arrived at through mathematical or scientific formulas. Both Faust and Don Giovanni were engaged in a quest for emotional truth and succeeded in unleashing the infernal forces that eventually consumed them.

Such, in brief, were the social, ideational, and emotional impulses that defined the horizon before which the panorama of the 18th-century arts unfolded.

PART V

THE REVOLUTIONARY PERIOD

I7 - THE NEOCLASSICAL STYLE

PARIS, EARLY 19TH CENTURY

Some books, some archeological discoveries, and some social upheavals brought to Paris many radical changes in intellectual orientation, in styles of art, and in forms of government during the latter part of the 18th and early part of the 19th century. Stuart and Revett, two Englishmen who had visited Greece, published in 1762 *Antiquities of Athens*, which made a clear differentiation between Greek and Roman architecture. Two years later, J. J. Winckelmann's *History of Ancient Art*, the equivalent of a modern best seller, similarly distinguished between sculptures. "The principal and universal characteristic of the masterpieces of Greek art is a noble simplicity and a quiet grandeur," he declared. "As the depth of the sea remains always at rest, however the surface may be agitated, so the expression in the figures of the Greeks reveals in the midst of passion a great and steadfast soul." These words provided the critics of the rococo style with the needed aesthetic ammunition, and verbal volleys were fired at Boucher and Fragonard because of the frivolous content of their paintings. During Revolutionary times, the voice of Diderot, moral philosopher and apostle of the Enlightenment, continued to echo, especially his dictum that the function of art was to make "virtue adorable and vice repugnant."

The wave of enthusiasm for antiquity that then swept France made that country into a kind of classical phoenix rising from the volcanic ashes of Pompeii and Herculaneum. News of the excavation of these ancient cities was eagerly followed by the French, before whose eyes an image of a widespread high standard of living seemed to be unfolding. Luxury previously had been associated with a decadent aristocracy, and it came as something of a revelation for the French middle class to learn that the ordinary inhabitants of these old Roman resort towns had lived so well. Classicism, which hitherto had meant temples, forums, and great monuments, now could be associated with an unpretentious but luxurious domestic architecture and ideals of comfort that people like themselves could live with and understand.

The French Revolution, for all its fury, was essentially a bourgeois movement in which the rights of property remained unquestioned. The excavation of these ancient ruins gave the people something worth striving for at precisely the time when they were able to do something about it.

Ancient Rome now became a symbol for the revolutionary protest. In politics, this at first meant

(above) JEAN-PIERRE CORTOT. *Fame*, detail of *Apotheosis of Napoleon*. 1838. Stone relief. Arc de Triomphe de l'Étoile, Paris. (See also Fig. 519.)

General Events

	1748	Excavations begun at Pompeii and Herculaneum
	1762	*Antiquities of Athens* published by Stuart and Revett
	1764	*History of Ancient Art* published by Winckelmann (1717–1768)
	1766	*Laocoön* published by Lessing (1729–1781)
	1774	Gluck's *Orfeo* produced at Paris Opera
1785–	1820	Federal style in the United States
1788–	1791	Brandenburg Gate in Berlin built by Langhans
	1789	French Revolution began
1792–	1794	First French Republic
	1796	Napoleon's first Italian campaign
	1798	Napoleon's campaign in Egypt
		Battle of the Pyramids
	1799	Napoleon became First Consul
	1802	Napoleon made Consul for life
	1803	Napoleonic Code of Laws issued
	1804	Napoleon crowned emperor
		Beethoven finished *Eroica* Symphony
	1806	Temple of Glory (later La Madeleine) begun by Vignon
		Arc du Carrousel begun by Percier and Fontaine
		Arc de Triomphe begun by Chalgrin
	1814	Napoleon abdicated; Bourbons restored to French throne
1814–	1821	Louis XVIII, king of France
	1815	Napoleon defeated in Battle of Waterloo
		Elgin Marbles exhibited in London
	1816	Elgin Marbles purchased by Parliament, placed in British Museum
	1821	Napoleon died
1824–	1830	Charles X, king of France
	1830	July Revolution
1830–	1848	Louis Philippe, king of France; constitutional monarch

Painters

1716–	1809	Joseph-Marie Vien
1746–	1828	Francisco Goya
1748–	1825	Jacques-Louis David
1771–	1835	Antoine-Jean Gros
1780–	1867	J. A. D. Ingres
1791–	1824	Théodore Géricault

Sculptors

1757–	1822	Antonio Canova
1770–	1844	Bertel Thorwaldsen
1798–	1880	P. J. H. Lemaire

Architects

1733–	1808	Karl Gotthard Langhans
1739–	1811	Jean Francis Chalgrin
1743–	1826	Thomas Jefferson
1753–	1837	John Soane
1762–	1820	Pierre-Alexandre Vignon
1762–	1853	Pierre F. L. Fontaine
1764–	1838	Charles Percier
1784–	1864	Leo von Klenze

Musicians

1714–	1787	Christopher Willibald Gluck
1741–	1813	A. E. M. Grétry
1741–	1816	Giovanni Paisiello
1760–	1837	Jean-François Lesueur
1760–	1842	Salvador Cherubini
1770–	1827	Ludwig van Beethoven
1774–	1851	Gasparo Spontini

a republican instead of a monarchical form of government. In religion, it was associated with a tolerant paganism as opposed to a dogmatic form of Christianity. (For a brief time, in fact, the Cathedral of Notre Dame in Paris was rededicated to the Goddess of Reason.) Heroism and self-sacrifice, rugged resolve and Spartan simplicity became manifestations of the Revolutionary spirit, and reflections of these qualities were readily found in Roman literature and art. The political writings of Cicero and Seneca were widely read and quoted to confirm the principle that sovereignty resided in the people and that government should be based on a voluntary agreement among citizens. Political pamphlets came to be studded with quotations from Tacitus, Sallust, and Horace, and the oratory of the period was modeled on that of Cicero. The convention hall where the revolutionary legislators met was lined with laurel-crowned statues of Solon, Camillus, and other ancient statesmen, and in debates the speakers relied on apt phrases from Cicero to clinch important points. They referred to their partisans as Brutuses and Catos and to their opponents as Catalines; their postures and gestures were studied imitations of Roman statues, and their oaths were sworn on the head of Brutus or by the immortal gods. (The painter David designed a costume for these representatives of the people that combined the ancient tunic with a togalike cape draped over the shoulders. It did not catch on.)

Everyone who could read became biography-conscious and spoke like living characters out of Plutarch's *Parallel Lives*. (On the day she murdered Marat, Charlotte Corday had spent her time reading Plutarch.) Never before had public personalities seemed so obviously to have walked straight out of books. Surely Oscar Wilde must have had this Revolutionary period in mind when he wittily twisted the old Greek aesthetic doctrine by saying that nature, especially human nature, imitates art.

Many of the symbols of the French Revolution too were borrowed directly from the ancients. The cap of liberty was a copy of the Phrygian cap worn by the liberated slaves in Rome. The *fasces*, or bundle of sticks with the protruding ax tied together with a common bond, was once again the symbol of power. The calendar was reorganized, and the months of the year given Latin names. The rainy month became Pluviôse; planting time, Germinal; the month of blossoms, Floreal; midsummer, Thermidor; and harvest time, Fructidor. Façades of houses featured classical columns; rooms were furnished with Roman couches, lighted by bronze lamps, and decorated with replicas of ancient statuary.

When Napoleon Bonaparte rose to political power, he too shared the popular enthusiasm for all that was ancient. His chosen models were Alexander the Great and Julius Caesar, especially the latter since Caesar's career and Napoleon's had so many parallels. Napoleon became first a republican consul; later he ruled France through a tribune; and then, after a plebiscite, he became the modern incarnation of a Roman emperor. The *fasces* became his emblem of authority; the eagles of the old Roman legions he made into the insignia of the French battalions, and eventually he was crowned with the laurel wreath, that ancient symbol of immortal fame.

Such a manipulation of the forms and images of ancient glory had a vast appeal to this man of modest birth. Coming to power so soon after the demise of an unpopular monarchy, Napoleon had to emphasize that many of the Roman emperors were of equally plebian backgrounds, and that the imperial toga had not necessarily been hereditary. But his hold on the people was indisputable and his elevation was made with full popular consent. Napoleon's mission was to bring order to what had been political chaos and to consolidate the social gains that had been made. His meteoric career was the success story of the 19th century, embodying as it did the ideal of the emancipated individual rising to leadership through his own efforts rather than by an accident of birth. In it, members of the parvenu society of his time could find substance for their fondest materialistic daydreams. The truth was that now, with the reins of power in their hands, the middle class did not know quite how to manage them. Napoleon did.

Napoleon's achievement of these ancient prerogatives of power, however, was not made with antiquated methods, and the highly modern means he employed make a fascinating study in contrasts. Never could Napoleon have risen to power had he not forged a mighty war machine, and this was possible only by the application to industry and agriculture of all the latest technological and scientific knowledge. By employing universal conscription to populate his armies and by his undoubted administrative ability, he was able to regiment all the various parts of his state into efficient cogs in his wheel of victory. Further, he had inherited the popular classical vocabulary, and he proceeded to use it. The ancient symbols that served his state by upholding the ideals of heroism and self-sacrifice and by awakening latent national ambitions were both useful and decorative. Consequently, Napoleon cast himself in varying roles at different times: when he was crossing the Alps, he was Hannibal; on a far-off battlefield, he was Alexander; burdened with administrative affairs at home, he was Caesar. And those around him had their assigned roles also. When David requested a sitting for a portrait, Napoleon dismissed the thought with a wave of his hand, instructing the astonished artist to paint his genius, not his likeness, and asking rhetorically if Alexander had ever posed for Apelles.

Like its Roman prototype, Napoleon's empire was international in scope, and its intellectual and artistic life transcended national boundary lines. What Greece had been to Rome, Italy was now to France. Napoleon brought the Italian sculptor Canova to Paris for various commissions, and his musical preferences were for such composers as Paisiello and Spontini. His proclamation to the Italian people on the eve of his invasion of their country points up this internationalism. "We are the friends of all nations," he protested, perhaps too much, "especially the descendants of Brutus, the Scipios, and of the great men we have chosen for our own model." And he took frequent pains to point out that he was embarking on a cultural as well as a military mission. Here was no barbarian Attila storming the citadel, but a conqueror who came to sack Rome in the company of a group of art experts who were well aware of the value of everything they took. A petition signed by all the important French artists actually had been sent to the Directory in 1796, pointing out how much the Romans had become civilized by confiscating the art of ancient Greece and how France would likewise flourish by bringing original works to Paris to serve as models. While this returning Caesar

491. Place de la Concorde, Paris (aerial view).

brought back with him no human captives, his victory celebration was livened by the presence of such distinguished prisoners of war as the *Apollo Belvedere* (Fig. 78), the *Discobulus* (Fig. 35), the *Venus de' Medici* (Fig. 291), the paintings of Raphael, and the rare treasures he had pilfered from the Vatican and other Italian museums.

As an Italian himself, Napoleon knew the value of such pomp and circumstance, and his life was consciously conditioned by these visions of ancient splendor. Inevitably, however, the tables were turned, and he sometimes found that his critics also could find apt parallels from the past. When things began to go from bad to worse, Chateaubriand, his ambassador in Rome, compared him with Nero. Yet even when his cause was hopelessly lost, Napoleon added one final flourish of Plutarchian grandeur to adorn his letter of surrender. "I throw myself," he wrote, "like Themistocles upon the mercy of the British people."

ARCHITECTURE

With the reorganization of the government, the remaking of the constitution, and the recodification of the laws on the model of his reincarnated Roman Empire, Napoleon was determined that Paris should be replanned as a new Rome. He therefore undertook the ordering and commissioning of buildings with the same incredible vigor that marked his activities in other fields. The heart of the new city was still to be the spacious center designed around the old Place Louis XV, which

under the Directory had been renamed the Place de la Concorde (Fig. 491). Its axis began on the left bank of the Seine River with the old Palais Bourbon, now the Chamber of Deputies, which was to have its face lifted by a Corinthian colonnade. It continued across the river, by the bridge that had been begun in early revolutionary days, to the center of the Place, where some statuary was to cover the spot where the guillotine had done its grim work. The termination was to be the unfinished Church of La Madeleine at the end of the Rue Royale, which was to be rebuilt in the form of a Roman temple. To complete his scheme, Napoleon commissioned Percier and Fontaine, his favorite architects, to redesign the Rue de Rivoli, which intersected the axis at right angles and ran parallel to the Seine. Elsewhere throughout the city, triumphal arches and monumental columns were to proclaim to the world the presence of a new Caesar and Trajan.

Napoleon showed his interest in these projects by frequently conferring with his architects and engineers, by visiting construction sites, and by dreaming up new ideas while on distant battlefields. It was in Poland that he signed the decree for the building of his Temple of Glory, La Madeleine (Fig. 492). According to his express wish, the unfinished church was to be transformed and bear a dedicatory inscription: "From the Emperor to the soldiers of the Grande Armée." The building was not to look like a church but like such a temple as one would find in Athens or Rome. The interior was to contain marble tablets that were to be inscribed with the names of all the troops who had partici-

(left) 492. Pierre-Alexandre Vignon. Façade, La Madeleine, Paris. 1762–1829. 350′ long, 147′ wide, podium 23′ high.

(below) 493. La Madeleine, plan.

pated in the battles of Ulm, Austerlitz, and Jena; silver panels that would list their names again according to the departments of France which had sent their sons to the grand army; and gold plaques that would bear the names of those who had fallen on the field of battle. Around the room were to be bas reliefs of the regiments with their insignia; statues of the marshals were to occupy niches; and elsewhere trophies, regalia, banners, and drums were to be displayed. Each year on the anniversaries of the three battles the temple was to be illuminated and a grand concert given. Preceding the music, there were to be odes and eulogies stressing the virtues necessary for a soldier's life; and in a magnanimous mood of self-renunciation, Napoleon expressly forbade any mention of himself in these commemorative poems and orations. The grand council of the Legion of Honor was to be entrusted with the annual ceremonies, choosing the best poetry and music from the works submitted and rewarding the authors with gold medals. The minister of the interior, who was commissioned to carry out the order, promptly issued an artistic call to arms, summoning all the architects, sculptors, and painters to submit designs of a grand and noble character.

Napoleon personally selected an architectural plan by Pierre-Alexandre Vignon, because it fulfilled his conditions by looking sufficiently ancient and pagan. The building is indeed a pagan Corinthian temple, and, except for the sculptural details, it was completed according to Vignon's plan. In the Roman manner, it stands on a podium 23 feet high and is approached by a flight of steps in the front.

Running completely around the building is a series of Corinthian columns about 63 feet in height, 18 on each side, 8 on each end, and an additional row of 4 in front that supports the cornice. Since its rededication for religious purposes, this pagan temple of glory has had a large sculptural group by Lemaire on its pediment, representing the Last Judgment. In the center stands the figure of Christ, 17 feet high, with the repentant Mary Magdalene at His feet. To His left are allegorical figures representing the sins of Envy, Hypocrisy, and Avarice, while on His right are an angel of mercy and personifications of the virtues of Faith, Hope, Charity, and Innocence.

The interior cella of an ancient temple was never intended as a gathering place and always remained dark and mysterious. Hence, of necessity, Vignon had to depart from precedent and come up with something new (Fig. 493). The surprise that awaits the visitor as he passes through the massive bronze doors is complete, for the interior and exterior actually amount to two different buildings.

494. PIERRE-ALEXANDRE VIGNON. Interior, La Madeleine, Paris. 1762–1829.

The aisleless nave (Fig. 494) is divided into three long bays and a choir, which are not roofed in timber as in a Greek temple or vaulted in the Roman manner but are crowned with three low saucer domes on pendentives. The nave terminates in a semicircular apse that is roofed over by a semidome. Chapels are located in the recesses created by the buttresses that support the domes, and two classical orders—the Corinthian and Ionic—form the basis of the decorative scheme. Rich use is made of marble paneling, and the domes are coffered in the manner of the Roman Pantheon. What little light there is in this windowless interior comes from skylights at the tops of the domes, an idea derived from the Pantheon's oculus. The best that can be said about this method is that it keeps the exterior roof line intact. The exterior, as a study in classical design, has a certain dignity in its archeological faithfulness to such older models as the Maison Carrée (Fig. 91), though it excels its prototypes only in its larger proportions. The interior, however, does have a certain originality as an early example of the 19th-century eclectic style.

From its letters of foundation in 1757 to its final dedication in 1845, La Madeleine had a checkered history, to say the least. When Louis XV laid its cornerstone in 1764, he proclaimed it a monument to the piety of the French royal family. Work on it ceased during the Revolution, and it served during the days of the Terror as a morgue for the headless victims of the guillotine. The old unfinished pile was cleared off under Napoleon to become a temple to his cult of military glory. The word *glory*, however, began to have a hollow ring even before the end of the Empire, and after

Waterloo the building reverted to its status as a church of the Magdalene. Under the Bourbon restoration it became an expiatory monument to atone for the execution of Louis XVI and his family, which lasted until the Revolution of 1830. After its completion in 1842, it was finally dedicated by Louis Philippe, somewhat anticlimactically, as one of the parish churches of Paris.

In 1806, after winning military victories in Germany and Austria, Napoleon entrusted to Percier and Fontaine the building of a triumphal arch. Now known as the Arc de Triomphe du Carrousel (Fig. 495), it was designed as a gate of honor to the Tuileries Palace. It turned out to be a rather slavish imitation of the Arch of Septimus Severus in Rome, though of more modest proportions, but standing on the platform above it was one of Napoleon's proudest battle trophies—the group of four bronze horses taken from St. Mark's in Venice (Fig. 333). Owing to the shifting fortunes of war, Venice later got back the horses as a result of a peace treaty, and a triumphal chariot drawn by horses of a considerably later vintage was installed in their place to celebrate, somewhat ironically, the restoration of Louis XVIII. The face of the arch is decorated with rather undistinguished bas reliefs depicting such scenes as the Battle of Austerlitz, the surrender of Ulm, the peace of Tilsit, and Napoleon's triumphal entries into Munich and Vienna.

When finished, the result was too meager to measure up to Napoleon's imperial ambitions, and so another and still grander arch was commissioned for the Place de l'Étoile (Fig. 496). In this familiar Paris landmark, the architect Jean Francis Chalgrin achieved more life and elasticity by freely adapting

495. Charles Percier and Pierre F. L. Fontaine. Arc de Triomphe du Carrousel, Paris. 1806. 63½' wide, 48' high.

496. Jean Francis Chalgrin. Arc de Triomphe de l'Étoile, Paris. 1806–1835. 160' high.

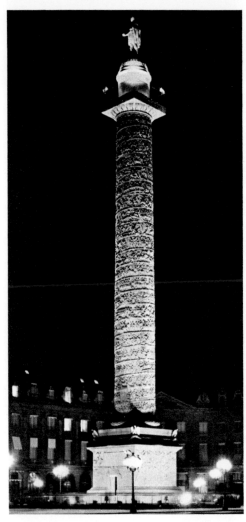

497. CHARLES PERCIER and PIERRE F. L. FONTAINE. Vendôme Column, Paris. 1810. Marble with bronze spiral frieze.

statue at the top originally was to have been of Charlemagne, but Napoleon yielded to flattery and allowed himself to be portrayed in the manner of a Roman emperor crowned with the laurel wreath and holding an orb surmounted by winged victory. This statue was carried off to England by the British army of occupation that entered Paris in 1814. Louis XVIII replaced it with one of Henry IV, but Louis Philippe put Napoleon back on top, this time as Citizen Bonaparte. In 1865, Napoleon III thought this statue an affront to his uncle and predecessor, and so Citizen Bonaparte came down and Napoleon in the imperial toga went up again. In 1871, under the Commune, the whole column was pulled down with ropes and pulleys by a group that included the painter Courbet, but under the Third Republic it was reassembled. Today it stands substantially as it was in the time of Napoleon III.

The wave of enthusiasm for classical architecture was by no means confined to Paris. Germany, England, and the United States had each experienced classic revivals in the 18th century. During the early 19th century, the Roman revival was strongest in the countries identified with Napoleon's Empire, while the Greek revival was accented in the nations of the anti-Napoleonic coalition, notably England and Germany. In England, such a public building as the British Museum (Fig. 498) was strongly Greek in character. In Berlin, an early example is the Brandenburg Gate (Fig. 499), modeled after the Athenian Propylaea. In Munich, two museums were based on the same model, one of which is the Glyptothek (Fig. 500), and near Regensburg, there is a Hall of Fame, called Valhalla, that is an archeologically exact reproduction of the Parthenon. In the United States, the classical revival period corresponded generally to the federal style, which ran its course from c.1785 to 1820. Buildings that show the Roman influence are the Virginia state capitol, which Thomas Jefferson designed after the Maison Carrée, and the Rotunda (Fig. 501), the original library of the University of Virginia, which was modeled after the Pantheon (Fig. 101).

rather than copying a known model. In it, French baroque precedents, Roman classical inspiration, and academic correctness of execution are combined in a harmonious manner. For his monumental effect, Chalgrin relied on bold proportions and a grand scale. Later, after Napoleonic times, the severity of the general outline was relieved by the skillful placement of high-relief sculptures of Cortot and Rude (Figs. 519, 520), works on a scale comparable to the immense size of the arch itself.

Still not content, Napoleon ordered a monumental Doric column to be erected in the Place Vendôme (Fig. 497). In size and style of ornamentation, it was a conscious copy of Trajan's Column in Rome (Fig. 105), the main difference being that its spiral reliefs are done on a bronze strip made from the guns and cannons captured from the defeated Prussian and Austrian armies. The sculpture recounts the story of the campaign of 1805 in scenes, such as Napoleon's address to his troops, the capture of Ulm, the meeting of the three emperors, and the conquest of Istria and Dalmatia. The

PAINTING

The most articulate artistic spokesman for this stern world of revolutionary fervor and ancient Roman heroism was destined to be Jacques-Louis David, a painter whose temperament and technique were ideally suited to the spirit of the times. A reformer by nature and a classical enthusiast by nurture, David painted pictures the austerity of

498. SIDNEY SMIRKE. British Museum (south front), London. 1823–1847.

499. KARL GOTTHARD LANGHANS. Brandenburg Gate, Berlin. 1789–1793.

500. LEO VON KLENZE. Glyptothek, Munich. 1830.

501. THOMAS JEFFERSON. Rotunda, University of Virginia, Charlottesville. 1819–1826.

502. JACQUES-LOUIS DAVID. *Oath of the Horatii.* 1784.
Oil on canvas, 10′ 10″ × 14′. Louvre, Paris.

which was a conscious reaction to the rococo extravagances exemplified in the work of his grand uncle, Boucher. By virtue of his studies in Rome, David had absorbed all that was necessary for the exploitation of the classical enthusiasms of the readers of Plutarch's *Parallel Lives* and Winckelmann's *History of Ancient Art.* Harkening to Diderot and other earnest voices, a picture for David was never a mere painting; it had to have a manifestolike message pointing in the direction of political and social action. It was inevitable that the high moral purposes of the French Revolution would be reflected in some kind of didactic art, and David's immediate success can be attributed to the fact that his style extolled the same stalwart ideas that the revolutionists espoused. Bourgeois by birth and upbringing, David frankly addressed his art to the newly established middle-class social order.

David's first great success was the *Oath of the Horatii* (Fig. 502), finished in Rome while Louis XVI was still on the French throne. The subject, one of the legends of the founding of the ancient Roman republic, was suggested by Corneille's ballet *Les Horaces.* The three arches of the severely simple setting separate the figures like niches for statuary. In the center stands Horatius

Proclus dedicating the swords of his three sons, who swear to defend the Roman republic against the plotting Curatii, one of whom was betrothed to their grief-stricken sister on the right. Baroque precedents can be cited for this important painting. "If I owe my subject to Corneille," said David, "I owe my picture to Poussin." Clarity of contour, sculpturesque sharpness of modeling, harsh but clear handling of light and shadow, characterize this stark but heroic canvas.

Over and beyond his work as a painter and the intrinsic value of his painting, David assumed the role of power politician in the field of art with far-reaching effects. In a period when it was something of a triumph for a man to keep his head on his shoulders, David showed a political shrewdness and sense of timing that would have done credit to a prime minister. After accepting many commissions from Louis XVI and election to the Academy of Painting and Sculpture, established under Louis XIV, he went over to the side of the Revolution at the opportune moment. As a member of the Convention, he not only voted for the execution of his former patron but succeeded in abolishing the Academy and establishing in its stead the École des Beaux-Arts, which he reoriented from the tradi-

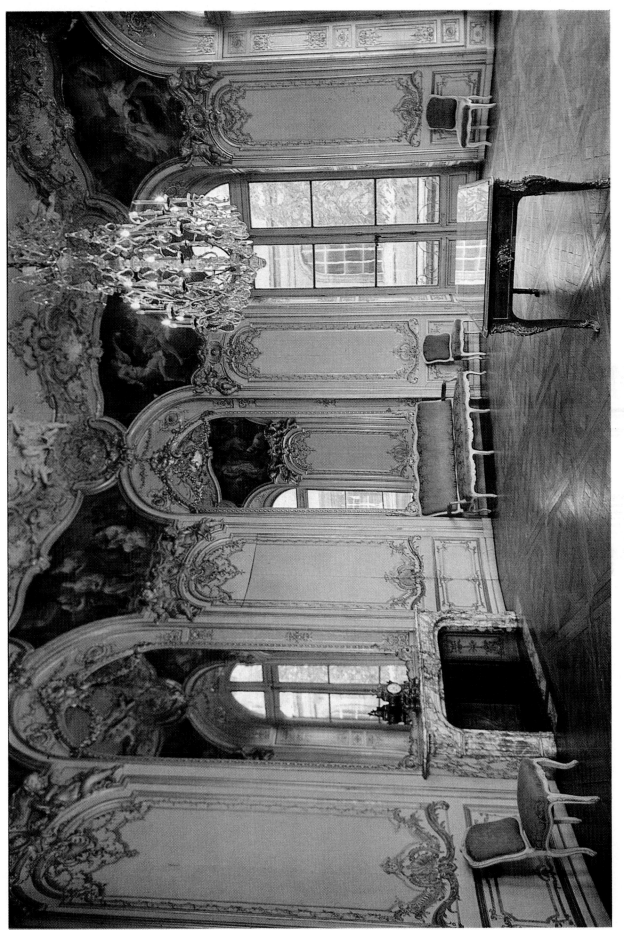

Plate 43. GERMAIN BOFFRAND. Salon de la Princesse, Hôtel de Soubise, Paris. c. 1740.
Oval, c. 33 × 26′. (See p. 423.)

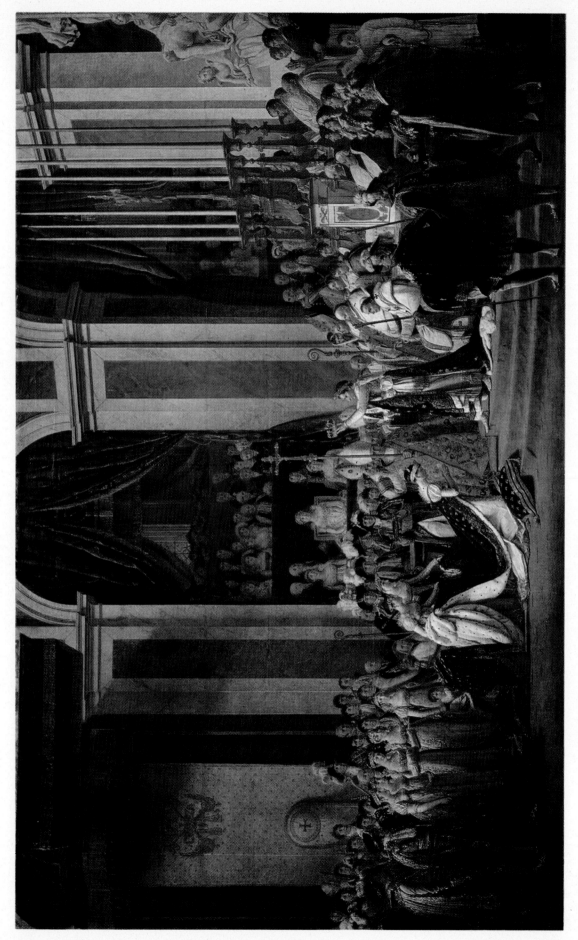

Plate 44. Jacques-Louis David. *Le Sacre (Coronation)*. 1805–1808. Oil on canvas, 20′ × 30′6½″. Louvre, Paris. (See p. 440.)

503. JACQUES-LOUIS DAVID. *Lictors Bringing Back to Brutus the Bodies of His Sons.* 1789.
Oil on canvas, 10′ 8″ × 13′ 10½″. Louvre, Paris.

tional baroque and rococo styles toward the study of Roman antiquity. He then blandly hitched his wagon to Napoleon's rising star. When Napoleon assumed the title of Emperor, David was given the title of First Painter of the Empire, a commanding position that he proceeded to exploit to the fullest. His activities included the organization of official ceremonies, coordination of the system of state museums, and the granting of licenses to the artists who wished to show their works in the annual public exhibitions. More academic than the former academicians, he succeeded in laying the foundations of official art that endured for the rest of the 19th century. While his theories and subject matter are still a matter of controversy, David's craftsmanship was on a par with any of the master painters of the past, and many distinguished painters of the present have been well aware of his style and manner of execution. The technique of Salvador Dali and the 20th-century neoclassicism of Picasso, for instance, owe much to the cool objective draftsmanship of their 19th-century predecessor.

David's picture of the *Lictors Bringing Back to Brutus the Bodies of His Sons* (Fig. 503) bears the date of the fateful year of 1789. It is both a reminder that his career had its inception during the latter days

of the monarchy and that he was attempting to continue the subject and substance of his earlier spectacular success, *Oath of the Horatii.* In it one finds the same stern spirit of self-sacrifice, the same severity of style that had appealed so much to the eyes that were weary of the fussy rococo, the same somber type of setting, which had interested those who were reading about the archeological discoveries at Pompeii and Herculaneum. With remarkable boldness, David was able to flaunt the dour, do-or-die virtues of Roman republicanism right under the noses of his aristocratic patrons. These two pictures were not only the manifesto of a new style in art but of a new image of society as well, and their unparalleled success was owed in no small measure to the fact that they appeared at precisely the right moment.

For his subject David again chose an incident from the days soon after the founding of the ancient Roman republic. Lucius Junius Brutus, one of the consuls, had discovered that his own sons were involved in a plot to restore the recently overthrown monarchy. Having ordered their executions, he is shown as an isolated figure in the statuesque shadow of the goddess Roma. Behind him are the lictors bearing the bodies of his sons, while a third group is formed by his grieving wife and daughters. Many who were living through the trying times of the Revolution could see something of themselves in that figure of stoical resolution, torn between his public duty to the state and his private paternal grief.

Equally melodramatic but with more of the violent action of the Revolution was the picture that followed a decade later, *Battle of the Romans and Sabines* (Fig. 504). Romulus, the legendary founder of Rome, and his warriors had taken the women of the Sabines by violence, as pictured by Rubens and Poussin (Figs. 418, 419). Here David depicts the sequel when the Sabine fathers and brothers came to avenge the rape of their womenfolk. By this time, however, the women had become Roman wives and mothers and are shown rushing outward from the city gates with their children and throwing themselves between the combatants to stop the bloodshed. Again the subject is one of conflicting loyalties, brought out by the principal protagonists in the foreground. Romulus is about to throw his spear at the king of the Sabines, while the king's daughter Hersilia, now the wife of Romulus, rushes between them, begging them to desist. In keeping with his aesthetic theory of placing principles above reality, David idealizes his figures and minimizes detail by showing the men almost nude and the horses without harness. For all its sound and fury, however, the composition as a whole tends to become almost as cold and hard as the carved stone relief that inspired it.

In his portraiture, David reveals himself an expert appraiser of personality, and his viewers find in this genre a certain relief from his more heroic efforts. A sensitive example is the unfinished portrait of *Madame Récamier* (Fig. 505), one of the most fascinating and intelligent women of the period. In her, David found a promising subject, who furnished her salon in the fashionable Pompeian style he had done so much to popularize. Here she reclines in the classical manner on an Empire chaise longue just as she might have done on the days she received her guests. Her white gown is draped with deep folds reminiscent of antique statuary. The only other pieces of furniture are the footstool and bronze lamp, which were drawn from Pompeian originals. The clarity with which David handles the outlines of the figure and the silhouette of the head combine with the austere setting to give a general effect of orderliness and elegance.

David did many portraits of Napoleon, mostly in official attitudes, but in his *Bonaparte on Mount St. Bernard* (Fig. 506) he captures something of the essence of Napoleon the conqueror. Shortly after the conclusion of the successful Italian campaign,

504. JACQUES-LOUIS DAVID. *Battle of the Romans and Sabines.* 1799. Oil on canvas, 12′8″ × 17′. Louvre, Paris.

(above) 505. JACQUES-LOUIS DAVID. *Madame Récamier*. 1800. Oil on canvas, 5′ 8″ × 7′11¾″. Louvre, Paris.

(right) 506. JACQUES-LOUIS DAVID. *Bonaparte on Mount St. Bernard*. 1800. Oil on canvas, 8′11½″ × 7′ 7½″. Versailles Palace.

the artist told the First Consul that he wanted to paint him sword in hand on the field of battle. Napoleon is reported to have replied: "No, it is not with the sword that battles are won—paint me calm and serene on a fiery steed." Lest one be swept away by this disarming touch of honesty on Napoleon's part, let him recall that the actual crossing was made on the back of a sure-footed mule. In addition to the use of such poetic license, David makes doubly sure that no one would miss the point by providing the observer with a history lesson. Written on the rocks in the foreground are the names of the great former transalpine conquerors, Hannibal and Charlemagne, beside that of Bonaparte.

To commemorate his assumption of the imperial dignity, Napoleon in 1804 commissioned David, as First Painter, to execute four grandiose pictures. Since the Empire was destined to last but a decade, David had time to complete only two of them: the *Coronation*, or *Le Sacre* (Plate 44), and the *Distribution of the Eagles,* those ancient standards of the Roman imperial legions that Napoleon had adopted as his own. Both were historical canvases in the grand tradition of Poussin and Lebrun, but in these paintings David extended that genre to include contemporary events.

Napoleon's coronation had taken place in the choir of the Cathedral of Notre Dame in Paris, where his decorators, Percier and Fontaine, had designed a special setting for the occasion. The ancient Gothic architecture had been camouflaged with imitation marble arches and pilasters that frame the boxes and galleries for distinguished guests. David originally proposed to paint the moment after Pope Pius VII had blessed the crown and Napoleon had taken it from the altar to place it on his own head. But the emperor preferred the more gallant pose when he put the crown on the brow of his kneeling empress. Aside from this bit of incidental activity, David's painting amounts to a stately group portrait on a grand scale. As a piece of official art, the placement and attitude of every personage in it had to be passed on by the master of protocol and ratified by Napoleon himself, even to the inclusion of his mother who had made a particular point of being away from Paris that day. David, however, had been there and had made sketches on the spot. But when he drew Pius VII with hands resting on his knees as the artist had actually observed him, David was told by Napoleon that the successor of St. Peter had not come so far to do nothing. Consequently, David had to revise his drawing to show the Pope extending his hand in benediction.

In such circumstances, it is a minor miracle that David was able to get as much elasticity into the composition as he did. His achievement is all the more remarkable when one reflects how easily the whole thing could have become nothing more than a fancy-dress ball, with Napoleon as the middle-class messiah standing in the midst of the members of his family whom he had made kings, princes, cardinals, and so on. But David, by his masterly grouping, commanding postures, and sure handling of the wealth of detail, preserves the uncluttered spaciousness of the setting and the proportions of the whole. The scene also provided the painter of classical austerity with a chance to exploit the element of color, and David made rich but not lavish use of the medium. In all these ways the versatile David was able to adapt his art to Napoleon's dreams of imperial Roman grandeur.

The immense 20- by 30-foot canvas contains some 150 lifesize portraits, and it took several years before each of these individuals had visited the church where David set up his studio to sit for his or her likeness. The assemblage is made up mostly of beplumed marshals of the imperial army, maids of honor to the empress, court chamberlains, and members of the diplomatic corps. The United States ambassador is included, but the English delegation is conspicuous by its absence. Napoleon's mother and other members of his family occupy the center box, while in the gallery above is a group of artists and intellectuals, including the composer Grétry. As a signature, David painted himself sitting and sketching, accompanied by his wife and daughters, favorite pupils, and his teacher Vien.

The symbolism in *Le Sacre* calls for comment, because it underscores Napoleon's problem of holding a coronation that would not evoke memories of the hated aristocracy and yet have an aura of legitimacy, of striking a balance between the luxury and elegance of the old regime and the Spartan simplicity of the Revolutionary period. This he had managed to achieve in the form of government when, figuratively speaking, he set ahead the hands of the clock of history to point to the hour of the prosperous Roman Empire instead of the austere Roman republic, and it was this image that the pomp and circumstances of the coronation must confirm. Past coronations had been designed primarily to impress other aristocrats, but Napoleon, as a popular ruler, was concerned with impressing the populace. In both the actual coronation and in David's painting, he let them savor the taste of glory and quickened their pulses with a sense of destiny. The crimson coronation robes of the emperor and empress are embroidered all over with golden bees, Napoleon's chosen symbol for the integrated state in which all members had their appointed place and worked for the good of the hive in order to produce the honey of prosperity. Elsewhere in the painting,

507. Jean-Auguste Domi-
nique Ingres. *Apotheosis
of Homer.* 1827. Oil on
canvas, 12′8″ × 16′10¾″.
Louvre, Paris.

the sheaves of wheat and cornucopias are symbols of imperial plenty; palm branches and figures of victory symbolize triumph; and Napoleon's laurel-wreath crown is the ancient symbol of literary immortality. The papal coat of arms below the canopy at the left gives a touch of historical continuity so necessary to Napoleon's regime, but the throne that had stood under a triumphal arch festooned with curtains of imperial purple and facing the high altar was omitted from the painting. The supreme symbol on the actual occasion was Napoleon's act of crowning himself to signify the break with the past and his derivation of authority from the people by a plebiscite. By this dramatic touch, Bonaparte also proclaimed the existence of the free individual who recognized no authority superior to himself and the fact that his power was derived through his own efforts and those of the people and not from above. In the painting, this symbolism was transferred to Napoleon's act of crowning Josephine.

No presentation of this revived Roman Empire would be complete that showed only the histrionic attitudes of the conqueror. The sufferings of a subjugated people, which invariably follow in the wake of an invading army, found vivid expression in the scenes painted by Francisco Goya after the French campaign in Spain in 1808. His *Executions of the Third of May, 1808* (Plate 45), which Goya finished some years later, accents the reverse side of the Napoleonic coin. Goya saw nothing of the heroic aspect of warfare, only the desolation of his country and the accompanying horrors and bloodshed. In this picture, both the technique and the subject

matter are quite the opposite of the cold and correct presentations of David. Goya, whose compassionate art was the very antithesis of French neoclassicism, further explored the miseries that trail in war's wake in his cycle of 85 etchings, *Disasters of War.* Here, through his incisive mind and biting wit, a carnival of carnage, fearful bestialities, and demonic destruction is revealed.

After David, the leading light of the academic art world was his pupil, Jean-Auguste Dominique Ingres. Like his teacher, Ingres realized the importance of championing the arts in official circles; eventually he became a senator of France. The Academy had been reestablished after Napoleon's downfall, and the idea of placing the official stamp of approval on writers and painters finds full expression in the *Apotheosis of Homer* (Fig. 507). Commissioned as a ceiling mural in the newly established Charles X Museum in the Louvre, the painting is well adapted to its museum setting, for it is impressive in content as well as in its large proportions. Ingres treats his subject as if it were some supreme session of an academy of arts and letters for the immortals. In their midst sits the enthroned Homer, the greatest of them all. Behind him is the façade of an Ionic temple; winged victory holds the laurel wreath above his brow; at his feet are the personifications of his brain children, the *Iliad* and the *Odyssey*; and about him are his successors who have carried the torch for poetry and art throughout the ages. In this exclusive society, Aeschylus is seen unfolding a scroll listing his tragedies; the poet Pindar holds up his lyre in tribute; Vergil and

Dante (extreme left) represent epic poetry; Longinus is standing up for philosophy, Boileau for criticism; at the lower right Racine and Molière, in the courtly wigs of the time of Louis XIV, make an offering of tragic and comic masks; and Raphael, the profiled figure in the upper left, is the proxy for Renaissance painting. Below him in the foreground is Poussin, and behind him, Shakespeare.

Ingres' source seems to have been a Hellenistic relief, now in the British Museum, showing a simplified version of the same subject with allegorical representations of the *Iliad* and *Odyssey* as well as personifications of Time and the muses of History, Poetry, Drama, and Mythology. Ingres' virtuosity in drawing is seen in the sharply delineated figures. Like his contemporaries, he accepted the Greek aesthetic of art as a representation of nature, with the reservation that it was the artist's function to endow nature with orderliness through the process of rearrangement and editorial excision. In this case, he builds his composition by means of precise lines, which he then organizes into a series of receding planes. Color for him, as it was for David, was always secondary.

SCULPTURE

The sculptor Antonio Canova, who in his day enjoyed a reputation second to none, was summoned from Rome to Paris by Napoleon to execute statues of the emperor and his family. Through his neoclassical spectacles, the Italian artist saw Napoleon's mother as the matronly Agrippina of old, his sister Pauline—not without some justification—as Venus Victorious, and Napoleon himself, most obligingly, as a Roman emperor (Fig. 508). Canova was accompanied to Paris by his brother, who recorded the conversations between artist and patron from which we learn that Napoleon had a few qualms about being portrayed, as the saying goes, in the "heroic altogether" and suggested an appropriate costume. To this Canova grandiosely replied: "We, like the poets, have our own language. If a poet introduced into a tragedy, phrases and idioms used habitually by the lower classes in the public streets, he would rightly be reprimanded by everybody. In like manner, we sculptors cannot clothe our statues in modern costumes without deserving a similar reproach." The sculptor's arguments prevailed, and, except for the suggestion of a toga draped over his shoulder, Napoleon stands there in all his marble glory, holding in his right hand an orb surmounted by winged victory and in his left, a staff of authority in lieu of a scepter. The head is idealized but recognizable; the body with the shifting of the weight to-

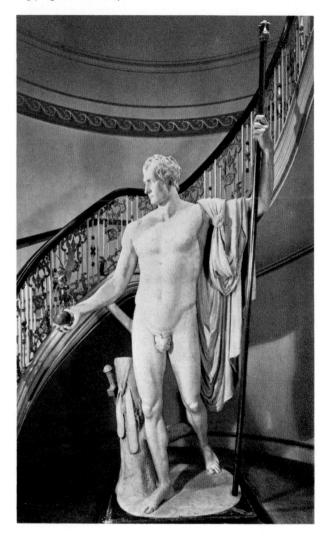

508. ANTONIO CANOVA. *Napoleon.* 1802–1810. Marble, *c.* 11'8" high. Wellington Museum, London (Crown copyright reserved).

ward one side points directly to Praxitelean models as does the inevitable Hellenistic tree trunk.

The reclining statue of *Pauline Bonaparte as Venus* (Fig. 509) is another example of the use of a Hellenistic prototype, for Canova, like David, had come under the sway of Winckelmann. While it is almost an exact sculptural counterpart of David's *Madame Récamier* (Fig. 505), the statue conveys much less of the individuality of its subject than does the painting. Both Canova statues show how much more a sculptor was restricted in his expression than a painter was during this wave of classical enthusiasm, simply because of the wealth of well-known antique models. While practically nothing of ancient painting was known to David, museums filled with well-preserved ancient statues were open to Canova. While the one was free to create a new style, the other had to conform to existing models. Like a good academician, Canova advised his stu-

509. ANTONIO CANOVA. *Pauline Bonaparte as Venus.* 1808. Marble, lifesize. Borghese Gallery, Rome.

dents on a "scrupulous adherence to rules" so as to guard against "arbitrary and capricious errors."

Judicious deviation from the "rules" was possible, however, when it could be justified on rational grounds. In Canova's aesthetics, everything was defined by classical canons. Hence when he did a portrait of a contemporary figure, the body, its pose, and the drapery were taken directly from antique models, and the head was idealized just enough to fit the subject. In theory, Canova accepted the Greek idea of art as an imitation of nature, but in practice his art became an imitation of art. For his observations of human nature, he was content to look about the Vatican collections instead of going out on the highways and byways. Furthermore, his constant self-conscious striving to create objects of art too often led to artificial works. In the mind and hands of a greater artist, Canova's aesthetic might possibly have produced more significant results, but in his own case it had a definitely stultifying effect.

Because of the great demand for his work, Canova employed a large number of assistants in his studio. His large output, plus the use of some modern devices and methods that were unknown to Praxiteles, gave his workshop something of the aspect of a factory. Among other things, he used chemical solutions to achieve the extraordinary smoothness of his surface textures, and he employed a pointing machine to make exact copies of ancient sculptures. Despite murmurings from less successful sculptors, nothing in Canova's lifetime diminished his glittering reputation. The many young Americans who were attracted to Rome by his fame returned from their studies to do things like Horatio Greenough's colossal statue of George Washington as Zeus (Fig. 510), which outgrew its intended set-

510. HORATIO GREENOUGH. *George Washington.* 1832–1841. Marble, 11′ 4″ high. Smithsonian Institution, Washington, D. C.

ting in the Capitol and is now in the Smithsonian Institution.

The British Parliament invited Canova to London to pass on the value of the Parthenon sculptures before it purchased them from Lord Elgin. One would have thought that, after feeling the full force of these originals, the Italian sculptor might have realized their superiority to his previous models. Instead, he smugly found in them the justification of his own life's work and seized the opportunity to point out how wrong his critics had been. He did show good judgment, however, in refusing to attempt a restoration and in some of his observations on the differences between the real Greek sculpture and the works designed for the Roman market.

MUSIC

"Among all the fine arts, music is the one which exercises the greatest influence upon the passions and is the one which the legislator should most encourage." So wrote Napoleon to the inspector of the conservatory soon after he became a consul. Napoleon's interest in music, or in any of the arts for that matter, was always conditioned by its effect on the people at large and its function in the service of the state. His personal band, for instance, stood in readiness for a parade or a public celebration; and the popular side of the art, especially military music, was never neglected. The welfare of composers, opera singers, and orchestra musicians was also a matter of much concern to all the post-Revolution governments. Since the aristocrats had fled the country, patronage had now to come from other sources. Napoleon, therefore, interested himself in the affairs of the Paris Opera, insisting that all budgetary matters and commissions for new works be submitted to him even when he was away on his military campaigns. He attended public performances whenever possible and took special pleasure in the popular demonstrations his appearances usually provoked. The beneficial effects of this interest, however, must be equated with a control over all aspects of stage production that amounted to a strict form of state censorship.

Napoleon's attempts to win over the French artists and those of the conquered countries extended into the field of music. His personal preferences leaned rather strongly to the Italian vocal style, especially that of Paisiello, whose gentle lyricism was congenial to his taste. It was Paisiello who received the commission to compose the *Te Deum* for the national celebration of the concordat with the Vatican, and the appointment as first conductor of the Imperial Chapel Orchestra.

Second in charge was the French composer Lesueur, who had written the music for the coronation ceremonies and a successful opera on Macpherson's *Ossian*, one of Napoleon's favorite books. The production that most closely caught the spirit of the new Empire, however, was Spontini's opera *La Vestale*. Appearing as it did in 1807 at the height of Napoleon's military successes, it had the necessary pomp and pageantry to whip public enthusiasm to a pitch of frenzy. It had the requisite Roman setting, and the spectacle of a vestal virgin's struggle between her desire for personal happiness and her vows of service to the state was sufficient to ensure more than 100 performances in its first season in Paris. The libretto stressed the gaining of glory on the battlefield, and Spontini supplied the necessary triumphal marches. His music is full of the sounding brass and the trumpet's blare, singing in the grand style, and the declamation of massive choruses. One of his contemporaries wrote that "his *forte* was a hurricane, his *piano* a breath, his *sforzando* enough to wake the dead." It was none other than Berlioz who attributed to him the invention of the "colossal crescendo."

Unknown to Napoleon, however, the essence of the heroic ideal had been distilled in musical form in one of the countries he had conquered. Ludwig van Beethoven's *Third Symphony*, which the composer himself called the *Eroica*, or Heroic, was never heard by the man whose career had suggested it; nor was it played in Paris until 1828, a quarter of a century after it was composed. Yet a French writer of later times, Romain Rolland, could declare with the full weight of history on his side: "Here is an Austerlitz of music, the conquest of an empire. And Beethoven's has endured longer than Napoleon's." The inception of this mighty work apparently took place in 1798 when General Bernadotte, as an emissary of France, visited Vienna. The general was enough interested in music to have the French violinist Rodolphe Kreutzer in his suite, and Beethoven soon came to his attention. It is Bernadotte who is credited with the suggestion that Beethoven write a work honoring Consul Bonaparte, although he probably had in mind little more than a dedication. For four years Beethoven thought about the suggestion, and eventually the *Eroica* bore the desired dedication. But the year that the symphony was completed was the year in which Napoleon accepted the title of Emperor. Beethoven, feeling that the erstwhile apostle of liberty had become both a traitor and a new tyrant, erased the name from the title page and inscribed it instead "to the memory of a great man." This memory indeed had stirred Beethoven deeply, and from the days of his youth he had been a lifelong partisan of the ideals of liberty, equality, and fraternity. It was Napoleon's espousal of these principles, his implacable opposition to hereditary privilege, his will and ability to translate these ideals into action, that had moved Beethoven profoundly as it had so many other artists and writers of the time. The *Third Symphony* is not, and never was, narrowly Napoleonic, but more generally an elaboration of the heroism of one who, for a time at least, rallied the progressive and freedom-loving people of all nations around his standard.

The music Beethoven wrote for the theater was invariably based on themes involving the quest for individual liberty and the cause of popular freedom. His *Prometheus* ballet, for instance, was about two statues that were brought to life by the divine fire of knowledge and human creativity. The overtures and incidental music he wrote for plays had to do, in the case of Collin's *Coriolanus*, with an inner struggle for freedom, and in the case of Goethe's *Egmont* as well as Kotzebue's *Ruins of Athens* and *King Stephen*, with the liberation of an oppressed people. While he admired the music of Mozart's *Marriage of Figaro* and *Don Giovanni*, Beethoven was shocked by the immorality of the plots and some of the characters. In his only opera, *Fidelio*, he insisted on a libretto that would reflect high moral purpose and steadfast resolve.

In Beethoven's instrumental compositions, these ideals of liberty, equality, and fraternity attained their most abstract and universal expression in his fluid forms. Beethoven used the power of his art to convey the spirit of these great human declarations, and, by so doing, he illuminated the path of man as he works toward his ultimate destiny of progress and perfectibility. His achievement was all the greater because he was able to do this without programmatic dilutions, thereby strengthening rather than weakening his art. Through the *Eroica*, Beethoven was giving tangible shape to the aspirations of a large segment of mankind during those stirring times. In it, he mirrored the titanic struggle between the opposing attitudes of submission and assertion, between passivity and activity, and between acceptance and challenge. Through it, he gave flesh to the word of the triumph of spirit over matter, will over negation, and the victorious human drive against the forces of suppression. Though the length of the symphony is unprecedented and the orchestra somewhat expanded, Beethoven never fell into the trap that many of the French composers of the Revolutionary period did when they equated colossal size with grandeur of utterance. While the revolutionists wrote their choruses for 1,000 voices, accompanied by cannons and three or four combined orchestras, Beethoven added just one horn to his usual brass section. He clothed his ideas in rich folds of lustrous sound that grow out of the poetic idea itself. Furthermore, by raising the level of musical content and making it commensurate with his instrumental forces, he succeeded in producing an organic work of art where the others failed. While the symphony as a whole can be criticized on formal grounds and for a certain lack of unity in the four separate movements, the fiery spirit of creation when Beethoven was at the height of his mature powers has never been surpassed. The *Eroica* was as much a revolution in the musical field as the French Revolution was in that of political thought and action.

Each of the four movements was in its way precedent-shattering. The first is distinguished by its restless surging character and its enormous expansion of first-movement form to encompass a development section of 245 bars. The mobilization of such forces, as well as the transformation of the coda into a terminal development 140 measures in length, caused Romain Rolland to call it a "Grand Army of the soul, that will not stop until it has trampled on the whole earth." A cogent formal analysis of this opening movement by Donald F. Tovey can be found in the *Encyclopaedia Britannica* under "Sonata Forms."

A Funeral March as the second movement of a symphony was another innovation, though Beethoven had included one in his earlier *Sonata for Piano*, Op. 26, which bears the inscription "on the death of a hero." Its heroic proportions here, as well as its poetic conception as an apotheosis of the hero, link it with the first movement. While such an apotheosis is a fairly common idea for a painting, statue, poem, play, or opera, its incorporation into the more abstract symphonic form is unique. The effect is that of a glowing elegy for the heroic among mankind who give up life itself so that the ideals for which they fought may live. It is, in this case, a collective rather than an individualized expression, though it emphasizes that every great advance of mankind is accompanied by personal tragedy. The stately measured rhythms and muffled sonorities also reminded the listener of Beethoven's time that contemporary heroes, as well as such ancient ones as Socrates and Jesus, often suffered martyrdom at the hands of an uncomprehending society.

The title Scherzo over the third movement also appears for the first time in a formal symphony, though again it had been used earlier in piano sonatas and chamber music. Beethoven once more reveals himself a man of the Revolutionary period by the substitution of this robust humor for the traditional minuet, but in such a grand design he hardly had any other alternative. Berlioz has referred to its energetic rhythms as a kind of play, "recalling that which the warriors of the *Iliad* celebrated round the tombs of their chiefs."

For his Finale, Beethoven writes such a monumental set of variations that it becomes a veritable musical arch of triumph through which the image of a liberated humanity joyfully passes in review. To comprehend its full meaning, one needs to look both backward and forward to other landmarks in Beethoven's work. The theme itself is taken from the last dance of his ballet music for *Prometheus*. Its frequent appearance in his notebooks, and its existence in two other versions—a simple country dance and a set of piano variations—show that it figured prominently in his musical thought for several years. For him the theme had definite Promethean associations and a certain buoyant optimism. The figure of Prometheus represented for Beethoven, as for Shelley, "the type of the highest perfection of moral and intellectual nature impelled by the purest and truest motives to the best and noblest of ends." It was Prometheus who first defied the gods in order to bring the divine fire of the arts and sciences from the Olympian hearth to animate the spirits of men and release them from the bondage of ignorance. Prometheus thus became a symbol of creative power through which Beethoven was able to convey his conviction of the ultimate perfectibility of mankind. The fiery and precipitous descent of the opening bars had also been heard in the ballet music in a more literal sense. Here it serves as a mighty preparation for the emergence of the skeleton theme.

What is heard at first is simply a structural outline derived from the bass of the Promethean dance, which defines a tonal center together with the upper and lower dominant limits of the tonality. This harmonic vacuum is gradually populated by the addition of a second, third, and fourth voice, while simultaneously the rhythmic divisions are quickened by similar subdivisions. Not until the 76th bar is the Promethean melody joined to its previously heard skeletal bass.

The form of the Finale is a series of variations unequal in length and strongly contrasted in style. What had before been but a pleasant little dance tune now assumes the imposing shape of a triumphant melody, which Beethoven, by his additive process, is able to build into the cumulative structure he needs for his victory finale. Here the great idea springs fully grown and fully armed from the brain of its creator. The heroic image is later continued in the finales of the *Fifth* and *Ninth Symphonies*, and the amplification in these later works contributes to a more profound understanding of the earlier *Eroica*.

All three finales envision the emergence of a strong and free human society, and all three start with quasi-popular themes. In the *Eroica*, it is a modest little country dance; in the *Fifth*, a simple marching tune; and in the *Ninth*, an unpretentious hymn. One and all, they are built up to epical proportions. By the use of an immense variety of styles, episodic deviations, a wide range of keys, and shifting orchestral color, they become collective rather than individual expressions. Instead of being restricted to one side of life, they embrace a cross section of musical levels and reach out to encompass the entire human panorama. Some variations are aristocratic in sound, while others are rough and ready. Compare, for example, the elegant sonorities of bars 175–197 in the *Eroica* finale with the boisterous band music heard in bars 211–255. A similar open-air episode to that heard in bars 211–255 occurs in the finale of the *Ninth*, where Beethoven inserts a popular "Turkish" march, scored in a bizarre manner for bassoons, horns, trombones, cymbals, triangle, and drums. Further contrasts in the *Eroica* finale can be heard in the fugal episodes (bars 117–174, and 266–348), which employ sophisticated contrapuntal devices, such as the inversion of the skeleton theme (277–280) and the rather stolid German chorale (249–364) that begins at the point where the tempo is slackened to a *Poco andante*. All this vast variety of forms— dances, songs, fugues, chorales—are arranged sequentially in the manner of a procession that eventually leads up to the rousing triumphant climax heard in bars 381—395. At this point, Beethoven throws in all his orchestral forces, including the brasses and drums, to bring about the image of ultimate achievement of the heroic idea. Afterward there remain only the quieter anticlimax (396–430), in which the whole awesome spectacle is contemplated retrospectively, and the whirlwind *presto* that terminates the movement.

THE ARCHEOLOGICAL IDEA

The Napoleonic era was a paradoxical mixture of progressive and retrogressive tendencies. At the very time when the social aspirations of the Revolutionary period were about to be realized in democratic forms, Europe was confronted with a militant revival of ancient Roman imperial autocracy. The 18th-century individualism that had led to the struggle for freedom was engulfed in a 19th-century regimentation disguised as a movement to maintain the social gains that had been made. Revolutionary ideals were partially eclipsed by Napoleonic actualities; the desire for freedom collided with the need for order; the rights of man conflicted with the might of man; and spiritual well-being was pitted against material considerations.

New scientific and technological advances competed for attention with revivals of ancient glories. Napoleon boasted of a new culture, yet he clothed it in a Roman toga. The architecture of La Madeleine's interior was modern by early 19th-century standards, but the exterior was a cold archeological study. Canova, in his portrait sculpture, matched the heads of his clients with bodies copied from antique statues. And painters, trying to express new ideas, ran into the strength of established academic tradition. Voltaire, in the previous century, had said that the voice of the people was the voice of God; and Mengs, in his *Thoughts on Beauty* (1765), had said that the beautiful was that which appealed to the majority. Now came David, with strong governmental support, to dictate to the majority what they should enjoy. At a time when emotionalism was rampant, David insisted on a rational system of rules for the pictorial arts. Such a cleavage between feeling and thinking, however, must be seen as a necessary reaction to the excessive passion of Revolutionary times.

The early 19th century was by no means unique in its revival of a bygone era. Every period in Western art since Greco-Roman days has revived classical ideas and motifs in one manner or another. From the 1,000-year span of Greco-Roman civilization, many choices have been made by succeeding centuries. Dramas and operas have been set in Athens, in Sparta, the Alexandrian empire, the Roman republic, and the West and East Roman empires, and their characters have been lofty Olympian deities and rugged Roman heroes. Dramatists have chosen the Roman playwright Seneca as a model, as did Quinault and Racine in the baroque period, and the Athenians Aeschylus and Euripides, as did Shelley and Goethe. Architects in the 17th century, such as Bernini and Perrault, built then-modern palaces that they decorated with classical motifs, while the neoclassicists Vignon, Percier, and Fontaine constructed almost precise models of Greek and Roman temples. Forms of government, likewise, ranged from the democratic city-state and republic to the autocratic kingdom and empire. Aside from the shape and spirit a revival assumes, it is largely a matter of selectivity.

Each period has tended to choose from the past those elements that harmonized with its specific ideals and aspirations. Florentine Renaissance humanists, in their reaction to medieval scholastic thought and the traditional Church interpretation of Aristotle, turned to the pagan beauties of antiquity in general and to the philosophy of Plato in particular. The Renaissance revival of classicism, however, was confined to a few intellectuals and artists. Neoclassicism, on the other hand, was mirrored in forms of government, became the officially approved art style, and rested on a base of broad popular acceptance. Baroque classical interests reflected an aristocratic image of man and were restricted to courtly circles. Louis XIV and his associates identified themselves with the gods of Mt. Olympus, and their moral standards, like those of the ancient deities, were the ethics of a highly privileged class. Napoleonic neoclassicism, by contrast, was oriented toward the comfortable middle class, which saw a congenial hedonistic image in the living standards of ancient Pompeii and Herculaneum but tempered luxury with the stricter moral standards of a revolutionary regime. The new interest in classical architecture, sculpture, and painting was also a bourgeois criticism of the artificiality and extravagance of courtly life as mirrored in the 18th-century rococo. Without the moral connotations of this revived interest in the art of the ancient world, the choice of conservative classical art forms would have been extremely odd for the Revolutionary period.

The principal difference between early 19th-century artists and their predecessors was in the desire for faithfulness to antique models. Archeological correctness was now possible, owing to a more detailed knowledge of the past. Winckelmann and his generation had made classical archeology a science, and the excavations at Pompeii and Herculaneum had provided the material and stimulus for authenticity. For neoclassical success, a building had to be archeologically accurate. The Vendôme Column was planned as a replica of Trajan's Column and the Arc du Carrousel preserved the proportions and shape of the Arch of Septimus Severus, even if reduced somewhat in size. When variations were made, as in the instance of the Arc de Triomphe and La Madeleine, the results were more interesting. The first two may be likened to a pair of competent academic theses, while the latter pair approximate the livelier style of good historical novels. Archeological correctness meant lifting an ancient building, which had been designed for a now-antiquated purpose, out of its context, period, and century and putting it down bodily into another period where it had no practical reason for being. This transposition would never have occurred in the rational Enlightenment period. While Palladio, Mansart, and Wren had been concerned with adapting classical principles to the needs of their times, Vignon, Percier, and Fontaine were busy trying to fit activities of the Napoleonic period into ancient molds. The use of a Roman portico over a baroque period doorway was one thing; Napoleon's invention of a cult of glory as an excuse to build a Roman temple was quite another. If such antiquarianism were carried to its logical conclusion and architecture were to become the handmaid of archeology, a city eventually would be turned into a museum. While people occasionally visit museums, they do not necessarily want to live in one—and, fortunately, the Napoleonic period was not that logical.

Likewise, in the neoclassical style, a successful statue had to be accurate. And since such a profusion of antique models existed, the sculptors were limited in their creative freedom. Their desire for exactitude often led them to the point of absurdity. They omitted carving the irises and pupils of the eyes and left them blank, because they did not know that the Greeks had painted in such details. The prevailing whiteness made their works resemble mortuary monuments, since they had overlooked the fact that the ancients had designed their friezes for the strong light and shadow of the open air and not for the dim interiors of museums. While Praxiteles and Michelangelo had turned marble into flesh, Canova and Thorwaldsen converted the living flesh of their models into cold stone.

Enthusiasm for antiquity sometimes led David into similar predicaments. For the heads of figures in his early pictures he used ancient Roman portrait busts instead of live models. In the baroque period, when Poussin and Claude Lorrain painted Rome, they did so usually in terms of picturesque ruins, but David painted archeological reconstructions. Madame Récamier was a 19th-century Parisian socialite, but David made her into a fancy-dress reincarnation of a Pompeian matron. The *Battle of the Romans and Sabines* was inspired by the reproduction of an ancient relief David had come across as an illustration in a book. On this occasion, while he did use living models, he said that his desire was to paint the ancient walls and drape his figures with such exactness that if an ancient Roman were to come to life, he would find himself right at home. David's adherence to lines and planes was often so strict that the effect of his paintings was almost as severe as that of relief sculpture. David was saved, however, from the major pitfalls of his architectural and sculptural colleagues because so few examples of ancient painting were known at the time. As a consequence, he was forced to divert his considerable talent as a painter in the direction of a new style.

In poetry, a similar motivation can be found in the reforms of André Chénier, which were based on his studies of the Latin and Greek originals. For the forms of his odes and elegies, his pastoral idylls and epics, he drew directly on Homer, Pindar, Vergil, and Horace. "Let us upon new thoughts write antique verses," he had declared; and to a considerable degree his enthusiasm helped him to carry out his announced objective.

In this archeological era, however, the musicians fared the best of all because they had no examples surviving from antiquity to emulate. An opera, to be sure, could get some authenticity into its plot, decor, and costumes; and such productions of 1807 as Persuis and Lesueur's *Triomphe de Trajan*, their *L'Inauguration du Temple de la Victoire*, and Spontini's *La Vestale* tried to make the grade in this respect. All this, however, was on the surface and could hardly be compared with the type of authenticity represented by the Vendôme Column or the Napoleonic arches of triumph. Since the musicians had to evolve their own style, the music of the period has overshadowed the other contemporary arts and its vitality has given it a lasting general appeal. Just as the fussy rococo had brought about a countermovement in the pre-Revolutionary neoclassicism, so a reform in music had been carried out in the 18th century under Gluck. By reducing the number of characters in his operas, omitting complicated subplots, strengthening the role of the chorus, transferring much of the lyrical expression to the orchestra, writing simple unadorned melo-

dies, and avoiding Italianate coloratura cadenzas, Gluck had brought about a musical revolution similar to David's in painting and paved the way for a new style. His ideas were based partially on a reinterpretation of Aristotle's *Poetics*, and in his Preface to *Alceste* (1767) he had stated that his music was designed to allow the drama to proceed "without interrupting the action or stifling it with a useless superfluity of ornaments." Echoing Winckelmann, he added that the great principles of beauty were "simplicity, truth and naturalness."

These principles found their ultimate expression in the sinewy music of Beethoven, who, by impatiently brushing aside ancient precedents, achieved an expressive style that was genuinely heroic and not merely histrionic. Of all the artists of the neoclassical persuasion, Beethoven emerges as the most truly representative, and his art is the outstanding expressive accomplishment of his time.

511. BERTEL THORWALDSEN. Salon, Villa Carlotta, Cadenabbia, Lake Como, Italy. *c.* 1829–1831.

18 - THE ROMANTIC STYLE

PARIS, 1830

Well before the romantic Revolution of July, 1830, new ideas were stirring the minds and imaginations of the intellectuals and artists of Paris. In 1827, as the new movement was gaining momentum, Victor Hugo published his *Cromwell*, a drama with a Preface that served as a manifesto of romanticism. Guizot was lecturing at the Sorbonne on the early history of France. François Rude, destined to be the principal sculptor of the period, returned from his Belgian exile. And the painter Delacroix wrote in his journal that when he went to the Odéon Theater to see Shakespeare's *Hamlet*, he met the writers Alexandre Dumas and Victor Hugo. The Ophelia in that production was Harriet Smithson, later to become the wife of the composer Hector Berlioz. Gérard de Nerval's translation of Goethe appeared that autumn and inspired Berlioz to compose *Eight Scenes from Faust*, which later reached popularity in the revision called the *Damnation of Faust*. Delacroix, who had just exhibited his *Death of Sardanapalus* (Fig. 512) in the Salon, was already at work on his famous *Faust* lithographs to illustrate the edition of Goethe's drama that was published in 1828.

All in all, the 1820's were an inspiring time, and when Théophile Gautier later came to write

his history of romanticism, he looked back on his youthful years with nostalgia. "What a marvelous time," he wrote, "Walter Scott was then in the flower of his success; one was initiated into the mysteries of Goethe's *Faust*, which as Madame de Staël said, contained everything. One discovered Shakespeare, and the poems of Lord Byron: the *Corsair; Lara; The Gaiour; Manfred; Beppo;* and *Don Juan* took us to the orient, which was not banal then as now. All was young, new, exotically colored, intoxicating, and strongly flavored. It turned our heads; it was as if we had entered into a strange new world." Romanticism was swept in on a wave of political unrest culminating in the July Revolution of 1830, and it was to be the dominant French style until the February Revolution of 1848.

Nowhere is there a better example of the mating of an artistic genius with the spirit of his time than in the life and work of Eugène Delacroix set in the Paris of 1830. His *Liberty Leading the People* (Plate 46) brought those glorious July days to incandescent expression. The canvas, in which he distilled the essence of that revolution, is dominated by the fiery allegorical figure of Liberty, here seen as the

(above) FRANÇOIS RUDE. *Head of Bellona*, detail of *Departure of Volunteers of 1792*. 1833–1836. Stone relief, Arc de Triomphe de l'Étoile, Paris. (See Fig. 519.)

512. Eugène Delacroix. *Death of Sardanapalus.* 1827. Oil on canvas,
12′11 ¼″ × 16′2 ¾″. Louvre, Paris.

spirit of the French people whom she leads onward
to triumph. No relaxed Mediterranean goddess but
a virile, energetic reincarnation of the spirit of 1789,
her muscular arms are strong enough to hold with
ease both a bayoneted rifle and the tricolored banner of the Republic. Though bare-breasted, she
betrays no sign of softness or sensuality, and her
powerful limbs stride over the street barricades as
she leads her followers forward through the on-
coming barrage. Though an allegorical figure, she
is treated by Delacroix as a living personality. Only
the Phrygian cap and the almost-classic profile,
serene in the face of danger, indicate her symbolic
significance. She does not hover over the action on
wings, as so many other artists depicted her; instead, with her feet on the ground, she is in the
midst of action.

Liberty's motley followers include both impetuous students and battle-scarred soldiers who
have heeded her call rather than that of their reactionary king. The boy on the right is recruited from
the Paris streets. Too young to understand the
significance of the events, he is there, a pistol in
each hand, joining in the general excitement. In
the background are the remnants of the old guard
from revolutionary days still carrying on the
struggle. Two main social classes are represented—
in the shadows on the extreme left, the man armed

with a saber is an obviously proletarian figure,
while in front of him toward the center the more
prominent figure in the modish frock coat, top hat,
and sideburns is a bourgeois gentleman who has
grabbed his musket and joined in the general confusion. It was his class that controlled the fighting and derived the benefits from it by stamping
its image on the new monarchy represented in the
person of Louis Philippe, the Citizen King. Though
the July Revolution was essentially a palace revolt
replacing a reactionary Bourbon with his more
liberal cousin, no aristocrats are represented as
taking part. In the shadow below, the wounded and
dying are strewn on the loose cobblestones looking
toward Liberty, for she is both their inspiration and
their reason for being. Through smoke at the right
the towers of Notre Dame are discernible.

Because of the contemporary frame of reference in which one recognizes the familiar shirts,
blouses, trousers, rifles, pistols, and other 19th-
century paraphernalia, the picture sometimes has
been called realistic. But, because the spirit of the
work transcends the event itself, and because the
artist has rendered feeling rather than actuality,
the picture surely is in the romantic style. By in-
fusing reality with the charge of an electric emotional attitude, Delacroix raises his picture to the
level of an idealized though highly personal

General Events

	1814	Fall of Napoleon
		Restoration of the monarchy under Louis XVIII
	1821	Napoleon died
	1824	Louis XVIII succeeded by Charles X
	1830	July Revolution overthrew old line of Bourbons
		Louis Philippe began reign as limited monarch
	1837	Commission for the Preservation of Historical Monuments founded by Louis Philippe
	1840	Guizot, French historian and statesman, became prime minister
	1848	February Revolution overthrew Louis Philippe's government
		Second Republic proclaimed; Louis Napoleon, nephew of Napoleon I, elected president
	1852	Louis Napoleon elected emperor; reigned as Napoleon III
	1870	Napoleon III abdicated after unsuccessful conclusion of Franco-Prussian War
		Third Republic proclaimed

Architects

1726–	1796	William Chambers
1748–	1813	James Wyatt
1752–	1835	John Nash
1790–	1853	François Christian Gau
1795–	1860	Charles Barry
1802–	1878	Richard Upjohn
1814–	1879	Eugène Viollet-le-Duc
1817–	1885	Théodore Ballu
1818–	1895	James Renwick
1824–	1881	George Street

Sculptors

1784–	1855	François Rude
1787–	1843	Jean-Pierre Cortot
1796–	1875	Antoine-Louis Barye

Painters

1771–	1835	Antoine Jean Gros
1775–	1851	J. M. W. Turner
1776–	1837	John Constable
1780–	1867	J. A. D. Ingres
1791–	1824	Théodore Géricault
1796–	1875	Camille Corot
1798–	1863	Eugène Delacroix
1808–	1879	Honoré Daumier
1814–	1875	François Millet

Writers

1717–	1797	Horace Walpole
1749–	1832	Johann Wolfgang Goethe
1766–	1817	Germaine de Staël
1768–	1848	Chateaubriand
1771–	1832	Walter Scott
1774–	1843	Robert Southey
1783–	1842	Stendhal (Henri Beyle)
1787–	1874	François Guizot
1788–	1824	Lord Byron
1788–	1860	Arthur Schopenhauer
1792–	1822	Percy B. Shelley
1795–	1821	John Keats
1797–	1856	Heinrich Heine
1799–	1850	Honoré de Balzac
1802–	1870	Alexandre Dumas
1802–	1885	Victor Hugo
1803–	1870	Prosper Mérimée
1804–	1876	George Sand
1811–	1872	Théophile Gautier

Musicians

1782–	1871	Daniel Auber
1782–	1840	Niccolo Paganini
1784–	1859	Ludwig Spohr
1786–	1826	Carl Maria von Weber
1791–	1864	Giacomo Meyerbeer
1803–	1869	Hector Berlioz
1809–	1849	Frédéric Chopin
1809–	1847	Felix Mendelssohn
1810–	1856	Robert Schumann
1811–	1886	Franz Liszt
1813–	1883	Richard Wagner
1813–	1901	Giuseppe Verdi
1818–	1893	Charles Gounod
1833–	1897	Johannes Brahms
1838–	1875	Georges Bizet

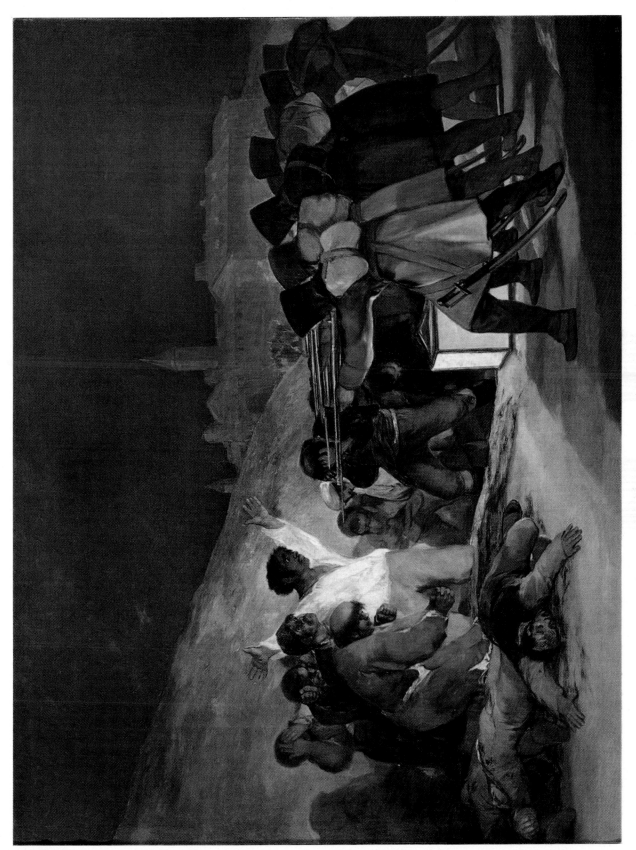

Plate 45. FRANCISCO GOYA. *Executions of the Third of May, 1808.* 1814–1815. Oil on canvas, 8'9" × 13'4". Prado, Madrid. (See p. 441.)

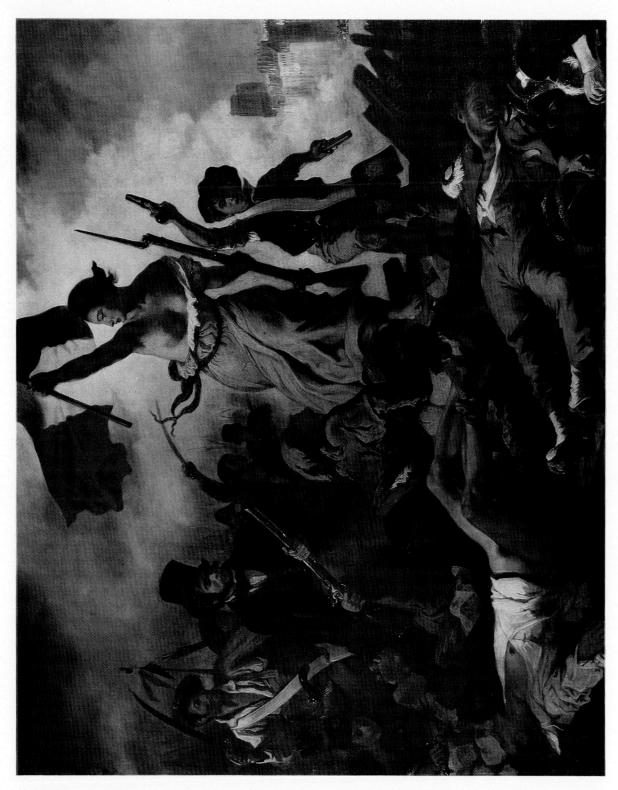

Plate 46. Eugène Delacroix. *Liberty Leading the People, 1830.* 1830. Oil on canvas, 8'6" × 10'10". Louvre, Paris. (See p. 450.)

expression, so that all who see it seem to be experiencing the event for themselves. More eloquent than any page in a history book, the canvas has captured the feeling as well as the facts that make up the incident. It is as if all the noise had awakened the artist from his dreams of the past, and now suddenly wide awake, he has applied his expressive techniques consciously to one of the stirring happenings of his own time.

As always with Delacroix, color plays an important part in the communication of mood. Here, a striking instance of the use of color is seen in the way he takes the red, white, and blue of the banner (the symbol of patriotism) and merges them into the picture as a whole. The white central strip, signifying truth and purity, blends with the purifying smoke of battle; the blue, denoting freedom, matches the parts of the sky visible in the top corners through the smoke; while the red in the flag high above balances the color of the blood of those below who have fallen for the ideal of liberty. Thus the symbolism of the banner blends into the color scheme, and both combine with the dramatic lighting to define the emotional range. All these, in turn, expand the patriotic theme into a formal pictorial unity of concentrated intensity. With the purchase of this picture in the name of the state by the new bourgeois king at the time it was shown in the Salon of 1831, the seal of official approval was stamped on the romantic style.

PAINTING

It was characteristic of romantic painting that Delacroix, its leading representative, should look to the fantasy of the literary world for the sources of his pictorial visions rather than to the world of appearances. His choice of subjects as well as his treatment of them makes this immediately apparent. The *Death of Sardanapalus* (Fig. 512), *Mazeppa*, *Giaour and the Pasha*, and the *Shipwreck of Don Juan* all point to their inception in the poetry of Byron. His interest in Shakespeare is shown in his drawings of scenes from *Hamlet* and the witches' scene

(top) 513. EUGÈNE DELACROIX. *Witches' Scene* (illustration for *Macbeth*, Act IV, Scene 1). 1825. Lithograph, 11¾ × 9¾". Metropolitan Museum of Art, New York.

(center) 514. EUGÈNE DELACROIX. *Mephistopheles in the Air* (illustration for Goethe's *Faust*, Part I, lines 1709–19 and 2078–89). 1828. Lithograph, 10¾ × 9". Metropolitan Museum of Art, New York.

(right) 515. EUGÈNE DELACROIX. *Witches' Kitchen* (illustration for Goethe's *Faust*). 1828. Lithograph, 12¾ × 10¼". Metropolitan Museum of Art, New York.

(left) 516. EUGÈNE DELACROIX. *Margaret in Church* (illustration for Goethe's *Faust*, Part I, lines 3449–82 and 4095–4124). 1828. Lithograph, 10 ½ × 8 ¾". Metropolitan Museum of Art, New York.

(above) 517. EUGÈNE DELACROIX. *Faust and Mephistopheles Galloping* (illustration for Goethe's *Faust*). 1828. Lithograph, 11 × 8". Metropolitan Museum of Art, New York.

from *Macbeth* (Fig. 513). His *Abduction of Rebecca* steps directly out of Chapter 31 of Scott's *Ivanhoe*, and his illustrations for Goethe's *Faust* (Figs. 514–517) won the complete admiration of the author himself, who felt that for clarity and depth of insight they could not be surpassed.

Delacroix' imagination had been haunted by *Faust* since he first saw it in London, and, in a letter to a friend in Paris, he had commented particularly on its diabolical aspect. The lithographs that eventually resulted show his mastery of illustration and prove Delacroix as adept in works of small dimensions as in epical pictures. In spite of his close kinship with Byron and Goethe, Delacroix was not always in sympathy with the work of his romantic Parisian contemporaries. In his diary he spoke of Meyerbeer's opera *Le Prophète* as "frightful" and referred to Berlioz and Hugo as those "so-called reformers." "The noise he makes is distracting," he wrote about Berlioz' music, "it is an heroic mess." Of all musicians he admired Mozart the most, and among his contemporaries only Chopin had the requisite polish and craftsmanship to measure up to his standards.

Delacroix' color technique was a means of conveying a highly emotional and turbulent subject matter. For him, color was dominant over design, and as he declared, "gray is the enemy of all painting... let us banish from our palette all earth colors... the greater the opposition in color, the greater the brilliance." His admitted models in painting were the heroic canvases of Rubens and the dramatic pictures of Rembrandt with their emphasis on the dynamics of light, and among his contemporaries he admired the mellow landscapes and subtle coloring of Constable (see Plate 47). His own art was built on an aesthetic of color, light, and emotion rather than on line, drawing, and form. This is nowhere better illustrated than in his early masterpiece, *Dante and Vergil in Hell* (Fig. 518), the first of his pictures to attract wide attention when it was exhibited in the Salon of 1822.

Stemming from the predilection for the medieval and macabre, the interest in Dante was one of the main facets of the romantic style. What Homer had been to neoclassicism, the Tuscan poet was to romanticism. Shelley and the Pre-Raphaelites were making England Dante-conscious; and while Schlegel and Schelling were translating and interpreting him for the Germans, Chateaubriand and Sainte-Beuve were doing the same for the French.

In his picture, Delacroix enters the realm of pure pathos. The central figure is that of Vergil in the crimson robe of a Florentine crowned with the laurel wreath, standing with impassive monumentality as a symbol of classic calm. On his left is Dante with a red hood on his head, expressively human in contrast to the serenity of his immortal companion and emotionally involved with his grotesque and gruesome surroundings. He looks with terror on the damned who swirl about him in the water below. The wake of the boat is livid with the writhing forms of the condemned, who hope eternally to reach the opposite shore by trying to attach themselves to the bark. One attempts to clamber aboard, the gnashing teeth of another bite into the edge of the boat, but in vain as they are plunged again into the dark waters. Distress and despair are everywhere. On the right is Phlegyas, the sepulchral boatman, seen from the rear as he strains at the rudder to guide the boat across the River Styx to the flaming shores of the city of Dis, visible in the distant background between the clouds of sulfurous fumes. The lurid coloration serves to create the illusion that the picture has been painted in blood, phosphorus, and flame.

When Delacroix was at work on it, he had a young friend read Dante's *Divine Comedy* to him and, as he says in his journal: "The best head in my Dante picture was swept in with the greatest speed and spirit while Pierret was reading me a canto from Dante which I knew already but to which he lent, by his accent, an energy that electrified me.

That head is the one of the man behind the boat, facing you and trying to climb aboard, after throwing his arm over the gunwale." The particular passage that inflamed the artist's imagination and on which he built the picture is from the eighth book of the Inferno.

When first exhibited, the picture brought down storms of protest and vituperation on Delacroix' head, which helped immeasurably to bring the young artist to critical attention. One defender of David's academic tradition called it a "splattering of color," and another thought he had "combined all the parts of the work in view of one emotion." While its expressive intensity was novel then, the work now easily falls into place as part of the macabre aspect of the romantic style. Even the nude figures, as muscular as those of Michelangelo and Rubens, function here more as color masses than as forms modeled three dimensionally. As Delacroix once declared, color *is* painting, and his development of a color palette capable of eliciting specific emotional reactions from his viewers was destined to have a far-reaching effect on impressionistic and postimpressionistic painting.

518. EUGÈNE DELACROIX. *Dante and Vergil in Hell*. 1822. Oil on canvas, 6' 1 ½" × 7' 10 ½". Louvre, Paris.

519. François Rude. *Departure of the Volunteers of 1792 (La Marseillaise).* 1833–1836. c. 42 × 26′. Right stone relief, Arc de Triomphe de l'Étoile, Paris.

SCULPTURE

One of the dominating sculptural works of the romantic style is the *Departure of the Volunteers* (Fig. 519) by François Rude. It achieved its stature by its vehement expression and sustained heroic mood, and by its prominent location on one side of the Arc de Triomphe (Fig. 496) in Paris that assured it the largest possible audience. Sculptured in the boldest high relief, the dimensions of the composition alone—rising to a height of almost 42 feet and spreading laterally 26 feet—make it of truly colossal proportions. Its conception and commission date from the wave of patriotic emotion associated with the Revolution of July, 1830, and the memories that stirred of earlier struggles for freedom. This common source of inspiration was shared by both Delacroix and Rude, whose design certainly owes much to Delacroix' *Liberty Leading the People* (Plate 46). It took Delacroix but a year to get his painting of Liberty before the public, but a sculptural work of these proportions took Rude six years to execute.

The scene depicted is that of a band of volunteers rallying to the defense of the newly established French Republic when it was threatened by foreign invasion in 1792. The five resolute figures in the foreground are coming together to meet the common danger and are receiving mutual inspiration from the figure of Bellona, the Roman goddess of war (p. 450), who hovers over them, inciting them onward with the singing of *La Marseillaise*. A fine rhythmical mood is established by the compact grouping of the figures, reinforced by the repeated motif of the legs that combine in a neat marchlike manner with the arms of the soldier stooping to tie his sandal. This rhythm serves to weld the composition together as a whole in the manner of a lively yet majestic march. These representatives of the humanity so recently liberated by the French Revolution are self-motivated protectors of their newly won liberty, equality, and fraternity. The full manhood of four of the volunteers is balanced by the potential strength of the finely realized nude figure of the impetuous youth and the waning ability of the old man behind him who can only point out the

520. JEAN-PIERRE CORTOT. *Apotheosis of Napoleon*. 1838. 42′ high. Left stone relief, Arc de Triomphe de l'Étoile, Paris.

direction to the others and wave them on. The surging power, directed by the common ideals, impels the volunteers onward with irresistible force and momentum.

Because Rude designed the *Departure* for a Napoleonic arch of triumph, his motifs are of Roman derivation. The soldiers are outfitted with Roman helmets and shields, though the coats of mail and weapons in the background recall those of the medieval period. The avoidance in the costumes and symbols of any contemporary reference in this representation of an event that had taken place less than a half-century before links the composition with the tendency to draw on the past for inspiration. Popularly, and quite properly, called the "*Marseillaise* in stone," it represents a most ingenious sculptural use of a musical motif in suggesting the great Revolutionary song, which serves to unify the patriotic spirit of the group. The anthem, composed by a young lieutenant in the Revolutionary army, Rouget de Lisle, was practically forgotten during the days of Napoleon's empire, and under the Bourbon restoration was, of course, officially

banned. Credit for its rediscovery and revival goes to Berlioz. Stirred to patriotic frenzy by the events of July, 1830, though avoiding direct participation, this erratic genius contented himself with scoring the song for double chorus and orchestra, characteristically asking "all who have voices, a heart, and blood in their veins" to join in. The final stanza begins dramatically with three unaccompanied voices; then, as Berlioz gradually marshals his vocal and orchestral forces, a big crescendo leads up to the refrain: "To arms, O citizens." This version received many performances, the most notable being a large benefit with the proceeds going to the families of the victims of the July Revolution. Later, the song was officially adopted as the French national anthem, though not with Berlioz' orchestration, and has become one of the world's best-known tunes.

Rude's treatment of the subject, the momentum of his composition, and the impassioned facial expressions, especially of the war-goddess Bellona (p. 450), make the *Departure* an odd contrast to its companion piece, *Apotheosis of Napoleon* (Fig. 520), which Jean-Pierre Cortot executed at the same time. Rude had made a complete design for the decoration of the arch, but he was commissioned to do only the *Departure of the Volunteers*. Public taste and official circles still leaned toward neoclassicism, and Cortot's group shows a typical academic approach. While the neoclassical style continued throughout the century, the vitality it had shown during Napoleon's heroic days already was definitely waning. With Rude, all is passion and movement, and his composition seems almost to burst its bonds in its dynamic forward tendency. With Cortot, all is balanced and rigidly poised in a static equilibrium centering on the standing figure of Napoleon. Clothed in the toga of a Roman emperor, Bonaparte is being crowned by a seminude personification of the spirit of France, looking as if she were the Venus de Milo, with arms happily restored for the occasion, who had just walked over from the Louvre Museum. Other allegorical figures, including one representing History, make up the rest of the group. The best that can be said about Cortot's work is that it has a certain stateliness and avoids the pitfall of pomposity. These two

examples standing opposite each other on the same monument show clearly the difference between the neoclassical and romantic styles, as well as the continuation of the rather stilted academic tradition and the assertion of the movement, action, and emotion characteristic of the vigorous new romantic style.

In a later work, *Joan of Arc Listening to the Voices* (Fig. 521), Rude combines emotionalism and medieval subject matter. Executed originally in 1845 for the gardens of the Luxembourg Palace, it later found its way into the Louvre. Rude represents the Maid of Orleans in peasant costume with a suit of armor at her side, thus indicating both her rural origin and her heroic mission. The mystic element is suggested as she lifts her hand to her ear in order to hear the angelic voices that guide her. By trying to capture the intangible sounds of these heavenly voices as Joan listens quiveringly with upraised head, Rude strains his marble medium to its expressive limits.

Rude, who had grown up in Revolutionary times, was always thoroughly in sympathy with the liberal spirit. He accepted exile in Belgium in 1815 rather than live under a Bourbon ruler. Action was his aesthetic watchword. "The great thing for an artist," he once said, "is to *do*." Some critics find his *Departure of the Volunteers* overcrowded, overloaded, and unbalanced. Others feel that this crowding and imbalance is justified by the subject of a concerted uprising of the masses and that unity is achieved by the direction of its movement. Clearly it shows no will toward classical repose, and its sheer energy makes a clean break with academic tradition. By thus liberating sculpture from many outworn idioms and clichés, Rude revealed himself as a true romanticist.

ARCHITECTURE

Romantic architecture received its initial impetus from the popularity in the late 18th century of the so-called "Gothic" novels. Romances and plays of this type published in England were variously entitled: *The Haunted Priory; The Horrid Mysteries; Banditti,* or *Love in a Labyrinth; Raymond and Agnes,* or *The Bleeding Nun of Lindenberg;* and *Castle of Otranto,* Horace Walpole's famous novel, subtitled *A Gothic Tale.* The settings for these stories were large baronial halls or decayed abbeys, liberally equipped with mysterious trapdoors, sliding panels, creaking postern gates, animated suits of

521. FRANÇOIS RUDE. *Joan of Arc Listening to the Voices.* 1845. Marble, lifesize. Louvre, Paris.

522. James Wyatt. Fonthill Abbey (no longer standing), Wiltshire. 1796–1807. Tower 278′ high. Contemporary lithograph.

armor, and sepulchral voices emanating from ancient tombs. Such scenes served as backdrops for the injured innocence of fragile and helpless heroines and the intrepid, if somewhat reckless, courage of dashing heroes. These tales played their part in the redefinition of the word *Gothic*—which Voltaire had called a fantastic compound of rudeness and filigree—into something more redolent of the mystical, tinged with weirdness and bordering on the fantastic.

These imaginary castles of the novels first took on concrete form in England as the architectural whims of wealthy eccentrics. Walpole, the well-to-do son of a powerful prime minister, had indulged his fancy in a residence that gave its name to one aspect of the romantic style, "Strawberry Hill Gothick." William Beckford, whom Byron called "England's richest son," had the architect James Wyatt construct him a residence he called Fonthill Abbey (Fig. 522). Its huge central tower rose over a spacious interior hall that was approached by a massive staircase (Fig. 523). The rest of the interior was a labyrinth of long drafty corridors that provided the wall space for the proprietor's collections of pictures and tapestries as well as a suitable setting for his melancholy musings. In his frenzy to have it completed, Beckford drove the workers day and night to the point where, in their haste, they neglected to provide an adequate foundation for the tower; and only a few years after its completion, the tower of Beckford's dream castle fell to the

523. James Wyatt. Interior, Fonthill Abbey. 1796–1807. *c.* 25′ long, *c.* 35′ wide. Contemporary lithograph.

ground, taking most of the building with it. Since ruins were greatly admired as residences at the time, this catastrophe only served to enhance the abbey's picturesqueness and make it all the more desirable.

In the early 1820's, Fonthill Abbey became so enormously popular that newspapers wrote of the "Fonthill mania." Visitors numbering up to five hundred a day made the pilgrimage to see it. Beckford's spectacular landscaping, which had involved transplanting over one million trees to create a picturesque setting, commanded the admiration of the painter Constable who lived nearby, as well as that of such poets as Lord Byron and Edgar Allan Poe. To the popular imagination Fonthill Abbey was a Walter Scott novel in stone.

The Gothic novel in literature and the Gothic revival in architecture steadily gained momentum. Jane Austen's *Northanger Abbey*, a delicious satire on the movement, was published just as Sir Walter Scott's historical novels were bringing their author such huge acclaim. Scott's novels were translated into French beginning about 1816, and they, in turn, paved the way for the popular romances of Hugo and Dumas. Among the surviving English architectural expressions of this literary phase are the Houses of Parliament (Fig. 524), begun by Sir Charles Barry in 1839, and the New Law Courts by George Street, both of which are familiar landmarks in the London of today. In Germany, as early as 1772, the young poet Goethe, under the guidance of his university mentor Gottfried Herder, was writing in praise of the builder of the Stras-

(above) 524. CHARLES BARRY and A. WELBY PUGIN. Houses of Parliament, London. 1840–1860. 940' long.

(below) 525. Castle Neuschwanstein, Bavarian Alps. Begun 1869.

bourg Cathedral, Erwin von Steinbach. The book significantly was entitled *Von Deutscher Baukunst (On German Architecture)*. Later, Goethe placed his drama on the medieval Faust legend in a Gothic setting. In the 19th century, German literary interest in neomedievalism became the background for Richard Wagner's operas *Tannhäuser, Lohengrin,* and *Parsifal*. Wagner's most enthusiastic patron was King Ludwig II of Bavaria, who helped the composer build his opera house at Bayreuth. To stimulate his own Gothic fancies, the king built Castle Neuschwanstein (Fig. 525) amid picturesque alpine scenery.

In France, architectural energies at first were diverted toward the preservation of the many medieval monuments still in existence. Less than a year after the July Revolution, Victor Hugo had published his *Notre Dame de Paris* (known to the English-speaking world as the *Hunchback of Notre Dame*). The fact that the real hero of the novel is Paris' Gothic cathedral fanned into flames the popular enthusiasm for the restoration of churches, castles, and abbeys. Support for the reconstruction of Notre Dame was soon forthcoming in official circles from Guizot the historian, who was then prime minister. It was he who founded in 1837 the *Commission pour la Conservation des Monuments Historiques*. In France, as previously in England and Germany, romantic architecture was associated with the resurgence of patriotic and nationalistic sentiment. At last, the Gothic revival had arrived on home soil, channeling French national energies into new flights of the imagination and providing French minds with an escape from recent dreams of Roman imperial glory that had turned into the nightmare of the Napoleonic defeat.

The precise scholarship of the French academic minds found a ready outlet in the establishment of the new science of medieval archeology, which resulted in the restoration of such buildings as Ste. Chapelle and the Cathedral of Notre Dame in Paris; and in Viollet-le-Duc's skillful reconstructions of Carcassonne Castle on the Pyrenees border (Fig. 209) and the Church of La Madeleine at Vézelay (Plate 9). In his essays on medieval architecture, Eugène Viollet-le-Duc called attention to the engineering logic of medieval builders and demonstrated the organic unity of the Gothic structural system in which each stone played its part, and in the period of Gothic florescence even the decorative details served useful purposes. That everything was necessary and nothing was used merely for effect not only revised 19th-century architectural thought but laid one of the bases for the 20th-century return to functional building.

As comparative latecomers on the medieval revival scene, the French architects were in no hurry to leave their reconstructions and design new buildings. The advantage was theirs when they did so, however, because they could review all the previous experiments and avoid the follies and excesses that characterized the movement elsewhere. Though planned at the same time Victor Hugo, Delacroix, and Berlioz were active, it was not until 1846 that ground was broken for the Church of Ste. Clotilde (Fig. 526). Designed by François Christian Gau, a native of Cologne but a naturalized Frenchman, the project was completed after his death by Théodore Ballu. Although Ste. Clotilde was built principally of white stone, the use of cast-iron girders in the vaulting to assure strength and durability was a distinctive technical innovation. To be sure, the girders were disguised by blocks of stone, but the fact that a building of medieval design used materials developed by the 19th-century Industrial Revolution was sufficient to arouse great interest among contemporary architects.

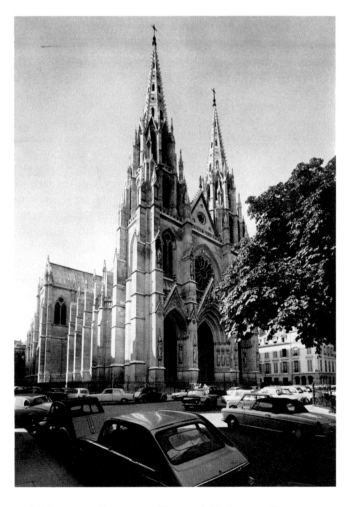

526. François Christian Gau and Théodore Ballu. Ste. Clothilde, Paris. 1846–1857. 105′ wide, 216′ high.

Based on Gothic models of the 14th century, the church has the usual features of a nave with side aisles, transept, choir, and apse with radiating chapels. The space of the richly ornamented façade is divided by four buttresses into three parts, each with an entrance portal. Those on the sides have tympanums showing in sculptured relief the martyrdom of St. Valéry and the baptism of Clovis. The approaches to the portals have niches containing standing figures of the Merovingian saints who were associated with the earliest history of French nationhood, including Clovis' queen Ste. Clotilde and Ste. Geneviève, patroness of Paris.

The interior is lighted by a clearstory with as many as sixty stained glass windows, which carry out the iconographical scheme promised by the sculptures of the façade. The representations tell the legendary stories of Ste. Clotilde and some of her contemporaries, St. Valéry, St. Martin of Tours, St. Remi, and two of her children who were canonized, St. Cloud and Ste. Bathilde. The choir is the setting for a large three-manual organ with a case elaborately carved in the Gothic manner. It was here that the distinguished composer César Franck presided from the year 1872 until his death, and here that he made his famous improvisations.

The dedication of a church to a Merovingian saint connected with the early history of Paris was entirely in the spirit of that part of the Gothic revival movement which appealed so strongly to nationalistic sentiment. While an account of Clotilde's life is to be found in the writings of Gregory of Tours and other medieval chronicles, she was known to the Paris of this time through Guizot's widely read *History of France*, a book based on his lectures of 1827–1830 at the Sorbonne, which told of the country's evolution from the 5th century A.D. With the growing knowledge of the 19th-century historians, the beginnings of French nationhood could be traced to the early conquests of Clovis, who united the remnants of the Roman Empire in Gaul into one kingdom. Furthermore, local civic pride was touched by the fact that, even at this early date, Clovis and Clotilde had considered Paris as their royal seat. The dedication of an important new church to Ste. Clotilde and of the Sorbonne library to Ste. Geneviève (Fig. 557) and the awakening interest in St. Joan of Arc point to an increasing awareness of France's national medieval glory. The choice of female saints can be linked to the revival of the spirit of chivalry, which had been expressed in the form of numerous Lady churches, such as Notre Dame of Paris, of Chartres, and of Rheims. When the Church of Ste. Clotilde is compared with these original Gothic monuments, however, it seems studied, overly symmetrical, and academically frigid. But when it is viewed in the con-

text of its times and combined with the reflections of medieval fervor of Victor Hugo, the moving craftsmanship of Rude, the lively chromaticism of Delacroix' painting, and the fantastic imagery of Berlioz' music, it catches some rays of their glowing warmth and becomes at once both their worthy architectural companion and an important incident in the unfolding of the romantic style.

POETRY

Of the three great literary figures who influenced the writings of Victor Hugo at this time, Dante and Shakespeare were out of the past, and only his elder contemporary Goethe came from his own time. These three writers, as he states in the Preface to *Cromwell*, pointed out the sources of the grotesque elements that were to be found everywhere, "in the air, water, earth, fire those myriads of intermediate creatures which we find alive in the popular traditions of the middle ages; it is the grotesque which impels the ghastly antics of the witches' revels, which gives Satan his horns, his cloven feet and his bat's wings. It is the grotesque, still the grotesque, which now casts into the Christian hell the frightful faces which the severe genius of Dante and Milton will evoke...." Needless to say, understanding of his great predecessors involved a high degree of selectivity. It was the Inferno section that Hugo extracted out of Dante's *Divine Comedy*. His poem of 1837—*Après une lecture de Dante*—closely parallels Delacroix' picture of Dante: "When the poet paints the image of hell," he wrote, "he paints that of his own life." The substance of the poem continues: "Beset by shades and specters, the poet must grope blindly through mysterious forests as weird forms bestrew his dark voyage. Lost amidst indecisive fogs, with each step he hears lamentations and the faint sounds of the grinding of white teeth in the black night. All the vices such as vengeance, famine, ambition, pride and avarice darken the scene still more. Farther on, the souls of those who have tasted the poison of cowardice, fear and treason are mingled with the grimacing masks of those whom hatred has consumed. The only light amidst this general gloom is the voice of the eternal artist, Vergil, who calls, 'Continue onward.' ..."

In Petrarch, it was the Triumph of Death that Hugo admired; in Boccaccio, the vivid descriptions of the black plague; in Shakespeare, the macabre scenes from *Hamlet* and the boiling and bubbling of the witches' caldron in *Macbeth*; and in Goethe's *Faust*, the descriptions of the Walpurgis Night. Collectively, these constitute a veritable carnival of the macabre, the horrible, and the lugubriousness of doom and damnation.

Hugo's transition to this new psychology is apparent as early as 1826 when he brought out a new edition of his *Odes* to which he added 15 *Ballades*, No. 14 of which was entitled "Witches' Sabbath." This new orientation he explains in his introduction. The odes, he wrote, included his purely religious inspirations and personal expressions, which were cast in classical meters. Those bearing the title of ballad have the character of caprice, and include pictorial fantasies, dreams, and legends of superstition. He tells of the latter coming to him under the inspiration of the repertoire of medieval troubadours, especially those Christian rhapsodies of epical nature that were chanted by the minstrels to the accompaniment of their harps as they wandered from one castle to another.

The ballad begins with a description of a Gothic church at midnight; the clock in the belfry tolls 12, and the witching hour begins. Strange lights flash, the holy water begins to boil in the fonts; shrieks and howls are heard, as from all directions come those who answer Satan's call—specters, dragons, vampires, ghouls, monsters, and the souls of the damned from their fresh-emptied tombs. While Satan sings a Black Mass, an imp reads the Gospel, and the whole fantastic congregation performs a wild dance.

All in unison moving with swift-circling feet
While satan keeps time with his crozier's beat,
And their steps shake the arches colossal and high,
Disturbing the dead in their tombs close by.

The last two lines serve as a refrain and are repeated after each of the ten verses, two of which will suffice as samples.

Come, he-goats profane,
Come, lizards and snails,
Come, serpents with scales,
So fragile and frail.
Burst into the fane!
Let discord take wing,
With melodious swing,
Come, enter the ring,
And repeat the refrain.

And their steps shake the arches colossal and high,
Disturbing the dead in their tombs close by.

From his tomb with sad moans
Each false monk to his stall
Glides, concealed in his pall,
That robe fatal to all,
Which burns into his bones.

Now a black priest draws nigh,
With a flame he doth fly
On the altar on high
He the curst fire enthrones.

The dawn whitens the arches colossal and gray,
And drives all the devilish revellers away;
The dead monks retire to their graves 'neath the halls,
And veil their cold faces behind their dark palls.

For his introduction and refrain Hugo uses a dual rhyming scheme, *aa, bb, cc,* and so on. That of the intervening verses, however, is based on a variant of an old medieval triple-rhyming pattern recalling that of the 13th-century *Dies Irae* (p. 224), which is still an important part of the requiem mass. The first, fifth, and ninth lines rhyme, while two groups of triple rhyme are placed between them to make a pattern of *a, bbb, a, ccc, a.* The *Dies Irae* had made an earlier appearance in the church scene of Goethe's *Faust,* where Margaret, aware of her forthcoming doom, hears the chorus intone the awesome lines (Fig. 516). Both the technique and imagery of Hugo's ballad are related to the fantastic sections of *Faust,* and both poems, in turn, have a common ancestor in the witches' scene from Shakespeare's *Macbeth.* The similarity of metrical plan and black-magic imagery is unmistakable. One finds the same lilting language that is designed to charm the ear and stimulate the imagination rather than make logical sense, especially in the Walpurgis Night scene from *Faust.* The scene is filled with witches riding he-goats and giant owls; the earth crawls with salamanders and coiling snakes; while bats fly around and glittering fireflies provide the illumination. As Mephistopheles describes the ghostly dance, all manner of gruesome and awsome night creatures—

. . . crowd and jostle, whirl, and flutter!
They whisper, babble, twirl, and splutter!
They glimmer, sparkle, stink, and flare—
A true witch-element! Beware!

The sources of Hugo's inspiration are thus clear, but while he must be counted among the masters of language and the outstanding literary figures, he was never a prime mover or noted for his originality. Highly skilled as a manipulator of symbols and a master of poetic forms, he was able to give articulate expression to the changing voices of his time. In spite of all this verbal virtuosity and the uniformly high quality of his output, he never succeeded in producing a poetic masterpiece that stood out above all others. In his work all the ideas of his time are mirrored in his unparalleled rhetoric, and his voice is as typical as any within the framework of this period. The brief but pungent reply of a modern critic pretty well sums it up. When asked whom he considered the greatest French poet of the 19th century, he answered, "Unfortunately, Victor Hugo."

527. GUSTAVE DORÉ. *Berlioz Conducting*. 19th-century caricature.

MUSIC

The salons of Paris during the days of the romantic dawn were populated with poets, playwrights, journalists, critics, architects, painters, sculptors, musicians, and utopian political reformers without number. Heinrich Heine, poet and journalist from north Germany, Chopin from Poland, Liszt from Hungary—all mixed freely with such homegrown artists and intellectuals as Victor Hugo, Théophile Gautier, Lamartine, Chateaubriand, de Musset, Dumas, George Sand, and others. Social philosophers like Lamennais, Proudhon, Auguste Comte, and Saint-Simon, gave a political tinge to the heated aesthetic debates. In this supercharged atmosphere Hector Berlioz must have appeared as an authentic apparition, embodying in the flesh the wildest romantic dreams and nightmares. One contemporary described him as a young man trembling with passion, whose large umbrella of hair projected like a movable awning over the beak of a bird of prey. The German composer Robert Schumann saw him as a "shaggy monster with ravenous eyes"; his personality as that of a "raging bacchant"; and spoke of his effect on the society of his times as being "the terror of the Philistines." The suave and polished Felix Mendelssohn, on the other hand, found his French col-

league completely exasperating, and he continually reproached Berlioz because, with all his strenuous efforts to go stark raving mad, he never once really succeeded.

In one striking personality, Berlioz combined qualities that made him a great composer, the ranking orchestral conductor of his day, a brilliant journalist, and an autobiographer. As a conductor, the painter Gustave Doré caricatured him as the mad musician (Fig. 527). At the first performance of one of his overtures, when the orchestra failed to give him the effect he demanded, he burst into tears, tore his hair, and fell sobbing on the kettledrums. His *Memoirs* are stylistically a literary achievement of the first magnitude and rank with the few top autobiographies of world literature. From this lively source one gathers that Berlioz' development proceeded in a series of emotional shocks which he received from his first contacts with the literature and music of his time. One after the other, the fires of his explosive imagination were ignited by Goethe's *Faust*, which resulted in his oratorio the *Damnation of Faust*; by the poetry of Byron, which became the symphony for viola and orchestra, *Harold in Italy*; and by Dante's *Divine Comedy*, which was sublimated into his great *Requiem*. In music it was first Gluck, then Weber, and he said that he had scarcely recovered from these two when he "beheld Beethoven's giant form looming over the horizon. The shock was almost as great as that I had received from Shakespeare, and a new world of music was revealed to me by the musician, just as a new universe of poetry had been opened to me by the poet." It was, of course, the Beethoven of the *Eroica*, *Pastoral*, and *Ninth* symphonies. To a milder extent, the literary figures of Vergil, Walter Scott, and Victor Hugo made up the more distant claps of thunder in his creative brainstorms.

Berlioz even insisted on actually living out his enthusiasms to an alarmingly realistic degree. He fell violently in love with the Irish actress who was playing the feminine leads in the Shakespearean troupe that was so successful in the Paris season of 1827. After a desperate romance leading both to the brink of suicide, he finally married the beautiful feminine package whom he thought of as Juliet and Ophelia wrapped up in one. When his wife turned out to be merely the actress Miss Harriet Smithson, now Mme H. Berlioz, he wrote with acute anguish to a friend: "She's an ordinary woman." The cold dawn of disillusionment brought years of personal misery, compensated for by some happier results on the musical side. For all his external flightiness, his literary, musical, and human loves were completely enduring; and he carried them with him to the end of his life. There one finds him still musing on the "mild, affable, and acces-

espressivo   *poco sf*   *sf*

sible" figure of Vergil; on Shakespeare, "that mighty indifferent man, impassable as a mirror"; on Beethoven, "contemptuous and uncouth, yet gifted with such profound sensibility"; and on Gluck, "the superb."

Berlioz' autobiographical *Fantastic Symphony*, first performed in the year 1830, contains a complex of many ideas he gathered from the musical and literary atmosphere that surrounded him. In the detailed programmatic notes he wrote for it, it is clear that he took the idea of poisoning by opium in the first movement from De Quincey's *Confessions of an English Opium Eater*, which had appeared shortly before in a French translation by Alfred de Musset. The musical form of this movement, with its *Largo* introduction and the *Allegro agitato e appassionato assai* continuation, is in the Beethovenian symphonic tradition. Its principal claim to technical originality is the use of an *idée fixe*, or fixed idea (above), by which Berlioz conveys the idea of his beloved who is everywhere present and colors his every thought. The metamorphosis of the theme on its appearance in each of the movements fulfills a dual purpose—that of providing a semblance of unity in the sequence of genre pieces, and that of expressing, by its mutations, the necessary dramatic progress. The theme is varied in each of its reappearances and provides the listener with the necessary continuity to build up the image of a dramatic character through the associative process. All evidence, however, points to the fact that this specific programme was written later than most of the music, which apparently was conceived for quite another purpose.

Gérard de Nerval's prose translation of Goethe's *Faust* had appeared late in the year 1827 and was the direct inspiration for Berlioz' *Eight Scenes from Faust*. Since most of the movements of the *Fantastic Symphony* were being written at the same time, this alone would indicate a connection in the creative process. Berlioz was among the earliest to attempt a realization of Goethe's great drama in music. An opera by Spohr had appeared in 1816,

but the well-known one by Gounod came many years later. A secular oratorio by Schumann, a *Faust Symphony* by Liszt, and a *Faust Overture* by Wagner are but a few of the many subsequent works on this theme. The subject of Faust was in the wind, and the stages of London, Paris, and other Continental cities rang with the echoes of the many versions of this subject in dramatic and ballet form. The Paris Opera alone had accepted no less than three librettos that were waiting to be commissioned. It is known that Berlioz was angling for one of these, and this fact further fortifies the case for the common source of inspiration for the *Damnation of Faust* and the *Fantastic Symphony*. Since the desired commission was not forthcoming, those parts projected for a Faust ballet became instead the movements of the *Fantastic Symphony*.

The reveries and passions of the first movement are certainly Faustian in a general, if not specific, sense. Every Faust ballet of the time contained a gay dance sequence for "Auerbach's Cellar" scene, and the second movement of the *Fantastic Symphony*, called the "Scene at the Ball," was probably first written for "Auerbach's Cellar." The external and internal storms of the third movement, the "Scene in the Country," bring out the benign as well as the malignant aspects of the Faustian conception of nature. The closest correspondence, however, comes in the climactic final movements where the relationship is quite unmistakable. The fourth, the grim "March to the Scaffold," was probably composed first as the execution scene where Margaret pays the penalty for the dual crimes of matricide and infanticide. In the *Symphony*, it becomes a musical nightmare of the first order in which the hero (autobiographically Berlioz himself) marches in grotesque rhythms to his own doom. As other writers have pointed out, this scene may well have been suggested to Berlioz by the unfortunate execution of the gifted young poet André Chénier, who met death on the guillotine under Robespierre and thus became the martyred poet of the Revolution. In the final bars of this movement, the fixed melodic idea is sounded in the high piercing register of the clarinet. It is suddenly cut off to suggest the fall of the blade and the decapitation of the hero. After a dull thud and a roll of the drums, the grimacing crowds roar their bloodthirsty approval of the execution.

The last movements of both the *Eight Scenes from Faust* and the *Fantastic Symphony* have to do with the triumph of the exultant diabolical forces as they claim the souls of their victims. The endings to Berlioz' early works are often the most wild and dissonant parts. No anticlimactic calms after the storms, no carefully planned resolutions, no safe havens after the shipwrecks. The *Symphony* ends with a diabolical "Witches' Sabbath," just as *Harold in Italy* ends with an "Orgy of the Brigands." The grisly scene here is both the climax and the unresolved end, and the movement that most fully justifies the title "Fantastic." It is divided into three distinct sections. The first is introductory and begins with wild shrieks for the piccolo, flute, and oboe, accompanied by the ominous roll of the kettledrums in bars 7 and 8, which is echoed softly by the muted horns in bars 9 and 10 to suggest distance. After a repetition, the tempo changes from *Larghetto* to *Allegro* and the *idée fixe* is heard (21–28). The ghostly appearance of the fixed melodic idea associated with Berlioz' beloved in this final movement undoubtedly was derived from the witches' kitchen scene of Goethe's drama where Faust has gone to have his form changed from that of old age back to young and lusty manhood, and where the conjuring up of the image of Margaret is a part of the process (Fig. 515). It is also related to the Walpurgis Night scene where Margaret again puts in a brief appearance. Surely it is a novel notion that the winsome heroine, exemplified in previous mutations as the embodiment of desirability, should now appear at the witches' sabbath. Was she a witch all along and disguised only in his imagination in desirable human form? Or is this merely another manifestation of her "bewitching" power? The entrance at this point of his beloved on her broomstick, accompanied by a pandemonium of sulfurous sounds, is therefore somewhat unexpected. The hero, obviously Berlioz, gives a shriek of horror (29–39) as he listens to her modulate from the previously chaste C major to the more lurid key of E flat. Her instrumental coloration, while still that of the pale clarinet, descends now in pitch to a new low and more sensuous register. After this shocking revelation, she executes a few capers and subsides for the time being as the introduction concludes with bar 101.

The second section is labeled *Lontano* ("in the distance") and begins with the tolling of the chimes recalling the opening lines of Hugo's ballad. After this signal for the unleashing of the infernal forces, the foreboding *Dies Irae* is solemnly intoned, first by the brass instruments in unison octaves. In bars 127–146, it is in dotted half notes; next, in bars 147–157, the rhythm is quickened into dotted quarters; then it becomes syncopated in triplet eighths (157–162) and ends with an abrupt upward swish of the C scale. With the appearance here in syncopation and in such surroundings of this ancient and honorable Gothic liturgical melody, a solemn part of every Roman Catholic requiem mass, Berlioz fulfills the promise of his programme that he will make a "burlesque parody" on the *Dies Irae*. Besides serving Berlioz as a symbol conjuring up all the fire-and-brimstone aspects of medieval Christianity, it also introduces at this point a form of macabre humor. This parody of a sacred melody caused considerable comment at the time. Schumann attributed it to romantic irony, one of the few forms of humor tolerated in a style practiced by artists who took life and themselves with deadly seriousness. Another explanation, however, seems more logical and is to be found by applying a remark that Hugo made in his Preface to *Cromwell*. "When Dante had finished his terrible Inferno," he wrote, "and naught remained save to give his work a name, the unerring instinct of his genius showed him that multiform poem was an emanation of the drama, not of the epic; and on the front of that gigantic monument, he wrote with his pen of bronze: Divina Commedia." Thus if Dante was justified in conceiving his Inferno as a comedy, albeit a divine one, then Berlioz could include the *Dies Irae* in this context. Even the devil is conceded to be a clever theologian, and in Goethe's drama he is found in the sacred precincts of the church, whispering in Margaret's ear as she listens to the choir chant the *Dies Irae*. This scene was also one Delacroix chose for the subject of a lithograph (Fig. 516); and the image of Satan saying mass at midnight in the Gothic setting of Hugo's poem relates all these works to the same idea.

The title of the final section of Berlioz' *Symphony*, which begins with bar 241, is *Ronde du Sabbat*, the same as that of Hugo's poem, again showing the connection with that ballad. A dance fragment hinted at previously now becomes the "Rondo of the Sabbath" theme and a four-bar phrase forming a fugue subject. The first entrance is for the 'cellos and double basses (241–244); this is followed by the violas (248–251); next, for the first violins fortified by the bassoons (255–258); and the final entrance is scored for the woodwind section and horns. These successive entries, each with a different instrumental combination, mark Berlioz' departure from the academic tradition of the linear fugue. Here he introduces the element of instrumental coloration into the usually austere fugal exposition. Other color combinations follow with melodic and chromatic variants of the subject in a fugal development that has won the composer wide admiration. It must be noted that when Berlioz is writing his wildest images, his mind is always in command; and at the climax of such a work as this, he writes a fugue without either violating the rules or sacrificing his expressive intentions. After the fugue on the dance theme has come to its climax with the entire string section playing an extension of the subject (407–413), the *Dies Irae* makes a reappearance, and the two themes are woven together with great skill from bar 414 to the end. Some of Berlioz' enthusiastic admirers have called this contrapuntal section a double fugue. There is only one fugue, however, with the *Dies Irae* melody running concurrently. With the final blood-curdling shrieks and flying images, a composer, perhaps for the first time in music history, has written a fugue that fulfills its literal meaning— that is, a flight.

After the *Fantastic Symphony*, the use of the *Dies Irae* became a symbol of the macabre, and it has been used countless times since. Liszt's *Totentanz* for piano and orchestra is a set of variations on it, while it appears again in Gustav Mahler's sym-

528. GUSTAVE COURBET. *Hector Berlioz.* 1850. Oil on canvas, 24 × 19″. Louvre, Paris.

phonies and in some of Rachmaninoff's variations on a theme of Paganini. With this final movement, Berlioz also established a style that brought the demonic element—and a chain of harmonic and psychological dissonances—into music to stay. Both Moussorgsky's *Night on Bald Mountain* and Saint-Saëns' *Danse Macabre* are cut from the same cloth. One writer has even called this movement of Berlioz' the first piece of Russian music. Some of Stravinsky's wilder moments in his *Fire Bird* and *Rite of Spring* would certainly seem to bear this out. Anyone, in fact, who knows this movement well can hardly be shocked by the dissonances of modern music.

Berlioz was one of the first composers to build up his musical forms by the use of tone color. The only way to understand his music is to hear it in all the full richness of its instrumental sound, because his scores can never be transcribed successfully for piano or any other instrumental medium. In addition to the incomparable richness of his orchestral palette, the sheer quantitative weight he added to the ensembles of his day is nothing short of spectacular. Seldom composing in any but the largest forms, he delighted in the use of orchestral and choral combinations of extraordinary complexity. To assemble all the necessary forces for a Berlioz performance is always a challenge, and the demands his works make on the time and effort of the performers are considerable. In his gigantic *Requiem*, he employs an immense principal orchestra, a chorus of 500, a tenor soloist, and 4 huge brass bands. The latter were placed facing the 4 points of the compass, so as to suggest vast space and to enhance their acoustical effect when they sound the call for Judgment Day. All this, plus such additional effects as a battery of 16 kettledrums, caused the newspapers to comment the day following the first performance that Paris had not heard such a volume of sound since the fall of the Bastille.

There was always something of the conqueror about Berlioz as he marshaled his orchestral forces in such a composition. Each orchestra had its own conductor, and the choruses were signaled by commanders of lesser rank, with all of them taking their cues from the generalissimo himself, who appeared in the role of a musical Napoleon storming over the battlefield. Berlioz was the first of the great orchestra conductors and the prototype of the great maestros of our day. No wonder his contemporaries did not know how to take him and found both his personality and his compositions somewhat difficult to absorb. He always reminded them of something monstrous, and it remained for Heinrich Heine to find the most apt way of putting this into words. "Here is the wingbeat that reveals no ordinary songbird," he wrote, "it is that of a colossal night-

529. Francisco Goya. *Witches' Sabbath.* c. 1819–1823. Oil on canvas, 4' 7 1/8" × 14' 4 1/2". Prado, Madrid.

ingale, a lark the size of an eagle, such as must have existed in the primeval world." In 1850 when his extravagant youthful energies were spent, the painter Courbet depicted him as a man of thought and contemplation (Fig. 528).

IDEAS

The dynamics of the Revolutionary period, with its social, political, and industrial upheavals, confronted artists with the image of a rapidly changing world. The shift of responsibility and wealth from the aristocracy to the middle class brought about a corresponding change in the patrons for whom the buildings were built, the statues carved, the pictures painted, and the music composed. No longer were the arts produced only for a small sophisticated group of aristocrats; instead, they were addressed to a larger and more anonymous public mainly of the bourgeois class. Finesse, subtlety, and intellectual grasp of complex forms could not be anticipated in audiences. Artists now had to charm, exhort, and astonish. Under the new system an architect could not count on one patron for a single monumental project but had to cater to many clients with smaller buildings involving many different tastes and styles.

The consequences in the arts were profound and far reaching. Artistic media were brought closer together, and painting and music in particular became allied with literature for poetic allusions and programmatic interpretations. Color in painting, as well as tone color in instrumentation, became important in the vocabulary of romanticism. It was not sufficient, moreover, for an artist to be a fine craftsman. He had now to be a great personality and espouse epic causes. Above all, perhaps, romanticism involved the psychology of escapism from an increasingly industrialized and mechanized world. The mainstream of romantic ideas, then, flowed from the alliance of the arts, colorism, individualism and nationalism to the various escape mechanisms: revivals of the past, back to nature, and exoticism.

Alliance of the Arts and Colorism

Painters and sculptors began to work in a greater variety of forms than before, while poets and musicians likewise revealed the fragmentation of their world view by writing shorter works and generally showing an inability to conceive or present their world as a systematic whole. Even when such a composer as Berlioz did write symphonies, the results were no longer the all-embracing universal structures of Beethoven but sequences of genre pieces strung together by a literary programme or some recurrent motive that gave them a semblance of unity.

New also was the idea that an artistic opus was not a self-contained whole but something that shared many relationships internally as well as externally with other works of art. This idea began with the attempts by certain individual artists to overcome many of the arbitrary limitations and technical rules of their separate crafts. The literature of the period was filled with musical allusions, and musicians for their part were drawing on literature with full force for their programme pieces. The architects were called upon to build dream castles out of the novels of Walpole, Scott, and Hugo; and it is difficult to think of Delacroix' painting or Berlioz' music without Vergil, Dante, Shakespeare, Goethe, and Byron coming to mind. The effect on music was a host of new and hybrid forms, such as the programme symphony and the symphonic poem. The tonal art had been associated from its beginnings with words, and programme music was

Plate 47. JOHN CONSTABLE. *Hay Wain*. 1821. Oil on canvas, 4'2 ½" × 6'1".
National Gallery, London (reproduced by courtesy of the Trustees). (See p. 454.)

Plate 48. JEAN-AUGUSTE DOMINIQUE INGRES. *The Turkish Bath. c.* 1852–1863.
Oil on canvas, diameter 42 ½″. Louvre, Paris. (See p. 476.)

by no means an invention of the 19th century. No other period, however, built an entire style on this mixture. There is also a considerable distinction between the setting of words to music, as in a song, or the musical dramatization of a play, as in an opera, and basing a purely instrumental form on the spirit of a poem or the sequential arrangements of episodes taken from a novel. Berlioz wrote overtures not only to operas but to such novels as Scott's *Waverly* and *Rob Roy*. Mendelssohn wrote *Songs Without Words* for the piano leaving the imagination to supply the text, and Berlioz' *Fantastic Symphony* and *Harold in Italy* became operas without words. In such later works as the "dramatic symphony" *Romeo and Juliet* and the "dramatic legend" *Damnation of Faust*, which are scored for soloists and chorus as well as orchestra, he was, in effect, writing concert operas in which the costumes and scenery are left to the listener's imagination. This tendency continued until it reached a climax in Richard Wagner's music dramas, which he conceived as *Gesamtkunstwerke*—that is, complete, consummate, or total works of art.

Among the important innovations of the time was an increasing emphasis on color in the various artistic media, both for its own sake and for its capacity to convey symbolic meaning. For the architects and sculptors, color was associated with the picturesque and local color. Poetry began to depend on the sounds of words and their appeal to the senses more than to the mind. Hugo's "Witches' Sabbath" with its patterns of repeated sounds and colors would be practically meaningless if this literary tone color were omitted. To Delacroix, more than line or composition, color was the dimension on which he depended for intensity of expression. "When the tones are right," Delacroix wrote in his journal of 1847, "the lines take care of themselves." Berlioz can be understood only when his musical ideas are heard in the original instrumentation. He is a composer who defies transcription. If the English horn solo in the "Scene in the Country," the third movement of the *Fantastic Symphony*, were to be played by a flute or clarinet, Berlioz' expressive intention would vanish instantly. Such an example reveals the extent Berlioz relied on the tone color of specific instruments; and in his hands instrumentation becomes a musical dimension in itself, capable of carrying its own expressive weight independent of melody and rhythm. Both Delacroix and Berlioz based their styles principally on color.

Romantic Individualism and Nationalism

The romantic period was also the age of the emancipation of the individual and the era of the great man who attained the heights on his own efforts. Napoleon had stamped his image on his era with his preeminence in the realm of military glory and statecraft, thus giving rise to the idea of similar dominating figures in the smaller worlds of letters, painting, sculpture, architecture, and music. Artists vied with each other for the top rung of the ladder in their respective fields. For sheer virtuosity in letters it would be difficult to surpass Victor Hugo, who could write with mastery in any style. Viollet-le-Duc and other architects could duplicate any building in the history of architecture; and the names of such bravura composer-performers as Paganini and Liszt are legendary. All this was, perhaps, a positive assertion of the diminishing self in the face of growing social collectivization. Each work of art was associated with the personality of a distinctive individual. It was no longer enough for an artist to be a master of his craft, no matter how high the degree of his skill; he had also to be a great man, a prophet, a leader. It was consequently an age of autobiography, confessions, memoirs, portraiture, and showmanship. The will to biography, the necessity of living a "life," often took so much time that it was actually a handicap to artistic production. More than in any other period there was an obligation for the artist to be a personality in the worldly sense in addition to his artistic activities. The place of the artist in society had been a matter of vital concern to such men as David and Beethoven, who combined the moralistic fervor of revolutionary thought with a sense of social responsibility. David's championship of the cause of art in the French legislature, and Beethoven's behavior toward his patrons as their social equal, reveal both men as modern artists who placed the aristocracy of genius on a higher plane than that of birth.

The great individual, however, could not exist in a social or political vacuum. Byron, Delacroix, and others felt compelled to bend their energies and talents to the cause of liberating the oppressed Greek people from the Turkish tyrant's yoke. Whether an artist conceived of himself in classical terms as a Prometheus or in the medieval vocabulary as a knightly champion of the weak against the strong was not too important. He simply needed a geographical sounding board, local color, and a linguistic medium suited to his creative needs. Some could find it in folk tales and ballads of a particular locale; others in collections and variations of Spanish epics, Scottish ballads, German fairy tales; still others in the writing of Italian symphonies, Hungarian rhapsodies, and Polish mazurkas. In this light, nationalism, like the medieval revival, was a northern declaration of cultural independence from the Mediterranean tradition, tied up in the immediate sense in England and Germany with the opposition to Napoleon as a latter-day Caesar. Berlioz' nationalism is expressed in a more subtle way, but his operas without words, concert operas, and music dramas were as distinct a departure from the prevailing Italian operatic tradition as were those of Weber in Germany.

Escapism

During the romantic period there was a growing gulf between the realities of the early industrial age and the escapist tendencies in the arts. In recognition of the new technologies an École Polytechnique had been established in 1794 by the Revolutionary government. Napoleon, however, yielded to the advice of David and others and allowed the establishment of a separate École des Beaux-Arts in 1806. By thus educating engineers in one school and architects in another, the construction techniques of building tended to be divorced from the stylistic aspects of architecture. When the architects did begin using cast iron, it was to build dream castles and neomedieval cathedrals; and when musicians began to write for the improved horns and trombones, it was to sound the call of Judgment Day and introduce a rain of neomedieval fire and brimstone into their symphonies. In general, then, the full significance of the Industrial Revolution remained for a later age to exploit.

The American and French revolutions, which had held out such high initial hopes and promised the imminent liberation of man, were followed by a reaction bordering on pessimism when the results did not live up to the overly optimistic expectations. Then when the Revolution of July, 1830, had overthrown the last of the old line of Bourbons, the French middle class was finally confronted by a king cast in its own image. As the bourgeoisie beheld Louis Philippe in his frock coat, umbrella in hand, walking down the boulevard to the Bourse, they were somewhat dismayed to find that their monarch was—like themselves—stouter of figure than of heart and—again like themselves—engaged in the pursuit of causes more materialistic than ideal. A bit appalled at what they saw, is it any wonder that they sought psychological compensation in dreams of the more dashing royal personalities of the past, whose recklessness consisted of more hazardous adventures than buying and selling shares on the stock exchange? How could King Louis Philippe, living in a palace replete with the bourgeois comforts of modern plumbing, compare in popular fancy with Joan of Arc's dashing dauphin, living dangerously while being pursued by his remorseless enemies from one dank and drafty castle to another?

The activities of Darwin's earthworms, for instance, were infinitely more useful than the sublime spectacle of one of Delacroix' lions in mortal combat with a stallion. But how could the worms capture the popular imagination as the lions did? A highly productive factory or an ingenious city sewer system made infinitely duller pictures and poetry than the interiors of Oriental harems and the palm-lined shores of the River Ganges. While willing to use the fruits of the Industrial Revolution as aids in the production and dissemination of their artistic wares, the artists of the time were quite convinced that the new technologies were not making their world more beautiful. Thus the rift between usefulness and beauty widened. Refusing to reconcile themselves to reality, the artists sought ever more fanciful ways and means of avoiding the issue. Certainly they knew what was going on in their world. As intellectuals, they were better educated and better informed than similar groups in other times had ever been.

When employing their escape mechanisms, they were fully aware of what they were escaping from. "Any time but now, and any place but here" became the battle cry of romanticism. The yearning for past periods—whether ancient Greco-Roman or medieval—was expressed in the various revivals. Since the classic and medieval revivals were accepted as official styles, and since they lingered longer than other aspects of romanticism, they have been dwelt upon in these pages at greater length. But the fuller vocabulary of romantic escapism included the "Back to Nature" movement, a longing for the lost paradise of a simple, pastoral life, and exoticism, with its fantasies of life in far-off places.

Revivals of the Past. Neoclassicism had been the earliest of the revivals of the past, and the passion for exactitude soon had divided it into separate Greek and Roman revival movements. Through historical novels and romantic imaginations, interest in medieval times was awakened; and as medieval scholars extended their studies, artists delved deeper into the Middle Ages. Revivals of Gothic, Romanesque, and Byzantine styles followed next. The romantic affinity for times past was then expanded into admiration for the Renaissance and baroque periods. The Library of Ste. Geneviève in Paris (Fig. 557) and the Boston Public Library, in their exteriors at least, were revivals of Renaissance architecture, and—shades of the French Revolution—the Paris Opera, begun in 1861, revived Louis XIV's Versailles. Wagner composed the opera *Rienzi* after a novel by Bulwer-Lytton about a ruler of the Roman Renaissance, and Mendelssohn rediscovered the greatness of Bach's oratorios and in 1829 performed the *St.*

Matthew Passion for the first time since the composer's death.

In retrospect, the 19th-century antithesis of classic and romantic has been resolved, because both now are seen as component parts of the same broader revival idea. The artists who lived on into the post-Napoleonic period drew their inspiration from Greco-Roman or medieval times with equal facility. John Nash, for example, built himself a neoclassical town house in London and a romantic Gothic castle in the country; Rude made statues of Roman nymphs and of Joan of Arc; Ingres painted the *Apotheosis of Homer* and later a picture of the Maid of Orleans; Keats wrote "Ode on a Grecian Urn" and also "St. Agnes' Eve"; Victor Hugo included neoclassical odes in the same volume with his medieval ballads. Berlioz admired Vergil quite as intensively as he did Dante and wrote the *Trojans at Carthage*, an opera based on the *Aeneid*, as well as the *Requiem*, based on the medieval hymn *Dies Irae*. After neoclassicism and romanticism had run their courses, the revival idea led, in the later 19th century, to a broad eclecticism, whereby a virtuoso architect could build in any past style, a painter could do a portrait or historical canvas à la Titian or Rubens, a poet could employ any form or metrical organization with facility, and a composer could pull out at will a Renaissance or baroque stop on his organ.

England and Germany both claimed the Gothic style as their own, and to them it was a conscious departure from the Greco-Roman ideals of antiquity as well as their rebirth in the Renaissance, baroque, and neoclassical styles. In England especially, the Gothic revival was bound up closely with the wave of prosperity caused by a great industrial expansion, a glowing national pride, and a reaction against the Napoleonic Empire that had threatened their own. A reassertion of the separation of the Church of England from Rome took shape in the Oxford movement, which demanded veering away from Greco-Roman architectural forms as essentially pagan, and restoration of medieval liturgies that, in turn, needed appropriate settings.

In Germany, the Gothic revival took the form of a vision of past national glory associated with that country's entrance upon the European scene under Charlemagne, whom the Germans adopted as their national hero Karl der Grosse. The relative security and eminence of Germany under the rule of the Holy Roman Empire had continued intermittently up to the reign in the 16th century of the Hapsburg Charles V, the last of the powerful emperors. The past thus played an important role in the 19th-century revival of German power, based as it was on the memory of an empire dominated by the north. Stung into action by its abolition under Napoleon, German nationalism fermented during the 19th century until it matured into the heady wine of Bismarck's statesmanship, the aroma of which reminded Teutonic connoisseurs of the heroic bouquet of such ancient vintages as those of Attila, Alaric, and Frederick Barbarossa.

From the Renaissance on through the aristocratic baroque tradition and the 18th century, French art was closely bound to traditional Greco-Roman forms. During the Revolution of 1789 and its aftermath, a wave of anticlericalism led to the actual destruction of some medieval buildings to protest against Church influence and herald the new freedom. The neoclassicism of the First Empire continued through the early years of the 19th century and, though weakened under the Bourbon restoration, had at least official approval right up to the Revolution of July, 1830. Underneath the political surface, however, the destruction of medieval monuments had indirectly stimulated certain groups to preserve parts of these works in museums. When the glories of their own medieval past were bought to the attention of some Frenchmen, at a time when the popular wave of neomedieval enthusiasm was gathering such momentum in England and Germany, this was bound to have consequences in France. Unlike Protestant England and Germany, France had broken its ties with Roman Catholicism only briefly during the first wave of Revolutionary fervor. Even Napoleon had found it politically expedient to make a concordat with the Vatican and to be crowned in the sacred precincts of Notre Dame in Paris in the presence of the Roman pontiff.

Since the power of the French state was such that it was able to withstand foreign pressure even at the time of the Revolution and, later, to embark on the conquest of the continent under Napoleon, there was no national inferiority complex to be taken into account. Very significantly, it was not until French national power had been thoroughly subdued under the coalition which defeated Napoleon that the romantic style took a firm hold on the French mind and imagination. Even then, it endured officially less than a generation—that is, between the revolutions of 1830 and 1848.

The medieval revival is also found on the American scene. In New York the Gothic spires of Trinity Church (Fig. 530) rise among lower Broadway's skyscrapers. Two churches by Renwick furnish further examples—Grace Church (Fig. 531) and St. Patrick's Cathedral, both dating from the mid-19th century. Many American colleges and universities, in their zeal to be identified with ancient and honorable causes, were also built in the neomedieval style. And scattered throughout the country are half-timbered houses (for a Gothic precedent, see Fig. 234), castle residences, railroad stations, and other public buildings show the wide influence of the medieval revival on 19th-century American architecture.

Back to Nature.   Rousseau had already sounded the clarion call of "back to nature" in the late 18th century. By so doing, he challenged the urbane, civilized, aristocratic image of man with his projection of the noble savage type whose rustic charm was achieved by shunning society and communing with a nature unspoiled by human hands. For his own part, Rousseau was perfectly willing to be received in courtly circles, and his rustic little

531. JAMES RENWICK. Grace Church, New York. 1845.

opera *Le Devin du Village (The Village Soothsayer)* was performed for Louis XVI at Versailles with great success. His ideas were partly responsible for the country cottage, complete with a dairy and mill, that Queen Marie Antoinette had built for herself amid the formal gardens of the royal palace (Fig. 532).

The back-to-nature idea took root and became one of the more popular 19th-century escape mechanisms with that segment of the population which lived in cities and dreamed of an idyllic country life they had no intention of living. These people delighted, however, in reading poetry full of nature imagery as well as folk ballads and fairy tales. They hung landscapes by Corot (Fig. 533) and the now all-too-familiar peasant scenes of Millet on the walls of their apartments and town houses. Beethoven's *Pastoral Symphony* and Wagner's *Forest Murmurs,* as well as dozens of piano pieces and songs,

530. RICHARD UPJOHN. Trinity Church, New York. 1839–1846.

sounded the proper bucolic note in music. Weber's opera *Der Freischütz*, which had been the success of the 1826 season in Paris, brought out some of the darker aspects of nature. In it, much is made of the sinister powers of the night, and the forces over which it rules are effectively presented in the eerie Wolf's Glen scene. Nature, here, as well as in Goethe's *Faust*, included malignant and benign aspects, and both works unleashed terrifying elemental forces as well as powers of a magical and fantastic character.

Outstanding among landscapists was John Constable with his quiet studies of the English countryside, such as *Hay Wain* (Plate 47), and picturesque views, such as *Salisbury Cathedral from the Bishop's Garden* (Fig. 534). In comparison with the Claude Lorrain landscapes that Constable admired (see Fig. 420), the composition of *Hay Wain* is as relaxed and informal as a casual English garden

534. JOHN CONSTABLE. *Salisbury Cathedral from the Bishop's Garden.* 1836. Oil on canvas, 34 ¼ × 43 ⅝". Frick Collection, New York (copyright).

535. ANTOINE JEAN GROS. *Napoleon Visiting the Pesthouse at Jaffa.* 1804. Oil on canvas, 17'5" × 23'7". Louvre, Paris.

when placed beside a formal French one. Constable's major pictorial interests were in rendering mercurial changes of atmosphere; the infinitely varied intensities of light on clear, showery, or foggy days; sunshine filtered through translucent green leaves; and the constantly changing reflections of the varicolored sky and passing clouds on water. To capture these effects Constable made innumerable oil sketches in the open air and later finished his pictures in his studio. When his paintings were exhibited in Paris, their freshness, warmth, and spontaneity created a considerable stir. Delacroix admired Constable's bold use of color, and his descriptive powers and technical innovations had an important influence on the later impressionists.

Exoticism. The heady perfumes of the Orient also were wafted into the nostrils and thence to the fancies of romantic patrons, intellectuals, and artists. While shrewd businessmen were opening up new foreign markets, and missionaries were going forth from Europe to try to bridge the Christian and pagan worlds, artists were busy capturing the popular imagination with scenes of exotic mysteries associated with far-off lands and peoples. As early as 1759, Arthur Murphy in the Prologue of a play called *Orphans of China* had proclaimed: "Enough of Greece and Rome: Th'exhausted store of either nation now can charm no more." So the Oriental world was added to the imaginative repertory, and its changing image in one guise or another has been mirrored in the arts up to the present time. Reflections of this early phase can be found in such operas

as Gluck's *The Unforeseen Meeting* or *The Pilgrims to Mecca* (1764) and Mozart's *Abduction from the Seraglio* (1785), with its setting in a Turkish harem, and in William Beckford's Oriental novel *Vathek* (1786). Kew Gardens in London was studded with fanciful structures revealing a wide imaginative range. Some paths led to little rococo pavilions, others to Greek temples or Gothic chapels. Among them were a Moslem mosque, a Moorish palace, and a house of Confucius. A pagoda, built by the conservative Palladian architect William Chambers, is the only one of these bagatelles that has survived.

Only a short time later, Napoleon was fighting his Battle of the Pyramids (1798), and Gros was commissioned to paint *Napoleon Visiting the Pesthouse at Jaffa* (Fig. 535) depicting an incident in the Near East campaign. In England, a tale entitled *Thalaba the Destroyer* (1799) by Robert Southey included chapters called "The Desert Circle" and "Life in an Arab Tent." Drawing rooms were hung with wallpapers depicting scenes of mandarin China, and fashionable hostesses were pouring tea at Chinese Chippendale tables. The Prince Regent of England, like Kubla Khan in Coleridge's poem, did,

> A stately pleasure-dome decree:
> Where Alph, the sacred river, ran
> Through caverns measureless to man
> Down to the sunless sea.

Less poetically though no less fancifully, this was the Oriental pavilion the Prince Regent commissioned his architect to build at his favorite seaside resort of Brighton. John Nash, who had previously built an exotic country house for a gentle-man who had lived in India, came up with an Arabian Nights extravaganza in a style that was then referred to as "Indian Gothic." The exterior (Fig. 536) is an exotic fantasy of minarets and cupolas, pinnacles and pagodas, all constructed over cast-iron frames. A domed ceiling painted like a spreading palm tree covers the dining hall (Fig. 537). Waterlily chandeliers suspended from the cast-iron claws of scaly dragons, lotus-blossom lamps, Oriental lacquerware, and Chinese Chippendale furniture complete the decor.

Schopenhauer's *World as Will and Idea*, based on the Oriental philosophy of the negation of the will, saw the light of day in 1819. Byron wrote his poetic drama *Sardanapalus* in 1821, which he based on Alexander the Great's conquest of the East; Delacroix depicted one of its scenes in his *Death of Sardanapalus* (Fig. 512), while Berlioz took the last part for a cantata written in 1830. Hugo published a series of poems called *Les Orientales* in 1829; Louis Philippe established the French Foreign Legion in 1831; and Barye was modeling wild-animal figures, such as his *Lion Hunt* (Fig. 538). Delacroix, after returning from a visit to North Africa, painted exotic scenes such as his *Algerian Women in Their Harem* (Fig. 539), which was shown in the Salon of 1834.

(above) 536. JOHN NASH. Royal Pavilion, Brighton. 1815–1821. Lithograph. Metropolitan Museum of Art, New York.

(left) 537. JOHN NASH. Dining Hall, Royal Pavilion, Brighton. 1815–1821. Lithograph. Metropolitan Museum of Art, New York.

538. ANTOINE-LOUIS BARYE. *Lion Hunt.* Date unknown. Bronze, 15″ high. Corcoran Gallery of Art, Washington, D.C.

The colorful Japanese prints that found their way to Europe after Admiral Perry's voyage of 1852–1854 had an important effect on painting. Gautier published a book called *L'Orient* in 1860, which was based on his travels, and the following year an opera by Auber called *La Circassienne* was performed. At this same time, Delacroix was painting one of his last pictures, *The Lion Hunt*, which vividly portrayed the violent struggle of men and horses against the unbridled ferocity of wild animals. Gounod's opera *The Queen of Sheba* was produced in 1862 at about the same time Ingres was finishing his fleshscape *The Turkish Bath* (Plate 48). The search for exotic settings eventually culminated in two of the greatest works of the lyrical repertory—Verdi's *Aïda*, written in 1871 for the Cairo Opera in celebration of the opening of the Suez Canal, and Bizet's *Carmen*, which, based on a short story by Mérimée, was first performed in 1875. Toward the end of the century exoticism had begun to pall, and the realistic novelist Zola was making fun of his romantic colleague Gautier because "he needed a camel and four dirty Bedouins to tickle his brains into creative activity."

539. EUGÈNE DELACROIX. *Algerian Women in Their Harem.* 1834. Oil on canvas, 5′ 9″ × 7′ 5″. Louvre, Paris.

19 - THE REALISTIC
AND IMPRESSIONISTIC STYLES

PARIS, LATE 19TH CENTURY

While neoclassicism and romanticism were dominated by flights from reality, realism and impressionism tried to come to terms with the contemporary world. One measure of the force of social progress is the rapid rise and overthrow of the various forms of government in France during the period from 1789 to 1852. Between the absolute monarchy of Louis XVI and the empire of Napoleon III, Paris experienced a Revolutionary reign of terror, a republic, the Napoleonic empire, a royal restoration, a constitutional monarchy, and a socialist commune. While these upheavals were making headlines, even more powerful and radical changes were being initiated by the Industrial Revolution. The growth of factories employing the new machine methods of production meant the shift from an agrarian to an urban economy and the migration of large numbers of people from the farms to the cities. While the 18th-century worker had been able to weigh the tangible produce of his farm or take satisfaction in the completion of a handsome, handmade pair of shoes, his 19th-century counterpart exchanged the intangible elements of his time and labor for a precarious and fragmentary living.

The application of modern scientific knowledge to industrial progress opened up many novel possibilities in the arts. Such new materials as cast iron facilitated the rapid construction of buildings and furnished the means whereby complicated decorative devices, hitherto made laboriously by hand, could be produced quickly and cheaply to satisfy the demand for the practical or the picturesque. Painting, likewise, was indebted to modern science for the development of chemical pigments. Synthetic products began to replace the old earth pigments and ground minerals and often resulted in greater brilliancy and intensity than the genuine product. Low-cost reproductions, such as the lithograph and other prints, made it possible for artists to find a wider distribution for their pictures and a new public. The facilities provided by the mechanical printing press brought about the mass distribution of newspapers, novels, and sheet music. Cast-iron instead of wooden frames for pianos meant that pianists could have larger and more durable instruments as well as ones that stayed in tune over longer periods of time. The invention of new valve mechanisms for brass instruments and the comparative standardization of their manufacture gave composers a reasonable assurance of getting the complex instrumental effects they now demanded in their orchestrations.

(above) AUGUSTE RODIN. *Three Shades*. 1880. Bronze, 38 ¾″ high, 35 ½″ wide, 17 ¾″ deep. Rodin Museum, Paris.

477

General Events

1830–	1848	Louis Philippe, constitutional king
1837–	1901	Victoria, queen of England
	1839	Daguerre and Niepce published findings on photography; daguerreotype process resulted
	1848	February Revolution; Louis Philippe overthrown
		Second French Republic proclaimed
		Communist Manifesto issued by Marx and Engels
	1851	Great Exhibition of All Nations in London; Crystal Palace by Paxton was one of buildings
		Louis Napoleon, president of Second Republic, made *coup d'état*, and became dictator
1852–	1870	Louis Napoleon reigned as Emperor Napoleon III
	1853	Admiral Perry opened Japan
1856–	1866	*Physiological Optics* published by Helmholtz (1821–1894); *On the Sensation of Tone as a Physiological Basis for the Theory of Music* (1863)
	1857	*Les Fleurs du Mal (Flowers of Evil)* published by Baudelaire
1858–	1868	Bibliothèque Nationale built by Labrouste
	1859	*Origin of Species* published by Darwin
	1863	*Life of Jesus* by Renan
1870–	1871	Franco-Prussian War; Napoleon III abdicated; Third French Republic established; Germany united as empire
	1871	*Descent of Man* published by Charles Darwin
	1874	First impressionist exhibit held
	1889	*La Grande Exposition Universelle* held in Paris; Eiffel Tower was one of buildings
	1892	*Pelléas et Mélisande* by Maeterlinck presented in Paris
	1896	*Matter and Memory* published by Henri Bergson
	1902	Debussy's opera on Maeterlinck's *Pelléas et Mélisande* produced in Paris

Painters

1808–	1879	Honoré Daumier
1819–	1877	Gustave Courbet
1832–	1883	Édouard Manet
1834–	1903	James A. McN. Whistler
1834–	1917	Edgar Degas
1839–	1906	Paul Cézanne
1840–	1926	Claude Monet
1841–	1919	Pierre Auguste Renoir
1848–	1903	Paul Gauguin
1853–	1890	Vincent van Gogh
1859–	1891	Georges Seurat
1864–	1901	H. M. R. de Toulouse-Lautrec

Sculptors

1827–	1875	Jean-Baptiste Carpeaux
1840–	1917	Auguste Rodin

Architects

1801–	1865	Joseph Paxton
1801–	1875	Henri Labrouste
1809–	1891	Georges-Eugène Haussmann
1832–	1923	Gustave Eiffel

Musicians

1813–	1883	Richard Wagner
1822–	1890	César Franck
1833–	1897	Johannes Brahms
1835–	1921	Camille Saint-Saëns
1838–	1875	Georges Bizet
1842–	1912	Jules Massenet
1845–	1924	Gabriel Fauré
1860–	1956	Gustave Charpentier
1862–	1918	Claude Debussy
1875–	1937	Maurice Ravel

Writers and Philosophers

1798–	1857	Auguste Comte
1799–	1850	Honoré de Balzac
1809–	1865	Proudhon (Pierre-Joseph)
1812–	1870	Charles Dickens
1820–	1903	Herbert Spencer
1821–	1867	Charles Baudelarie
1821–	1880	Gustave Flaubert
1828–	1906	Henrik Ibsen
1840–	1902	Émile Zola
1842–	1898	Stéphane Mallarmé
1844–	1900	Friedrich Nietzsche
1850–	1893	Guy de Maupassant
1859–	1941	Henri Bergson
1862–	1949	Maurice Maeterlinck
1870–	1925	Pierre Louÿs
1871–	1922	Marcel Proust

From the mid-19th century onward, governments were seeking constitutional formulas that would strike a just balance between social rights and material progress; religious denominations were trying to reconcile time-honored Scriptural truths with the new scientific knowledge; social theories were concerned with how political liberalism could evolve side by side with religious orthodoxy; and philosophies were attempting a new resolution between the static absolutes of idealism and the dynamic thought underlying the theories of evolution. Architects were wondering how their work could still remain in the realm of the fine arts and yet make use of the new materials and technological methods they now commanded. Sculptors, such as Rodin, were asking whether the traditional mythological and historical themes could be replaced by more contemporary subjects. The realistic and impressionistic painters were seeking a formula for the incorporation into the accepted framework of pictorial art of the new physical discoveries concerning the nature of light and its perception by the human eye. Novelists, such as Zola, were trying to establish an alliance between scientific and literary methods. Poets and playwrights, such as Mallarmé and Maeterlinck, were looking for a middle ground between the realities of the Revolutionary age and the traditional limitations of poetic expression. And composers, such as Debussy, were endeavoring to harmonize the new acoustical discoveries involving the physics of sound with the accepted concepts of tonality and musical form.

Governments and rulers settled down from high-flown heroics and histrionics into the drab but necessary routine of bureaucratic officialdom. The energies of artists were diverted from historical and exotic subjects into everyday life and seemingly trivial occurrences. The novels of Balzac and Dickens were concerned with social comment and criticism, as was the art of Honoré Daumier. *Le Ventre Législatif* (*Legislative Paunch*, Fig. 540) is one of the many biting political satires on the governmental institutions and social conventions of his time that Daumier published as journalistic cartoons. The people of Daumier's Paris live on in such genre works as *Third-Class Carriage* (Fig. 541), where the artist's sense of social criticism is muted and his deep understanding and human compassion come to the fore. Ugliness, violence, and shock techniques, however, were intended to arouse but not to insult or alienate potential patrons. Some artists, though, found life so disillusioning that art became the sole compensation for the miseries of their existence. These painters and poets eventually severed their ties with their potential middle-class patrons altogether and retreated into a private world of art, where the painters painted pictures for a limited

(above) 540. HONORÉ DAUMIER. *Le Ventre Législatif* (*Legislative Paunch*). 1834. Lithograph. Art Institute of Chicago.

(left) 541. HONORÉ DAUMIER. *Third-Class Carriage*. *c.* 1862. Oil on canvas, 26 × 35 ½″. Walters Art Gallery, Baltimore.

479

(below) 542. JACQUES-LOUIS DAVID. *Death of Marat.* 1793. Oil on canvas, 5′5″ × 4′2½″. Royal Museums of Fine Arts, Brussels.

(bottom) 543. THÉODORE GÉRICAULT. *Raft of the Medusa.* 1818–1819. Oil on canvas, 16′1″ × 23′6″. Louvre, Paris.

audience of other painters of similar persuasion and the poets put down their inspirations principally for the eyes and ears of other poets. They thus led the insecure lives of an underprivileged social group and tended to band together in desperate little societies within society. In general, however, the artists turned toward the new world of the great city for their material and inspiration. The artificial replaced the natural, and urban entertainments eclipsed the delights of nature. The usual was dominant over the unusual, and the here-and-now was definitely in ascendance over the there-and-then.

Neoclassical and romantic artists had been quite as willing as their successors to use the new technological processes for the distribution of their pictures, poetry, novels, and musical compositions in order to reach as wide an audience as possible. And even the most ardent advocates of ancient and medieval glories had, on occasion, emerged from the past to participate in then-present events. David had portrayed Revolutionary incidents in his *Oath of the Tennis Court,* and in the stark horror of his *Death of Marat* (Fig. 542). Delacroix' *Massacre at Scio (Chios)* had brought the Greek struggle for independence to a large audience, just as his *Liberty Leading the People* (Plate 46) had dramatized the Revolution of 1830.

An artist far ahead of his time was Théodore Géricault whose *Raft of the Medusa* (Fig. 543) created a furor when first exhibited in the Salon of 1819. Taking his subject from a recent disaster at sea, Géricault told the tale of the shipwrecked sailors of the French merchant marine whose vessel had foundered off the African coast without lifeboats or other safety provisions. From the flotsam and jetsam the hapless men fashioned a raft and floated for days on end without food and water until rescued by the ship seen on the horizon. To heighten this incident of suffering, insanity, starvation, and even cannibalism, Géricault interviewed the few survivors, studied madmen in asylums, sketched dying men in hospitals, and the dead in morgues. The artist was as much interested in creating a social document designed to remedy an intolerable situation as he was in painting a great work of art. The storm of criticism the picture stirred up was almost as furious as the tempest that wrecked the *Medusa*. "This is not art," cried the academicians, "it is life."

PAINTING

About the middle of the 19th century, the most important younger painters rejected romantic flights of the imagination and academic glorifications of the heroic past. Gustave Courbet was in the vanguard of those who styled themselves "realists," defined painting as a physical language, and ruled out the metaphysical and invisible. The saints and miracles of the 19th century, according to Courbet, were mines, machines, and railroad stations. With a keen eye and a desire to record accurately what he saw about him, Courbet consciously set out to build an art on the commonplace. His painting was concerned with the present, not the past; with the momentary, not the permanent; with bodies, not souls; with materiality, not spirituality. His nudes suggested no nymphs or goddesses; they were merely the models who posed in his studio. The villagers attending the *Burial at Ornans* (Fig. 544) are there out of a sense of duty. The priest routinely reads the committal service, and the gravedigger casually waits to complete his job. No one betrays any great grief, and the skull and bone at the grave's edge add a realistic rather than a macabre touch. Courbet, however, sometimes became almost as passionate about the ugly as his predecessors had about the beautiful. Both Courbet and his younger colleague Édouard Manet, who came under his influence, were sometimes betrayed into an emotional interest in their subjects in spite of themselves; at times they even tried to induce shock reactions in their audiences much in the manner of the novelists Balzac and Dickens.

Only occasionally did Courbet venture beyond the bounds of the immediate material world as in *The Artist's Studio*, subtitled *A Real Allegory Summarizing a Phase of My Artistic Life that Lasted Seven Years* (Fig. 545). From his own fragmentary comments on this paradoxical "real allegory," several layers of meaning can be read. It is realistic in the sense of being an autobiography on canvas, a personal document derived from his travel sketches, pictorial subjects, and attitudes

544. GUSTAVE COURBET. *Burial at Ornans.* 1849. Oil on canvas, 10′ 3″ × 20′ 10″. Louvre, Paris.

545. GUSTAVE COURBET. *The Artist's Studio*. 1854–1855. Oil on canvas, 11′ 10″ × 19′ 7″. Louvre, Paris.

toward art during seven productive years. The grouping of the lifesize figures suggests the flow of time mirrored in Courbet's past, present, and future. On the left, as he explained, he placed all the negative forces, or "those who deal in death"— a hunter and peasant from his native village Ornans, an undertaker's assistant, a Catholic priest, a Jew he had sketched in London, the crucified thief on the cross, a discarded dagger and guitar symbolizing romantic poetry, a skull resting on a copy of *Le Journal des Débats*, and the faces of those burdened by the miseries of life. On the right are "the people who live on life"—his Parisian contemporaries, including two lovers, the seated critic Champfleury, his patroness and patron, the social philosopher Proudhon, and the poet Baudelaire (extreme right). Behind Courbet, seated at his easel and painting one of his numerous landscapes, is an enigmatic undraped woman, who may be his model, his realistic muse, a personification of Nature, or the Naked Truth. Looking up at the landscape in the making is a boy, "the Innocent eye" that can appraise without prejudice, the audience of the future.

The artists that followed Courbet sought for even greater closeness to nature in order to develop an art based on immediacy of expression. They took their easels out of doors and tried to do as much of their painting on the spot as possible rather than to work in their studios from sketches. They were against painting a picture that carried any

moral, any message, or any literary associations whatsoever, and they cultivated a calculated indifference toward pictorial content. Optical realism was pursued to the point of separating visual experience from memory and avoiding any associations the mind normally calls into play. In 1874, Claude Monet exhibited a picture called *Impression—Sunrise*, which gave the new movement its name. At first, *impressionism* was picked up as a term of critical derision. The word has remained, and it does have a certain appropriateness, implying the unfinished, the incomplete, an affair of the moment, an act of instantaneous vision, a sensation rather than a cognition.

It is impossible, of course, to substantiate any claim of a direct cause-and-effect relationship between science and art in this period or any formal connection between optical physics and painting. It is equally impossible to state that painters were unaware of or indifferent to such things as the invention of the camera, the scientific discoveries about the nature of light, and the new knowledge about the physiology of the eye. Joint researches of Daguerre and Niepce on the making of photographic images on prepared metal plates, which resulted in the daguerreotype process, had been published as early as 1839. The revelation that visual imagery was primarily dependent on minute gradations of light intensities was bound to have an effect on painting. Physicists, including Helmholtz, made discoveries about the component prismatic parts of white light, and pointed out that the sensation of color has more to do with a retinal reaction in the eye than with objects themselves. The color wheel also demonstrated that two separate hues of a wheel at rest are fused by the eye into a third hue when the wheel is in rapid motion. And when all the colors of the spectrum are rotated, the eye sees them as tending toward white.

Painters also did some speculation of their own on the nature of the visual experience. Form and space, they reasoned, are not actually seen but implied from varying intensities of light and color. Objects are not so much entities in themselves as they are agents for the absorption and refraction of light. Hard outlines, indeed lines themselves, do not exist in nature. Shadows, they maintained, are not black but tend to take on a color complementary to that of the objects that cast them. The concern of the painter, they concluded, should therefore be with light and color more than with objects and substances. A painting should consist of a breakdown of sunlight into its component parts, and brilliance should be achieved by the use of the primary colors that make up the spectrum. Instead of greens mixed by the painter on his palette, separate daubs of yellow and blue should be placed close together and the mixing left to the spectator's eye. What seems confusion at close range is clarified at the proper distance. By thus trying to step up the luminosity of their canvases so as to convey the illusion of sunlight sifted through a prism, they achieved a veritable carnival of color in which the eye seems to join in a dance of vibrating light intensities. As a result of this reexamination of their technical procedures, the impressionists discovered a new method of visual representation. Since, however, it was concerned so exclusively with the world of appearances, impressionism was more the ultimate phase of realism than a new style in itself.

Édouard Manet painted *Rue de Berne* (Fig. 546) late in his career with the impressionistic theory in mind. In it, he builds a cityscape out of a configuration of interrelated planes. By his subtle use of color intensities more than by linear perspective, he achieves the effect of recession and depth. In other versions of this scene, he painted some road menders in the foreground, and his choice of such a casual street scene is in keeping with the general preference for subjects that can be taken in at a glance rather than those that must be studied carefully and in detail. It also exemplifies the conscious cultivation of the accidental—the random scene in which emotional involvement with the subject is impossible.

Manet's last large-scale work, *Bar at the Folies-Bergère* (Plate 49), is a technical tour de force of major magnitude. At first glance the viewer him-

546. ÉDOUARD MANET. *Rue de Berne*. 1878. Oil on canvas, 25 ½ × 31 ½". Collection Paul Mellon.

self would seem to be the customer the barmaid is waiting to serve, but her client apparently is the top-hatted, goateed gentleman who is seen in mirror image behind the girl's reflection at the upper left. For correctness the maid would have to stand almost sidewise to cast such a reflection, but with poetic license Manet lets her face forward. The composition is tightly structured, with the double image of the pensive waitress and the bottles of the stunning still life in the foreground defining the vertical rise, and the marble counter at the picture plane, the table behind, and the mirrored ledge of the balcony taking care of the horizontal balance. The Bohemian scene is bathed in garish gaslight, glints of which are caught by the crystal chandeliers, assorted bottles, the vase and compote dish, and the balcony scene reflected in the shimmering expanse of the mirror. Except for the barmaid, all the figures are suggested rather than defined. With a few bold strokes Manet creates girls with opera glasses, ladies in colorful costumes, bearded men in stove-pipe hats, and above all captures the mood of an evening's diversion.

Renoir, Manet's younger contemporary, had already painted a similar scene set in a popular outdoor Paris café, *Le Moulin de la Galette* (Plate 50), that had been shown in the 1877 impressionist exhibit. The full force of impressionistic color is felt in the rainbow of brilliant hues, especially the variations of blue, and the marvelous quality of filtered sunlight that Renoir had at his command.

His obvious intention was to evoke the atmosphere of carefree gaiety and the whirling movement of the dance, as well as to revel sensuously in an intangible world of color and light.

More than any other painter, Claude Monet was the central figure of impressionism, and his picture the *Old St. Lazare Station* (Fig. 547) is among his most typical works. The rendering of the humid atmosphere, the mixture of steam and smoke, the hazy sunlight filtering in from the open background and the transparent roof, the contrast between the open spaces and the closed forms of the engines and railroad cars are the things that concern him most.

There is no hustle and bustle, no drama of arriving or departing people, no crowds or excitement, no interplay of men and machines, such as one might expect in such a setting. Instead, his people merely file from the waiting room toward the train, and the workmen go about their tasks in a matter-of-fact way. The picture therefore becomes an atmospheric study in blues and greens.

The full development of Monet's broken-color technique is even more clearly discernible in the *Garden at Giverny* (Fig. 548), his suburban home. In it, he breaks his light up into a spectrum of bright colors that delights the eye by forming shimmering

547. CLAUDE MONET. *Old St. Lazare Station*. 1877. Oil on canvas, 23 ½ × 31 ½". Art Institute of Chicago.

548. CLAUDE MONET. *Garden at Giverny*. c. 1899. Oil on canvas, 35 × 39". Art Institute of Chicago.

patterns in and around the leaves and lilies. Water imagery repeatedly recurs in impressionistic painting. Its iridescence, its fluidity, its surface reflections, the perpetual play of changing light, make water ideal for conveying the conception of the insubstantial, impermanent, fleeting nature of visual experience. Figure 548 is but one of many versions Monet painted of the same subject, and his method of work reveals that the objects he painted were of less concern than the light and atmosphere surrounding them. In order to capture the moment he wanted, he would take up in a single day a succession of canvases—one showing the garden at dawn, another in full morning light, and a third in a late-afternoon glow. The following morning he would take up the dawn scene where he had left off the day before and, when the light changed, set it aside for the next canvas, and so on. With scientific detachment, he tried to maintain the constancy of his subject matter by painting series of *Haystacks*, *Rouen Cathedral*, and *Old St. Lazare Station*, so as to focus the interest on the variables of light and atmosphere. Each version varies according to the season, day, or hour. Monet might even be called the "weather man" of painting were it not that, in spite of himself, his genuine involvement with nature usually overcame his objective detachment. As Cézanne one remarked: "Monet, he's only an eye, but my God what an eye!"

Impressionism is clearly an art of the urban man who sees himself in terms of temporal flow, mounting tensions, and sudden change. His volatile life is ruled by impermanent rather than permanent forces, and becoming is more real to him than being. Impressionistic painters purposely chose everyday subjects, such as street scenes, children at play, and life in a night café. When they did go to the country, it was to the suburbs in the manner of city folk on a holiday. As a result, the general effect of impressionist painting is bright, cheerful, and lighthearted rather than heavy or somber. The artists were intoxicated by light rather than life, and they saw the world as a myriad of mirrors that refracted a constantly changing kaleidoscope of color and varying intensities of light. They lived therefore in a visual world of reflections rather than substances, and one in which visual values replaced the tactile. To reproduce the fugitive atmospheric effects the impressionists desired, they had to work directly from nature. This led to a speeding up in the process of painting to a point where working with oils approached the more rapid technique of watercolor. The criticism of hasty work and careless craftsmanship that the impressionists incurred from their contemporaries was sometimes quite justified. But when their intentions are fully taken into account, one finds no lack of technical skill on the part of the style's most important practitioners. They wanted their paintings to seem spontaneous and to have an improvised, fragmentary look. Beauty, like color, they felt was in the eye of the beholder, not in the picture itself. They intended to paint not so much what is seen but how it is seen. Instead of composing, which implies a placing together, they sought to isolate one aspect of experience and explore it to the utmost. Their art therefore becomes one of analysis more than synthesis, sensation more than perception, sight more than insight. As such the cool objectivity of impressionism represents the triumph of technique over expression.

In their total immersion in the two-dimensional world of appearances, the impressionists consciously neglected the other dimensions of psychological depth and emotional involvement. As a consequence, they soon began to chafe under the arbitrary restrictions of such a limited theory. Nor were their audiences happy with the role of innocent bystander they had been assigned. Both artist and spectator had, in effect, resigned the active role for that of the aloof observer of life who lets the river of experience go by without attempting to divert its flow in any significant direction. In scarcely more than a dozen years after Monet had shown his *Impression—Sunrise*, the movement had lost its momentum. Even though no one painted an *Impression—Sunset* to commemorate the event, impressionism in its pristine form was at an end, to all intents and purposes, with the last impressionist exhibit in 1886. Many of the discoveries that had been made, however, survived in variously modified forms in the work of the postimpressionist painters.

Sunday Afternoon on the Island of La Grande Jatte (Plate 51) by Georges Seurat shows how the impressionistic theory was carried to a logical, almost mathematical, conclusion. Light, shadow, and color are still the major concerns, and the subject is also that of an urban scene, this time of a relaxed group of middle-class Parisians on a Sunday outing. Instead of informal casual arrangements, however, everything here seems as set as an old-fashioned family portrait. Instead of misty nebulous forms, such details as a bustle, a parasol, or a plug hat are as stylized and geometrical as in a Renaissance fresco. Instead of improvising his pictures out of doors, Seurat carefully composed his large canvas in his studio over a period of years. Instead of hastily painted patches of broken color, Seurat worked out a system called *pointillism* by which thousands of dots of uniform size were applied to the canvas in such a calculated and painstaking way that the most subtle tints were brought under the painter's control. The whole picture, moreover, was subdivided into areas, and a scheme of grad-

549. VINCENT VAN GOGH. *Père Tanguy*. 1887–1888. Oil on canvas, 25 ½ × 20″. Private collection.

uating shades blended tonalities into one another to achieve an over-all tonal unity.

Vincent van Gogh's *Starry Night* (Plate 52) demonstrates how colors can be used to achieve intensely expressive effects. The deep purple sky, the yellow light of the stars, the green upward-curling silhouette of the cypress tree all stem from impressionism. Broken color, however, has here become a myriad of dark swirling vertiginous lines used as a means toward revealing an inner ecstatic vision. The many portraits Van Gogh painted are among the most discerning in the history of this art. *Père Tanguy* (Fig. 549) is a warm and penetrating portrayal of the art-supply dealer who had befriended both Van Gogh and Cézanne in their Paris days, and who sold the Japanese prints that had inspired Van Gogh and his contemporaries, one of whom was Paul Gauguin. In *Mahana No Atua*, or *Day of the God* (Plate 53), Gauguin also shows how the brilliant color of the impressionists can be adapted to make quiet two-dimensional decorative designs.

In the 1870's, Paul Cézanne was using the prismatic color palette of the impressionists, but he soon discovered the expressive limitations of the theory. His solution of some of the pictorial problems it posed became a turning point in the history of painting. For him, the superficial beauty of impressionism did not provide the firm base on which to build a significant art. The delight in the transitory tended too much to exclude the more permanent values. Instead of severing connections with the past, he said that he wanted "to make of impressionism something solid like the art of the museums." Poussin was the old master he chose to emulate, and his expressed desire was to re-create Poussin in the light of nature. The cultivation of instantaneous vision, according to Cézanne, ruled out the participation of too many other important faculties. His pictures, unlike those of the impressionists, were not meant to be grasped immediately, and their meaning is never obvious. For Cézanne, painting should be not only an act of the eye but also of the mind. If painting aimed only at the senses, any deeper probing of human psychology would be eliminated. Light is important in itself, but it can also be used to achieve inner illumination. Color as such is paramount, but color is also a means of describing masses and volumes, revealing form, creating relationships, separating space into planes, and producing the illusion of projection and recession. Primary colors produce brilliance, but judicious mixtures can run a whole gamut of subtle effects. Cézanne, therefore, retained both light and color as the basis of his art, but not to the extent of eliminating the need for line and geometrical organization. Cézanne's interests are not so much in the specific as in the general. Analysis is necessary for simplification and to reduce a picture to its bare essentials, but for Cézanne composition and synthesis are still the primary processes of the pictorial art. His canvases therefore tend to be more austere than voluptuous, more sinuous than lush. His pictures have order, repose, and a serene color harmony, yet they are capable of rising to high points of tension and grandeur. In one landscape everything is cool and shadowy; in another the heat of the southern sun seems almost to burn the canvas.

The forms Cézanne chose were from his daily experience—apples, mountains, houses, trees—constants by which it is possible to measure the extent of his spiritual growth. "You must paint them to tame them," he once remarked. Mont Ste. Victoire, a rising rocky mass near his home in Aix-en-Provence, was for Cézanne a recurring motif. Just as Goethe wrote his *Faust* throughout his entire creative career, so Cézanne painted his mountain again and again until it became a kind of symbol of his ambitions and aspirations. The contrast of an early and a late version provides an interesting index to his artistic growth. The first *Mont Ste. Victoire*, subtitled *Landscape with Via-*

duct (Fig. 550), dates between 1885 and 1887. Another version with no subtitle (Fig. 551) was done between 1904 and 1906. Both are landscapes organized into a pattern of planes by means of color. Both show his way of achieving perspective not by converging lines but by intersecting and overlapping planes of color. In the first version, there is a complementary balance between the vertical rise of the trees and the horizontal line of the viaduct. In the second, these details are omitted, and a balance is achieved between the dense-green foliage of the lower foreground and the purple and light-green jagged mass of the mountain in the background. In the earlier, the mountain descends in a series of gently sloping lines; in the later, it plunges precipitously downward. In the former, such details as the road, houses, and shrubs are readily recognizable. In the latter, all is reduced to the barest essentials, and only such formal contours as the cones, cubes, and slanting surfaces remain. Both pictures, however, are landscapes interpreted by the same sensitive and highly individual temper-

550. PAUL CÉZANNE. *Mont Ste. Victoire*. 1885–1887. Oil on canvas, 25 ³/₈ × 31 ⁷/₈″. Metropolitan Museum of Art, New York.

551. PAUL CÉZANNE. *Mont Ste. Victoire*. 1904–1906. Oil on canvas, 27 ⁷/₈ × 36 ¹/₈″. Philadelphia Museum of Art (George W. Elkins Collection).

487

ament. Both show Cézanne's lifelong desire to mold nature into a coherent pattern in order to unite the inanimate world of things and the animate world of the human mind.

In such a still life as *Basket of Apples* (Plate 54), Cézanne, like Chardin before him (see Plate 42), works in a more intimate vein. The search for pure formal values, however, still continues. In one of his letters, he remarked that nature reveals itself in the forms of the cylinder, the sphere, and the cone. Here his cylinders are the horizontally arranged biscuits, his spheres the apples, and his cone the vertically rising bottle. They are balanced in this case by the forward-tilting ellipse of the basket and the receding plane of the tabletop. An almost imperceptible feeling of diagonal motion is induced by the distribution of the fruit from the upper left to the lower right, which is brought to an equally imperceptible stop by means of the pear-shaped apple at the extreme right. Such a simple geometrical arrangement of familiar forms imparts a feeling of comfort as well as one of order and clarity. Cézanne painted these still-life compositions so slowly and carefully that he usually found it necessary to use artificial flowers and fruits so that he could study their arrangement for weeks at a time. While he treats his cones and cubes as abstractions, his warm color saves them from frigidity, and he never fails to relate them in a subtle and expressive way to living forms.

Cézanne never overlooked the human values in his art, and the stolid peasants he found in the cafés of his native Provence often served him as models. His *Card Players* (Fig. 552) are every bit as impassive and monumental in their way as are his mountains. They are posed with the same stability and equilibrium as his still lifes; and their lines, volumes, masses, and textures are conceived with the same simplicity as one of his landscapes.

Cézanne set himself such severe limitations that his pictures fall mainly within the classifications of landscapes, still life, figure compositions, and portraits. Even within these categories, he kept his themes constant so that each picture could be a separate experiment. By such means he tried to bring form and stability into a visual world where everything was change and transition. If he succeeded only at times and failed at others, each result must be equated with the immensity of the task that he set for himself. Like all great masters, he realized in his mature years that he had made only a beginning, and he once remarked that he would forever be the primitive of the method he had discovered. His historical position may indeed be just this, but his work may be said to form the bridge between impressionism and modern painting.

552. PAUL CÉZANNE. *Card Players. c.* 1890–1892. Oil on canvas, 25 ½ × 32″. Collection Stephen C. Clark, New York.

553. AUGUSTE RODIN. *The Bronze Age.* 1876. Bronze, 5′11″ high. Rodin Museum, Paris.

SCULPTURE

Among the sculptural exhibits at the Paris Salon of 1877 was a statue of a nude youth entitled *The Bronze Age* (Fig. 553). Too lifelike, said the academic critics. Too good, thought his fellow sculptors as they started rumors that Auguste Rodin was trying to pass off a statue taken directly from plaster casts of a living model. In official quarters the gossip was given sufficient credence to cause the hasty withdrawal of the work. To refute one and all, Rodin had casts and photographs made of the model who had posed for him, and the following year, with official explanations and apologies *The Bronze Age* was again on exhibition. A short while later it was bought by the state for placement in the Luxembourg Gardens. Such was the gulf, however, between art and life, between a monument and a

reality, that in academic circles a statue which looked too real, too lifelike, or natural was considered a disgrace.

Like his forward-looking contemporaries in other fields, Rodin had veered away from the heroic toward the natural. Although he admired Gothic sculpture and wrote a book about French cathedrals, his work contains few sermons in stone. Though he admired Dante and drew almost all his later subjects from an early project for the *Gates of Hell* (Fig. 554), his conceptions show little of the escapism that motivated his immediate predecessors. Intended as door panels for a projected building to house the Paris Museum of Decorative Arts, Rodin's gates had as their points of departure the portals of the Florence Baptistry, notably Ghiberti's *Gates of Paradise* (Plate 18), and the writhing nudes of Michelangelo's *Last Judgment* (Fig. 366). The literary source was an odd combination of Dante and Baudelaire. "Dante is not only a visionary but a sculptor," wrote Rodin. "His expression is lapidary in the good sense of the word." Above the actual doors broods the Michelangelesque figure of *The Thinker*—man, not Christ, is here to judge. Rodin's figures are bodies not souls, his damned suffer more from sensuous than spiritual

554. AUGUSTE RODIN. *Gates of Hell.* 1880–1917. Bronze, 18′ high, 12′ wide, 33″ deep. Rodin Museum, Philadelphia.

longings. Most details were worked out between 1880 and 1887, except for readjustments that went on until 1917. *The Thinker*, Rodin's best-known work, and *Three Shades* (p. 477), *Adam*, and *Eve*, three of Rodin's later large-scale sculptures, were derived from the original germ cell of his inspiration for the *Gates of Hell*.

For Rodin, the process of forming supersedes that of form itself. The *Hand of God* (Fig. 555) exemplifies this, both in the method of execution and in the subject itself. Out of an indefinite mass of uncut stone, symbolic of the formless void, the hand of the Creator arises. Divine omnipotence is suggested by the scale of the hand in relation to that of the human figures which are emerging from a lump of uncarved marble. The significance of the work was caught by the philosopher Henri Bergson, author of *Creative Evolution*, who called it "the fleeting moment of creation, which never stops." It is the implication that nothing is ever quite complete, that everything takes place in the flow of time, that matter is the womb which is continuously giving birth, that creation is a never-ending process rather than an accomplished fact—in short, the acceptance of the theory and philosophy of evolution—which gives Rodin's conception its daring quality.

Rodin always acknowledges his material frankly, seeks neither to disguise it nor to escape from it, and creates the feeling that his figures are just emerging out of their original stone or clay state. This is not, however, the mighty Michelangelesque struggle of man against his material bonds. Rather it is a sensuous love of material as such, a reveling in the flesh or stone, and a desire to explore all its possibilities and potentialities. If Michelangelo left his figures incomplete and still dominated by their material medium, it was largely because circumstances prevented his finishing them. With Rodin, the incompleteness is a conscious and calculated part of his expressive design. Like the symbolist poets, the novelist Proust, and the dramatist Maeterlinck, Rodin went one step beyond mere description. For Rodin, as for his literary contemporaries, events were nothing in themselves. Only when conjured up later in memory did they acquire the necessary subjective coloration; and only then, paradoxically, could the artist treat them with the needed objective detachment.

Rodin always preferred to work from a memory image rather than directly from a model in the flesh. When he did work with a model, it was

(above) 555. AUGUSTE RODIN. *Hand of God.* 1898. Marble, 29″ high. Rodin Museum, Paris.

(left) 556. AUGUSTE RODIN. *The Kiss.* 1896. Marble, lifesize. Rodin Museum, Philadelphia.

usually to make a quick sketch, a wash drawing, or an impression in wax or soft clay. He could then allow his figures to take plastic shape in this preliminary stage at the moment of inspiration and thus to promote the feeling that they were products of improvisation. The process of transferring his figures into marble or bronze was left until the forms had been refined in memory and had assumed a more subjective and personal quality.

Rodin defined sculpture as an art of hollows and projections, or the hole and the lump, a sculptural equivalent of architecture's void and mass. Light and shadow thus become the principal means of animating his material. His figures do not displace volume so much as they cast shadows, and they seem to exist more in time than in space. His choice of subjects also reveals this preoccupation with the transitory: *The Kiss* (Fig. 556), *The Dream, Fugit Amor, The Wave, Dawn, Twilight, Night and Day*. The surface play of light and his greater concern with the atmosphere which envelops his forms than with the figures themselves link Rodin's art with that of the impressionist painters. His intentions are so close to those of pictorial art that it sometimes seems that oil and canvas would have been the proper medium for his transitory and impermanent visions. Through memory and introspection, however, Rodin was able to give his compositions some three-dimensional plausibility, and by the projection of psychological depth into his work, he raised his art above the commonplace.

ARCHITECTURE

Throughout the 19th century there was a sharp division of thought about the work of an architect. Was he primarily an artist or a builder? A designer or engineer? Should he concern himself more with decoration or with structure? Was his place in a studio making drawings or in the field working with his materials? The champions of the pictorial viewpoint achieved such virtuosity that at practically a moment's notice they could produce on their drawing boards a design based on any known building from the past. Late in the century, all the historical styles had been so carefully catalogued and documented that the range of choices was almost unlimited. What had begun as the revival of special periods had now been broadened to include all. The term for such a freedom of choice is *eclecticism*, and if a name is to be chosen for the architectural style of the period this is the only one possible. The sole limitation on this eclecticism was the generally accepted appropriateness of the styles of certain periods to special situations. The classical was considered best for commemorative buildings and monuments, but classicism now could be anything from Mycenaean Greek to late imperial Roman. Medieval was the preference for churches, but this might mean Byzantine, Romanesque, early or late Gothic. For public buildings, Renaissance was thought most suitable, though here again the choice could be from the 15th century on.

The industrial age, however, had produced new methods and materials that opened up novel possibilities. The potentialities of cast iron, for example, had been perceived by engineers and industrialists long before architects began to speculate on the creative applications it could make to their art. The structural use of iron actually dates from the latter part of the 18th century, although at first it was found in bridges, cotton mills, and other utilitarian buildings, where it usually was combined with brick, stone, or timber or else used as a substitute for one or more of them. Nevertheless, the first steps toward a revolution in the art of building had been taken. The century was eventually to see the spanning of broader widths, the enclosure of more cubic space, and projections toward greater heights than had hitherto been thought possible. The new materials and structural principles were both a threat and challenge to the traditional pictorial designers, and the more they were incorporated into building plans, the more progressive architecture became.

It has already been noted how iron columns and girders had been used quite openly by John Nash in the exotic Brighton Pavilion (Figs. 536, 537), marking one of the first instances of their use in a large residential building. In Paris, François Gau had used iron girders masked with stone facings to reinforce his Gothic-revival Church of Ste. Clotilde (Fig. 526). Now Henri Labrouste, with an even more penetrating insight into the possibilities of the new material at his command, went one step farther in his Library of Ste. Geneviève. A first glance at its exterior (Fig. 557) reveals simply a well-executed Renaissance-revival building—as such it is indebted to a 15th-century Italian church in Rimini designed by Alberti—with the usual festoons of garlands adorning the space above its seriate windows. A closer inspection, however, shows that the ground floor is conceived as a solid space, while the bold arcade of windows above gives promise of light and air within. Since the building is a library, there is a working relationship between the closed storage space for the books below and the open reading room above. This is as far as the exterior goes toward a unity of means and ends, however, and the stone on the outside gives no hint that the interior is constructed of iron.

By utilizing the strength of metal, Labrouste was able to replace the massive masonry ordinarily

557. HENRI LABROUSTE. Library of Ste. Geneviève, Paris. 1843–1850. 336' long.

558. HENRI LABROUSTE. Reading Room, Library of Ste. Geneviève, Paris. 1843–1850. 330 × 66', 42' high.

required for such a large reading room (Fig. 558) and at the same time provide for a maximum of open space and brilliant illumination. The room is vaulted with two series of arches made of cast iron, supported by tall, thin, fluted cast-iron columns, which form two parallel barrel vaults. An open foliated pattern related to the classical acanthus leaf is used as a decorative motif, and the vaults are supported by tall, thin, fluted Corinthian colonettes, also made of iron. Labrouste thus managed his material so that he brought out its full structural possibilities. But by allowing his iron colonettes to assume a form associated with carved stone, he compromised with tradition and let the expressive potentialities lag somewhat behind.

What Labrouste began in the Library of Ste. Geneviève, he brought to a brilliant fulfillment in

his later masterwork, the stacks of the Bibliothèque Nationale (Fig. 559). This storage space for books is conceived as the very heart of the library, and it is now brought out into the open alongside the reading room itself. Though closed to the public, a full view of it is obtained through a glass-enclosed archway. All superfluous ornamentation is omitted in favor of the function for which it was designed. Except for the bookcases and the glass ceiling, everything is of cast iron. By dividing his space into five stories, four above and one below the ground level, Labrouste provided for the housing of about a million volumes. The floors are of open grillwork, which permits a free flow of light to reach all levels. Frequent stairways provide rapid communication between floors, and the strategically placed bridges allow freedom of access between the two wings. As

Plate 52. VINCENT VAN GOGH. *Starry Night.* 1889. Oil on canvas, 29 × 36 ½".
Museum of Modern Art, New York (acquired through the Lillie P. Bliss Bequest). (See p. 486.)

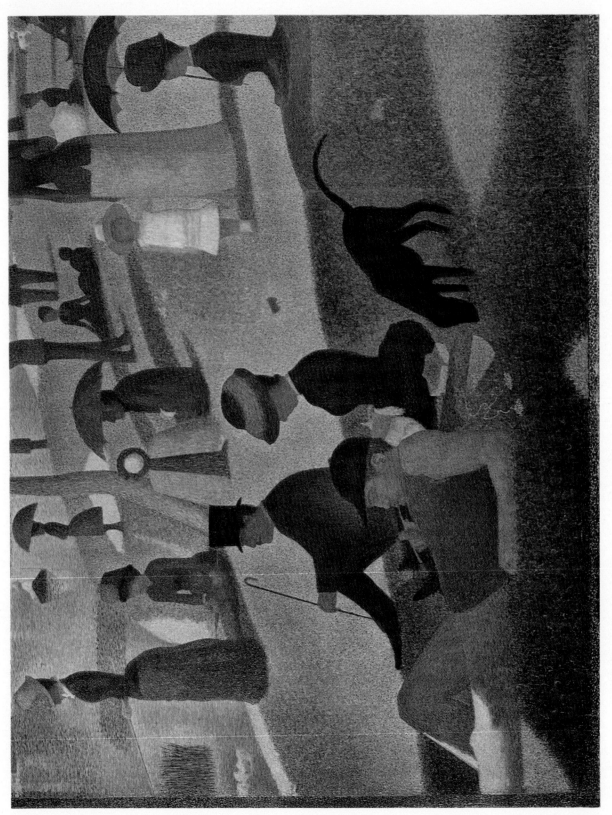

Plate 51. GEORGES SEURAT. *Sunday Afternoon on the Island of La Grande Jatte* (detail). 1884–1886. Oil on canvas, 6'9" × 10'6". Art Institute of Chicago. (See p. 485.)

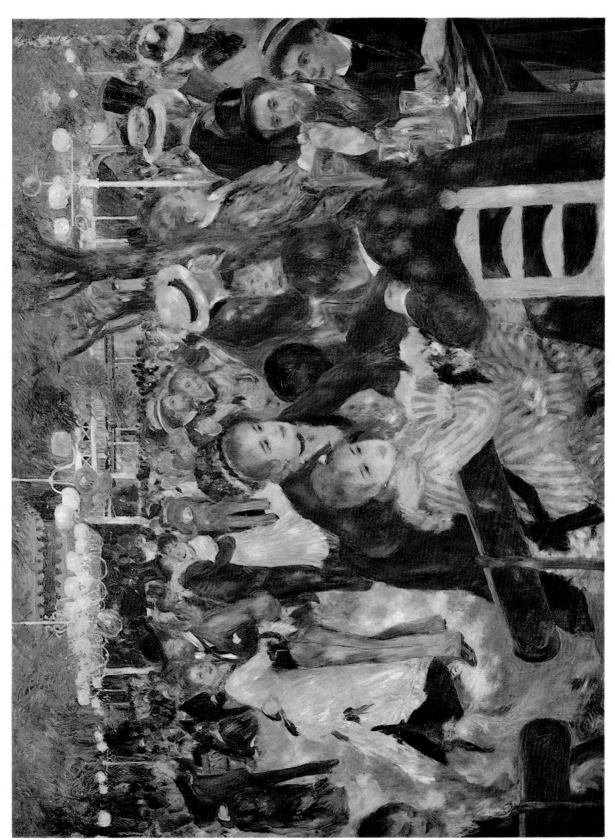

Plate 50. AUGUSTE RENOIR. *Le Moulin de la Galette.* 1876. Oil on canvas, 4′3 ½″ × 5′9″.
Louvre, Paris. (See p. 483.)

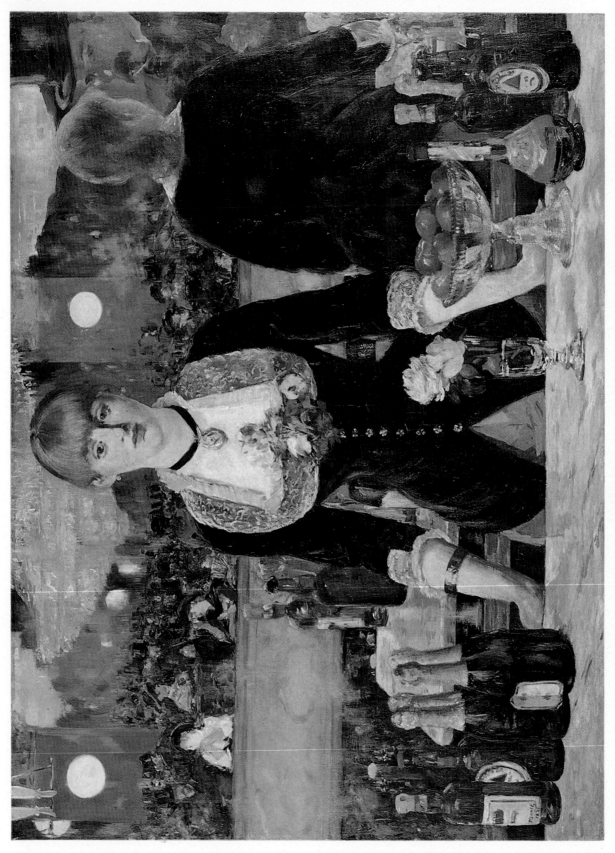

Plate 49. Édouard Manet. *Bar at the Folies-Bergère.* 1881–1882. Oil on canvas, 37 ½ × 51″. Courtauld Institute Galleries, London. (See p. 483.)

a composition, they present a pleasing visual pattern of vertical and horizontal intersecting planes. In both these libraries, it is evident that Labrouste has taken a bold stride toward the realization of the potentialities of the modern materials and that his work as a whole represents a positive contribution to the development of a new architecture.

The same year that Labrouste was completing his first library, a new and original structure was going up in London that made no pretensions whatsoever of being either a Roman bath or a Renaissance palace. The London *Times* referred to it as Mr. Paxton's "monstrous greenhouse"; and, to be sure, it was conceived and carried out by a landscape gardener skilled in the construction of conservatories and nurseries. The occasion was the Great Exhibition of the Works of Industry of All Nations, where the latest mechanical inventions as well as raw materials were to be brought together with the finished products of industry. Machinery of all sorts was to take its place beside the manufactured arts and crafts that were being turned out by the new factories. The Crystal Palace (Fig. 560) that Joseph Paxton constructed to house the exposition was destined to eclipse the exhibits themselves and to find for itself a unique place in the history of modern architecture. His light and airy structure was rectangular in shape, 408 feet in width and—with a neat bit of symbolism to coincide with the year of the exhibition—1,851 feet in length. It rose by means of a skeleton of cast-iron girders and wrought-iron trusses and supports, all bolted together with mathematical precision. Its walls and roof enclosed 33 million cubic feet of space in a transparent sheath of glass. The rapidity of its construction was no less remarkable than its form. Previously, the whole structure had been accurately analyzed into a multiplicity of prefabricated parts, and so well planned was it that 18,000 panes of glass were put in place by 80 workmen in one week. Begun the end of September, 1850, it was easily ready for the grand opening, May 1, 1851.

Contrary to expectations, the Crystal Palace turned out to be a thing of surprising beauty and brilliance, as inexpensive in its construction as it was daring in its use of materials. No applied decoration of any sort marred the forthright character of the exterior. And while the iron columns of the interior paid lip service to their classical ancestors, the enormous scale made such details incidental.

560. JOSEPH PAXTON. Crystal Palace, London. 1851. Cast iron and glass, 1,851' wide. Lithograph.

At the inauguration ceremonies (Fig. 561), Albert, the Prince Consort, stood by a crystal fountain and restated the purpose of the exhibition: to present "a living picture of the point of development at which the whole of mankind had arrived,... and a new starting point from which all nations will be able to direct their further exertions." Nothing seemed impossible to the machine age, and the engineers were indeed the prophets of the new order. Everything now seemed set for Victorian man to step out of his self-created pseudo-Gothic gloom into the new and shining age of industrial prosperity. Mr. Paxton and his greenhouse, however, had to wait more than half a century before the architects fully caught up with them.

Back across the Channel meanwhile, Georges-Eugène Haussmann was replanning the city of Paris on a scale commensurate with its growth into one of the first great 19th-century industrial cities. The new method of cast-iron construction, the need for wide and long streets to facilitate the flow of traffic, and the accessibility of railroad stations were all taken into account in his designs. If the taste of his patron, Napoleon III, ran somewhat to festoons of floral garlands and bulbous terracotta statuary, these were only a camouflage for the really fundamental changes that were going on beneath the surface. The expositions devoted to the wonders of modern industry, which were held at regular intervals, reached a climax in the International Exhibition of 1889. Its Gallery of Machines, by employing steel and glass, achieved a span of 375 feet, the widest ever made up to that time. Even more spectacular, however, was the tower (Fig. 562) that soared more than 1,000 feet above ground. Gustave Eiffel, an engineer who had made his reputation in bridges and industrial buildings,

was entrusted with a contract for this unprecedented structure, which he conceived as a bridge into the sky. It was to be built by means of an assembly of small machine-manufactured parts riveted together with precision down to a tenth of a millimeter. In just 17 months, Eiffel was able to boast that he had engineered a structure that would stand forever against earth, wind, and weather.

From its four foundation members, the Eiffel Tower makes a series of three spectacular upward leaps to a platform 984 feet above the ground, where all of its elegant lines converge. A lantern then carries the height still farther to a point more than 1,000 feet in the sky. A spiral staircase and a system of elevators corresponding to the above stages allow visitors to mount as far as the base of the lantern. Except for a few nonfunctional decorations about the base, Eiffel's design resulted in a masterpiece of structural integrity and honest use of material. Before it was built, however, a violent protest in the form of a petition had been received by the exposition authorities. "We the writers, painters, sculptors, and architects," it began, "come in the name of French good taste and of this menace to French history to express our deep indignation that there should stand in the heart of our capital this unnecessary and monstrous Eiffel Tower." What was to have been but a temporary exhibition building, however, turned out to be such a rousing success that it was assured a permanent place in the Parisian scheme of things. Uses quite unanticipated at the time it was built were subsequently found. Successively and simultaneously, it has served as a lookout point, a weather observation post, a beacon tower for air traffic, a radio tower, and a television transmission station. It was at once the prototype of the modern steel skyscraper and a symbol of the modern metropolis.

562. GUSTAVE EIFFEL. Eiffel Tower, Paris. 1889. 984′ high to base of lantern.

LITERATURE AND MUSIC

The desire on the part of writers to come to terms with their own world rather than to explore the avenues of escape was responsible for the literary movements known as realism and naturalism. In some cases, writers cultivated a kinship with the scientific materialism that dominated the thought of the period following the February Revolution of 1848. In others, notably with Zola and Ibsen, they allied themselves with sociology and wrote their novels and plays much as a social worker might handle a case history. Somewhat earlier, Balzac had proved himself far too sophisticated a

writer to see much in the medieval period beyond ignorance, poverty, and rustic village life and was able to write glowingly of the beauty of factories and big cities. The subject matter of his novels was drawn from the complex moral and psychological trials of middle-class life in the large metropolitan centers that he knew. This did not imply complete acceptance of the bourgeois image of man; on the contrary, it often meant violent opposition to his accepted values. Attitudes toward their writing varied with the temperaments of individual writers. Flaubert, for one, felt compelled to withdraw from life in order to describe it with the necessary objectivity; and he was convinced that such scientific detachment alone qualified the artist as well as the scientist. Zola, on the other hand, could not write without a passionate self-identification with the oppressed subjects of his novels. In the spirit of a reformer, he found it a necessity to bring social sores out into the sunlight of public exposure in order to effect a cure. With him, the novelist becomes a social research worker, and the novel a documentary case history.

This scientific objectivity was obviously better adapted to the writing of novels than to poetry or music. Some realism, to be sure, can be found in the vivid instrumentation of Berlioz, and his opera *Benvenuto Cellini* had included a forging scene. Wagner's *Ring of the Nibelung* also had a scene that calls for anvils to be hammered backstage, while the fire glows and sparks fly during the forging of a sword. In spite of its exotic setting, Bizet's conception of the character of Carmen was realistic enough to cause a certain sensation when it was first performed; and some time later the whir of sewing machines could be heard in the sweatshop scene of Charpentier's opera *Louise*. In general, however, music as well as poetry found a far more congenial sphere of operation in the intangible realm of the imagination. Another movement arose in the 1880's under the leadership of the poet Mallarmé, which tried to give freer reign to the imaginative process through a new use of symbolism.

The art of the symbolist is one of the fleeting moment; everything rushes past in an accelerated panorama. With the metaphor as a starting point, a symbolist prose poem flows by in a sequence of images that sweeps the reader along on a swift current of words with a minimum of slowing down to ponder on their meaning. Like the impressionistic painters, the symbolists reveled in sense data, and, like the realistic novelists, they looked for their material among the seemingly inconsequential occurrences of daily life. But in their endeavor to endow such happenings with profundity, and in their effort to attach to them a deeper symbolic significance, they went one step beyond their colleagues.

While the painters had found a new world in the physics of light, and the novelists another new world in the social sciences, the symbolists looked to the new discoveries in psychology. By purposely leaving their poetry in an inconclusive and fragmentary state, they were making use of the psychological mechanism of reasoning from part to whole. Since the poets did not define the whole, the reader's imagination was allowed full scope.

Just as the impressionist painters had left the mixing of color to the eye of the observer, and the relationship of the subject matter to the viewer's mind, so Mallarmé and the symbolists left the connection, order, and form of their verbal still lifes to be completed by the reader. They also found a new world to explore in "listening" to colors, "looking" at sounds, "savoring" perfumes, and in all such mixtures of separate sensations known to psychology as synaesthesia. By developing a hypersensitive tonal palette, Claude Debussy, like his symbolist colleagues, was able to sound a gamut of images from volatile perfumes *(Sounds and Perfumes on the Evening Air)*, fluid architecture *(Engulfed Cathedral)*, sparkling seascapes *(La Mer)*, exotic festivities *(Iberia, Fêtes)* to gaudy fireworks *(Feux d'Artifice.)* The symbolists pushed outward to the threshold limits of perception in order to develop more delicate sensibilities and stimulate the capacities for new and peripheral experiences. They moved about in a twilight zone where sensation ends and ideation begins. The very word *symbolism*, however, implies that their images are revelations of something surpassing sense data. And it is here that they parted company with the objective techniques of the realists and impressionists, who were largely content with careful description.

Maurice Maeterlinck made an interesting attempt to translate the aims of the symbolist poets into dramatic form. His *Pelléas et Mélisande*, a play first performed in 1892, effects a synthesis of the material world and the world of the imagination. In it, he denies the importance of external events and explores the quiet vibrations of the soul. His symbols function as links between the visible and invisible, the momentary and the eternal. The tangible fragments of common experience, the seemingly trivial everyday occurrences, however, furnish clues to the more decisive stuff of life. "Beneath all human thoughts, volitions, passions, actions," he writes in one of his essays, "there lies the vast ocean of the Unconscious, the unknown source of all that is good, true and beautiful. All that we know, think, feel, see and will are but bubbles on the surface of this vast sea." This sea, then, is the symbol of the absolute toward which all life is reaching out but which can never quite be grasped. What is heard is only the ripples on the surface. "The shallows murmur," as Maeterlinck puts it "while the deeps are dumb." A play by its very nature must unfold through the medium of speech, but Maeterlinck felt that "it is in silence that true life lies."

In his drama, the sea, the forest, the fountain, the abyss are the *dramatis personae* in a profounder sense than the human characters, who at best are but shadowy reflections of real people. In spite of the settings in which they appear, Maeterlinck's characters belong neither to the past nor to the future but hover in an extended now. They seem to have no spatial extension, no volume, but exist more as creatures of duration. They grope their way through the impenetrable forest of symbols that surrounds them and mysteriously controls their destinies. Daytime is never more than a shadowy twilight, and at night even the moon is veiled and its light, pale. Maeterlinck is the master of the enigmatic, the indefinite, and paradoxical. Wise old Arkel is blind, but he is the only one in the cast who can "see" what is going on. Philosophical profundities flow more naturally from the child Yniold than from the more "mature" members of the family. And on her deathbed, Mélisande declares sonorously that she was never in better health. A book without a subject had once been projected by Flaubert, but it was never written. *Pelléas and Mélisande*, however, comes perilously close to being a play without a plot. So little is externalized that the progress of what plot there is seems to unfold within the characters. One overhears rather than hears the dialogue, and, in the ordinary sense, so little happens that a kind of dramatic vacuum is created which can be filled only by the imaginations of the spectators. Just as the eye must mix the colors in an impressionistic painting, so the observer's imagination in a Maeterlinck play must connect the metaphors, must unite the separate tableaux into a flow of images, must fill each pregnant pause with projections from his own experience, and must supply the emotional depth to its surface play of symbols.

Such a fragile theory is too flimsy a foundation on which to build a very substantial dramatic art, and it is not too surprising that Maeterlinck's audiences were somewhat baffled. A period that knew Zola's realistic novels and Ibsen's problem plays found it hard to enter into this shadowy world of the spirit. Maeterlinck's good fortune, even though he never quite realized it, was to find a composer who could fill his silences with the necessary nebulous sounds, who could give voice to the "murmur of eternity on the horizon," and who could write the music that provided the link from dream to dream. It was, indeed, as if the music of Debussy had been created for the very purpose of providing the tonal envelope to enclose Maeterlinck's "ominous silence of the soul." Debussy was able to make the sea sing "the mysterious chant of the infinite." In his score, the references to the ocean on which all the characters are floating toward their unknown destinies are handled with special sensitivity. In one guise or another, its waters are present in practically every scene, either in the fragmentary form of a spring in the forest, a well in a courtyard, a fountain in a park, or the stagnant, fetid pools of underground caverns. This ever-present water imagery is used as the symbol of the flowing, fleeting nature of experience. As an unstable medium without form of its own, it becomes the means of capturing vague atmospheric effects and reflecting subtle changes of mood. The course of Mélisande's life is conveyed by means of these changing waters. She comes from over the sea, is found by a dark pool in the forests, discovers her love for Pelléas at a fountain in the park, and as she dies she asks that the window be opened so that she can once more be with the sea.

Debussy was conversant with the literary figures and developments of his time, especially the work of Mallarmé and Pierre Louÿs. He had entered into their discussions and sought the technical means of translating their poetic theories into the medium of music. His style first took shape in the songs he wrote on texts by the symbolist poets, but Maeterlinck's drama provided him with the necessary lyric material to ripen it and bring it to maturity. Like the poets, his musical methods were in many ways the opposite of conventional operatic techniques. He followed Wagner in giving the orchestra the main task of carrying on the sequence of the drama; and, as a result, his work became more of a symphonic poem with running commentary by the singers than a conventional opera. With characteristic insight, Debussy saw that melody, in the sense of a set operatic aria, impeded rather than promoted the dramatic progress. "I wished—intended, in fact—that the action should never be arrested; that it should be continuous, uninterrupted," he commented. "Melody is, if I may say so, almost anti-lyric, and powerless to express the constant change of emotion or life. Melody is suitable only for song [chanson], which confirms a fixed sentiment."

In thus considering recitative as the most important element of the lyric drama, Debussy allies himself with his illustrious predecessors Lully and Rameau. But while their characters spoke in the highly inflected accents of baroque theatrical grandiloquence, his speak in cadences more closely approximating modern conversational French. "The characters in this drama endeavor to sing like real persons," the composer wrote; and by bringing their language closer to everyday speech, and allowing the flow of dramatic action to proceed without interruption, his opera assumes a plausibility seldom achieved in such a highly artificial medium. By using modes other than the traditional major and minor, his recitative takes on the flexible character of psalmodic chant. The rhythms are free, and the absence of regular accentuation allows the words to flow with elasticity. Debussy's musical motives parallel the literary symbols and are often just broken fragments of melody, which suggest rather than define atmospheric effects or are associated with the mood of a character. While used with greater subtlety, they nevertheless are much closer to Wagner's system of leitmotifs than Debussy was willing to admit. His harmonic method likewise was well suited to the rendition of the ambiguities and obscurities of the symbolist poets. His key centers lose their boundaries; progressions move about freely in tonal space; the predominance given to the tritone interval accents the indefinite drift; and everything is in a state of flux, always on its way but never arriving. Debussy's sensitivity to the timbre of sounds borders on the uncanny. He thought of Mélisande's voice as "soft and silky," and the woodwinds dominate the orchestral coloration with their peculiarly poignant and penetrating quality. Above all, performers must know how to make this intangible music live and breathe, how to render its rhythms with the proper elasticity, and how to fill its silences with meaning.

Debussy's evocation of Maeterlinck's pallid world is one of those rare instances of the indissoluble union of literature and music that make it impossible for later generations to think of them as separate entities. Debussy worked on *Pelléas* over a period of ten years and was constantly worrying about the audience reaction to his fragile lyric drama. Maeterlinck's play had not been a success, and in a letter dated August, 1894, Debussy anxiously asks a friend, "How will the world get along with these two poor little beings?" In an obvious reference to the popularity of Zola's writing, he goes on to express his hatred of "crowds, universal suffrage, and tri-colored phrases." Even after the opera had been accepted for performance in 1897

and rehearsals had begun, he withdrew it again for another five years of revision. Contrary to expectation, however, the opera was a success and was widely performed. His elusive music ultimately proved its capacity to cast a spell over the most indifferent of audiences. After this it dropped out of sight for a while, but recent revivals have assured it a permanent place in the international repertory.

IDEAS

Any interpretation of the complex interplay of forces that underlies and motivates the divergent tendencies of the latter part of the 19th century faces the usual danger of oversimplification. Two of the most salient ideas, however, are chosen principally because they provide significant insights into the relationship of the several arts. These are: the influence of the scientific method on the arts and the interpretation of experience in terms of time.

Alliance of Art and Science

Artists in all fields were aware of the extraordinary success of the scientific method. Realism and impressionism brought a new objective attitude into the arts, together with an emphasis on the technical side of the crafts and a tendency for artists to become specialists pursuing a single aspect of their various media. Architects began to look toward engineers for the more advanced developments in building. A painting for an impressionist was a kind of experiment, an adventure in problem solving. Cézanne thought of each of his pictures as a type of visual-research problem. In sculpture, Rodin was seeking for a new synthesis of matter and form. The literary realists were cultivating a scientific detachment in their writing and developing a technique that would enable them to record the details of their minute observations of everyday life with accuracy and precision. Zola, by means of his experimental novel, introduced a modified social-scientific technique to fiction. In addition to his poetic dramas, Maeterlinck wrote popular nature studies, such as *Life of the Bee* and the *Magic of the Stars*. Debussy, when writing to a friend, spoke about some of his compositions as his "latest discoveries in musical chemistry."

Many of the actual discoveries of scientific research opened up new vistas in the various arts. Experiments in optical physics revealed secrets of light and color that painters could explore. New chemical syntheses provided more luminous pigments for their canvases. Increased knowledge of the physiology of the eye and the psychology of perception led to a reexamination of how an observer looks at a picture and what he perceives. New metal alloys and processes of casting were a boon to sculptors. The theories of evolution gave Rodin some poetic ideas on how form emerges from matter, the animate from the inanimate. Helmholtz' book *On the Sensation of Tone as a Physiological Basis for the Theory of Music* stirred Debussy and other composers to speculate on the relation of tone to overtone and consonance to dissonance in their harmonic procedures.

The impressionistic painters were convinced that pictures were compounded of light and color, not line and form; the symbolists claimed that poetry was made with words, not ideas; and composers felt that music should be a play of varied sonorities rather than a means of evoking programmatic associations. By pursuing this general line of thought, Monet revealed a new concept of light and color and their interdependence; Rodin, an atmospheric extension of solid three-dimensional form; the symbolists, a new world of poetry; Debussy, a new concept of sound; and Paxton and Eiffel, by incorporating light and air into their designs, achieved a new architectural relationship between inner and outer space. This mechanistic phase, however, could lead just so far, and artists were soon trying to push beyond it into paths that would lead to deeper psychological insights. Each of the postimpressionists in his own way was probing to find how the new discoveries could be used as a means toward new modes of expression. Cézanne's path led into a new concept of pictorial geometry that became an important anticipation of 20th-century art, and the point of departure for cubism. Maeterlinck attempted to humanize science and describe it in poetical terms. In his case, the result was a kind of animism in which stones, fountains, and objects spoke a language and felt a soul life of their own. In an essay on the "Intelligence of Flowers," he tried to establish more sympathetic ties between man and nature. In his stage fantasy *The Bluebird*, Sugar and Bread are among the live characters. Cézanne also felt the living force of the objects he placed in his still lifes, and in a conversation with a friend remarked that there are people who say a sugar bowl has no soul, yet it changes every day. The symbolists also tried to effect a synthesis between the phenomenal world and that of the creative imagination. Their metaphors were material in the sense that they received expression through the senses, but they hinted at the existence of a more profound ideational world and were definitely based on a view that life was something more than the sum of its molecular parts. Debussy also veered away from the exploration of the physical elements of sound toward the deeper psychological implications of tonal symbolism.

Continuous Flux

The arts of the late 19th century were also bound together by their common tendency toward the interpretation of experience in terms of time. Progress was an idea that was carried over from the late 18th century. Material progress continued to be an indisputable fact, but what was rapidly becoming apparent was that it did not go hand in hand with moral, spiritual, and aesthetic progress. With industrialization came a specialization in which men were concerned more with fragments than with wholes. Industrial man was rapidly forfeiting to the machine his place as the primary productive unit. With this loss of control came a corresponding shift from a rational world view toward an increasingly irrational one. With industrialization also came a capitalistic economy in which the lives of workers were controlled by intangible forces beyond themselves, such as the fluctuations in foreign markets and on the stock exchange. Two centuries previously, baroque man had been shaken by the Copernican revolution in which the notion of a static earth in the center of the universe was replaced by that of a freely moving satellite around the sun. Late 19th-century man was similarly rocked by the Darwinian and other evolutionary theories, which taught that creation was an ever-continuing process rather than an accomplished fact. As a result of such forces and ideas, the onward-and-upward notion of progress was revised downward to one of continuous flux and change.

The literary and visual realists concentrated on the momentary, the fragmentary, the everyday occurrence. Even when they planned their works in more comprehensive schemes, the effect was more that of a broad cross section than a coherent three-dimensional structure. For twenty years, Balzac worked on parts of his *Human Comedy*, Wagner on his Ring Cycle, Rodin on his *Gates of Hell*, and Proust on his *Remembrance of Things Past*. None, however, is a systematic, organic, or logical whole or a single perfected masterpiece. Instead of an all-embracing unity, they are easily broken down into a collection of fragments, motifs, genre scenes, scraps, and pieces. The late 19th century produced no grandiose metaphysical systems, such as those of Thomas Aquinas, Leibniz, Kant, or Hegel, each of whom tried to encompass all experience in a single universal structure.

The thinker who came the closest to making a coherent picture of this turbulent age was Henri Bergson, a lecturer at the École Normale in Paris.

His point of departure was a remark made by the pre-Socratic philosopher Heraclitus, who had said that one cannot step into the same river twice. Bergson cited Heraclitus in support of his theory that time was more real than space, that the many were closer to experience than the one, and becoming was closer to reality than being. Bergson was critical of the intellect because it tended to reduce reality to immobility. He therefore ranked intuition as a higher faculty than reason, because through it the perception of the flow of duration was possible, and through it static quantitative facts were quickened into the dynamic qualitative values of motion and change. Existence is never static but a transition between states and between moments of duration. Experience, he taught, is durational, "a series of qualitative changes, which melt into and permeate one another, without precise outlines...." Art for Bergson is the force that sets man free and through which he can grasp "certain rhythms of life and breath," which compel him even against his will "to fall in with it, like passers by who join in a dance. And thus they compel us to set in motion, in the depth of our being, some secret chord which was only waiting to thrill."

Bergson was thus convinced that reality is mobility, tendency, or "incipient change of direction." Looking at or listening to a work of art is perceiving the mobile qualities of the objects or sounds presented. The aesthetic experience is essentially temporal and involves an "anticipation of movement," which permits the spectator or auditor in various ways "to grasp the future in the present." His theory of art is based on what he calls his "spiritualistic materialism" by which finely perceived material activity elicits spiritual echoes. All is based on the "uniqueness of the moment"; and perception of the temporal flow is synonymous with an awareness of the pulsation of life, something that is quite apart from the mechanical or inert matter. Past, present, and future are molded into an organic whole as "when we recall the notes of a tune melting, so to speak, into one another." Time, therefore, is "the continuous progress of the past, which gnaws into the future and which swells as it advances." But Bergson's concept of time is not clock time with its divisions into seconds, minutes, and hours, nor is it concerned with the usual groupings of past, present, and future. These are just arbitrary conveniences, like the points on a clock past which the hands move. Time cannot be spatialized and measured in such a quantitative way; it is a quality, not a substance.

The application of Bergson's theory of time to the arts of the late 19th century can be very illuminating. The philosopher often cited the motion picture as an example of what he meant by the perception of duration. The pictures in themselves are static, but through mobility the separate states are melted together by the mind into a continuous temporal flow. So also are the separate colors on an impressionistic canvas, the separate metaphors in a symbolist poem, the separate scenes in a Maeterlinck play, the separate chords in a Debussy progression, molded by the mind into a temporal continuum. In visual impressionism, the eye mixes the colors; in a symbolist poem, the mind supplies the connecting verbs for the nominal fragments; in a Maeterlinck play, the imagination makes the irrelevancies of speech and action into a dramatic sequence; and in Debussy's music, the ear bridges over the silences.

In all the arts, this ceaseless flux leads toward the improvisatory, the consciously incomplete; and each work tries to be a product of inspiration rather than calculation. With the visual impressionists, all pictorial substance is atomized into an airy mixture of color sprays, fleeting shadows, and momentary moods. Cézanne sometimes paints so thinly that parts of the canvas are actually bare, and at other times the texture is so thin as to be almost transparent. Rodin likewise leaves parts of the stone surrounding his figures uncut; and it is by no means an accident that some of the most important buildings of the time were open to the air and sky and were conceived as temporary exposition structures, such as the Crystal Palace, the Gallery of Machines, and the Eiffel Tower. In *Pelléas et Mélisande*, the characters are only outlined or sketched, and what they really feel has to be inferred by the spectator. The imagination actually supplies the emotional depth to what is but a surface play of forms. In all instances the audience, through perception, imagination, and memory, actively participates in the creative activity.

Both the awareness of science and the accentuation of the temporal flow became important means by which the arts at the end of the 19th century established the basis for the transition to the various modern styles. Cézanne has with justification been called the first great modern master; the functional architecture of Labrouste, Paxton, and Eiffel has become the foundation stone of contemporary architecture; Rodin's convex and concave surfaces and his preoccupation with the atmospheric problems of light and shadow have led to important new developments in sculpture; the fragmentary style of the symbolists anticipated the "stream-of-consciousness" and other techniques of modern literature; and Debussy's concept of relative rather than absolute tonality, together with his harmonic experimentation, have pointed toward some of the significant musical developments of the 20th century.

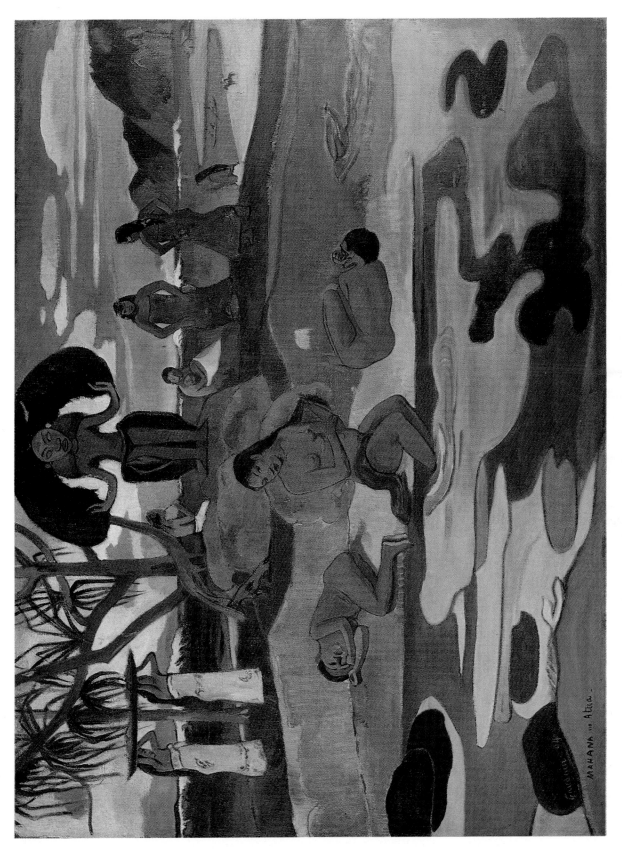

Plate 53. PAUL GAUGUIN. *Mahana No Atua (Day of the God)*. 1894. Oil on canvas, 26 × 34 ½".
Art Institute of Chicago. (See p. 486.)

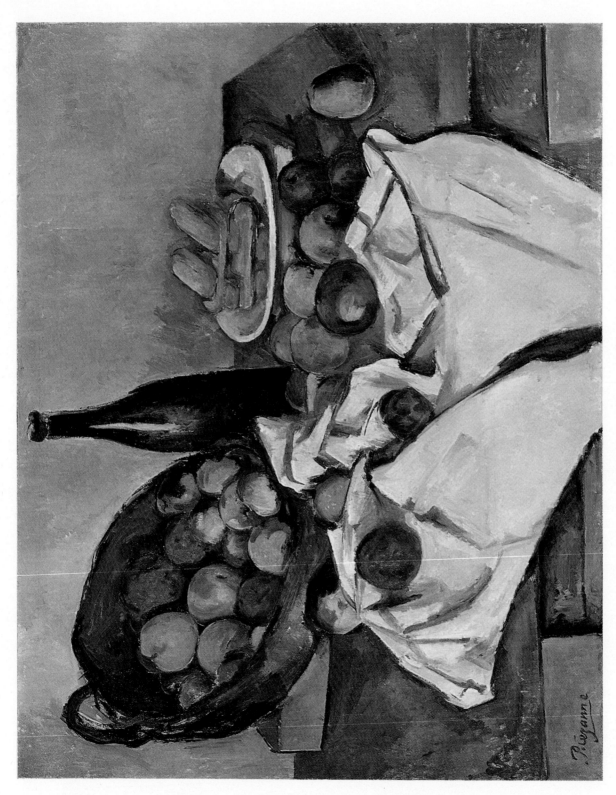

Plate 54. PAUL CÉZANNE. *Still Life: Basket of Apples.* 1890–1894. Oil on canvas, 25 ¾ × 32″. Art Institute of Chicago. (See p. 488.)

20 - CONTEMPORARY STYLES

THE AGE OF ISMS AND SCHISMS

Wars, revolutions, social upheavals, displacement of peoples, the release of atomic energy, computers and automation—all have proceeded at such a pace that 20th-century man has difficulty keeping up with himself. While new means of communication and transportation have shrunk his globe, the vast expansion of knowledge has made it impossible for him to view his world as a whole. The completion of the Industrial Revolution, the progress of electronic technology, and the necessity for specialization have further fragmented his vision. Clashes and discord for him are more usual than concord: disunity is ascendant over unity; discontinuity is more familiar than continuity; and a multiverse has replaced the universe. In their quest for meaning and reality, today's angry young man and modern organizational man exist in their lonely crowds—bombarded on all sides by the mass media of television, radio, motion pictures, newspapers, and magazines. And they must decide whether to conform or reform, suppress or express themselves, look within or without for enlightenment, and yet attempt to close the ever-widening gap between the actual and ideal.

The 19th century, somehow, had been able to contain the forces of liberty and authority, democracy and dictatorship, individualism and collectivism, free enterprise and economic monopoly, scientific advances and orthodox religious beliefs, freedom of thought and anti-intellectual tendencies. The 20th century, however, has seen these smoldering disputes break out into open conflict. The clashes of rival colonialisms were followed by revolutions in the wake of two world wars that brought communism to Russia, China, and eastern Europe; nazism to Germany and Austria; civil war, totalitarianism, and cold war to most of the world; and the rise of a host of new nations out of the ashes of old disintegrating colonial empires. Revolutions and wars, however, are but one aspect of man's strife; art movements are another. Above all the clangor and confusion, the voice of the present century can be heard, for pens and paint brushes are also weapons in the social and spiritual struggle for survival.

Since the arts are forms of action, artists as well as social reformers and revolutionaries shout their battle cries, issue their manifestoes, propose their panaceas, and formulate their own isms and

(above) R. BUCKMINSTER FULLER. United States Pavilion at Expo 67, Montreal. Geodesic dome constructed of steel pipes and transparent acrylic, 250′ in diameter.

501

CHRONOLOGY: 20th Century

General Events

1891 Wainwright Building, St. Louis, first skyscraper

Motion-picture camera patented by Thomas Edison; sound recording developed

1903 Aviation age begun by Wright brothers

1905 Sigmund Freud founded psychoanalysis

First motion-picture theater opened in Pittsburgh

"Fauve" exhibit in Paris, with paintings by Derain, Rouault, Matisse

Die Brücke exhibit in Dresden; included paintings by Nolde, Kirchner (movement lasted till 1913)

1907– 1914 Cubism developed in Paris by Braque and Picasso

1908 Model T (touring car) introduced by Henry Ford

1909 Wireless radio developed by Marconi

Peary reached North Pole; 1911, Amundsen the South Pole

1909– 1915 Futurist movement in Italy

1910 Einstein's general theory of relativity

1911 *Der Blaue Ritter* (Blue Rider) group formed in Munich with Kandinsky and Marc

1911– 1912 Chirico and Chagall exhibited protosurrealist pictures in Paris

1913 New York Armory Show brought advanced controversial European art trends to United States; vogue for modern art began in America

1914– 1918 World War I

1916– 1922 Dadaism founded in Zürich, Switzerland; spread quickly to Berlin, Paris, New York

1917 Russian revolution began

1917 *De Stijl* magazine published in Holland; gave name to International Style with Mondrian, Gropius, Miës van der Rohe, Le Corbusier, J. J. P. Oud

1922 Fascist revolution in Italy

1924 Surrealist manifesto promulgated in Paris; movement later included Miró, Dali

1927 Lindbergh's solo flight across Atlantic

1928 First complete talking film

1929 New York stock marked collapsed; Great Depression began

1933 Nazi revolution in Germany

1936– 1939 Spanish Civil War

1939 Television begun under commercial license

1939– 1945 World War II

1945 First atomic bomb exploded

United Nations organized at San Francisco

1950– 1953 Korean War

1957 First earth satellite put into orbit by USSR; U.S. satellite, 1958

1961 First manned satellite by USSR; U.S. manned satellite, 1962

1962 Telstar, American communications satellite, launched

Architects

1856–	1924	Louis Sullivan
1869–	1959	Frank Lloyd Wright
1874–	1954	Auguste Perret
1883–		Walter Gropius
1886–		Miës van der Rohe
1887–	1965	Le Corbusier (Charles-Édouard Jeanneret-Gris)
1890–		J. J. P. Oud
1891–		Pier Luigi Nervi
1995–		Buckminster Fuller
1806–		Philip Johnson
1910–	1961	Eero Saarinen

Painters

1844–	1910	Henri Rousseau *(le douanier)*
1863–	1944	Edvard Munch
1866–	1944	Vasily Kandinsky
1867–	1956	Emil Nolde
1869–	1954	Henri Matisse
1870–	1954	John Marin
1871–	1958	Giacomo Balla
1871–	1958	Georges Rouault
1872–	1944	Piet Mondrian
1879–	1940	Paul Klee
1880–	1916	Franz Marc
1880–	1966	Hans Hofmann
1881–	1955	Fernand Léger
1881–		Pablo Picasso
1882–	1916	Umberto Boccioni
1882–	1963	Georges Braque
1883–	1949	José Clemente Orozco
1883–	1966	Gino Severini
1884–	1920	Amadeo Modigliani
1884–	1950	Max Beckmann
1886–	1957	Diego Rivera
1886–		Oskar Kokoschka
1887–		Marc Chagall
1887–		Marcel Duchamp
1888–		Giorgio de Chirico
1889–		Thomas Hart Benton
1892–	1942	Grant Wood
1893–		Joan Miró
1894–	1964	Stuart Davis
1897–	1946	John Stewart Curry
1898–	1967	Charles Burchfield

1898–		Ben Shahn
1904–		Salvador Dali
1904–		Willem de Kooning
1910–	1962	Franz Kline
1910–		Francis Bacon
1912–	1956	Jackson Pollock
1917–		Andrew Wyeth
1925–		Robert Rauschenberg

Sculptors

1861–	1944	Aristide Maillol
1870–	1938	Ernst Barlach
1876–	1957	Constantin Brancusi
1883–	1962	Ivan Mestrovic
1885–		Paul Manship
1887–	1966	Jean (Hans) Arp
1890–		Naum Gabo
1891–		Jacques Lipschitz
1898–		Alexander Calder
1898–		Henry Moore
1901–	1966	Alberto Giacometti

Writers and Philosophers

1856–	1939	Sigmund Freud
1856–	1950	George Bernard Shaw
1863–	1938	Gabriele d'Annunzio
1869–	1951	André Gide
1871–	1945	Paul-Ambroise Valéry
1874–	1946	Gertrude Stein
1875–	1955	Thomas Mann
1876–	1944	Filippo Tommaso Marinetti

1878–	1967	Carl Sandburg
1882–	1941	James Joyce
1885–	1951	Sinclair Lewis
1887–	1962	Robinson Jeffers
1888–	1953	Eugene O'Neill
1888–	1965	T. S. Eliot
1889–	1963	Jean Cocteau
1896–	1966	André Breton
1897–	1962	William Faulkner
1899–	1961	Ernest Hemingway
1905–		Jean-Paul Sartre

Musicians

1860–	1911	Gustav Mahler
1864–	1949	Richard Strauss
1866–	1925	Erik Satie
1872–	1915	Alexander Scriabin
1873–	1943	Sergei Rachmaninoff
1874–	1951	Arnold Schoenberg
1875–	1937	Maurice Ravel
1876–	1946	Manuel de Falla
1881–	1945	Bela Bartok
1882–		Igor Stravinsky
1883–	1945	Anton Webern
1885–	1935	Alban Berg
1885–	1965	Edgar Varèse
1891–	1953	Serge Prokofiev
1892–	1955	Arthur Honegger
1892–		Darius Milhaud
1895–	1963	Paul Hindemith
1898–	1937	George Gershwin
1899–	1963	Francis Poulenc

---

schisms. In the late 19th century such relatively simple aesthetic creeds as realism, naturalism, symbolism, and impressionism had their flocks of faithful followers. By comparison the 20th century has become an angry Tower of Babel in which such gospels as contructivism, dynamism, intimism, orphism, parallelism, purism, suprematism, synthetism, and vorticism have been promulgated. Still in common currency are the movements known as cubism, dadaism, fauvism, and surrealism. Too often these organized art movements have been so preoccupied with their doctrines they have produced little art. Their principal purpose has been to provoke lively discussion, attract attention, arrange for exhibits, concerts, and publications. The passions associated with these isms have usually generated more heat than light, more confusion than clarification; and the groups responsible have rarely spoken or written about them very sensibly. Often these isms and schisms have led to dead ends, sometimes to significant breakthroughs. Ultimately, what matters is whether their pictures, pieces, or poems are worth looking at, listening to, or reading.

The volatility and violence of the 20th century are of explosive proportions. In addition to atomic explosions, modern man has to contend with the population and cultural explosions. The revolution in electronic communications is more far reaching than the invention of Gutenberg's printing press in the 15th century. At no other time has it been possible to witness the construction of so many buildings, read so much literature, or hear so much music. The facility of modern travel, the flood of picture books, paperbacks, and recordings, the proliferation of television, radio, and motion-picture performances have brought greater accessibility to the arts for an infinitely larger audience than any previous age has known.

Through high fidelity sound recording, the entire literature of music—past and present—has become available, and every home is a potential concert hall. Through television, every living room can be both a theater and an opera house, as well as a sports arena and political forum. And picture books and prints have become what André Malraux has called museums without walls. So all works of art, whether poetry or plays, paintings or piano pieces, are now within grasp. However, as with any other positive advance, there is a corresponding negative aspect. The flood gates have been opened, and 20th-century man is inundated with literature both written and spoken, music that flows by day and night without stopping, art exhibits and picture books that create log jams in the stream of experience. Ruthless exploitation of the arts in the mass media for commercial purposes has brought about corresponding vulgarizations and has bred the insidious attitudes of casualness and indifference when great experiences are available with too little effort.

With the mass media there are so many publics, so many degrees of sophistication, so many levels of education, so many frames of national and international reference, that an artist can no longer be sure which audience he is addressing. Unlike past times when a direct relationship existed between artist and patron, the contemporary creator can only cast his art on the wave lengths of sight and sound and hope somewhere and somehow to reach a sympathetic segment of his anonymous audience. There is also a concomitant confusion in the choice of media. Knowing that a wider public may be reached, a novelist may well write a book with the expectation that it will be staged or filmed, a painter or sculptor produce works that will photograph well for a picture book, and a composer or performer adapt his style to make a successful recording.

In approaching the art of the 20th century, one has much to keep in mind. Modern art, like the art of the past, must be understood in terms of its own frame of reference and what the artist is trying to do. The contemporary artist may intend to delight or irritate, to exhort or castigate, to surprise or excite, to soothe or shock. He may be trying deliberately to achieve disorder rather than order, chaos rather than a cosmos. The act of creating sometimes replaces the importance of the object created. Chance happenings and random selections tend to make some recent art a performance or an activity. Improvisation, as formerly practiced in baroque or rococo concertos and their cadenzas, now characterizes much modern music. As in rococo art, some modern painting has become the handmaiden of interior design. Finding poetry where no one saw it before is the eternal role of the artist, whether his quest carries him to the ruins of antiquity, skid row, or the junk yard. A painter may plan his picture as a visual sock in the eye, a composer may intend his music as aural assault and battery. Judging from the reactions to Picasso's early exhibits and the riot that greeted Stravinsky's *Rite of Spring* ballet, some artists have succeeded beyond their wildest expectations. But sheer shock

values soon diminish, and artists have learned that they can blow Gabriel's trumpet of Judgment once, but not every day.

The tempo of change has been so swift that 20th-century man cannot keep pace with his scientists and artists. The span of time between innovations and their understanding and popular acceptance is often referred to as cultural lag. Fashions, fads, and fancies succeed each other with bewildering speed. This season's "in group" is next year's outcast. Alongside the passing fads, however, are found the solid accomplishments of artists of major stature. The discoveries of Frank Lloyd Wright, Gropius, and Le Corbusier in architecture, of Picasso, Kandinsky, and Mondrian in painting, of Schoenberg and Stravinsky in music rank as major breakthroughs in the history of art. These artists now enjoy the status of old masters of modern art. The younger generation of artists, as well as their public, today are passing through a period of consolidating the gains that have been made and preparing the ground for future discoveries.

Modern materials and methods have opened up new possibilities in the arts. Ferroconcrete, structural steel, glass, and laminated wood have taken their place alongside bricks and mortar, while cantilevering has joined the post and lintel. With the growth of cities, modern architects have had to construct facilities ranging from airline terminals, suspension bridges, and low-cost public housing to such entirely new capital cities as Brasilia and Chandigarh. Side by side with the steel-and-glass office buildings and urban-planning projects of the industrialized society, 20th-century architects have been called upon to build a host of new churches and temples in imaginative and daring designs.

The sculptor now uses the welding torch as well as the chisel, and his materials are fiberglass, stainless steel, and plastics as well as bronze and marble. His statues no longer seem dedicated to preserving the enduring image of man, and their static monumentality has often given way to mobility and machine propulsion. Painters work on masonite surfaces and in mixed media as well as the traditional oil on canvas, and with palette knife and dripping techniques as well as with the brush. Along with the invention of such new art forms as the motion picture, kinetic sculpture, and happenings, the ancient arts of mosaic, fresco, and stained glass have reasserted their expressive power. And a new pictorial category of abstract and fantastic pictures has been added to the traditional classifications of historic paintings, genre scenes, portraiture, landscape, and still life.

The graphic arts have been expanded to include many new media, among them silk-screen

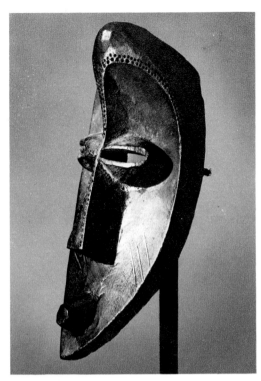

563. *Mask*, from Itumba, former French Congo. Wood, 14″ high. Museum of Modern Art, New York.

printing and color photography. The arbitrary distinction between the so-called "major and minor arts," fine arts and crafts, beauty and utility has narrowed to the point where architect and engineer, sculptor and furniture designer, a cathedral and a suspension bridge—once thought to be poles apart—have been brought together in the modern unity of form and function. Drama has expanded from the live theater to include the motion picture and television media. New concepts of language are being explored with words used as syllabic sounds in an abstract poetry, and composers are experimenting with electronically generated sound.

EXPRESSIONISM AND ABSTRACTIONISM

Pablo Picasso's *Les Demoiselles d'Avignon* (Plate 55) incorporated so many of the ideas of the early 20th century that it became a landmark of the modern-art movement. At the turn of the century Paris was alive with young artists, new notions, and stimulating exhibits. Picasso was impressed in turn by the great Cézanne retrospective of 1907; with a showing of pre-Roman Iberian sculpture which, as in most archaic art, represented the human body in angular geometrical patterns; and with expositions of African tribal sculpture. As a result he began to

reexamine his pictorial approach, turned away from representational conventions toward tighter geometrical controls, and acquired the first pieces of his collection of primitive African sculpture.

Les Demoiselles d'Avignon had begun as an allegory. A man seated amidst fruit and women was to have symbolized Vice, while his opposite number entering on the left holding a skull in his hand was to have been Virtue. Under the new influences, however, the original plan was abandoned and the picture developed in another direction by blending the figures, the background drapery, and the still life below into an abstract design. The girl on the left who is pulling back some curtains became a series of overlapping planes and geometrically arranged contours. The head of the figure in the upper right resembles a mask from Itumba in the old French Congo (Fig. 563), while the head of the woman just below and the profile of the figure on the left also show African tribal influence. Picasso's preliminary drawings reveal his fascination with the oval-shaped heads, the long noses, small mouths, and angular bodies that characterize the sculpture of the Ivory Coast. The color, with its spectrumlike shading of bright hues one into another, contributes to the effect of an emotional crescendo, while the formal arrangement of the figures suggests the angular rhythms of a primitive dance.

Les Demoiselles is thus a pivotal picture. The heightened postimpressionistic colors combined with the violence and energy of primitive art make it a summary of the avant-garde Paris school of painting at the turn of the century. It also marks Picasso's intuitive invention of cubism, that most important step toward abstraction. When Georges Braque, one of the fauve painters, first saw *Les Demoiselles*, he perceived that both he and Picasso had been assimilating Cézanne's geometry of cones, spheres, and cylinders and his principles of formal construction. Together over the ensuing four years they worked out the rules of cubism.

In sorting out the developments in contemporary art, one has basically but two ways of looking at the world—from within or without, subjectively or objectively, through emotion or reason. These outlooks are by no means mutually exclusive, since mind is necessary for emotional awareness, and without emotional drive even the most rational proposition would be empty and devoid of meaning. For purposes of the present study the arts in which emotional considerations are dominant have been grouped under expressionism; those in which logical and analytical processes are uppermost are under abstractionism. Here a note of caution must be sounded, because all art is expressive to some degree, just as all art is abstract to a certain extent.

Expressionism looks within to a world of emotional and psychological states rather than without on a fluid world of fugitive realism, as with impressionism. In their zeal to develop a style with greater emotional force, the expressionist artists turned away from naturalism. With Van Gogh and Gauguin as their point of departure, these painters distorted outlines, applied strong colors, and exaggerated forms to convey their ends. Expressionism in its limited sense applies to the German art movements of the pre-World War I period, *Die Brücke* and *Der Blaue Reiter*. A broader definition, however, includes parallel developments in all major centers where artists were concerned primarily with the emotional approach to art and with their passionate involvement in all phases of contemporary life.

The expressionist is fully conscious of the visible world, but, leaving behind the classical idea of art as an imitation of nature, he closes his eyes to explore the world of the mind, spirit, and imagination. He would agree with Goethe's dictum that feeling is all, and he welcomed Freud's delving into the subconscious, which revealed a new world of emotion in the dark drives, hidden terrors, and mysterious motivations underlying human behavior. The expressionist is well aware that he inhabits a number of complex overlapping worlds, and he knows too that there are worlds to be explored which are not seen by the eye and which are not subject to logical interpretation. Expressionistic pictures are in psychological rather than natural focus, describing intangible worlds with new techniques and new symbols, discordant colors and distorted shapes. The clashing dissonances of expressionistic music are intended to arouse rather than soothe the listener, and expressionistic literature intends to startle the reader with subjective revelations of neurotic, psychical, often psychotic, states.

As James Joyce phrased it, the artist should strive "constantly to *express*, to *press out again*, from the gross earth or what it brings forth, from sound, shape and colour which are the prison gates of our soul, and image of the beauty we have come to understand—that is art." To describe his reactions to physical, psychical, and spiritual events, the expressionist alters, distorts, and colors his images according to the intensity of his feelings. Expressionism, then, may range from quiet nostalgic moods, through sudden shock reactions and hysterical outbursts, to screaming nightmares. The results of such expressionistic excursions into the subconscious may be quite uneven, but the artists' passports to such nether regions are nonetheless valid. Over the years, expressionism has embraced such movements as neoprimitivism, dadaism, surrealism, and social realism.

Abstractionism implies analyzing, deriving, detaching, selecting, simplifying, geometrizing, before distilling the essence from nature and sense experiences. The heat generated by the contemporary psychological and political revolutions of the 20th century was felt in expressionism, but the light of the new intellectual points of view is mirrored in the various forms of abstractionism.

In previous centuries, a picture was a reflection, in one way or another, of the outside world. In 20th-century abstractionism, the artist frees himself from the representational convention. Natural appearances play little part in his design that reduces a landscape or a group of objects to a system of geometrical shapes, patterns, lines, angles, and swirls of color which achieve his desired abstract imagery. Choosing his pictorial content from nature, the abstract artist eliminates the unimportant minutiae of the observed world, and refines the haphazardness of nature and ordinary visual experience. His imagination and his invention are concentrated on pictorial mechanics and the arrangement of patterns, shapes, textures, and colors. From the semiabstract cubist art, in which objects are still discernible, abstractionism moves toward nonobjectivism in which a work of art has no representational, literary, or associational meaning outside itself, and the picture becomes its own referent.

In the early years of the century, physicists were at work formulating a fundamental new view of the universe, which resulted in the concepts of space-time and relativity. In the arts, meanwhile, new ways of seeing and listening were also being worked out. In painting, for example, the cubist canon of multiple-visual viewpoints was developed, whereby several sides of an object could be presented at the same time. In sculpture, a new theory of volume was worked out, whereby open holes or gaps in the surface suggested the interpenetration of several planes, and the existence of other sides and surfaces not immediately in view. In architecture, the international style, using steel and glass, was able to incorporate in a structure the simultaneous experience of outer and inner space. Literature and music found new ways of presenting materials in the temporal dimension. In literature, the stream-of-consciousness technique merged objective description and subjective flow of images; and in music, the so-called "atonal" method of composition was formulated, by which fixed tonal centers were avoided in favor of a state of continuous flux and constant variation.

Such novel organizations of space and time demanded new ways of thinking about the world, new ways of looking at it, listening to it, and reading about it. Abstractionism thus includes such developments as cubism, futurism, the mechanical style, nonobjectivism, the 12-tone method of musical composition, and the international style of architecture.

Neoprimitivism

As the great conflagration of 20th-century expressionism burst into flame, the spark that set fire to that movement called neoprimitivism was the 19th-century discovery of the primitive arts of the South Sea Islanders and the wood carvings of African tribes. As the term is used here, *neoprimitivism* is limited to the conscious adaptations by sophisticated artists of authentic specimens of primitive art. The first major artist to employ the exotic patterns and motifs in his woodcuts and paintings had been Gauguin, and such pictures as his *Mahana No Atua* (Plate 53), painted during his extended sojourn in Tahiti, clearly reflect the native influence. Examples of Polynesian craftsmanship, such as oars, arrows, and harpoons, had been collected by traders on their voyages and were shown in the Paris expositions of 1878 and 1889. Later, when expeditions went to the interior of the dark continent, wooden objects carved by Negro tribesmen were brought back for display; and the ethnological museums, founded in Paris and Dresden to house these collections, commanded considerable interest among scholars, artists, and the general public. Articles and books on African sculpture soon appeared, and in 1890 James Frazer began publishing *The Golden Bough*, a monumental 12-volume compendium of primitive customs and beliefs, folklore, magical practices, and taboos.

Primitive art, with its complete negation of the notion of progress, seemed to be the promise of a new beginning. Especially appealing was the animistic attitude of the primitive carvers who divined the spirit of wood and stone and expressed it in the grains, textures, and shapes of their materials. So also was the emotional power and hypnotic state induced by the repetitive rhythms of tribal rituals as seen in Picasso's *Dancer* (Fig. 564), which is from the same period as *Les Demoiselles d'Avignon*. German expressionists were fascinated by the strange weird forms and anti-intellectualism of African images; French artists, among them Matisse, found in their simplified geometrical forms a new wealth of decorative motifs and a justification for their abstract designs.

The impact of primitive art also affected the course of 20th-century sculpture. When the young painter Modigliani came to Paris in 1906, he fell so completely under the spell of African Negro sculpture that for a while he traded the brush for the chisel. One of these works, *Head* (Fig. 565), is in the same Ivory Coast style that Picasso had adopted,

564. PABLO PICASSO. *Dancer*. 1907. Oil on canvas, 59 × 39 ¼". Collection Walter P. Chrysler, Jr.

565. AMEDEO MODIGLIANI. *Head*. c. 1913. Stone, 24 ¾" high. Tate Gallery, London (by courtesy of the Trustees).

and, in his paintings, he later used stylized oval faces and elongated forms such as those in his *Yellow Sweater* (Plate 56).

The sources of Henry Moore's powerful sculpture are prehistoric primordial forms, Stonehenge, ancient Etruscan tombs, pre-Columbian Mexican carvings, African and Oceanic art, the way wind and water shape trees and erode jutting boulders, and, above all, his own fertility of formal invention. "Truth to material," Moore wrote, "[is] one of the first principles of art so clearly seen in primitive work.... The artist shows an instinctive understanding of his material, its right use and possibilities." His recumbent figures are like mother earth or some fertility goddesses of a forgotten cult. The curves and convolutions transcend the human form and become part of the heaving hills and plunging valleys of a rolling landscape. Many of Moore's figures are pierced by holes and hollows so that his sculpture has an interior as well as exterior existence. With the *Reclining Figure* (Fig. 566) at Lincoln Center, in New York City, Moore expanded his holes by dividing the figure so he could shape, metaphorically, not only his monumental masses but also the space around and between. The two parts are related but separate with the head and body at one end and the legs at the other. "But between them,"

Moore remarked, "I am trying to make a kind of mixture of the human figure and of landscape."

The elemental simplicity of Brancusi's sculpture has its formative inspiration in the power of primitive forms and the bold innovations of the fauve painters. Brancusi's objective was to free sculpture from everything extraneous and get down to ultimate essences. One egg-shaped marble piece, for instance, is called *Beginning of the World*. Like the neoprimitives, he accepts his materials for what they are—marble for its smoothness and roughness, metal for its hardness or softness. Whatever the material, he tries to divine its nature and realize its potentialities without forcing it to simulate something else. "What is real," Brancusi once remarked, "is not the external form, but the essence of things." In his *Bird in Space* (Fig. 567) he is dealing with a bronze that has such a high copper content it approaches the brilliance of gold. By molding it into a graceful curvilinear form and giving it a high polish, he releases the metal medium into a form of energy. It is the abstraction of a movement, a feather in flight. Brancusi has sometimes tried to increase the sense of motion in sculpture by placing his figures on slowly rotating turntables. In this way, his glistening surfaces catch the light and his forms seem to float through space.

Knowledge of non-European musical systems had likewise increased rapidly during the late 19th century. The orchestrations of Debussy and Ravel had been influenced by the strange and exotic sounds of the gamelan orchestras from Java, which both composers had heard at the International Exposition of 1889. By far the strongest of these new influences, however, was American jazz music, which had its beginnings in New Orleans and Chi-

568. PABLO PICASSO. *Stravinsky*. 1920. Pencil drawing, 24 ½ × 19". Collection the artist.

cago and which was heard in Europe through the traveling Negro bands. In his group of piano pieces called *The Children's Corner* (1908), Debussy included a number called "Golliwog's Cake Walk." The Golliwog was an eccentric comic-strip character in the Paris newspapers who was born out of an ink blot. Obviously a popularization of the interest in primitivism, he delighted grownups as well as children with his antics. The cakewalk was, of course, a favorite dance in the American Negro minstrel shows and one of the ancestors of the foxtrot.

Stravinsky (Fig. 568), whose music reflects many style trends, achieved the neoprimitive musical counterpart of Picasso's *Les Demoiselles d'Avi-*

Rite of Spring (Dance of the Adolescents)   IGOR STRAVINSKY

569. HENRI MATISSE. *Blue Window. c.* 1911. Oil on canvas, 51 1/2 × 35 5/8″. Museum of Modern Art, New York (Mrs. John D. Rockefeller, Jr., Purchase Fund).

gnon in the ballet *Rite of Spring*, which he wrote for the Diaghileff company in 1913. Subtitled *Scenes from Pagan Russia*, the opening "Dance of the Adolescents" uses repetitive rhythms and syncopated accents similar to those of American jazz. The sharply angular melodics, the complex polyrhythmic textures, the brutal accentuations, and the geometrical movements of the dancers are a masterly realization of the spirit of savagery.

The primitive, hypnotic, repeated rhythms first exploited by Stravinsky are found in the works of many contemporary composers—Prokofiev's *Scythian Suite* (1914) and the "Ritual Fire Dance" from Manuel de Falla's ballet *El Amor Brujo (Love the Sorcerer)*, produced in 1915 with stage sets and costumes by Picasso. The entrance of jazz idioms into serious musical forms is also one of the familiar aspects of contemporary music. Stravinsky published some ragtime music for piano in 1922, with a cover designed by Picasso; and George Gershwin's *Rhapsody in Blue* (1924) and his jazz opera *Porgy and Bess* (1935) have achieved a wide popular success.

Wild Beasts, The Bridge, Blue Rider, and Operatic Uproars

The expressionist deals with intensities of feeling rather than intensities of light. For him, the heat of creation supersedes the coldness of imitation, and he presents subjective reactions instead of representing objective realities, reasserting the supremacy of the human imagination over the representation of nature. About the time Picasso was discovering primitive sculpture, other groups were championing expressionism in painting as a reaction to the cool atmospheric effects and objective detachment of impressionism. Van Gogh had pointed the way with his frenzied canvases, passionate pictorial outbursts, saturated colors, and evangelical fervor. Such a painting as *Starry Night* (Plate 52), with the dark-green flames of the cypress trees, rolling rhythms of the hills, and cosmic explosion of the Milky Way, was enough to set imaginations on fire. The barbaric splendor of Gauguin's color harmonies was seized upon as a useful means for producing lively emotional responses, while the expressionists looked more distantly at the luminous colors of medieval stained glass and the imaginative inventiveness of Romanesque sculpture. Primitive arts of Polynesia and Africa played their parts here too.

The violent color clashes and visual distortions of the French painters of expressionistic persuasion earned for them the designation of *Les Fauves* (Wild Beasts), from a chance remark by a critic at the 1905 Paris Salon d'Automne who thought the room looked like a cage of wild animals. The early work of Matisse, that most civilized of painters, was so classified, though in retrospect it is difficult to understand why. If there was ever anything "wild" about Matisse, it has to be found in his reveling in brilliant color for its own sake, a subtle resourcefulness of invention, and a quality of Oriental splendor, which make him a *fauve* but a *fauve* devoid of ferocity.

The *Blue Window* (Fig. 569), which he painted about 1911, shows his concern with formal aesthetic problems, vibrant color harmonies, and arabesque-like decorative motifs. The picture is composed as an abstract still-life study merging subtly into a stylized landscape. The hatpins in the cushion on the left unite with the empty vase behind them; the flowers in the other vase grow into the foliage and the roof of the painter's studio outside; the Oriental idol in the axial center leads the eye to the vertical division of the casement window; while the lines formed by the contours of the lamp continue with those of the tree trunk in the garden. The bedroom table and its objects are thus united with the trees and sky beyond, and the interior and exterior elements become parts of one design. Depth and recession are suggested only by a slight lessening of the color intensities. In this picture, Matisse came close to realizing his dream of an "art of balance, of purity and serenity devoid of depressing subject matter."

Matisse's discriminating eye for subtle color harmonies and delicate curvilinear design is revealed in the *Roumanian Blouse* (Plate 57). For Matisse, expressionism did not apply to the content of his canvases or to the communication of an emotional message but rather to the entire formal management of his pictorial pattern. "Expression to my way of thinking," he once remarked, "does not consist of the passion mirrored upon a human face or betrayed by a violent gesture. The whole arrangement of my picture is expressive...."

German expressionism in the decade before World War I was mainly associated with two groups that developed simultaneously with the fauves: *Die Brücke* (The Bridge) and *Der Blaue Reiter* (The Blue Rider). The Bridge was a loose association of Dresden painters who took this name because they wished to form links with all artists of the expressionistic persuasion, as well as a bridge to the future. They acknowledged their debt to Van Gogh, Gauguin, and especially to the Norwegian Edvard Munch. From the latter's *The Scream* (Fig. 570), it is easy to see his appeal to the young emotionalists. Stark terror and nightmarish fears haunt this picture. The lines radiating outward from the hysterical woman's head seem to continue her piercing cry in a pattern of shattering shock waves.

Emil Nolde was among the most articulate members of *Die Brücke*, and *Dancing Around the Gol-*

den Calf (Fig. 571) was one of his many Biblical subjects. Violent color dissonances of blood-red and orange-yellow plus distorted drawing carry his message of the primitive fury and demoniac energies of his tormented dancers. *Der Blaue Reiter* was the title of a painting by Kandinsky that became the manifesto of the southern German expressionist movement. It was also the name of a book of 1912 edited by Franz Marc and Kandinsky that reproduced paintings shown at a Munich exhibit of the previous year by some of the French fauves and Paul

(above) 570. EDVARD MUNCH. *The Scream.* 1893. Lithograph on red paper. Museum of Fine Arts, Boston (Mrs. Serai W. Mosby–William Francis Warden Fund).

(left) 571. EMIL NOLDE. *Dancing Around the Golden Calf.* 1910. Oil on canvas, 34 ¾ × 39 ½". Bavarian State Picture Collection, Munich.

511

Klee, as well as by Marc and Kandinsky. The book also contained articles on modern art, while the Viennese composer Arnold Schoenberg contributed a chapter on parallel expressionistic developments in music. Marc's art, as seen in his *Tower of Blue Horses* (Fig. 572), is one of vibrating, pulsating rhythms, curvilinear design, and lyrical undulating movement.

Kandinsky was an international figure, who first painted in his native Russia, worked in the postimpressionistic and fauve styles in Paris, and then joined in founding the Blue Rider group in Munich. Works of his Blue Rider period, such as *Improvisation on a Warlike Theme* (Plate 58), still contained natural, human, and animal figures. In this case, the artist mentions that he painted it "subconsciously and in a state of strong tension" in 1913 when rumors of war were rife. This, he added, explains the presence of the two cannons in the lower right and the explosive forms.

By eliminating objects and figures, dissolving material forms, and improvising according to his moods, Kandinsky reached the frontiers of nonobjective art (see pp. 530–531) and set the stage for the abstract-expressionists of the 1940's and 1950's (see pp. 531–532), in which painting is "liberated" from nature. His *Picture with White Edge, No. 173* (Fig. 573) shows what he can express with lines, colors,

572. FRANZ MARC. *Tower of Blue Horses.* 1912. Oil on canvas, 6'8" × 4'3 ¼". Formerly State Museums, Berlin (present whereabouts unknown).

573. VASILY KANDINSKY. *Picture with White Edge, No. 173.* 1913. Oil on canvas, 4'7 ¾" × 6'7". Solomon R. Guggenheim Museum, New York.

and shapes. Commenting on his completely abstract paintings, Kandinsky stated that their content is "what the spectator *lives* or *feels* while under the effect of the *form and color combinations* of the picture"—which may or may not coincide with what the artist had in mind when he painted it.

Kandinsky, who published poetry, plays, and an autobiography, also recognized the affinity of his work to music. According to his own account, he strove to reproduce on his canvases the "choir of colors which nature has so painfully thrust into my very soul," and he believed that a painting should be "an exact replica of some inner emotion." Works that required "an evenly sustained pitch of inner emotional uplift sometimes lasting for days" he called "compositions." Spontaneous shorter works, sketches, and watercolors that "do not last the span of a longer creative period" he designated "improvisations."

Some of the earliest and most violent outbursts of musical expressionism are found in Richard Strauss' operas *Salome* (1905) and *Elektra* (1909), which he wrote in Munich while the Blue Rider movement was developing. Taking off from Richard Wagner's *Tristan und Isolde*, Salome's "love death" is an operatic excursion into the realm of abnormal psychology. In *Salome*, Strauss lures his listeners with sensuous sounds and a rainbow of radiant orchestral colors, and at the same time horrifies them with the gruesome spectacle of Salome's amorous soliloquy to the severed head of John the Baptist. This simultaneous attraction and repulsion is bound to produce emotional excitement and elicit truly expressionistic reactions. The sensational nature of Oscar Wilde's libretto, together with the famous Dance of the Seven Veils, caused the opera to be banned in New York, Boston, and London. *Elektra* is a dramatically effective version of Sophocles' tragedy (as adapted by Hugo von Hofmannsthal) filled with emotional climaxes, bloodcurdling shrieks, and lurid orchestral sounds.

Arnold Schoenberg's expressionistic song cycle *Pierrot Lunaire* (1912) explores the weird world of Freudian symbolism, and in his monodrama of 1913 *Die Glückliche Hand (The Lucky Hand)* the dissonances of the musical score are reinforced by crescendos of colored lights. Something of a climax is achieved in Alban Berg's opera *Wozzeck* (1925), a musical dramatization of big-city low life, in which a ballet of beggars, drunkards, and street girls pursue the murderer as he vainly tries to escape from himself. Whereas Wagner had worked up his climaxes over a considerable period of time, generally starting low in pitch and volume and mounting upward in an extended melodic, harmonic, and dynamic crescendo, Schoenberg and Berg telescoped the process. Their music became all

climax, with the extremes of low and high, soft and loud following each other suddenly and by leaps instead of in a gradual progression. Dissonances with Wagner existed in chains of sequences that eventually resolved. With Schoenberg and Berg, dissonance exists freely for its own sake with little or no relation to consonance.

Cubism

Just as the discovery of the rules of linear perspective had revolutionized the expression of the Florentine Renaissance, so cubism brought about a new way of looking at things in the 20th century. First worked out in painting, the reverberations of cubism were felt directly in sculpture and architecture, and indirectly in literature and music. A strong shove in the direction of abstraction came from the large retrospective exhibit of Cézanne's paintings held in Paris in 1907, where the young painters who saw it were struck by the artist's pictorial architecture. In the catalogue, they noted a quotation from a letter in which Cézanne remarked that natural objects can be reduced to the forms of the cylinder, the sphere, and the cone. Art, they reasoned, is not an imitation of nature in the usual sense but an imposition upon nature of geometrical forms derived from the human mind. As a result, cubist painting became a play of planes and angles on a flat surface. Cézanne's famous sentence, it should be pointed out, never mentioned cubes at all. His cylinders, spheres, and cones are rounded forms, presupposing curvilinear drawing; cubist drawing, on the contrary, is mainly rectilinear.

The Renaissance ideal had been the complete description of a pictorial situation from a single point of view; another vantage point would imply another picture. The cubist theory of vision took into account the breaking up and discontinuity of the contemporary world view in which objects are perceived more hastily in parts rather than more leisurely as wholes. The world, as a consequence, was seen fragmentarily and simultaneously from many points of view rather than entirely from a single viewpoint. In Picasso's *Demoiselles d'Avignon* (Plate 55), for instance, the faces of the second and third figures from the left are seen frontally, while their noses appear in profile. Picasso and Braque, as the coinventors of cubism, therefore undertook a new definition of pictorial space in which objects were represented simultaneously from many visual angles, in wholes or in parts, opaque and transparent. Just as the Crystal Palace and the Eiffel Tower had pointed the way to the interpenetration of the inner and outer aspects of architectural space, the art of the cubists undertook to move inside as

574. GEORGES BRAQUE. *Oval Still Life*. 1914. Oil on canvas, 36 ³/₈ × 25 ³/₄″. Museum of Modern Art, New York (gift of the Advisory Committee).

well as outside an object, below and above it, in and around it.

The cubists also were convinced that pictorial space, limited as it is by the two dimensions of the flat canvas, was something quite apart from natural space. From the Renaissance onward, the accepted procedure had been to produce the illusion of three dimensionality by some form of linear perspective derived from the principles of Euclidean geometry. The cubist painter, however, approached his canvas as an architect in order to construct his picture. Instead of trying to create the illusion of depth, he built his picture on the straight lines of the triangle and T-square by which he defined the planes of his surface. The expression of volume, as achieved by the modeling of objects in light and shade, was also modified, and so was the tactile feeling and structural solidity of Renaissance painting. Instead of representing objects in the round, the cubists analyzed them into their basic geometrical forms, broke them up into a series of planes, then collected, reassembled, tilted them at will into a new but strictly pictorial pattern of interlocking, interpenetrating, and overlapping surfaces and planes. Cubist color at the beginning was purposely

confined to the rather neutral tones of gray, green, olive, and ochre. The emphasis was on design and texture, and unity was found in the picture itself rather than in the objects represented. The technique in its earliest stages can be observed in Plate 55 in the way Picasso renders the bodies of the figures on the extreme left and upper right. Braque's *Oval Still Life* (Fig. 574) shows cubism in its more developed form after the rules had been worked out. Typical is its use of natural objects as a point of departure. Such still-life components as the table, violin, and sheet music are then broken up so that they can be reassembled in a design devised by the artist.

In their early doctrinaire stages, cubist pictures tended to be rather cold, impersonal studies in abstract design, but modifications of this pure state began to appear, such as Picasso's *Three Musicians* (Fig. 575). The flat two-dimensional arrangement is retained, but the bright coloration gives the canvas a gaiety not found earlier. The three masked figures sitting at a table are the same *commedia dell' arte* figures that regularly recur on Picasso's canvases, cubist or otherwise, and that come from his love of circus and theatrical performances in which clowns and other performers dress in gay carnival costumes. The figure on the left playing a violin is a Harlequin, the center one with the clarinet is a Pierrot, while the more solemn monk on the right plays what appears to be an accordion.

Picasso's *Woman's Head* (Fig. 576) is a translation of cubist principles into the three-dimensional medium of sculpture. It presents a geometrical analysis of the structure of the human face and emphasizes the most important planes and surfaces. By this process of disintegration, the head can be organized into a number of different facets, each of which can cast its own shadow and thus bring variety and a sense of movement to the composition.

The sculptures of Jacques Lipschitz are three-dimensional adaptations of cubism in its mature phase. The *Man with Mandolin* (Fig. 577) creates a repetitive pattern of rough stone textures, diagonal lines, tilted planes, irregular rectangles and triangles. From the side (Fig. 578), variants on the main theme appear, and curved shapes are accented to provide contrasts for the dominant rectilinearity of the design. In other works Lipschitz breaks down the traditional distinction between solids and voids, convex and concave surfaces, wholes and parts in intricately contrived interlocking designs.

The musical aspect of this new concept of space-time is found in the breaking up of traditional tonality as well as in the search for new musical resources and mediums of expression. Stravinsky, as a strict adherent of the principles of order, had said that "tonal elements become musical only by (left) 575. PABLO PICASSO. *Three Musicians*. 1921. Oil on canvas, 6′8″ × 6′2″. Philadelphia Museum of Art (Gallatin Collection).

(above) 576. PABLO PICASSO. *Woman's Head. c.* 1909. Bronze, 16 ¼″ high. Albright–Knox Art Gallery, Buffalo.

(left) 577. JACQUES LIPSCHITZ. *Man with Mandolin*. 1917. Stone, 29 ¾″ high. Yale University Art Gallery, New Haven, Conn. (Collection Société Anonyme).

(right) 578. JACQUES LIPSCHITZ. *Man with Mandolin* (side view).

515

Original Row

Retrograde

Inversion

Retrograde Inversion

virtue of their being organized." The 12-tone system of musical composition that Schoenberg evolved about 1915 was an answer to the need for a new order and one of the stricter forms of tonal organization. Schoenberg, who preferred to be called a constructor rather than a composer, begins a work by setting forth a basic row of 12 different tones. This row can be played in normal order, upside down by melodic inversion, backward in retrograde motion, and upside down once more in retrograde inversion (see above). Furthermore, it can be presented successively in sequences or simultaneously as in the various species of counterpoint. It can also be played in whole or in part simultaneously as in a chord or tone cluster, or it can be played serially as in a melody.

A row can be used either as an entity or broken up into several shorter themes or motives. It has been estimated that around half a billion different combinations are possible, which certainly is no limitation on its possibilities. The system provides a wealth of material as well as a certain freedom within an orderly framework. The 12-tone method has generally been referred to as atonality (that is, without tonality), but Schoenberg called it simply a method of composing with 12 tones that are related only with one another. Tonality is thus relative rather than an absolute, since there is no single tonal center. Tonality in the usual sense, however, is not excluded; rather, it is encompassed and transcended.

One of the most accessible works in the 12-tone repertory is Alban Berg's *Violin Concerto* of 1935. The row, in this case, is a straight ascending vertical series without repetition that can easily be followed by the alert, attentive ear. Ingeniously contrived, the first six tones contain the four triads of tonal music—notes one to three being the minor triad, two to four the augmented, three to five the major, four to six the diminished. A combination of four tones (one to four, two to five, etc.) forms types of seventh chords, while the top four notes make a series of whole tones resembling the scale favored by Debussy and the musical impressionists. Berg's tonal space thus includes traditional and impressionistic melody and harmony as a point of departure into nontonal or atonal music in which tones are relative only to each other rather than to a single tonal center.

Futurism and the Mechanical Style

The movement known as futurism was begun in Italy under the leadership of the poet and dramatist Marinetti prior to World War I. Agreeing with Nietzsche, who said that history was the pro-

579. GIACOMO BALLA. *Dog on Leash.* 1912. Oil on canvas, 35 × 42 ½″. George F. Goodyear and the Fine Arts Academy, Buffalo.

Plate 58. VASILY KANDINSKY. *Improvisation No. 30 (on a Warlike Theme).* 1913.
Oil on canvas, 43 ¼″ square. Art Institute of Chicago. (See p. 512.)

Plate 57. HENRI MATISSE. *Roumanian Blouse.* 1940.
Oil on canvas, 36 ¼ × 28 ¾″. Musée d'Art Moderne, Paris. (See p. 511.)

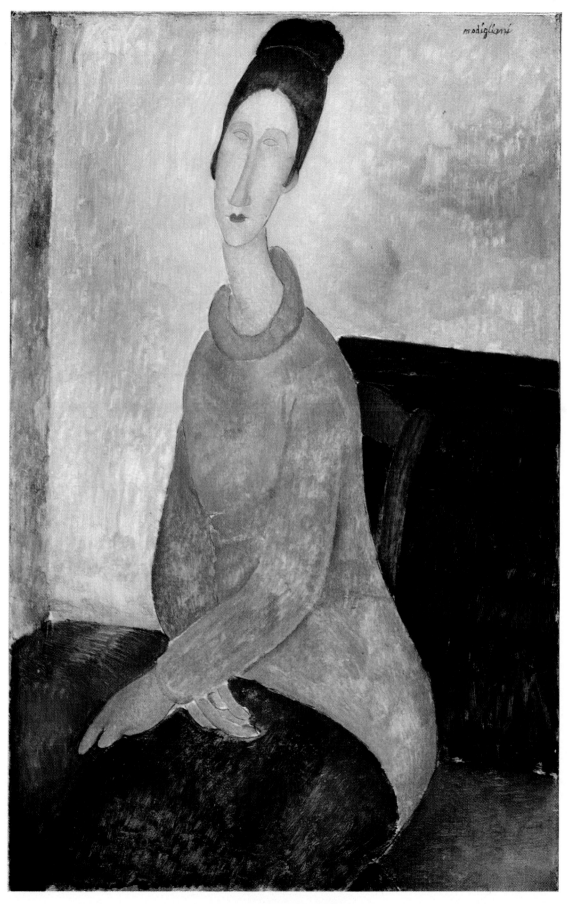

Plate 56. AMEDEO MODIGLIANI. *Yellow Sweater (Portrait of Mme Hébuterne)*. 1919.
Oil on canvas, 39 ³/₈ × 25 ¹/₂″. Solomon R. Guggenheim Museum, New York. (See p. 508.)

Plate 55. PABLO PICASSO. *Les Demoiselles d'Avignon.* 1907.
Oil on canvas, 8′ × 7′8″. Museum of Modern Art, New York
(acquired through the Lillie P. Bliss Bequest). (See p. 505.)

cess by which the dead bury the living, Marinetti said in his *Manifesto* of 1909 that futurism was being founded to "deliver Italy from its plague of professors, archeologists, tourist guides and antique dealers." The futurists wanted to destroy the museums, libraries, academies, and universities in order to make way for their particular wave of the future. "A roaring motor-car, which runs like a machine gun," they said, "is more beautiful than the Winged Victory of Samothrace." Theirs was a vision of a state ruled by a mechanical superman, in which the people would be reduced to cogs in the gigantic wheel of a fully mechanized society. War was praised as "a motor for art," and their social thinking was completely antidemocratic. Mussolini frankly acknowledged his indebtedness to the group for some of the ideas and symbols that were later to serve the interests of the Italian fascist movement.

"We go out. We swallow fog. The city is full of phantoms. Men cloaked in the mist walk silently. The canals exhale vapors." So goes in part a poem by Gabriele d'Annunzio, who was close to the movement. In architecture, futurists admired factories, skyscrapers, grain elevators, railway terminals, and triple-decked bridges. A manifesto on the "Aesthetics of Machinery" was written by one futurist painter to celebrate the beauty and spiritual qualities of gears, pulleys, pistons, locomotives, steam shovels, flywheels, and pinions.

Above all, the futurists projected an art for a fast-moving, machine-propelled age. They admired the motion, force, velocity, and strength of mechanical forms, and in their pictures they wanted more than anything else to include the dynamic sensation of motion. A galloping horse, they said, has not four legs but twenty. Giacomo Balla, in a picture called *Dog on Leash* (Fig. 579), paints a dog with each of its legs in several positions spreading out fanwise. Deriving his inspiration from automobiles, airplanes, trains, and machine guns, Severini paints *Armored Train* (Fig. 580) with its diagonal lines and plumes of smoke suggesting speed, while the gunfire adds the dimension of action and violence.

Boccioni, the most distinguished futurist painter, was also the only sculptor of the group. His *Unique Forms of Continuity in Space* (Fig. 581) captures the dynamics of motion in the turbulent hurrying stride of a moving figure. The body itself is felt only in the implied massive muscular tensions. Boccioni's subject is speed as expressed in a continuum of swirling, spiraling lines and the rushing currents of air as the figure cuts his path through space.

Futurism was influential chiefly in the formation of the "mechanical style." Its members were a bit too noisy and exhibitionistic to produce endur-

580. GINO SEVERINI. *Armored Train.* 1915. Oil on canvas, 46 × 34 ½". Collection Richard S. Zeisler, New York.

581. UMBERTO BOCCIONI. *Unique Forms of Continuity in Space.* 1913. Bronze, 3′ 7 ½″ high. Museum of Modern Art, New York (acquired through the Lillie P. Bliss Bequest).

ing art, and their activities ran more to manifestoes than to significant works. As a result, their future was all too soon behind them.

By taking some ideas from the cubists and others from the futurists, Fernand Léger developed an individual style of his own. Such a picture as *Mechanical Elements* (Fig. 582) has the visual hum of well-oiled machinery. As in *The City* (Plate 59), each part fits into its appointed place, and everything is neat and precise. Léger loved crankshafts, cylinder blocks, and pistons, which he painted in gleaming primary colors of enamellike brightness. Because he took Cézanne's statement about cylinders, spheres, and cones far more literally than the cubists did, his drawing was curvilinear rather than rectilinear, and he modeled his forms in light and shade. His buildings are structural steel skeletons populated by robots with spheres for heads, cylinders for legs, pipes for arms, and tubes for fingers. There is no room in Léger's world for sentiment, and such human forms as do occur, he introduces only for their "plastic value"; for this reason they remain "purposely inexpressive." In 1924, Léger made an abstract motion-picture film called *Ballet Mécanique*, in which machine forms and motorized movements replaced human beings and their activities.

Stravinsky, meanwhile, had composed an *Etude for Pianola* in 1917, and the French composer Arthur Honegger, using the normal symphonic complement, gave voice in 1924 to the triumphant song of the machine in a work called *Pacific 231*. Its name is an allusion to that year's model of an American locomotive, and the piece was designed to evoke the sounds of the railroad, complete with the grinding of the wheels and the shriek of the steam whistle. Perhaps the most successful musical realization of the mechanical style is found in the works of Edgar Varèse. Technically trained in two fields, Varèse was as much a physicist as a musician, and the titles of his works sound as if they came from a laboratory: *Intégrales*, *Density 2.15* (the specific gravity of the platinum of the flute for which it was composed), and *Ionization*. The last is constructed in a series of interlocking planes of sound that suggest, but are not directly imitative of, the rhythms of modern city life. Varèse's expressed aim was to build a music that would face the realities of the contemporary industrial world rather than attempt to escape from it.

582. FERNAND LÉGER. *Mechanical Elements*. 1918–1923. Oil on canvas, 6′11 1/8″ × 5′6 1/8″. Art Museum, Basel.

Dadaism, Neodadaism, and Surrealism

In their Paris exhibits of 1911 and 1912, the Italian Giorgio de Chirico and the Russian Marc Chagall anticipated the development of dadaism and surrealism. The latter term, in fact, was coined at that time by the French critic and playwright Guillaume Apollinaire to describe the dream fantasies, memory images, visual paradoxes, and assorted incongruities of their pictures. Chirico's dreamscape *The Disquieting Muses* (Fig. 583) takes expressionism into an introspective world of free associations. "Everything," according to this artist, "has two aspects: the current aspect, which we see nearly always and which ordinary men see, and the ghostly and metaphysical aspect, which only rare individuals may see in moments of clairvoyance and metaphysical abstraction." On a visit to Versailles Palace, as he says in his autobiography, he realized that "every corner of the palace, every column,

every window possessed a spirit, an impregnable soul.... At that moment I grew aware of the mystery which urges men to create strange forms." His intention was to break down the barriers of childhood and adulthood, the sleeping and waking states, the unbelievable and the believable, the illogical and the logical, the fantastic and the familiar. *The Disquieting Muses* is filled with an ominous silence and an all-pervading emptiness that are heightened by the mystery of deep perspective. Other Chirico pictures bear the deliberately ambiguous but evocative titles, couched in Freudian psychoanalytic terms, of *Nostalgia of the Infinite*, *Melancholy and Mystery of a Street*, and *Enigma of an Autumn Afternoon*. They are filled with sundials casting lengthened shadows, arcaded galleries, empty vans, factory chimneys, and spacious city squares populated only with strange statues. These elusive fantasies are based on Chirico's memories of his youth spent in Greece and Italy, and they are painted with a meticulous academic brush technique.

I and My Village (Fig. 584) grows out of Chagall's memories of Russia. In one of his childhood reveries he remembered the ceiling of his parents'

585. ROBERT RAUSCHENBERG. *Tracer.* 1964. Oil on canvas, 7 × 5'. Collection Mr. and Mrs. Frank Titelman, Altoona, Pa.

crowded cottage suddenly becoming transparent. "Clouds and blue stars penetrated along with the smell of the fields, the stable and the roads," he writes, and "my head detaches itself gently from my body and weeps near the kitchen where the fish is being prepared." In *I and My Village*, as in a dream, one image is superimposed on another, the houses are topsy-turvy, the farmer going to the fields is right side up, the peasant woman upside down, and the cow seems to be dreaming contentedly about a milkmaid.

The melancholy emptiness of Chirico and the nostalgic longing of Chagall's dream world find a remarkable parallel in Gustav Mahler's *Song of the Earth* (1911) and Thomas Mann's short novel *Death in Venice* (1913). In both, there is the same attempt to synthesize the contradictory tendencies of the time, the same juxtaposition of banal and fanciful elements, the same weary lyricism, a similar

longing for the unattainable, the same elusive ideals hovering on the distant horizon.

Dadaism was the product of the disillusionment, defeatism, and insane butchery of World War I. Anguished artists felt that the civilization that had brought about such horrors should be swept away and a new beginning made. To christen their movement, they chose at random a childish word out of the French dictionary—*dada*, a hobby-horse. Dadaism, consequently, was a nihilistic movement, particularly distrustful of order and reason, a challenge to polite society, a protest against all prevailing styles in art; it was, in fact, anti-art. Dada artists worked out an ism to end all isms, painted nonpictures compounded of the contents of wastebaskets, concocted nonsense for the sake of nonsense, wrote manifestoes against manifestoes, and their political expression was anarchy. Their bitter humor and iconoclasm, however, helped to explode hypocritical pomposities, to prick the balloons of pretentiousness, and, by reducing the role of art to absurdity, cleared the air of the postwar period.

The original dadaism did not last long. It was soon absorbed into surrealism, which has aptly been described as the "dadaism of the successful." After half a century in limbo, however, the vocabulary has been revived in the 1960's with a vengeance. The paraphernalia of neodadaism still comprises the same combinations of banality and the commonplace, the same assemblages of debris from attics and junkyards. But while dadaism grew out of the disillusionment and despair of a bankrupt society during World War I, neodadaism is nurtured by a joyous acceptance of modern materialism and the techniques of mass media; while the former was a desperately and deadly serious movement, the latter revels in nonsense for the sake of nonsense and laughs with the world, not at it.

As Robert Rauschenberg has disarmingly remarked, he just wants to live in the world, not reform it. His pictures, *Tracer* for example (Fig. 585), are what he calls "combines" of trash objects placed in incongruous juxtapositions. Because he uses actual automobile tires, umbrellas, bicycle wheels, stuffed birds, his combines are often as much sculptures as paintings. Other neodadaists of the "Pop Art" persuasion share Rauschenberg's enthusiasm for the trivia of everyday experience, have worked up a passion for packaging, and found their poetry in the supermarket by using soup cans, cola bottles, and the bright crisp containers for detergents. Rauschenberg and other neodadaists have joined in group adventures in improvised art known as *happenings*. In these chance and random creations, smells, weird electronic sound effects, moving pictures, blaring radios, vacuum cleaners, athletes running around in track suits, nonsense dialogue—are all combined into an improvised spectacle resembling controlled chaos.

The surrealist manifesto of 1924 proclaimed that the style was based on "pure psychic automatism by means of which one sets out to express, verbally, in writing or in any other manner, the real functioning of thought without any control by reason or any aesthetic or moral preoccupation." Surrealism, literally superrealism, implies a greater reality underlying the world of appearances, an illogical, subconscious, metaphysical dream world beyond the logical, conscious, physical one. Members of the group believed in the superior reality of the dream to the waking state, of fantasy to reason, of the subconscious to the conscious. André Breton,

author of the manifesto, also spoke of the "convulsive beauty" of dreams, and Paul Eluard said, "a poem should be the debacle of the intellectual."

The painter Salvador Dali associated himself with the group in 1929 and became one of its leading advocates. He described his pictures as "hand-painted dream photographs" and adorned them with symbols of various phobias, delusions, complexes, and other trappings of abnormal psychology. Like Chirico and Chagall, Dali was haunted by the mystery of time, and his *Persistence of Memory* (Fig. 586) suggests images of evolutionary, geological, and archeological as well as dream time. Dali also experimented with double images and psychic transformation as seen in his *Paranoic Face* (Fig. 587), where the viewer may see either some figures

586. SALVADOR DALI. *Persistence of Memory.* 1931. Oil on canvas, 9 ½ × 13″. Museum of Modern Art, New York.

587. SALVADOR DALI. *Paranoic Face.* 1935. Oil on wood, 7 ½ × 9″. Collection Edward James, London.

521

sitting before a mound and trees or the apparition of a strange face.

Today Paul Klee is generally accepted as one of the most significant pictorial talents of the 20th century. Such pictures as *Diana* (Plate 60) have caused many to dismiss him with a shrug, a scoff, or a smile. His disarming childlike innocence, however, is a highly deceptive simplicity and usually masks infinitely subtle meaning. His inventiveness outdoes even Picasso. He can delight the eye, tickle the fancy, or repel the observer with images straight out of nightmares. *Apparatus for Magnetic Treatment of Plants, Twittering Machine, A Cookie Picture, Moonplay, Idol for Housecats, Child Consecrated to Suffering, A Phantom Breaks Up*—so the titles run. The symbolism in his *Diana* will show the extraordinary complexity of Klee's art. The title identifies the figure as the mythical goddess of the chase, while the arrow is equipped magically with an eye to insure unerring accuracy. The broken contours of Diana's body suggest hurried flight through space,

(below) 588. JOAN MIRÓ. *Personages with Star.* 1933. Oil on canvas, 6′6 1/4″ × 8′1 1/2″. Art Institute of Chicago (gift of Mr. and Mrs. Maurice E. Culberg).

and the wheel under the goddess' foot is derived from Romanesque sculpture where it signified miraculous transportation. The color and surface treatment recall impressionism and Seurat's pointillism.

Klee consciously set out to look at the world through the eyes of a child in order to achieve a spontaneity untroubled by reason. "I want to be as though new-born, knowing nothing," as he put it. With Klee, as with Freud, the child was father of the man. By experimenting with hypnotic suggestion and psychic automatism, he gives his drawings the casual quality of doodles or the impulsiveness of improvisations. His mastery of line is so complete, however, that his work should never be confused with carelessness. By sticking mainly to small forms and to the techniques of watercolor and ink, pencil and crayon, he produces pictures with a refreshing unpretentiousness. He also has an element of genial humor that is notably missing in so much of modern art.

Joan Miró, like Klee, essayed an art of pure imagination existing outside logic or reason. His *Personages with Star* (Fig. 588) uses the technique of automatic drawing in a trancelike state and shows (left) 589. ALBERTO GIACOMETTI. *Palace at 4 A. M.* 1932–1933. Wood, glass, wire, string; 25″ high. Museum of Modern Art, New York (Purchase).

(below) 590. JEAN (HANS) ARP. *Relief.* 1938–1939. Wood, 19 ¾″ square. Museum of Modern Art, New York (gift of the Advisory Committee).

the influence of Kandinsky. While much of surrealism is preoccupied with morbid and abnormal psychological states, Miró lightens his fantasies with whimsy. His pictures have such fanciful titles as *Persons Magnetized by the Stars Walking on the Music of a Furrowed Landscape*, and they teem with abstract insects that buzz silently and geometrical worms that squirm statically.

Giacometti and Hans Arp represent surrealism's sculptural dimension. Giacometti's *Palace at 4 A.M.* (Fig.589) uses a geometrical, cagelike framework containing spectral and skeletal forms. The phantom figures in their interpenetrating open and closed spaces produce a haunting sensation of human isolation and loneliness. Arp, who was a member of both the dadaist and surrealist movements, is also associated with abstract sculpture. His *Relief* (Fig. 590) is typical of his abstract work in wood, which he cuts with a jig-saw. In the manner of the African Negro carvers, he accepts the nature of his material with its curved shapes, knots, grain, and other distinguishing characteristics, and then sets himself the problem of bringing out its beauty by varying its contours and by cutting and refining its surfaces and textures.

The attempts by the doctrinaire surrealists to work in the arts of sculpture, literature, and music have not been successful, and significant parallels can be found only outside the movement. James

Joyce and Gertrude Stein tried to establish a method for subconscious or automatic writing as a way to tap the reservoir of the subconscious mind. The result was the stream-of-consciousness technique, notably exemplified in Joyce's *Ulysses* (1922). The more irreverent iconoclastic tendencies of surrealist painting have their musical parallels in such compositions as Erik Satie's three piano pieces of

1913. Entitled *Desiccated Embryos*, they have semi-sarcastic expression marks, such as that which calls upon the pianist to play a melody "like a nightingale with a toothache." There is also the biting satire of Prokofiev's brilliant fairy-tale opera *Love of Three Oranges* (1921) and the weird symbolism of Bela Bartok's legendary opera *Bluebeard's Castle* (1922). Paul Klee's world of childhood fantasy finds a charming lyrical counterpart in Maurice Ravel's opera *The Child and the Sorceries (L'Enfant et les Sortilèges)* of 1925. In Colette's libretto, a child breaks some bric-a-brac and toys in a temper tantrum. In a dreamlike sequence, the objects then come to life to seek revenge. A Wedgewood teapot and a china cup, appropriately enough, carry on a conversation in broken English while dancing a fox-trot; a little old man pops up out of nowhere and sings multiplication tables and story problems with erroneous answers; two cats sing a hilarious mewing duet; and all that is left of the torn picture of the fairy princess in the story book is "a golden hair and the debris of a dream." Ravel's ingenious orchestration adds whistles, wood blocks, and friction instruments to the usual ones and cheese graters for certain bizarre effects.

Neoclassical Interlude

No century would be complete without its bow before the shrines of Greece and Rome, and just as the Renaissance, the 18th, and the 19th centuries did, the 20th century has its neoclassicism. While works with classical allusions abound in the present century, the neoclassic movement came into sharpest focus in the 1920's. The comparative calm before the storm of World War I had been broken by the emotional extremes of pictorial expressionism and such neoprimitive outbursts as Stravinsky's *Rite of Spring*. In the aftermath of war, order and clarity seemed more important than violent expression. And after the abstractions of cubism and futurism, the reassertion of the human figure in art seemed in order.

In 1917, Picasso had made a trip to Italy where he was impressed by the Pompeian wall paintings and stimulated by meetings in Rome with Stravinsky and Serge Diaghileff, who were there with the latter's Russian ballet company. One direct result was their three-way collaboration on a ballet with song called *Pulcinella*, which was first performed in Paris in 1920. Stravinsky's score was based on the form of the classical dance suite of the early 18th century with music adapted from Pergolesi. Picasso's costumes were designed in the manner of the stylized Pierrot and Harlequin *commedia dell'arte* figures, while his scenery included a backdrop filled with angular distortions showing a street in Naples with a view of the bay and a moonlit Mt. Vesuvius. In 1922, an adaptation of Sophocles' *Antigone* by Jean Cocteau was mounted in Paris. Picasso designed the scenery and masks, while the incidental music for harp and oboe was supplied by Arthur Honegger. An opera called *The Eumenides* by Darius Milhaud, based on Paul Claudel's translation of the tragedy by Aeschylus, was written in the same year. *Mercury* was the title of still another ballet brought out by the Diaghileff company in 1924, with music by Erik Satie and costumes and scenery by Picasso. Three years later, Stravinsky completed his opera-oratorio *Oedipus Rex*. Diaghileff again was the producer, and Jean Cocteau's text, based on Sophocles' tragedy, was translated into Latin so that it would be in a "petrified" language and thus would be reduced to mere syllabic material. The motionless stance of the actors was intended to make them as static as Greek columns, and the chorus was placed back of a bas relief where only their heads were visible. Such productions continued sporadically throughout the 1930's when Stravinsky was once more found collaborating with André Gide on a work for orchestra, chorus, and tenor called *Persephone* (1934).

Picasso's pictures in the 1920's, such as the *Three Graces* (Fig. 591), also reflect this neoclassicism and are characterized by elegance of line, sculpturesque modeling of bodies, and reduction of pictorial elements to the barest essentials. Others, such as *Pipes of Pan* (Fig. 592), are beach scenes in which the figures appear statuesquely against geometrically organized backgrounds and chaste colors of white and blue. While his painting took another tack after the *Three Graces*, his many book illustrations continued to show classical influences. Picasso had long admired the linear technique of Ingres, especially the pencil drawings. Even in such an austere medium as etching, his illustrations for a new edition of Ovid's *Metamorphoses* (1930) and for Gilbert Seldes' version of Aristophanes' *Lysistrata* (1934) show his capacity for effective expression.

In the neoclassical interlude, the statues of Maillol and Despiau reassert the expressive importance of the nude figure both in the round and in relief. Maillol's static, stable, calm figures are a welcome relief in a turbulent century. His neoclassicism is creative not imitative, free not academic. The *Torso of Venus* (Fig. 593), with its Praxitelean curve and stance, its antiquity and modernity, achieves a quiet monumentality that is both universal and timeless.

One of the most consistent patterns of contemporary literature, especially in France, is the reinterpretation of Greek myths in highly sophisticated terms as a subtle device for pointing out modern (left) 591. PABLO PICASSO. *Three Graces*. 1924. Oil and charcoal on canvas, 6'6 7/8" × 4'11". Collection the artist (courtesy Museum of Modern Art, New York).

(below left) 592. PABLO PICASSO. *Pipes of Pan*. 1923. Oil on canvas, 6' 8 1/2" × 5' 8 5/8". Collection the artist (courtesy Museum of Modern Art, New York).

(below) 593. ARISTIDE MAILLOL. *Torso of Venus*. 1925. Bronze, 3'9" high. Courtesy Galerie Dina Vierny, Paris.

moralistic or political parallels. This tendency runs regularly through the works of André Gide from his early *Prometheus Drops His Chains* (1899) to his autobiographical story *Theseus* (1946). It can also be found in Franz Werfel's antiwar play *The Trojan Women* (1914) and in Jean Paul Sartre's *The Flies* (1943). The latter was staged in Paris during the Nazi occupation, and the allusion to the plague of flies that sucked Orestes' blood in Aristophanes' bitter comedy could have escaped no one. Poets have sometimes found classical subjects a convenient way of leaving their works in a fragmentary state like antique ruins. Paul-Ambroise Valéry's trilogy of 1922, for instance, contains a poem called *Fragments of Narcissus*. T. S. Eliot's *Sweeney Agonistes* (1932) in which the grandeur of the past is contrasted with the banality of the present, likewise is incomplete and bears the subtitle *Fragments of an Aristophanic Melodrama*. Freud's use of the names of characters from Greek literature—Oedipus, Electra, Narcissus—as symbols of recurrent subconscious drives also found its way into literature.

James Joyce's novels *A Portrait of the Artist as a Young Man* (1916) and *Ulysses* (1922) use classical allusions as a frame of reference but avoid the logic and order of Greek forms. The author's admitted inspiration for *Ulysses* was Homer's *Odyssey*. With his adoption of the stream-of-consciousness technique, the classical molds became convenient devices to hold the nebulous, dreamlike sequences in some semblance of unity. They also provide the bewildered reader with a few recognizable straws to grasp when he begins to founder on the sea of such an unfamiliar style of writing. The entire action of *Ulysses* occurs in Dublin in a single 24-hour period to preserve the classical unities of place and time. The plot, concerns a wanderer who voyages through the terrors and temptations of the labyrinth of Dublin's streets while on his way home to his wife and son, which is reminiscent of Odysseus' search for Penelope and Telemachus. In the larger sense, the book is concerned with man's eternal search for a meaning for life. In Joyce's manuscript, the titles of chapters were based on quotations from the *Odyssey*, but these were omitted when it was printed. Most of the work is obscure and cryptic, but the juxtaposition of the heroic past helps to heighten the squalid picture of the present that he paints.

Social Realism

Social realism represents the artist's protest against the intolerable conditions that beset mankind. In the tradition of Goya, Hogarth, and Daumier, many contemporary painters have championed the cause of the weak against the strong, the poor against the rich, the oppressed against their oppressors. In their search they have explored the dregs of society, the urban excrescences of skid row, and the ugliness of the lower depths. In so doing they have discovered that the paint brush and the pen are often mightier than the sword.

This Will Be the Last Time, Little Father (Fig. 594) is the title of the print by Georges Rouault that describes the heartbreaking farewell of a son as he leaves for war and almost certain death. Rouault's art is visionary, but his tragic clowns, comical lawyers, static acrobats, and active landscapes reveal his broad compassion for and passionate protests against human exploitation and degradation. His pictures often mirror the grimacing masks of those who presume to sit in judgment on their fellowmen, and the insensitive countenances of people in positions of power who are indifferent to human suffering. His series of 100 etchings and aquatints for two projected portfolios entitled *Miserere* (Have Mercy on Us) and *Guerre* (War), with text by a literary friend, occupied him intermittently in the years following World War I. Though the portfolios as

594. Georges Rouault. *This Will Be the Last Time, Little Father.* 1914–1927. Copperplate engraving, 28 1/2 × 16 7/8". Museum of Modern Art, New York.

such were never published, 58 prints have been issued separately. The title page of the war volume in which Figure 594 was to have appeared reads: "They Have Ruined Even the Ruins."

Orozco, one of the Mexican muralists deeply involved in his country's revolution, identified himself with the struggle of the illiterate masses as they tried to break the chains of their landowning and capitalist exploiters. His grim satire also extends to the academic community as pictured in *Gods of the Modern World* (Fig. 595). This macabre comment on the sterility of higher education depicts a skeleton giving birth, while one professor acts as a midwife and others witness the ghastly event.

The New York artist Ben Shahn is an ardent champion of minority groups and the eloquent portrayer of the anonymous city dweller who has lost his sense of community identity. The stark setting and grim countenances of *Miners' Wives* (Fig. 596) express the anxiety, fear, and desolation of the families of men connected with a hazardous occupation. Man's inhumanity to man is the general theme, as Shahn pleads the cause of the downtrodden and victims of social injustice.

In his *Guernica* (Fig. 597), Picasso used a combination of expressionist and abstract techniques as a violent protest against a cruel and inhuman act by modern barbarians. What lighted the fuse that set off this pictorial explosion of carnage and terror was the first saturation air raid of the century—the horrible "experiment" by the German air force

(above) 595. José Clemente Orozco. *Gods of the Modern World*. 1932–1934. Fresco, 10'6" × 14'8". Dartmouth College, Hanover, N. H.

(below) 596. Ben Shahn. *Miners' Wives*. 1948. Oil on canvas, 48 × 36". Philadelphia Museum of Art.

597. PABLO PICASSO. *Guernica*. 1937. Oil on canvas, 11′ 6″ × 25′ 8″. Collection the artist (on extended loan to the Museum of Modern Art, New York).

carried out against the defenseless Basque town of Guernica, an incident in General Franco's successful rebellion against the legally elected government of the Spanish Republic. Picasso, a loyalist partisan, was in Paris with the commission to paint a mural for the Spanish pavilion of the World's Fair of 1937. Just two days after the news of the bombing reached Paris, he began work. The huge canvas, accomplished in a matter of weeks, took up one wall of the Spanish pavilion, where it made an unforgettable impression on the thousands who saw it. The attention it attracted and the measure of understanding accorded it have been altogether in proportion to *Guernica's* value as one of the century's most important paintings.

Guernica, a picture in the great tradition of historical painting, is one of those rare incidents of the right artist painting the right picture at the right time. Its purpose was frankly propagandistic; its intent, to horrify. But besides recalling the apocalyptic visions of Romanesque Last Judgments, it is a work of social protest in the manner of Goya and Daumier. The principal action begins in the lower right where a woman dashes forward, clutching her hands in an attitude of despair. The triangular composition then mounts to its apex at the point where the lamp, horse's head, and the eye of day, with the electric bulb of night as its pupil, converge. From this climax, the eye moves downward to the head of the dismembered warrior in the lower left.

Guernica, according to Picasso, is allegorical, and he has explained some of the symbolism. The horse with the spear in his back, the inevitable victim of bullfights, signifies victimized humanity succumbing to brute force. The motif of the shrieking mouth is repeated in that of the screaming woman with her dead child at the left, the face of the soldier below, and the victim of the flames at the right. The bull standing for brutality is the only triumphant figure in this symbolic struggle between the forces of darkness and light, between barbarism and civilization. Above, an arm reaches forward to hold the lamp of truth over the whole gruesome scene.

Guernica appeared at a time when many earlier pictorial experiments could be combined. It employs all the exaggerations, distortions, and shock techniques developed by expressionistic drawing, but it omits lurid coloration in favor of the somber shades of mourning—black, white, and gradations of gray. The abstract design, the overlapping planes on a two-dimensional surface, and the absence of modeling all derive from cubism. So also does the simultaneous principle of the day-and-night symbol; the head of the bull, which is seen both from the front and the side at the same time; and the sensation of inner and outer space by which the observer is at once both inside and outside the burning buildings. The elongation of the heads to express headlong motion coincides with the photography of movement made with stroboscopic light.

598. FRANCIS BACON. *Painting (The Butcher).* 1946. Oil and tempera, 6′6″ × 4′4″. Museum of Modern Art, New York (Purchase).

The screaming, nightmarish subject matter is similar to that of expressionism. Picasso usually paints so rapidly and prolifically that he often has difficulty resisting the temptations of his own facile technique. Consequently, much of his work is uneven. Here, however, after making 100 sketches, he worked in a disciplined and selective manner that shows the artist in complete command of his medium. Thus, his successful synthesis in *Guernica* of so many of these divergent 20th-century techniques, as well as the vivid dramatization of his subject, has given powerful expression to the chaos and conflicts of this tortured century.

Bitter satires on the junglelike conditions of urban life and the dismal effects of mass media on the popular mind preoccupy the English painter Francis Bacon. In his *Painting* (Fig. 598), subtitled *The Butcher,* he speaks with the vocabulary of expressionism and surrealism as he depicts his nightmarish apparition. Less bitter but nonetheless poignantly expressive are Andrew Wyeth's muted evocations of the social decay as well as the unfulfilled aspirations of life on the American scene (Fig. 599).

The eminent Jugoslav sculptor Ivan Mestrovic characteristically used the human figure to achieve his expressionistic effects. *Job* (Fig. 600), after he has lost his family and flocks, sits down among the ashes and cries out, "Let the day perish wherein I was born, and the night in which it was said, there is a man child conceived" (Job 3:3). By this allusion to the age-old personification of human misery, and by the twisted and tortured posture of the emaciated body, Mestrovic created a symbol of the plight of mankind crying out to the heavens in a protest against needless suffering.

Nonobjectivism, Abstract-Expressionism, and Op Art

Abstractionism was carried to its logical geometrical conclusion by Piet Mondrian just as ex-

599. ANDREW WYETH. *Mother Archie's Church.* 1945. Tempera on panel, 25 × 48″. Addison Gallery of American Art, Phillips Academy, Andover, Mass.

pressionism had reached its point of pure abstraction in the work of Kandinsky. The pictures of these two artists are, of course, poles apart. Both artists, however, are *nonobjective* in that they are nonfigurative and nonrepresentational and that the pictorial content of their canvases bears no reference to recognizable objects or to anything outside the actual pictures. All subject matter, all associational meanings, are studiously avoided. The picture with its lines, shapes, and colors is its own referent.

Mondrian's art, like Kandinsky's, evolved gradually from the concrete to the abstract. In his early years, Mondrian painted landscapes and quiet interior scenes in the tradition of his native Holland, and his later style (Fig. 601), though completely abstract, owes much to the cool geometrical precision of his great predecessor Vermeer. Mondrian could well be describing his *New York City* (Plate 61) when he wrote: "The new style will spring from the metropolis." He delighted in the criss-cross patterns of city streets, architect's blueprints, gaunt structural steel skeletons of skyscrapers under construction, and simple faces of buildings of the international architectural style (see pp. 536—539). The new art, he continued, would not be individual, but collective, impersonal, and international. All references to the "primitive animal nature of man" should be rigidly excluded in order to reveal "true human nature" through an art of "balance, unity, and stability." This objective he strove to realize by using "only a single neutral form: the rectangular area in varying dimensions." His colors are likewise abstract—black lines of various widths against white backgrounds, relieved occasionally by a primary color "climax"—red, blue, or yellow—in as pure a state as possible. In his opinion, a work of art should be "constructed," and he approached a canvas with all the objectivity of a draftsman making a blueprint. The result of this pictorial engineering is the series of chaste, two-dimensional spatial studies for which he is best known. His visual patterns have a repose that rests on a precise balance of horizontal and vertical elements, and they are clean to the point of being prophylactic. His pictures are far more complex than they may seem to the casual eye; and they have had a great influence on modern design, especially of advertising layouts, posters, rugs, and linoleum.

Abstract-expressionism, a tense, explosive movement that had its inception in New York after World War II, combines the characteristics of cubist abstraction and nonobjectivism with expressionistic intensity and surrealist automatic painting. The act of painting is often considered more important than that which is painted. The "old master" of the style was the German Hans Hofmann who had absorbed the fauve and cubist techniques

600. IVAN MESTROVIC. *Job.* 1946. Bronze, 4' high. Syracuse University, New York.

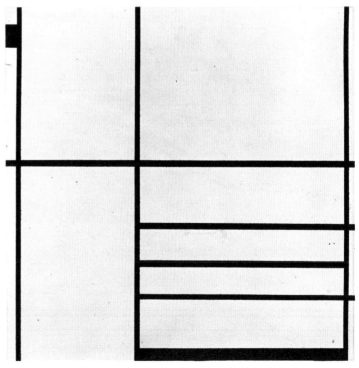

601. PIET MONDRIAN. *Composition in White, Black, and Red.* 1936. Oil on canvas, 40 1/4 × 41″. Museum of Modern Art, New York (gift of the Advisory Committee).

in Paris at the turn of the century. Late paintings, such as *Proprie Moto* (Fig. 602), consist of blocks of strong colors that activate his canvases with surprising energy. At other times Hofmann painted all-black canvases, others with awninglike stripes, or swirling vortices of vivid hues in which the pictorial content becomes nothing more than the color and texture of the paint.

Jackson Pollock, an American abstract-expressionist, was an "action painter," who laid the canvas on the floor so he could move bodily into the orbit of his restless pictures. With commercial paints he used dribbling, splattering, and flinging techniques to get the textural effects he desired. Paintings like *Convergence* (Plate 62) have no predetermined pattern, and the actual act of painting became the content—a kind of pictorial choreography in which the spectator is invited to join.

Op Art, or optical art, is also a form of action painting, except that the action takes place in the viewer's eye. Optical art, which painters of that persuasion have called "perpetual abstraction," developed out of geometrical abstraction and optical illusionism. These artists are allied with mathematicians, physicists, and psychologists in their experiments and exploration of optical phenomena. Instead of seeing is believing, with Op Art seeing is deceiving. Like the impressionists, optical artists are concerned primarily with the work of art as an act of the eye. But unlike the impressionists, they avoid all association with the outside world and concentrate on the way the eye and brain respond to optical data. By activating the responsive eye, by the impact on perception of color dissonances and the juxtaposition of geometrical patterns, optical art has produced startling effects of constant motion and ceaseless change that amount to a new way of seeing.

Bridget Riley's *Current* (Fig. 603) illustrates how stable lines seem to shift and equivocate. Since it is impossible to apprehend the whole picture at once, different responses are induced as the eye moves over partial sectors of the surface so that the illusions of faster-slower, forward-backward movement occurs. The sense of perception, in other words, is confused as the eye and brain signals get their wires crossed. In the process the viewer feels sensations varying from disorientation to depression, from giddiness to exhilaration.

ARCHITECTURE

More than any of the other 20th-century arts, architecture has exhibited a greater sense of responsibility, reached a more homogeneous crystalliza-

tion of style, and achieved a wider popular acceptance. A building, unlike a painting, has to stand up; unlike a sculptural group, it has to fulfill some practical purpose. Experimental architecture is possible, but the discipline of sound engineering has kept architects from some of the wilder flights of fancy seen in painting, sculpture, literature, and music. Today's architect is no mere stone mason—he is an engineer of society, a social philosopher, a poet and idealist, as well as a practical builder.

The needs of a complex, modern, urbanized society and the availability of new materials and structural methods have made a new architecture both possible and necessary. *Ferroconcrete*, or cement reinforced by embedding wire mesh or iron rods in it, leads the procession of new materials. It has the strength of both steel and stone without their weaknesses or expense, it can span broader spaces than marble, and carry the weight of steel. The *cantilever*—the extension of a slab or beam horizontally into space beyond its supporting post—is an ancient principle that had to await its large-scale use until the development of ferroconcrete.

Frank Lloyd Wright, Walter Gropius, and Le Corbusier are the old masters of contemporary architecture. Each was a leading representative of one or the other of two schools of thought once considered to be polar extremes. Wright with a romantic turn spoke in terms of the union of nature and man through his "organic architecture." Gropius and Corbusier were exponents of the international style with the emphasis on building for the Machine Age. In the course of the century the noisy argumentation has been muted, and a synthesis of the two viewpoints has been effected in some of the notable buildings of the 1960's.

Today's architect has once again become the partner of the painter, sculptor, and mosaicist. From the bleak utilitarianism of the early international style, architecture has turned once more to the principle of ornamentation—not, however, extraneous embellishment or mere architectural embroidery, but the inclusion of sculptures and murals as integral parts of the larger architectonic statement. Well-placed sculptural groups, frescoes, or mosaics as points of interest can always give definition to exteriors and interiors; serve as symbols of human involvement or images of social activities; and an unexpected turn here or twist there can create an element of fantasy, whimsy, warmth, and delight. In such a complex as Lincoln Center in New York City, architects have called upon the sculptors Moore (Fig. 566) and Lipschitz, as well as the painter Chagall, to provide a handsome setting for the performing arts and an educational center that would vie with an ancient acropolis or forum for completeness of expression.

Plate 59. FERNAND LÉGER. *The City.* 1919. Oil on canvas, 7′7″ × 9′8½″. Philadelphia Museum of Art (A.E. Gallatin Collection). (See p. 518.)

Plate 60. PAUL KLEE. *Diana*. 1931. Oil on wood, 37 $\frac{1}{2}$ × 23 $\frac{5}{8}$″.
Collection William Bernoudy, St. Louis. (See p. 522.)

602. HANS HOFMANN. *Proprie Moto*. 1965. Oil on canvas, 5′ × 4′4″. André Emmerich Gallery, New York.

603. Bridget Riley. *Current*. 1964. Synthetic polymer paint on composition board, 4′ 10 ³/₈″ × 4′ 9 ⁷/₈″. Museum of Modern Art, New York (Philip C. Johnson Fund).

604. Louis Sullivan. Wainwright Building, St. Louis. 1890–1891.

Organic Architecture: Sullivan, Wright

Sullivan's slogan "form follows function" is subject to a variety of interpretations, but the line of thought it provided led to an important reevaluation of architectural forms in relation to human activities and to a reexamination of basic architectural methods, materials, and purposes. Sullivan's disciple Frank Lloyd Wright, and the architects identified with the international style, accepted the principle that stone should behave like stone, wood like wood, and steel like steel, and that the design should be modified by the materials used. Both also pointed to the absurdity of people catching trains in Roman baths, working in Renaissance office buildings, banking money in Doric temples, living in English Tudor houses, and going on Sunday to Gothic churches. The criterion for a successful building, then, is no longer what it looks like, but how well it fulfills its purpose.

The skyscraper, among the earliest and boldest instances of modern architecture, was made possible by steel-skeleton construction and the elevator. It came out of the American Middle West as an answer to the need for commercial centralization. In the hands of Louis Sullivan, who put up the Wainwright Building in St. Louis in 1891 (Fig. 604), the skyscraper was a "proud and soaring thing," reflecting the pride of the businessman in his work, as well as the drive and power of a technologically oriented people. The principal drawback to skyscrapers, however, is their contribution to congestion in already overcrowded areas. From a human standpoint, their value has thus far been less spectacular than their engineering.

Wright, picking up where Sullivan left off, saw both the advantages and drawbacks of the skyscraper. With characteristic romanticism, he spoke of his buildings in naturalistic terms. His 18-story skyscraper in Bartlesville, Oklahoma, has a "taproot" foundation, grows upward like a tree, with its floors and walls cantilevered outward like branches from its central trunk. Skyscrapers, he was convinced, did not belong in already congested cities but in the open, where they could breathe and have room to cast decent shadows. Wright's philosophy of architecture was that of a liberating force, and his creative freedom allowed for decorative motifs to grow organically out of his basic designs, the relations of masses to voids, the fenestration, the colors and grains of wood, and the textures of stone. Through his masterly articulation, space for living and working comes to life and breathes. "Nothing," he observed, "is complete in itself, but is only complete as the part is merged into the larger expression of the whole."

The architect, according to Frank Lloyd Wright, is the poet who imagines the ideal life and fashions the forms, shapes, and spaces that guide men to live it. His organic architecture was based on the unity of site, structure, and decoration, and the early houses he built in and around Chicago were his first claim to fame. For him a dwelling had to be a home for the human spirit as well as for the human body. A man's house, he thought, should express warmth, protection, and seclusion. The heart of the home, according to Wright, is the hearth in the form of a massive fireplace, and all the other rooms should be built around this. Interior space, moreover, should not confine but expand without interruption from the inside out to bring men closer to the earth, plants, trees, and water.

"Falling Water" (Fig. 605), which Wright built for Edgar J. Kaufmann at Bear Run, Pennsylvania, is an expressive combination of reinforced concrete material, cantilevered construction, and a dramatic site. The house comes close to realizing Wright's ideal of a structure growing organically out of its site. In this case, his client loved the waterfall and wanted to live near it. "Falling Water" therefore embraces both the stream and the waterfall; and by means of the cantilevered slabs that project from the rock embankment on which they rest, Wright carried the living space outward over the water itself. The ledge of natural rock under the water is paralleled by the concrete shelf above, while the jutting slab on top is placed at right angles to repeat the direction of the moving water. The site as well as the building is a series of terraces proceeding outward from a stone core. The interior is one large room opening out onto the terraces and porches. The horizontal planes of these porches, in turn, are balanced by the vertical volumes of the fireplace. The local stone used in this chimney mass is related both in color and texture to the natural rock of the river bank. The cantilevering here allows the several stories the independence to develop their own fluid floor plans. As on the outside, the inside space radiates around the central core, with advancing and receding areas promoting what Wright called the "freedom of interior and exterior occupation."

In the closing years of his notable career, this dean of American architects finally received a commission to construct a building in his country's largest city—the Guggenheim Museum (Fig. 606), an art gallery for abstract painting and sculpture in

605. FRANK LLOYD WRIGHT. "Falling Water" (Kaufman House). 1936–1937. Reinforced concrete and stone. *c.* 64′ deep × 62′ wide. Bear Run, Pa.

(below) 606. FRANK LLOYD WRIGHT. Solomon R. Guggenheim Museum, New York. 1957–1959. Reinforced concrete, diameter at ground level *c.* 100′, at roof level 128′, dome 92′ high.

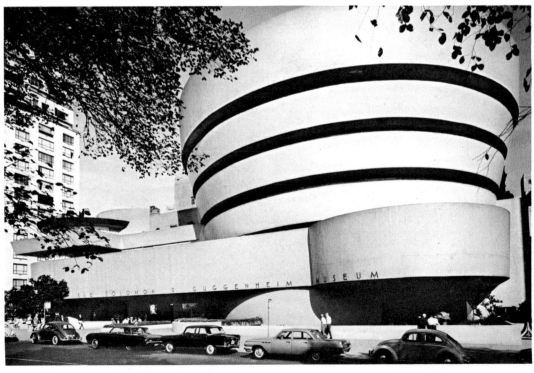

New York City. To Wright, a museum should never be a group of boxlike compartments but a continuous flow of floor space in which the eye encounters no obstruction. To achieve this ideal, he designed a single, round room of reinforced concrete nearly 100 feet in diameter, with a hollow cylindrical center core surmounted by a wire-glass dome 92 feet above ground (Fig. 607). Spiraling upward around the room, traversing a distance of a quarter of a mile, is an open 6-story cantilevered ramp rising at a 3-percent grade and broadening from a width of 17 feet at its lowest level to almost 35 feet at the top. Throngs of spectators can be accommodated without congestion as they move easily up or down the ramp. The visitor can take the elevator to the top level and wind downward at leisure, or he can start at the bottom and walk up. He can inspect part of the exhibit at close range and at eye level or view three levels simultaneously across the open room.

607. FRANK LLOYD WRIGHT. Interior, Solomon R. Guggenheim Museum, New York. 1957–1959. Ramp over ¼ mile long.

International Style: Gropius, Le Corbusier, Miës van der Rohe

The international style crystallized in Germany with the work of Walter Gropius and Miës van der Rohe, in France with Le Corbusier, and in the Netherlands with J. J. P. Oud. When Gropius was commissioned to reorganize a German art school after World War I, he renamed it the Bauhaus (Building Institute) and made it a technical school of design with special emphasis on the industrial arts and the study of modern materials and methods. For the plant he brought together the complex of studios, machine shops, administrative offices, and professors' houses into a single masterly group of interlocking and interrelated cubes. Smaller units had chaste Mondrianlike façades; others, like the Machine Shop, were open structures with glass-curtain walls.

As an exponent of the international style, Gropius started with the open box as the basic unit of space, varied its volume, and grouped several in a related pattern of cubes. The Machine Shop (Fig. 608) shows how the building is treated as an open volume rather than as a closed mass. By the method of cantilevering, Gropius allowed the building to project several feet outward over its supporting piers. The horizontal emphasis thus established is then carried out in the concrete base and repeated at the roof level. Between these parallel lines hang the glass-curtain walls that bear no structural weight. This transparency permits detail, such as the spiral staircase and the skeletal structure of the interior, to remain open and visible from the exterior. By thus allowing the interior and exterior of the building to be seen at the same time, Gropius achieved the architectural equivalent of the cubist painters, who presented simultaneously the front view and profile of a human face or several different sides of an object. The Bauhaus group has proved to be one of the most important and influential buildings of its decade.

At the Bauhaus all the visual arts were included in the curriculum but without the traditional distinctions between fine and useful arts. By making furniture design and photography as respectable as sculpture and painting, Gropius hoped to break down the artificial cleavage between artist and craftsman. In the 19th century, Ruskin and William Morris had made a similar effort to bring the world of art and the world of work back together again, but in their romanticism they thought only in terms of handicrafts and shunned the machine. Gropius, however, regarded the machine as the normal tool of modern civilization, a tool to be mastered as any other and made to serve, not enslave. His objective for the Bauhaus was to accomplish a marriage of beauty and utility within the framework of the Machine Age.

The Bauhaus exploration of materials and industrial processes led to many new approaches in printing, pottery, metalwork, weaving, and stagecraft. Students were taught never to forget the purposes their products were designed to serve. A chair, in other words, was made to sit in, a lamp to give efficient lighting. As a result, the Bauhaus became the fountainhead of the new industrial design. Such innovations as tubular steel chairs, indirect lighting fixtures, and streamlined appliances were accepted for mass production and are parts of every household today. In order to counterbalance the utilitarian side, however, Gropius added the painters Kandinsky, Klee, and Lyonel Feininger to his distinguished faculty to uphold the expressive and creative aspects of drawing and painting. Mondrian and the architect Miës van der Rohe also maintained close relations with the Bauhaus.

Le Corbusier, unlike Wright's naturalistic approach, thought of houses variously as machines for living, containers for families, extensions of public services. His commissions included a range from country villas to entire cities, private dwellings to apartment blocks, temporary exposition structures to pilgrimage churches. For him, architecture was the masterly and magnificent play of masses brought together in the light. Cubes, cones, spheres, cylinders, pyramids, he said, are the great

(above) 608. WALTER GROPIUS. Bauhaus Machine Shop, Dessau, Germany. 1925–1926. 167 × 49′.

primary forms that reveal themselves in sun and shadow. While Wright's buildings embraced the earth in harmony with nature, Le Corbusier raised his structures on piers to assert the "independence of things human." Wright, rather tartly, called Le Corbusier's cubistic buildings "boxes on stilts."

Le Corbusier's L'Unité d'Habitation (Plate 63) is an apartment house in Marseilles that brings together in a single structure a community of 1,600 persons with complete facilities for living, shopping, and recreation. Remembering the dismal mass dwellings in Paris, which he called "disastrous architectural fortifications where thousands of families never see the sun," he set out to build apartments vibrating with color, light, and air. To do so he cantilevered a gigantic structure of rough-textured concrete over a double row of massive pylons. The outside staircase is both functional and decorative in sculpturesque fashion. Set at an oblique angle to the horizontal axis, it relieves the rectangular masses with its rising motion. The exterior is honeycombed with shallow balconies, which have sunbreaks tinted in polychrome shades on the inner sides. These sunbreaks proved so effective in protecting the tall living rooms from the sun's glare that they have since become architectural clichés in warm climates. Each floor has duplex apart-the designers of Lever House created a small public garden and an open passageway at the street level for pedestrians.

The Seagram Building (Fig. 610) has been called by its designers, Ludwig Miës van der Rohe and Philip Johnson, the "Tower of Light." The open ground level allows the essential structure to be seen, while providing space for outdoor pools and gardens set in a pink granite platform. The amber-gray glass and bronze tower is cantilevered over stainless-steel piers that give lightness and

ments served by a skip-stop elevator system. At the halfway point an entire floor is allotted to shops, while a day school for children, a gymnasium, and a theater are found on the roof level.

The steel, glass, and concrete creations of Gropius and Le Corbusier are also found in New York skyscrapers, of which two striking examples are Lever House (Fig. 609) and the Seagram Building (Fig. 610). Here the pronounced vertical tendency of the early skyscrapers is offset by limiting the number of stories, setting the structure back from the street, and adding a horizontal base that becomes the pedestal on which the skyscraper is balanced. Lever House is cantilevered outward beyond the structure, a device that, together with the blue-green translucent glass walls which reflect the city and sky, contributes notably to the effect of spaciousness and openness, and its sparkling spic-and-span exterior is as clean as the products its owners sell. By omitting the ground floor and reducing the supporting steel shafts to a minimum,

(above left) 609. GORDON BUNSHAFT, with Skidmore, Owings, and Merrill. Lever House, New York. 1952. 300′6″ high.

(above) 610. LUDWIG MIËS VAN DER ROHE and PHILIP JOHNSON. Seagram Building, New York. 1958. 520′ high.

openness to the soaring masses. Structurally spare, Miës went beyond mere practicality and delighted in the proportions of his buildings as well as reveled in the beauty of his materials. "The less is more," declared the architect, a dictum that applied to decoration as well as structure. While baser metals would be equally practical, Miës shows extreme sensitivity to the qualities and inherent beauty of his materials. He chose bronze for his vertically rising beams, which are alternately smooth and textured to provide an interesting linear pattern.

Synthesis: Nervi, Saarinen

Pier Luigi Nervi and Eero Saarinen have achieved notable results in their imaginative solutions to contemporary building. Nervi's *Palazzetto dello Sport* (Figs. 611, 612) is a sports palace erected in Rome originally for the 1960 Olympic games. The Y-shaped ferroconcrete columns recall human forms as they bend forward to support the massive concrete shell. The possibilities inherent in dome construction have been greatly expanded with

(above) 611. PIER LUIGI NERVI. Palazzetto dello Sport, Rome. 1960.

612. PIER LUIGI NERVI. Interior, Palazzetto dello Sport, Rome. 1960.

539

613. EERO SAARINEN. Trans World Flight Center, Kennedy International Airport, New York. 1962.

the new technology. Buckminster Fuller, who developed the principle of the geodesic dome (see p. 501), has proposed one large enough to enclose, air-condition, and control the climate of a two-mile area in midtown Manhattan. Recent 20th-century architects are thus thinking in expanded terms that run a gamut from exploiting forms made possible by the new technology to urban planning for a vastly increasing industrialized society.

For his Trans World Flight Center (Fig. 613), Saarinen with his flowing concrete forms and dynamic stresses conveys the idea of flight while providing an airline terminal facility. Four large concrete shells resting on abstract-shaped supports enclose an interior remarkable for its spatial elasticity and sculpturesque plasticity (Fig. 614). The complete absence of angularity makes both the interior and exterior a carnival of curvilinear forms. In his Gateway Arch for the Jefferson Westward Expansion Memorial at St. Louis (Fig. 615), Saarinen threw a sublimely simple, gleaming stainless steel arch soaring 630 feet into space to mark the movement toward the western frontier. Technically it is a *catenary curve*—the shape of a chain suspended freely between two points with height equal

to width. The hollow triangular legs enclose elevator shafts and a winding stairway leading to an observatory at the apex. Set in an 85-acre park on the banks of the Mississippi, this highest arch in the world is visible at a distance of 30 miles.

IDEAS: RELATIVISM

The only thing that is permanent is change. This seeming paradox points its finger at the very heart of 20th-century thought, whether expressed in philosophical, scientific, or aesthetic terms. No static, unchanging absolute can possibly provide a satisfactory view of the moving world of today. Even the age-old principles of mathematics can no longer be regarded as eternal truths but, like art, man-made expressions relative to the time and place of their creation. So also the firmest dogmas of religious faiths and political doctrines are subject to far more commentary and modification from time to time than their followers would care to admit.

The shift from a static world order to the present dynamic view of the universe, which began

Plate 61. PIET MONDRIAN. *New York City*. 1942.
Oil on canvas. 10 × 12′. Courtesy Sidney Janis Gallery, New York. (See p. 531.)

Plate 62. JACKSON POLLOCK. *Convergence*. 1952. Oil on canvas, 7'10" × 13'.
Albright-Knox Art Gallery, Buffalo (gift of Seymour H. Knox). (See p. 532.)

Plate 63. Le Corbusier. *L'Unité d'Habitation*, Marseilles. 1947–1952.
550′ long, 79′ wide, 184′ high. (See p. 537.)

Plate 64. PABLO PICASSO. *Girl before a Mirror*. March, 1932. Oil on canvas, 5′3¾″ × 4′3¾″.
Museum of Modern Art, New York (gift of Mrs. Simon Guggenheim). (See p. 542.)

with Copernicus and Galileo, has swept all before it. Those who believe in orderly progress toward a definable objective interpret this flux as some form of evolution; those who accept it at face value, as most scientists do, believe simply in change. Both would agree with Nietzsche when he said that truth has never yet hung on the arm of an absolute; both must of necessity describe the world in relative terms. In his observations of physical phenomena, Albert Einstein saw that, in a world where everything moves, any calculation or prediction, to be valid, must be based on the relative position of the observer. Newton's absolute space, which was immovable, and his absolute time, which flowed on uniformly—both of which were "unrelated to any outward circumstances"—had to be discarded and replaced by the theory of relativity. All space, in the modern view, has to be measured by mobility and change of relative position, and all time by the duration of movement in the space traversed. The world thus becomes a spatio-temporal continuum, in which all matter, energy, and events are related in the four dimensions of space-time.

The study by anthropologists of the life and customs of primitive peoples has shown how ethical considerations are relative to tribal customs as well as social and economic conditions. In Tibet, a woman may have several husbands because one man may be too poor to support a wife. In Africa, some tribes permit a rich man to have as many wives as he can afford. The pragmatic philosophers William James and John Dewey took a long look at history and a wide view of the world and came to the conclusion that when an idea is useful and effective it is true; when it ceases to work, its truth is no longer valid and another solution must be found.

Such a relative world, in which all things appear differently to each person and each group, depending on educational, geographical, historical, ethnic, and psychological backgrounds, can be understood only in terms of many frames of reference. Any absolutism—such a totalitarian society as Plato's *Republic*, for instance—insists on a maximum of conformity; a relativism—such as that of a modern democracy—allows for many different images of man. This relative world, moreover, is populated by men who see themselves in multiple images and express themselves in a multiplicity of styles. In it can be found Marx' proletarian man, speaking in some form of social protest and bent on bringing about the ultimate triumph of the working classes and masses. Darwin's jungle man is there, beating on his neoprimitive tom-toms and discoursing in existentialist vocabularies on the survival of the fittest. Nietzsche's superman, determined to impose his mighty will on an unwilling world, has been thwarted in two world wars. The voice of Freud's psychological man is heard coming from couches and canvases as he tries to share his surrealistic nightmares with the world at large. Mechanical man, the spawn of the Industrial Revolution and the Machine Age, walks robotlike at large, thinking mechanistic thoughts in his electronic brain and expressing futuristic principles in his mechanical style. There, too, is Einstein's scientific man of relativity, drawing abstract pictures of his space-time world in slashing angular lines organized by the multifocus perspective of cubism. Modern art as the mirror of this relativistic world thus assumes many shapes and reflects a multiplicity of human images.

Small wonder, then, that this world, which has produced scientists who analyze and synthesize and physicists who work with fission and fusion, has also given birth to revolutionists who want to destroy a social order so as to reconstruct it in a different way; to warring nations who hope to break down one international order so as to build up a new balance of power; to iconoclasts who feel compelled to shatter certain images men live by so that they can remake the world in their own image; and to artists who dissolve and distort tangible solid objects so as to shape them into new forms that exist solely in their imaginations and on their canvases.

In this relative world, therefore, the cubist disintegrates the objects in his paintings so that he can reintegrate them in patterns of his own choosing. Since each picture creates its own spatial relationships, space is relative to the mind and mood of the painter rather than an absolute as in Euclidean geometry. It is both impossible and undesirable to make any precise analogy between cubist principles and the mathematics of space-time. A relationship, however unsystematic it may be, can nevertheless be found in the cubist concept of the simultaneity of several viewpoints, in the presentation of objects from many sides at once, in the use of multifocus perspective, and in the symbolic emphasis on abstract geometrical forms. By representing bodies at rest or in successive stages of motion, a futurist or mechanical-style picture sets up a space-time continuum of its own. By showing a figure simultaneously from the front and side, clothed and in the nude, opaque and transparent as in an X-ray view, Picasso in the *Girl Before a Mirror* (Plate 64) creates his own pictorial theory of relativity. Similarly,

Chirico in *The Disquieting Muses* (Fig. 583), representing ancient Greek statues in a space bounded by a medieval castle, a modern factory, and a futuristic tower, creates a simultaneous image of time in which past, present, and future coexist in an extended now.

Concurrently with this new conquest of two-dimensional space, architecture developed many new ways of molding its three-dimensional equivalent. Frank Lloyd Wright ruled out such self-contained absolutes as the Greek temple in favor of an architecture specifically related to the changing aspects of human living and working space. He thus evolved the flexible floor plan with its advancing and receding areas and its freedom of interior and exterior occupation. The international stylists also came up with their version of the simultaneous perception of inner and outer space by means of the glass-curtain wall and the organizing of such multibuilding complexes as apartment houses and the United Nations group into systems of related cubes of varying volumes.

In music, the experience of dissonance is emancipated from its dependence on consonance, so that it demands neither preparation, anticipation, nor resolution. The absolutes of tonality, rhythmical regularity, and musical form have yielded to a host of tonal relativisms. Instead of an insistent reiteration of a single meter, a modern musical score can use polymetrical sequences in which a measure of 4/8 is succeeded by one of 7/8, then 2/8, 9/8, and so on. The same principle can be used simultaneously with several rhythms going on at the same time, as in the polyrhythmical textures of Stravinsky's *Rite of Spring*. Instead of organizing a work around a single key center, some composers have employed two tonalities simultaneously in the technique known as bitonality, while others have gone one step farther into polytonality. This, in turn, led to Schoenberg's method of composing with 12 tones that are related not to a central tonality but only to one another. Within the internal organization of the work, the sequence of tones known as the row can be played forward or backward, normally or upside down, simultaneously as in a chord, or fragmented into shorter motives. The 12-tone method emphasizes change and discourages repetition, and the principle of constant variation creating a perpetual state of tonal flux is its ideal.

In *Ulysses*, James Joyce found his answer by making a simultaneous cross section of the life of a city. In this labyrinthine literary space-time continuum, all events, whether memories of the past or premonitions of the future, flow together into a kind of extended present. As in a dream, there is no distinction between before and after. While the single day and night and city in which all takes place have some relation to the Greek unities of time, place, and action, there is no Aristotelian beginning, middle, or end to his structureless literary structure. The reader can begin at almost any place in the book, and the continuity will not be broken. The series of fleeting images are simply recorded, and the door to the dream world of free association of words and thoughts is left open so that the reader can move in and supply the transitions between moods, the union of the fragments, and thus, in turn, create his own relative order; and its end, like the title of the final chapter of a Samuel Johnson novel, is a conclusion in which nothing is concluded.

Many of the forms of expressionism are also relative to the individual psychology of the artist, just as a Frank Lloyd Wright building is relative to the need of the human situation. Expressionism presupposes the free associational techniques of psychological relativism. Somewhat like the romantic revolt of a century earlier, the expressionistic artist reasserts the primacy of the imagination over the intellect and takes flight from reality in order to find a superior reality in the world of mystery and fantasy. The tendency is anti-intellectual in the

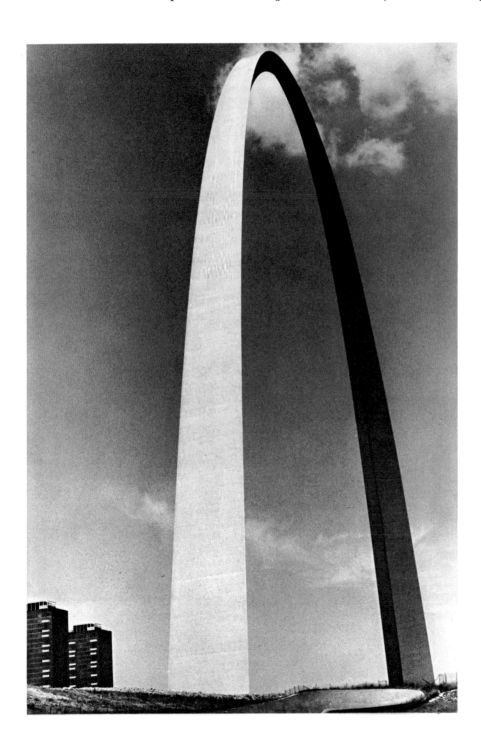

615. EERO SAARINEN. Gateway Arch, Jefferson Westward Expansion Memorial, St. Louis. 1967. Stainless steel, 630' high, span 630' at base.

extreme, though the symbols and vocabulary are evolved by highly rationalistic procedures. The emotional content poured on their canvases, pages, and musical scores derives from a particular human imagination and hence is relative to the infinite number of unsolved conflicts and suppressed passions of many different private worlds.

Historical relativism has provided the modern artist with an unparalleled number of choices of styles and techniques from the past as well as the present. The artist of the 20th century is the heir of all the ages. A Picasso exhibit or a Stravinsky concert can mean a bewildering assortment of styles. Inspiration for the one can be drawn from ancient Iberian sculpture, African tribal masks, Romanesque wall frescoes, and medieval stained glass, as well as from contemporary sources. Picasso's paintings also include provocative variations on Velázquez' *Las Meninas*, Delacroix' *Pietà*, and other masterpieces that have caught his eye. His media may include pencil drawings, collages constructed of cloth and paper, ceramics, and woodcuts, as well as oils and watercolors. Sources for Stravinsky may be drawn from the free rhythms of Gregorian chant, the dissonant counterpoint of the 14th century, the operas of Mozart, or the polyrhythmic practices of African tribal music. When Picasso said, "I do not search, I find," he implied that his freedom of approach was unlimited. He can accept for the moment any style that comes along without becoming its dogmatic prisoner. Both Picasso and Stravinsky have repeatedly demonstrated that a new work can be based on an aesthetic theory diametrically opposed to the one that preceded it. This does not mean, however, that they must repudiate or burn up that which has gone before. To these master craftsmen, historical rela-

tivism provides a complete freedom of choice without the necessity of sacrificing either their originality or their principles.

Philosophers of history, such as Spengler and Toynbee, through their sweeping historical panoramas have shown that the past still exists within the living present. From the point of view of historical relativity, tradition is usually a more potent factor than innovation, and at all times, including the present, evolution has been a stronger force than revolution. Most 20th-century ideas and problems are variations on old themes that have bothered men ever since the 5th century B.C. Those that in the past led to sharp dissonances have never been resolved; instead, they have become outmoded, outgrown, temporarily forgotten, or they are bypassed, circumvented in one way or another, or assume new shapes and forms. "Ideas have never conquered the world as ideas," as Romain Rolland remarked in his novel *Jean Christophe*, "but only by the force they represent. They do not grip men by their intellectual contents but by the radiant vitality which is given off from them at certain periods in history.... The loftiest and most sublime idea remains ineffective until the day when it becomes contagious, not by its own merits, but by the merits of the groups of men in whom it becomes incarnate by the transfusion of their blood." More important than the solutions or lack of them have been the emotional forces these notions have generated and the good fruits they have yielded. All the workable ideas eventually have been embodied in the buildings men erect to house their activities, the statues and pictures that reflect their human images, the words that express their innermost thoughts, and the music that gives voice to their strivings and aspirations in a constantly changing world.

INDEX

Certain features of a glossary are combined with the Index. When a technical term is defined in the text, reference is made to that page; in other instances, a short definition (in parentheses) is given after the entry. Color-plate and figure references are cited in the form Pl. 1, Fig. 23, or p. 44, so that terms may be clarified by looking at the illustrations. Each work of art has been listed by title as well as by artist and, in addition, is listed under the city and building in which it is presently located. Each building is also listed under its city and under the architect, with a cross-reference made from its title to the city of location. General events as well as birth and death dates of persons are given in the Chronologies at the beginning of chapters and have not been indexed.

Ave Maria, Josquin des Prez, 284–285; excerpt from, 285

Avignon, France, as papal center, 209, 210; international style of, 210

axis, architectural, related to man, 127; of centralized church, 109, 124; of oblong basilicas, 104, 109; of Roman Forum, 75–76; of Place de la Concorde, 430, Fig. 491; of Versailles Palace, 350, Figs. 403–405

Bacchants, The, Euripides, 27, 30, 32, 38

Bacchus, Michelangelo, 266, 288, Fig. 303

Bacchus and Ariadne, Titian, 307, Fig. 356

Bach, C.P.E, 419

Bach, Johann Sebastian, 321, 386, 402, 403, 404, 419; revival of, 470–471; *Art of the Fugue*, 424; *St. Matthew Passion*, 470–471; *Well-Tempered Clavier*, 424

"Back to Nature" movement, 468, 470, 472–474

Bacon, Francis, *Painting (The Butcher)*, 530, Fig. 598

Bakers, Chartres, 197, Fig. 230

Baldacchino, Bernini, 331, Pl. 30

Baldpate. See *Zuccone, Lo*

Balla, Giacomo, *Dog on Leash*, 517, Fig. 579

Ballades, of Victor Hugo, 463, 466

ballata, 256

ballet, 30; 19th-century, 445–446; under Lully, 364–365; with song, 524; 20th-century, 504, 510, 524

ballet de cour, French, 349, explained, 363; English version of, 399

Ballet Méchanique, Léger, 518

Ballu, Théodore, 461–462

Baltimore, Maryland
  Walters Art Gallery
    Daumier, *Third-Class Carriage*, 479, Fig. 541

Balzac, Honoré de, 479, 481; subjects of novels, 495; *Human Comedy*, 499

Banquet of Officers of the Civic Guard of St. George at Haarlem, Hals, 372–373, 378, Pl. 37

Baptism of Christ and Procession of Twelve Apostles, 110, Fig. 129

baptistries, at Naples, 112; Christian, 127; Christian octagonal, 110. *See also* Florence; Pisa; Ravenna

Bar at the Folies-Bergère, Manet, 416, 483, Pl. 49

Bar-sur-Aube, France
  Church of St. Maclou
    Phylactery Reliquary of Tooth of St. Maclou, 146, Fig. 176

Barber of Seville, Beaumarchais and Mozart, 413–414

baroque architecture, aristocratic, 349–355; Austrian Counter Reformation 411–412; bourgeois, 369–370, 387; early examples of, 296–304, Figs. 351–352; English, 389, 391, 392–398; origins of, 296; Roman Counter Reformation, 325–327, 345; Spanish Counter Reformation, 333–337, 342; transition to, 296

baroque classicism, 447–448

baroque music, aristocratic, 349, 363–365; bourgeois, 371–372, 382–386, 388; early, 315–317, Spanish, 343; transition to, 321

baroque painting, aristocratic, 357–363; bourgeois, 371, 372–383, 387; Roman Counter Reformation, 328–331, 345; Sp. Counter Reformation, 325, 338–342, 345

baroque rationalism, 403–404, 407

baroque sculpture, aristocratic, 355–357; bourgeois, 312; Roman Counter Reformation, 331–332, 345

baroque style, academic, *vs.* free, 363, 367; dates of, 404; of interiors, Versailles, 353, Pl. 33; mannerist devices in, 311, 318–319; and Renaissance compared, 345; roads to, 320–321; rococo phase of, 409–414; summary of, 404–405; synthesis of, 296, 393, 404–405; Titian's influence on, 307; and Velázquez, 342; and Venice, 296

barrel vault, Byzantine, 112, Fig. 136; highest ribbed, 139; Norman, 173, Fig. 204; Renaissance, 238, Fig. 269; Roman use of, 81, 86, Figs. 94, 104; Romanesque, Figs. 155, 161–162; of Sistine Chapel, 273

Barry, Charles, Houses of Parliament, 460, Fig. 524

Bartok, Bela, *Bluebeard's Castle*, 524

Barye, Antoine, *Lion Hunt*, 475, Fig. 538

Basel, Switzerland
  Art Museum
    Léger, *Mechanical Elements*, 518, Fig. 582

basilica, defined, 76; central-type, 108–114; centralized *vs.* oblong, 109; Christian, and Greek temple compared, 102; early Roman Christian, 104–105, 132, 157; early Roman Christian *vs.* Romanesque, 139; oblong, 102, 104–105, 121, 125; Palladio quoted on, 298; symbolism of, 105

Basilica of St. Francis. *See* Assisi

Basilica of St. Peter. *See* Rome, St. Peter's Basilica

Basilica Ulpia, 76, 78, 80, 87, 93, Figs. 85, 88–89

Bassano, Jacopo, in Veronese's painting, 310, Fig. 358

baths, in Bithynia, 91; imperial Roman, 80–81, 82, 86–87 263; Pergamene, 44

Baths of Caracalla, 81, 85–86, Figs. 95–96

Baths of Diocletian, 81

Baths of Titus, uncovered, 263

Baths of Trajan, 80–81, 86

battle of gods and giants, in Parthenon frieze, 22; in Pergamene frieze, 44, 49, 50–54, 66, Figs. 57–60

Battle of Hastings. *See* Hastings, Battle of

Battle of Issus, depicted in mosaic, 57, detail, Fig. 66

Battle of the Romans and Sabines, David, 438, 448, Fig. 504

Battle of Roncesvalles, 167–168

Battle of San Romano, Uccello, 248–249, Fig. 287

Battle of Ten Nude Men, Pollaiuolo, 259, Fig. 298

Baudelaire, Charles, in Courbet's painting, 482, Fig. 545

Bauhaus Machine Shop, 536–537, Fig. 608

Bayeux, France
  Cathedral, 161, 163, 167, reliquaries of, 176
  Town Hall Museum
    Bayeux Tapestry, 161, 163–166, 167, 175–178, 256 Pl. 11, Figs. 194–196, 198; compared to *Song of Roland*, 175–178; influence on, 90; stylization in, 166, 177

bays, architectural, 138, Fig. 161

bead-and-reel motif, 13, Fig. 14

Beaulieu, France
  Abbey Church, 141

Beaumarchais, *Barber of Seville*, 413–414; Mozart's adaptation of *Marriage of Figaro*, 419

beauty, Aquinas' definition of, 204; Burke on, 424; classical ideal, 26; impressionists' view of, 485; Mengs on, 447; Michelangelo on, 287–288; and the rococo, 423, 424; Winckelmann's idea of, 449

Beauvais, France, 181
  Cathedral of, 183, 186, 206, Fig. 213

Beckford, William, residence of, Fonthill Abbey, 459–460, Figs. 522–523; *Vathek*, 474

Beethoven, Ludwig van, 424, 444–447, 468; influence on Berlioz, 464, 465; as neoclassical artist, 449; patrons of, 469; *Coriolanus*, 445; *Egmont*, 445; *Fidelio*, 445; *Fifth Symphony*, 446; *King Stephen*, 445; *Ninth Symphony*, 446–447, 464; *Prometheus*, 445, 446; *Ruins of Athens*, 445; *Sixth Symphony (Pastoral)* 464, 472; *Sonata for Piano*, Op. 26, 445; *Third Symphony (Eroica)*, 444–447, 464

Beggars Receiving Alms, Rembrandt, Fig. 447

Bellini, Gentile, *Procession in St. Mark's Square*, 291–292, 294, Fig. 331; 314–315, details, Figs. 361–362

Belvedere Palace. *See* Vienna

Bendel, *Rococo Angel*, p. 406

Benedictine Order, and Cluny, 136; tradition of copying, 146–148

Benedictine Rule, 131, 133

Benevento, Italy
  Arch of Trajan, 71, 74–75, 86, Fig. 81, detail, Fig. 82

Benvenuto Cellini, Berlioz, 495

Benjamin Franklin, Houdon, 418, Fig. 489

Berg, Alban, *Violin Concerto*, 516, excerpt from, 516; *Wozzeck*, 513

Bergson, Henri, on Rodin, 490; on time and art, 499–500; *Creative Evolution*, 490

Berlin, Germany
  Brandenburg Gate (Langhans), 434, Fig. 499
  Charlottenburg Palace
    Watteau, *Gersaint's Signboard*, 415, Pl. 41
  Pergamon Museum, 46
    Altar of Zeus, 44–45, 46, 48–54, 66–67, 69, 70, Figs. 50, 55–61; Hephaiston, mosaic from Palace of Attalus II, 57, Figs. 64–65
  State Museums
    Douris, *Instruction in Music and Grammar*, 31, Fig. 44; *Kore* from Samos, 25, Fig. 36; Lippi, *Nativity*, 248, Pl. 19; *Orpheus among the Thracians*, 31, Pl. 3

Abbot Suger's visit to, 180; ambulatory columns and capitals, 140, 141, 150–152, 153, 158, Figs. 165, 179–182; apse painting, 148; arches in, 186; decoration of, 140; dedication of, 201; Galilee portal of, 137–138, Fig. 156; music in, 150–153, 199

Ochier Museum
Medallion with Lamb, p. 130; *First Tone of Plainsong*, 151, Fig. 179; *Second Tone*, 151, Fig. 180; *Third Tone*, 151, Fig. 181; *Fourth Tone*, 151–152, Fig. 182

Romanesque house, 159, Fig. 193
coat of arms, of Medici family, 240, Figs. 270, 271; papal, 441, Pl. 44; royal Spanish, 334
Cocteau, Jean, 524
Cœur, Jacques, House of, 202, Fig. 235
coffers or coffering, defined, 85, Fig. 103; of dome, 327, Fig. 372
Colbert, Jean-Baptiste, 347, 349, 350, 362, 366, 392
Coleridge, Samuel Taylor, *Kubla Khan*, quoted, 474
Colette (Sidonie Gabrielle Claudine Colette), 524
Colleoni, Bartolommeo, Verrocchio's equestrian monument of, 244, Fig. 282
colonettes, cast-iron, 492, Fig. 558; of Chartres, 186, Pl. 13, Fig. 216; Renaissance, 239, Fig. 270
colonnade, defined, 9; used by Bernini, 331, Fig. 324; circular Doric and Corinthian, 14; Doric, Fig. 6; double Corinthian, 78, Fig. 89; of Hagia Sophia, 112, Fig. 136; Hellenistic, 45; Ionic, 50, Fig. 55; paired Corinthian, 350, Fig. 401
color, abstract use of, 531; and arts, allied, 468–469; in Bayeux Tapestry, 166; Cézanne's use of, 486–488; cubists' use of, 514; Delacroix on, 454; Delacroix' use of, 453, 454, 455, 469; eyes' reaction to, 483; of Les Fauves, 510; Gauguin's use of, 486, Pl. 53; used for depth, Giotto, 216–217; El Greco's use of, 338, 340, 341; impressionists' use of, 483–485; Matisse's use of, 510; Picasso's use of, 505, Pl. 55; and pointillism, 485–486, Pl. 51; 19th-century use of, 468, 469; of Romanesque frescoes, 148–149; Rubens' use of, 358; of spectrum, 483; in stained glass, 195–196, 198; in Van Gogh's use of, 486; in Venetian painting, 304; Vermeer's use of, 380–381, Pl. 38
color perspective (the art of using colors of higher and lower intensity to suggest receding planes from foreground to background), of Cézanne, 487–488; of Giotto, 216–217; of impressionists, 483; of Matisse, 511
Colosseum. *See* Rome
column, caryatid as, 12, Fig. 13; cast-iron, 492, 493, Figs. 558, 561; clustered, 186, Fig. 216; Composite, 74, 93; Corinthian, 14, 82, Figs. 16–18; Doric, 9–10, 14, 39, 45, 50, Figs. 9–10; Doric

and Ionic compared, 12–13, Fig. 10; and entasis, 11; Greek construction of, 11; Ionic, 12–13, 82, Figs. 10–12; Norman, 173, Fig. 204; painted, Hellenistic, 55; Tuscan, 82, Fig. 97
Column of Trajan. *See* Rome
Column of Marcus Aurelius, influence of, 90
Combat of Tancred and Clorinda, Monteverdi, Preface quoted, 317
Combat of Two Demons, 145, Fig. 174
comédie-ballet, of Molière, 363–364
commedia dell'arte figures, 514, 524, Fig. 575
Commentaries, Ghiberti, 241, 242, 258, 261
Communion, symbol for, 119, Fig. 146
Compagnie dei Laudesi (singing societies), 224
Compleat Gentleman, The, Peacham, Henry, quoted, 383
Composite order of architecture, 93, 302, 394; columns, 74, Fig. 81; 337–338, Fig. 387; pilasters, 238, Fig. 268; 410, Fig. 470
composition, pyramidal, 250, 266, Pl. 22, Figs. 288, 305; triangular, 216, Fig. 245; Veronese's unity of, 309, Pl. 28; Venetian decentralization of, 317–318
Composition in White, Black, and Red, Mondrian, 531, Fig. 601
Compostela, Spain, tomb of St. James, 157
Cathedral of Santiago de Compostela Master Matteo, Pórtico de la Gloria, 145, Fig. 168; *Self-portrait*, 145, Fig. 189
Comte, August, 464
Conant, Kenneth J., 130. *See* Figs. 117, 156, 157, 161, 164, 165
Concert, Giorgione and Titian, 310, Fig. 363
Concert, Vermeer, 382–383, Fig. 445
Concert Champêtre, Giorgione, 304, 317, Pl. 25
concerto and concertato style, 313
concrete, Roman use of, 82, 84, 85, 95; Gothic use of, 188; reinforced, 534, 536. *See also* ferroconcrete
concretion, defined, 36
Condorcet, Marie Jean, *Progress of the Human Spirit*, 424
Confessions of an English Opium Eater, De Quincey, 465
Confessions, St. Augustine, 122–123
Conques, France
Abbey Church of Ste. Foy, 145
Reliquary Statue of Ste. Foy, 146, Pl. 10
Consolations of Philosophy, Boethius, 121
Constable, John, 460, 474; *Hay Wain*, 454, 473–474, Pl. 47; *Salisbury Cathedral from the Bishop's Garden*, 473, Fig. 534
Constantine, Emperor, 83, 99, 104; mausoleum for daughter of, 109, Fig. 153–154
Constantinople, 108, 112, 115, 125, 128, 130; as capital of East Roman Empire, 179; fall of, 295; music of, 123; named, 99; rites of at Ravenna, 102. *See also* Byzantium; Istanbul
Contemplative Life, 194, Fig. 228
Contest of Apollo and Marsyas, 59–60, Fig. 68

Contest of Athena and Poseidon for the Land of Attica, 12, 19, 23, Fig. 26
continuo, described, 383; aria, 401
continuous flux, 499–500
continuous method of visual narration, earliest example of, 53; explained, 89; list of examples of, 90; of Masaccio, 246, Fig. 284; of Pisano's pulpit, 218, Figs. 249–250; of Trajan's Column, 87–90, Figs. 106–108
Convergence, Pollock, 532, Pl. 62
Conversion of St. Paul, Caravaggio, 328–329, Fig. 376.
Copernicus, 541; quoted, 346; theory of, 323, 403, 499; *Revolution of the Planets in Their Orbits*, 323
Corbaccio, Boccaccio, 217
Corbusier. *See* Le Corbusier
Corday, Charlotte, 429
Corinthian order of architecture, introduced, 14, Figs. 16–18; Figs. 89–90; of Pantheon, 84, Figs. 102–103; capital variant, 118, Fig. 141; Renaissance use of, 238, Figs. 266, 268; colonnade of Louvre, 350, Fig. 401; of St. Paul's, 394, Fig. 457; of La Madeleine, 431, Fig. 492
Coriolanus, Collin, Beethoven's music for, 445
Cornaro Chapel, Santa Maria della Vittoria, Rome, 331, Fig. 379. *See also* Rome, Church of Santa Maria della Vittoria
Corneille, Pierre, *The Cid*, quoted, 366; *Les Horaces*, 436
cornice, 10, Fig. 10; baroque, p. 389; Renaissance, 239, Fig. 270; raking, 10, Fig. 10
cornu, defined, 92; Roman, 92, Fig. 109
Coronation. See Sacre, Le
Coronation of Poppea, Monteverdi, 317
Corot, Camille, *Washerwomen in Willow Grove*, 472, Fig. 533
corporation pictures, explained, 294, Fig. 331; Dutch, 371, 372–374, 378, Pls. 36–37
Cortot, Jean-Pierre, 434; *Apotheosis of Napoleon*, 457–458, Fig. 519, detail, p. 427
Council of Trent, 281; effect on art, 282, 325; reforms of, 323, 342–343
counterpoint, Berlioz' use of, 467; of Des Prez, 284; Gothic, 199–201; *punctus contra punctum*, 199; Purcell's, 402, 403; Renaissance, 284–285; traditional *vs.* polychoral, 343; in twelve-tone music, 516; Venetian, 315, example of, 316. *See also* fugues; polyphony
Counter Reformation, 281, 296, 307, 322–325; effects of on arts, 325, on St. Peter's dome, 282; personification of spirit of, 340, Fig. 394; mysticism of, 343–345
Counter Reformation baroque architecture, Austrian, 411–412, Figs. 472–473, 475–477; Roman, 325–327, 345, Figs. 367–369, 370–373; Spanish, 333–337, 342, Figs. 381–389
Counter Reformation baroque music, 342–343, 345; example of, 343
Counter Reformation baroque painting, Roman, 328–331, 345, Pl. 29, Figs. 375–378; Spanish,

deus ex machina, defined, 29; 365; Purcell's use of, 401
Devin du Village, Le, Rousseau, 472
Dewey, John, 541
Diaghileff, Serge, 524; company of, 509–510, 524
diakonikon, defined, 109
dialectics, 40; in Gothic sculpture, 193
Diana, Klee, 522, Pl. 60
"Diana, House of." *See* Ostia, Italy
Dickens, Charles, 416, 479, 481
Diderot, Denis, 436; on art, 416, 427; *Encyclopédie*, 407, 423; *The Natural Son*, 415
Dido and Aeneas, Purcell and Tate, 400–402, 405; excerpts from, 400, 401
Dies Irae, 204, 223–224; example of, 224; in 19th-century literature, 463; in 19th-century music, 466, 467, 471; rhyme pattern of, 463
Dignity of Man, The, Pico della Mirandola, 261, quoted, 275
dimension, of cubists, 514; in early Christian sculpture, 117; in early Roman Christian and Byzantine compared, 121; in Hellenistic painting, 55; of illuminated manuscripts and Bayeux Tapestry, 166; in Mondrian's painting, 531; of relief sculpture, 241; of stained glass, 195; in Venetian arts, 318
Dionysiac technites, explained, 61
Dionysian Procession, 28, Fig. 43
Dionysus, 21, Fig. 28
Dionysus, altar to, in Athens, 32; altar at Pergamon, 45; Aristotle on, 37; cult of, 27–28, 39; and Greek drama, 6, 27–28, 39; and musical instruments, 59, 61; statues of, 21, Fig. 28; 24, Pl. 1, Fig. 32; theaters of, 6, 28, Figs. 3, 42
Dioskourides of Samos, *Street Musicians*, 92, Fig. 110
discant *(discantus)*, defined, 200; 203; example of, 200
Discobolus (Discus Thrower), Myron, 24–25, 34, Fig. 35; captured by Napoleon, 430
Disembarkation of Cleopatra at Tarsus, Lorrain, 362, Fig. 420
Disembarkation of Queen Maria de' Medici at Marseilles, Rubens, 358, Pl. 34
Disquieting Muses, The, Chirico, 519, 542, Fig. 583
dissonance, in Des Prez' music, 284; of Schoenberg and Berg *vs.* Wagner, 513; 20th-century, 542
Distribution of the Eagles, David, 440–441
Divine Comedy, Dante, 66, 168, 226–227, 232, 466; influence of, 455, 462, 464
Dr. Tulp's Anatomy Lesson, Rembrandt, 372, Fig. 427
Dog on Leash, Balla, 517, Fig. 579
Doge's Palace. *See* Venice
dome, and central-type church, 109-110, 114; decorations of, 110, Fig. 129; early Christian use and developments of, 109–114, Figs. 130–131, 136; geodesic, 540, p. 501; later solutions for, 233, 237, Figs. 263, 265; 282, 283, 288, Figs. 326–327, 330; 286, Fig. 328; of San Carlo alle Quattro Fontane, 327, Fig. 372; 395,

Fig. 453; 540, p. 501; psychological effects of, 114; Roman development and use of, 74, 84–86, Fig. 103; support of, 84, 111–112, Figs. 130, 131; 20th-century use of, 539–540, p. 501, Figs. 611–612; as unifying device, 114, 239, 260, 394
domestic architecture, and basilicas, 76, 104; early baroque, 298–299, Figs. 339–340; Gothic, 202, Figs. 234–235; Gothic revival, 459–460, 461, Figs. 522, 523, 525; half-timbered, 202, 472, Fig. 234; Hellenistic, 64, Fig. 74; neoclassical, 427; Renaissance, 239–240, Figs. 270–271; Roman, 83, 86, 93, Figs. 99, 100; Romanesque, 159, Fig. 193; 17th-century Dutch, 370, Fig. 423; 20th-century, 534–535, Fig. 605; 537–538, Pl. 63
domesticity, Dutch bourgeois, 386–388
Dominican Order, 209, 236
Don Giovanni, Mozart, 415, 419–422, 424, 445; excerpts from, 421
Donatello, 236, 241, 242–244, 245, 257, 260, 283; as artist, 242; *David*, 243, 260, Fig. 277; *Gattamelata*, 244, 260, Fig. 279; *Prophet (Lo Zuccone)*, 242–243, 260, Fig. 276; *Repentant Magdalene*, 243–244, Fig. 278; *St. John the Evangelist*, 271
Doré, Gustave, *Berlioz Conducting*, 464, Fig. 527
Dorian mode, 60–61; mixed, example of, 224; tradition of, 58–59
Doric column, 10, Figs. 10, 21; and Ionic, compared, Fig. 10; of Propylaea, 9, Fig. 7; manneristic use of, 303, Fig. 349; Napoleon's monumental, 434, Fig. 497; Roman version of, 82; Trajan's, 87, Fig. 105
Doric frieze, 10, Fig. 10; example of, Figs. 19–21; unity of, 53
Doric order of architecture, 9-10, 14, Fig. 10; baroque use of, 334, 335, Fig. 383; and Ionic compared, Fig. 10; Renaissance use of, 286, Fig. 328; Venetian use of, 298, 302, Fig. 337
Doric temple, Parthenon as example of, 9–11, 14, Fig. 9
Doryphorus (Spearbearer), Polyclitus, 23, 24, 34, Fig. 31
Douris, *Instruction in Music and Grammar*, 31, Fig. 44
drama, bourgeois, 415; Greek, 6, 27–30, 31, 32, 35, 36, 37, 39; and 19th-century symbolism, 496–497; Restoration, 389, 398–403; Roman, 28; 20th-century, 505. *See also* opera
drapery (as represented in art), in Bernini's sculpture, 332, Fig. 380; 355, 356, Fig. 411; classical influence of, on Renaissance sculpture, 242, Fig. 276, on neoclassical sculpture, 443, Fig. 509; in David's painting, 438, Fig. 505; in early Christian mosaic, 108, Fig. 124; 115, Pl. 8, Fig. 137; in 14th-century Italian painting, 220, Figs. 252–253; in El Greco's painting, 339, Fig. 392; in Gothic sculpture, 194,

Fig. 229; in Hellenic sculpture, 13, Fig. 13; 21, Fig. 28; 25, Fig. 33; 25–26, Fig. 36; 27, Figs. 39, 41; in Hellenistic sculpture, 56, Pl. 4; 48, Figs. 53, 54; of Michelangelo's sculpture, 266, Fig. 304; 271, Fig. 312; in Renaissance painting, 253, Fig. 292; in Titian's painting, 307, Fig. 356; used symbolically, 89
Dresden, Germany, as center for "Die Brücke," 511
Albertinum
Athena Lemnia (body of), 26, Fig. 37
Gemäldegalerie
Rembrandt, *Self-portrait with Saskia*, 375, Fig. 432
The Zwinger, 406
drum (section of a column), defined, 11
drum (musical), in Roman mosaic, 92, Fig. 110; in Romanesque sculpture, 151, Fig. 180
Drunkenness of Noah, Michelangelo, 277–278, Fig. 318
Dryden, John, 389, 392, 393, 398–400, 402, 403; compared to Wren and Purcell, 402–403; influence of, 403; quoted, 398–399; *Albion and Albanius*, Preface quoted, 399–400; *King Arthur*, 400, 402, Preface quoted, 402
dualism, Gothic, 202–203; of Abelard, 203
Duccio di Buoninsegna, 219; *Maestà*, 230–231, Fig. 262, detail, *Pietà*, Fig. 261; *"Rucellai" Madonna*, 220, Fig. 253
Dufay, Guillaume, 236, 237, 255, 256, 259, 284; *Nuper Rosarum*, motet, 236–237, 256
Dumas, Alexandre, 450, 460, 464
duplum, explained, 199; examples of, 199, 200; use of, 199–201
Dutch architecture, 369–370, 387, Fig. 424
Dutch arts, summarized, 371–372
Dutch music, 371–372, 382–383, 386, 388; performance depicted, Fig. 445; English influence on, 383
Dutch painting, 371, 372–382, 383, 387, Pls. 36–38, Figs. 423–425, 427–428, 430–445, 448
Dutch Reformed Church, 370–371
Dying Gaul, 47–48, 53, Figs. 51, 52

early Christian style, and authoritarianism, 124–127; and decline of sculpture, 116–117; and early Roman Christian and Byzantine, differentiated, 101; in formative stage, 121; influence of liturgy on, 128–129; summarized, 124
early Italian Renaissance, architecture of, 212, 217, Figs. 240–242, 248; ideas of, 227–232; literature of, of Dante, 226–227, 232; music of, 210, 223–225, 229, 230, 231, excerpts from, 224, 225; painting of, 210, 212–217, 219–223, 226, 229–231, Pl. 17, p. 209, Figs. 243–247, 252–262; of Giotto, 209, 210, 212–217, 220–221, 223, 226, 230–231, Pl. 17, Figs. 243–247, 254, 257, 259, 260; sculpture of,

Portrait of Dante, 226, Fig. 257; *St. Francis Renouncing His Father*, 215–216, Fig. 245; *Scrovegni Family Donating Chapel*, p. 209; *Sermon to the Birds*, 214, 215, 228–229, Fig. 244

"Giotto's Tower." *See* Florence, Campanile

Giovanni Arnolfini and His Wife, Jan van Eyck, 253, Pl. 21, Fig. 293

Giovanni di Simone, Campo Santo, 217, Fig. 248

Girardon, François, 357

Girl Before a Mirror, Picasso, 542, Pl. 64

Giselbertus, *Last Judgement*, 145, Fig. 169

Gladatorial Contest, 91–92, Fig. 109

Glareanus (Heinrich Loris), quoted, 284

glass, in Crystal Palace, 493, Figs. 560, 561; Gothic use of, 195; Roman substitute for, 81; 20th–century use of, 536, Fig. 608; 538, Figs. 609–610

Glorious Revolution, 392

Gluck, C.W., 402; influence of, 464, 465; music reforms of, 449; operas of, 406, 419; *Alceste*, Preface quoted, 449; *The Unforseen Meeting*, or *The Pilgrims to Mecca*, 474

glyphs (grooves), 10

God, Byzantine concept of, 125; Romanesque concept of, 154; in feudalistic society, 176; and Neo-Platonism, 274

God Dividing Light from Darkness, Michelangelo, 279, Fig. 321; *ignudi* in, 277

Goddess Adjusting Her Sandal, 27, Fig. 41

Goddess Throwing Jar of Snakes, 52–53, Fig. 60

Gods of the Modern World, Orozco, 527, Fig. 595

gods and goddesses, and Greek sculpture, 37; Hellenic, 6, 12, 19, 21–22, 26, 27, 33, 34, 35, 39; Hellenic *vs.* Hellenistic, 66; Hellenistic, 64; on Altar of Zeus, frieze, 44, 49, 50–54; personified in Greek drama, 36; Roman, 74, 79, 84, 88

Goethe, Johann Wolfgang von, 407, 447, 454, 506; on architecture, 460–461; on Mozart, 420; *Egmont*, 445; *Faust*, 287, 424, 450, 463, 466, 473, illustrations for, 453–454, Figs. 514–517, influence of, 462, 464, music based on, 465–466, quoted, 463, translations of, 450, 465; *Von Deutscher Baukunst*, 461

"*Gold-Weigher, The*," Fig. 426

Golden Bough, The, Frazer, 507

golden section, principle of, 11

"Golliwog's Cake Walk," Debussy, 509

Gombrich, E. H., 251

Gomez de Mora, Juan, Casa de las Conchas and La Clérica, 336–337, Fig. 387

Good Government, Ambrogio Lorenzetti, 221, detail, Fig. 255

Good Shepherd, 117, 127, Fig. 144

Good Shepherd Separating the Sheep from the Goats, 106, Fig. 121

Goslar, Germany
Imperial Palace and Chapel of St. Ulrich, 159, Fig. 190

Gothic, 19th-century redefinition of, 459

Gothic architecture, diversity of, 205; domestic, 202; English tradition of, 394–397; expression and symbolism of, 181; feudal, 175; French, 179–189; Italian, 209, 211–212, 233, 237, 291–292; minimum of symmetry in, 188; Norman developments incorporated in, 174; opposing factors in, 202; revival of, 458–462, 471–472; and use of stained glass, 198; Suger's book on, 180; synthesis in, 180; system of thrusts and counterthrusts, 187, 206; vaulting of, 183, 186–187, 233, 237, Figs. 216, 218; Viollet-le-Duc on, 461

Gothic cathedrals, capitals of, 190; chapels of, 188–189; interiors of, 114, 189; Italian, 209; lighting of, opposed to Romanesque abbeys, 189; as liturgical setting, 198; locations of, 181–182; prototype of, 179–181; psychological effect of, 114; religious enthusiasm of builders of, 183; and Renaissance church compared, 260; and Romanesque church compared, 190; Romanesque forerunner of, 139; sculpture of, 190, 202; seven-spired cathedral, 181, Fig. 211; spires of, 182; stained glass in, 185, 189, 195–196; symbolism of, 181; synthesis in, 205–206; width of, 112. *See also* Chartres; Paris, Cathedral of Notre Dame

Gothic crafts and journeymen, 190

Gothic dualism, 202–203

Gothic literature, 191–192, 202

Gothic liturgy, 198; setting for, 188

Gothic music, 198–201, 202–203, 225; examples of, 199, 200; as branch of mathematics, 204–205; Chartres, important center of, 194; minnesingers, 169, Pl. 12, Fig. 199; modified polyphony of, 284; School of Notre Dame, 199–201; secular, 201; as synthesis, 206; use of isorhythm in, 237

"Gothic" novels, 458–459

Gothic revival, 471–472; architecture of, 458–462, 471–472; Figs. 522–526, 530–531

Gothic sculpture, 154, 190–194, 218, Fig. 251; naturalism of, 229; opposing factors in, 202; and Romanesque compared, 190. *See also* Chartres

Gothic style, 101, 179–206; appeal of, 206; forerunner of, 139; origin of, 181; understanding of, 202

Gounod, Charles, *Faust*, 465; *The Queen of Sheba*, 476

Governors of Old Men's Home at Haarlem, Hals, 367, Fig. 439

Goya, Francisco, 367, 416, 441, 526, 528; *Disasters of War*, 441; *Executions of the Third of May, 1808*, 441, Pl. 45; *Witches' Sabbath*, Fig. 529

Gozzoli, Benozzo, 236, 240, 250, 260; *Journey of the Magi*, 248 256, detail, Fig. 286

Grabu, Nicholas, 400

Grace Church (Renwick), 471, Fig. 531

Grammar, 193, Fig. 225

Grande Écurie, 363, 364

graphic arts, 17th-century, 374–375; 20th-century, 505. *See also* etching; lithograph

Grave Stele of Hegeso, 35, Fig. 46

Greater Panathenaea, 16, 23

Greco, El (Domenicos Theotocopoulos), 294, 325, 338–341, 343, 345, 367, 381, 404; as a mannerist, 333; influence of, 360; influence on, 307, 321; style of, 341; *Burial of Count Orgaz*, 339, Pl. 31, Fig. 392; *Cardinal de Guevara*, 340–341, Fig. 394; *Dream of Philip II*, 338; *Expulsion from the Temple*, 339–340, Fig. 393; *Martyrdom of St. Maurice*, 338, Fig. 390; self-portrait, and son's portrait, 339, Pl. 31

Greek architecture, compared to Roman, 427; Hellenic, 6–14, 28, 35, 37, 38–39, 66, Figs. 1–18, 42, 47; Hellenistic, 42–46, 49–50, 54, 64, 66, Figs. 48–50, 55, 72, 74; 19th-century book on, 427; rationalism of, 38–39; space in, 35, 50, 93

Greek art, as imitation of nature, 36; Winckelmann on, 427

Greek chorus, 28, 33, 39; and music, 29, 32; Nietzsche on, 28, 32

Greek-cross church plan, examples of, 111, Figs. 113, 114; 157, Fig. 185; 282, Fig. 325; 291, Figs. 331, 332; 334, Fig. 383; 394, Fig. 454; placement of choir in, 313

Greek drama, 6, 27–30, 35; Aristotle on, 30, 37; compared to Christian liturgy, 127; compared to Roman drama, 92; function of, 37; heroes in, 28, 29, 30, 36, 37; humanism of, 36; and music, 28, 29, 30, 31, 32; patron of, 6; rationalism of, 39; and time, 36; unity of, 39; writers of, 6

Greek music, Aristotle on, 60–61; and drama, 28, 29, 30, 31, 32; in education, 31, 61; Hellenic, 30–33, 58; Hellenistic, 58–62, example of, 62; and idealism, 37; "new," 33; Plato on, 31, 36, 60; and rationalism, 38; Roman adaptation of, 92–93; Roman survival of, 94; Socrates on, 31

Greek painting, 55; of Apelles, 251, 429; Hellenistic, 55–56, 58; Plato on, 38; surviving Roman copies of, Pl. 4, Fig. 63; of vases, 55, Pl. 3, Fig. 44

Greek poetry, 29, 61

Greek rationalism, 37–40; *vs.* baroque, 403

Greek revival, 19th-century, 434, 470

Greek sculpture, archaic, 23, 25, Figs. 30, 36; Hellenic, 23–27, 67, Pls. 1, 2, Figs. 31–35, 37–41, 43, 45, 46; Hellenic architectural, 14–23, Figs. 13, 19–29; Hellenistic, 46–49, 53–54, 63, 64, 66–68, Figs. 51–54, 62, 68–71, 73, 75–78; Hellenistic architectural, 49–54, Figs. 55–61; and idealism, 37; and rationalism, 38, 39; realism in, 66–67; Winckelmann on, 427

Greek temple, altar of, 102; *vs.* Christian church, 102; and Palladio's churches, 300, 304;

Harlot's Progress, 418; *Marriage à-la-Mode*, Scenes I, IV, and V from, 416–418, 424, Figs. 485–487; *Rake's Progress*, 418
Holy Roman Empire, 295, 296, 322–323, 387, 404, 471; and the papacy, 202, 209, 322–323
home, the, and Dutch arts, 371–372, 386–387, 388; as music center, 372, 382–383, 386, 388, Figs. 445, 446
Homer, 22, 35, 168; Aristotle on, 37; in Ingres' painting, 441, Fig. 507; quoted, 12; *Odyssey*, 526, quoted, 5, 35
Honegger, Arthur, *Antigone*, 524; *Pacific 231*, 518
honeysuckle motif, 13, Fig. 14
Honorius, Emperor, 99
Hooch, Pieter de, 388; *Mother and Child*, 378–379, Fig. 440
Horace, 90, 428; quoted, 45
horns (cornu), Roman, 92; pictured, Fig. 109
Horsemen, 16, Fig. 22
Hospicio de San Fernando (Ribera), 337, Fig. 389
Houdon, Jean-Antoine, *Benjamin Franklin*, 418, Fig. 489; *Voltaire*, 418, Fig. 488
"House of Diana." *See* Ostia, Italy
houses. *See* domestic architecture
Hugh of Semur, Abbot, 133, 136–137, 141, 148, 153, 154
Hugo, Victor, 460, 464, 469; Delacroix on, 454; influence of, 464; influences on, 462; and the revivals, 462, 471; *Après une Lecture de Dante*, quoted, 462; *Cromwell*, 450, Preface quoted, 462, 466; *Notre Dame de Paris (Hunchback of Notre Dame)*, 461; *Odes* and *Ballades*, 463; *Les Orientales*, 475; "Witches' Sabbath," 469, influence of, 466, quoted, 463
human figure, anatomy of, 244, 258–259, 372, 387; Byzantine *vs.* early Roman Christian treatment of, 108; as caryatids, 12, 13; in Giotto's painting, 215; in Gothic sculpture, 194; Greek ideals of, 34; in Hellenistic sculpture, 66–68; *ignudi*, 277; Polyclitus' canon for, 24, 39; proportions of, Ghiberti on, 258; Renaissance personalizing of, 260–261; in Roman sculpture, 87; Romanesque contortion of, 154; Venetian ideal of, 318. *See also* nudes
humanism, classical, 256, 257–258; of Enlightenment, 424; Florentine, 232, 236, 250–251, 255, 285, 286, 447; Hellenic, 33–36, breakdown of, 62; Roman Renaissance, 232, 285–288; revolt against, 323
humanitarianism, Franciscan, 228, 229–232
Humfrey, Pelham, 391
Hunchback of Notre Dame, Hugo, 461
"Hundred Guilder Print," Rembrandt, 374–375, Fig. 429
Huxley, Aldous, 66; quoted, 360
Huygens, Constantijn, 369
hydraulus or hydraulic organ, 91, 92; pictured, Fig. 109
hymns, Arian, 122; early Christian, 122, 123–124; Calvinist, 382; Franciscan, 223–225; Gothic, 201;

harmonizations of 386; preludes and fugues on, 382; Roman, 94; of St. Ambrose, 123; of St. John, 150; syllabic, 123–124

I and My Village, Chagall, 519–520, Fig. 584
Ibsen, Henrik, 495, 496
iconography, defined, 110; of cathedrals dedicated to Notre Dame, 182; of Chartres' sculpture, 190–192; of Chartres' stained glass, 196; of early Christian mosaics, 124; Giorgione's break with, 304, 320; of Gothic and Romanesque sculpture, 190; and Romanesque sculpture, 142–143, 149; of St. Denis' windows, 180; of the Sistine Chapel ceiling, 273–274; Veronese's treatment of, 311
Ictinus, 6; Parthenon, 11, Fig. 9
idealism, Hellenic, 6, 33, 36–37, 38, 40; decline of, 62, 64, 66
idealism in art, defined, 36
ideas, archaeological, 447–449; aristocratic baroque, 366–367; baroque synthesis, 403–405; bourgeois baroque, 386–388; Counter Reformation, 343–345; domesticity, 386–388; early Christian, 124–129; early Italian Renaissance, 227–232; 18th-century, 422–424; feudal Romanesque, 175–178; Florentine Renaissance, 256–261; Gothic, 201–206; Hellenic, 33–40; Hellenistic, 62–70; humanism, 285–289; late 19th-century, 498–500; mannerism, 317–320; militant mysticism, 343–345; monastic Romanesque, 153–158; neoclassical, 447–449; relativism, 540–544; Roman, 93–96; Roman Renaissance, 285–289; romantic, 468–476; 20th-century, 540–544; Venetian mannerism, 317–320
idée fixe, defined, 465; Berlioz' use of, 465–466; example of, 465
ignudi, of Michelangelo, 277, Fig. 321
Ile-de-France, The, 179–181; music of, 198
Iliad, Homer, personified in Ingres' painting, 441, Fig. 507
illuminated manuscripts, 147–148, 154, Fig. 177; 169, Pl. 12, Fig. 199; 188, Pl. 14; influence of, 143, 163, 166
imagery, heroic, in Beethoven's *Eroica*, 444–446; in Dante's *Divine Comedy*, 227; in music, 317, 400, 497; in photography, 482; religious, 344
Immaculate Conception, Murillo, 342, Fig. 396
immortality, symbolized, 110, 118, 119, Fig. 146
Imperial Baths, Roman, 80–81, 82, 86, 87, 263
Imperial Procession, Fig. 79
Impression—Sunrise, Monet, 482, 485
impressionism, in the arts, 498; in painting, 477, 482–485, 499, Pls. 49, 50, Figs. 546–548, influence of, 485–486, influence on, 455; in sculpture, 491; and postimpressionism, 485–488, Pls. 51–54, Figs. 549–552

Improvisation No. 30 (on a Warlike Theme), Kandinsky, 512, Pl. 58
In ecclesiis, Gabrieli, 314–315; excerpt from, 316; text of, 315
individualism, Hellenistic, 62–66; 19th-century romantic, 468, 469; Renaissance, 256, 258, 260–261
industrial design, 537
Industrial Revolution, and the arts, 470; effects of, 461, 477, 499
Ingres, Jean-Auguste Dominique, 441–442, 524; *Apotheosis of Homer*, 441–442, 471, Fig. 507; *Turkish Bath*, 476, Pl. 48
Inquisition, Congregation of the, 281; censorship by, 323; and Spain, 340–341, 380; and Veronese, 310–311
Institutes of Oratory, Quintilian, 90
Instruction in Music and Grammar, Douris, 31, Fig. 44
instrumental music, Boethius' view of, 121; Hellenic, 31; Roman, 91–92, Fig. 109. *See also* music; individual composers
instrumentation, development of, 313–314; of Berlioz, 466–467, 469; of Debussy, 498; Oriental influences on, 509; of Purcell, 400; of Ravel, 524; realism in, 495; of romantic music, 468–469; and standardization of instruments, 477
instruments. *See* musical instruments
intonazione, 313
intercolumniation, defined, 9; Hellenic *vs.* Hellenistic, 50
international style of architecture, 507, 532, 534, 536–539, 542, Pl. 63, Figs. 608–610; influence of, 531
intervals, Greek ideal of, 37; mathematical concept of, 32, 39; perfect, 152
Ionic column, 9, 14, Figs. 11, 15; compared to Doric, 12–13, Fig. 10
Ionic order of architecture, 12–13, 14, Figs. 10, 11, 15; of Escorial Palace, 335; of La Madeleine, 432; Venetian use of, 296, 298
Ionic temple, 12–14, Figs. 11, 15
Iris, 21, Fig. 28
iron, Renaissance use of, 233. *See also* cast-iron construction
irrationalism, 407, 424
Isaac, Heinrich, 255–256, 260, 265, 342; compared to Des Prez, 284; carnival song *Un dì lieto* of, 256
Isaiah, sculpture, 154, Fig. 183
Isidore, *Etymologies*, 143
Isidorus of Miletus. *See* Fig. 134
isocephaly, defined, 16; at Ravenna, 108
isorhythmic musical principles, 237
Istanbul, Turkey
  Church of SS. Sergius and Bacchus, 112, Fig. 133
  Hagia Sophia (Anthemius of Tralles and Isidorus of Miletus), 86, 112–114, 116, 125, Figs. 134–136; music of 123; Byzantine capitals of, 116, 118, Fig. 140
Italian Renaissance. *See* early Italian, Florentine, and Roman Renaissance
Italy, in 14th century, 209–211; Napoleon in, 429–430. *See also* Roman Empire; Florence; Rome
Ivanhoe, Scott, Delacroix' illustrations for, 454

ivory carvings, early Roman Christian, 120–121, Figs. 147–150

Jacopone da Todi, 225, 231; *Stabat Mater Dolorosa*, 225, 231
James I of England, 391, 399
James II of England, 392
James, William, 541
jazz, 509, 510
Jefferson, Thomas, 86, 304, 418, 434; University of Virginia Rotunda, 86, 304, 434, Fig. 501
Jerusalem, 43, 143; in Roman sculpture, 74, Fig. 83
Jesuit Order. *See* Society of Jesus
Jewish Graveyard, Ruisdael, 379–380, Fig. 441
Joachim Returning to the Sheepfold, Giotto, 214–215, 230, Fig. 259
Joan of Arc Listening to the Voices, Rude, 458, Fig. 521
Job, Mestrovic, 530, Fig. 600
John XXII, Pope, 230
John of the Cross, 323, 333; quoted on mysticism, 344
John of Salisbury, 199
Johnson, Philip, Seagram Building, 538–539, Fig. 610
Johnson, Samuel, 543
Jonah Sarcophagus, 118, Fig. 145
Jones, Inigo, 304, 321, 397; as set designer, 399, Fig. 465; Banqueting House at Whitehall, 391, Fig. 450, detail, p. 389
jongleurs. *See* minstrels
Jonson, Ben, *Masque of Blackness*, 399
Journey of the Magi, Gozzoli, 246, 248, 256, detail, Fig. 286
journeymen craftsmen, 190, 210, 211
Joyce, James, quoted on art, 506; *A Portrait of the Artist as a Young Man*, 526; *Ulysses*, 523, 526, 542
Judgment Angel, sculpture, 145, Fig. 170
Julius II, Pope, 258, 262, 263, 267, 281, 286; choir of, 263; and Michelangelo, 265, 266–267; 271, 273; Raphael's portrait of, 263, Fig. 301; statue of, 273; symbol of, 263; tomb of, 263, 266–269, 271, 273, 274, 282, Figs. 306–312
July Revolution of 1830, 450–451, 453, 471; painting inspired by, 450–451, 453, Pl. 46; sculpture inspired by, 456–458, Fig. 520, detail, p. 450
Justinian, Emperor, 99, 102, 105, 108, 112, 114–115, 119, 121, 123, 125; mosaic portrait of, 114–115, Fig. 137; *Digest of Laws*, 115

Kandinsky, Wassily, 504, 511–512, 522, 530, 537; quoted on abstract painting, 513; quoted on music, 513; *Der Blaue Reiter*, 511; *Improvisation No. 30 (on a Warlike Theme)*, 512, Pl. 58, quoted on, 512; *Picture with White Edge*, 512–513, Fig. 573
katharsis, defined, 30
Kaufmann, Edgar J., home of, 534–535, Fig. 605
Keats, John, 471; "Ode on a Grecian Urn," quoted, 33
Kepler, Johannes, 403, 405
keyboard instruments, baroque, 313; Gothic innovations in, 200; hydraulic organ, 91, 92; in Venetian painting, 313

keyboard music, 313, 382, 386, 424
Kierkegaard, Sören, 420
King Arthur, Dryden, 400; legend of, 191–192
Kiss, The, Rodin, 491, Fig. 556
Klee, Paul, 511–512, 524, 537; quoted, 522; painting titles of, 522; *Diana*, 522, Pl. 60
Klenze, Leo von, Glyptothek, 434, Fig. 500
Knife Sharpener, 59–60, Fig. 69
Kore from Samos, 25–26, Fig. 36
Kotzebue, August von, *King Stephen* and *Ruins of Athens*, 445
Kouros from Sounion, 23, 24, Fig. 30
Kreutzer, Rodolphe, 444

Labrouste, Henri, 491–493, 500; Library of Ste. Geneviève, 491–492, 493, Figs. 557, 558; National Library, Paris, 492–493, Fig. 559
La Fontaine, Jean de, 366
Lamb, Charles, quoted on Hogarth, 418
Lamentation. See *Pietà*
landscape painting, 56–57; of Cézanne, 486–488, Figs. 550, 551; Dutch, 371, 379–380, Figs. 423, 441; of Lorrain, 362, Fig. 420; romantic, 473–474, Pl. 47, Fig. 534
Landscape with Three Gabled Cottages, Rembrandt, p. 368
Langhans, Karl Gotthard, Brandenburg Gate, 434, Fig. 499
languages, ancient Greek, 29, 69, Renaissance study of, 257; French vernacular, 168; and humanism, 286; Italian vernacular and Dante, 226; Latin in the Gothic period, 202, 206; Latin for literature, 226; Latin in the Renaissance, 257, 286; Latin *vs.* vernacular French, 201, 206; Latin *vs.* vernacular Italian, 228; and linguistic reform, 403; modern French, 498; old French, 166, 168; Provençal French, 224; Umbrian dialect, 224, 225
Laniere, Nicholas, 391
lantern tower, of Florence Cathedral, 233, Figs. 263, 265; of St. Paul's, 394, 395, Fig. 453; of St. Peter's, 282, 283, Figs. 324, 326; of St. Sernin, 137, Fig. 159
Laocoön Group, Agesander, Athenodorus, and Polydorus of Rhodes, 64–66, 80, 263, Fig. 75; influence of, 269; Versailles copy, 357
Lapith and Centaur, Phidias(?), 16, Fig. 20
La Rochefoucauld, François de, quoted, 66
Lasso, Orlando di, 285, 343
Last Judgment, Giotto, 223, Pl. 17, detail, p. 209
Last Judgment, Giselbertus, 145, Fig. 169
Last Judgment, Michelangelo, 280, 281, 288, 320, 323, 325, detail, Fig. 366; influence of, 489
Last Judgments, early Christian allusion to, 106; and medieval thought, 191; Romanesque, 66; neoclassical, 431; theme for Traini's fresco, 221
Last Supper, Leonardo, 287, 311, Fig. 329
Last Supper, mosaic, 106, Fig. 122

Last Supper, Tintoretto, 308, Fig. 357
Last Supper, Veronese. See *Feast in the House of Levi*
Latin-cross church plan, choir placement in, 313; and Greco-Roman temple combined, 300; of St. Peter's, 282–283, Fig. 325; symbolism of, 104–105; typical of basilica, 104, Fig. 118
lauds (*laudi spirituali*), 223–225, 255; examples of, 224, 225
lavabo, explained, 132
Lawes, Henry, 399
lay, 168
Lay of the Last Minstrel, Scott, quoted, 224
leaf-and-tongue motif, 13, Fig. 14
learning, Gothic representations of, 193–194; medieval divisions of, 191
Lebrun, Charles, 347, 349, 354, 362, 366, 367, 412; *Alexander the Great Entering Babylon*, 362, Fig. 421; Hall of Mirrors, Versailles, 353–354, Fig. 409
Le Corbusier (Edouard Jeanneret), 504, 532, 536; influence of, 538; Wright on, 537; *L'Unité d'Habitation*, 537–538, Pl. 63
Legend of the Three Companions, 214, quoted, 224
Léger, Fernand, 518; *Ballet Mécanique*, 518; *The City*, 518, Pl. 59; *Mechanical Elements*, 518, Fig. 582
Legislative Paunch, Daumier, 479, Fig. 540
Leibniz, Gottfried von, 403
leitmotif, 498
Lemaire, Philippe, La Madeleine pediment sculpture, 431, Fig. 492
Le Nôtre, André, 355; plan of Versailles gardens, 354, Fig. 410
Leo X, Pope, 255, 258, 262, 263–264, 268, 281; as art patron, 265; as humanist, 266; and Michelangelo, 265; Raphael's portrait of, 265, Fig. 302
Leo X with Two Cardinals, Raphael, 265, Fig. 302
Leonardo da Vinci, 245, 246, 260, 262, 287; as court artist, 357; as epitome of Renaissance man, 261; notebooks of, 258; and the mannerists, 319; pyramidal composition of, 266, Pl. 22, Fig. 305; in Raphael's painting, 280, Pl. 24; and scientific naturalism, 259; *Adoration of the Magi*, 259, Fig. 299; *Last Supper*, 287, 311, Fig. 329; *Madonna and Child with St. Anne*, 266, 320, Fig. 305; *Madonna of the Rocks*, 266, Pl. 22
Leonin, 199, 200; *Magnus Liber Organi*, 199, 200, 201
Lessing, Gotthold, *Miss Sara Sampson*, 415
Lesueur, J. F., 444; operas by, 449
letter writing, of Cassiodorus, 121–122; of Debussy, 498; of Michelangelo, 267, 273; of Mozart, 419, 423; of Napoleon, 430; of Pliny the Younger, 90–91; Roman art of, 90–91, 95
Le Vau, Louis, Versailles Palace, Fig. 406, Marble Court of, 364, Fig. 422
Lever House, New York City, 538, Fig. 609

liberal arts, the seven, 30, 203; in Gothic sculpture, 193–194, Figs. 225–227; Gothic view of, 191; patroness of, 182, 191, 193
Liberty Leading the People, Delacroix, 450–451, 453, 480, Pl. 46; influence of, 456
libraries, of Alexandria, 45; of Escorial Palace, 335–336, Fig. 386; Labrouste's building developments for, 470, 491–493, Figs. 557–559; of the Medici, 240; at Pergamon, 45, 46, 68; of the Sorbonne, 462; of Trajan's Forum, 78, 87, 90, 94; of Venice, 291, 292, 294
Library of Ste. Geneviève. *See* Paris
Library of St. Mark. *See* Venice
Lictors Bringing Back to Brutus the Bodies of His Sons, David, 437–438, Fig. 503
life after death, Greek idea of, 35
Life of the Virgin Mary, 192, Fig. 224
light, in Caravaggio's painting, 329; in Dante's *Divine Comedy*, 227; in De Hooch's painting, 378–379; in Rembrandt's etchings, 375; in Van Eyck's painting, 253; in Velázquez' painting, 342; and visual arts, 195
light and color, Cézanne's use of, 486; in Delacroix' paintings, 454; impressionists' use of, 483, 484–485; 19th-century experiments with, 482–483, 498
light and shadow, Apollodorus' use of, 55; architectural use of, 296, 298, 327, 350, 411; in Bernini's sculpture, 357; early foundations for, 228; in Piero della Francesca's painting, 250; in Giotto's painting, 221; in Gothic sculpture, 190, 194; in Hellenistic sculpture, 53, 66; in Masaccio's painting, 246, 249; Plato on, 38; in Ravenna mosaics, 106; in Rembrandt's painting, 372, 373; in Rodin's sculpture, 491; and sculpture location, 117; in Uccello's painting, 248–249; in Venetian painting, 304; in Vermeer's painting, 380–381
lighting, in abbey church, 139; of early Christian basilicas, 104; in Gothic cathedrals, 114, 189, 206; in Hagia Sophia, 114; in Italian Gothic church, 212; of mosaics, 108; Norman use of, 173, 174; in Pantheon, 85; polychromatic, 195; in Roman architecture, 81, 87, 93; and sculpture location, 14, 117, 332; and Sistine Chapel ceiling, 274–276; through stained glass, 195, 198
Lincoln Center for the Performing Arts. *See* New York City
Lindau Gospels, 146, Fig. 175
linear perspective, defined, 248; of cubists, 513, 514; foundation for, 228; Ghiberti's attempts at, 241; Leonardo's and Raphael's solution of, Pl. 24, Fig. 329; of Piero della Francesca, 249; of Polygnotus, 55; Renaissance use of, 259, 260; Uccello's treatise on, 249; Veronese's liberties with, 311

lintel, defined, 9, Fig. 15; of Arch of Trajan, 74, 93; of Erechtheum, 13, Fig. 14; of Vézelay portal, 143, Figs. 166, 167
Lion Hunt, Barye, 475, Fig. 538
Lion Hunt, Delacroix, 476
Lippi, Filippo, 236, 240, 260; *Nativity*, 248, Pl. 19
Lipschitz, Jacques, 532; *Man with Mandolin*, 514, Figs. 577, 578
Lisle, Rouget de, *La Marseillaise*, 457
Liszt, Franz, 464, 469; *Faust Symphony*, 465; *Totentanz*, 467
literature, early Italian Renaissance, 226–228; feudal, 166–168; Hellenic, 31; Hellenistic, preservation of, 69; late 19th-century, 479, 495–498; Roman, 90–91; romantic, 458–461, 462–463; romantic and music, 464–467; romantic, Oriental influence on, 474, 475; stream of consciousness, 506, 523, 526; surrealist, 523; 20th-century neoclassical, 524, 526
lithograph (a printed impression transferred to paper from a drawing on a stone surface made with crayons or greasy pencils), 477; examples of, Figs. 513–517, 540, 560, 561
liturgical sequence, defined and example of, 224; in requiem mass, 224
liturgy, Ambrosian, 122–124; Anglican in Venice, 314; Arian, 122; Byzantine, 109, 115, 123–124, 125, 129; Christian *vs.* Greek drama, 127; Cluniac, 138–139; early Roman Christian, 125, 128–129; Gothic, 198–199; requiem mass, 224; Roman Renaissance, 284; symbols for, 119; Venetian, 321
Locke, Matthew, 389
Lombardy, architecture of, 157, Fig. 187; groins of, 212
London, Canaletto, 398, Fig. 464
London, England, 161; Great Exposition at, 493–494; Great Fire of, 389, 392, 394; opening of the King's Theater, 398; 17th-century, 389, 391–393; skyline of, 392, 398, Fig. 464; Wren's plan for rebuilding of, 392, 396, Fig. 458
  British Museum (Smirke), 434, Fig. 498
  Mausolus, 63, Fig. 73; Parthenon sculptures (Elgin marbles): *Demeter and Persephone*, 21, Fig. 28, *Dionysus*, 21, Fig. 28, *Iris*, 21, Fig. 28, *Lapith and Centaur*, 16, Fig. 20, *Moon Goddess' Horse*, 21, Fig. 29, *Presentation of Peplos*, 19, Fig. 25, *Sun God's Horses*, 21, Fig. 28, *Three Goddesses*, 21, Fig. 29
  Collection of Her Majesty the Queen
  Canaletto, *London*, 398, Fig. 464; Van Dyck, *Children of Charles I*, 391, Fig. 452
  Courtauld Institute
  Manet, *Bar at the Folies-Bergère*, 416, 483, Pl. 49
  Hampton Court Palace (Wren), 397–398, Figs. 462–463
  Houses of Parliament (Barry), 460, Fig. 524

Kew Gardens, 474
National Gallery
  Botticelli, *Venus and Mars*, 251, 287, Pl. 20; Constable, *Hay Wain*, 454, 473–474, Pl. 47; Hogarth, *Marriage-à-la-Mode: Countess' Levee*, 416, Fig. 486, *Death of the Earl*, 416, 418, Fig. 487, *Marriage Contract*, 416, Fig. 485; Leonardo, cartoon for *Madonna and Child with St. Anne*, 266, 320, Fig. 305; Titian, *Bacchus and Ariadne*, 307, Fig. 356; Van Eyck, *Giovanni Arnolfini and His Wife*, 253, Pl. 21, detail, Fig. 293
New Law Courts (Street), 460
Palladium, 301
St. Martin-in-the-Fields (Gibbs), 397, Fig. 460
St. Mary-le-Bow (Wren), 397, Fig. 459
St. Paul's Cathedral, (Wren) 86, 392–396, Figs. 453–457
Tate Gallery
  Modigliani, *Head*, 507–508, Fig. 565
Tower of London, 161, 171–173, 174, 175, 177–178, Figs. 201–203
  St. John's Chapel, 173, Fig. 204
Victoria and Albert Museum
  Houdon, *Voltaire*, 418, Fig. 488
Wallace Collection
  Fragonard, *The Swing*, 414, Pl. 40; Watteau, *Music Party*, 412–414, Fig. 478
Wellington Museum, Apsley House
  Canova, *Napoleon*, 442, Fig. 508; Velázquez, *Water Carrier of Seville*, 341, Fig. 395
Whitehall Banqueting House (Jones), 391, Fig. 450, detail, p. 389
  Rubens, ceiling paintings, Fig. 451
Longhena, Baldassare, 315; Church of Santa Maria della Salute, 303–304, Figs. 351, 352
Lorenzetti, Ambrogio, 219; *Good Government*, 221, Fig. 255
Lorenzetti, Pietro, 212, 219, 221
Lorenzo de' Medici, Verrocchio's workshop, 254–255, 261, Fig. 295
Lorrain, Claude, 362, 448, 473; painting titles of, 362; *Disembarkation of Cleopatra at Tarsus*, 362, Fig. 420
Louis VIII of France, 194
Louis IX of France, 188, 194, 205; portrayed, 188, Pl. 14
Louis XIII of France, 358, 360, 366
Louis XIV of France, 329, 362, 389, 391, 404, 448; and absolutism, 346–349, 366; and the arts, 347; art collection of, 362–363; bust of, 355–356, Fig. 411; death of, 406; equestrian statue of, 356, Fig. 412; music of, 363–365; musicians of, 321, 363–365, 392, 405; and the Louvre, 349–350, 392; as a monarch, 346–349; portrait of, 346, Fig. 398; quoted, 347; relief of, 353, Pl. 33; social and personal life of, 347; as Sun King, 347, 354, 356, 363, 366, p. 346; symbol of, 347; and Versailles, 350–355
Louis XV of France, 432
Louis XVI of France, 418, 432, 436, 473

Louis XVIII of France, 432, 434
Louis Philippe of France, 432, 434, 451, 470, 475
Louise, Charpentier, 495
Louvre. *See* Paris
Louÿs, Pierre, 497
love, Platonic theory of, 306
Love of Three Oranges, Prokofiev, 524
low relief, defined, 16; examples of, Figs. 21–25, 105–108
Loyola, Ignatius, 281, 333, 344; canonization of, 323; German College, founded by, 343; Society of Jesus, founded by, 281, 323, 344; *Spiritual Exercises*, 325, 344
Lucian, 252, quoted, 26
Lucretius, 90, quoted, 280
Ludovisi throne, 26–27, Fig. 39, p. 3
Ludwig II of Bavaria, 461
Lully, Jean-Baptiste, 347, 349, 360, 365, 367, 391, 400, 498; as music director for Louis XIV, 363, 364–365, 366; *Alceste*, 364–365, excerpt from, 365, performance of depicted, Fig. 422
lute, in painting, 304, Pl. 25; in sculpture, 151, Fig. 179; as Christian symbol, 151; species of, 382, Fig. 445
lute tablature, 383, Fig. 446
Luther, Martin, 322
Lutheran Reformation, 310, 386
Luxembourg Palace. *See* Paris
lyre and lyre playing, 59, 60, 62, 122, 127, 166, 168; as Christian symbol, 151; depicted, Figs. 68, 181; Roman, 92
lyrical tragedy, 364
Lysicrates, Choragic Monument of, 14, Figs. 16, 17
Lysippus, *Apoxomenos (Scraper)* 34, Fig. 45; Roman copy of "*Farnese*" *Hercules* of, 54, 242, 357, Fig. 62
Lysistrata, Aristophanes, quoted, 9; Picasso's illustrations for Seldes' version of, 524

macabre, in literature, 462–463; in music, 464–466
Macbeth, Shakespeare, Delacroix' illustration for, 453, Fig. 513; influence of, 462, 463
Machiavelli, 286; *History of Florence*, 258; *The Prince*, 258, 261
Macpherson, James, *Ossian*, 444
Madame Récamier, David, 438, 448, Fig. 505
Madeleine, Church of La. *See* Paris; Vézelay
Maderno, Carlo, 104, 323; and St. Peter's, 282, 283, Figs. 324–325, 327
Madonna and Child with St. Anne, Leonardo, 266, 320, Fig. 305
Madonna Enthroned, Cimabue, 218–219, Fig. 252
Madonna Enthroned, Giotto, 220–221, Fig. 254
Madonna in Majesty. See *Maestà*
Madonna of the Rocks, Leonardo, 266, Pl. 22
Madrid, Spain, as capital city, 333
Hospicio de San Fernando (Ribera), 337, Fig. 389
Prado Museum
Goya, *Executions of the Third of May, 1808*, 441, Pl. 45; *Witches' Sabbath*, Fig. 529; Murillo,

Immaculate Conception, 342, Fig. 396; Rubens, *Garden of Love*, 358, 412–413, Fig. 417; Titian, *Venus and the Organ Player*, 304, 317, Fig. 354; Velázquez, *Las Meninas (Maids of Honor)*, 341–342, Pl. 32
madrigals, development of 313; English style of, 401; forerunner of, 256; Monteverdi's *Eighth Book of Madrigals*, 315–316; Renaissance, 170
Maestà, Duccio, 230–231, Fig. 262, detail, Fig. 261
Maeterlinck, Maurice, 479, 490, 500; nature studies of, 498; quoted, 496; *The Bluebird*, 499; *Pelléas et Mélisande*, 496–498, 500, excerpt from, 497
Maillol, Aristide, *Torso of Venus*, 524, Fig. 593
Magic Flute, The, Mozart, 424
Magna Charta, 205
Magnus Liber Organi, Leonin, 199, 200
Mahana No Atua, Gauguin, 486, 507, Pl. 53
Mahler, Gustav, 467; *Song of the Earth*, 520
Maison Carrée. *See* Nîmes
Mallarmé, Stéphane, 479, 495–496
Malraux, André, 503
Malton, Thomas. *See* Fig. 457
man, Balzac's view of, 495; baroque, 323, 403–404, 499; Byzantine, 125, 127; classical man, 127; early Christian, 127; the Enlightenment's view of, 424; in feudal society, 228; Franciscan attitude toward, 228–229; and Greek humanism, 33–34; Greek idea of, 3; Hellenic, 66; Hellenic and Hellenistic compared, 66; Hellenistic, 64, 66; industrial, 499; late 19th-century, 499; medieval, 230; Michelangelo's view of, 269, 271, 272, 274–275; Pico della Mirandola's view of, 274–275; Plato's view of, 274, 287; Platonic ascent of, 275; Protagoras and Sophocles on, 33; Renaissance attitude toward, 260–261; Romanesque, 130, 154–155, 228; 20th-century, 501, 503–504, 541–542; Victorian, 494
Man with Mandolin, Lipschitz, 514, Figs. 577, 578
mandorla, 148, Fig. 178
Manet, Édouard, 416, 481; *Bar at the Folies-Bergère*, 416, 483, Pl. 49; *Rue de Berne*, 483, Fig. 546
Mann, Thomas, *Death in Venice*, 520
mannerism, academic, 319; and architecture, 302–303; and the baroque, 311, 320; explained, 296, 318–319; free, 307–308, 319–320; influence of, 341; and painting, 304; and religious reforms, 323; of Tintoretto, 307–308
Mansart, Jules Hardouin, 366, 367, 448; Versailles Palace, 353–354, 410, Figs. 405–406, 409
Manteneia, Greece, relief from, 59, Fig. 68
Mantua, Italy, 322
Palazzo del Tè (Giulio Romano), courtyard detail, 303, Fig. 349

manuscripts, at Escorial Library, 336; illuminated, 147–148, 154, 169, 188, Figs. 177, 199, Pls. 12, 14; influence of, 143, 163, 166; music, 32, 54, 225, 382; of *Song of Roland*, 159
Marat, Jean Paul, 429
marble, Istrian, 110; Parian, 6, Fig. 6; Pentelic, 6, 10, Figs. 6, 9, 11, 15–16, 18; polychrome, 78, 108, 115, 291; quarries of, 267; used as glass, Roman, 81
Marble Court at Versailles During a Performance of Lully's Opera, Alceste, 364, Fig. 422
Marc, Franz, 511–512; *Tower of Blue Horses*, 512, Fig. 572
Marcellinus, quoted on music, 92
Marcus Aurelius, Emperor, 71, 91; column of, 90; equestrian statue of, 76, 244, Fig. 86; *Meditations*, 76
Margaret in Church, Delacroix, 454, Fig. 516
Marie Antoinette, Cottage of, "Le Hameau," 472, Fig. 532
Marinetti, Filippo, 516; *Manifesto* of, quoted, 517
Marriage-à-la-Mode, Hogarth, 416–418, 424, Figs. 485–487
Marriage of Bacchus and Ariadne, Tintoretto, 318, Fig. 364
Marriage at Cana, Veronese, 309–310, Pl. 28, detail, Fig. 358
Marriage Contract, The, Hogarth, 416, Fig. 485
Marriage of Figaro, The, Mozart and Beaumarchais, 419, 420, 423, 445
Marseillaise, La, De Lisle, 457; as sculpture motif, 456–458, Fig. 520
Marseilles, France
L'Unité d'Habitation (Le Corbusier), 537–538, Pl. 63
Marsila, King of Spain, 167, 176
Marsyas, contest with Apollo, 59–60, Fig. 68; punishment of, 59–60, 66, 269, 357, Fig. 70
Martini, Simone, 210, 212, 219; frescoes of, 229; *Annunciation*, 221, Pl. 16; *St. Martin before Emperor Julian*, 229–230, Fig. 258
Martyrdom of St. Maurice and the Theban Legion, El Greco, 338, Fig. 390
Marx, Karl, 541
Mary, Queen of England, in Veronese's painting, 309, Pl. 28
Masaccio, 236, 245–246, 259; use of atmospheric perspective and chiaroscuro, 246, 249; *Expulsion from the Garden*, 246, 278–279, Fig. 283; *The Tribute Money*, 246, Fig. 284
Mask, from Itumba, 505, Fig. 563
masks, of Greek actors, 28–29
masque, English court, 399, 401; drawing for scenery, 399, Fig. 465
Masque of Blackness, Jonson, 399
mass media, 501, 504
mathematics, and the arts, 258; Hellenistic, 68; and human body, 39; and music, 32, 37, 121, 204–205, 237, 259; and number symbolism, 204; Plato on, 38; proportions and art, 39; symbolism of in *Divine Comedy*, 226
Matilda, Queen, 176; church of, 173
Matisse, Henri, 416, 507, 510; quoted, 511; *Roumanian Blouse*, 511, Pl. 57

matroneum, defined, 112, Fig. 132
Matteo, Master, Pórtico de la Gloria, 145, Fig. 168; *Self-portrait*, Fig. 189
mausoleum, circular, 109–110
Mausoleum of Galla Placidia, 101, 111, Figs. 113, 114
Mausoleum at Halicarnassus, 63, Fig. 72
Mausolus, 63, Fig. 73
Maximian, Archbishop, 108; cathedra of, 119–121, 129, Figs. 147–150; mosaic portrait of, 114-115, Fig. 137
Mazarin, Cardinal, 346–347, 363
mechane, defined, 29
Mechanical Elements, Léger, 518, Fig. 582
mechanical style, in music, 518; in painting, 506, 517–518; Pl. 59, Fig. 582
Medallion with Lamb, p. 130
Medici, Cosimo de', as art patron, 236, 248, 260; in Botticelli's painting, 250, Fig. 289; as Florentine ruler, 236, 255; in Gozzoli's painting, 248, Fig. 286; library, of, 236, 240; and Neoplatonic Academy, 236; palace of, 239–240, Figs. 270–271
Medici, Giovanni, Arnolfini, Van Eyck's portrait of, 253, Pl. 21, Fig. 293
Medici, Giovanni de', 257; in Botticelli's painting, 250, Fig. 289
Medici family, as art patrons, 250, 253–254; as bankers, 236; coat of arms of, 240, 248, Figs. 270, 271, 286; driven from Florence, 253, 262; library of, 286; musician to, 236; palace of, 239–240, 244, Figs. 270, 271; sculptor to, 244; under Spanish power, 322; tombs of, 272, 274, 303, 320, Fig. 313
Medici, Giuliano de' in Botticelli's painting, 250, Fig. 289; in Gozzoli's painting, 248, Fig. 286
Medici, Giuliano de', Duke of Nemours, Michelangelo's tomb for, 272, 274, 303, 320, Fig. 313
Medici, Lorenzo de', 257–258, 263, 358; in Botticelli's painting, 250, Fig. 289; *canti carnascialeschi*, quoted, 255, 256; death of, effect on arts, 253; education of, 255; in Gozzoli's painting, 248, Fig. 286; as humanist, 250, 255; as "Il Magnifico," 254; and Michelangelo, 274; music and poetry of, 254, 255–256; as Neo-Platonist, 285; as papal banker, 254–258; and Simonetta Cattaneo, 251; son of, 263; Verrocchio's bust of, 254–255, 261, Fig. 295; *San Giovanni e Paolo*, 256
Medici, Maria de', Queen of France, Rubens' paintings of, 358, Pl. 34, Fig. 416
Medici, Pierfrancesco di Lorenzo de', 250, 251
Medici, Piero de', 248; in Botticelli's painting, 250, Fig. 289; in Gozzoli's painting, 248, Fig. 286
Medici-Riccardi Palace. *See* Florence
medicine, personified in Gothic sculpture, 194
medieval period. *See* Byzantine, early Roman Christian, feudal Roman-

esque, Gothic, monastic Romanesque, and Norman entries. *See also* chivalry; feudalism; monasticism; and so on
medieval revival, 458–462, 469, 470, 471–472; architecture of, 458–462, 471–472, Figs. 522–526, 530–531; music of, 461
medieval styles, transition to, 102, 127
medievalism. *See* medieval revival
Mediterranean world, Athens in, 3; and Northern Europe, compared, 179; Rome in, 74–75
melismatic music, defined, 124, 127; melisma of, 124, 200
Melk, Austria
Benedictine Abbey Church (Prandtauer), 412, Figs. 475–477
melodic intervals. *See* intervals
melodrama, defined, 29
melody, applied to oratory, 95; Beethoven's use of, 446; *cantus firmus*, 199–200; of *chanson de geste*, 170; Debussy quoted on, 497–498; of *Dies Irae*, 224; and discant, 200; Greek, 30, 37; Gregorian, 199–200; Phrygian, 58, 60; Socrates' view of, 31
Memmi, Lippo. *See* Pl. 16
Mendelssohn, Felix, 464, 470–471; *Songs Without Words*, 469
Mengs, Raphael, *Thoughts on Beauty*, 447
Meninas, Las, Velázquez, 341–342, 544, Pl. 32
Mephistopheles in the Air, Delacroix, 454, Fig. 514
Merchant of Venice, The, Shakespeare, quoted, 32
Merry Family, Steen, 387–388, Fig. 448
Merry Lute Player, Hals, 376, 378, Fig. 437
Mesomedes, 94
Mestrovic, Ivan, *Job*, 530, Fig. 600
Metamorphoses, Ovid, Picasso's illustrations for, 524
Metastasio, Pietro, 406; libretto of, 419
metope, defined, 10, Fig. 10; of Parthenon, 14, 16, 22, Figs. 19, 20
Mexico City, Mexico
Cathedral, 345, Fig. 397
Meyerbeer, Giacomo, *Le Prophète*, 454
Michelangelo Buonarroti, 102, 104, 246, 260, 262, 284, 286, 319, 333, 393, 394, 404, 448; artistic ancestor of, 242; and central-type church, 260; compared to Des Prez, 284; and Counter Reformation, 325; death of, 282; in El Greco's painting, 340, Fig. 393; on Ghiberti's bronze doors, 236; as humanist, 245; individualism of, 261; influence of, 302–303, 307, 357–358; influences on, 239, 266; and Julius II, 265, 273; and Neo-Platonism, 258, 268, 271, 274–275, 279, 287, 288; quoted, 267, 273, 287–288; compared to Rodin, 490; sculptural methods of, 271; signature of, 266; sonnets of, 288, quoted, 271, 279–280; style characteristics, 271; Tolnay's monograph on, 274; as transition to baroque, 285; use of triple division, 288; Vasari quoted on,

272; in Veronese's painting, 311, Fig. 359; view of man, 269, 271, 274–275; *Ancestor of Christ*, 275, Fig. 317; *Bacchus*, 266, 288, Fig. 303; "*Boboli Captives*," 271, Fig. 310; *Bound Slave*, 269, Fig. 307; *Bruges Madonna*, 266; *Creation of Adam*, 279, Pl. 23; *Creation of Eve*, 279; *Creation of the Sun and the Moon*, 279, Fig. 320; *David*, 257, 266, 271, Fig. 296; *Delphic Sibyl*, 276–277, Fig. 316; *Drunkenness of Noah*, 277–278, Fig. 318; *Fall of Man and Expulsion from Paradise*, 278, Fig. 319; Farnese Palace, 281, Fig. 323; *God Dividing the Light from Darkness*, 279, Fig. 321; *Last Judgment*, 280, 281, 288, 320, 323, 325, Figs. 314, 366, influence of, 489; Medici tombs, 272, 274, 303, 320, Fig. 313; *Moses*, 268–269, 271, 288, Fig. 312; *Noah's Sacrifice*, 278; Pauline Chapel frescoes, 281; *Pietàs*, 266, 272, 284, 288, 325, Fig. 304; *Rebellious Slave*, 269, Fig. 308; St. Peter's Basilica, 281–283, 288, 325, 334, Figs. 324–327, 330; self-portrait, Fig. 366; Sistine Chapel ceiling, 90, 273–280, 288, details, Pl. 23, Figs. 315–321; statue of Julius II, 273; *Study for the Libyan Sibyl*, p. 262; tomb of Julius II, 263, 266–269, 271, 273, 274, 282, Figs. 306–312; *Victory*, 269, 271, Fig. 309
Michelozzo, 236, 246; Medici-Riccardi Palace, 239–240, Figs. 270–271
middle class. *See* bourgeoisie
Miel, Jan, *Urban VIII Visiting Il Gesù*, 325, Fig. 369
Miës van der Rohe, Ludwig, 536, 537; quoted, 539; Seagram Building, 538–539, Fig. 610
Milan, Italy, 122, 123
Brera Gallery
Tintoretto, *Finding St. Mark's Body*, 308, 318, Pl. 27
Church of Sant' Ambrogio, 157, Fig. 187
Church of Santa Maria delle Grazie, Leonardo da Vinci, *Last Supper*, 287, 311, Fig. 329
Miletos, Turkey, 42
Milhaud, Darius, *The Eumenides*, 524
militant mysticism, 343–345
Millet, François, 472
Milo of Crotona, Puget, 357, Fig. 414
Milton, John, 389; *Comus*, 399
mimêsis, defined, 34
minarets, 475, Figs. 134, 536
Miners' Wives, Shahn, 527, Fig. 596
miniator, defined, 147
miniature painting, 146–148, Pl. 12, Figs. 177, 199
Minneapolis, Minnesota
Institute of Arts
El Greco, *Expulsion from the Temple*, 339–340, Fig. 393
minnesingers, depicted, 169, Pl. 12; forerunners of, 168
minor nave, defined, 137
minstrels, 166, 168–170; at Battle of Hastings, 167; of God, 224–225; in medieval period, 166, 168
minuet, 445

musical contests and festivals, of Apollo and Marsyas, 59–60; at Eumenaia, 62; at Tralles, 62

musical instruments, construction of, 404–405; in *Don Giovanni*, 422; early Christian, 122; in early Italian Renaissance fresco, 222, Fig. 256; in 18th-century painting, 413, Fig. 478; Florentine use of winds, 236; Gothic organ, 200; in Gothic sculpture, 193, Fig. 227; Hellenic, 31, 32, 59; Hellenistic, 59–61, Figs. 68, 71; manufacture of, 382; of minstrels, 168; of Renaissance, 260, in painting, 304, Pl. 25, Fig. 354; Roman, 91–92, Figs. 109, 110; in Romanesque sculpture, 145, Fig. 170; 151–152, Figs. 179–182; romantic period, 469; 17th-century Dutch, 371–372, in painting, 381, 382–383, Figs. 444–445; 17th-century English, 389, 404–405; standardization of, 477; *See also* instrumentation; names of instruments

musical notation, ancient, 122; earliest effective version of, 150; Greek, 32, 62; Guidonian principles of, 150; omission of in copying, 54, 225; of 17th-century lute tablature, *see* Fig. 446; on staff, developed, 150; teaching of, 61

musical patronage, 18th-century, 415; feudal, 169; Florentine Renaissance, 260, 265; of Louis XIV, 363–365; 19th-century, 461; 17th-century Dutch, 388

musical theory, ancient, in the Renaissance, 250, 257; Gothic, 204; Hellenic, 32; Poliziano's treatise on, 286; Romanesque, of Guido, 150

musicians, in Gentile Bellini's painting, 314, Figs. 361, 362; Byzantine, 123, 125; Hellenic, 19, 32; Hellenistic, 59–61, Figs. 68, 71; of Louis XIV, 363–365; poetsinger, 122; professional Dutch, 371; in Renaissance sculpture, p. 233; Roman, 91–92, Figs. 109, 110; in Romanesque sculpture, 145, Fig. 170; 150–152, Figs. 179–182; in 17th-century Dutch painting, 382, Fig. 445; 376, 378, Fig. 437; in Veronese's painting, 310, Fig. 358. *See also* minstrels

musketeer pictures, 372–373, Pl. 37

Musset, Alfred de, 464, 465

Mussolini, Benito, 517

Myron, 6, 24–25, 34, 36, 59, 69; *Discobolus*, 24–25, 34, 430, Fig. 35

Mystic Mill: Moses and St. Paul Grinding Corn, 145, Fig. 172

mysticism, and Counter Reformation, 323; early Christian, 124, 127–129; medieval, 229; militant, 343–345

mythology, Bernini's sculpture, 356, Fig. 413; Botticelli's paintings, 251–252, Pl. 20, Fig. 290; in early baroque sculpture, 296, Fig. 336; in Florentine Renaissance, 250; and Greek drama, 27; in Greek painting, 55, 56–57; Hellenic book on, 35; Hellenistic on Altar of Zeus, 51–54, 69; on Parthenon, 22; and Poussin, 360;

in Renaissance painting, 286; Roman, 27–28, 74; in Rubens' paintings, 358, 360, Pl. 34, Fig. 416; in Titian's painting, 307, Fig. 356; 20th-century reinterpretation of, 524, 526

Naples, Italy, 57, 210
National Museum
Defeated Persians under Darius, 57–58, Fig. 66; Dioskourides of Samos, *Street Musicians*, 92, Fig. 110; *"Farnese" Hercules*, 54, 242, 357, Fig. 62; *Hercules Finding his Infant Son, Telephus*, 56, Pl. 4; Polyclitus, *Doryphorus (Spearbearer)*, 23, 24, 34, Fig. 31; *Three Graces*, 55, Fig. 63

Napoleon, Canova, 442, Fig. 508

Napoleon I of France, 90; as patron of arts, 429; coronation of, depicted, 440–441, Pl. 44; and David, 429, 438, 440; in Gros's painting, 474, Fig. 535; and music, 444; painter for, 437; portrait of, 438–440, Fig. 506; quoted, 429, 430, 440, 444; and redesign of Paris, 430–434; rise to power, 429; Roman models and symbols for, 429; statues of, 434, Fig. 497; 442, Fig. 508; 458, Fig. 519; and the Vatican, 471

Napoleon III of France, 434, 477, 494

Napoleon Visiting the Pesthouse at Jaffa, Gros, 474, Fig. 535

narthex, defined, 102; 141, Fig. 166

Nash, John, 470; Royal Pavilion, 474–475, 491; Figs. 536–537

nationalism, beginning of, 202, 205; German, 471; 19th-century romantic, 423, 468, 469–470

Nativity, Filippo Lippi, 248, Pl. 19

Nativity and Annunciation to the Shepherds, G. Pisano, 218, Fig. 251

naturalism, in early Italian Renaissance painting, 229; early Roman Christian, 121; in Flemish painting, 253; Franciscan, 258; in literature, 495; medieval, 228; Renaissance, 291

nature, cubists' view of, 513; Franciscan view of, 228; Ghiberti's treatment of, 242; Greek art as imitation of, 36, 66; and Greek humanism, 34; and late 19th-century artists, 482; Romanesque stylizations of, 166, 177; and Rousseau's movement, 468, 472–474

Naumburg, Germany
Naumburg Cathedral
Naumburg Master, *Uta*, Fig. 239

nave, defined, 102; circular, 108; derivation of word, 104; minor, defined, 137; short longitudinal, 326; symbolism of, 104–105; examples of, Pls. 9, 13, Figs. 118, 161, 162, 216, 242, 494

necking of a column, defined, 10, 13, Fig. 10

neoclassical architecture, 430–434, Figs. 491–501

neoclassical literature, 20th-century, 524, 526

neoclassical music, 19th-century, 444–447; 20th-century, 524

neoclassical painting, 19th-century, 434–442, 448, Pls. 44, 45,

Figs. 502–507; 20th-century, 524, Figs. 591, 592

neoclassical sculpture, 19th-century, 442–444, 448, 457–458, Figs. 508–510, 519; 20th-century, 524, Fig. 593

neoclassicism, 18th-century, 367; early 19th-century, 447–449; late 19th-century, 458, 470; 20th-century, 524, 526

neodadaism, 520–521, Fig. 585

neomedievalism, 461

Neonian Baptistry, 110

Neoplatonic Academy, Florence, 236

Neo-Platonists, Florentine, 251, 257–258; and Michelangelo, 268, 271, 274–275, 279; reaction against, 323; Roman Renaissance, 277, 279, 287; in Titian's *Sacred and Profane Love*, 306, Pl. 26

neoprimitivism, defined, 507; in music, 509–510; in painting, 505, 507, 508, Pls. 53, 55, 56, Fig. 564; in sculpture, 505, 507–509, Figs. 563, 565–567

Nero, Emperor, 91, 263

Nerval, Gérard de, 450, 465

Nervi, Pierluigi, Palazzetto dello Sport, 539–540, Figs. 611–612

New Haven, Connecticut
Yale University Art Gallery
Lipschitz, *Man with Mandolin*, 514, Figs. 577–578

New York City
Columbia University
Low Memorial Library, 86
Cooper Union Museum
Watteau, *Drawing*, 409, Fig. 467
Frick Collection
Constable, *Salisbury Cathedral from Bishop's Garden*, 473, Fig. 534; Ruisdael, *Quay at Amsterdam*, 368–369, 370, 379, Fig. 423; Vermeer, *Officer and Laughing Girl*, 380–381, Fig. 443
Grace Church (Renwick), 471, Fig. 531
Kennedy International Airport
Trans World Flight Center (Saarinen), 540, Figs. 613–614
Lever House (Bunshaft, of Skidmore, Owings, and Merrill), 538, Fig. 609
Lincoln Center for the Performing Arts, 532
Moore, *Reclining Figure*, 508–509, 532, Fig. 566
Metropolitan Museum of Art
Boucher, *Toilet of Venus*, 414, Fig. 479; Cézanne, *Mont Ste. Victoire*, 486–488, Fig. 550; Clodion, *Nymph and Satyr*, 414, Fig. 482; El Greco, *Cardinal de Guevara*, 340–341, Fig. 394; *Old Market Woman*, 67, Fig. 76; Piranesi, *Pantheon, Interior*, Fig. 103; Poussin, *Rape of the Sabine Women*, 360–361, 438, Fig. 419; Rembrandt, *Christ Healing the Sick*, 374–375, Fig. 429
Museum of Modern Art
Arp, *Relief*, 523, Fig. 590; Bacon, *Painting (The Butcher)*, 530, Fig. 598; Boccioni, *Unique Forms of Continuity in Space*, 517, Fig. 581; Braque, *Oval Still Life*, 514, Fig. 574; Chagall, *I and*

236, 274–275, 310; on the arts, 38, dialogues of, 36, 39, 250, 286; on music, 30; on musical instruments, 60, 310; Pergamene Academy of, 44; quoted, 31, 36; on the soul, 277; in Raphael's painting, 280, Pl. 24; Renaissance interest in, 257; theories of, 279, 288, 306; and triple divisions, 274, 277; *Laws*, Ficino on, 257; *Republic*, 255, 285, 541, Ficino on, 257, quoted, 31, 36; *Symposium*, 287, Ficino on, 251; *Timaeus*, 32, 287, quoted, 274, depicted, 280, Pl. 24

Pliny the Elder, on mosaics, 58

Pliny the Younger, 90, 95; on art, 91; on music, 122; quoted, 90, 92; villas of, 90–91; *Panegyric*, 91

Plotinus, *Enneads*, 250

Plutarch, 360; on music, 61; on Pericles, 6; quoted, 33; *Parallel Lives*, 90, revival of, 429, 436

podium, defined, 49; 79, Fig. 91

Poe, Edgar Allen, 460

Poetics, Aristotle, 30, 449; quoted, 36–37

poetry, of Dante's *Divine Comedy*, 226–227; epic, 159, 166–169, 170, 177; Florentine Renaissance, 254–256, 265; Franciscan, 223–225; Gothic, 191, and Romanesque compared, 177; of Greek drama, 29, 30; and Greek music, 31, 61; medieval Latin, 224; neoclassical, 448; of Petrarch, 221–223; Plato on, 38; Roman, 91; Romanesque, 159, 166–169, 170, 177; romantic, 462–463; Spanish, 332, 345; of the symbolists, 495–496

pointillism, explained, 485–486, Pl. 51

Politics, Aristotle, 33, 449, quoted, 36–37

Poliziano, Angelo, 250, 251, 255, 274, 286; in Gozzoli's painting, 248, Fig. 286

Pollaiuolo, Antonio, 244–245, 256, 257, 259; *Battle of Ten Nude Men*, 258–259, Fig. 298; *Hercules Strangling Antaeus*, 244, Figs. 280–281

Pollock, Jackson, *Convergence*, 532, Pl. 62

polychoral style of music, for organ, 382; Spanish, 343; Venetian, 313, 315, 318, example of, 316

polychrome marble, 78, 108, 115, 291

Polyclitus, 6, 23–24, 39; canon of, 24, 39; quoted, 39; *Doryphorus*, 23, 24, 34, Fig. 31

Polydorus of Rhodes, *Laocoön Group*, 64–66, 80, 263, 269, 357, Fig. 75

Polygnotus, 6, 55; Aristotle on, 37

polyphony, defined, 198; beginnings of, 152–153; Gothic, 198, 199–200, 203; of Netherlands, 313; Renaissance developments in, 237, 283–285; spread of, 284; Venetian developments in, 313–317, 321

Pompeii, Italy, 55–56, 57; excavations of, 427, 448; frescoes from, 524; mosaic from, 57, Fig. 66

Pont du Gard. *See* Nîmes

Ponte, Lorenzo da, 419–420

Pop Art, 520

porches, of Erechtheum, 12, 13, Fig. 12; of Gothic cathedrals, 182, Fig. 222

Porcia and Cato (?), 80, Fig. 93

Porta, Giacomo della, 323; Church of Il Gesù, 326, Fig. 367–368; St. Peter's dome, Fig. 324

portal, defined, 9; of cathedrals, 182; Galilee, 137; Gothic of Chartres, 188, 194, Figs. 222–223; of Parthenon, 23

portico, defined, 9; of Erechtheum, 12, Fig. 12; Roman, 79, Fig. 91; 85, Fig. 101

Porticó de la Gloria, Master Matteo, 145, Fig. 168

Portinari, Tommaso, 253–254

Portinari Altarpiece, Van der Goes, 253–254, Fig. 294

Portrait of Dante, Giotto(?), 226, Fig. 257

Portrait of Jan Uytenbogaert, Receiver General, Rembrandt, 371, Fig. 426

portraiture, in Bayeux Tapestry, 166, Pl. 11; in Byzantine mosaics, Pl. 8, Fig. 137; in etching, Fig. 426; in manuscript illuminations, Pl. 14; in painting, Pls. 21, 28, 34, 39, 44; Figs. 257, 301–302, 331, 358–359, 393, 398, 416–417, 438, 505, 528, 545, 549; Rembrandt's psychological depths in, 372, 375–376; in sculpture, Figs. 92, 93, 411, 412, 488

Poseidon, contest with Athena, 12, 19, 23, Fig. 26

Poseidon(?), (Zeus), 24, 25, Pl. 2, Fig. 34

Poseidon and Apollo, 19, Fig. 24

post-and-lintel construction, 9, 10, 38–39; at Pergamon, 46

postimpressionism, 485–488, 499, Pls. 51–54, Figs. 549–552; colors of, 505; Delacroix' influence on, 455

pottery, Pergamene, 44; survival of, 54–55

Poussin, Nicolas, 360–363, 367, 381, 404, 438; and Cézanne, 486; and classicism, 448; compared with Rubens, 360–361, 363, 367; influence of, 362; in Ingres' painting, 442, Fig. 507; and French academicism, 363; *Et in Arcadia Ego*, 361–362, Pl. 35; *Rape of the Sabine Women*, 360–361, 438, Fig. 419

Pozzo, Andrea, 329, 345; *St. Ignatius in Glory*, 325, 331, Fig. 377, detail, *America*, Fig. 378

Prandtauer, Jakob, Abbey Church at Melk, 412, Figs. 475–477

Praxiteles, 257, 448; sculpture of school of, 59, Fig. 68; *Aphrodite of Cnidos*, 26, Fig. 38; *Hermes and the Infant Dionysus*, 24, Pl. 1, Fig. 32

preludes and fugues, of Bach, 424; of Sweelinck, 382

Presentation of Peplos, 19, Fig. 25

Priene, Turkey, 42, 43; plan of, Fig. 48

Priestess Burning Incense, p. 3

Prima Porta, Italy, statue of Augustus of, 79, Fig. 92; wall painting from, 93, Pl. 6

Primavera (Allegory of Spring), Botticelli, 251, 287

primitive art, 505, 507, 510, Fig. 563

Prince, The, Machiavelli, 258, 261

printing, of Bible, 370; effects of, 407; of music, 321, 382, 383, 386, 17th-century example of, Fig. 446; press for, 404, 477, 503

Procession in St. Mark's Square, Gentile Bellini, 291–292, 294, Fig. 331; details of, 314–315, Figs. 361–362

Procession of Maidens, 19, Fig. 23

Procession of Virgin Martyrs, 107–108, Fig. 124

Procopius, 114, 115; on Hagia Sophia, 114

Procuratie Nuove. *See* Venice, Library of St. Mark

program music, 468–469

Projected Tomb of Julius II, Michelangelo, 267, Fig. 306

Prokofiev, Serge, *Love of Three Oranges*, 524; *Scythian Suite*, 510

prologue, in Greek drama, 28

Prometheus, Beethoven, 445, 446

Prometheus Drops His Chains, Gide, 525

Prophet, 154, Fig. 184

Prophet (Lo Zuccone), Donatello, 242–243, 260, Fig. 276

proportions, of the body, Ghiberti on, 258, Polyclitus' canon for, 24, 39; manneristic violations of, 296; of Masaccio's figures, 246; Michelangelo's liberties with, 266; of Parthenon, 39; Plato on, 38; of Renaissance buildings, 258; spatial, 85, 215; Vitruvius quoted on, 24

Proprie Moto, Hofmann, 532, Fig. 602

Propylaea. *See* Athens

prosody, defined, 31; of Debussy, 497–498; of representative style, 400

protagonist, defined, 29; 30

Protagoras, quoted, 33

Protestant churches, and the arts, 371–372; music of, 321, 382, 386

Protestant Reformation, 281, 296, 322

Protestantism, 343, 370–371, 386–387, 404; foreshadowing of, 101

prothesis, defined, 109, Figs. 125–126

Proudhon, Pierre-Joseph, 464; in Courbet's painting, 482, Fig. 545

Proust, Marcel, 490; *Remembrance of Things Past*, 499

psalmody, 122–123; in monastic life, 131, 150; Protestant, 382; responsorial, 123; tones of, symbolized in Romanesque sculpture, 150–152, Figs. 179–182

psaltery, in Gothic sculpture, 193, Fig. 227; in Romanesque sculpture, 151, Fig. 181

Ptolemy, in Gothic sculpture, 193; in Raphael's painting, Fig. 322

Puget, Pierre, 349; *Milo of Crotona*, 357, Fig. 414

Pugin, A. Welby, House of Parliament, Fig. 524

Pulcinella, Stravinsky, 524

pulpit, of cathedral, 182; of Pisa Baptistry, 217–218, Figs. 249–250; of Pisa Cathedral, 218, Fig. 251

Purcell, Henry, 389, 391, 393; and concept of space in music, 405; musical style of, 403–404; *vs.* Wren and Dryden, 402–403; *Dido and Aeneas*, 400–402, 405, excerpts from, 400, 401; *King Arthur*, 402; *The Libertine*, 420

putti, defined, 57

Pythagoras, 193–194, Fig. 226

Pythagoras, 32; in Gothic sculpture, 193–194, Fig. 226; musical theory of, 152, symbolized, 193, Fig. 227; quoted, 37; reform of, 39

Rheims, France, 181, 186, 193, 199
Cathedral, 188, 191
Visitation, p. 179
rhetoric, personified in Gothic
sculpture, 193
rhythm, of *Ars Nova*, 230; in Debussy's
music, 498; Dionysian, 61,
Fig. 71; of frottola, 256; and
Greek humanism, 36; of Greek
music, 31; of isorhythmic motet,
237; polyrhythm, 542; of
Stravinsky's music, 510, example of, 509; of tribal rituals,
depicted in painting, 507, Fig. 564
ribbing, of Chartres, 186; of Florence
cathedral dome, 233; of Gothic
vaults, 187, Fig. 219. *See also* cross
vaulting; barrel vaulting
Ribera, Pedro de, Hospicio de San
Fernando, 337, Fig. 389
ricercare, 313
Richelieu, Cardinal, 346, 360, 366
Rigaud, Hyacinthe, *Louis XIV*, 346,
Fig. 398
Riley, Bridget, *Current*, 532, Fig. 603
Ring of the Nibelung, Wagner, 495, 499
Rite of Spring, Stravinsky, 467, 504,
509–510, 524, excerpt from, 509
ritornel, 364, 365
Robbia, Luca della, 248; *Choristers*,
p. 233
rococo, the, 409–414; in architecture,
410–412, Figs. 470–477; and
aristocratic baroque style, 406–
407, 422; dates of, 407; in design
and decor, 409–410, 412, Pl. 43,
Figs. 467–469, 476–477, 490,
p. 406; development of, 406;
location of style, 423; and modern
art compared, 504; in painting,
412–414, Pl. 40, Figs. 478–479;
in sculpture, 414, 418, Figs. 480–
482, 488, p. 406; summarized,
422–423
Rococo Angel, Bendel, p. 406
Rodin, Auguste, 479, 489–490, 498,
499, 500; on Dante, 489; and
Michelangelo compared, 490; on
Michelangelo's *Moses*, 271; on
sculpture, 491; *Adam*, 490; *The
Bronze Age*, 489, Fig. 553; *Eve*, 490;
Gates of Hell, 489–490, 499,
Fig. 554; *Hand of God*, 490,
Fig. 555; *The Kiss*, 491, Fig. 556;
The Thinker, 489–490; *Three
Shades*, 490, p. 477
Roger II of Sicily, dining hall of, 159,
Figs. 191–192
Roland. See *Song of Roland*
Rolland, Romain, quoted, 444, 445;
Jean Christophe, quoted, 544
Roman architecture, 71, 73–87, Pl. 5,
Figs. 84–85, 87–91, 94–104, 111;
Christian adaptations of, 102,
110, 127; contributions of, 84,
86–87, 93; *vs.* Greek, book on,
427; influence of, 238, 239, 240,
250, 301; utilitarianism of, 94–96
Roman Catholic Church, baptism in,
110; belief in Immaculate
Conception, 342; and censorship,
296; and Council of Trent, 323;
and Counter Reformation, 322–
323, 333; early customs in, 107–
norm of architecture for, 304;
and Protestant Reformation, 311;
psalmody in, 123; and Romanesque hierarchism, 155–157

Roman Counter Reformation, baroque
architecture of, 325–327, 345,
Figs. 367–369, 370–373; baroque
painting of, 328–331, 345, Pl. 29,
Figs. 375–378; baroque sculpture
of, 331–332, 345, Figs. 374, 379–
380
Roman couple, portraits of *Porcia and
Cato(?)*, 80, Fig. 93
Roman drama, and music, 92
Roman Empire, 71, 74–75, 87, 94; and
Christianity, 108, 125; conquest
of Dacia, 87–89; conquest of
Greece, 41; cultural influences on,
42, 101; decline of, 124; East and
West, 99, 101, 102; effect of
decline of on arts, 101; and
utilitarianism, 94–96
Roman imperial baths, 80–81, 87, 263,
Figs. 95–96; in Bithynia, 91;
vaulting in, 117; water for, 82
Roman literature, 90–91, 95; 19th-
century revival of, 428
Roman liturgy, 123, 124
Roman mosaics and mosaicists, 91–92,
105, 108, Figs. 109–110
Roman music, 91–93, 94, 95, Figs. 109–
110
Roman people, abilities of, 71; burial
place of, 118; cultural traditions
of, 91; entertainment of, 80, 82,
90–91, 92; and Hellenistic arts,
68, 70; life of a patrician, 90–91;
organizing genius of, 93–94;
popular arts of, 90, 94; taste of,
47; utilitarianism of, 94–96
Roman religion, 80; and Pantheon, 84
Roman Renaissance, architecture of,
281–283, Figs. 323–327, 330;
music of, 263, 265, 283–285, 286;
painting of, 263, 265, 273–280,
Pl. 22–24, Figs. 301–302, 305,
315–322, 329; sculpture of, 266–
272, Figs. 303–304, 307–313
Roman revival, 96, 434, 470. *See also*
classical revival
Roman de Rou, quoted, 167
Roman sculpture, 71, 74, 79–80, 87–90,
Figs. 82–83, 86, 92–93, 106–109,
p. 71; bronze horses of St. Mark's,
244, 291, 432, Fig. 333; copies of
Hellenic originals, Figs. 31, 35,
37, 38, 45; copies of Hellenistic
originals, Figs. 51–54, 62, 70–71,
77–78, p. 41; influence of, 218,
232, 238, 242–243, 244, 428; realism and symbolism in, 74, 89–90
Roman style, and Greek compared,
93; influence of, 96, 257, 333
Romance of the Rose, 191
Romanesque architecture, church,
136–141, 153, 156, 157–158,
Figs. 156–166, 185–188; feudal,
159, 177–178, Figs. 190–193, 200;
monastic, 130–141, Figs. 156–
166; Norman, 171–175, 177–178,
Figs. 201–208; structural developments of and Gothic style, 180–
181
Romanesque ideas, 153–158, 175–178
Romanesque life, and feudal system,
175–176; house at Cluny, 159,
Fig. 193; and jongleurs, 168–169;
monastic, 130–135, 146–147, 149,
153–154; and religious faith and
thought, 154–155; society of, 202
Romanesque music, church, 150–153;
secular, 168–170

Romanesque painting, fresco, 148–
149, 154, Fig. 178; miniature,
146–149, 154, Fig. 177
Romanesque sculpture, 154–155,
Figs. 183–184, 189, p. 130; of
capitals, 140, Fig. 165; 145,
Figs. 170–174; 150–152, Figs. 179–
182; and Gothic compared, 190;
of Last Judgments, 66; placement
of, 190; purpose of, 146; stone
and metal, 146, Figs. 175–176;
on tympanums, 138; 141–143,
Figs. 166–167; 145, Figs. 168–169
Romanesque style, developed, 153–
154; inventiveness of, 157;
summarized, 177–178
Romano, Giulio, 320; Palazzo del Tè,
303, Fig. 349
romantic architecture, 458–462,
Figs. 522–526; influence of nature
movement on, 472, Fig. 532;
Oriental influence on, 474–475,
Fig. 536–537; teaching of, 470
romantic individualism, 468, 469
romantic literature, 458–461; alliance
of with arts, 468–469; Oriental
influence on, 474, 475; poetry,
462–463; and the revivals, 471
romantic music, 457, 461, 462, 464–
468, 469, 470, excerpt of, 465;
alliance of with arts, 468–469;
Delacroix on, 454; and nature,
472–473, Oriental influence on,
474, 475, 476
romantic nationalism, 468, 469–470
romantic painting, 450–455, Pls. 46–
47, Figs. 512, 518; alliance with
arts, 468; and back-to-nature
movement, 472, 473–474, Pl. 47,
Figs. 533–534; Oriental influence
on, 474, 475, 476, Pl. 48, Figs. 535,
539, and the revivals, 471
romantic sculpture, 456–458,
Figs. 520–521, p. 450; Oriental
influence on, 475, Fig. 538
romanticism, and alliance of arts and
colors, 468–469; anticipation of,
380, 407; and back–to–nature
movement, 472–474; beginning
of, 450–453; effects of, 468; and
escapism, 470–476; and exoticism,
474–476; and individualism and
nationalism, 469–470; and
revivals of the past, 470–472
Rome, Italy, 57, 74, 75, 82, 96, 122,
128, 130, 155, 156; apartments
and residences in, 83, 86, as
artistic capital, 262; Figs. 99–100,
under Augustus, 96; as
Christianity's capital, 96; founder
of, 79; as gateway of art styles,
96; imperial capital moved from,
99, 101; in late Antonine Age, 94;
in late 16th and early 17th
centuries, 322–323, 325; music in
ancient, 92–93; "new," 99; and
Pergamon, 45, 70; port of, 83;
as Roman city, 75; Schola
Cantorum of, 150; sewer system
of ancient, 86, 95; in 16th
century, 262–266; sacks of, 99,
322–323; as symbol for
revolutionary protest, 427–428
Arch of Septimus Severus, 432, 448
Arch of Titus, 71, 74, 90, 296,
detail, Fig. 83
Augustus' Altar of Peace, 70, Figs.
79–80, detail, Fig. 112

491; Roman, 74, 76, 79–80, 87–90, 95; Roman Counter Reformation, 331–332, 345; Roman Renaissance, 266–272; romantic, 456–458; "school," 190; and social realism, 530; survival of, 54–55; and theory of volume, 506; 20th-century materials for, 504; Winckelmann's book on, 427. *See also* architectural sculpture; high relief; frieze; low relief; and so on

scuola(e), of Venice, 294, 308, 320
Seagram Building (Miës van der Rohe and Johnson), 538–539, Fig. 610
Second Tone of Plainsong, 151, Fig. 180
secular music, Romanesque developments in, 168–170. *See also* music
sedes, defined, 119–120
see, defined, 120
Seikolos, skolion of, 62
Seldes, Gilbert, *Lysistrata*, 524
Selene and horses, 22, Fig. 29
Self-portrait at Easel, Rembrandt, 376, Fig. 435
Self-portrait with Saskia, Rembrandt, 375, Fig. 432
self-portraiture, Botticelli, 250, Fig. 289; David, 440, Pl. 44; Ghiberti, 241, Fig. 275; Gozzoli, 248, Fig. 286; El Greco, 339, Pl. 31; Matteo, Fig. 189; Michelangelo, 323, Fig. 366; Piero della Francesca, 250, Fig. 288; Raphael, 280, Pl. 24, Fig. 322; Rembrandt, 375–376, Figs. 430–436; Renaissance, 261; Rubens, 357, Fig. 415; Steen, 387–388, Fig. 448; Van Eyck, 253, Pl. 21, Fig. 293; Velázquez, 341, Pl. 32; Vermeer, 381, Fig. 444; Veronese, 310, 311, Figs. 358–359
sequences, musical, medieval, 224; of Purcell, 404
Seneca, on music, 92; writings of, 427
Sermon to the Birds, Giotto(?), 214, 215, 228–229, Fig. 244
Seurat, Georges, *Sunday Afternoon on the Island of La Grande Jatte*, 485–486, detail, Pl. 51
seven liberal arts. *See* liberal arts
Severini, Gino, *Armored Train*, 517, Fig. 580
"shadow painter" (Apollodorus), 55
Shadwell, Thomas, *The Libertine*, 420
Shahn, Ben, *Miners' Wives*, 527, Fig. 596
Shakespeare, William, 424; Berlioz on, 465; Delacroix' illustrations for *Hamlet* and *Macbeth*, 453, Fig. 513; influence of, 462; in Ingres' painting, 442, Fig. 507; quoted, 32; *Taming of the Shrew*, forerunner of 265
Shelley, Percy B., 447, 454; quoted, 446; *Hellas*, quoted, 3
sibyls, of Michelangelo, 276–277, 288, Fig. 316, p. 262
Sicily, 41, 62, 157
Siena, Italy, art traditions of, 218–219; and Black Death, 217, 221
  Cathedral Museum
    Duccio, *Maestà*, 230–231, Fig. 262, detail *Pietà*, Fig. 261
  Palazzo Pubblico
    Lorenzetti, A. *Good Government*, 221, Fig. 255
Simonides, quoted, 33

simultaneous narration. *See* continuous narration
sinfonia, 313, 386; of Gabrieli motet, 315, excerpt from, 316
singing. *See* music, opera, psalmody, and so on
singing societies, 224
Singspiel, 419
Sistine Chapel. *See* Rome, Vatican
Sistine Chapel Choir, founded, 284, named, 263; under Des Prez, 283–285; and Palestrina, 325
Sixtus IV, Pope, 263, 273, 284
skene, defined, 28
Skidmore, Owings & Merrill, Lever House, 538, Fig. 609
skolion, defined, 62; of Seikolos, 62
skyscrapers, 534, Fig. 604; 538–539, Figs. 609–610; prototype of, 494; tallest building before, 283
Smirke, Sir Robert, British Museum, 434, Fig. 498
Smithson, Harriet, 450, 464
social realism, in 20th-century art, 506; in painting and graphics, 526–530, Figs. 594–599; in sculpture, 530, Fig. 600
Society of Jesus, 323, 344, 345, 404, 407, 420; churches of, 325–326, 331; papal sanction of, 281, 333
Socrates, 3, 6, 33, 39, 62, 68, 257; and beauty, 36; on education 37; idealism of, 37, 64; on music, 31, 60; quoted, 127; and truth, 38
solmization, Guido's system of, 150
sonata, of Beethoven, 445; Italian trio, 386
song, Boethius on, 121; from a *chantefable*, 170; Greek, 62, accompaniment for, 59, in drama, 29, 30, 32; Roman, 92. *See also* airs and arias; music; opera; and so on
Song of the Earth, Mahler, 520
Song of Roland, 164, 166–168, 170, 256; and Bayeux Tapestry and feudalism compared, 175–178; music for, 170
sonnets, of Michelangelo, 271, 279–280, 288; of Petrarch, 228
sophists and sophistry, 6
Sophocles, 6, 27, 29; music of, 33; quoted, 33; plays of, 29–30, 39; *Antigone*, 524; *Elektra*, 513, *Oedipus Rex*, 29, 30, 38, 524
Sortie of Captain Banning Cocq's Company, Rembrandt, 372–374, Pl. 36
Sosus, *Unswept Dining Room Floor*, 58, Fig. 67
Souillac, France
  Church of Notre Dame, west portal, *Isaiah*, 154, Fig. 183
soul, Greek idea of, 31; Platonic and Neo-Platonic idea of, 268, 271, 274, 275, 277, 279
Southey, Robert, *Thalabor the Destroyer*, 474
space, baroque sense of, 338, 404–405; and cubists, 513–514, 542; defined by Rembrandt, 372; dome's effect on, 260, 395; early Christian concept of, 127; Giotto's use of, 221, 229; and Gothic architecture, 205–206; Greek humanization of, 35; Greek and Roman ideas of compared, 93; in Hagia Sophia, 112; Hellenic use of, 16, 22; Hellenic and Hellenistic concepts of compared, 50;

Hellenistic use of, 54, 55, 66; inner and outer, 366, 499, 506, 529, 542; interior, Wright's concept of, 534, 535; Michelangelo's use of, 274–275; Palladio's treatment of, 298, 300–301; Renaissance concepts of, 238–239, 246, 258, 259, 260, 345; Roman enclosure of, 93; and stained glass, 196; tonal, 498; 20th-century treatment of, 499, 506, 513, 534, 535, 541; van der Goes distortion of, 253; Velázquez' use of, 342; Venetian, 317; Vermeer's use of, 380
space-time, 506, 514, 541, 542
Spanish architecture, Counter Reformation baroque, 333–337, 342, Figs. 381–389; Romanesque, 139, Figs. 162–163
Spanish painting, Counter Reformation baroque, 325, 338–342, 345, Pls. 31–32, Figs. 390–396; 19th-century, 441, Pl. 45
Spanish sculpture, Romanesque, 145, Figs. 168, 189
Spear Bearer, Polyclitus, 23–24, Fig. 31
Speculum Majus, Vincent of Beauvais, 190–191
Spinoza, Baruch, 369, 387
spiral frieze, of Trajan's Column, 87–90, 95, Figs. 105–108; of Vendôme Column, 434, Fig. 497
Spohr, Ludwig, *Faust*, 420, 465
Spoils of Jerusalem, 71, 74, Fig. 83
Spontini, Gasparo, 429; *La Vestale*, 444, 449
Squarcialupi, Antonio, 236, 255, 260, 286
squinch, defined, 112, Fig. 131
Stabat Mater Dolorosa, Jacopone da Todi, 225, 231
staff notation. *See* musical notation
stage settings, English 17th-century, 399, Fig. 465; Greek, 29, 32; for Lully's *Alceste*, 364, Fig. 422; Picasso's for *Antigone* and *Pulcinella*, 524, for *El Amor Brujo*, 510
stained glass, of cathedrals, 182, 462; of Chartres, 195–198, Pl. 15, Figs. 230–233; design prototypes, 148; dimension of, 196; and interior space, 196, 198; and lighting, 195, 196, 198; making of, 195–196; 20th-century, 504
stainless steel, 538, Fig. 610; 540, Fig. 615
Starry Night, Van Gogh, 486, 510, Pl. 52
stasimon, defined, 32
Steen, Jan, *Merry Family*, 387–388, Fig. 448
steeples, of parish churches, 393, 396–397, Figs. 459–460
Stein, Gertrude, 523
stele, defined, 35, of Hegeso, Fig. 46
stile antico and *moderno*, 285, 313
Still Life: Basket of Apples, Cézanne, 416, 488, Pl. 54
Still Life: Bowl of Plums, Chardin, 415–416, Pl. 42
still-life painting (formal arrangements of objects including fruits and flowers), 371, Fig. 425; 415–416, Pl. 42; 416, 488, Pl. 54; 510–511, Fig. 569; 514, Fig. 574
stoa, defined, 44; of Attalus II, Fig. 2
stoicism, 44, 64, 66, 68; Roman, 76, 94

Storm-and-Stress movement, 407, 420, 424
Story of Adam and Eve, Ghiberti, 241, Fig. 274
Story of Joseph, 121, Figs. 149–150
Strauss, Richard, *Elektra, Salomé*, 513
Stravinsky, Igor, 504, 509–510, 516, 544; and Picasso, 524, portrait of, 509, Fig. 568; quoted on tonality, 514, 516; *Étude for Pianola*, 518; *Fire Bird*, 467; *Perséphone*, 524; *Pulcinella*, 524; *Oedipus Rex*, 524, *Rite of Spring*, 467, 504, 509–510, 524, 542, excerpt from, 509
Stravinsky, Picasso, 509, Fig. 568
stream of consciousness technique, 500, 523
Street in Delft, Vermeer, 380, Fig. 442
Street, George, New Law Courts, 460
Street Musicians, Dioskourides of Samos, 92, Fig. 110
strophe, defined, 28
Stuart and Revett, *Antiquities of Athens*, 427
stylobate, defined, 9, Fig. 10; Ionic, 13; optical distortion of, 11
Styx, river, in Delacroix' painting, 455, Fig. 518; in Michelangelo's painting, 325; water spirit, in sculpture, 52, Fig. 60
Sublime, the, 424
Suetonius, *Lives of the Twelve Caesars*, 90
Suger, Abbot, 145, 179–180, 195; quoted, 198
Sullivan, Louis, Wainwright Building, 534, Fig. 604
Summa Theologiae, Aquinas, 203; quoted, 193
Sun God's Horses, 21, Fig. 28
Sun King Medallion, 347, p. 346
Sunday Afternoon on the Island of La Grand Jatte, Seurat, 485–486, Pl. 51
Suppliants, The, Aeschylus, 32
surrealism, 503, 506, 523; in literature and music, 523–524; in painting, 521–523, Pl. 60, Figs. 586–588; in sculpture, 523, Figs. 589–590
Sweelinck, Jan Pieterszoon, 321, 372, 382, 386
Sweeny Agonistes, Eliot, 526
Swift, Jonathan, *Beggar's Opera*, 416; *Gulliver's Travels*, 416
Swing, The, Fragonard, 414, Pl. 40
symbolism, of basilica, 104–105; in Bayeux Tapestry and *Song of Roland*, 176; Byzantine, 108, 109, 114, 115; in Chartres sculpture, 192–193; of the Chrismon, 115, 119; of Christian church, 110; of circular tombs, 110; of Cluny capitals, 150–151; through color, 250; in David's painting, 440–441; in Delacroix' paintings, 450–451, 453; in *Divine Comedy*, 226; early Christian, 117, 118, 119, 121, 127–129; of Escorial Palace, 333; of Klee's paintings, 522; of Louis XIV, 346, 347; medieval breakdown of, 228; in music, 152, 343, 497; of monks, 154; and numerology, 204; in 19th-century poetry and drama, 495–497, 499; in Picasso's *Guernica*, 529; of popes' tombs, 268; in *Portinari Altarpiece*, 253; Renaissance, 310; in Romanesque sculpture, 143, 145; of seven liberal arts, 193–194; of Sistine

ceiling, 274–279; in Trajan's Column frieze, 89, 90; in Vermeer's painting, 381
symbolist poets and poetry, 495–496, 499
Symphoniae Sacrae, G. Gabrieli, 313, 314–315; excerpt from, 316; text, 315
symphonic music, 30, 419, 468–469; of Beethoven, 444–447; of Berlioz, 465–468. *See also* specific symphonies
synthesis, baroque, 404–405; Mozartian, 419–422; of 20th-century architecture, 539–540, Figs. 611–615, p. 501; of 20th-century styles in *Guernica*, 530
Syracuse, New York
Syracuse University Collection Mestrovic, *Job*, 530, Fig. 600

Tacitus, 90, 428
Tannhäuser, Wagner, 169, 461; castle of, 159, Fig. 200
Tasso, Torquato, *Jerusalem Delivered*, 317
Tate, Nahum, *Dido and Aeneas*, 400–402, 405
technites, Dionysiac, 61
Telephus, 51, 55; in painting, 56, Pl. 4; in sculpture, 53, Fig. 61
Telephus Being Suckled by a Lioness, 53, Fig. 61
Telephus frieze, 53, 66, detail, Fig. 61
"Tellus Panel," Fig. 112
temenos, defined, 49
tempera painting, defined, 148; and oil, 254; and Venetian climate, 304
Tempest, Giorgione, 304, 317, Fig. 353
Tempietto (Bramante), 286, Fig. 328
temple, classical, and basilica combined, 300; classical, Renaissance use of, 286; Corinthian, 431, Figs. 492–494; Greek, typical, 9–10, unity of, 39; and Greek ideals, 37; of heroes, 63; octastyle, 10; pagan *vs.* Christian churches, 102
Temple of Glory. *See* Paris, Church of La Madeleine
tenor, defined, 199; 200
Terborch, Gerard, 388
Teresa of Avila, 323, 333, 343; Bernini's statue of, 331–332, Fig. 380; canonized, 323; chapel dedicated to, 331–332, Fig. 379; mysticism of, 344; writings of, 332, 336, 345
terracotta, use of, 58, 414
tessera, defined, 57, 108
terza rima, 204
theater, church used as, 326; of 18th-century Italy, 406; Elizabethan *vs.* Greek, 29; Hellenic, 28–30, at Athens, Fig. 3, at Epidaurus, Fig. 42; Hellenistic, 61, at Pergamon, 45; King's, London, 398; Marble Court of Versailles used as, 364, Fig. 422; Palladio's Olympic, 301, Figs. 346–347; patronage of, 389. *See also* stage settings
Theodora, Empress, 114, 115; mosaic portrait of, Pl. 8
Theodore, Archbishop, 114–115; sarcophagus of, 119, Fig. 146
Theodoric, 99, 102, 107, 108; and music, 121, 122; palace of, 107,

Fig. 123; quoted, 102, 105; and Sant' Apollinare Nuovo, 102, 105; tomb of, 109–110, Fig. 127
Theodoric's Palace, 107, Fig. 123
Theodorus of Thocaea, Tholos, 14, 109, Fig. 47
theology, Aquinas' synthesis of, 203; and Council of Trent, 323; early Christian, 101, 112, 125, 127; of Enlightenment, 424
Theophilus, quoted, 149–150
theorbo, 382, 413, Figs. 445, 478
Theotocopoulos, Domenicos. *See* Greco, El
thermae. *See* Roman imperial baths
Theseum. *See* Athens, Hephaesteum
Theseus, Gide, 525
Thinker, The, Rodin, 489–490
Third Symphony (Eroica), Beethoven, 444–447
Third Tone of Plainsong, 151, Fig. 181
This Will be the Last Time, Little Father, Rouault, 526–527, Fig. 594
tholos, defined, 109; 14, Fig. 47
Thomas of Celano, and *Dies Irae*, 223–224
Thorwaldsen, Berthel, 448; Villa Carlotta, Fig. 511
Three Goddesses, 21, Fig. 29
Three Graces, ancient painting, 56, Fig. 63
Three Graces, Picasso, 524, Fig. 591
Three Musicians, Picasso, 514, Fig. 575
Three Philosophers, Giorgione, 310
Three Shades, Rodin, 490, p. 477
Three Trees, Rembrandt, Fig. 449
Thucydides, 35; method of, 258
tibia, defined, 92, Fig. 110
Timaeus, Plato, 32, 287; quoted, 274; in Raphael's painting, 280, Pl. 24
time, Bergson's view of, 500; Greek concept of, 35, 36; in Greek drama, 30, 36; and 19th-century arts, 499–500; Platonic concept of, 306; and Roman sculpture, 93–94; and space, 506, 514, 541, 542; and surrealism, 521
Timgad, Algeria, Roman city, 42, Fig. 49
Timotheus, 33
Tintoretto (Jacopo Robusti), 294, 304, 307–308, 313; influence of, 321, 357, 358; in Veronese's painting, 310, Fig. 358; *Finding St. Mark's Body*, 308, 318, Pl. 27; *Last Supper*, 308, Fig. 357; *Marriage of Bacchus and Ariadne*, 318, Fig. 364; *Paradise*, 318, detail p. 291
Titian (Tiziano Vecellio), 294, 307, 310, 313, 340; influence of, 307, 321, 357, 358; in El Greco's painting, 340, Fig. 393; patron of, 295; in Veronese's painting, 310, Fig. 358; *Assumption of the Virgin*, 306–307, 317–318, 338–339, Fig. 355; *Bacchus and Ariadne*, 307, Fig. 356; *Concert* (with Giorgione), 310, Fig. 363; *Sacred and Profane Love*, 305, 306, 318, Pl. 26; *Venus and the Organ Player*, 304, 317, Fig. 354
Titus, Arch of. *See* Rome
toccata, 313, 382
Toilet of Venus, Boucher, 414, Fig. 479
Toledo, Juan Bautista de, Escorial Palace, 333–336, Figs. 381–384

Toledo, Spain
Church of San Domingo el Antiguo, painting for, 338–339, Fig. 391
Church of San Tomé
El Greco, *Burial of Count Orgaz*, 339, Pl. 31, Fig. 392
Tolnay, Charles de, 274
tomb, in altar, 111; of Costanza, 109, Fig. 153–154; of Galla Placidia, 101, 111, Figs. 113–114; of Hadrian, 109, Fig. 111; of Mausolus, 63, Fig. 72; of popes, 262, 268; of St. Peter, 282; of Theodoric, 109–110, Fig. 127. *See also* mausoleum; sarcophagus
Tomb of Giuliano de' Medici, Duke of Nemours, Michelangelo, 272, Fig. 313
Tomb of Julius II, Michelangelo, 263, 266–269, 271, 273, 274, 282, Fig. 311
tonality, and Debussy's symbolism of, 496–498; 20th-century, 514, 516, 542
tone color in music, 467. *See also* instrumentation
tones, Greek discoveries with, 32; Odo's arrangement of, 150; of plainsong, in sculpture, 151–152, 153, Figs. 179–182; and tonal center, 62
Torso of Venus, Maillol, 524, Fig. 593
Toulouse, France
Church of St. Sernin, 137, Figs. 159–160
Tovey, Donald F., 445
Tower of Blue Horses, Marc, 512, Fig. 572
Tower of London. *See* London
towers, bell (campanile), Figs. 263, 332; of Chartres, 184–185; of Gothic cathedrals, 182; Norman, 174. *See also* lantern towers
Toynbee, Arnold Joseph, 544
tragedy, French *tragédie lyrique*, 364–365; Greek, 29–30, 36, 37
Traini, Francesco, *Triumph of Death*, 221–223, Fig. 256
Trajan, Emperor, 71, 80, 81, 82, 83, 84, 87, 90; accession of, 75, 91; burial place of, 87; campaigns of, 74, 75, 87–89, 94; letter quoted, 91; projects of, 71, 74, 75, 80, 82, 83; statues of, 76, 79–80, 87, p. 71; temple to, 45, 78–79. *See also* Arch of Trajan; Baths of Trajan; Forum of Trajan; Trajan's Column
Trajan, 79–80, p. 71
Trajan Accepting Surrender of Decebalus, 88, Fig. 108
Trajan Addressing Troops, 88, Fig. 107
Trajan Sacrificing, 74, Fig. 82
Trajan's Campaign against the Dacians, 87–88, Fig. 106
Trajan's Column, 76, 78, 87–90, 94, Figs. 85, 88, 90; copy of, 434, Fig. 497; influence of, 232; inscription on, 76; spiral frieze of, 87–90, 95, Figs. 105–108, forerunner of, 53, influence of, 90
Tralles, Turkey, music of, 61–62
transept, defined, 104; of Chartres, 186, Fig. 217; of Cluny, 137, 140–141, Figs. 156, 158, 164
Transworld Flight Center (Saarinen), 540, Figs. 613–614
Tribute Money, Masaccio, 246, Fig. 284

triforium, defined, 104; of Chartres, 186, 187, Figs. 217–218; Norman, 173; matroneum, 112, Pl. 7, Fig. 132
triglyph, defined, 10, Fig. 10; 13; of Parthenon, 16, 39; manneristic use of, 303
Trinity, The, dispute over, 101; symbol of, 119, 204, 226, 331, Fig. 146
Trinity Church (Upjohn), 471, Fig. 530
triplum, 199, 201; example of, 200
Tristan und Isolde, Wagner, 513; legend of, 191
Triumph of Death, Traini, 221–223, Fig. 256
Triumph of Venice, Veronese, 311, 318, Fig. 360
triumphal, arch, defined, 104; of Il Gesù, 326, Fig. 367; of St. Paul's, 395; of San Vitale, 109
Trivium, 193
Trojan Women, The, Werfel, 526
troubadours, 168, 169; music of, 170; and St. Francis, 224
trouvères, forerunners of, 168, 169
true arch, 86, Fig. 104
trumeau, 194, Fig. 229
trumpet, in Hellenistic sculpture, 47, Fig. 51; in painting, 381, Fig. 444; in Roman mosaic, 91–92, Fig. 109; in Roman sculpture, 74, Fig. 83; in Romanesque sculpture, 145, Fig. 170
truth, Hellenic and Hellenistic search for, 63–64, 68; medieval disputes over, 203; Socratic notion of, 40
tuba (trumpet), Roman, 91–92, Fig. 109
Tubal-Cain, in Gothic sculpture, 194
tunnel vaulting. *See* barrel vaulting
Turin, Italy
Guarini, Church of Santa Sidone, p. 322
Turkish Bath, The, Ingres, 476, Pl. 48
Turpin, Archbishop, 164, 167, 176
Tuscan order of architecture, 302; columns of, 82
twelve-tone method of musical composition, 507, 514, 516, 542; example of, 516
tympanum, defined, 138; archivolts of, 143; Gothic, 192–193, 194, Figs. 223–227; Romanesque, 142–143, 145, Figs. 166–169

Uccello, Paolo, 233, 240, 248, 249; *Battle of San Romano*, 248, Fig. 287
Ulm, Germany
Cathedral, 205, Fig. 237
Ulysses, Joyce, 523, 526, 542–543
Un dì lieto, Isaac and Lorenzo de' Medici, 256; excerpt from, 256
Unique Forms of Continuity in Space, Boccioni, 517, Fig. 581
L'Unité d'Habitation (Le Corbusier), 537–358, Pl. 63
United States Pavilion Expo 67 (Fuller), 540, p. 501
unity, of arts in Romanesque liturgy, 158; of Chartres' façade, 184, Fig. 214; defined by dome, 114, 239, 260, 282; in Giotto's painting, 216; Gothic, 206; in government, 333, 346–349, 366; in Greek drama, 30, 36, 39; of Greek temple, 39; Hellenic, 16, 22, 33,

38, 50, 66; Hellenistic, 50, 53, 66; in music, 465; of Norman interiors, 174; Roman, 74, 89, 93; of St. Paul's, 393; in Venetian painting, 318; in Veronese's compositions, 309; of Versailles Palace, 366. *See also* classical unities
universities, Dutch, 369, 387; Gothic, 205; of Paris, 193
University of Virginia, Charlottesville Rotunda (Jefferson), 86, 434, Fig. 501
Unswept Dining Room Floor, Sosus, 58, Fig. 67
Upjohn, Richard, Trinity Church, 471, Fig. 530
Urban II, Pope, 136
Urban VIII, Pope, quoted, 328; in Sacci and Miel's painting, Fig. 369
Urban VIII Visiting Il Gesù, Sacchi and Miel, Fig. 369
Uta, Naumburg Master, 205, Fig. 239
utilitarianism, Roman, 94–96
Uylenburch, Saskia van, in Rembrandt's painting, 375, Fig. 432
Uytenbogaert, Jan, Rembrandt's portrait of, 371, Fig. 426

Valéry, Paul-Ambroise, "Fragments of Narcissus," 526
Valhalla (Hall of Fame), Regensburg, 434
Van de Velde, Jan Jansz, *Still Life*, 371, Fig. 425
Van der Goes, Hugo, *Portinari Altarpiece*, 253–254, Fig. 294
Van der Heyden, *City Hall at Amsterdam*, 369, Fig. 424
Van Dyck, Anthony, 321, 367, 391; *Charles I of England*, 391, Pl. 39; *Five Children of Charles I*, 391, Fig. 452
Van Eyck, Jan, oil medium of, 254; *Giovanni Arnolfini and His Wife*, 253, Pl. 21, self-portrait detail, Fig. 293
Van Gogh, Vincent, 506, 511; *Père Tanguy*, 486, Fig. 549; *Starry Night*, 486, 510, Pl. 52
Van Wesel, Andries. *See* Vesalius
Varèse, Edgar, *Density 2.15, Intégrales, Ionization*, 518
variations, musical, 386, 446
Vasari, Giorgio, 261, 319; quoted, 272
vase painting, 31, 55, Pl. 3, Fig. 44
vaulting. *See* barrel vaulting, cross vaulting
Velázquez, Diego, 307, 341–342, 367, 381, 404; and El Greco compared, 341; *Las Meninas*, 341–342, 544, Pl. 32; self-portrait, 341, Pl. 32; *Water Carrier of Seville*, 341, Fig. 395
Vendôme Column. *See* Paris, Place Vendôme
Venetian architecture, 296–304, 317, 318, Figs. 332, 334–348, 351–352
Venetian music, 313–317, 318, 319; in Spain, 343; as transition to baroque, 321
Venetian painting, 291–292, 294, 304–311, 313, 317–318, 319, Pls. 25–28, Figs. 331, 353, 364, p. 291
Venetian style, spread of, 320–321; summarized, 317–319

Veneziano, Domenico, 249
Venice, Italy, condottiere of, 244, Figs. 279, 282; city's growth, 294–295; doges of, 295; as musical center, 313; patron saint of, 292; religious freedom in, 295, 296, 313, 314; *scuole* of, 294 308, 320; 16th-century life in, 291–292, 294–296; and Vicenza, 296
  Academy
    Bellini, *Procession in St. Mark's Square*, 291–292, 294, Fig. 331, details, 314–315, Figs. 361–362; Giorgione, *Tempest*, 304, 317, Fig. 353; Veronese, *Feast in the House of Levi*, 310–311, Fig. 359
    Campanile, 291, Fig. 332
    Loggietta (Sansovino), 296, Fig. 336
  Campo SS. Giovanne e Paolo
    Verrocchio, *Equestrian Monument of Bartolommeo Colleoni*, 244, Fig. 282
  Church of the Frari
    Titian, *Assumption of the Virgin*, 306–307, 317–318, 338–339, Fig. 355
  Church of Il Redentore (Palladio), 300–301, Figs. 342–345
  Church of San Giorgio Maggiore (Palladio), 300, Fig. 341
    Tintoretto, *Last Supper*, 308, Fig. 357
  Church of Santa Maria della Salute (Longhena), 301-304, Figs. 351–352
  Doge's Palace, 291, 292, 294, Figs. 331–332
    Tintoretto, *Marriage of Bacchus and Ariadne*, 318, Fig. 364, *Paradise*, 318, detail, p. 291; Veronese, *Triumph of Venice*, 311, 318, Fig. 360
  Library of St. Mark (Sansovino), 291, 292, 294, 296, Figs. 331–332, 334–335
  Scamozzi's Procuratie Nuove for, 291, 302–303, Fig. 348
  St. Mark's Cathedral, 157, 291–292, 294, 295, Figs. 331–332; music in, 313–317, 318; horses of, 244, 291, 432, Fig. 333; square of, 291–292, 294, 315, Figs. 331–332
Le Ventre Législatif, Daumier, 479, Fig. 540
Venus, 27; ideal type, 251; as lover of antiquity, 251, Pl. 20; symbol of, 79, Fig. 77
Venus and Adonis, Blow, 400
Venus and Mars, Botticelli, 251, 287, Pl. 20
Venus and the Organ Player, Titian, 304, 317, Fig. 354
Venus de' Medici, statue, 251, 430, Fig. 291
Venus of the Vatican, statue, 263
Verdi, Giuseppe, *Aïda*, 476
Vergil, 79, 90, 127, 168, 232; in Delacroix' painting, 454–455, Fig. 518; in *Divine Comedy*, 226, 232; influence of, 464, 465; in Ingres' painting, 441–442, Fig. 507; revival of, 471; *Aeneid*, 277, 402, 471, quoted, 95
Vermeer (van Delft), Jan, 367, 376, 383, 388, 404, 531; and

Rembrandt compared, 381–382; *Artist in His Studio*, 381, Fig. 444; *Concert*, 382–383, Fig. 445; *Officer and Laughing Girl*, 380–381, Fig. 443; *Street in Delft*, 380, Fig. 442; *View of Delft*, 380, Pl. 38
vernacular languages, and Dante, 226, 231; Franciscans use of, 211, 224; in French music, 201; and Latin, 201, 206; of minstrels, 168; Renaissance, 255
Veronese, Paolo, 304, 308–311, 313, 319; and academicism, 294; and the Inquisition, 310–311; and mannerism, 311; quoted, 308, 311; *Feast in the House of Levi*, 310–311, Fig. 359; *Marriage at Cana*, 309–310, Pl. 28, detail Fig. 358; self-portraits, 310, 311, Figs. 358–359; *Triumph of Venice*, 311, 318, Fig. 360
Verrocchio, Andrea del, 245, 257, 258, 259; *Equestrian Monument of Bartolommeo Colleoni*, 244, Fig. 282; (workshop of), *Lorenzo de' Medici*, 254–255, 261, Fig. 295
Versailles, France
  Versailles Palace (Mansart), 350–355, 470, Pl. 33, Figs. 403–410; Chirico quoted on, 519; closing of, 406; former garden sculpture, 357, Fig. 414; gardens of, 353, 354, Fig. 410; influence of, 355, 393, 404, 406; interior decoration of, 353–354, 362, Pl. 33, Figs. 407–409, 421; music and drama at, 363–365, 472, Fig. 422; as symbol of absolutism, 355, 366
  Bernini, *Louis XIV*, 355–356, Fig. 411; David, *Bonaparte on Mount St. Bernard*, 438–440, Fig. 506; Hall of Mirrors (Mansart and Lebrun), 353–354, 410, Fig. 409; "Le Hameau" (Mique), 472, Fig. 532; Louis XIV's State Bedchamber (Mansart), 352, 353, Fig. 407; Marble Court (Le Vau), 352, 364, Fig. 422; Petit Trianon, Grand Gallery (Gabriel), 423, Fig. 490; Queen's Bedchamber (Mansart), 353, Fig. 408; Salon de Guerre (Mansart and Lebrun), 353, 357, 409, Pl. 33
Vesalius (Andries van Wesel), *Anatomy*, 372, 387
Vespucci family, Amerigo, Marco and Simonetta, 251
Vézelay, France
  Abbey Church of La Madeleine, 141–145, 461, Pl. 9; capitals of, 145, Figs. 170–174; central portal of narthex with tympanum, 142–143, 155, 168, 177, Figs. 166–167; fresco of, 148; interior of, Pl. 9; narthex and nave, 138, 141–142, Pl. 9, Fig. 166
Via Traiana, 71
Vicenza, Italy, 296
  Basilica (Palladio), 296, 298, Figs. 337–338
  Olympic Theater (Palladio), 301, Figs. 346–347
  Villa Rotonda (Palladio), 86, 298–299, 304, 318, Figs. 339–340

Victoria, Tomás Luis de, 285, 333, 343, 345; *O vos omnes*, excerpt from, 343
Victory, Michelangelo, 269, 271, Fig. 309
Vienna, Austria
  Austrian National Library
    Great Hall (Erlach), 412, Fig. 474
  Belvedere Palace (Hildebrandt), 410–411, Figs. 470–471
  Hofburg Palace, salon, 409, Fig. 468
  Karlskirche (Erlach), 411, Figs. 472–473
  Kunsthistorisches Museum
    Cellini, *Saltcellar of Francis I*, 320, Fig. 365; Rembrandt, *Self-portrait*, 376, Fig. 434; Rubens, *Self-portrait*, 357, Fig. 415; Vermeer, *Artist in His Studio*, 381, Fig. 444
  Schönbrunn Palace, 406
    Grand Gallery (Erlach and Picassi), 410, Fig. 469
View of Delft, Vermeer, 380, Pl. 38
View of a Garden, 93, Pl. 6
Vignola, Giacomo, 323; Church of Il Gesù, 326, Fig. 367
Vignon, Pierre-Alexandre, 431, 447, 448; Church of La Madeleine, 430–432, Figs. 492–494
Vikings, 171; ships of, 165, Fig. 197, detail, p. 159
Villa Carlotta (Thorwaldsen), salon of, Fig. 511
Villa of Livia, wall painting from, 93, Pl. 6
Villa Rotonda. *See* Vicenza
Vincent of Beauvais, quoted, 228; *Speculum Majus*, 190–191
Vingt-quatre Violons, 363, 364, 392
viol, medieval use of, 166, 168; in Gothic sculpture, 193, Fig. 227
viola da braccia, depicted, 310, Fig. 358
viola da gamba, depicted, 382–383, Fig. 445
Violin Concerto, Berg, 516; excerpt from, 516
Viollet-le-Duc, Eugène, 141, 461, 469; drawing of seven-spired cathedral, 181, Fig. 211; restoration of Carcassonne Castle, 461, Fig. 209
Virgin Mary, attributes of, 182, 191, 193; cathedrals to, 182, 183, 191; and Chartres stained glass iconography, 196; cult and relic of, 188; in 14th-century Italian art, 231, and Gothic music, 201; life of in Chartres' sculptures, 182, 192–193, Figs. 224, 229
Virgin Portal, Chartres, 192, Fig. 224
virtù, Renaissance trait of, 261
virtues, Christian, 168; in Greek thought, 35, 38; of monks, 153; in *Song of Roland*, 167
Visitation, sculpture, p. 179
Vitruvius, 11, 32, 258, 286; influence of, 296, 335, 361; on Polyclitus' Canon, 24; treatise of, 242
Voltaire, François M. A., 406, 415, 447, 459; Houdon's bust of, 418, Fig. 488; *Candide*, 416, 424
Voltaire, Houdon, 418, Fig. 488
volutes, Fig. 10; Corinthian, 14; Ionic, 13
voussoir, defined, 86

PHOTOGRAPHIC SOURCES

References are to figure numbers unless indicated Pl. (plate).

A.C.L., Brussels (542); Adelys, Paris (553, 555, illus. p. 477); Aero-Photo, Paris (229); Alinari-Art Reference Bureau, Ancram, N.Y. (16, 38, 43, 46, 53, 66, 68, 79, 80, 93, 101, 106, 110, 112, 125, 138, 145, 151, 192, 241, 243, 244, 245, 249, 251, 255, 256, 257, 258, 259, 260, 261, 262, 266, 268, 269, 272, 273, 281, 282, 283, 284, 297, 299, 300, 301, 302, 303, 306, 311, 314, 317, 323, 324, 328, 329, 333, 344, 357, 358, 370, 372, 375, 376, 377, 378, 380, 411, 413, 414, 416, 421, 466, 509, 539); Anderson-Alinari-Art Reference Bureau (67, 81, 82, 115, 121, 122, 132, 137, 149, 246, 315, 316, 318, 320, 321, 334, 335, 354); Anderson-Art Reference Bureau (113, 285, 286, 331, 356, 360, 366, 390, 417); Anderson and Spiers. *Architecture of Ancient Rome.*

London: B.T. Batsford, 1927 (96); Andrews, Wayne, Grosse Point, Mich. (530); Archives Photographiques, Paris (19, 155, 158, 159, 166, 167, 169, 170, 171, 172, 173, 174, 176, 178, 183, 184, 185, 193, 194, 195, 196, 197, 208, 218, 220, 221, 223, 224, 233, 235, 307, 308, 398, 399, 400, 401, 402, 403, 404, 407, 409, 410, 420, 424, 435, 438, 481, 483, 484, 489, 490, 494, 495, 496, 498, 502, 503, 504, 505, 506, 507, 512, 518, 519, 520, 521, 526, 528, 532, 535, 543, 544, 557, 558, 559, 562, illus. pp. 291, 427, 450); Art Institute of Chicago (582); Austrian State Tourist Office, New York (468, 469, 470, 471, 474, 477); Barsotti, Signor S.R., Florence (271); Bavarian State Picture Collection, Munich (418); Beville, Henry B., Alexandria, Va.

MEDIEVAL AND MODERN EUROPE

NORWAY

SCOTLAND

NORTH SEA

Edinburgh

N. IRELAND

DENMARK

Durham

IRELAND

Dublin ◉

York •

ATLANTIC OCEAN

ENGLAND

Gloucester • Oxford •

THE NETHER-LANDS

Hamburg

Haarlem • ◉ Amsterdam

London ◉

Exeter • Salisbury •

The Hague • • Delft • Utrecht

GERMA

Canterbury •

Bruges •

Goslar •

Leip

Hastings •

Ghent • Antwerp •

St. Omer •

Aachen •

Naumburg

Brussels

BELGIUM

• Cologne

Weima

Bayeux •

Rouen • • Amiens

Rhine R.

Caen •

• Beauvais

Frankfurt-am-Main

Mt. St. Michel •

Seine R.

◉ Paris • Rheims

Nürnberg

Chartres •

Loire R.

Vézelay •

Strasbourg •

Ulm •

Danu

Tours •

• Bourges

Poitiers •

• Autun

SWITZER-LAND

Munic

FRANCE

• Cluny

Santiago de Compostela •

• Périgueux

Milan •

Vicenza •

V

• Souillac

Turin •

Mantua •

Padua

Garonne R.

• Moissac • Conques

Salamanca •

• Toulouse

Bologna •

Avila • • Escorial

Roncesvalles •

Carcassonne •

Nîmes • • Avignon

• Arles

Pisa • Florence •

PORTUGAL

◉ Madrid

Barcelona •

Marseilles •

Nice •

Siena •

Peru

Lisbon ◉

• Toledo

CORSICA

As

SPAIN

◉

• Cordova

TYRRHE

• Seville

BALEARIC IS.

SARDINIA

SEA

Granada • Murcia •

MEDITERRANEAN

Mon

AFRICA